# Introductory

## 4TH EDITION

# COMPUTERS

## UNDERSTANDING TECHNOLOGY

## FLOYD FULLER

APPALACHIAN STATE UNIVERSITY, RETIRED
BOONE, NORTH CAROLINA

## BRIAN LARSON

MODESTO JUNIOR COLLEGE
MODESTO, CALIFORNIA

Paradigm
PUBLISHING

St. Paul • Los Angeles • Indianapolis

Senior Developmental Editor: Christine Hurney
Production Editor: Donna Mears
Cover Designer: Leslie Anderson
Text Designer and Page Layout: David Farr, ImageSmythe; Ryan Hamner; Petrina Nyhan
Illustrator: Precision Graphics

Care has been taken to verify the accuracy of information presented in this book. However, the authors, editors, and publisher cannot accept responsibility for Web, e-mail, newsgroup, or chat room subject matter or content, or for consequences from application of the information in this book, and make no warranty, expressed or implied, with respect to its content.

**Trademarks:** Some of the product names and company names included in this book have been used for identification purposes only and may be trademarks or registered trade names of their respective manufacturers and sellers. The authors, editors, and publisher disclaim any affiliation, association, or connection with, or sponsorship or endorsement by, such owners.

**Image Credits: Chapter 1.** Page 2: Corbis; Page 3: Dex Images/Corbis; Page 4: (top) PhotoDisc/Getty Images, (middle) Corbis, (bottom) AP Photo/Peter M. Fredin; Page 6: (top) © Intel Corporation, (bottom) Corbis; Page 7: Bettman/Corbis; Page 8: T. Kevin Smyth/Corbis; Page 9: (top) Corbis, (bottom) Courtesy of the National Human Genome Research Institute; Page 10: © Paradigm Publishing, Inc.; Page 12: (top) © Paradigm Publishing, Inc., (bottom) screen shot reprinted with permission from Microsoft Corporation; Page 13: Screen shots © Google Inc.; Page 16: © Paradigm Publishing, Inc.; Page 18: Courtesy of ASUSTek Computers Inc.; Page 19: (top left to right, bottom left) Courtesy of Dell Inc., (bottom right) © Hewlett-Packard Company; Page 20: (left to right) Courtesy of FujiFilm Inc., © Maxell Corporation Inc., © Memorex Products Inc., © Memorex Products Inc.; Page 22: AP Photo/Karsten Thielke; Page 25: (top) Corbis, (bottom) Rainer Holz/zefa/Corbis; Page 26: (top) © Ed Kashi/Corbis, (bottom) Toshiyuki Aizawa/Reuters/Corbis; Page 27: Royalty-Free/istockphoto.com; Page 28: © Motorola, Inc.; Page 29: Courtesy of Dell Inc.; Page 30: AP Photo/Hewlett Packard Company; Page 31: (top) Courtesy of Dell Inc., (bottom) Royalty-Free/Corbis; Page 32: Kimberly White/Reuters/Corbis; Page 33: Markowitz Jeffrey/Corbis Sygma. Image Credits continue following Index.

We have made every effort to trace the ownership of all copyrighted material and to secure permission from copyright holders. In the event of any question arising as to the use of any material, we will be pleased to make the necessary corrections in future printings. Thanks are due to the aforementioned photographers and agents for permission to use the materials indicated.

ISBN 978-0-76383-927-7 (Text & CD)
ISBN 978-0-76383-926-0 (Text)

© 2011 by Paradigm Publishing, Inc.
875 Montreal Way
St. Paul, MN 55102
E-mail: educate@emcp.com
Web site: www.emcp.com

Printed in the United States of America

19 18 17 16 15 14 13 12 11 10     2 3 4 5 6 7 8 9 10

# CONTENTS

## CHAPTER 7
# The Internet and the World Wide Web 303

# PREFACE

**F**OR MILLIONS OF PEOPLE WORLDWIDE, the computer and the Internet have become an integral and essential part of life. In the home, we use computers to communicate quickly with family and friends, manage our finances more effectively, enjoy music and games, shop online for products and services, and much more. In the workplace, computers have become an indispensable tool. With them, workers can become more efficient, productive, and creative, and companies can connect almost instantly with suppliers and partners on the other side of the world.

Studying this book will help prepare students for the workplace of today—and tomorrow—in which some level of computer skills is often an essential requirement for employment. Employees who continually try to improve their skills have an advantage over those who do not. Some would even argue that understanding technology has become a survival skill. This book will help students become survivors.

## Textbook Overview

As with the previous editions, the goal of this new edition of *Computers: Understanding Technology* is to introduce students to the key information technology concepts and the vital technical skills that can help improve their personal and professional lives. The book has evolved through various editions with the help of instructors participating in reviews and focus groups. We have used that feedback to create a state-of-the-art computer concepts product that will enhance the teaching and learning experience.

This textbook is offered in three divisions of identical chapter content to match the three most common computer concepts course lengths. The Comprehensive book consists of Chapters 1–15, the Introductory book consists of Chapters 1–9, and the Brief book includes Chapters 1–5. The topic order is as follows:

Chapter 1, Our Digital World
Chapter 2, Input and Processing
Chapter 3, Output and Storage
Chapter 4, System Software
Chapter 5, Application Software
Chapter 6, Telecommunications and Networks
Chapter 7, The Internet and the World Wide Web
Chapter 8, Security Issues and Strategies
Chapter 9, Database and Information Management
Chapter 10, Information Systems
Chapter 11, Electronic Commerce

Chapter 12, Programming Concepts and Languages
Chapter 13, Multimedia and Artificial Intelligence
Chapter 14, Computer Ethics
Chapter 15, Information Technology Careers

**Tech Insight Special Features** To more precisely meet the needs of the varied computer concepts courses across the country, each text contains a set of Tech Insight special features that present essential information on topics of particular interest. Table 1 shows the Tech Insight titles and indicates the book version in which each appears. These succinct overviews appear following the last chapter in the text.

**Additional Application Exercises: Windows and Internet Tutorials** Recognizing the crucial need for students to be able to use Windows efficiently and effectively, we have developed a set of 15 Windows 7 tutorials that teach the core computer management skills. Students can work through the group of tutorials in one sitting, or they can work through them one at a time as the first activity in the end-of-chapter exercises. The Windows 7 Tutorials appear with the six Internet tutorials at the end of the book. All of the tutorials are included in the three versions of the text.

**Table 1 Tech Insight Special Features**

| Tech Insight Title | Comprehensive | Introductory | Brief |
|---|:---:|:---:|:---:|
| Adding Software and Hardware Components to Your PC | | ✔ | ✔ |
| Bioinformatics | ✔ | | |
| Buying and Installing a PC | ✔ | ✔ | ✔ |
| Computer Ethics | | ✔ | ✔ |
| History of Computers Timeline | ✔ | ✔ | |
| The Internet and the World Wide Web | | | ✔ |
| Telecommunications and Networks | | | ✔ |
| Using XML to Share Information | ✔ | | |
| Working with PDF Files | ✔ | ✔ | |

Note: All of the Tech Insight special features are available on the Internet Resource Center at www.emcp.net/CUT4e.

## Chapter Features

Chapters have been designed around a set of engaging elements to help students learn the concepts presented.

**Cyber Scenarios** Cutting-edge developments related to the chapter topic are illustrated in a realistic portrayal of how technology may affect students' lives now and in the near future. These practical scenarios allow students to connect with the concepts that will be covered in more depth in the chapter.

**CyberScenario**

JENNA WINBON IS AWAKENED BY UPBEAT MUSIC playing and her window blinds opening to let in the morning sunshine. The smell of fresh-brewed coffee gradually makes it to her end of the house as she ponders her upcoming day at the office. A computer system called a home information infrastructure manages the MP3 player and stereo system, window blinds, and coffee-

instead of her normal Peachtree Center office.

Opening the door from the utility room to the garage automatically starts Jenna's car and opens the garage door simultaneously. As she backs out of the garage,

**Interesting and Informative Topic Boxes** The intra-chapter topic boxes have been updated for this edition to reflect new technical developments or new information about the subject. All of these boxes expand the text discussion and present high-interest applications of the topic. Chapters contain four to six topic boxes of varying types.

- Hot Spot focuses on wireless technology and the interesting twists, perspectives, and uses of wireless technology and related communications and community-building issues.
- Tech Visionary honors the current drivers and prominent pioneers in IT.
- Cutting Edge showcases hot new technologies.
- Globe Trotting features innovative IT applications worldwide.
- e-THICS highlights ethical issues and situations in IT.

**Expanded Content** Throughout the book, icons appear in the textbook's margins identifying where additional, related content can be found to enrich chapter study. Each chapter is supported by animated, Flash-based Tech Demos on the Encore CD as well as articles and related activities on the Internet Resource Center.

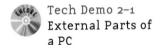 Tech Demo 2-1
External Parts of
a PC

Go to this title's
Internet Resource
Center and read the
article titled "Internet
Social Networks."
www.emcp.net/CUT4e

**On the Horizon** Each chapter ends with a brief overview of some exciting new developments to watch.

## OnThe**Horizon**

**SCIENTISTS, COMPUTER ENGINEERS, AND ENTREPRENEURS OF ALL KINDS** are working feverishly to develop new and improved hardware devices that will make information access faster and easier. After all, much is at stake—the millions and billions of dollars in revenue to be shared by successful individuals and companies. Inventors are also motivated by the great satisfaction that comes with creating something new and better. Several trends are worth watching.

**Chapter Summaries and Key Terms Listings** To help students review the concepts and terminology presented in the text, the chapter summaries include questions and answers that directly relate to the main concepts presented in each chapter. These summaries are also available in an interactive format on the text's Internet Resource Center, hotlinked with corresponding terms and definitions. Key terms are grouped, allowing students to better understand the relationships between the terminology and the larger, organizing concepts in the chapter.

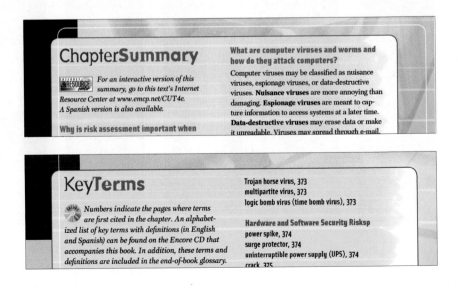

### Chapter**Summary**

*For an interactive version of this summary, go to this text's Internet Resource Center at www.emcp.net/CUT4e. A Spanish version is also available.*

**Why is risk assessment important when**

**What are computer viruses and worms and how do they attack computers?**

Computer viruses may be classified as nuisance viruses, espionage viruses, or data-destructive viruses. **Nuisance viruses** are more annoying than damaging. **Espionage viruses** are meant to capture information to access systems at a later time. **Data-destructive viruses** may erase data or make it unreadable. Viruses may spread through e-mail,

### Key**Terms**

*Numbers indicate the pages where terms are first cited in the chapter. An alphabetized list of key terms with definitions (in English and Spanish) can be found on the Encore CD that accompanies this book. In addition, these terms and definitions are included in the end-of-book glossary.*

Trojan horse virus, 373
multipartite virus, 373
logic bomb virus (time bomb virus), 373

**Hardware and Software Security Risksp**
power spike, 374
surge protector, 374
uninterruptible power supply (UPS), 374
crack 375

**End-of-Chapter Concepts Exercises** As in previous editions, this text includes end-of-chapter exercises that assess the students' comprehension of the chapter content using a variety of approaches to maintain interest, foster creative and critical thinking, and address different learning styles. These exercises are also available on the Internet Resource Center at www.emcp.net/CUT4e along with supplemental information there and on the text's Encore CD. Icons identify where the student can find additional content.

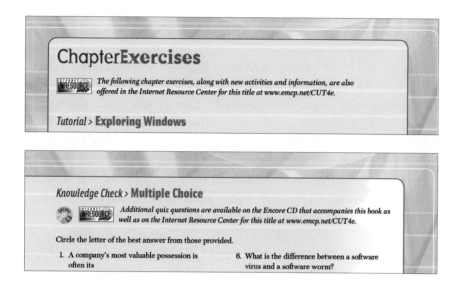

## Student Courseware

Additional content to support the textbook is offered through a multimedia CD, a companion Web site, and hands-on tutorials. An eBook is also available. These ancillaries help address the different learning styles of students.

**Using the Encore CD** The CD packaged with the textbook adds an experiential and interactive dimension to the learning of fundamental computer concepts. For every chapter, the Encore CD offers the following features.

- **Tech Demos:** These brief, animated Flash segments bring key topics to life. To highlight them for the instructor and student, the text includes a margin note and Encore CD icon next to the related chapter discussion.
- **Quizzes:** The Encore CD includes a rich bank of multiple-choice quizzes available in both practice and reported modes. In the practice mode, students receive immediate feedback on each quiz item and a report of his or her total score. In the reported mode, the results are e-mailed to both the student and instructor. Book-level and chapter-specific quizzes are available.
- **Glossary:** Key terms and definitions, with audio support, are combined with related illustrations from the text. The glossary terms and definitions are also available in Spanish.
- **Image Bank:** Illustrations of concepts and processes are accompanied by the related terms and definitions.
- **Key Terms Flash Cards and Acronyms Flash Cards:** Flash cards are a fun way to learn terms and acronyms, and each chapter is supported by this interactive, game-like feature.

Additionally, the Encore CD includes a comprehensive set of computer literacy tutorials called Tech Tutors, which are accessible at any time and within any chapter.

The Encore CD may be used as a preview or as a sequel to each chapter—or both. That is, a student can play each chapter's Flash animations to get an overview of what is taught in the book and then study the text chapter before returning to the CD for its enriching content and interactivity. Or, a student can complete the reading of a chapter and chapter exercises and then work through the corresponding chapter on the CD. Either way, students will benefit from working with this integrated multimedia CD and will find an approach that suits all learning styles.

**Using the Internet Resource Center**  Students will find other useful learning aids on the Internet Resource Center at www.emcp.net/CUT4e. At this site, students can access chapter-specific Lecture and Study Notes documents, PowerPoint presentations, quizzes, interactive chapter summaries (in English and Spanish), terminology crossword puzzles, and key terms and acronyms flash cards. To further address the dynamic and ever-changing nature of computer technology, the site provides additional readings, projects, and activities for each chapter. Icons on the text pages identify articles and activities found on the Internet Resource Center that correspond to chapter content.

**Learning to Use Microsoft Office 2010, Windows, and Internet Explorer**
A CD consisting of 160 tutorials is available for students who want to learn the essentials of Microsoft Office 2010, Windows, and Internet Explorer. Using realistic simulations, which come with audio, students can quickly learn the basic operations of Word, Excel, Access, and PowerPoint 2010 as well as recent versions of Windows and Internet Explorer.

**Studying with an eBook**  For students who prefer studying with an eBook, *Computers: Understanding Technology, Fourth Edition* is available in an electronic form. The Web-based, password-protected eBook features dynamic navigation tools including bookmarking, a linked table of contents, and the ability to jump to a specific page. It also supports helpful study tools such as highlighting and note taking. Through the eBook, students have access to the full Encore CD contents.

## Instructor Resources

The Instructor Resources CD is an all-in-one resource that includes planning resources such as lesson plans (called Lesson Blueprints), teaching suggestions, and sample course syllabi; presentation resources such as lecture notes, student study notes, PowerPoint presentations, and additional discussion questions and enrichment activities; and assessment resources including an overview of available assessment venues, answer keys for end-of-chapter exercises, chapter test banks, and sample midterm and final exams. All of the resources on the Instructor Resources CD are also available on the password-protected instructor section of the Internet Resource Center for this title at www.emcp.net/CUT4e.

The Instructor Resources CD also includes the **EXAM**VIEW® Assessment Suite. Instructors can use the bank of over 1,500 multiple choice, true/false, short answer, and graphics-based items to create customized, Web-based or print tests.

Instructors can use SNAP Web-based Training and Assessment to access banks of concept items for each chapter, or to build new test items. Exams delivered by SNAP over the Web are reported and graded automatically. Tutorials teaching the basics of Office and Windows are also available on the Microsoft® Office 2010 Essential with Windows and Internet Explorer Tutorials CD.

## Acknowledgements and Appreciation

Writing and publishing a book is a complex and expensive task that requires the dedicated efforts of many people. Throughout this project, we authors have had the pleasure and privilege of working closely with the highly skilled and quality-focused professionals at EMC Corporation.

We offer our sincere appreciation to Christine Hurney, Senior Developmental Editor, and Donna Mears, Production Editor, for their diligence and for their many contributions to this book. Their excellent editorial efforts and their attention to detail contributed greatly to the successful completion of this work Working closely with Christine and Donna has been a privilege and a pleasure. A special thanks is in order to Sonja Brown, Editorial Director, for her professional insights and contributions. Also, we thank Sarah Kearin for her work writing the new topic boxes. To the entire staff at Paradigm Publishing, we offer our sincere gratitude.

We are indebted to technical writer and consultant Alec Fehl, whose careful attention to accuracy and relevancy proved invaluable. Thank you to Robertt Neilly for updating the Windows 7 and Internet tutorials.

Our families deserve special credit. Our wives, Edith and Alma, and our children, Cindy and Michael, and Amanda and Keith, were constant sources of love, support, and encouragement. Although we can never repay them for their sacrifices on our behalf, we are truly grateful to each, without whose support we could not have written this book.

**Consultants and Reviewers** We are indebted to three individuals who served as technical consultants and reviewers for the first edition, which provided the solid foundation for this and future editions:

David Laxton, industry consultant, Cincinnati, Ohio
Deborah Merz, technical writer and consultant, West Bloomfield, Michigan
Mary Kelley Weaver, instructor, St. Johns River Community College

Additionally, we thank the instructors and other professionals who participated in shaping the revision plan for this edition. As instructors who teach introductory computer courses, and as practicing professionals who are knowledgeable about the latest computer technologies, they brought a real-world perspective to the project.

Roberta Baber
Fresno City College
Fresno, California

Lynn Bowen
Valdosta Technical College
Valdosta, Georgia

Joy Bukowy
Robeson Community College
Lumberton, North Carolina

John P. Cicero, PhD
Shasta College
Redding, California

Bruce Collins
Davenport University
Holland, Michigan

Reet Cronk, PhD
Harding University
Searcy, Arkansas

Heather Crosthwait
Enersource Hydro Mississauga
Information Systems
Mississauga, Ontario

Marvin Daugherty
Ivy Tech Community College
Indianapolis, Indiana

Joan Davis
Centennial College
Toronto (Scarborough), Ontario

Phillip Davis, PhD
Del Mar College
Corpus Christi, Texas

Angie Davison
Lake Land College
Mattoon, Illinois

Mary Beth Graham
Carroll Community College
Westminster, Maryland

Wade T. Graves, EdD
Grayson County Community College
Denison, Texas

Saeed Molki
South Texas College
McAllen, Texas

William Schlick
Schoolcraft College
Livonia, Michigan

Pam Silvers
Asheville-Buncombe Technical
Community College
Asheville, North Carolina

Joyce Thompson
Lehigh Carbon Community College
Schnecksville, Pennsylvania

Kenneth Weimer
Kellogg Community College
Battle Creek, Michigan

## Dedication

The moment I met the young lady who would later become my wife, I knew that my life would be changed forever. And, it has been. She has been my devoted companion, my closest friend, the mother of our children, and my enduring source of encouragement and inspiration. For her devotion to our family and to so many others to whom she has given so freely of her time and energies, I dedicate this book to my wife, Edith Mizelle Fuller.

—Floyd Fuller

For all the times the kids climbed on the computer or poured juice on the keyboard, for all the times she took care of things while I typed, and for all the times she was understanding and thoughtful, I dedicate this book to my wife, Alma Larson.

—Brian Larson

# CHAPTER 1

# Our Digital World

# CyberScenario

**IT'S 8:30 A.M. AND MARC HANSON'S FLIGHT** has just taken off from Dallas, heading for Chicago's O'Hare International Airport. After the Boeing 767 reaches its cruising altitude, the flight attendant announces that passengers are now permitted to use personal electronic devices, including their computers.

Marc reaches under his seat to retrieve his notebook computer, and a few keystrokes later, his computer is connected to the Internet. Marc logs into his company's network and reviews the sales presentation he will be making today. He makes a few updates and e-mails it to his Chicago contact in preparation for the meeting.

Marc sends an e-mail message to remind his supervisor that he will not be in the office today. He sends another e-mail to Steve Reminger at Teledex Company in Chicago confirming their meeting at 3 p.m. He sends four more messages during the next few minutes, each one to a branch office in another part of the country.

He carefully reviews his investment portfolio by accessing his broker's Web site. Caterpillar is down $0.50, Dell Computer is up $1.25, Microsoft Corporation is up $2.21, and Disney is up $1.13. All in all, not bad! After placing an order to buy 100 more shares of Disney, Marc moves on to check the news.

Marc scans the latest headlines by accessing *USA Today's* Web site. One article announces that a major competitor is having difficulty with its proposed acquisition of a smaller company. From another article,

Marc learns about the latest alternative-fuel vehicles being introduced next year. Before he shuts down his computer, he pays his electric bill and checks the current price of an item he is selling in an online auction.

Returning the laptop to his briefcase, Marc retrieves his smartphone and sends an instant message to Helen Ramirez to notify her of the flight's updated arrival

## Immersed in Digital Technology

Tech Demo 1-1
Digital Lifestyle

Computers and other digital devices permeate our daily lives. High-definition televisions (HDTVs) display amazingly clear and colorful images of sports events, reality TV shows, and other popular programs. Electronic coffeemakers, digital alarm clocks, and cell phones quicken and simplify daily routines. Automobile manufacturers use computerized robots to build cars and trucks. Businesses increasingly rely on electronic mail (e-mail) to communicate internally and with vendors and customers. Electronic freeway information signs and traffic monitor-

Shelly sends a photo of her softball team after a victory while Marc has been traveling. Marc saves the picture on his phone and promises to be at her next game.

Marc's e-mails are among the billions of e-mail messages sent daily throughout North America. The Web sites he accessed are part of the millions of Web sites on the Internet in the year 2007, which has grown exponentially since the World Wide Web's birth less than two decades ago. During the hour and a half it took Marc to fly from Dallas to Chicago, he accomplished the following tasks:

- updated a sales presentation and distributed it for a same-day meeting
- communicated with at least six different people at diverse locations
- reviewed his appointments for the day
- read the latest national and regional news
- checked the day's trading prices of his stock investments and placed a trade
- transferred money from his bank account to the electric company
- checked the status of an auction item
- viewed a photo taken at his daughter's school while he was traveling

In the not too distant future, Marc and millions of other consumers will regularly use the Internet from anywhere, at anytime, using smaller and smaller Internet-enabled devices. Business, household, and personal activities are becoming more accessible from any location through devices that connect through the Internet without wires.

time. She responds that she will meet him upon his arrival at 10:30 a.m. Marc looks for updates to his schedule and sees that after a quick debrief over coffee, it will be time for lunch with Mirax Corporation's purchasing agents, when he will present his company's marketing suggestions. Following the Teledex appointment in the afternoon, his busy day will end with dinner at the Lough Bispo Restaurant on Chicago's North Side before he takes an evening flight back home.

Marc then calls his daughter, Shelly. When she answers, her image appears in color on the small LCD screen of Marc's phone, as does his image on hers.

ing devices help drivers navigate our busy highways and alert drivers to emergencies, such as missing or abducted persons. And some 72 percent of U.S. residents use the Internet from home, school, or some other location, according to a report from the International Telecommunications Union. In today's world, living even a day without some type of digital interaction is highly unlikely for most people. What about you? How digital is your life? Complete the survey in Figure 1-1 to get a sense of the number of digital interactions you have every day. Place a check mark next to each activity you have experienced in the past 24 hours.

Digital coffeemakers offer options for start time, temperature, and even varied flavors for different days of the week.

Cell phones have become so common in everyday life that most people would be lost without them.

ROAD MAY BE
ICY
IN AREAS

Sharing up-to-date information with morning commuters allows drivers to take alternate routes or make other plans.

Like most people, you are probably aware that you interact with electronic devices every day, but perhaps you were surprised by the large number of your digital experiences. The extent to which computers and digital technology drive daily life has led historians to characterize today's world as a "digital world." You know the term *digital* has something to do with computers. But what does the term mean and why is it important?

- driving a car
- tracking appointments on a personal digital assistant (PDA)
- calling or text messaging (also called texting) on a cell phone
- depositing or withdrawing money at an ATM
- working on a desktop computer or laptop
- sending information via a fax machine
- filling up the gas tank in your car
- creating copies with a photocopier
- riding an elevator
- shopping online
- playing video games
- answering a telemarketing call
- manipulating numbers with a calculator
- buying groceries in the self-serve checkout line
- riding on the subway
- retrieving a voice mail message
- snapping a photo on a digital camera or a camera phone
- watching a movie on a DVD player
- cooking with a microwave
- operating an electronically controlled dishwasher
- adjusting an electronic thermostat
- buying food or soda from an electronic vending machine
- entering a locked building with a security card
- purchasing an item with a debit card
- researching airline ticket prices on the Internet
- buying or selling an item on eBay
- downloading music from a Web site

**Figure 1-1  Digital Interaction Survey**
Check all of the activities that you have experienced in the last 24 hours.

## Digital Information

**Digital** refers to a type of electronic signal that is processed, sent, and stored in discrete parts (bits), rather than an analog signal, which is a series of electronic pulses in a continuous wave. These discrete parts are represented by "on" and "off" electrical states, which in turn correspond to the digits 1 (on) and 0 (off). In a computer, this system of 1s and 0s corresponding to on and off electrical currents represents all information. Thus, computers use digital information, and computer technology in general is considered digital technology. You will learn more about this fundamental information technology concept in the chapters that follow, but for now, remember that *digital* refers to information represented by numbers and that all of the interactions listed in the survey in Figure 1-1 used digital information.

Tech Demo 1-2
Analog vs. Digital

Tech Demo 1-3
Digitizing
Information

## Computerized Devices vs. Computers

Digital processing occurs within miniature electrical circuits etched onto a tiny square of silicon (or another material) called a **chip**, and digital cameras, cell phones, electronic coffeemakers, and computers all contain electronic chips.

The first dual-core Itanium processor was released by Intel in July, 2006. Intel and its partners claim the processor increases performance by a factor of two, while reducing power comsumption by approximately 20 percent compared with the previous single-core version.

However, the chips within computerized devices differ considerably from the chips within computers in terms of power and capability, a distinction that separates electronic devices into two broad groups: special-purpose, or embedded computers, and general-purpose computers, or simply computers. The manufacturer has programmed the chip within an **embedded computer** to perform a few specific actions. For example, an embedded chip in a digital camera automatically controls the speed of the camera's lens so the right amount of light enters through the lens. An embedded chip in a bar code scanner reads the bar code on clothing tags and identifies the item and its price. A tiny computerized chip in a digital thermometer determines the body temperature of patients at a medical clinic.

The electronic chips within a **general-purpose computer**, on the other hand, contain programs that allow the user to perform a range of complex processes and calculations. For example, a computer containing a word processing program allows a user to create, edit, print, and save various kinds of documents, including letters, memos, and brochures. A **computer**, therefore, is defined as an electronic device that:

- operates under the control of a set of instructions, called a **program**, that is stored in its memory
- accepts data that a user supplies
- manipulates the data according to the programmed instructions
- produces the results (information)
- stores the results for future use

A digital thermometer is an example of an embedded computer, which contains a chip that the manufacturer programs to perform a specific function.

# The Computer Advantage

Prior to the early 1980s, computers were unknown to the average person. Many people had never even seen a computer, let alone used one. The few computers that existed were relatively large, bulky devices confined to secure computer centers in corporate or government facilities. Referred to as mainframes, these computers were maintenance intensive, requiring special climate-controlled conditions and several full-time operators for each machine. Because the early mainframes were expensive and difficult to operate, usage was restricted to computer programmers and scientists, who used them to perform complex operations, such as processing payrolls and designing sophisticated military weaponry. Other than a few researchers or technicians having security clearances, most employees were prohibited from entering areas where the computer was housed and operated.

Beginning in the early 1980s, the computer world changed dramatically with the introduction of the **microcomputer**, also called the personal computer (PC) because this computer was intended to be operated by an individual user. These relatively small computers were considerably more affordable and much easier to use than their mainframe ancestors. Within a few years, ownership of personal computers became widespread in the workplace, and today, the personal computer is a standard appliance in homes and schools. A 2005 U.S. Census Bureau report stated that, by 2003, 76 percent of U.S. households with school-aged children owned a computer, and 83 percent of children had access to a computer at school. In terms of business spending, the information technology (IT) sector now accounts for more than 50 percent of capital expenditures.

 Tech Demo 1-4, 1-5, and 1-6 History I, II, and III

Today's computers come in a variety of shapes and sizes and differ significantly in computing capability, price, and speed. For example, a powerful business com-

Early mainframe computers, such as the one shown above, were large, bulky devices that were difficult to operate.

puter capable of processing millions of customer records in a few minutes may cost millions of dollars while an office desktop computer used for creating correspondence and budget forecasts may cost less than a thousand dollars. Whatever their size, cost, or power, all computers offer advantages over manual technologies in the following areas:

- speed
- accuracy
- versatility
- storage capabilities
- communications capabilities

## Speed

Computers operate with lightning-like speed, and processing speeds are increasing as computer manufacturers introduce new and improved models. Contemporary personal computers are capable of executing billions of program instructions in one second. Some larger computers, such as supercomputers, can execute trillions of instructions per second, a rate important for processing the huge amounts of data involved in forecasting weather, monitoring space shuttle flights, and managing other data-intensive applications.

## Accuracy

People sometimes blame human errors and mistakes on a computer. In truth, computers are extremely accurate when accurate programs and data are entered and processed. A popular expression among computer professionals is **garbage in, garbage out (GIGO)**, which means that if inaccurate programs and/or data are entered into a computer for processing, the resulting output will also be inaccurate. It is the user's responsibility to make certain that programs and data are entered correctly.

Computers, such as those found on communication satellites, can process information with speed and accuracy.

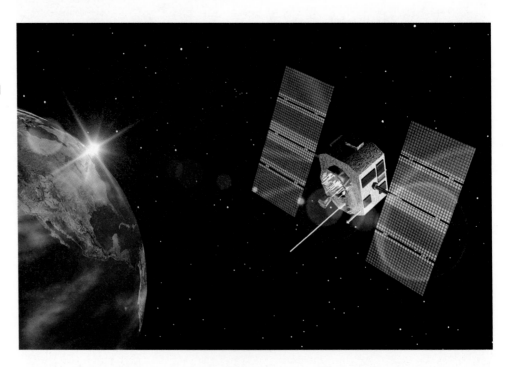

## Versatility

Computers are perhaps the most versatile of all machines or devices. They can perform a variety of personal, business, and scientific applications. Families use computers for entertainment, communications, budgeting, online shopping, completing homework assignments, playing games, and listening to music. Banks conduct money transfers and account withdrawals via computer. Retailers use computers to process sales transactions and to check on the availability of products. Manufacturers can manage their entire production, warehousing, and selling processes with computerized systems. Schools access computers for keeping records, conducting distance-learning classes, scheduling events, and analyzing budgets. Universities, government agencies, hospitals, and scientific organizations conduct life-enhancing research using computers. Perhaps the most ambitious computer-based scientific research of all time is the Human Genome Project, which was completed in April 2003, more than two years ahead of schedule and at a cost considerably lower than originally forecast. This project represented an international effort to sequence the 3 billion DNA (deoxyribonucleic acid) letters in the human genome, which is the collection of gene types that comprises every person. Scientists from all over the world can now access the genome database and use the information to research ways to improve human health and fight disease.

Members of a family may use computers for a varity of purposes, including entertainment, communications, budgeting, online shopping, paying bills, completing homework assignments, viewing and printing photos, playing games, and listening to music.

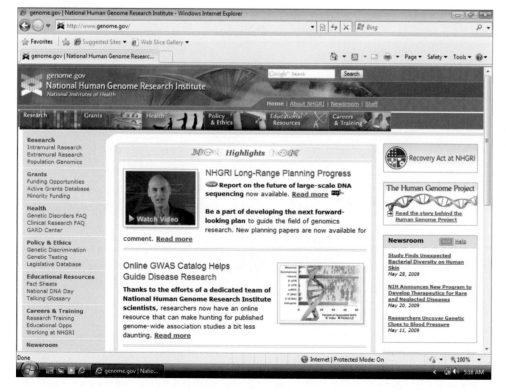

The National Human Genome Research Institute funds genetic and genomic research, studies the related ethics, and provides education to the public and to health professionals.

A flash drive can hold a large amount of data in a very small amount of physical space. Flash drives are portable, allowing users to easily move information from one computer to another.

## Storage

Storage is a defining computer characteristic and is one of the features that revolutionized early computing, for it made computers incredibly flexible. A computer is capable of accepting and storing programs and data. Once a program is stored in the computer, users can access it again and again to process different data. For example, a user repeatedly can access a spreadsheet program such as Microsoft Excel to track budget expenditures and to project possible outcomes if income and expenses change. Computers can store huge amounts of data in comparably tiny physical spaces. For example, one compact disc can store about 109,000 pages of magazine text, and the capacities of internal storage devices are many times larger.

## Communications

Most modern computers contain special equipment and programs that allow them to communicate with other computers through telephone lines, cable connections, and satellites. Computers having this capability are often linked together so users can share programs, data, information, and equipment such as a printer. The structure in which computers are linked together using special programs and equipment is called a **network**, as shown in Figure 1-2. Newer communications technologies allow users to exchange information over wireless networks using wireless devices such as personal digital assistants (PDAs), notebook computers, cell phones, and pagers.

A network can be relatively small or quite large. A **local area network (LAN)** is one confined to a relatively small geographical area, such as a building, factory,

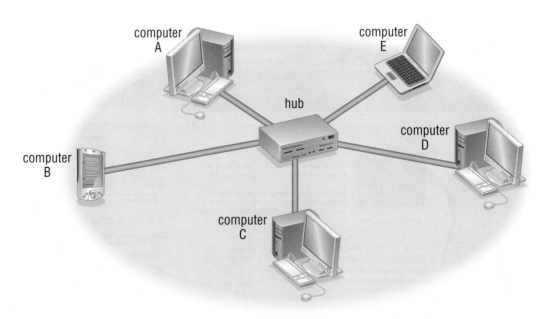

**Figure 1-2  A Network**
This type of network, called a star network, is a collection of computers and devices linked together by software and communications devices and media.

or college campus. A **wide area network (WAN)** links many LANs and might connect a company's manufacturing plants dispersed throughout the United States. Constant, quick connections along with other computer technologies have helped boost productivity for manufacturers such as Timken Company, an industrial bearing maker headquartered in Canton, Ohio. All of its tooling machines are networked, and the factory itself is networked to 76 other company locations in the United States and worldwide. Using digital designs and networked machines, the company can produce a customized bearing product in 15 to 30 minutes, which took half a day using older methods.

**The Internet: A Super Network**   The network you are most likely familiar with is the Internet, which is the world's largest network. The **Internet**, also called the Net, is a worldwide network made up of large and small networks linked together via communications hardware, software, telephone, cable, and satellite systems for the purpose of communicating and sharing information (see Figure 1-3).

In 2005, research firms reported that an exciting milestone was achieved: One billion people around the world were using the Internet for various purposes, including:

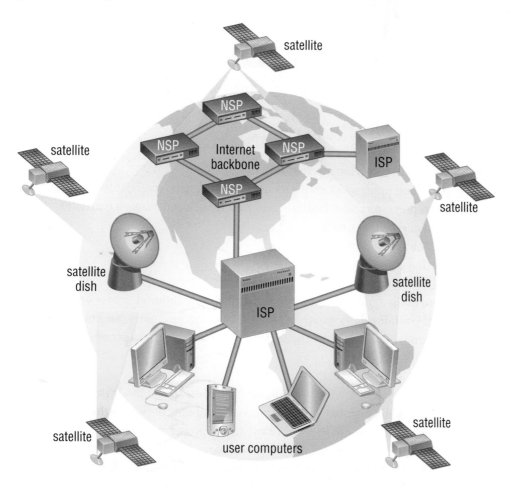

**Figure 1-3  The Internet**
The Internet is a worldwide network of large and small networks linked together via communications hardware, software, and media for the purpose of communicating and sharing information.

An online service such as MSN provides users with Internet access, daily weather reports, stock quotes, and other types of information.

- sending and receiving electronic mail (e-mail)
- researching information, such as weather forecasts, maps, stock quotes, news reports, airline schedules, and newspaper and magazine articles
- buying and selling products and services
- taking online college courses
- accessing entertainment, such as online games and music

There are many online service providers that offer Internet access and provide a portal that contains daily weather reports, stock quotes, news, and other types of information. Users can leave the service provider's portal to access other Web sites of interest.

**The World Wide Web**   A widely used part of the Internet is the **World Wide Web** (**WWW** or the **Web**), a global system of linked computer networks that allows users to move from one site to another by way of programmed links on Web pages. A **Web page** is an electronic document stored on a computer running the Web site. The document may contain text, images, sound, and video, and it may also contain links to other Web pages and other Web sites. Web visitors find information using a **search engine**, which is a software program that locates and retrieves requested information. For example, suppose you entered the topic of "feeding habits of brown bears" into the program's search box. Within moments, the search engine would display a list of information sources on the Web.

A search engine such as Google is a software program that enables a user to search for, locate, and retrieve information available on the World Wide Web.

All network and Internet activities begin with individual computers, and it is at the computer level where the information that drives our economy originates. Understanding the broad steps in the processing of information is key to recognizing the significance of computer technology.

# How Computers Work

Computers are designed to accept data a user enters, process the data according to program instructions, and then output the processed data in a useful form—as information. Note that data and information are not the same thing. Information is a product of a recurring series of events called the information processing cycle.

## Data and Information

**Data** is raw, unorganized facts and figures. By itself, a piece of data may be meaningless. For example, the fact that an employee has worked 40 hours in one week may be useless to the payroll department staff. However, by entering additional data, such as the employee's pay rate, number of exemptions and deductions, and then processing the data, department personnel can generate useful information, including paychecks, earnings statements, and payroll reports. Therefore, **information** is defined as data that has been processed (manipulated, organized, or arranged) in a way that converts it into a useful form. Once created, information can be displayed on a computer screen or printed on paper. It can also be stored for future use, such as for processing periodic payroll reports.

Data entered into a computer can be one type or a combination of two or more of the following types, illustrated in Figure 1-4:

- **Text data** consists of alphabetic letters, numbers, and special characters. These data are typically entered to produce output such as letters, e-mail messages, and reports.
- **Graphic data** consists of still images, including photographs, mathematical charts, and drawings.
- **Audio data** refers to sound, such as voice and music. For example, using a microphone a person can enter a voice message that the computer stores in digitized form. Or, a user can download music from a Web site and listen to the songs over speakers connected to the computer.
- **Video data** refers to moving pictures and images, such as a videoconference, film clip, or full-length movie. For example, a user may record a home movie using a digital video camera. The user then connects the camera to a computer, which plays the video and displays it on the computer screen.

**Figure 1-4 Types of Data Combined to Provide Information**
Combining types of data can improve the level of presentation quality of a message. Text data and graphic data are combined to create a professional business letter (left). Audio data and video data are combined to create a movie (right).

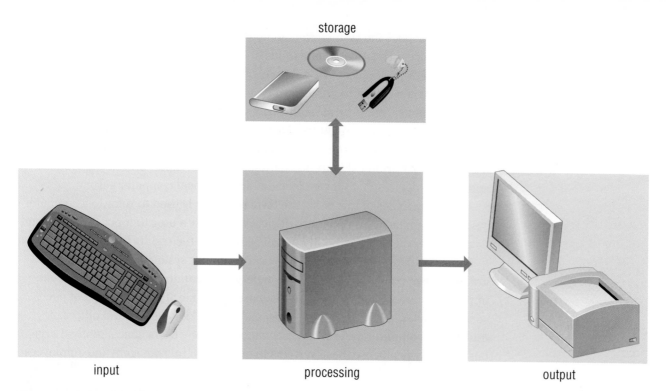

storage

input            processing            output

**Figure 1-5 Information Processing Cycle**
During the information processing cycle, data is entered into a computer, processed, sent as output, and stored (if required for future use).

## The Information Processing Cycle

Using a computer to convert data into useful information is referred to as **information processing** (also called data processing). Processing data into information involves four basic functions: input, processing, output, and storage. During processing, these four functions are often performed sequentially, but not always. The steps of input, processing, output, and storage are collectively known as the **information processing cycle**, which is illustrated in Figure 1-5.

Data entered into a computer is called **input**, which also is the name of the first step in the information processing cycle. Once entered through an input device such as a keyboard or mouse, the data is manipulated, or processed, according to the programmed instructions. **Processing** occurs in a computer's electrical circuits. This results in the creation of information called **output**. Output is then sent to one or more output devices, such as a monitor or a printer. Usually, it is also sent to **storage** media such as a hard drive, compact disc, or flash drive for future use. Information a computer processes can be output in a variety of forms:

- written, or textual form, as in research reports and letters
- numerical form, as in a spreadsheet analysis of a company's finances
- verbal or audio form, as in recorded voice and music
- visual form, such as photos, drawings, and videos

## Computers and Computer Systems

Technically, the term *computer* identifies only the **system unit**, the part of a computer system that processes data and stores the information. A **computer system**, however, includes the system unit along with input devices, output devices, and storage devices. The number and kinds of devices included are a matter of individual need or preference. For example, a buyer shopping for a new personal computer would expect to purchase an entire system, including the system unit, keyboard, mouse, monitor, storage devices, and perhaps a printer. An engineer in a structural design firm might need a more powerful system unit capable of running building design software, along with a larger monitor, a plotter, and a standard document printer. Figure 1-6 shows a variety of input, processing, output, and storage devices that may be included in a personal computer system.

In the remainder of this book, the term *computer* is used to refer to a computer system that includes all necessary devices that allow a user to input programs and data, process the data, output the results, and store the results for future use.

Some computer systems are single-user computer systems whereas others are multi-user computer systems. A **single-user computer system**, as the name implies, can accommodate a single (one) user at a time. This is the type of personal computer system found in homes and in small businesses and offices. A **multi-user computer system** can accommodate many users concurrently. Large businesses typically use these systems to enable several managers and employees to simultaneously access, use, and update information stored in a centrally located system. For example, using computers at their respective workstations, a payroll clerk can access and view an employee's payroll record while a shipping clerk is tracking a customer's shipment. In addition, the users can interact with each other

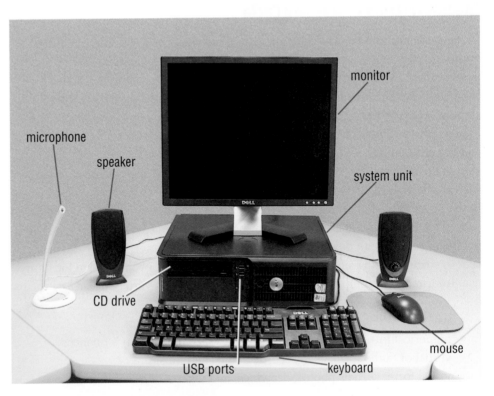

### Figure 1-6  A Personal Computer System
At a minimum, a computer system consists of more than just the system unit. It also includes a monitor, keyboard, mouse, a hard disk drive, videoprocessor, CPU, motherboard, and power supply. Users can add a variety of other input, output, and storage devices.

# Pick-Up the Phone

**THE YEAR 2000 MARKED THE BEGINNING** of the new millennium, a good time to set up resolutions for the future. In that spirit, the United Nations established lofty goals to improve the lives of people around the globe: to diminish poverty and hunger, reduce infant mortality, increase gender equality, fight disease, and establish universal primary education.

Thanks to tremendous innovations in science and communication, solutions seem to be close at hand. The difficulty remains in getting the technology that could be a lifeline to those who need it the most. It may be hard to believe, but one in six people worldwide still does not even have access to a telephone. That means 800,000 villages—1 billion people—are without any type of connection to the outside world.

The gap between developing countries who are being empowered by access to a global network of knowledge and those that are still virtually in the dark is widening. Getting even the remotest village connected will be essential to meeting the United Nations' Millennium Goals.

As then Secretary-General Kofi Annan stated, "...we are truly the first generation with the tools, the knowledge and the resources to meet the committment ... to making the right to development a reality for everyone and to freeing the entire human race from want."

easily and quickly. The main focus of this book is on general-purpose, single-user computers—personal computers—that enable users to complete a variety of computing tasks. These are the computers you will most likely work with in your home, in your school's computer lab, and on the job.

## Components of a Computer System

A computer system consists of two broad categories of components: hardware and software. The combination of hardware and software that makes up a particular system depends on the user's requirements, and given the number of hardware devices and software programs available in the marketplace, users can configure all kinds of possible setups. Manufacturers typically offer a system unit, monitor, and keyboard package, leaving the choice of mouse, printer, and other hardware devices up to the buyer. PC system units are usually preloaded with the Microsoft Windows operating system software plus some basic programs such as a word processing program.

### Computer Hardware: An Overview

**Hardware** includes all of the physical components that make up the system unit plus the other devices connected to it, such as a keyboard or monitor. These connected devices are referred to as **peripheral devices** because they are outside, or peripheral to, the computer. Examples include a keyboard, mouse, camera,

Go to this title's Internet Resource Center and read the article titled "Major Advances in the History of Computing."
www.emcp.net/CUT4e

and printer. Some peripheral devices, such as a monitor and hard disk drive, are essential components of a personal computer system. Hardware devices are grouped into the following categories:

- system unit
- input devices
- output devices
- storage devices
- communications devices

**The System Unit**   The system unit is a relatively small plastic or metal cabinet housing the electronic components that process data into information. Inside the cabinet is the main circuit board, called the **motherboard**, which provides for the installation and connection of other electronic components (see Figure 1-7). Once installed on the motherboard, the components can communicate with each other, thereby allowing data to be processed into information.

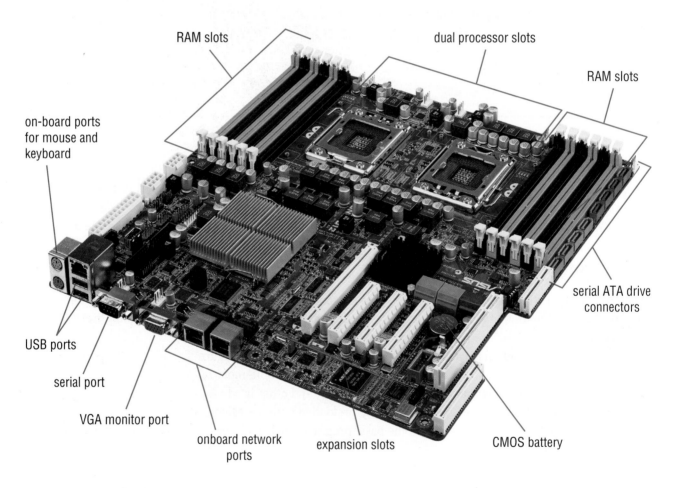

**Figure 1-7  Parts of a Motherboard**
This empty motherboard is ready for the chips and cards to be placed in the open slots.

The microphone, keyboard, and mouse are common types of input devices.

The main components of the motherboard are the **central processing unit (CPU)**, also called the microprocessor (or simply processor), and internal memory. The CPU processor consists of one or more electronic chips that read, interpret, and execute the instructions that operate the computer and perform specific computing tasks. When a program is executed, the processor temporarily stores the program's instructions and the data the instructions need into the computer's memory. **Main memory**, also called primary storage or random access memory (RAM), consists of small electronic chips that provide temporary storage for instructions and data during processing.

Go to this title's Internet Resource Center and read the article titled "Enterprise Computing Trends." www.emcp.net/CUT4e

**Input Devices**   An **input device** is a hardware device that allows users to enter program instructions, data, and commands into a computer. The program or application being used determines the type of input device needed. Common input devices are the keyboard, mouse, and microphone.

**Output Devices**   An **output device** is a device that makes information available to the user. Popular output devices include display screens (monitors), printers, television screens, and speakers. Some output devices, such as a printer, produce output in **hard copy** (tangible) form, such as on paper or plastic. Other output devices, such as a monitor, produce output in **soft copy** (intangible) form that can be viewed, but not physically handled.

Monitors and printers are the most common output devices for personal computers.

Most new personal computers contain a combination CD/DVD drive that can read a variety of CD and DVD formats.

**Storage Devices**   Unlike memory that stores instructions and data temporarily during processing, a **storage device**, often called storage medium or secondary storage, provides for the permanent storage of programs, data, and information. Once stored, information can be retrieved, modified, displayed, imported, exported, copied, or printed.

A storage device itself records programs, data, and/or information to a storage medium and retrieves them from the storage medium. For example, a CD drive (storage device) would write data to a CD (storage medium), and the CD drive would retrieve data from the CD later.

**Communications Devices**   A **communications device** makes it possible for a user to communicate with another computer and to exchange instructions, data, and information with other computer users. The most popular communications device is a **modem**, an electronic device capable of converting computer-readable information into a form that can be transmitted and received over communications systems, such as standard telephone lines. Due to increased speeds, broadband Internet access (via cable and DSL) has been replacing dial-up acess over the past few years. Nielson Online reported that as of June 2008, only 9.5 percent of U.S. Internet users connecting from home had a dial-up connection, while 90.5 percent had a broadband connection.

## Computer Software: An Overview

**Software** consists of programs containing instructions that direct the operation of the computer system and programs that enable users to perform specific applications, such as word processing. The three main classifications of software are system software, application software, and communications software.

**System Software**   **System software** tells the computer how to function and is divided into two categories: operating system software and utility software. The **operating system** is the most important piece of software in a computer system. It contains instructions for starting the computer and coordinates the activities of all hardware devices. Most personal computers use one of the Microsoft Windows operating systems, while Apple Macintosh computers use either the Macintosh operating system or Microsoft Windows.

**Utility software** consists of programs that perform administrative tasks, such as checking the computer's components to determine whether each is working properly, managing disk drives and printers, and checking for computer viruses.

Macintosh OS X is the most common operating system for the Macintosh platform.

**Application Software**   **Application software** consists of programs that perform specific tasks, such as word processing, spreadsheet preparation, database searching, and slide show presentation. Thousands of commercially prepared application programs are currently available for managing personal and business activities.

**Communications Software**   **Communications software** makes it possible for a computer to transmit and receive information to and from other computers. To communicate over the Internet, a user needs an account with an **Internet service provider (ISP)**, a company that has a permanent connection to the Internet and

Windows Vista is an operating system that can be used on the PC platform.

## INVENTOR OF THE FIRST COMPUTER
# Konrad Zuse

**MANY SCHOLARLY SOURCES CREDIT** Howard Aiken and his team of researchers for building the first computer in 1944. American researchers such as Aiken would find out only after World War II ended that a German engineer had finished building a computer almost three years ahead of them. What took a *team* of researchers in the United States to accomplish was finished three years earlier by one man named Konrad Zuse. Most researchers were unaware of his achievements for many years due to the poor communication between Germany and the rest of world. This confused the issue of where and by whom the first computer was actually built. Now most scholars agree that Zuse's Z3 was the first reliable, freely programmable computer based on binary floating-point number and switching systems. Essentially, the world's first computer!

Zuse was born June 22, 1910, in Berlin, Germany, and graduated with a degree in civil engineering from the Technical University of Berlin in 1935. His distaste of the routine, but complex, calculations he encountered as an engineering student led him to dream of a machine capable of automatic calculation.

In 1938 he quit his job with the Henschel aircraft factory and moved in with his parents so he could work full time on creating his dream machine. In their living room he first built the Z1, a prototype for the Z3. The Z1 was a binary, electrically driven mechanical calculator that used thin metal sheets instead of relays. The method of storing data on metal sheets was entirely novel and considerably cheaper than relays. The only electrical unit was a small engine used to provide 1 Hertz.

From the beginning, Zuse believed that computers should be freely programmable. He also realized they should work in a binary number system. This would allow binary switching elements to run the whole computer. This semi-logarithmic mechanism allowed the machine to compute very small and large numbers with precision. He also developed a punch tape memory to accompany these systems. These tools were all used in the Z1, leading to a very sophisticated machine. The Z3 used generally the same architecture as the Z1, but instead of punch-tape-controlled memory it used electronic relays, which are much more reliable.

The Z3 utilized the binary number system and could perform floating-point arithmetic at a time when the rest of the world was still speculating about it being theoretically possible. He also started a company in 1941 called Zuse-Ingenierbüro Hopferau and created the Z4, the first commercially sold computer, beating the commercial Harvard Mark I to market by five months. The Z4 was a fully functional, automatic, digital computer.

In 1986, Zuse decided to rebuild the Z1. He was 77 when he started, and the project ran from 1987 to 1989. The first Z1 was financed by Zuse, his family, and his friends. The reconstruction project required about 800,000 Deutsche Marks; a group of companies interested in the project financed it. The replica is now on display in the Museum for Transport and Technology in Berlin, Germany. Zuse died December 18, 1995, but left behind a world reshaped by his innovations.

provides temporary access to individuals and others, usually for a fee. Some ISPs provide communication software that is installed on a subscriber's computer to enable the user to send and receive electronic mail messages to other similarly equipped computers. The software also provides access to the massive storehouse of information on the Internet and the World Wide Web. Other ISPs allow subscribers to simply use standard e-mail software and a **Web browser**, a special program for viewing Web pages, to accomplish the same functions.

## Categories of Computers

Go to this title's Internet Resource Center and read the article titled "Enterprise vs. Personal Computing." www.emcp.net/CUT4e

Rapid advances in computer technology often blur the differences among types of computers, and industry professionals may disagree on how computers should be categorized. Typically, they use criteria based on differences in usage, size, speed, processing capabilities, and price, resulting in the categories named in Table 1-1:

- personal computers
- handheld computers
- workstations
- midrange servers
- mainframe computers
- supercomputers

Note, however, that personal computers and midrange servers both may be used for the same purpose in networking and that the processing capabilities

**Table 1-1  Categories of Computers**

| Category | Size | Instructions Executed per Second | Number of Accommodated Users | Approximate Price Range |
|---|---|---|---|---|
| personal computer | fits on a desk, in a briefcase, on a laptop, or is worn | 600 million to about 3 billion, or more | a single user, or a part of a network | a few hundred to thousands of dollars |
| handheld computer | fits in hand(s); some may be carried in a pocket | depending on device, a few hundred | a single user, or a part of a network | depending on the model, $99 to several hundred dollars |
| workstation | similar to a desktop PC, but larger and more powerful | depending on the type, 3 to 5 billion | a single user, or a part of a network | a few thousand up to several thousands of dollars |
| midrange server | fits into a large cabinet or a small room | billions of instructions | hundreds of users concurrently | $5,000 to hundreds of thousands of dollars |
| large server or mainframe computer | with needed equipment, occupies a partial or full room | billions of instructions | hundreds or thousands of users concurrently | several thousands up to millions of dollars |
| supercomputer | with equipment, occupies a full room | trillions of instructions | thousands of users concurrently | several million dollars |

# Nano City

**INDIA'S ECONOMY IS ON FIRE. IT IS SECOND ONLY TO CHINA** in growth and is set to become one of the largest markets in the world. The cities of Hyderabad and Bangalore have evolved into Eastern-version Silicon Valleys, but unplanned growth has stunted their ability to evolve into world-class technological centers. Now a native son has set his sights on creating a technological Oz from the ground up.

Sabeer Bhatia, the founder of Hotmail, will be overseeing the creation of a planned city offering world-class infrastructure, the highest level of Internet connectivity, and all the high-tech bells and whistles needed to attract and nurture entrepreneurs, technology workers, venture capitalists, and world-class educational research institutes.

Because nanotechnology represents the future of IT and biotechnology, the techno-metropolis has been dubbed "Nano City." Located in Haryana, near New Delhi, Nano City is estimated to cost $2.5 billion, primarily financed by the state government.

Bhatia realizes that it may take up to fifteen years before any quality research and products come out of Nano City, but he has big dreams for its future. He predicts that Nano City will someday have not just the highest per capita income of any city in India, but of any city in the world.

among the different groups may overlap. Handheld computers are given their own category, although technically they are a subset of personal computers. Their growing market and importance for business and home users warrants treating them as a separate category.

Go to this title's Internet Resource Center and read the article titled "Continuing Evolution of Personal Computing Technology." www.emcp.net/CUT4e

## Personal Computers

A **personal computer (PC)** is a self-contained computer capable of input, processing, output, and storage. A personal computer must have at least one input device, one storage device, one output device, a processor, and memory. The processor, or microprocessor, is contained on a single chip. Recall that the chip is a thin piece of silicon containing electrical circuitry. About the size of a postage stamp, the processor chip serves as the computer's central processing unit (CPU), performing calculations and processing data. Think of the CPU as the "brain" of the computer. The three major groups of PCs are desktop computers, portable computers, and handheld computers.

**Desktop Computers** A **desktop computer** is a PC designed to allow the system unit, input devices, output devices, and other connected devices to fit on top of, beside, or under a user's desk or a table. This type of computer may be used in the home, a home office, a library, or a corporate setting. Desktop computers are

A desktop computer, as the name suggests, is designed to fit on top of a user's work area. Users can place tower-type system units on the floor.

typically connected to a network (or an Internet connection) with cables. Wires or cables also connect keyboards, monitors, speakers, printers, and other peripheral devices to the system unit.

Although wires and cables are likely to be a feature of the computer world for some time to come, newer computing technologies that communicate wirelessly, without physical connections, increasingly are replacing them. The mobility of today's workforce and the need for Internet access anytime, anywhere have driven the demand for portable computers.

**Portable Computers**   A **portable computer** is a personal computer that is small enough to be moved around easily. As its name suggests, a **laptop computer** can fit comfortably on the lap. As laptop computers have decreased in size, this type of computer is now more commonly referred to as a **notebook computer**.

One type of portable computer, a netbook, is offered as a low-cost alternative to a full notebook. A **netbook** is smaller and has less power than a full-size notebook with its main purpose being e-mail and Internet access.

In 1989, GRID Systems released the first commercially available tablet-style portable computer, which has evolved into the current-day **tablet PC**. A tablet PC has a liquid crystal display (LCD) screen on which the user can write using a special-purpose pen, or **stylus**. The handwriting is digitized, and the tablet PC can convert it to standard text or it can remain as handwritten text. Tablet PCs also typically have a

A notebook computer is a portable computer designed for mobile users, people who frequently move about in their work.

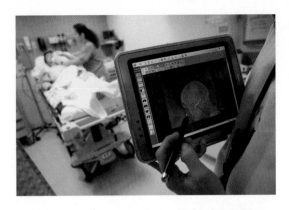

A tablet PC is a type of notebook computer that has a liquid crystal display (LCD) screen on which the user can write using a special-purpose pen, or stylus.

keyboard and/or a mouse. Tablet PCs rely on **digital ink technology**, where a digitizer (a grid of tiny wires) is laid under or over an LCD screen to create a magnetic field that can capture the movement of the special-purpose pen and record the movement on the LCD screen. The effect is like writing on paper with liquid ink. Once captured, the digitized information can be entered into a computer for processing. In the past, tablet PCs use a special operating system designed for tablet PC technology, such as Microsoft Windows Vista includes tablet PC functionality.

Another type of portable computer, the **wearable computer**, is in its early stages. As the name implies, a wearable computer is worn somewhere on the body, thereby providing a user with access to mobile computing capabilities and information via the Internet. Futurists predict that wearable computers may be incorporated into clothing items such as the Java Jacket invented in 2000 by Doug Sutherland, a staff engineer at Sun Microsystems. His jacket computer lets him monitor his e-mail, adjust the water temperature in his aquarium, and operate the lights at his home. A six-button keypad is embedded in the cuff.

A wearable computer, such as this portable eyewear viewer, allows for hands-free computing capability.

Cutting Edge

# A Computer in Your Eye

**HAVE YOU EVER THOUGHT** about what super power you would want to have, if such a thing were possible? If bionic eyesight tops your list, it may be closer to reality than you think, thanks to engineers at the University of Washington in Seattle. The team of researchers is developing an electronic contact lens that, when completed, could have a major impact on both the medical and computer technology industries.

The lens is still in its early stages, but the team has developed a prototype with an electronic circuit and red light-emitting diodes (LEDs). Although the prototype is not yet functional, its creation represents a breakthrough for the engineers, who eventually hope to outfit each lens with several types of

circuits and antennas, hundreds of LEDs, and a wireless signal. Wearers of the lens would use it like a regular computer, but the images would appear in front of the eye rather than on a traditional screen.

As for its medical capabilities, the lens would use the biomarkers present on the surface of the eye to monitor how the body's systems are functioning and transmit the information directly to doctors. This could lead to quicker and more accurate diagnoses and greatly reduce the need to take blood samples.

While the design of the lens is still far from completion, researchers are moving forward—they are currently studying how to power and mass produce the device.

Zion Lennox

**Handheld Computers**  Even smaller personal computers can fit into the hand. This type of computer is known as a **handheld computer**, also called a handheld, pocket PC, or palmtop. The display and keyboard of this type of computer is quite small due to space limitations. Some handheld computers contain chips in which both programs and data are stored, eliminating the need for disk drives.

Handheld computers are popular with business travelers. Once back in the office, a user can connect a handheld computer to a larger computer for exchanging information. In recent years a type of handheld computer called a **personal digital assistant (PDA)** has become widely used. With a PDA, a user can perform calculations, keep track of schedules, make appointments, and write memos. Some PDAs use wireless transmitting technology (in the form of radio waves), which allows Internet access from almost any location.

A handheld computer is small enough to fit in the palm of a user's hand.

# Fly-by-Wireless Technology

**ENGINEERS IN PORTUGAL** have successfully carried out test flights of the AIVA, an aircraft that, when complete, will rely entirely on a wireless network to connect its engines, navigation system, and onboard computers. The unmanned, nine-foot-long prototype uses Bluetooth technology to send messages between its critical systems. Older aircraft use mechanical links and cables to connect components, but the "fly-by-wireless" approach will allow planes to use less power and be lighter in weight.

Number one for the engineers is to make the wireless aircraft safe from electromagnetic interference or jamming caused by chance or by terrorist design. The world will probably see wireless used for brakes and steering in cars long before it is fine-tuned enough to meet the high standards of aviation regulations and nervous fliers.

A variety of Internet-enabled devices allows users to access the Internet, send and receive e-mail messages, and browse the World Wide Web.

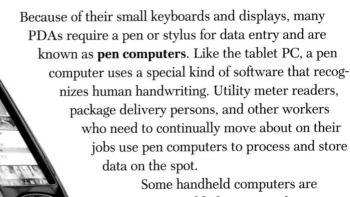

Because of their small keyboards and displays, many PDAs require a pen or stylus for data entry and are known as **pen computers**. Like the tablet PC, a pen computer uses a special kind of software that recognizes human handwriting. Utility meter readers, package delivery persons, and other workers who need to continually move about on their jobs use pen computers to process and store data on the spot.

Some handheld computers are Internet-enabled, meaning they can access the Internet without wire connections. For example, a **smartphone** is a cell phone that connects to the Internet to allow users to transmit and receive e-mail messages, send text messages and pictures, and browse through Web sites on the phone display screen. Some PDAs with similar Internet capabilities also have built-in phone capabilities. The similar capabilities of multifunction PDAs and smartphones illustrate the convergence that is occurring as different types of devices take advantage of Internet technology.

## Workstations

Workstations resemble desktop personal computers but provide users with more processing power and greater capability. A **workstation** is a high-performance single-user computer with advanced input, output, and storage components that can be networked with other workstations and larger computers.

A workstation is a high-performance, single-user computer with advanced input, output, and storage components that can be networked with other workstations and larger computers.

Workstations are typically used for complex applications that require considerable computing power and high-quality graphics resolution, such as computer-aided design (CAD), computer-assisted manufacturing (CAM), desktop publishing, and software development. Workstations generally come with large high-resolution graphics displays, built-in network capability, and a high-density storage device. Like personal computers, workstations can serve as single-user computers. However, they are typically linked to a network and have access to larger computers, often midrange servers or mainframes.

## Midrange Servers

Linked computers are typically connected to a larger and more powerful computer called a **network server**, sometimes referred to as the host computer. Although the size and capacity of network servers vary considerably, most are midrange rather than large mainframe computers (discussed later). Sun Microsystems, Inc., and Hewlett-Packard Corporation are leading manufacturers of servers.

A **midrange server**, formerly known as a minicomputer, is a powerful computer capable of accommodating hundreds of client computers or terminals (users) at the same time. Users can access a server through a terminal or a personal computer. A **terminal** consists of only a monitor and keyboard, with no processing capability of its own. Because it has no processing power and must rely on the processing power of another computer, terminals are often referred to as dumb terminals. Midrange servers are widely used in networks to provide users with computing capability and other resources available through the network, such as Internet access, software, data, printers, scanners, and other peripherals.

## COFOUNDERS OF HEWLETT-PACKARD CORPORATION
# William Hewlett and David Packard

**FEW INDIVIDUALS, IF ANY,** have had a greater impact on the computer industry than William Hewlett and David Packard. The business they founded together in Hewlett's garage in 1939 spawned the California high-tech corridor that became known as Silicon Valley. The business was the Hewlett-Packard Corporation, which designs and builds a variety of state-of-the-art computer products, perhaps the best-known being computers and printers. Today, a visitor to almost any computer store will quickly spot Hewlett-Packard products ranging from electronic calculators to Web servers and systems. The "Hewlett" name appears first in the corporate name and on HP products as the result of a coin toss when the two men formed their original partnership.

Hewlett was born May 20, 1913, in Ann Arbor, Michigan. Packard was born September 7, 1912, in Pueblo, Colorado. Both attended Stanford University and were awarded bachelor of arts degrees in 1934. Packard stayed at Stanford to earn a master's degree in electrical engineering, while Hewlett received his master's in electrical engineering at the Massachusetts Institute of Technology.

HP's first product was a resistance-capacitance audio oscillator based on a design developed by Hewlett when he was a graduate student. This first product was sold to Walt Disney, who used eight of them in the production of *Fantasia*. The company's first "plant" was a small garage in Palo Alto, California, with an initial capital investment of $538.

Through the years, both Hewlett and Packard held various corporate offices and government positions and also served as trustees on corporate and college boards. Each received numerous awards both in this country and abroad. In 1993, Packard retired as chairman of the board at Hewlett-Packard Corporation at which time he was named Chairman Emeritus, a title he held until his death in 1996. Hewlett served as company president and vice-chairman of the board and was named Director Emeritus in 1987. He died in July 2000 at the age of 87.

Both men leave behind a remarkable legacy of technological innovation and business strategy. Together they built a company known worldwide for innovation and for computer products that, through the years, have been models widely envied among computer engineers.

William Hewlett (left) and David Packard

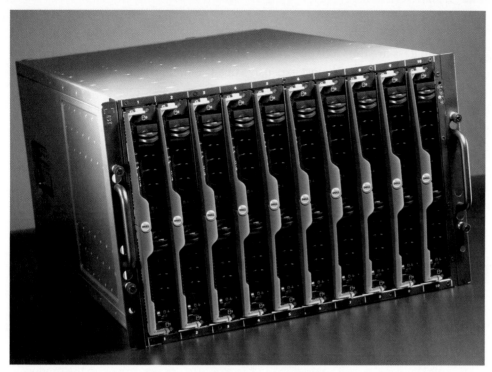

A midrange server is a powerful computer that can accommodate (serve) multiple users in a network. Midrange servers come in a variety of shapes and sizes, but even the smallest ones are several times more powerful than a personal computer.

## Mainframe Computers

In a small business environment, a personal computer can be used as a server. Large businesses needing more powerful servers may use mainframe computers. Larger, more powerful, and more expensive than midrange servers, a **mainframe computer** is capable of accommodating hundreds of network users performing different computing tasks. A mainframe's internal storage can handle hundreds of millions of characters. Mainframe applications are often large and complex. These computers are useful for dealing with large, ever-changing collections of data that can be accessed by many users simultaneously. Like midrange servers, a mainframe computer can also function as a network server. Government agencies, banks, universities, and insurance companies use mainframes to handle millions of transactions each day.

A mainframe computer is a large, powerful, and expensive computer system that can accommodate multiple users at the same time. Mainframes and midrange servers are differentiated by their processing capabilities.

## Supercomputers

Supercomputers are the Goliaths of the computer industry. A **supercomputer** is the fastest, most powerful, and most expensive of all computers. Many are capable of performing trillions of calculations in a single second. Performing the same number of calculations on a handheld calculator would take a person two million years.

Supercomputer designers achieve stunning calculation speeds by joining hundreds of separate microprocessors. Many of the machines provide enough disk storage capacity for hundreds of terabytes of data (1 **terabyte** is the equivalent of 1 trillion alphabet letters, numbers, or special characters). In a move to expand supercomputing into the realm of the unimaginable, IBM continues developing the BlueGene supercomputers. BlueGene/L, currently the fastest computer in the world, processes at a peak speed of 596 teraflops. (A **teraflop** equals about 1 trillion calculations per second.) BlueGene/L and BlueGene/P hold the number 4 and number 5 positions respectively in the Top500 supercomputer list, announced in November 2008 by Top500.org. The next system, BlueGene/Q, is targeted for speeds of 3 petaflops. (A **petaflop** is equilivant to 1 quadrillion calculations per second.) Primary applications include weather forecasting, comparing DNA sequences, creating artificially intelligent robots, and performing financial analyses.

Supercomputers are the world's fastest, most powerful, and most expensive computers, capable of processing huge amounts of data quickly and accommodating thousands of users at the same time. IBM's BlueGene supercomputer was completed in 2005 and is at the top of the TOP500 supercomputer list.

# OnThe**Horizon**

**COMPUTERS, NETWORKS, THE INTERNET, AND THE WEB** are unquestionably among the most important technological developments in history. Cell phones, wireless personal digital assistants, and the use of the Internet for communications are becoming commonplace. But what about the future? Where is computing technology heading? Social thinkers, futurists, and computer experts may not agree on specific predictions, but their thoughts tend to converge in the area of technology trends we can expect to occur in the first decade of the twenty-first century.

## Embedded Computers Everywhere

The rapid increase in embedded computers in all areas of personal and work life will continue. Consumers will be able to scan foods and other types of products embedded with special chips to get information on product content, age, and freshness. Before long, every citizen will probably carry a small plastic card housing a tiny microchip that contains complete medical, credit, military, and driving records. Many more "smart highways" embedded with millions of tiny sensors will alleviate driving worries because they will guide cars speeding along at 120 mph, all the time aware of surrounding traffic.

Futurists predict that before long, people will carry a "personal history" card embedded with a microchip that contains one's medical, credit, military, and driving records.

## On-Demand Computing

Some computer industry leaders, including strategists at IBM and American Express, contend that information technology is maturing and entering a phase in which corporations will buy computing resources the way they purchase utilities—paying only for as much as they use. No doubt the downturn in IT spending in the early 2000s helped pave the way for this buy-as-you-go approach, but the ready availability of computing resources over the Internet has also played a role. Called "on-demand computing," the trend means reduced fixed costs and greater flexibility for businesses.

## Convergence

Convergence is the combining of separate technologies into a single package, resulting in a product featuring all the benefits of the individual technologies as well as additional benefits derived from the merger of the component technologies. The trend towards convergence in computer technologies is driven by companies eager to attract customers by offering products with novel features and one-stop shopping.

The Voice over Internet Protocol (VoIP) network known as Skype offers a perfect example of the trend toward convergence in computer technologies. When Skype first appeared it offered computer-to-computer telephony using a peer-to-peer networking arrangement. Since its debut, Skype has rapidly incorporated different technologies in order to offer its users a number of additional features, including video calls and conferencing, group chats, SMS, call forwarding, and the ability to call ordinary telephones. Convergence has allowed Skype to continue to attract customers and maintain its status as the leading VoIP network. You can expect to see similar examples in the coming years as companies pursue convergence to produce more feature-laden products.

## Faster Communication and a Shrinking Global Community

Within the present decade, almost-instant Internet connections will become the norm throughout the United States and worldwide, allowing information to be accessed in fractions of a second. Broadband penetration to U.S. households is predicted to exceed 77% by 2012, with the rate of growth increasing rapidly. This rapid growth is not limited to the U.S.—China's broadband connectivity growth rate is now twice that of the U.S.

Faster Internet connections affect the way we use the Internet. High-speed Internet facilitates synchronous (real-time) distance eduction through the Internet, now frequently known as online learning. Within the next 10 years one expert has predicted that the number of college students taking courses online will increase from the current 7% to 25%.

High-speed Internet connections will increase the number of online shoppers as well. Experts predict that by the year 2010, the dollar amount of online shopping will represent more than 40 percent of all sales.

Eventually almost everyone in the world will have access to high-speed Internet. For the twenty-first century, it is safe to say that *virtually* anything is possible.

# Chapter**Summary**

 *For an interactive version of this summary, go to this text's Internet Resource Center at www.emcp.net/CUT4e. A Spanish version is also available.*

## How has digital technology infiltrated your daily life?

We are living in a **digital** world in which computer technology increasingly powers the devices of daily life, including high-definition televisions (HDTVs), microwave ovens, watches, cell phones, and automobiles. Embedded chips, computers, networks, and the Internet and World Wide Web enable us to communicate globally. No digital device has exerted a greater impact on our lives than computers. A **computer** is an electronic device that operates under the control of programmed instructions stored in its memory, accepting data (input) that is manipulated (processed) according to the instructions and output as information, which may be stored for future use.

## What advantages do computers offer?

Computers offer advantages in the areas of speed, accuracy, versatility, storage, and communications. As a result, they are widely used in homes, schools, the workplace, and in society for communicating, managing finances, analyzing data, planning, researching, and for hundreds of other purposes and applications. The **Internet** and the **World Wide Web**, in which networks of computers around the world are linked together, continue to play a dominant role in all areas of human activity.

## How do computers convert data into useful information?

**Data** is raw, unorganized facts and figures. Data entered into a computer consists of one or more of the following types: **text**, **graphic**, **audio**, and **video**. **Information** is data that has been processed (manipulated, organized, or arranged) in a way that converts the data into useful forms.

Using a computer to convert data into useful information is called **information processing** (also called data processing). The **information processing cycle** involves the actions of **input**, **processing**, **output**, and **storage**.

## What is the difference between a computer and a computer system?

The term *computer* identifies only the **system unit**, the part of a computer system that processes data into information. A **computer system** includes the system unit along with input, output, storage, and communications devices.

## What are the primary components of a computer system?

Computer system components can be divided into two broad groups: hardware and software. **Hardware** includes all of the physical components of the computer and the **peripheral devices** connected to it. The main hardware components are the **system unit**, **input devices**, **output devices**, **storage devices**, and **communications devices**.

   **Software** consists of programs containing instructions that direct the operation of the computer system and programs that enable users to perform specific applications. The main types of software are **system software**, consisting of the **operating system** and **utility software**; **application software**; and **communications software**.

## What are the basic categories of computers and their distinguishing characteristics?

A **personal computer** is a self-contained computer capable of input, processing, output, and storage. A **handheld computer** fits comfortably in a user's hand. A **workstation** is a high-performance single-user computer with advanced input, output, and storage components that can be networked with other workstations and larger computers. A **midrange server**, is a powerful computer capable of accommodating hundreds of client computers or terminals (users) at the same time. A **mainframe computer** is capable of accommodating hundreds of network users

performing different computing tasks. A **supercomputer** is the fastest, most powerful, and most expensive of all computers.

# Key Terms

*Numbers indicate the pages where terms are first cited in the chapter. An alphabetized list of key terms with definitions (in English and Spanish) can be found on the Encore CD that accompanies this book. In addition, these terms and definitions are included in the end-of-book glossary.*

# Chapter**Exercises**

 *The following chapter exercises, along with new activities and information, are also offered in the Internet Resource Center for this title at www.emcp.net/CUT4e.*

## *Tutorial >* **Exploring Windows**

Tutorial 1 demonstrates how to start up a Windows-based PC and log in with a user name, if required. It also explains the proper way to shut down the PC to avoid data loss and file corruption. (See the Exploring Windows tutorials section at the end of the book.)

## *Expanding Your Knowledge >* **Articles and Activities**

*Visit the Internet Resource Center for this title at www.emcp.net/CUT4e, read the articles related to this chapter, and complete the corresponding activities. The article titles include:*

- Topic 1-1: Major Advances in the History of Computing
- Topic 1-2: Enterprise Computing Trends
- Topic 1-3: Enterprise vs. Personal Computing
- Topic 1-4: Continuing Evolution of Personal Computing Technology

## Terms Check > **Matching**

 *For additional practice, go to the Internet Resource Center for this title at www.emcp.net/CUT4e for a chapter crossword puzzle.*

Write the letter of the correct answer on the line before each numbered item.

a. network
b. Web page
c. Internet
d. data
e. software
f. personal computer
g. information
h. computer
i. operating system
j. hardware

_____ 1. A collection of raw, unorganized content in the form of words, numbers, sounds, or images.

_____ 2. A worldwide network of computers linked together via communications software and media for the purpose of sharing information.

_____ 3. Data that is organized to be meaningful and potentially useful.

_____ 4. The most important piece of software in a personal computer system.

_____ 5. An electronic document stored at a location on the Web.

_____ 6. A computer designed for use by a single individual and capable of performing its own input, processing, output, and storage.

_____ 7. Programs containing instructions that direct the operation of the computer system and the documentation that explains how to use the programs.

_____ 8. A computer's physical components and devices.

_____ 9. An electronic device that accepts input (programs and data), processes the data into information, stores programs and information, and delivers output (information) to users.

_____ 10. A group of two or more computers, software, and other devices connected by means of one or more communications media.

## Technology Illustrated > **Identify the Process**

What process is illustrated in this drawing? Identify the process and write a paragraph describing it.

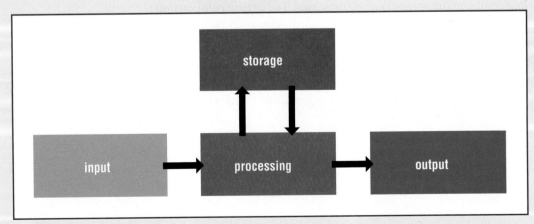

## Knowledge Check > **Multiple Choice**

  *Additional quiz questions are available on the Encore CD that accompanies this book as well as on the Internet Resource Center for this title at www.emcp.net/CUT4e.*

Circle the letter of the best answer from those provided.

1. A small electronic chip a manufacturer programs for use in another product, such as a digital camera or microwave oven, is called a(n)
   a. programmed chip.
   b. embedded chip.
   c. component chip.
   d. storage chip.

2. The usefulness of computers can be attributed to their speed, accuracy, versatility, reliability, storage, and
   a. communications capabilities.
   b. peripheral components.
   c. decreasing prices.
   d. connectability.

3. Technologies that consist of two or more computers, devices, and software connected by means of one or more communications media, such as telephone lines, are called
   a. computers.
   b. communications.
   c. information processing.
   d. networks.

4. A self-contained computer capable of performing its own input, processing, output, and storage is called a(n)
   a. embedded computer.
   b. digital chip.
   c. dual-purpose processor.
   d. personal computer.

5. A computer component contained on a single chip, or thin piece of silicon containing electrical circuitry, and serving as the computer's central processing unit is called a
   a. wired component.
   b. silicon chip.
   c. microprocessor.
   d. circuit chip.

6. The fastest, most powerful, and most expensive of all computers is the
   a. personal computer.
   b. supercomputer.
   c. mainframe computer.
   d. midrange server.

7. Data that has been processed into a useful form is called
   a. digital data.
   b. input.
   c. information.
   d. output.

8. According to this chapter's Cyber Scenario, which of the following activities did Marc perform using his smartphone?
   a. sending an instant message
   b. buying stock
   c. reading news headlines
   d. receiving a photo

9. The main circuit board inside the cabinet of a personal computer that provides for the installation and connection of other electronic components is the
   a. modem.
   b. secondary circuit board.
   c. motherboard.
   d. attachment board.

10. The most important piece of software in a computer system is the
    a. operating system.
    b. application software.
    c. utility software.
    d. communications software.

## *Things That Think* > **Brainstorming New Uses**

In groups or individually, contemplate the following questions and develop as many answers as you can.

1. Futurists hold that computers will be everywhere. For example, bridges will have computers that will alert city planners when part of a bridge is weakening or too stressed and in need of repair. What other objects can you think of that should have the same type of warning or notice capability built into the device?

2. Many futurists claim that we will be wearing computers in the future. What workplace dilemmas, problems, or limitations could be addressed if we start wearing computers that are capable of collecting and analyzing data (tracking inventory, for example)?

3. Computer literacy is extremely important as the use of computers has become commonplace in many occupations. What are some examples of how computers are used in your field of study or future career?

## *Key Principles* > **Completion**

Fill in the blanks with the appropriate words or phrases.

1. The term _____ refers to information represented by the numbers 1 (on) and 0 (off).

2. In a personal computer, the term *computer* identifies only the _____ , the part of a computer system that processes data into information.

3. A(n) _____ , also called the host computer, is a computer to which other computers are connected and on which programs, data, and information are stored.

4. Memory, also called _____ , consists of small electronic chips that provide temporary storage for instructions and data during processing.

5. A monitor produces output in _____ form, a type of output that can be viewed, but not physically handled.

6. Software that tells the computer how to operate is called _____ .

7. Software that consists of programs that perform administrative tasks, such as checking the computer's components to determine whether each is working properly, is called _____ .

8. A type of software program that locates and retrieves requested information from the Web is called a(n) _____ .

9. The processor and memory chips are housed on a computer's _____ .

10. CD drives and hard disk drives are examples of _____ devices.

## *Tech Architecture* > **Label the Drawing**

In this illustration of a computer system, label the devices as input, output, processing, or storage devices.

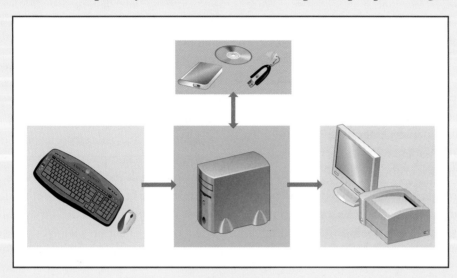

## *Techno Literacy* > **Research and Writing**

Develop appropriate written responses based on your research for each item.

1. Assume you are offered a free personal computer system of your choice and you are to select the input, output, and storage devices you want. Create a list of uses for your new computer. Then research various computer systems and components advertised in magazines and on the Internet. Choose a computer system that will meet your needs and write a paragraph explaining why you selected a particular personal computer system.

2. Knowing that handheld computers vary in operating system (Palm, PocketPC, etc.), memory, weight, price, and in other ways, create a table or chart that includes the manufacturer's name, handheld model, operating system, wireless capabilities, and price. Visit a computer store in your area and examine three handhelds. Using the chart you prepared, record information about each model. Based upon your analysis of the handheld computers

you examined, which would you prefer as your own? Are there additional features that affected your decision? Explain the reasons for your decision.

3. The Internet provides easy access to a wealth of information and is considered to be a time-saver for busy people. Prepare a written report explaining what aspects of your life have been simplified or improved by the use of the Internet. Include your predictions for additional Internet capabilities that you expect to use in the next five years.

4. Many projects are under way to expand the use of wearable computers in the workplace, in military applications, and for personal use. Using your school library or other sources of information, research the uses of wearable computers. Based on your findings, write an article describing the application of wearable computers to enhance our daily lives.

## Technology Issues > **Team Problem-Solving**

In groups, brainstorm possible solutions to the issues presented.

1. Today's classrooms are made up of more diverse students and students with a wider range of performance capabilities compared to previous decades. In fact, some theorists claim there is a 200 percent differential in the learning rate in our classrooms today. Imagine how computers will help instructors teach so many different types of students. Consider both traditional and distance learning modes.

2. Artificially intelligent robots are likely to play a large role in our future. What are some possible new applications of this technology in the areas of manufacturing, health care, and home maintenance?

3. Since computers were first introduced, there has been considerable debate concerning their effect on employment. For example, some people argue that computers have replaced many workers and are, therefore, a social evil. Others argue that the computer industry has created many new high-paying jobs in the technology field. In your group, discuss both sides of this issue: Have computers had an overall good effect or bad effect on society?

## Mining Data > **Internet Research and Reporting**

Conduct Internet searches to find the information described in the activities below. Write a brief report summarizing your research results. Be sure to document your sources, using the following format, which is recommended by the Modern Language Association (MLA):

- author's name (if known)
- title of document, in quotation marks
- title of Internet page or online periodical, in italics (if not titled, put Home Page or give the name of the organization that created and maintains the page)
- date of publication (for an article) or date site was last updated, if available
- date you accessed the site
- URL, in angle brackets ‹ ›

Example: Alexander, Sonja "NASA Selects 21 Tech Projects for Reduced-Gravity Flight Testing," *Features*, May 2009. June 2009 ‹http://www.nasa.gov/home/hqnews/2009/may/HQ__09-109__FAST__IPP__Awards.html›.

1. Using online news sources, select a specific event that occurred in one country (other than the United States) within the past year. Find three separate news reports of the event and describe how each media source perceived the event. What are the similarities? What are the differences? What are the possible reasons for the differences?

2. What kinds of information are available at the Web site of your state government? Your summary should discuss the information available on a particular date.

3. Research the topic of high-tech stock investments as discussed in online news sources. What is the current trend as of the date of your research?

## *Technology Timeline* > **Predicting Next Steps**

Look at the timeline below outlining the major benchmarks in the development of computing. Research this topic and fill in as many steps as you can. What do you think the next steps will be? Complete the timeline through the year 2030.

**1942** Dr. John Atanasoff and Clifford Berry design and build the first electronic digital computer.

**1958** Jack Kilby, an engineer at Texas Instruments, invents the integrated circuit, thereby laying the foundation for fast computers and large-capacity memory.

**1981** IBM enters the personal computer field by introducing the IBM-PC.

**1993** World Wide Web technology and programming is officially proclaimed public-domain and available to all.

**2004** Wireless computer devices, including keyboards, mice, and wireless home networks, become widely accepted among users.

**2006** Five million subscribers connect to BlackBerry Internet services for work and personal communications.

## *Ethical Dilemmas* > **Group Discussion and Debate**

As a class or within an assigned group, discuss the following ethical dilemma.

The term *plagiarism* refers to the unauthorized and illegal copying of another person's writing or creative work. For example, a student may copy an author's writing from a magazine article or from a Web page and submit the report without giving the original author credit. Also, an individual can illegally retrieve an artist's recordings from Web sites and replay the music again and again, thereby depriving the original artist of royalties.

In your group, discuss the issue of downloading commercial movies from the Internet for one's personal use. Should such practices be legal or illegal? Should the user be required to pay the production studio or the movie stars each and every time the movie is watched? Should there be legal penalties involved?

# CHAPTER 2

# Input and Processing

## Learning Objectives

> Define the terms *input* and *processing*

> Categorize input devices for personal computers and explain their functions

> Identify the main components of the system unit and explain their functions

> Explain the four basic operations of a machine cycle

> Describe the different types of computer memory and their functions

> Discuss the importance of expanding a computer's capabilities and explain how it can be accomplished

# Cyber**Scenario**

**JENNA WINBON IS AWAKENED BY UPBEAT MUSIC** playing and her window blinds opening to let in the morning sunshine. The smell of fresh-brewed coffee gradually makes it to her end of the house as she ponders her upcoming day at the office. A computer system called a home information infrastructure manages the MP3 player and stereo system, window blinds, and coffeemaker, along with many other appliances and electronic devices in her home.

Sitting at her bedside, she hears the shower start. She knows that in two minutes it will be ready for her at the temperature she programmed. Jenna glances at today's news headlines scrolling across the bottom of the flat-screen TV on the wall. Turning her attention to the morning show in progress, she sees that a segment on caring for aging parents is about to start. Walking toward the closet, Jenna instructs the TV to record the segment for her to view tonight. As Jenna opens the closet door, a voice informs her that today will be sunny and 78 degrees. She chooses a silk-blend suit and hangs it just outside the bathroom.

Before returning to her get-ready-for-work ritual, Jenna types a brief message on her smartphone. She wants to make sure that her company's purchasing manager orders new notebook computers for the three new sales associates before the local vendor's special offer expires.

Thirty minutes later, Jenna gathers her briefcase and smartphone and heads for the garage. As she passes the wall clock in the utility room, she is reminded on a digital display that she needs to go to the Marietta office today instead of her normal Peachtree Center office.

Opening the door from the utility room to the garage automatically starts Jenna's car and opens the garage door simultaneously. As she backs out of the garage, she notices the car's interior temperature is approaching the 72 degrees she had selected on

the Preferences menu of the controls system. Feeling a bit thirsty, Jenna asks her built-in navigation system to find the Starbucks closest to the Marietta office. After noting the location displayed on the retractable screen in the dashboard, she turns her attention to the satellite radio station she had selected, enjoying the music and anticipating the taste of a latte.

"Now," she thinks, "if only my appointments and meetings at the office will go as smoothly."

Computer systems similar to the one in Jenna's home may soon become a reality within reach of average consumers. Increasingly, builders are including high-speed cables in the walls of new houses to allow for networked media systems throughout the home. Called "structured wiring," this hidden cable system allows flexibility in room design and accommodates state-of-the-art technology such as video and audio monitoring and remotely controlled lighting, cooling, and heating.

In addition to having outdoor sprinklers that automatically shut off when it is raining, this technology can be used for safety and security. Alerting home occupants when someone enters the perimeter of the yard, viewing inside and outside video images of the home, and detecting motion (or lack of motion) in an elderly parent's house are examples of how houses will be able to communicate with their owners through smartphones or other communication technologies. Home systems such as these will add yet another dimension to the term *cyber space*.

# Input Technology

Chapter 1 explained that the process of turning data into useful information is called the *information processing cycle*, and that the four steps of the cycle are input, processing, output, and storage. Performing each step involves the use of specific components and devices, all of which are grouped under the term *hardware*. In this chapter you will learn about many of the devices for entering data and programs into the computer and about the computer itself—how it processes data into information and which hardware components are involved in that process. But first, it is important to better understand the first step in the information processing cycle and the technologies that support that function.

Tech Demo 2-1
External Parts of
a PC

The term *input* refers to any data or instructions entered into a computer enabling the computer to perform a desired task. Users can input data and instructions using a variety of methods and devices, such as typing on the keyboard or speaking into a microphone connected to a computer. In fast-food restaurants, workers input customers' orders by pressing a key that represents a food item or touching a picture of the item on the computer screen.

As defined in Chapter 1, an **input device** is a hardware device that allows users to enter programs, data, and commands into a computer system. The program or application being used determines the type of input device needed. For example, many computer games require a joystick, whereas writing a letter to another person requires a keyboard. Keyboards, point-and-click devices, and scanners are among the more popular input devices. Desktop and notebook computer systems usually include at least two input devices.

## The Keyboard

The most common input device is the **keyboard**, an electronically controlled hardware component used to enter alphanumeric data (letters, numbers, and special characters). A keyboard may be plugged into the system unit or connected wirelessly through **Bluetooth** or another radio-frequency (RF) technology. The two main keyboard types are alphanumeric and special-function.

The most common way to input data or instructions into a computer is with a keyboard.

### Alphanumeric Keyboards

The keys on most alphanumeric keyboards are arranged as they are on a typewriter, although computer keyboards typically contain additional keys. Keyboards for desktop computers contain from 101 to 105 keys that the user presses to enter data into the computer. Keyboards for smaller computers, such as notebook computers, contain fewer keys. In addition to keys for alphabet letters and symbols, most keyboards contain:

- function keys
- special-purpose keys
- cursor-control (arrow) keys
- numeric keys arranged in keypad form

Function keys, labeled F1, F2, F3, and so on, allow a user to quickly access commands and functions.

The numeric keypad, which performs the same functions as a calculator, is used for entering numbers quickly.

Special-purpose keys, such as Control, Alternate, and Delete, are used in conjunction with other keys to enter commands into the computer.

Cursor-control keys govern the movement of the cursor on the screen and include the Up Arrow, Down Arrow, Right Arrow, and Left Arrow keys on most keyboards.

**Figure 2-1 A Keyboard's Key Groupings**
A computer keyboard is organized into several different groups of related keys.

Figure 2-1 shows a typical keyboard with the special key groups and their functions. The placement of the specialty keys varies among hardware manufacturers.

**Special-Function Keyboards** A **special-function keyboard** is designed for specific applications involving simplified, rapid data input. For example, many fast-food restaurant cash registers are equipped with special-function keyboards. Rather than type the name and price of a specific sandwich, the employee need only press the key marked "Cheese Burger" to record the sale. Special-function keyboards enable fast-food employees, ticket agents, and retail clerks to enter transactions into their computer systems very quickly.

Many businesses use special-function keyboards to increase employee efficiency.

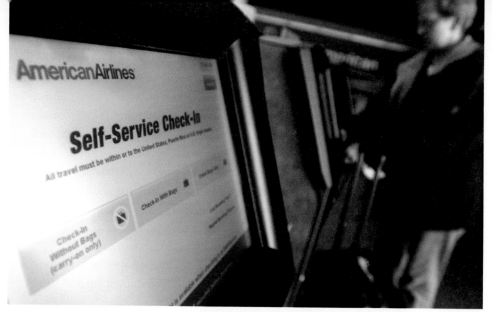

Touch screens are commonly used at airport check-in counters, allowing travlers to obtain boarding passes and check luggage.

## Touch Screens

A **touch screen** is another type of input device. Touch screens use sensing technology, allowing a user to make selections from among a group of options displayed on a screen by pressing a finger against the chosen option. For example, a bank customer can begin making a withdrawal by touching the *Withdraw* option on the automated teller machine (ATM) screen. Touch screens are widely used in ATMs, restaurants, airport check-in counters, and kiosks in buildings and stores. Many portable devices, such as cell phones and music players, also feature touch screens.

## The Mouse and Other Point-and-Click Devices

Operating systems such as Windows and Macintosh incorporate a **graphical user interface (GUI**, pronounced "gooey") containing buttons, drop-down menus, and icons to represent program features and commands visually. The user issues commands by pointing at an icon or menu item with a **mouse**, which after the

A mouse is an input device that, when moved about on a flat surface, causes a pointer on the screen to move in the same direction.

keyboard is the second most common input device. Moving the mouse causes the **mouse pointer** (cursor) on the computer screen to move in a corresponding way (see Figure 2-2). A pointer allows users to make selections from a menu and to activate programs represented by icons displayed on the screen. If you visualize the computer mouse as a small oval with a long cable tail, you can understand how it got its name.

A mouse plugs directly into the computer or is connected wirelessly. A mouse used on the Macintosh generally has one button, while a mouse used on a PC generally has two, although multibutton models are also available. The button on the left side is used to signal a choice by a single click or a double click, depending on the situation. The button on the right side is used to display special options and menus. The user can set up additional buttons to initiate special functions. A scroll wheel is often integrated into a mouse for easier movement up and down documents and Web pages.

On a traditional mouse, the underside of a mouse is a rubber-coated ball that glides over a rubberized pad with a smooth fabric surface, called a **mouse pad**. The most common mouse today, an **optical mouse**, uses a light sensor instead of a mouse ball to track movement. This type of mouse can be moved around on

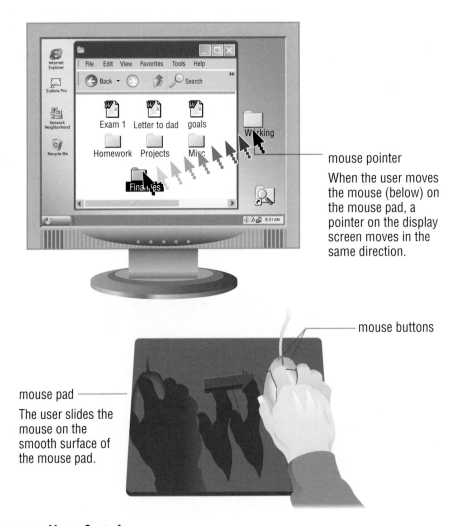

mouse pointer
When the user moves the mouse (below) on the mouse pad, a pointer on the display screen moves in the same direction.

mouse buttons

mouse pad
The user slides the mouse on the smooth surface of the mouse pad.

**Figure 2-2  Mouse Controls**
Every movement of the mouse corresponds to the movement of the mouse pointer on the display screen.

nearly any smooth surface except glass, so no mouse pad is necessary. A **foot mouse** allows people with carpal tunnel syndrome or other hand or wrist injuries to use a computer.

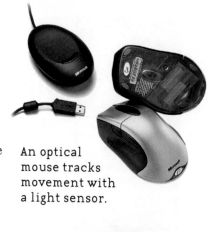

An optical mouse tracks movement with a light sensor.

**Trackballs** The trackball is an input device similar to a mouse. A **trackball** consists of a plastic sphere resting on rollers, inset in a small external case. The trackball is often described as an upside-down mouse, although unlike the mouse it remains stationary. Users move the ball with their fingers or palm. One or more buttons for choosing options are incorporated into the design of the trackball. The main advantage of using a trackball is that it requires less desk space than a mouse. A trackball is therefore a good choice for people working in confined areas. Trackballs also require less arm movement, making them useful to those with limited arm mobility.

The ball in a trackball is contained on top of the device or on the side. Rolling the ball moves the pointer on the screen.

**Touch Pads** A **touch pad**, also called a track pad, is a small, flat device that is sensitive to touch, pressure, or motion. Many portable computers have built-in touch pads, as shown in Figure 2-3. Notebook computers equipped with touch pads enable users to move the on-screen pointer by sliding a finger across the surface of the pad. A touch pad has two parts: One part incorporates two buttons, while the other functions like the smooth surface of a mouse pad. People with carpal tunnel syndrome, a painful condition caused by repetitive movements of the hand and wrist, find a touch pad or trackball easier to use than a mouse.

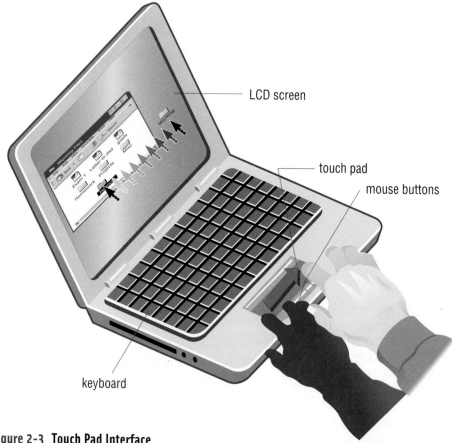

**Figure 2-3 Touch Pad Interface**
With a touch pad, the user traces a finger on the pad, moving the pointer on the screen. Below the touch pad, there are buttons for clicking commands.

# The Telepathic Typewriter

**IMAGINE THE FRUSTRATION OF BEING COMPLETELY PARALYZED,** unable to speak or motion to caretakers, family, or friends. It would take nothing less than a mind reader to find out your needs and feelings.

Telepathic technology may be in the future for those trapped without communication because of paralysis, disease, or stroke. Scientists in Berlin are working on brain-computer interfaces that would make it possible for a severely paralyzed person to voice thoughts without moving a muscle. Eventually, this research may even make it possible for people who are disabled to use brain signals to drive mechanical devices to move their limbs.

Brain waves are the electrical signals emitted by the firing of millions of nerve cells in the brain. To harness this electrical activity, a volunteer wearing a tight cap fitted with electrodes focuses on a computer screen containing letters. The electrodes pick up the activity and run the information through a computer program that identifies patterns in the brain signals. A la biofeedback, the volunteer learns how to manipulate brain waves into moving the cursor to select a letter.

Today, much research is being done using implanted brain sensors or wireless headsets that would allow mind control over the use of computers and talk on the telephone by people who are paralyzed, deaf, or mute.

A joystick is an input device used for moving objects about on the computer screen. Many types of computer games require a joystick.

**Joysticks** The **joystick** (named after the control lever used to fly fighter planes) is a small box containing a vertical lever that moves the graphics cursor correspondingly on the screen when pushed in a certain direction. It is often used for computer games. Some joysticks have a button in the tip for activation by the user's thumb. Pressing this button performs such actions as firing a game weapon at an object on the screen. Notebook computer users have recently become accustomed to a unique type of joystick, called a "pointing lever," or simply a "pointer." It is about the size of a pencil eraser and fits between the G and H keys of the keyboard. By placing the index finger on top of the lever, users can slightly push or pull it to adjust the pointer on the screen. This type of joystick eliminates a bulky external mouse or joystick and allows the hand to remain close to the keyboard.

## Pens and Tablets

Some people complain that drawing with a mouse is like drawing with a bar of soap, although exquisite computer art has been generated using a mouse. Artists, engineers, and others who need precise control over an input device may choose instead to use a **digitizing pen** and a **drawing tablet** to simulate drawing on paper.

A **graphics tablet** is a flat tablet mapmakers, engineers, and digital artists use to trace or create precise drawings. Hundreds of tiny intersecting wires forming an electronic matrix are embedded in the tablet surface. The intersection of two wires represents a specific location, or address, each of which has a value of "0." To capture an image, users grasp a stylus or crosshair cursor and trace an image or drawing placed on the tablet surface. As the user draws on the tablet surface with the pen, the values of intersections the pen touches change to "1"s. During the process, the exact locations of the 0s and 1s are stored in the computer's memory and can be saved on a storage medium. When the drawing is displayed on the screen or on paper, all "1" bits are displayed as tiny dots, which collectively represent the image. After tracing streets, parks, highways, or other images, users can input location labels with the keyboard.

Engineers, drafters, and others who need to create precise, detailed drawings use graphics tablets. Portable graphics tablets may be connected to a desktop or laptop computer as a replacement for the standard mouse.

**COFOUNDER AND CHAIRMAN EMERITUS, INTEL CORPORATION**

# Gordon E. Moore

**IN 1965 GORDON MOORE PREDICTED** that the number of transistors the industry would be able to squeeze onto a computer chip would double every year, while the price per transistor would drop just as dramatically. This prediction, now known as Moore's Law, held true until 1975, when he updated the prediction to a doubling every two years. The performance increase is unprecedented in any other industry in human history and plays a large part in driving our modern economy. The total number of transistors on a chip has gone from hundreds to billions since 1970, an improvement making today's chips more than 5,000 times more powerful.

Essentially, Moore's Law still holds and will continue to do so for the immediate future. Experts debate how long we can continue to shrink transistors, as some components of the newest transistors (not yet in production) are only three atoms wide. Logically, the smallest possible transistor could be measured in the space of a few atoms, but what will Intel do for an encore after this goal is achieved within the next 10 to 20 years?

Moore was born in San Francisco, California, in 1929. He earned a B.S. in chemistry from the University of California at Berkeley and later a Ph.D. in chemistry and physics from the California Institute of Technology. He is considered a founding father of Silicon Valley, as he was a cofounder of chip maker Intel Corporation in 1968 and originally served as executive vice president. He became president and CEO in 1975, then chairman and CEO in 1979. Currently, his title is Chairman Emeritus.

## Optical Scanners

An **optical scanner** (or scanner) is a light-sensing electronic device that uses lasers to read and capture printed text and images, such as photographs and drawings. The scanned text or picture is created and stored as an image rather than as a paper document. Once scanned, the text or image can be displayed, edited, printed, stored on a disk, inserted into another document, or sent as an attachment to an e-mail message. Figure 2-4 shows how a scanner converts a picture into a digital image.

The scanned material is stored as a matrix of rows and columns of dots, called a **bitmap**. Each dot consists of one or more bits of data. The greater the number of bits making up a dot, the clearer the scanned image. The density of each dot helps determine the quality of the captured image. Modern scanners can capture text and images at resolutions ranging from 30 to 48 bits per dot. A scanned picture is often as clear as the original image.

Resolution also depends on the number of pixels per inch. A **pixel** is the smallest picture element (or dot) that a monitor can display. The higher the number of pixels, the sharper and clearer the captured image when displayed or printed.

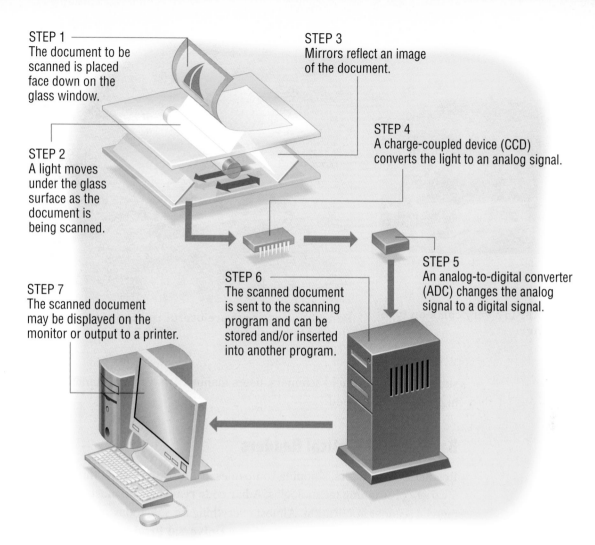

**STEP 1**
The document to be scanned is placed face down on the glass window.

**STEP 2**
A light moves under the glass surface as the document is being scanned.

**STEP 3**
Mirrors reflect an image of the document.

**STEP 4**
A charge-coupled device (CCD) converts the light to an analog signal.

**STEP 5**
An analog-to-digital converter (ADC) changes the analog signal to a digital signal.

**STEP 6**
The scanned document is sent to the scanning program and can be stored and/or inserted into another program.

**STEP 7**
The scanned document may be displayed on the monitor or output to a printer.

**Figure 2-4 The Scanning Process**
A scanner captures text and/or graphic images and converts them into a format the computer can understand for display and storage.

**Resolution** is measured in **dots per inch (dpi)** and expressed as the number of rows and columns. For example, a scanner with a dpi of 600 ∞ 1,200 has a capacity of 600 columns and 1,200 rows of dots. Most modern scanners for home or office use a resolution of at least 1,200 dpi. Commercial scanners offer higher resolutions and are more expensive.

Scanners can process information in two different ways. A **dumb scanner** can only capture and input scanned text and images. Once entered into a computer, the text or image cannot be altered. By contrast, an **intelligent scanner** uses **optical character recognition (OCR)** software that allows captured text or images to be edited with a word processor or other application program. Depending on the scanner model, the OCR software may be included in the package, or it may need to be purchased separately.

The two most popular types of scanners are page scanners (flatbed scanners) and handheld scanners. Personal computer users often use page scanners to capture text, graphics, and other data from printed documents. Pages are either laid face down on the scanner's glass surface or fed through the scanner by means of a side-feed device. While the page scanner remains stationary, the scanning device inside moves back and forth to capture an image of the material on the glass

A flatbed scanner is a very common type of image scanner.

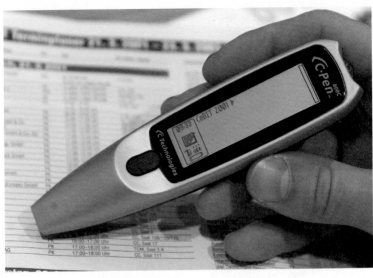

Pen-style scanners are useful in scanning and storing text quickly.

surface. With handheld scanners, users manually move the scanner across the material to be scanned.

## Bar Code and Optical Readers

Retailers, wholesalers, shipping companies, banks, hotels, and other businesses use a variety of scanning technologies. A **bar code reader** is the most common commercial scanner application. Almost everything for sale today on the retail level is marked with a bar code, also known as a **Universal Product Code (UPC)**. The lines in a bar code contain symbols that can be read by a bar code reader. Sometimes the reader takes the form of a pen. At other times it is placed below a glass cover at the end of a conveyor belt. Bar code readers translate the lines into a number. The computer then uses this number to find information about the product in a database, such as its name and price. Using bar codes greatly increases accuracy in recording sales and enables retail stores to update inventory files automatically. Overnight shipping services such as FedEx and United Parcel Service (UPS) often use bar codes to identify packages.

Nurses use bar code readers to verify that they are giving the right medication to the right patient.

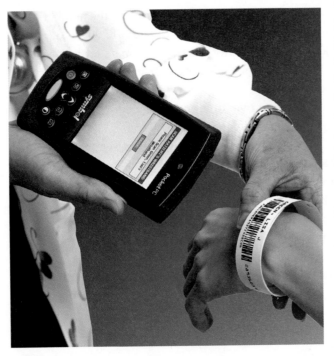

In addition to bar code readers, many retailers have also installed scanners known as optical readers at checkout stations. Similar to the use of credit or debit cards with magnetic stripes, a smart card can be inserted into a slot on an **optical reader**. A **smart card** contains electronic memory and an embedded microprocessor for accessing and updating the card's contents. This allows customers to pay for purchases, verify their identity, and access information such as personal medical records.

## Graphic and Video Input Devices

Graphic and video input devices can be directly connected to a computer to upload images and video in their original form. Today's graphic and video input devices are digital cameras and digital video cameras.

**Digital Cameras**  While conventional cameras record images on film, a **digital camera** captures images in a digitized form that a computer can use. In appearance, digital cameras resemble traditional film-based cameras, although digital cameras are often smaller in size. Most are portable, although some models are stationary and connect directly to a computer.

This bar code reader allows a customer to scan items as they are placed in the shopping cart, making the final checkout process quicker.

Several advantages that digital cameras have over conventional cameras have led to their increased popularity. With a digital camera, the picture is viewable right away, allowing the user to retake the photo if needed. Digital photos are also easier to retrieve, edit, duplicate, and share with others since they are just computer files.

Most digital cameras store captured pictures directly in flash memory (which will be discussed later in this chapter) for transfer to a computer as input. Users can then adjust the color and size of the image using photo-editing software. They can also print the picture, copy it into another document, post it on a Web site, or e-mail

A digital camera looks much like a standard camera but captures and stores an image in a digital format that users can view immediately or download to a computer.

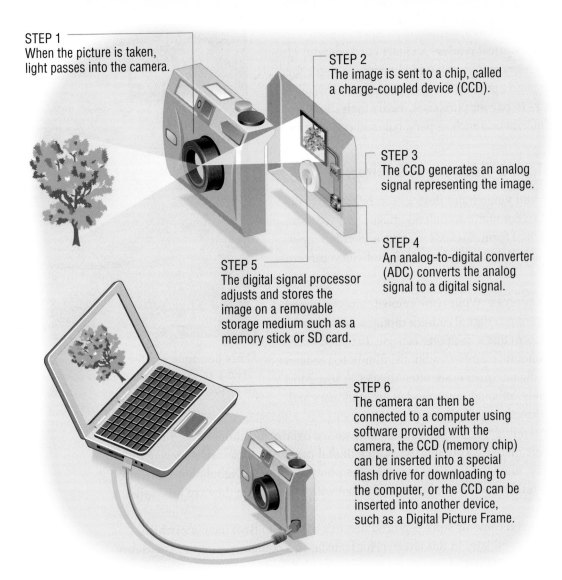

**STEP 1**
When the picture is taken, light passes into the camera.

**STEP 2**
The image is sent to a chip, called a charge-coupled device (CCD).

**STEP 3**
The CCD generates an analog signal representing the image.

**STEP 4**
An analog-to-digital converter (ADC) converts the analog signal to a digital signal.

**STEP 5**
The digital signal processor adjusts and stores the image on a removable storage medium such as a memory stick or SD card.

**STEP 6**
The camera can then be connected to a computer using software provided with the camera, the CCD (memory chip) can be inserted into a special flash drive for downloading to the computer, or the CCD can be inserted into another device, such as a Digital Picture Frame.

**Figure 2-5 How a Digital Camera Works**
A digital camera captures images by converting them from analog to digital format and storing them on a removable storage medium. Once users capture and store the pictures, they can print them or insert them into a document such as a sales brochure.

it. Many digital cameras can also be connected to a television for viewing or connected to a printer for printing. Figure 2-5 illustrates how a digital camera works.

As with scanners, digital photo quality is measured by the number of bits stored in a pixel, or dpi. The resolution of digital cameras is usually advertised in terms of megapixels (millions of pixels). A camera with a resolution of 4.0 or 5.0 megapixels produces high-quality pictures suitable for most consumers. However, professional photographers desire resolution of at least 4,096 × 4,096 pixels (about 16 megapixels), which is about twice the resolution of 35-millimeter film and approximately the same clarity achieved by high-end 4 × 5 film cameras.

Digital camera technologies are now common in cell phones as well. Many cell phone users are able to capture and transmit pictures taken by cameras inside their phones. For example, photographs of a newborn child can be instantly transmitted to family and friends, or a biology student on a field trip can take and store photographs of plants and animals for further study. Some cell phones are even equipped with digital video camera technology that can record short videos.

Many cell phones are equipped with digital camera technology, allowing users to capture and transmit pictures (and sometimes short videos).

**Webcams and Video Cameras** **Video input** occurs using a special type of video camera attached to the computer. Both webcams and digital video cameras (camcorders) are devices that capture video input. A **webcam** is a digital video camera that captures real-time video for transmission to others via a Web server or an instant messaging tool.

Most video input now involves the use of high-resolution digital video cameras and camcorders. These capture and store video in digital form that allows images, such as still photos and movies, to be displayed in clear and brilliant color. Unlike analog video cameras, digital video cameras do not require a digitizer. Instead, the video camera can be plugged directly into a computer's Universal Serial Bus (USB) port and used immediately (Figure 2-6). With video-editing software, it is possible to view each frame of the video and edit video sequences.

Businesses, government, and organizations are discovering numerous video-input applications. For example, book publishers can now include a small printed image on a book cover or within a magazine ad allowing an order to be placed

The SmileCam can automatically track motion and can be controlled remotely through an Internet connection.

An expansion video card provides improved graphics for high-resolution graphics applications such as digital photos and video.

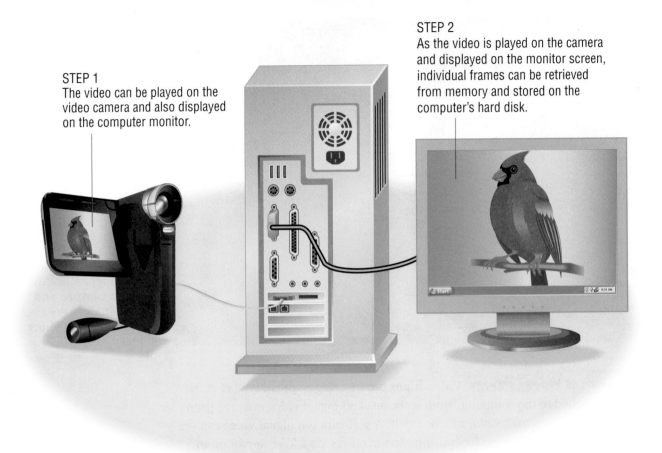

STEP 1
The video can be played on the video camera and also displayed on the computer monitor.

STEP 2
As the video is played on the camera and displayed on the monitor screen, individual frames can be retrieved from memory and stored on the computer's hard disk.

**Figure 2-6  Process for Viewing Digital Video**
Users can plug a digital video camera directly into a computer to display the recorded video.

when a person holds the image up to a video camera on the computer. The camera captures the printed image, enters it into the computer, and transmits the order over the Internet to the publisher.

Some banks have begun using advanced video-input systems to identify customers. A camera captures an image of a customer and quickly compares the image with those stored in a computer, eliminating the necessity of checking a driver's license or other identification. High-security situations that require quick identification, such as military installations, government facilities, and airports, use similar systems that store an image of a person's eye, fingerprints, or facial structure.

Manufacturers use video technology for quality control. For example, a product moving along an assembly line can be photographed and instantly compared with a stored photograph of the "perfect" product. If a missing or broken part is detected, the computer rejects the product before it is packaged for shipment.

Experimental unmanned military vehicles use a vision-input system to avoid obstacles while driving over rough terrain. Similar vision-input technologies may soon be commonly available for civilian vehicles. Vision-input offers great promise for safer driving in the future.

New facial recognition systems in airports can help security and law enforcement personnel identify terrorists by their facial structure.

## Audio Input Devices

The process of entering (recording) speech, music, or sound effects is called **audio input**. Personal computers must contain a sound card to record or play sound. They will also need speakers and a sound-capturing device, such as a microphone, audio CD player, or tape player plugged into a port (slot) on the sound card. Finally, special software is required, such as the Windows Sound Recorder utility.

**Voice input** technologies allow users to enter data by talking to the computer. Newer releases of word processing and spreadsheet applications commonly include voice input. Voice recognition and speech recognition are two types of voice input programs.

A **voice recognition program** does not understand or process speech. Instead, it recognizes only preprogrammed words stored in a database. A word database may contain only a few words, or many millions of words. Voice-activated ATMs, for example, allow customers to conduct financial transactions by speaking into the machine. Voice recognition capability also is included in the most recent releases

Computers equipped with appropriate hardware and software can record sound or respond to voice commands.

## COMPUTER PIONEERS

# John Eckert and John Mauchly

**JOHN P. ECKERT AND JOHN W. MAUCHLY** invented and improved computers through their original designs and profoundly impacted history through their work. They designed the Electronic Numerical Integrator and Computer (ENIAC), which was commissioned by the United States in 1943 to help the military compile tables for the trajectories of bombs and shells. The ENIAC used roughly 18,000 vacuum tubes and measured two-and-a-half meters tall and 24 meters long. It was 1,000 times faster than the electromechanical machines that preceded it, and was capable of up to 5,000 additions per second. The ENIAC was easily the most complex computer of its generation.

Mauchly was born August 30, 1907 in Cincinnati, Ohio, and studied physics while on scholarship at John Hopkins University. He graduated with a doctorate in physics in 1932. He did some work analyzing the weather and realized that weather forecasts would require compiling large sets of data very quickly. He developed an interest in electrical circuits for computation before beginning to teach at the University of Pennsylvania, where he would eventually begin to build the machines he envisioned.

Eckert was born April 9, 1919 in Philadelphia. He went to William Penn Charter School in Philadelphia and graduated in 1937 before going to the University of Pennsylvania to study electrical engineering. He started teaching there shortly after graduating in 1941. Mauchly, though 12 years his senior, took Eckert's training course in electronics designed for defense purposes, and they soon became interested in each other's work.

The University of Pennsylvania was already researching early computers. They specifically used a Bush analyzer designed by Vannevar Bush. The machine required too much manual work to be effective for smaller calculations, and Mauchly developed his own ideas on how to construct better computers. Mauchly and Eckert would discuss electronic computer designs for two years before Mauchly's report on the construction of a computer was accepted. Then they were approved by The Ballistic Research Laboratory in Aberdeen, Maryland, to start building the ENIAC. Eckert was appointed chief engineer on the project. The ENIAC was finished in 1946 after World War II ended, and was used chiefly on top-secret problems associated with the development of nuclear weapons.

of the Microsoft Office suite. A voice recognition program is a **speaker-independent program**, which means it can respond to words spoken by different individuals.

A **speech recognition program** provides another type of voice input in which words spoken by a user are stored in a database. A microphone and a type of speech recognition software, such as IBM's Via Voice or Dragon NaturallySpeaking, enable words spoken by the user to be stored in digital form in the computer. Once words are stored, the user can issue commands and enter data by speaking words that exactly match those recorded previously. A computer with speech recognition capability can continue to learn new vocabulary and commands from user voice input. A speech recognition program is usually a **speaker-dependent program**. The computer will recognize words only if they closely match the speech patterns of a

Eckert and Mauchly then started the Electronic Control Company together and received an order in 1946 to build the Binary Automatic Computer (BINAC). The major advancement of this machine

Eckert and Mauchly (center) with the ENIAC at the Moore School of Electrical Engineering in 1941.

was that instead of punched cards for data storage, it used magnetic tape. They changed their company name to the Eckert-Mauchly Computer Corporation and in 1950 developed the Universal Automatic Computer (UNIVAC), a computer capable of handling numbers and letters with equal ability and meant for business use. It was the

first commercial computer produced in the United States. They produced 46 UNIVACs before the Remington Rand Corporation bought them in 1950. Eckert stayed with the company as an executive until he retired in 1989. He continued to act as a consultant, however, until his death in 1995. After Mauchly left the company, he formed Mauchly Associates. He was president from 1959 until 1965 when he became chairman of the board. Later he was president of Dynatrend Incorporated from 1968 until his death in 1980.

Eckert and Mauchly both received various awards for pioneering the field of computer technologies and their amazing achievements. They shared the Harry M. Goode Memorial Award in 1966 and were elected to the National Academy of Engineering in 1967. Eckert won the U.S. National Medal of Science in 1969, and Mauchly was elected a life member of the Franklin Institute.

previously recorded word. If another person uses the computer, it may not understand verbal commands because of differences in speech patterns.

## Data Processing by Computers

All of the hardware devices discussed so far have dealt with input, the first phase of the information processing cycle. The second phase is processing, which involves another set of computer hardware components, most of which reside in the system unit. The purpose of inputting data into a computer system is to process data into a form that is useful. Recall that information processing, also called data processing or simply processing, refers to the manipulation of data according

Go to this title's Internet Resource Center and read the article titled "Processor Installation and Upgrades." www.emcp.net/CUT4e

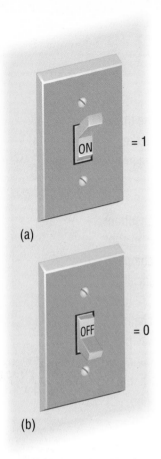

(a)

= 1

(b)

= 0

**Figure 2-7 Binary Number System Analogy**
The binary number system uses a condition that is similar to what happens when an electrical switch is turned on, causing current to flow. In the binary number system, a one (1) represents an "on" state in which there is an electrical charge (a), and a zero (0) represents an "off" state in which there is no electrical charge (b).

Go to this title's Internet Resource Center and read the article titled "Advances in Chip Architecture." www.emcp.net/CUT4e

to instructions in a computer program. The program used to manipulate the data may be written by the user or purchased from a software vendor. Data may be manipulated in various ways during processing. For example, a payroll program manipulates data by calculating employee gross pay, taxes to be withheld, deductions, and net pay. The results of those calculations can then be used to print employee paychecks and reports. A commercial word processing program such as Microsoft Word can be used to manipulate text and other data to produce letters, memos, and other documents.

All computers are electronic devices, which means they operate on electricity, and their programs and data are in electronic form. Programs and data are entered and stored in the computer's memory. When a program is executed, the processing unit retrieves the instructions and data as needed throughout the processing period. When processing is finished, the program and the processed data (information) are stored in the computer's memory until the information is output or saved for future use.

So what happens during processing? Physically, electrical currents representing programs and data are moving about very quickly through electronic circuits between components inside the system unit. The currents are created by tiny switches called transistors, which are either on or off, with "on" represented by the number 1 and "off" represented by the number 0. All data used in computers is represented by combinations of ones and zeros, each of which is considered a **bit** (an abbreviation for binary digit). As described in Chapter 1, electrical currents or signals within computers are therefore called digital signals, and data is referred to as digital data.

## Data Representation: Bits and Bytes

The first large computers made use of the decimal number system, in which numbers are indicated by the symbols 0 through 9. Engineers soon hit upon a much simpler system known as **machine language** for representing data with numbers. Machine language uses **binary numbers** ("bi" means two), which are constructed solely of the symbols 0 and 1. The **bit** (0 or 1) is the smallest unit of data in the binary system. By itself, a bit is not very meaningful. However, a group of eight bits, or a **byte**, is significant because a byte contains enough possible combinations of 0s and 1s to represent 256 separate characters. These characters include letters of the alphabet, numbers, and special symbols, such as a dollar sign ($), a question mark (?), and a pound sign (#).

To picture the concept of using binary numbers to represent data within the electrical circuits on a computer chip, consider an electric light switch. Flipping the switch to the "on" position causes the current to flow and turns on the light, while flipping the switch to the opposite position turns the light "off" (see Figure 2-7). Various patterns of "on" and "off" could therefore represent alphabet letters and numbers.

## ASCII and EBCDIC Coding Schemes

Two widely used data coding schemes based on the binary system are the **American Standard Code for Information Interchange (ASCII)** and the **Extended Binary Coded Decimal Interchange Code (EBCDIC)**. The ASCII data coding scheme is used on many personal computers and various midsize servers. The EBCDIC scheme is used mainly on IBM servers and mainframe computers. Figure 2-8 illustrates these two coding schemes and the combinations that represent specific characters. Coding schemes such as ASCII and EBCDIC make it possible for users to interact with a computer. For example, pressing a specific key on a keyboard, such as the letter "J," generates an electrical signal. The generated signal is converted into binary form (a byte) and is stored in memory. The computer then processes the digital signal and quickly displays an image (in this case, a "J") on the screen, as shown in Figure 2-9.

## Unicode

Although widely adopted as a standard for personal computers, the ASCII system has proved to be too limited because it cannot deal with certain languages, such as Chinese, which uses more complicated alphabets than does English. To accommodate a larger array of letters and symbols, computer scientists have developed a system called **Unicode**. Unicode uses two bytes, or 16 binary digits, and can represent 65,536 separate characters. Since the first 256 codes are the same in both ASCII and Unicode, existing ASCII-coded data is compatible with newer operating systems, including Windows Vista and Macintosh OS X, that use Unicode.

# The System Unit

The main part of a desktop computer, the **system unit**, houses the components that process data into information. System units for PCs come in various shapes and sizes. The modified system unit shown in Figure 2-10 illustrates various system unit components. From the outside, the system unit looks like a metal or plastic cabinet with several button switches and openings in the front and back. The inside is a maze of circuit boards, wires, and cables of various colors, a fan for cooling, and empty slots where more circuit boards can be added. The system unit comprises the power supply, storage bays, and the motherboard.

# The Power Supply

Like other electronic devices, a computer requires a **power supply** to supply energy to the computer. Many personal computers use a power cord that connects the computer into a standard alternating current (AC) 115 to 120 volt wall outlet. Because this type of power is unsuitable for use with a computer requiring

| SYMBOL | ASCII | EBCDIC |
|--------|----------|----------|
| 0 | 01100000 | 11110000 |
| 1 | 01100001 | 11110001 |
| 2 | 01100010 | 11110010 |
| 3 | 01100011 | 11110011 |
| 4 | 01100100 | 11110100 |
| 5 | 01100101 | 11110101 |
| 6 | 01100110 | 11110110 |
| 7 | 01100111 | 11110111 |
| 8 | 01101000 | 11111000 |
| 9 | 01101001 | 11111001 |
| A | 01000001 | 11000001 |
| B | 01000010 | 11000010 |
| C | 01000011 | 11000011 |
| D | 01000100 | 11000100 |
| E | 01000101 | 11000101 |
| F | 01000110 | 11000110 |
| . | . | . |
| . | . | . |
| . | . | . |
| X | 01011000 | 11100111 |
| Y | 01011001 | 11101000 |
| Z | 01011010 | 11101001 |
| ! | 00100001 | 01011010 |
| " | 00100010 | 01111111 |
| # | 00100011 | 01111011 |
| $ | 00100100 | 01011011 |
| % | 00100101 | 01101100 |
| & | 00100110 | 01010000 |
| ( | 00101000 | 01001101 |
| ) | 00101001 | 01011101 |
| * | 00101010 | 01011100 |
| + | 00101011 | 01001110 |

**Figure 2-8 ASCII and EBCDIC Coding Schemes**
ASCII is a coding scheme many computers, including personal computers, use. The EBCDIC coding scheme is used mainly on large computers such as IBM mainframe computers.

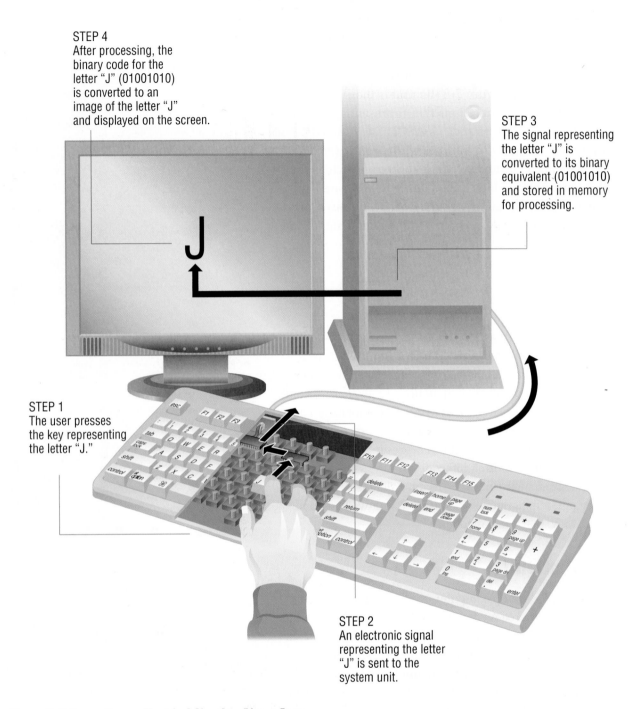

STEP 4
After processing, the binary code for the letter "J" (01001010) is converted to an image of the letter "J" and displayed on the screen.

STEP 3
The signal representing the letter "J" is converted to its binary equivalent (01001010) and stored in memory for processing.

STEP 1
The user presses the key representing the letter "J."

STEP 2
An electronic signal representing the letter "J" is sent to the system unit.

**Figure 2-9 Converting an Electrical Signal to Binary Form**
Pressing a specific key generates an electronic signal that is converted into binary form (a byte) and stored in memory. The computer then processes the digital signal and quickly displays the character on the screen.

a direct current (DC) between 3 and 12 volts, the power supply unit in the system unit converts the incoming current from AC into DC.

In addition to plug-in power, portable computers use battery power when plug-in power is unavailable or impractical. Most portable computer batteries are rechargeable, allowing the battery to be recharged for use again and again.

The power supply typically includes a fan for cooling of the entire system unit. Computer usage generates a lot of heat, but the components inside the system unit

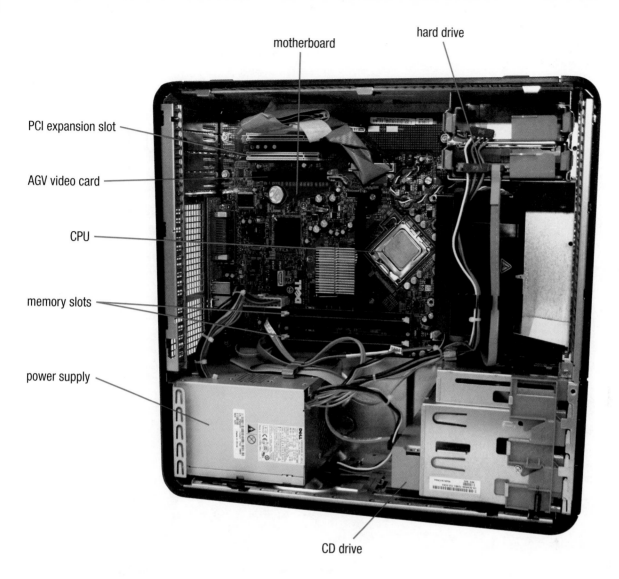

motherboard

hard drive

PCI expansion slot

AGV video card

CPU

memory slots

power supply

CD drive

**Figure 2-10 System Unit Components**
The system unit is the main part of a personal computer system, containing the components necessary for processing information.

need to stay cool. Some computers have additional fans for components such as the Central Processing Unit (CPU), but a single fan is usually sufficient.

## Storage Bays

A **storage bay** (often just called a bay) is a site where a storage device, such as a hard drive or CD/DVD drive, is installed. The number of bays in a computer determines the number of storage devices that can be installed, an important factor for buyers to consider when purchasing a PC. Figure 2-11 shows the bays in a typical desktop computer.

PC bays come in different sizes, the most common ones being a hard drive and a CD/DVD drive. An internal bay, such as one that houses a hard drive, is concealed entirely within the system unit. An exposed bay is used when direct access

 Tech Demo 2-2
Internal PC
Components

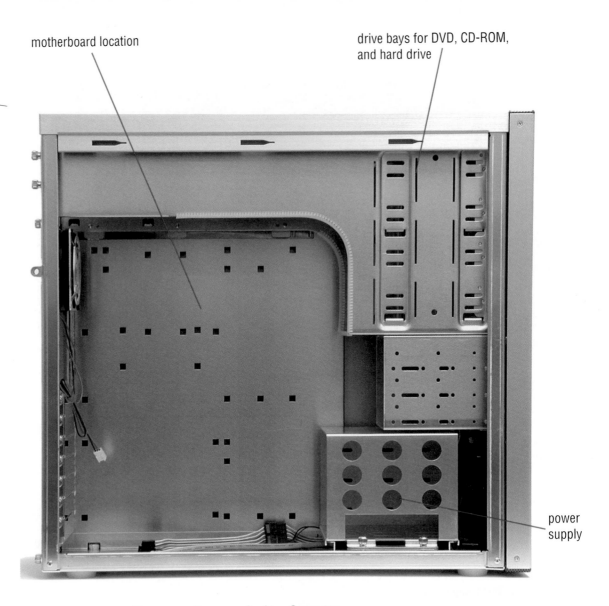

motherboard location

drive bays for DVD, CD-ROM, and hard drive

power supply

**Figure 2-11 Bays on a Desktop Computer**
The desktop computer shown above contains a CD/DVD drive bay and a hard drive bay.

is required to the device, such as insertion and removal of a CD or DVD in a CD/DVD drive.

## The Motherboard

Tech Demo 2-3
Motherboard

A **motherboard** is a thin sheet of fiberglass or other material with electrical pathways. Each **trace** is an etched pathway that connects a component soldered to the motherboard or attached to it by various wires or connectors. Figure 2-12 identifies components typically found on the motherboard in contemporary desktop computers, and their functions are as follows:

CPU    RAM

PCIE slot

PCI slot

CMOS battery

NIC chip

BIOS chip

parallel port

serial port    VGA video port

USB ports    NIC port

video chip

hard drive connector

motherboard power connector

SATA hard drive connector

audio ports

**Figure 2-12 Motherboard Components**
The motherboard holds the major processing and memory components, including the CPU, RAM, and ROM chips.

- central processing unit (microprocessor) for manipulating all types of data
- a system clock (and battery) to synchronize the computer's activities
- slots for connecting the random access memory (RAM) chips that contain the temporary memory where programs and data are stored while the computer is in use
- one or more read-only memory (ROM) chips that contain the computer's permanent memory where various instructions are stored
- expansion slots for attaching expansion cards that add various capabilities to the computer, such as the ability to access files over a network or to digitize sound or video
- ports for connecting input devices such as a keyboard, mouse, modem, and output devices such as speakers and a printer
- buses, which are electronic connections that allow communication between components in the computer

## The Central Processing Unit

Every computer contains a central processing unit (CPU). The CPU of larger computers often spans several separate microprocessor chips and various circuit boards, whereas in a personal computer the CPU is a single chip. This **microprocessor chip**, also called an integrated circuit, is a small electronic device consisting of tiny transistors and other circuit parts on a piece of semiconductor material. This material is known as a **semiconductor** because it is neither a good conductor of elec-

Go to this title's
Internet Resource
Center and read
the article titled
"Improvements
in Chip Materials
and Manufacturing
Processes."
www.emcp.net/CUT4e

# New Chip on the Block

**CELL PHONE TECHNOLOGY EVOLVES** so rapidly these days that it's surprising that one of the most important parts of cell phones, the memory chip, has remained relatively the same over the last twenty years. Since its development in the late 1980s, flash memory has been the standard way to store data in small electronics—but that may soon change. Samsung has begun producing a new chip that uses phase-change random access memory, or PRAM. PRAM is faster and more efficient than flash, and could one day replace it altogether.

The idea behind PRAM has been around for several decades. The chip contains a chemical compound called chalcogenide, which is heated to very high temperatures, changing the compound's physical state. The two resulting states serve as the ones and zeros of the binary code used for data storage. The benefit of this process is that PRAM chips do not need to erase a block of cells before writing new data; the bits can be changed individually. Because of this, PRAM chips can read and write data ten times faster than their flash counterparts and use less power in the process—PRAM memory chips could increase cell phone battery life by up to 20 percent.

PRAM is produced using the same technology that is used to produce flash memory, but Samsung has not revealed when the first cell phone with a PRAM chip will be released.

---

tricity (like copper) nor a good insulator (such as rubber). Semiconductor material therefore does not interfere with the flow of electricity in a chip's circuits. The most commonly used semiconductor material is silicon, a type of purified glass.

On a personal computer, all processing functions are contained on a single microprocessor chip. Because the functions are housed on a single chip, the terms *CPU* and *microprocessor* are used interchangeably. Recall from Chapter 1 that the CPU, or microprocessor, is often referred to as the "brain" of a personal computer system because it interprets and executes the instructions for most computer operations. The CPU consists of a control unit, an arithmetic/logic unit (ALU), and registers, as shown in Figure 2-13.

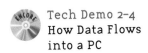

Tech Demo 2-4
How Data Flows
into a PC

These components of the CPU perform four basic operations that are collectively called a **machine cycle**. The machine cycle includes *fetching* an instruction, *decoding* the instruction, *executing* the instruction, and *storing* the result (see Figure 2-14). The machine cycle is the same whether you are using a midrange server or a personal computer.

**Control Unit** The **control unit** directs and coordinates the overall operation of the computer system. It acts as a traffic officer, signaling to other parts of the computer system what they are to do. It interprets program instructions and then initiates the action needed to carry them out. These are the *fetching* and *decoding* steps of the machine cycle. **Fetching** means retrieving an instruction or data from memory. **Decoding** means interpreting or translating the instruction into

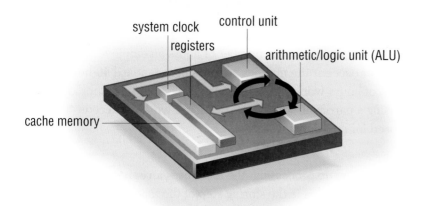

**Figure 2-13 Central Processing Unit**
The central processing unit (CPU) contains a control unit, arithmetic/logic
unit (ALU), and registers.

strings of binary digits (bytes) the computer understands. The time required to
fetch and decode an instruction is called **instruction time**, or **I-time**.

**Arithmetic/Logic Unit**  As shown in Figure 2-14, the **arithmetic/logic unit
(ALU)** is the part of the CPU that performs the *executing* step of the machine cycle.
**Executing** means carrying out the instructions and performing arithmetic and
logical operations on the data. The arithmetic operations the ALU can perform
are addition, subtraction, multiplication, and division. The ALU can also perform

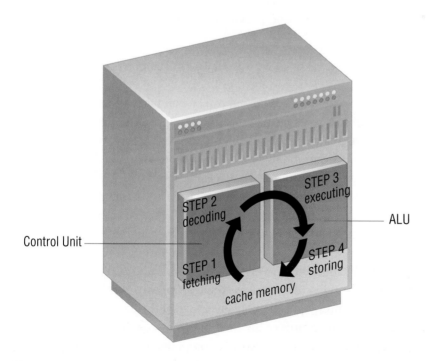

**Figure 2-14 Machine Cycle**
This process includes the four steps for reading and carrying out
an instruction: fetching, decoding, executing, and storing.

logical operations, such as comparing data items. For example, the ALU can determine if one data item, such as the number of hours an employee has worked, is less than, equal to, or exceeds the number of hours in a standard 40-hour work week. If the number of hours worked is less than or equal to 40, the employee's pay is calculated using a particular formula. If the hours worked exceeds 40, a different formula is used for calculating overtime pay.

**Registers**  To speed up processing, the ALU uses a **register** to temporarily hold instructions and data. This is the *storing* step of the machine cycle. **Storing** means writing or recording the result to memory. Registers are accessed much faster than memory locations outside the CPU. The time required to execute an instruction and store the result is called **execution time**, or **E-time**.

Various kinds of registers are used, each serving a specific purpose. Once processing begins, an **instruction register** holds instructions currently being executed. A **data register** holds the data items being acted upon. A **storage register** holds the immediate and final results of processing.

**Coprocessors**  In addition to the main processor, or CPU, a personal computer may also contain one or more coprocessors. A **coprocessor** is a special-purpose chip that assists the CPU in performing certain types of operations. The first mainstream coprocessor was a math coprocessor, which was used to perform mathematical computations more quickly for scientific, engineering, and statistical applications. Math coprocessors have now been integrated into most ALU components of microprocessor chips and are no longer separate chips. A **graphics coprocessor** is designed specifically for handling image-intensive applications, such as Web pages and computer-aided design programs. A **cryptographic coprocessor**, also called a crypto-coprocessor, provides encryption and related processing.

**Factors in Microprocessor Speed and Power**  The power and speed of microprocessor (CPU) chips are determined primarily by the number of transistors, the clock speed, and the number of bits that can be handled as a single unit. A variety of microprocessors with varying speeds and capabilities are available. Newer microprocessors are extremely fast and powerful and offer exceptional capabilities. For example, Intel Corporation's first Pentium 4 processor, introduced in 2000, contained 42 million transistors and had a clock speed of up to 1.7 gigahertz (GHz). Newer Intel microprocessors contain even more transistors and operate at speeds of  4.0 GHz or more. Contrast that capability with Intel's 80286 processor introduced in 1982, which had a clock speed of 6 to 12 megahertz (MHz) and a total of 134,000 transistors.

In 2003, Intel introduced the Pentium M chip for notebook computers. When packaged with an Intel Wi-Fi wireless adapter, the chip is called the Centrino. Notebook manufacturers quickly took advantage of the extended battery life and cooler operating temperatures of the Pentium M by offering several new ultralight notebooks that provide high-performance computing and wireless LAN capabilities. The Pentium M is especially useful for the Tablet PC, which needs a longer battery life and more processing power to manage handwriting recognition. Table 2-1 shows the clock speed and number of transistors for several microprocessors, and Table 2-2 lists similar statistics for mobile devices.

**Table 2-1   A Comparison of Desktop Personal Computer Processors**

| Processor Name | Manufacturer | Year of Introduction | Clock | Number of Transistors |
|---|---|---|---|---|
| 80286 | Intel | 1982 | 6–12 MHz | 134,000 |
| 68020 | Motorola | 1984 | 16–33 MHz | 190,000 |
| 80486DX | Intel | 1985 | 16–33 MHz | 275,000 |
| 68030 | Motorola | 1987 | 16–50 MHz | 270,000 |
| 68040 | Motorola | 1989 | 25–40 MHz | 1,200,000 |
| Pentium | Intel | 1993 | 75–200 MHz | 3,300,000 |
| Pentium Pro | Intel | 1995 | 150–200 MHz | 5,500,000 |
| Pentium II | Intel | 1997 | 233–450 MHz | 7,500,000 |
| Celeron | Intel | 1998 | 266–633 MHz | 19,000,000 |
| Athlon | AMD | 1999 | 1.1 GHz | 22,000,000 |
| Pentium III | Intel | 1999 | 1.0 GHz | 28,000,000 |
| Pentium 4 | Intel | 2000 | 1.3 GHz | 42,000,000 |
| Athlon XP | AMD | 2001 | 1.7 GHz | 77,000,000 |
| PowerPC 970 | IBM | 2003 | 1.8 GHz | 52,000,000 |
| Athlon 64 FX | AMD | 2005 | 2.8 GHz | 114,000,000 |
| Athlon 64 X2 | AMD | 2005 | 2.8 GHz | 233,000,000 |
| Pentium D (dual core) | Intel | 2005 | 2.8–3.2 GHz | 230,000,000 |
| Athlon 64 (dual core) | AMD | 2005 | 2.0–3.2 GHz | 233,000,000 |
| i7-950 | Intel | 2008 | 3.06 GHz | 731,000,000 |
| Phenom X4 | AMD | 2008 | 4.00 GHz | 463,000,000 |

**Table 2-2   A Comparison of Notebook Computer and Mobile Device Processors**

| Processor Name | Manufacturer | Year of Introduction | Clock Speed | Number of Transistors |
|---|---|---|---|---|
| Pentium Mobile | Intel | 1997 | 200 MHz | 55,000,000 |
| Celeron Mobile | Intel | 1999 | 266 MHz | 18,900,000 |
| Mobile Duron | AMD | 2000 | 1.3 GHz | 25,000,000 |
| Pentium M | Intel | 2003 | 1.3 GHz | 77,000,000 |
| Celeron | Intel | 2004 | 1.0 GHz | 55,000,000 |
| Turion 64 | AMD | 2005 | 2.4 GHz | 114,000,000 |
| Core 2 Extreme quad core | Intel | 2008 | 2.53 GHz | 820,000,000 |

# The Chip Debate

**LOYAL CUSTOMERS AT THE BAJA BEACH CLUB** in Barcelona can pay for a drink or get immediate access to the VIP lounge with just the wave of an arm—an arm that has been implanted with the VeriChip.

Employees at the Cincinnati video surveillance company CityWatch.com who need to get into the high-security database will now find it off limits unless they agree to have a VeriChip implanted under their skin.

The Pentagon is considering VeriChip implants in place of dog tags for its military personnel.

So what is this VeriChip? It is a glass-encapsulated radio frequency identification (RFID) tag about the size of a grain of rice. Dog and cat owners have used such "smart tags" to ensure that their pet can be tracked down if lost, and companies have used tags in consumer products to track sales and shipping. RFIDs have been promoted as a way to keep Alzheimer patients from wandering and as a way to literally keep medical records within arm's reach while traveling.

But the broadening use of RFIDs in humans has ignited an international debate. There are questions about security. The information on VeriChips is at present unencrypted, and anyone who attains access to it could easily read the data. Also, directions for making a cloning device that could easily swipe the ID number of a chip nearby are on the Internet.

In addition, to a lot of people the very idea of a "spy chip" smacks of Big Brother. These critics see the VeriChip as just another step toward an Orwellian world that already accepts government monitoring of cell phone calls, "black boxes" that collect data on driver behavior in automobiles, and public security cameras everywhere. When VeriChip Chairman Scott Silverman floated the idea on television of using his product to verify the whereabouts of guest workers, it only added to fears of VeriChips being used to control and monitor people. The debate is so heated that Wisconsin recently enacted a law making it a criminal offense to force an individual to have a chip implanted.

There is also the belief of some Christian leaders that the chip is a tool of the devil as prophesied in the Bible. The Book of Revelations tells of a time when no one can buy or sell without a mark on the right hand—the so-called "mark of the beast,"—and that connection could be a public relations nightmare for VeriChip.

---

A microprocessor's **word size** also affects its power and speed. In microprocessor terms, a **word** is a group of bits or bytes that a computer can manipulate or process as a unit. Some microprocessor chips are 32-bit chips, meaning they can handle 32-bit blocks of data at a time. Newer microprocessors are designed to handle 64-bit blocks of data at a time. For example, Intel's Pentium 4 chip is designed for 64-bit blocks of data, and the chip's main circuitry also accommodates 64-bit words. This means that a 64-bit data path leads from the CPU to RAM, which translates into faster processing.

**Microprocessor Performance Improvements** Since 1971, when Intel Corporation introduced the company's first microprocessor, chip designers have developed many techniques for improving the speed and performance of microprocessors. These techniques center on the raw materials used to make the chips, the density of the circuits on a chip, and changes in the way instructions are executed. Following is a summary of key advances in the development of micro-processors to date:

- **Reduced instruction set computing (RISC).** Many early computers and other devices used processors that contained a lengthy and complex set of instructions for processing data. Most modern computers now use a shortened set of instructions, called RISC, which increases their speed and efficiency.

- **Pipelining**. In older computers the CPU had to completely execute one instruction before starting a second instruction. Modern computers now use a technique called **pipelining**, which allows the CPU to execute instructions faster. Pipelining enables the computer to begin executing another instruction as soon as the previous instruction reaches the next phase of the machine cycle. Figure 2-15 shows the machine cycle with pipelining and Figure 2-16 shows the less efficient cycle without pipelining.

- **Closer circuits.** Newer computers contain chips with circuits packed much closer together than those in earlier chips, thereby decreasing the distance that instructions and data must travel. The closer packing makes them much faster and more efficient.

- **New and better materials.** Most chips consist of electrical circuits etched onto a piece of silicon. Some chip manufacturers are designing copper circuits to replace the aluminum circuits used today, because copper is a better conductor of electricity.

- **Parallel processing.** Despite the many performance improvements, most personal computers still use a single processor. This is primarily because a processor is the most expensive computer component, usually costing hundreds of dollars. With a single processor, instructions are executed *serially*, or one at a time. However, scientists have developed ways for two or more processors and memory components to work together simultaneously (in parallel). **Parallel processing** allows two or more processors to work

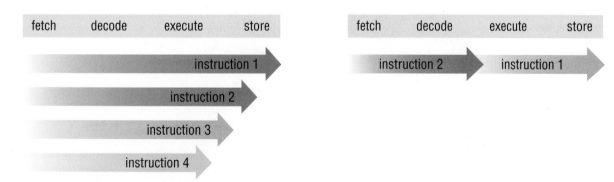

**Figure 2-15 Processing with Pipelining**
Computer processing speed is improved with pipelining. With pipelining, the computer begins executing a new instruction as soon as the previous instruction reaches the next phase of the machine cycle.

**Figure 2-16 Processing without Pipelining**
Older computers that did not use pipelining execute an instruction after the previous instruction completes the machine cycle. This is less efficient than when processing is done with pipelining.

concurrently on segments of a lengthy application, thus dramatically increasing processing capability.

- **Multithreading and hyperthreading.** Some newer microprocessors provide multithreading and hyperthreading capabilities that allow operating systems and applications software, such as Windows, to process applications faster. In programming, a thread is a part of a program that can execute independently of other parts. **Multithreading** refers to a carefully designed program that enables several threads to execute at the same time without interfering with each other. Intel has developed a technology called **hyperthreading**, which allows its Pentium series of microprocessors to execute multithreaded software applications simultaneously and in parallel rather than processing threads in linear fashion, thereby greatly increasing processing speed.

- **Dual-core and multi-core processors.** To speed processing, some processors now offer dual-core processors and multi-core processors for personal computers and servers. The word **core** refers to the essential processor components. A **dual-core processor** (Figure 2-17) is a CPU that includes two complete cores per physical processor, meaning a single integrated circuit (silicon chip) contains two processors and their cache memories (discussed later in this chapter). A **multi-core processor** contains more than two separate processors on a single chip. Dual-core and multi-core processors are well suited for multitasking environments in which a user can be working with multiple computing tasks concurrently.

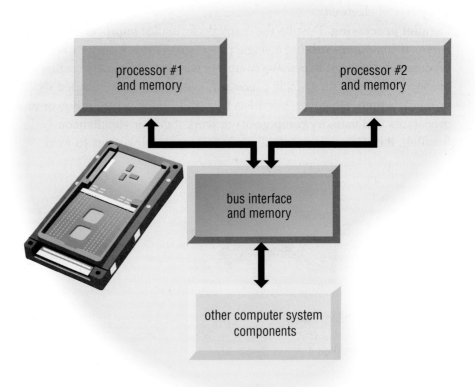

**Figure 2-17 Dual-Core Processor**
A dual-core processor is a CPU that includes two complete cores per physical processor, meaning that a single integrated circuit (silicon chip) contains two processors and their cache memories.

**NOBEL PRIZE WINNER**

# Jack S. Kilby

**THE 2000 NOBEL PRIZE IN PHYSICS** was awarded to 76-year-old Jack Kilby for his work on the integrated circuit, which paved the way for the technological revolution that became known as the "Information Age." The development of the integrated circuit permitted gigantic gains in computer power.

Kilby's first integrated circuit, about the size of a thumbnail, was built in 1958. His novel idea was to develop the numerous electrical transistors in the chip's circuit from a single block of material, rather than assembling them with wires and other components. Kilby's work led to the integrated circuits of today, shrunk in size and loaded with millions of transistors. Without the integrated circuit, the personal computers of today would not have been possible.

Also credited with coinventing the pocket calculator, Kilby worked for Texas Instruments until 1970 and then became a freelance inventor. He held more than 60 patents and has been awarded honorary degrees from three universities. Kilby said he had no idea how much his microchip would expand the field of electronics. Until his death in 2005, he still listened to music on a turntable and did not own a cell phone.

Kilby received half of the $915,000 Nobel prize. The other half was shared by two physicists who invented semiconductor heterostructures. The Nobel Prize is usually awarded for an abstract theoretical insight or an experimental

technique. This is the first time the award was given for engineering rather than pure science. As a nod to the worldwide impact of the Internet, the Royal Swedish Academy of Sciences gave the prize to three men whose work enabled the growth of computer technology.

## System Clock

A computer contains a **system clock** in the form of a small electronic chip that synchronizes or controls the timing of all computer operations. The clock generates evenly spaced electrical pulses that synchronize the flow of information through the computer's internal communication channels.

Pulses of the clock execute or "trigger" instructions. Since an instruction may direct the execution of other events either internal or external to the CPU, the clock pulse provides a way for these events to occur in harmony. Pulse speed is measured according to the number of clock pulses per second, called **hertz**. One hertz is equal to one pulse per second.

One **clock cycle** is equal to two ticks of the clock. A CPU uses a fixed number of clock cycles to execute each instruction. The faster the clock ticks, the faster the CPU can execute instructions. Some personal computers today operate at clock speeds faster than one gigahertz. The speed of the clock affects only the speed of the CPU. It has no effect on the operation of peripheral devices.

## Random Access Memory

**Random access memory (RAM)**, also called main memory or primary storage, is the temporary memory in which programs and data are stored while the computer is in use. Programs must first be entered, or input, into RAM before they are executed or data is processed. The CPU then moves information from RAM into its registers for processing. RAM performs these three functions:

- accepts and holds program instructions and data
- acts as the CPU's source for data and instructions and as a destination for operation results
- holds the final processed information until it can be sent to the desired output or storage devices, such as a printer or disk drive

Each memory location has its own unique address, just as each person has a postal mailing address. When the CPU needs an instruction or data from memory, an electronic message is sent to the appropriate address and the instruction or data is transferred to the appropriate register in the CPU.

The CPU must be able to find programs and data once they are stored in RAM. Therefore, program instructions and data are placed at a specific location within RAM, known as an **address**. Each location has its own unique address, just as each person has an individual postal mailing address. When the CPU needs an instruction or data from RAM, an electronic message is sent to the instruction's address and the instruction is transferred to the appropriate register in the CPU.

*Random* access means that because each RAM location has an individual address, the computer can go directly to the instructions and data it needs, rather than search each individual location one after another (sequentially). RAM memory is both readable and writable, meaning that the contents of any RAM location can be changed and/or read at any time. RAM memory is also **volatile memory**, meaning that it requires a constant charge to keep its contents intact. If a computer loses power, the contents of its memory are lost. Therefore, it is important to save any valuable work frequently to a permanent storage medium.

The temporary nature of RAM is its most important characteristic. When the computer is finished with one set of instructions and data, it can store another set in the first set's place. RAM is reusable, much like a chalkboard. Instructions and data can be written on the chalkboard (or into RAM) and then erased to make room for new instructions and data to be written in the same space.

**Types of RAM** Two types of RAM used with early PCs were **Dynamic RAM (DRAM**, pronounced dee-ram) and **Static RAM (SRAM**, pronounced ess-ram). Some personal computers contained either, or both, types. Without a continuous supply of electrical energy, DRAM chips eventually lose their contents. Because of this, DRAM chips must be constantly refreshed by receiving a fresh supply of energy. SRAM is a static type of RAM that is faster and more reliable (and more expensive) than the more common DRAM. The term *static* refers to the fact that SRAM doesn't need to be refreshed like DRAM and it therefore allows a faster access time.

Over the years, newer computers have been introduced that contain faster microprocessors. To accommodate the increased speed, chip manufacturers have designed and built faster RAM chips. **Synchronous DRAM (SDRAM)** divides RAM into two separate memory banks to increase the processing of memory requests. **Double Data Rate SDRAM (DDR SDRAM)** can transfer data twice as fast as SDRAM because it reads data twice during each clock cycle. DDR2 and DDR3 are newer versions of DDR SDRAM offering significant improvements in speed and performance.

The amount of main memory in a computer is important. Large programs, such as desktop publishing and computer-aided design applications, require a lot of main memory. A computer may be unable to use a program if the computer's main memory is insufficient. Additional RAM chips can be installed inside the system unit on most computers.

**Measuring RAM Capacities** RAM storage capacities are measured in bytes. Since most personal computers have enough memory to store millions or even billions, of bytes, it is common to refer to storage capacity in terms of **kilobytes** (equal to one thousand bytes), **megabytes** (equal to one million bytes), and even **gigabytes** (one billion bytes). Storage capacities of personal computers are typi-

**Table 2-3  Measures of Data Storage**

| Term | Abbreviation | Mathematical Notation | Approximate Number of Bytes | Exact Number of Bytes |
|------|-------------|----------------------|----------------------------|----------------------|
| bit | | | 0 or 1 | 1/8 |
| byte | | 1 | 1 | |
| kilobyte | KB | $2^{10}$ | 1 thousand | 1,024 |
| megabyte | MB | $2^{20}$ | 1 million | 1,048,576 |
| gigabyte | GB | $2^{30}$ | 1 billion | 1,073,741,824 |
| terabyte | TB | $2^{40}$ | 1 trillion | 1,099,411,627,7756 |
| petabyte | PB | $2^{50}$ | 1 quadrillion | 1,125,899,906,842,624 |
| exabyte | EB | $2^{60}$ | 1 quintillion | 1,151,921,504,606,846,976 |
| zettabyte | ZB | $2^{70}$ | 1 sextillion | 1,180,591,620,717,303,424 |
| yottabyte | YB | $2^{80}$ | 1 septillion | 1,208,925,819,614,629,174,706,176 |

cally quoted as 512 megabytes, or as one or more gigabytes. By contrast, today's mainframe computer storage is often measured in **terabytes**, or trillions of bytes, and the most powerful supercomputers offer storage capacities expressed in **petabytes**, each of which is approximately 1,000 terabytes. The prefix tera- is derived from the Greek word for monster, an apt association to the tremendous size of a terabyte. Table 2-3 displays the various measurements of storage. Table 2-4 shows the amount of memory typically contained in various types of computers.

**Cache Memory**  A type of processing storage used with RAM is cache memory. **Cache memory** (pronounced *cash*) is a holding area in which the data and instructions most recently called by the processor from RAM are stored. When a processor needs an instruction or data from RAM, it first looks for the instruction in cache memory. Because some instructions are called frequently, they are often found in cache memory, shortening processing time. Cache memory may be con-

**Table 2-4  Computer Memory Comparisons**

| Type of Computer | Number of Processors | Amount of Memory |
|------------------|---------------------|------------------|
| handheld computer | usually one | 64 MB or more |
| notebook PC | usually one | 256 MB or more |
| desktop PC | usually one or two | 512 MB or more |
| workstation | one or two | 128–1,024 MB or more |
| midsize server | several | hundreds of GB or more |
| mainframe | hundreds | hundreds of GB or more |
| supercomputer | hundreds to thousands | hundreds of TB to several petabytes |

tained on the CPU in the form of memory chips hardwired onto the motherboard, or as reserved space on a storage device such as a hard disk. Some operating systems also allow users to set aside a portion of RAM to be used as cache memory.

There are various types of cache memory. **Level 1 cache memory** is built into the architecture of microprocessor chips, providing faster access to the instructions and data residing in cache memory. **Level 2 cache memory** may also be built into the architecture of microprocessor chips, as is the norm for current processors. On older computers, it may consist of high-speed SRAM chips placed on the motherboard or on a card that is inserted into a slot in the computer. **Level 3 cache memory** is available on computers that have level 2 cache, or advanced transfer cache, and is separate from the microprocessor.

**Memory Access Time** **Memory access time** is the amount of time required for the processor to access (read) data, instructions, and information from memory. Access time affects the speed at which the computer can process data and therefore the overall performance of the computer. Access time is usually stated in fractions of a second, as shown in Table 2-5. For example, a millisecond (abbreviated as ms) is one-thousandth of a second, and a picosecond is one-trillionth of a second. A processor with a memory access time of 50 nanoseconds would be twice as fast as one with an access time of 100 nanoseconds. However, computer manufacturers usually describe memory in terms of the amount of memory, not its speed. Thus, a manufacturer may specify a computer as having 512 MB of memory that can be expanded to 2 GB.

## Read-Only Memory and Flash Memory

A computer's system unit has one or more **read-only memory (ROM)** chips that contain instructions or data permanently placed on the chip by the manufacturer. Figure 2-18 shows the location of RAM and ROM on the motherboard. The contents of a ROM chip can be read only by the user and cannot be altered or erased. ROM chips store nonvolatile memory. **Nonvolatile memory** is memory that is not lost if the power is interrupted. A typical PC contains ROM chips on which essential programs have been stored. One such program is the **basic input/output system (BIOS)**, the program that boots (starts) the computer when it is turned on. The BIOS also controls communications with the keyboard, disk drives, and other computer components. Also activated with the startup of the computer is a **power-on self test (POST) chip**, containing instructions that check the physical components of the system to make certain they are working properly.

## Table 2-5 Memory Access Times

| Term | Abbreviation | Speed |
|------|--------------|-------|
| millisecond | ms | one-thousandth of a second |
| microsecond | μs | one-millionth of a second |
| nanosecond | ns | one-billionth of a second |
| picosecond | ps | one-trillionth of a second |

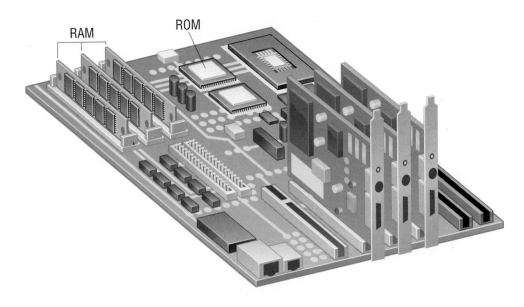

RAM

ROM

**Figure 2-18 Location of RAM and ROM on the Motherboard**
RAM chips temporarily store programs and data during the processing stage of the information processing cycle. On some small computers, ROM chips contain permanent storage of the operating system and the instructions for managing peripheral devices.

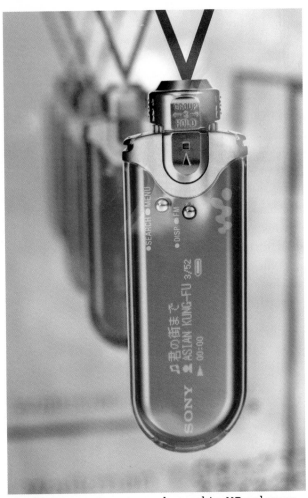

Flash memory is commonly used in MP3 players and digital cameras.

A computer also may have ROM chips containing permanent instructions that direct the operation of peripheral devices, including the keyboard, monitor, and disk drives. Without these ROM chips, users would need to enter complex instructions each time the devices are used.

**Flash memory**, also referred to as flash ROM, is a type of nonvolatile memory that can be erased and reused, or reprogrammed. Flash memory is used for storing programs and data on many handheld computers and devices, such as digital cameras, PDAs, cellular phones, and MP3 players. Some flash memory is portable. With digital cameras, a flash memory card can be removed and inserted into a printer or photo processing kiosk for instant printing. Portable flash drives are becoming increasingly common for transferring files between computers.

Several different types of removable flash cards are in use today, but they are physically different and incompatible with each other. The manufacturer and type of handheld device purchased will dictate the type of flash card used. Different types of flash cards include CompactFlash (CF), SmartMedia, Secure Digital (SD), MultiMediaCard (MMC), xD-Picture, and Memory Stick. The storage capacity of these flash cards typically ranges between 16 MB and 8 GB of data, and capacity is always increasing.

Flash memory is a small, portable card used to store various kinds of data and can be used in many different electronic devices.

## Expansion Slots and Expansion Cards

An **expansion slot** is an opening in the motherboard allowing the insertion of an **expansion card** (also called an adapter). Expansion cards are add-on components to required computer functions. These cards are used to either upgrade basic functionality such as graphics quality or they may be used to add new functionality such as networking.

Although a variety of expansion cards are available, the four main types typically found in today's computers as add-on components are sound cards, video or graphics cards, network interface cards, and modem cards. A **sound card** allows sound input, such as voice, by means of a microphone and sound output via speakers. A **graphics card** (also called a video card) enhances the quality of pictures and images displayed on the monitor. A **network interface card** allows for communication between the computer and a network. A **modem card** enables computers to communicate via telephone lines and other communications media. Newly purchased personal computers typically include many of the necessary cards already

An expansion card is a circuit board that can be installed inside a system unit, usually on the motherboard. Shown here are a graphics card (left), sound card (middle), and a network interface card (right).

**Table 2-6 Expansion Cards**

| Type of Card | Function |
|---|---|
| graphics card | enables a computer system to process and display high-quality graphics and video |
| modem card | enables a computer system to use telephone lines for communication between computers |
| network card | enables a computer system to participate in a local area network |
| sound card | allows high-quality sound input via a microphone and output via speakers |
| TV tuner card | allows a PC to pick up television signals |
| wireless network card | enables a computer to receive nearby wireless network signals |

installed, and additional expansion cards may be inserted into slots within a computer to add or upgrade some of the capabilities listed in Table 2-6.

Notebook and other portable computers are often too small to accommodate large motherboards, expansion boards, and other components. As a result, a type of expansion board called a **PC card** (or PCMCIA card) was developed specifically for smaller PCs. PC cards were replaced by **CardBus** technology, which was faster than PC cards, and CardBus has since been replaced by **ExpressCard**. The standards that are used to monitor these technologies have been developed by the Personal Computer Memory Card International Association (PCMCIA). The cards plug into the side of a notebook or portable computer. Most are about the size of a credit card, only thicker, and can be unplugged and removed when no longer needed.

CardBus (left) and ExpressCard cards are used primarily on laptop computers. They most commonly add wireless networking capability.

CHAPTER 2 Input and Processing

# Ports

A **port** (sometimes called an interface) is an external plug-in slot on a computer used to connect to a device such as a printer or a telephone line. Personal computers have ports that are "dedicated," meaning they are reserved for connecting a specific device. For example, a personal computer has a dedicated port for connecting a keyboard and another for connecting a mouse. Personal computers usually contain the following types of ports, as shown in Figure 2-19:

- Dedicated ports for connecting a mouse and a keyboard.
- A **Universal Serial Bus (USB) port** is widely used for high-speed modems, scanners, digital cameras, and other devices. Many keyboards and point-and-click devices are now available with USB ports as well. A single USB port can accommodate more than 100 peripheral devices connected together in sequence.
- A **serial port** (also called a communications [COM] port), is used for connecting some peripheral devices such as a keyboard, mouse, PDA, or external modem. A serial port can transmit data only one bit at a time. Most personal computers have at least one serial port, but dedicated ports and USB ports have largely replaced the use of serial ports.
- A **parallel port** is used for connecting a peripheral device to a computer. Older personal computers have at least one parallel port that is usually used for connecting a printer. Newer computers typically use USB ports to connect printers. A parallel port transmits data eight bits at a time. On personal computers, a parallel port uses a 25-pin connector.
- A **video port** connects a monitor and may be built into the computer or provided by a graphics card placed in an expansion slot.
- A **network port** connects a computer system to a local area network. The cable used to connect to a network has an RJ-45 connector, which is slightly larger than a telephone cable connector.
- A **modem port** connects a modem card to a telephone line. The cable used to connect to a telephone line is a standard telephone cable with an RJ-11 connector.
- An **audio port** connects a sound card to external devices such as speakers, microphones, and headsets.

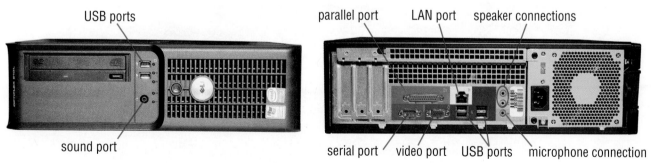

**Figure 2-19 Ports on a System Unit**
Ports are external plug-in slots that connect devices such as monitors, keyboards, and printers to the system unit. These ports are visible on the front and back of the system unit.

Due to size constraints, most personal computers have a limited number of ports, restricting the number of devices that can be connected. Some notebook computers can be inserted in a **docking station**, an accessory that provides additional ports plus (typically) a charger for the laptop's battery, extra disk drives, and other peripherals.

## Buses

Go to this title's Internet Resource Center and read the article titled "Bus Technology." www.emcp.net/CUT4e

How does data move from one component to another inside a computer? The answer is that every computer contains buses that connect various components and allow the transmission of data. A **bus** is an electronic path within a computer system along which bits are transmitted (see Figure 2-20). The size of a bus, referred to as **bus width**, determines the number of bits the computer can transmit or receive at one time. For example, a 32-bit bus can handle 32 bits at one time, whereas a 64-bit bus can handle 64 bits at one time. The larger the number of bits a bus can handle at one time, the faster the computer can transfer data. One way to visualize a bus is to think of it as a highway allowing data to travel from one location to another, with "bus stops" along the way where data is dropped off or picked up. The more lanes in the highway, the greater the number of "vehicles" ("0s" and "1s") that can travel on the highway at one time.

Computers contain two basic bus types: a system bus and an expansion bus. A **system bus** on the motherboard connects the processor (CPU) to main memory, providing the CPU with fast access to data stored in RAM. An **expansion bus** provides for communication between the processor and peripheral devices. For example, data traveling between RAM and a low-speed peripheral device, such as a printer or scanner, travels along an expansion bus.

A typical personal computer contains a variety of expansion buses. A **local bus** allows for the connection of high-speed devices such as hard drives. A **Peripheral**

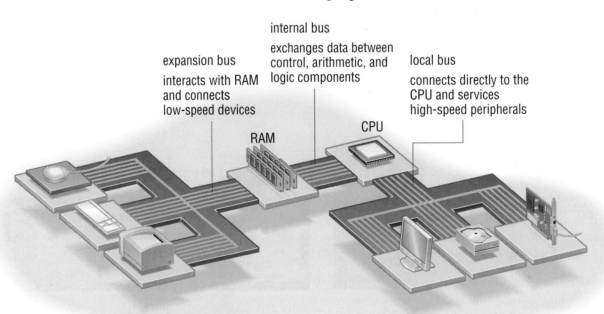

**Figure 2-20 Bus Connections**
Data in the form of bits travel along a bus to get from one location in a computer system to another, similar to the way vehicles travel along a highway. Bits travel along a bus from memory to the CPU, from input devices to memory, from the CPU to memory, and from memory to storage devices.

Component Interconnect (PCI) bus allows for the connection of sound cards, video cards, and network cards to a computer system. The speed at which data travels along a PCI bus is much faster than the speed at which data traveled in earlier bus technologies. Most personal computers now contain a PCI bus. An **Accelerated Graphics Port (AGP) bus** increases the speed at which graphics (including 3-D graphics) and video can be transmitted and accessed by the computer. Most newer processors, including Intel's Pentium processors, support AGP technology. For newer PCs, AGP is being replaced by the **PCI Express bus** standard for 3-D graphic cards. PCI-Express provides much faster data transfer rates than the original PCI, making it better suited for applications such as streaming video and computer games. The Universal Serial bus (USB) eliminates the need to install a board into a slot. This means that multiple external devices can be connected together and then connected to the computer's USB with a single cable. One device may be disconnected and another device connected while the computer is running, a capability known as **hot plugging** or hot swapping.

# OnThe**Horizon**

**THERE CAN BE LITTLE DOUBT** new and exciting computer technologies will continue to appear on the computing horizon. A variety of new input and processing technologies will increase the speed and capability of computers, making our lives more enjoyable and exciting. The following paragraphs identify some technologies we may expect to be introduced within a few years, if not earlier.

## Advances in Nanotechnology

Researchers in such fields as physics, chemistry, materials science, and computer science are using nanotechnology, which involves crafting machines from individual atoms, to build microscopic, massively parallel computers that are more powerful than the supercomputers of today. These computers could be programmed to replicate themselves and be injected into a human body to hunt down deadly viruses or cancers and destroy them. Scientists have already used the technology to create carbon nanotubes that are 100 times stronger and 100 times lighter than steel. Nanotubes can be used to develop semiconductors, aircraft, automobiles, and many other things. Nanotechnology robots (nanobots) could be used to clean up dangerous environmental spills and perform other tasks not suited well to humans.

Currently the U.S. government spends over 11 billion dollars on nanotechnology research and development, a figure that is undoubtedly exceeded by private sector R & D. These efforts have resulted in a number of real-world applications, and in 2005 sales of products incorporating nanotechnology exceeded 32 billion dollars, with

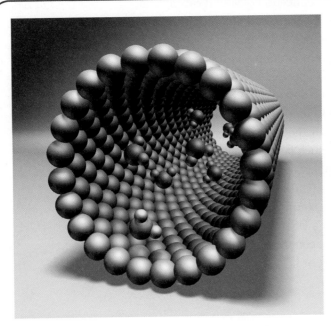

Nanotubes are at the core of nanotechnology, which builds computers at the atomic level.

predictions that sales will reach $2.6 trillion by 2014. Improvements brought about by nanotechnology are the reason for the rapid increase in sales figures. Intel predicts that its processor performance per watt will improve 300 percent by 2010 through the use of nanotechnology. The company is currently using 45 nanometers silicone technology, and plans to reduce that to 22 nanometers by 2011. To give an idea of how small these products are, a single nanometer is one billionth of a meter. The benefits of nanotechnology bring with them some dangers, particularly as the technology is employed in the health and environmental fields. Only 11 million of the 11 billion dollars the U.S. spends on nanotechnology R & D is devoted to studying the risks of the technology, a figure that many government and industry experts feel is far too low.

## Cell: A New Microprocessor Architecture

The Internet and Web have created a need for computers capable of handling massive amounts of information. Computers available now are relatively slow in accessing the Internet and downloading information. IBM, along with Sony and Toshiba, has created the first iteration of a new microprocessor architecture called Cell.

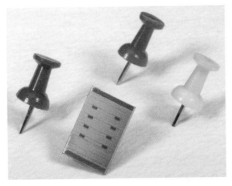

The Cell microprocessor, smaller than a quarter, debuted in the Sony Playstation 3.

Fashioned after supercomputing technology, the Cell microprocessor is based on cellular technology that will allow computers to run on tiny processors that are integrated directly with memory and communications circuits. IBM describes the future state as the equivalent of putting 32 desktop computers on a dime-sized chip. Each of these new chips will contain 32 to 36 cells, each of which will have a 1 GHz processor and up to 1 GB of memory. The expected result will be computers with computing capabilities equal to that of today's mainframe computers.

Cell has already been designed into the Sony Playstation 3, running ten times faster than the latest Intel Pentium chip. As Cell evolves, future applications may include smartphones, high-definition televisions, missile systems, radar, and medical imaging.

## Next-Generation Keyboards

Efforts to improve the ubiquitous keyboard continue apace. A Russian company recently announced a unique design featuring keys containing miniature display screens. Each key's screen can be instantly changed to show the function controlled by the key, whether it be alphanumeric characters or symbols. When a key's function changes its display will automatically change as well, making it an ideal keyboard for anyone needing to work with different character sets. The Optimus keyboard also can automatically display the function keys unique to many different programs, or display keys that control access to different software programs.

As computer devices continue to shrink the search for satisfactory input methods continues. Most solutions involve smaller keyboards or keypads, but several companies are now marketing laser keyboards that use both infrared and laser technology to project a virtual keyboard onto almost any surface, allowing users to type away on a full-size QWERTY Keyboard. The virtual keyboard is projected by a small battery-powered wireless device that can be rested in front of any flat surface, and can be attached to portable computers and mobile devices, including PDAs and cell phones.

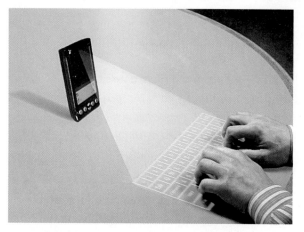

Virtual keyboards, or projection keyboards, are available as extensions to handheld computers for easier data entry.

## Smart Homes

Modern homes are full of labor-saving, entertainment, comfort, and security devices. The long-held dream of linking this equipment so that control can be automated is now being realized, and even updated to include the ability to control functions through the Internet. Homes equipped with the structured wiring and computerized control systems allowing intelligent control of household devices are known as Smart Homes. While it is possible for builders to install the required structured wiring into older homes, it is much easier to install it during the construction process, something that more and more builders are doing. As the technology proliferates the cost of equipping Smart Homes has dropped, and they are no longer confined to the upper levels of the real estate market.

While wiring still predominates as a connection method, home product wireless technologies such as Z-Wave are increasingly being employed. The Z-Wave Alliance is a consortium of independent companies who have adopted the Zensys' Z-Wave open standard. A key feature of Z-Wave products is their compatibility with other products operating to the Z-Wave standard. Current Smart Homes usually contain a combination of structured wiring and wireless technologies, but in the not too distant future it is likely that all household devices will be linked wirelessly.

# Chapter**Summary**

 *For an interactive version of this summary, go to this text's Internet Resource Center at www.emcp.net/CUT4e. A Spanish version is also available.*

## What is input?

The term input refers to data and instructions entered into a computer enabling the computer to perform the task desired by the user.

## What are some examples of input devices?

An **input device** allows programs, data, commands, and responses to be entered into a computer system. Types of input devices include **keyboards**, **touch screens**, **mice** (plural for mouse), **trackballs**, **touch pads**, **joysticks**, **pens** and **tablets**, **optical scanners**, **bar code readers** and **optical readers**, **microphones**, **digital cameras**, **video cameras**, and **webcams**.

## How do computers process data?

Also called data processing or simply processing, the term information processing refers to the manipulation of data according to instructions in a computer program. All computers are digital devices that use the *binary number system*. They are capable of recognizing only "off" and "on" ("0" and "1") states. Each of these "0" and "1" digits is called a bit. A **bit** represents the smallest unit of data in the binary system. A group of eight bits is called a **byte**. Combinations of 0s and 1s are used to represent letters, numbers, and special characters in coding schemes such as **ASCII**, **EBCDIC**, and **Unicode**.

## What are the main components of the system unit?

The **system unit** is the component that houses the processing hardware. It consists of the **power supply**, **storage bays**, and the **motherboard**. The power supply converts AC electricity into power that the computer can use. **Storage bays** are used

for installing additional devices such as hard drives and CD/DVD drives. The **motherboard** contains the **central processing unit (CPU)**, **system clock**, **random access memory (RAM)**, **read-only memory (ROM)**, **expansion slots**, and **expansion cards**, **ports**, and **buses**.

## What makes up the central processing unit?

The **CPU** within the system unit is the part of a computer where processing occurs. In a personal computer the CPU consists of a **microprocessor chip**, that processes the data. The CPU contains a control unit and an arithmetic/logic unit. The **control unit** controls activity within the computer. The **arithmetic/logic unit (ALU)** performs processing operations on the data. **Registers** are used for storing instructions and data until they are needed for processing.

## What types of memory does a computer need?

A computer needs both random access memory and read-only memory to function. **Random access memory (RAM)** chips inside the system unit are used to store programs while they are being executed, and data while it is being processed. The amount of RAM is measured in bytes. A specific type of RAM, called **cache memory**, provides for faster access to instructions and data, speeding up computer applications.

   **Read-only memory (ROM)** refers to chips on which instructions, information, or data has been prerecorded. Usually, once data has been recorded on a ROM chip, it cannot be altered or removed and can only be read by the computer. However, **flash memory** is a special type of ROM that can be erased and reprogrammed.

## What are expansion slots and cards?

An **expansion slot** is an opening in a computer where a circuit board, called an **expansion card**, can be inserted to add new capabilities to the computer. A **PC card** is a small expansion card that plugs into the side of a notebook or portable computer.

# Key**Terms**

*Numbers indicate the pages where terms are first cited in the chapter. An alphabet-ized list of key terms with definitions (in English and Spanish) can be found on the Encore CD that accompanies this book. In addition, these terms and definitions are included in the end-of-book glossary.*

**Input Technology**
input device, 47
keyboard, 47
Bluetooth, 47
special-function keyboard, 48
touch screen, 49
graphical user interface (GUI), 49
mouse, 49
mouse pointer, 50
mouse pad, 50
optical mouse, 50
foot mouse, 50
trackball, 51
touch pad (track pad), 51
joystick, 52
digitizing pen, 53
drawing tablet, 53
graphics tablet, 53
optical scanner (scanner), 54
bitmap, 54
pixel, 54
resolution, 55
dots per inch (dpi), 55
dumb scanner, 55
intelligent scanner, 55
optical character recognition (OCR), 55
bar code reader, 56
Universal Product Code (UPC), 56
optical reader, 57
smart card, 57
digital camera, 57
video input, 59
webcam, 59
audio input, 61
voice input, 61
voice recognition program, 61

speaker-independent program, 62
speech recognition program, 62
speaker-dependent program, 62

**Data Processing by Computers**
machine language, 64
bit, 64
binary numbers, 64
byte, 64
American Standard Code for Information Interchange (ASCII), 64
Extended Binary Coded Decimal Interchange Code (EBCDIC), 65
Unicode, 65

**The System Unit**
system unit, 65

**The Power Supply**
power supply, 65

**Storage Bays**
storage bay (bay), 67

**The Motherboard**
motherboard, 68
trace, 68
microprocessor chip (integrated circuit), 69
semiconductor, 69
machine cycle, 70
control unit, 70
fetching, 70
decoding, 70
instruction time (I-time), 71
arithmetic/logic unit (ALU), 71
executing, 71
register, 72
storing, 72
execution time (E-time), 72
instruction register, 72
data register, 72
storage register, 72
coprocessor, 72
graphics coprocessor, 72
cryptographic coprocessor (crypto-coprocessor), 72

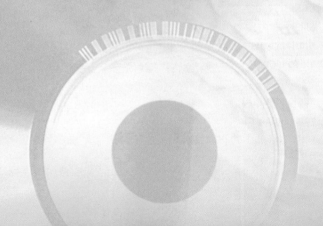

# ChapterExercises

## Tutorial > Exploring Windows

In Tutorial 2, you will explore new Vista features by opening the Help and Support Center and viewing an article describing the main features of Vista as well as viewing a demostration on security basics.

## Expanding Your Knowledge > Articles and Activities

 *Visit the Internet Resource Center for this title at www.emcp.net/CUT4e, read the articles related to this chapter, and complete the corresponding activities. The article titles include:*

- Topic 2-1: Processor Installation and Upgrades
- Topic 2-2: Advances in Chip Architecture
- Topic 2-3: Improvements in Chip Materials and Manufacturing Processes
- Topic 2-4: Bus Technology

## Terms Check > Matching

 *For additional practice, go to the Internet Resource Center for this title at www.emcp.net/CUT4e for a chapter crossword puzzle.*

Write the letter of the correct answer on the line before each numbered item.

a. motherboard
b. keyboard
c. arithmetic/logic unit
d. binary
e. port
f. fetching
g. system clock
h. register
i. expansion card
j. mouse

_____ 1. A number system that uses combinations of zeros and ones (0s and 1s) to represent letters, numbers, and special characters.

_____ 2. A circuit board that can be inserted into a computer to give the computer added capability.

_____ 3. Retrieving an instruction or data from memory.

_____ 4. The main circuit board inside the system unit.

_____ 5. A component of the ALU that temporarily holds instructions and data.

_____ 6. A small electronic chip that synchronizes or controls the timing of all computer operations.

_____ 7. An opening in the computer that allows an external component to be plugged into a circuit board.

_____ 8. A handheld point-and-click input device whose movement across a flat surface causes a corresponding movement of its on-screen pointer.

____ 9. The part of the CPU that carries out instructions and performs arithmetic and logical operations on the data.

____ 10. The most common input device used to enter alphanumeric characters into a computer.

## *Technology Illustrated* > **Identify the Process**

What process is illustrated in this drawing? Identify the process and write a paragraph describing it.

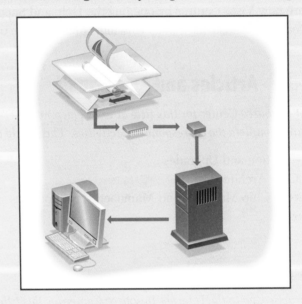

## *Knowledge Check* > **Multiple Choice**

  *Additional quiz questions are available on the Encore CD that accompanies this book as well as on the Internet Resource Center for this title at www.emcp.net/CUT4e.*

Circle the letter of the best answer from those provided.

1. Data and instructions entered into a computer that enable the computer to perform desired tasks are called
   a. processing.
   b. input.
   c. storage.
   d. controlling.

2. Data that has been processed in a manner that renders it meaningful and useful to the user is called
   a. input.
   b. information.
   c. a program.
   d. fetching.

3. A CPU contains
   a. a card reader and a printing device.
   b. an analytical engine and a control unit.
   c. a control unit and an arithmetic/logic unit.
   d. an arithmetic logic unit and a card reader.

4. The part of a computer that coordinates all of its functions is called its
   a. ROM program.
   b. system board.
   c. arithmetic/logic unit.
   d. control unit.

5. A byte is equal to
   a. four bits, or one nibble.
   b. six bits and one nibble.
   c. two bits.
   d. eight bits.

6. The system clock inside a computer ensures that the
   a. computer user will always know the correct time.
   b. computer will run faster than one without a system clock.
   c. activities of the computer will be properly synchronized.
   d. computer will be able to address a 32-bit data bus.

7. The parts of the information processing cycle are
   a. fetching, decoding, executing, and storing.
   b. fetching, comparing, interpreting, and outputting.
   c. inputting, interpreting, processing, and outputting.
   d. input, processing, output, and storage.

8. Processing speed in microprocessors is measured in
   a. megabytes.
   b. hertz.
   c. kilobytes.
   d. bits per second.

9. On a personal computer, all processing functions are contained on a single electronic chip called a
   a. microprocessor.
   b. data processor.
   c. calculation chip.
   d. BIOS chip.

10. A holding area that stores the data and instructions most recently called by the processor from RAM is called
   a. residual memory.
   b. nonvolatile memory.
   c. static memory.
   d. cache memory.

## Things That Think > Brainstorming New Uses

In groups or individually, contemplate the following questions and develop as many answers as you can.

1. Scientists have invented the first prototype of a computerized scalpel that can tell a surgeon when to stop cutting during surgery to remove cancerous tumors so that only the diseased tissue is removed. This technology would allow doctors to save healthy tissue, thus potentially improving the patient's odds for survival. What other fields could benefit from this development? Consider possible uses in various industries.

2. Computers can accomplish many tasks today, but there are still some things they cannot do. Think of some of the things you would like the computers of the future to be able to do. Which of the new uses will be the most popular and why?

## Key Principles > Completion

Fill in the blanks with the appropriate words or phrases.

1. A type of input device that allows a user to make selections from among a group of options displayed on a screen by pressing a finger against the chosen option is known as a(n) _____.

2. Material captured by a scanner is stored as a matrix of rows and columns of dots, called a _____.

3.  A computer language that uses binary numbers, which are constructed solely of the symbols 0 and 1, is known as _____.

4.  A type of code capable of accommodating certain languages having more complicated alphabets than English is called _____.

5.  Small electronic devices consisting of tiny transistors and other circuit parts on a piece of semiconductor material are called microprocessor chips or _____.

6.  A small electronic chip that synchronizes or controls the timing of all computer operations is the _____.

7.  A computer word is _____.

8.  Random access memory (RAM) is _____.

9.  Cache memory is _____.

10. The four steps or actions in the machine cycle are _____, _____, _____, and _____.

## *Tech Architecture >* Label the Drawing

In this illustration of a CPU, label the four basic operations of the machine cycle. Also, write a short description of the action taken in each step.

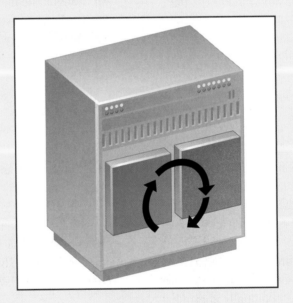

## *Techno Literacy >* Research and Writing

Develop appropriate written responses based on your research for each item.

1.  What is inside the computer case? Ask your instructor to allow you to open up a computer in the computer lab and look at the components inside. Using paper and pen, draw the components that you recognize and label each one. At a minimum, include the microprocessor chip, memory chips (RAM and ROM), expansion slots, expansion boards, and ports. Ask your instructor to explain other components you do not recognize. Label each one and write a brief summary of the component's function.

2. How many ways can users input data? Page through a computer magazine such as *PC World* or visit a computer store and select a personal computer that interests you. Research and describe all of the different input devices that could be used with that particular computer system.

3. What can you do with an expansion card? Describe the various types of expansion boards and their functions. What kind of expansion boards would you like to add to your computer? Why?

4. How do the kinds of computer memory differ? Describe the differences among RAM, ROM, flash memory, and cache memory. Is there any relationship between processing speed and the different types of memory? If so, what?

## Technology Issues > Team Problem-Solving

In groups, brainstorm possible solutions to the issues presented.

1. As our population ages, the number of Americans with disabilities will increase. Computers and computer technology offer the potential to make life easier for people who are disabled. What are some of the possibilities? What are some of the ways computer technology may be used to improve their lives in the future? Do you foresee any ethical problems with any of these solutions?

2. Even in today's computerized world there are still people who do not like computers and try to avoid them as much as possible. Why do you think people would feel that way? Do you see this attitude increasing or decreasing in the future? What can be done to combat this computer phobia (fear or dislike of computers), or should anything be done at all?

## Mining Data > Internet Research and Reporting

Conduct Internet searches to find the information described in the activities below. Write a brief report that summarizes your research results. Be sure to document your sources, using the MLA format (see Chapter 1, page 42, to review MLA style guidelines).

1. Moore's Law is a famous concept in the information technology industry. Developed around a prediction in 1965 by Gordon Moore, cofounder of Intel Corporation, the law holds that the computing capability of integrated circuits, measured by the number of transistors per square inch, doubles every two years (originally, Moore said 12 months). Research this topic and explain why Moore's Law continues to be accurate or why it has proved incorrect. What are industry leaders predicting for the future?

2. What is the most powerful supercomputer in the world? Where is it located? Who designed and manufactured the computer? What is it used for?

3. Research the topic of spying technologies that countries use to gather information on each other's activities. What are some of the newest devices and how successful are they?

## *Technology Timeline* > **Predicting Next Steps**

Look at the timeline below outlining the major benchmarks in the development of digital camera technology. Research this topic and fill in as many steps as you can. What do you think the next steps will be? Complete the timeline through the year 2030.

**1982**  Sony releases the first commercial electronic still camera, which was a video camera that took video freeze-frames.

**1989**  The first true digital camera that stores images with digital signals is introduced.

**1994**  The first digital cameras for the general consumer market are released.

**1995**  Sony debuts the first digital camcorder.

**2002**  Cell phones with digital cameras become available in the United States.

**2006**  The first feature film to be shot entirely with cell phones is completed.

## *Ethical Dilemmas* > **Group Discussion and Debate**

As a class or within an assigned group, discuss the following ethical dilemma.

As technology manufacturers look to cut costs, they often consider "outsourcing" production to an offshore company or moving production facilities to countries outside of the United States. Either of these options may result in savings due to lower labor and facilities costs.

In your group, discuss the issues of outsourcing production and moving production facilities to other countries. Are these practices illegal or unethical? Should such cost-cutting measures be considered more important than the employment of U.S. workers? Is it fair for companies to pay workers lower wages in another country? Should there be incentives for companies to maintain their facilities in the United States?

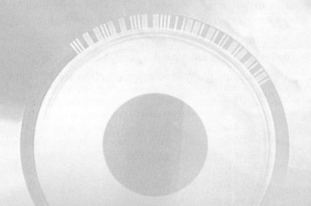

# CHAPTER 3

# Output and Storage

# CyberScenario

**ON THE DRIVE TO HER OFFICE, NELL BAKER,** vice-president of marketing at a New Jersey import company, contemplates her busy day ahead. First, she has a meeting with the company's district marketing managers, after which she will interview a candidate for a vacant district manager position in San Diego, California, and attend a board meeting via videoconference. Although she can't recall her other appointments, she will access her schedule when she arrives at the office. Pulling into her company's downtown parking deck, she parks in her reserved space, grabs her briefcase, locks her car, and takes the elevator to her office on the building's tenth floor.

As she approaches the door of her office suite, she remembers to pause while a security camera quickly photographs the iris of her right eye and compares the image to a previously captured image stored in the company's computer database. Within seconds a digitized voice greets her with the words, "Good morning, Ms. Baker," and the door to her suite is unlocked.

Entering her office, Nell is greeted by her administrative assistant and informed that her morning tea will soon be ready. Nell proceeds to her desk, settles into her chair, and presses a button underneath the desktop. A large screen connected to the information systems database descends from the ceiling as a voice from two hidden speakers says, "Good morning, Ms. Baker. What can I do for you?" Nell responds, "Get me the November sales reports for all marketing districts." Almost immediately, the report for the Northeast district appears on the screen, followed by the remaining district reports, each of which is displayed for 30 seconds. After a brief inspection of the information, Nell issues a voice command to print all the reports. Within minutes, the printer in the mahogany cabinet behind her desk has produced the documents.

Nell then issues a verbal command to display the application form and résumé of Charles Walker, whom she will interview at 10 a.m. for the vacant marketing position. Both documents are immediately displayed in the order in which they were requested. With Nell's command to print both documents, the laser printer quickly outputs the résumé and application, and Nell prepares to examine them more carefully. Finally, Nell issues a request to see her schedule for the day, which is promptly displayed on the drop-down screen above her desk. She spends the next few minutes carefully reviewing the marketing reports and Charles Walker's employment information.

All in all, it will be a typically fast-paced and productive day for Nell, made possible by modern state-of-the-art computer, storage, and output technologies that provide the information she needs to devise strategies and make decisions. Technologies similar to those Nell uses are rapidly becoming available in the workplace, allowing managers and employees to boost their productivity and enhance their employers' competitive position in the marketplace.

# Output

Recall from Chapter 1 that **output** is processed data that can be used immediately or stored in computer-usable form for later use. Output may be produced in either hard copy or soft copy, or in both forms. **Hard copy** is a permanent version of output, such as a letter printed on paper. **Soft copy** is a temporary version and includes any output that cannot be physically handled. For example, the information displayed on a bank teller's computer terminal screen during an account balance inquiry is considered soft copy. Voice output such as the telephone company's computerized directory assistance is another form of soft copy. We depend on all sorts of output in our daily lives.

## Types of Output

Computer output may consist of a single type of output or a combination of types. A properly equipped computer system is capable of outputting data in the form of text, graphics, audio, or video.

**Text** consists of characters and numbers used to create words, sentences, and paragraphs that compose various types of text-based documents including letters, memos, mailing labels, and newsletters. Web pages typically contain text and may also contain other forms of output including graphics, music, voice, and sound.

**Graphics** are computer-generated pictures produced on a computer screen, paper, or film. Also called graphical images, graphics range from simple line or bar charts to detailed and colorful images and pictures. Graphics are often seen on commercial Web page advertisements.

Soft copy output can be an effective way to share information quickly and efficiently. It can be more dynamic than hard copy output, and more portable as well.

It is common to see people listening to audio output.

Video and audio are often combined when home movies are made. Both the visual and audio components enhance the information that is output.

**Audio** is any sound, including speech and music. If a computer is equipped with a sound card and speakers, users can insert a CD or DVD into its drive and listen to music while relaxing or working on a project. Numerous Web sites provide sound that allows users to listen to a sales pitch describing a product or to sample selections from an advertised music CD.

**Video** consists of motion images, similar to those seen on a television or movie screen. Video is often accompanied by audio, making the output even more realistic and lifelike. A popular use of both audio and video is for creating home movies. By attaching a video camera to a computer, anyone can capture and play back movies of family members that record both images and conversation.

## Output Devices and Media

An **output device** is any hardware device that makes information available to a user. A computer produces output using the combination of output devices, media, and software available with a particular system. Popular output devices include displays (monitors), printers, plotters, televisions, and speakers. An **output medium** is any medium or material on which information is recorded. Examples of output media include paper, plastic film, and magnetic tape.

## Display Devices

A **monitor** is a fundamental component of every single-user computer system and is the most common soft copy output mechanism for displaying text, images, graphics, and video on a screen. Available in a variety of shapes, sizes, costs, and capabilities, monitors allow users to view information temporarily.

A monitor consists of a plastic case that houses a viewing screen and the electronic components that allow information to be displayed on the screen. Most mobile computers contain a monitor housed in the same case as the computer and other components. For example, the monitor of a notebook computer is attached to the case with hinges, allowing it to be viewed when the case is opened. The monitor of a handheld computer is also an integral part of the computer case.

Monitors are designed to operate smoothly with input devices, such as a keyboard. Information in the form of digital signals is entered into the processor, or CPU, by means of the keyboard or another input device. A **video card** (also called a graphics card or video adapter) converts digital signals into information, including text, pictures, and images, that is immediately displayed on the monitor screen.

While some older monitors displayed information in only one color, called monochrome, today's monitors are capable of displaying output in vivid color. Some are capable of displaying information in thousands of different colors and shades.

A computer monitor is a common soft copy output device.

Full-color displays are available in small, portable devices.

Monitors also come in a variety of sizes, from tiny two-inch screens for hand-helds and other mobile devices, to 21-inch (or larger) screens for PCs. Monitor sizes are measured diagonally, from one corner to the diagonally opposite corner. Common sizes for desktop PC monitors are 15, 17, 19, and 21 inches.

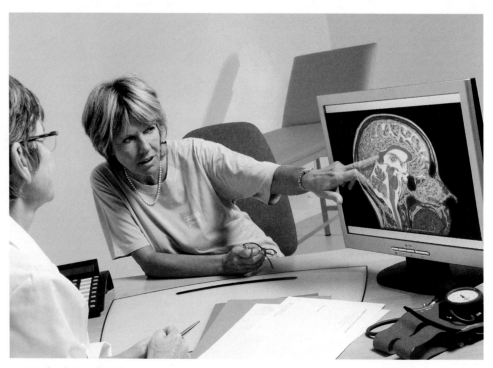

Large desktop displays can present vibrant, full-color images.

## Cathode Ray Tube (CRT) Monitors

The original type of monitor for desktop computers was the **cathode ray tube (CRT) monitor**. A CRT is a large, sealed glass tube housed in a plastic case. The front of the tube is the screen. A cable at the rear of the monitor plugs into a graphics adapter board on the motherboard inside the system unit. An electric cord on the monitor plugs into an electrical outlet. CRT monitors use the same cathode ray tube technology used in television sets, so most are fairly large and bulky. Smaller CRTs are used with terminals, such as those found in banks and retail establishments.

The screen of a CRT monitor is coated with tiny dots of phosphor material. An RGB monitor displays dots consisting of red, green, and blue phosphor. Red, green, and blue are primary colors, and they can be combined in various ways to produce a wide range of colors.

When information is sent to a CRT monitor, it is sent as an analog signal through a video card. A video card residing on the motherboard inside the system unit converts the digital signals produced by the computer into analog signals and sends them through a cable to the monitor. The type of display determines how the images appear on the screen.

## Flat-Panel Displays

A **flat-panel display** uses a technology that allows the screen to be smaller, thinner, and lighter than CRT monitors. An additional benefit of these lightweight compact screens is that they consume less power compared with CRT monitors. These features make them desirable among users of mobile devices, and they are increasingly found on desktop computers as well.

The majority of flat-panel displays use liquid crystals to produce information on the screen. In a **liquid crystal display (LCD)**, liquid crystals are sandwiched between two sheets of material. Electric current passing through the crystals causes them to twist. This twisting effect blocks some light waves and allows other light waves to pass through, creating images on the screen.

LCD monitors use digital signals, unlike CRT monitors that employ analog signals. Electronic circuitry converts analog signals coming from the video card back into digital signals. The cost of this technology has decreased to the point where LCD monitors are now inexpensive enough to include in new computer system packages sold by manufacturers. Very few CRT monitors are sold today.

LCD monitors feature active-matrix color displays. In an **active-matrix display**, also known as a thin-film transistor (TFT) display, separate transistors control each color pixel, allowing viewing from any angle. Large-size LCD monitors are now available that can be mounted on a wall in a video conferencing room.

Active-matrix displays produce clear, sharp images.

## Monitor Performance and Quality Factors

The quality and performance of monitors depend on three main factors:

- video card
- resolution
- refresh rate

## CEO, APPLE COMPUTER
# Steven Jobs

**STEVEN JOBS COULD SERVE AS THE PROTOTYPE** of America's computer industry entrepreneur. A college dropout fascinated with counterculture and Eastern thought, Jobs transformed himself into a millionaire by the age of 30. Additionally, he is credited with changing the way people think about technology and helping to ignite the personal computer revolution.

Jobs started his career as a video game designer at Atari. After spending time in college and traveling in the Middle East, Jobs returned to the United States and reconnected with friend and fellow technology enthusiast Steve Wozniak, who was working at Hewlett-Packard and building computers in his spare time. Jobs became convinced that Wozniak's latest computer, which became the Apple I, had market potential. Each sold a few prized possessions to raise $1,300, and together they started their computer business in Jobs' garage in 1976, naming the company Apple Computer based on Jobs' fond memories of a summer job in an Oregon orchard.

The Apple I was the first personal computer that appealed to a broad market of businesses, schools, and the public, and Apple Computer quickly became a $335 million company. But by 1981, IBM had joined the race for market dominance with the launching of the IBM PC, and Apple began losing ground. Meanwhile, Jobs was leading a development team that would soon change the face of personal computing. In December 1979, Jobs and his team visited the elite Xerox PARC research center, where they saw the Alto computer, a prototype that featured a graphical user interface and a mouse. Jobs' team rushed back to the office and modified specifications for the Lisa (a computer named after Jobs' daughter). Both the Lisa and its successor, the Macintosh, were launched with a mouse and a point-and-click interface.

Although the graphic user interface radically changed the way people use computers, the Macintosh fell short of its early sales predictions. In 1985, Jobs left the company. In 1986, he founded NeXT Software and purchased Pixar Animation Studios from filmmaker George Lucas. Under Jobs, Pixar produced *Toy Story* (the first wholly computer-generated film), *A Bug's Life, Toy Story 2,* and *Monsters Inc.,* all highly successful ventures.

In a strange twist, Jobs was invited back to Apple in 1996 when Apple bought NeXT for $400 million. Jobs became interim CEO, and helped turn around the company's dwindling market share with the introduction of the tremendously popular iMac and iBook computer lines in the summer of 1998.

In January 2000, Jobs was appointed permanent CEO of Apple Computers Inc. That same month, Apple also announced a $200 million investment in EarthLink, an Internet service provider that works with Apple to bring new online features to computer users. Under Jobs' direction, Apple continues to produce a variety of popular, innovative products, including the iPod and the iTunes music store.

**Video Card**   The display of graphics on a monitor is dependent on the memory and processor contained on the video card (or graphics card). Video cards usually have their own built-in video memory that is separate from the memory contained on the motherboard. Video memory is typically called Video RAM (or VRAM). The amount of VRAM on a video card determines the **bit depth** (also called color depth)—measured as bits per pixel—that drives the number of colors and the resolution of the display. It also dictates the speed at which signals are sent to the monitor. The amount of video memory ranges from 128 megabytes (MB) to 512 MB.

The number of colors a video card can display is determined by the number of bits used by the card to store information about each pixel (the bit depth). An 8-bit video card, often referred to as 8-bit color, uses 8 bits to store information about each pixel, whereas a 16-bit video card uses 16 bits. For example, an 8-bit video card can display 256 colors (28). A 16-bit video card can display 65,536 colors.

The greater the number of bits, the better and more clearly the image will be displayed on the screen. A 24-bit video card can display images more clearly than an 8-bit or 16-bit video card, and in true color. True color refers to any graphics device using at least 24 bits to represent each pixel. **True color** means that more than 16 million unique colors can be represented, a range that accommodates the complex shades and hues of our natural world (hence the term "true"). Since humans can only distinguish a few million colors, this is more than enough to accurately represent any color image.

**Resolution**   As with scanners and digital cameras, the number of pixels in the display determines the monitor's quality, or **resolution**. A **pixel** (short for picture element) is a tiny single point in anything being displayed on the screen. An electron beam moves back and forth across the rear of the screen causing the dots on the front of the screen to glow (see Figure 3-1). The glowing dots produce a character or

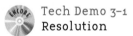

Tech Demo 3-1
Resolution

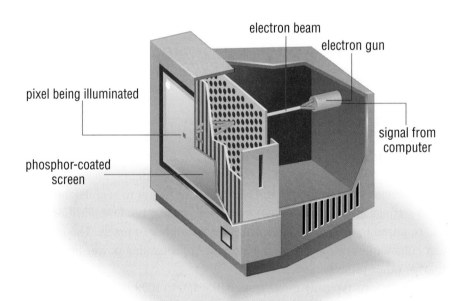

**Figure 3-1  CRT Monitor Mechanics**
An electron beam moves back and forth across a phosphor-coated screen, causing pixels to be illuminated.

**Figure 3-2  Resolution**
Images are displayed using pixels on the monitor screen. The greater the
number of pixels, the sharper the image.

image on the screen composed of pixels. Each pixel can be illuminated, or not illuminated, to produce an image on the screen, as shown in Figure 3-2.

The greater the number of pixels, the higher the resolution and the more
detailed the image. However, higher resolutions result in smaller displayed characters and images, which can be an advantage (more elements can be displayed)
or a disadvantage (smaller images and text may be difficult to see). Higher-
resolution settings also consume more processing power because additional
power is required to continually refresh a larger number of pixels. The increase
in power consumption slows down the amount of processing power immediately
available for other processing activities.

Screen resolutions typically range from 640 × 480 to 1600 × 1200 pixels or more.
Lower resolutions are suitable for displaying draft-quality text and images. Higher
resolution allows more accurate images to be displayed on the screen, and may be
desirable for users such as artists or Web page designers, who regularly work with
higher-quality text, graphics, and other detailed images. For a comparison, look
at Figure 3-3, which shows the same desktop displayed in a low-resolution and a

**Figure 3-3 Screen Resolution**
In the 800 × 600 pixels screen resolution (left), the desktop icons and the photo are larger than in the 1280 × 1024 pixels screen resolution (right).

high-resolution format. Most monitors sold today offer a range of resolution settings, which can be adjusted depending on the user's preference.

Another factor influencing image resolution is dot pitch. **Dot pitch** refers to the distance between the centers of pixels on a display. Less distance between pixels increases the quality of the displayed image. A smaller dot pitch makes text and graphics easier to read. Monitor dot pitch can range from 0.25 millimeters (mm) to 0.31 mm. A monitor having a dot pitch of 0.26 mm will display high-quality text and graphics and is suitable for most applications.

**Refresh Rate**  Refresh rate is yet another factor affecting monitor quality. Just as light from a flashlight becomes dimmer as the batteries run down, images displayed on a monitor screen become weaker as the current used to produce them diminishes. This causes the screen to flicker. To avoid this problem, power is continually being sent to the monitor to refresh the display. **Refresh rate** refers to the

Tech Demo 3-2
Refresh Rate

Wearable computers are well suited to today's mobile lifestyle.

number of times per second the screen is refreshed (redrawn). To avoid flickering, the refresh rate should be at least 72 hertz (Hz) or refreshed 72 times per second. High-quality displays have a fast refresh rate that produces a constant, flicker-free image that causes less eyestrain for the user.

Monitor controls are typically located on the front of the monitor and allow adjustment of the brightness, contrast, positioning, height, and width of images displayed on the screen. Monitors usually come with screen settings preset by the manufacturer. The Windows Vista operating system allows users to change monitor settings through the Control Panel options accessed by clicking the Office button (the Start button in previous Microsoft operating systems). Users can change the settings to meet their needs, or easily change back to the preset (default) settings.

## Monitor Ergonomics

**Ergonomics** is the study of the interaction between humans and the equipment they use. Extensive research has shown that the correct use of a monitor can greatly reduce eyestrain, fatigue, and other potential problems.

Many monitors have built-in features that address ergonomics issues. These features allow adjustment of the monitor to make viewing more comfortable, to minimize eye and neck strain, and to reduce glare from overhead lighting. Some have controls that allow adjusting the monitor for the brightness, contrast, height, and width of displayed images. Monitor brightness is a matter of individual preference. Some ergonomic specialists recommend the use of an antiglare screen to reduce glare from the screen. It is important for both users and monitors to be positioned correctly. Figure 3-4 illustrates the correct positioning to provide maximum comfort and ease of use.

## Wearable Computers

Some mobile workers need and use a hands-free **wearable computer** that allows them to perform their work without having to stop what they are doing to use a computer. Computers in the form of headsets, eyeglasses, watches, and other accessories are already in use by mobile workers. For example, a work crew can wirelessly connect to the corporate network to send and receive work-related data and information, such as a wiring diagram needed to locate a faulty electric outlet.

The use of wearable computers and displays is becoming widespread due to their cost-effectiveness and ability to eliminate work delays. Future improvements to wearable displays will render them smaller and even more adaptable to a greater variety of work-related, entertainment, and communications applications.

## Television Displays

Many home computer users take advantage of their television sets for displaying computer output. To use an older, CRT-style television as a display device for computer output, an electronic device called an NTSC converter was required. Named for the National Television System Committee, an NTSC converter device

line of sight to screen 10–20 degrees below horizontal

eye to screen 16"–24"

keyboard tilt 0–25 degrees

floor to typing surface 23"–28"

floor to seat 16"–19"

**Figure 3-4 Correct Monitor and Keyboard Position**
Correct positioning when using a monitor can reduce physical fatigue and discomfort.

converted the computer's digital signal into an analog signal that could be displayed on the television screen.

Newer television technology, **high-definition television (HDTV)**, does not require an NTSC converter. Because HDTV uses digital signals instead of analog signals, computers can be connected directly to the television set. HDTV sets typically include a wider screen and provide higher resolution than standard television sets. These features make HDTV attractive for presenting information to large groups.

The Federal Communication Commission (FCC) mandated that all television stations must cease analog transmissions and transmit all broadcasts in digital format only by June 12, 2009. This digital television transition freed up frequencies for public safety communications (police, fire, and emergency rescue). Consumers with analog televisions can watch digital broadcasts if they install a digital-to-analog converter, or subscribe to a digital service such as cable or satellite TV.

## Screen Projectors

A **screen projector** is a device that captures the text and images displayed on the computer screen and projects those same images onto a large screen so the audience can see the text and images clearly. It is often used in classrooms so students can see the instructor's presentation, and by speakers making presentations to a large audience at meetings, conventions, and conferences.

Two types of projectors are LCD projectors and DLP projectors. Most of the earlier computer projection systems were based on LCD technology which tends to produce faded and blurry images. A technology developed by Texas Instruments, called Digital Light Processing (DLP) uses tiny mirrors housed on a special kind of microchip called a Digital Micromirror Device (DMD). The result is sharp images that can be clearly seen even in a normally lit room.

Screen projectors help multiple people view the output on a computer screen.

# Printers

A **printer** is the most common type of device for producing hard copy output on a physical medium, such as paper or transparency film. Almost all printers are capable of printing in either portrait or landscape format (see Figure 3-5). In **portrait format**, a printed page is taller than it is wide. Portrait format is usually used for letters, memos, reports, and newsletters. In **landscape format**, a printed page is wider than it is tall. Landscape format is best suited for financial spreadsheets and other types of tabular reports. These types of reports typically include many columns of data, which the portrait format could not accomodate.

Printers are separated into two broad categories, based on how they interact with the print medium: impact and nonimpact. An **impact printer** prints much like a typewriter, by physically striking an inked ribbon against the paper. Dot-matrix printers and line printers are examples of impact printers. A **nonimpact printer** forms characters and images without actually striking the output medium, using electricity, heat, laser technology, or photographic techniques. Ink-jet printers, laser printers, thermal printers, and plotters are types of nonimpact printers.

Most older printers and computers connect via a parallel cable and port while newer printers and computers connect via USB. An electric cord at the rear of the printer plugs into an electrical outlet. Some printers have wireless capabilities, connecting them to a computer via Bluetooth or Wi-Fi.

(a)

(b)

**Figure 3-5 Portrait and Landscape Formats**
Portrait format's (a) name comes from the fact that traditional portraits are taller than they are wide. To represent a landscape (b), a wider-than-tall view is usually taken.

## Dot-Matrix Printers

A **dot-matrix printer** forms and prints characters in a manner similar to the way numbers appear on a football scoreboard. A close look at a scoreboard will reveal that each number consists of a pattern of lighted bulbs. For a dot-matrix printer, the "lighted bulbs" are tiny dots forming characters and images on the paper (the "scoreboard").

In dot-matrix printing, a print head strikes an inked ribbon and deposits ink on the page, which is why dot-matrix printers are classified as impact printers. Inside the print head are thin wires, and their impact produces tiny dots of ink arranged to represent text, symbols, or images, as shown in Figure 3-6.

The number of dots in a linear inch or dots per inch (dpi), is a measure of the resolution, or print quality. The print head of a dot-matrix printer may contain from 9 to 24 pins, depending on the printer model and manufacturer. The number of pins determines the number of dots the print head can print during one impact. More pins produce more dots in each character, resulting in higher-quality print. Dot-matrix printers print one character at a time. Their speed is measured by the number of characters per second (cps) the printer is capable of printing. These printers range in speed from a few characters to several hundred characters per second, with 450 cps being a typical rate.

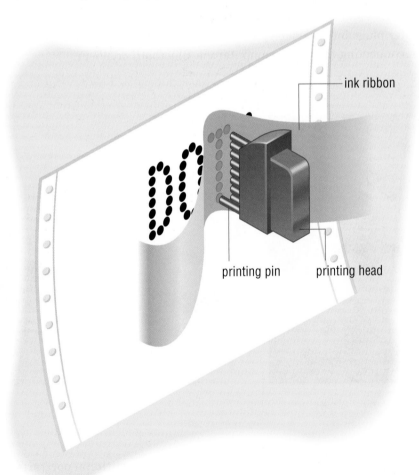

**Figure 3-6  Printing Using a Dot-Matrix Printer**
Before striking the ribbon, the printer extends the correct combination of pins to form a specific character. As with the display of pixels on a monitor, the more pins the printer uses, the sharper the printed letters.

The print quality of most dot-matrix printers is often inferior to higher-quality printers. The clarity of the printing may be described as **draft quality** (approximately 300 dpi), which is acceptable for some printing. For important business letters and documents, most users prefer **letter quality** (approximately 1200 dpi).

Because dot-matrix printers are impact printers, they are capable of printing multipart forms containing an original and carbon copies. For this reason they are more commonly found in businesses and schools. For example, colleges and universities may use dot-matrix printers for printing class rolls and grade reports. Individuals seldom use dot-matrix printers since they rarely need to print multipart forms and they usually prefer higher-quality print output.

## Line Printers

A **line printer** is a high-speed printer capable of printing an entire line at one time. A fast line printer can print as many as 3,000 lines per minute. A line printer contains a chain of rotating characters or pins that print an entire line at one time. They typically use 11 × 17-inch tractor-fed, continuous-form paper. Their fast speed makes them useful when large volumes of printing are needed, such as detailed company documents, reports, and invoices. The disadvantages of line printers are that they cannot print graphics, the print quality is low, and they are very noisy.

This line printer prints on continuous form paper that is tractor-fed.

## Ink-Jet Printers

For applications requiring letter-quality print, most people choose nonimpact printers, such as ink-jet and laser printers. Technological improvements and declining prices have made these two types the preferred printers among personal computer users. An **ink-jet printer** is a nonimpact printer that forms characters and images by spraying thousands of tiny droplets of electrically charged ink onto a sheet of paper as the sheet passes through the printer (see Figure 3-7). The printed images are in dot-matrix format, but of a higher resolution than images printed by dot-matrix printers. This is because the tiny dots produced by high-end printers are much closer together. In fact, the dots are so dense the printed characters and images may appear as letter-quality characters and images, rather than as a group of dots.

Tech Demo 3-3
Ink-Jet Printer's
Data Path

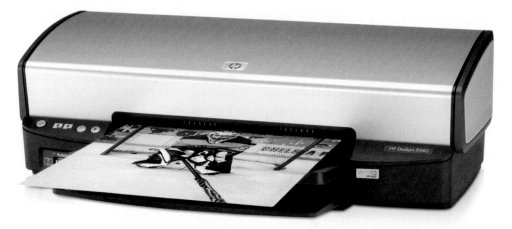

Ink-jet printers provide good-quality, inexpensive output.

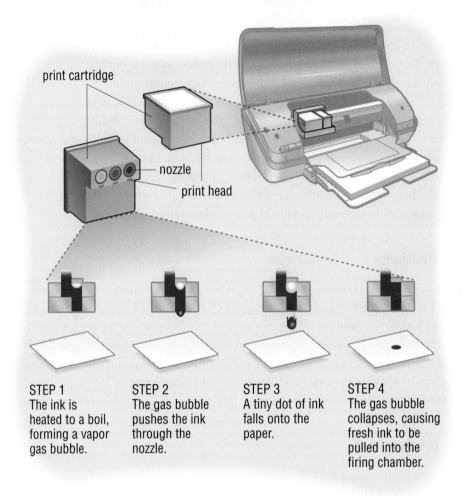

print cartridge

nozzle

print head

**STEP 1**
The ink is heated to a boil, forming a vapor gas bubble.

**STEP 2**
The gas bubble pushes the ink through the nozzle.

**STEP 3**
A tiny dot of ink falls onto the paper.

**STEP 4**
The gas bubble collapses, causing fresh ink to be pulled into the firing chamber.

**Figure 3-7  Printing Using an Ink-Jet Printer**
An ink-jet printer produces output by spraying tiny droplets of ink onto the paper or other medium to form text and images.

Typical resolutions are 600 dpi for black-and-white printing and 2400 dpi for color printing on high-quality paper. Higher resolution means higher-quality characters and images. Some high-end ink-jet printers are capable of producing photographic-quality output almost as detailed and colorful as photos processed using traditional darkroom methods.

Most ink-jet printers use two or more ink cartridges, one for black print and one or more for color printing. Each cartridge has multiple holes, called nozzles. During printing, combinations of tiny ink droplets are propelled through the nozzles by heat and pressure onto the paper, forming characters and images.

The number of pages per minute (ppm) a printer can produce determines an ink-jet printer's speed. Speeds currently range from 1 ppm to 16 ppm for draft-quality output. Printing color photos and other graphical images may slow the printing speed to as few as one or two pages per minute.

The cost of operating an ink-jet printer can vary greatly. A typical single page text document using only black ink may cost from $.02 to $.06 per page. By comparison, the cost of printing a combination of black and color characters and images may range from $.08 to $.20 per page. Printing a full-color photograph may cost $.90 or more.

Unlike dot-matrix printers, most ink-jet printers are relatively inexpensive. Prices of ink-jet printers range from less than $100 to $350. Their inexpensive price and versatility make them popular among personal computer users. They can be used for printing letters, memos, reports, spreadsheets, brochures, and a variety of other printing applications. Some computer manufacturers now bundle an ink-jet printer with each computer they sell.

## Laser Printers

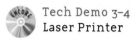

A **laser printer** is a nonimpact printer that produces output of exceptional quality using a technology similar to that of a photocopy machine. Laser printers are used for any printing application, including those requiring output of printing-press quality material. Their speed and ability to produce clear, crisp text and images have made them the fastest growing segment of the printer market. Prices range from under a hundred dollars for a black-ink laser printer (monochrome) to a thousand dollars and up for a color laser printer. Laser printers produce text and images of exceptional quality. Figure 3-8 illustrates the way a laser printer works.

A laser printer creates text and graphics on a rotating metal drum using a laser beam. During printing, components inside the printer read characters and relay them to a printer device called a laser mechanism. A laser beam produces characters and images on a rotating drum inside the printer by altering the electrical charge wherever the beam strikes the drum. The charges produce tiny magnetic fields (dots) on the drum, forming characters. As the drum rotates, it picks up an

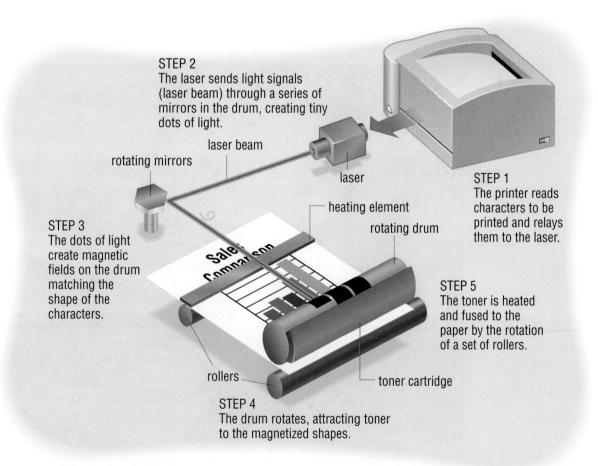

**STEP 2**
The laser sends light signals (laser beam) through a series of mirrors in the drum, creating tiny dots of light.

rotating mirrors

laser beam

laser

**STEP 1**
The printer reads characters to be printed and relays them to the laser.

**STEP 3**
The dots of light create magnetic fields on the drum matching the shape of the characters.

heating element

rotating drum

**STEP 5**
The toner is heated and fused to the paper by the rotation of a set of rollers.

rollers

toner cartridge

**STEP 4**
The drum rotates, attracting toner to the magnetized shapes.

**Figure 3-8 How a Laser Printer Works**
A laser printer produces output in a manner similar to that of a copy machine.

Laser printers produce output of exceptional quality and are among the most popular printers.

ink-like powder called **toner**, similar to copy machine toner. The sensitive dots on the drum are then deposited onto the paper. Using heat and pressure, a set of rollers fuses the toner onto the paper, forming the printed image. The circumference of the drum is approximately the same as the length of a standard sheet of paper. With one revolution of the drum an entire page is printed.

## Thermal Printers

A **thermal printer** is an inexpensive printer that uses heat to transfer an impression onto paper. Thermal printers are widely used in calculators and fax machines. There are three types of thermal printers: direct thermal, thermal wax transfer, and thermal dye transfer.

- A **direct thermal printer** prints an image by burning dots onto coated paper when the paper passes over a line of heating elements. Early fax machines used direct thermal printing.
- A **thermal wax transfer printer** adheres a wax-based ink onto paper. During the printing process a thermal printhead melts wax-based ink from the transfer ribbon onto the paper. When cool, the wax is permanent. Images are printed as dots, meaning the images must be dithered. Dithering creates the illusion of new colors and shades by varying the pattern of black and white dots. As a result, images are not quite photorealistic, although they are very good. Newspaper photographs, for example, are dithered. If you look closely, you can see that different shades of gray are produced by varying the

This thermal dye sublimation printer provides soft copy and hard copy output.

patterns of black and white dots. The more dither patterns that a device or program supports, the more shades of gray it can represent.

- A **thermal dye transfer printer**, also called a thermal dye sublimation printer, produces images by heating ribbons containing dye and then diffusing the dyes onto specially coated paper or transparencies. These printers are the most expensive and slowest type of thermal printer, but they produce exceptional high-quality, continuous-tone images similar to actual photographs. They require a special paper, which is quite expensive. A new breed of thermal dye transfer printers, called snapshot printers, produce small photographic snapshots and are much less expensive than other full-size thermal printers.

## Plotters

A **plotter** is a type of printer used to produce specialized kinds of large-sized high-quality documents, including architectural drawings, charts, maps, diagrams, and other images. Plotters are also used to create engineering drawings for machinery parts and equipment.

Depending on the type, plotters use a variety of technologies. For example, electrostatic plotters use a series of tiny dots tightly packed to produce a high-quality printed image. The printing mechanism consists of a row of tiny electrically charged wires. When the wires come into contact with the specially coated paper, an electrostatic pattern is produced that causes the toner to be fused onto the paper. When large, color images are needed, an ink-jet plotter—also called a wide-format ink-jet printer—may be used for printing a variety of materials. Most plotters are expensive, ranging in cost from hundreds to thousands of dollars.

## Special-Purpose Printers

There are several printers on the market that are made for specialized types of printing. These printers use ink-jet, laser, or thermal technology but are not general-purpose printers for everyday text and graphics. Photo printers, label printers, postage printers, and portable printers are examples of special-purpose printers.

Engineers often use plotters for producing high-quality, detailed prints of building, process, and machine designs.

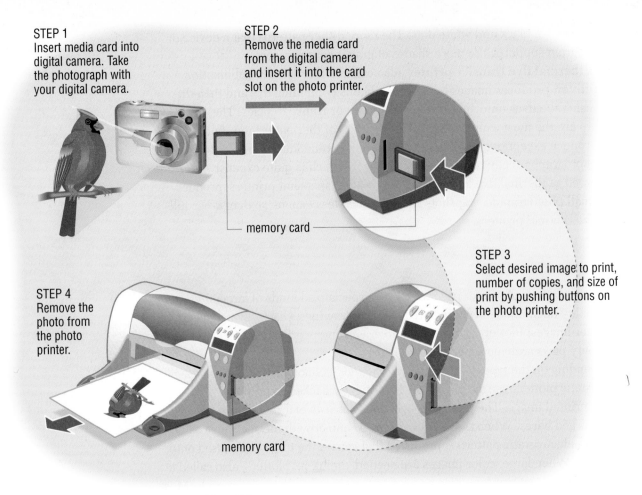

STEP 1
Insert media card into digital camera. Take the photograph with your digital camera.

STEP 2
Remove the media card from the digital camera and insert it into the card slot on the photo printer.

memory card

STEP 3
Select desired image to print, number of copies, and size of print by pushing buttons on the photo printer.

STEP 4
Remove the photo from the photo printer.

memory card

**Figure 3-9  Procedure for Using a Photo Printer**
A photo printer is a unique type of ink-jet printer used for printing high-quality photographs and other image printing needs.

**Photo Printers**   A **photo printer** is a unique high-quality ink-jet printer designed to print high-quality color photographs in addition to other types of print output. Most photograph printers can print photographs after they have been loaded (entered) from a digital camera into the computer and displayed on the screen. Some contain a slot for inserting a medium containing photographs, such as a **memory card** used with some digital cameras. Figure 3-9 shows the steps in taking a picture and printing it on a photo printer. Once the medium is inserted, the controls on the printer can be used to select a particular photograph, change its size, and choose the number of copies to print. Sizes for printed photographs range from 3 × 3 inches to 14 × 17 inches. The versatility of photograph printers makes them suitable for home and business use as they can be used for almost every printing need.

**Postage Printers**   A **postage printer** is similar to a label printer but also contains a weighing scale. Postage printers typically use thermal technology. Once an item is weighed, postage stamps are printed. To use a postage printer, the user purchases an amount of postage from an authorized postal service Web site. Each time a postage stamp is printed, the user's postage account is updated.

**Label Printers**    A **label printer** is a small printer that uses thermal technology to print information on an adhesive material that can be placed on various items including packages, envelopes, cabinet-type file folders, boxes, CDs, and other items. Most are capable of printing bar codes.

**Portable Printers**    A **portable printer** is a battery-powered, small, light-weight printer that can easily be transported by mobile workers and used with various types of computer and communications devices, such as notebook computers, personal digital assistants (PDAs), and smart phones. Most can fit easily into a standard-size briefcase. Many portable printers can be connected to a parallel of USB port, while others are capable of using wireless connections. The majority of portable printers use ink-jet printer technology.

## Multifunction Devices

A **multifunction device (MFD)**, also called an all-in-one device, is a piece of equipment that looks like a printer or copy machine, but which provides a variety of capabilities, including scanning, copying, printing, and usually faxing. The capabilities of multifunction devices vary according to the manufacturer and device model. Some print in black only, while others offer color printing. Most all-in-one devices use ink-jet or laser technology.

Multifunction devices offer several advantages over a combination of separate devices. They occupy less desktop space and they are usually less expensive than the combined cost of purchasing several devices. The main disadvantage is that all functions are lost if the device breaks down or becomes inoperable.

A **facsimile machine**, also called a fax machine, is an electronic device that can send and receive copies (a **fax**, or a facsimile) of documents through a telephone line. A fax device may be a stand-alone machine or a circuit board inserted into a slot inside a computer. The technology of faxing involves

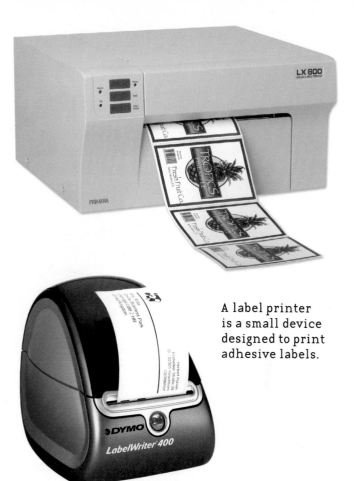

A label printer is a small device designed to print adhesive labels.

A portable printer is a small, lightweight battery-powered printer that mobile workers can easily transport and use with various types of computer and communication devices, such as notebook computers, PDAs, and smartphones.

A multifunction device is a device that provides multiple capabilities, such as scanning, copying, printing, and faxing.

scanning the page(s), converting the text and images into digitized data, and transmitting them. A fax device at the receiving end converts the digitized data into the document's original form that can be printed or stored.

Many personal computers come equipped with a **fax/modem card** that fits into an expansion slot. In addition to serving as a modem, the board provides many of the features of a stand-alone fax machine at a lower cost. A type of software called a **fax program** is needed to send and receive a fax. With fax programs, users can

Fax machines can send and receive copies of documents sent over communications media, such as telephone lines.

The fax/modem card allows communications with other fax machines.

compose, send, receive, print, and store faxes. Some of the better fax programs use optical character recognition (OCR) technology to convert a faxed transmission back into text so the document can be edited using any of the popular word processing programs.

## Audio Output

Computer users want to be able to hear the sounds included in Web sites, videos, and computer games. With audio output capabilities, it is now possible to listen to Web pages or watch television over the Internet. Certain software applications can read e-mail or Web pages out loud, which is of particular benefit to people who are visually impaired. The importance of audio capability is growing rapidly, and it is increasingly being seen as a required feature for personal computer systems.

### Speakers and Sound Systems

Most personal computers have built-in **speakers** that produce warning sounds to alert users to errors or other matters that require attention. A computer equipped with a powerful sound card like Creative Labs' Audigy SE can produce high-quality sound through attached speakers using CD-ROMs, MIDI (Musical Instrument Digital Interface) keyboards, or the Internet. Applications for which speakers are particularly important include computer games, multimedia distance learning programs, audio e-mail, and videoconferencing.

A **speaker headset** is a miniature version of larger speakers. Speaker headsets are already quite popular because they are frequently used with portable devices, including music CD players. As the name suggests, a speaker headset consists of two or more small speakers mounted at the tips of a flexible wire band that fits comfortably on the head, with the speakers positioned over the ears. Some computer users working in close proximity to other workers often use a speaker headset to minimize sound distractions.

Computer speakers allow users to hear sound effects from a computer game or an instructor's voice in a multimedia educational course.

# Techno Translation

**ALTHOUGH COMPUTERS TODAY ARE ABLE** to understand and even speak in human voices, one valuable application of computer voice technology still presents a major challenge: a universal voice translator.

No one understands the need to develop this technology better than the U.S. military, whose soldiers regularly need to communicate with citizens while stationed overseas and need a quick and accurate way to bridge the language gap. Enter the Defense Advanced Research Projects Agency (DARPA), which has created a portable English-to-Arabic translator that it is currently testing in Iraq.

The translator, which was developed using thousands of hours of real Iraqi conversations, is simple to use: a soldier speaks into it in English, waits for it to display an Arabic trans-

lation, and reads the screen as it translates the Arabic response into English. It is currently small enough to fit inside a backpack, but DARPA hopes to eventually shrink both its size and cost so that every soldier will be able to carry one. They also want to network the devices—that way, if one soldier discovers a translation error, every machine would receive an update.

The problem with the device is that it accurately translates only about 70 to 80 percent of the time, due in part to its inability to understand all the different regional dialects of Arabic. Research continues though, and once an acceptable rate of accuracy has been achieved in Arabic, the same translation technology can be applied to other languages.

## Voice Output Systems

Modern hardware and software technologies make it possible to produce synthesized human speech in the digital form a computer can understand and use. Most people have already experienced this technology when they have dialed a telephone number and heard a computerized voice say, "The number you have dialed is no longer in service," or, "The number you dialed has been changed." This same technology (**voice output**) is now available for use with all computers, and is becoming increasingly popular. Voice output can be used to listen to talk shows, news reports, athletic events, political speeches, interviews, and more.

## Storage Devices and Media

Go to this title's Internet Resource Center and read the article titled "Storage Resource Management." www.emcp.net/CUT4e

Information created and output on the devices discussed above can be stored for future use. Storage is the final phase of the information processing cycle. Earlier you learned that RAM memory provides temporary storage of programs and data during processing, and that this temporary storage is lost when the computer is turned off. To avoid losing programs and data every time the computer is turned off, all computers provide for permanent storage. **Permanent storage**, also known as secondary storage or auxiliary storage, consists of devices and media used for permanent recording. Stored information can later be retrieved, edited, modified, displayed, imported, exported, copied, or printed. Some secondary storage systems also allow users to make changes to the stored information and to permanently save the altered information.

# File Types

Almost all information stored in a computer must be in a **file**. There are many different types of files, including data, text, program, and graphics files. To distinguish among various files, the user gives each one a unique file name. A computer's operating system (operating systems are explained in Chapter 4) may impose restrictions on the format of file names. For example, earlier versions of Windows restricted the length of a file name to eight characters. Newer versions allow longer file names, but there are some characters that cannot be used in a file name.

A file name is followed by a period (.) and a set of characters called a file extension, which identifies the type of file. For example, the characters Payroll.xlsx identify a file named Payroll. The "xlsx" identifies the Payroll file as an XML-ready Microsoft Excel spreadsheet file. File names and file extensions must be separated by a period.

File extensions identify specific file types. Some are automatically added to a file by the operating system or program when a file is saved. However, in some situations a user can add an extension to a file to avoid confusion between similar files. Table 3-1 shows some examples of commonly used file extensions and the type of files they identify. In the Microsoft Office 2007 suite of programs, an x was added to some file extensions to indicate XML capabilities.

Go to this title's Internet Resource Center and read the article titled "Data Protection." www.emcp.net/CUT4e

**Table 3-1  Examples of Commonly Used File Extensions**

| File Extension | Full Name | Type of File |
|---|---|---|
| .bak | Backup | backup file |
| .bat | batch file | DOS file created in batch form |
| .bmp | Bitmap graphic | bit-mapped format for graphics |
| .com | command | executable command file (DOS) |
| .doc, .docx | document, xml | Microsoft Word (document) file |
| .eps | Encapsulated PostScript Vector graphic | graphics file format used by the PostScript language |
| .exe | executable file | executable file (DOS and Windows) |
| .htm | Hypertext Markup Language file | Web page |
| .jpg | Joint Photography Experts Group | compression format for graphical images |
| .mdb, .accdb | Access database | Microsoft Access database file |
| .pcx | PC Paintbrush | graphics file format |
| .pdf | portable document format | non-modifiable Adobe Acrobat Reader file |
| .ppt, .pptx | PowerPoint, xml | Microsoft PowerPoint file |
| .tif | tagged image format | type of bit-mapped image |
| .wbm | wireless bit-mapped | wireless bit-mapped graphic format for mobile computing devices |
| .xls, .xlsx | Excel spreadsheet, xml | Microsoft Excel spreadsheet file |

To be more useful, a storage device needs to be reliable and provide quick access to the data stored on the storage medium.

### Secondary Storage Systems

A secondary storage system consists of two main parts: A storage device and a storage medium. A **storage device** is a hardware component that houses a **storage medium** on which data are recorded (stored), similar to the way in which a VCR (the device) is used for recording a television program on the tape (the medium) inside a cassette. Some type of secondary storage device is usually built into a PC system, but is not visible unless the case housing the CPU and related components is removed. There are two main types of storage systems: magnetic and optical.

## Magnetic Storage Devices and Media

Go to this title's Internet Resource Center and read the article titled "Network Storage." www.emcp.net/CUT4e

A **magnetic storage device** is a commonly used type of secondary storage. This type is broadly classified into two categories: those using a fixed storage medium and those using a removable storage medium. A **fixed storage medium**, such as an internal hard disk, is permanently attached to the system unit. A **removable storage medium**, such as an external USB hard drive or digital tape cartridge, can be removed by the user and replaced by another medium. A **permanent storage medium** can be either fixed or removable.

Magnetic storage devices are also categorized by the way the data stored in them are accessed: sequentially (in the order in which data was stored) or *directly* (in any order, randomly). **Sequential access** can be compared to the way musical selections on a cassette tape are recorded and accessed one after the other. **Direct access** is comparable to the way songs are stored and selected on a CD player. Although the songs are stored one after another, any song can be played by selecting its number.

The speed of a disk storage device is measured by **access time**, the time a storage device spends locating a particular file. Recall that information in a computer's memory can be accessed quickly, in millionths of a second. However, accessing a file stored on a disk is slower. The access times of storage devices are measured in thousandths of a second. The speed at which data are transferred from memory or from a storage device is called the **data transfer rate**. As with access time, data transfer rates of storage devices are much slower than data transfer rates from memory.

A magnetic storage device works by applying electrical charges to iron filings on the surface medium. Specific particles are either magnetized (representing a 1-bit) or not magnetized (representing a 0-bit). Recall from Chapter 1 that a combination of 0 and 1 bits represents a byte, that is, a letter, number, or special character.

Magnetic storage devices are popular because they provide an inexpensive means for recording large amounts of information. The media used by magnetic storage devices can be read, erased, or rewritten, and can therefore be used over and over. The primary types of magnetic storage media are:

- hard disks
- tape cartridges

All modern personal computer systems have a built-in hard drive, and many users are opting for the convenience of a large capacity external USB hard drive as their removable storage device.

Portable external hard drives (top) are available in a variety of sizes, styles, and colors; fixed hard drives (bottom) are integrated into the computer system unit.

## Hard Disks and Hard Drives

Hard disks provide permanent storage for system software, application programs, and user files. A **hard drive** system consists of one or more rigid metal platters (disks) mounted on a metal shaft in a container that contains an access mechanism. The container is sealed to prevent contamination from dust, moisture, and other airborne particles, allowing the system to operate more efficiently. Hard drives range in size from 1 to 5.25 inches in diameter. Storage capacity ranges from less than 10 GB to more than 2 TB. Manufacturers usually format hard disks, but preformatted hard disks can be reformatted by users. Inexperienced users should never attempt to reformat a hard disk, since a PC's operating system is installed on the hard disk and reformatting destroys all of the previous contents.

People frequently use the terms *hard disk* and *hard drive* to mean the same thing, even though in technical terms the hard drive is the storage device and the **hard disk** is the magnetic storage medium. A hard drive unit may be either nonremovable (fixed) or removable (interchangeable). Most personal computers arrive from the factory with a fixed hard drive installed within the system unit housing. External hard drives can be added to a computer system as well. Figure 3.10 shows the inner workings of a hard drive.

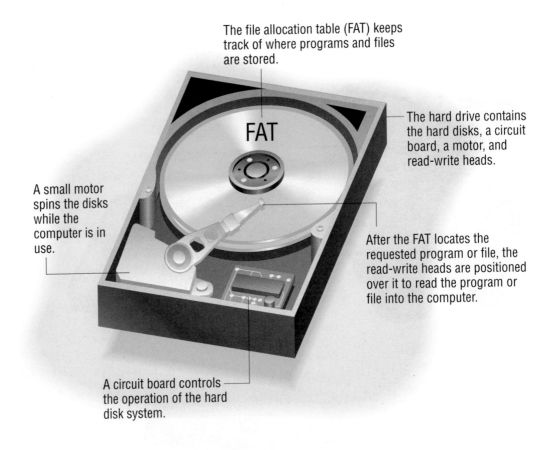

The file allocation table (FAT) keeps track of where programs and files are stored.

FAT

The hard drive contains the hard disks, a circuit board, a motor, and read-write heads.

A small motor spins the disks while the computer is in use.

After the FAT locates the requested program or file, the read-write heads are positioned over it to read the program or file into the computer.

A circuit board controls the operation of the hard disk system.

**Figure 3-10 Inner Workings of a Hard Drive**
A hard drive contains one or more hard disks on which data are stored. When activated, read/write heads move in and out between the disks to record and/or read data.

Data are stored along the tracks and sectors of hard disks. A **track** is a numbered concentric circle. A **sector** is a numbered section or portion of a disk similar to a slice of pie. A group of sectors is called a **cluster**, which is the smallest unit of storage space that is assigned a memory address. As programs or data are stored along the tracks on the disk, some computers automatically maintain a file directory, called a **file allocation table (FAT) file**, although some computers use other file allocation formats. FAT files on the disk keep track of the disk's contents. This directory shows the name of each file stored on the disk, its size, and the sector in which the file begins.

When in use, the disk spins and exposes its recording surfaces to the disk drive's read/write heads. As the disk rotates, the read/write heads move back and forth across the disk surface. When the user wants to access a particular file, the computer searches the file allocation table to find the requested file and its location on the disk. After learning the requested file's location, the computer locates and retrieves the requested file.

A hard disk rotates quickly and continues spinning while the computer is in operation, whereas a CD spins only when data is being stored or accessed. Continuous spinning of a hard disk provides faster access because it enables the disk surface(s) to move past the read/write heads faster. This speeds up the computer's operation because important system commands and functions are accessed and executed more quickly.

## Tape Cartridges and Tape Drives

One of the first types of secondary storage media for computers was magnetic tape. A **tape cartridge** is a small plastic housing containing a magnetically coated ribbon of thin plastic. Similar to a pocket-size tape recorder, a **tape drive** is used to read and write data to and from the tape.

Personal computer users do not usually use tape drives and tape cartridges since other forms of storage are available and inexpensive. Personal computer users will usually use optical storage (discussed later in this chapter) or USB flash drives. Tape storage is appropriate for storing large amounts of data that are no

Tape cartridges are used with personal computers mainly for backing up the contents of a hard drive. The tape is housed in a small plastic container that also contains a tape reel and a take-up reel.

longer actively used but need to be saved for historical purposes. For example, an administrator of a local area network might use magnetic tape cartridges to back up company data on a daily basis. Tape cartridges provide a relatively inexpensive, sequential-access type of storage.

## USB Flash Drives

A flash drive provides lots of storage in a small package.

A **USB flash drive** (also called a jump drive, thumb drive, and pen drive) is a storage device that plugs into a USB port on a computer or other mobile device. A flash drive is like a portable hard drive, except that it is completely electronic and has no moving parts. When the computer is turned on, it can immediately recognize the presence of the flash drive and store data in the drive's circuitry or retrieve previously stored data. A flash drive has nonvolatile memory, which means that it does not require power in order to maintain the information stored on it.

USB flash drives are popular among mobile users because they are small, lightweight, and transportable from one computing device to another. With a USB flash drive, a user can store large amounts of various kinds of information, including text, pictures, graphics, and spreadsheets. Once stored, the drive can be removed and transported to another device. New USB flash drives can store up to 128 GB.

Flash drives should be able to handle millions of cycles of writing and rewriting. The current life expectancy of most flash drives is about ten years, assuming that the drive receives the basic care and handling that any electronic component requires. The drive should not be dropped, subjected to weight or force, or opened, and it should be kept away from dust, and liquids.

## Optical Storage Devices and Media

An **optical disc** is a plastic disk 4.75 inches in diameter and about 1/20th of an inch thick. Both a **compact disc (CD)** and a **digital versatile (or video) disc (DVD)** are types of optical discs that are available in a variety of formats. Optical disc systems are widely used on computer systems of all sizes, and almost every new PC comes equipped with a **CD drive** or **DVD drive** (see Figure 3-11). The drive can read nearly any kind of data recorded on an optical disc, including text, graphics, video clips, and sound.

Laser technologies are used to store information and data on compact discs. A high-intensity laser records data by burning tiny indentations, each called a **pit**, onto the disc surface. A flat, unburned area on the disc is called a **land**. A low-intensity laser reads stored data from the disc into the computer by reflecting light through the bottom of the disc. Pits and lands reflect light slightly differently, so the computer can tell when the surface changes from a pit to a land and from a land to a pit. Pits and lands are both read as a series of binary 0s while the point at which a pit changes to a land (or vice versa) is read as a binary digit 1 (see Figure 3-12). The arrangement of 0s and 1s can thus represent data (see Figure 3-13).

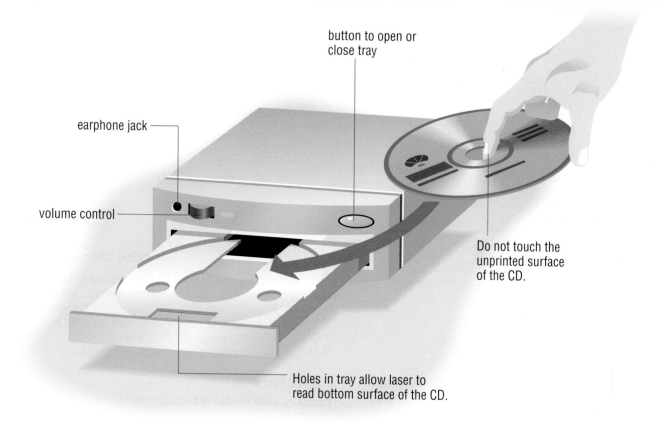

earphone jack

volume control

button to open or
close tray

Do not touch the
unprinted surface
of the CD.

Holes in tray allow laser to
read bottom surface of the CD.

**Figure 3-11  Parts of a CD Drive**
The CD is loaded printed side up, and the holes in the tray allow the laser to
read the bottom surface of the disc once the tray is closed.

Unlike hard disks, which store data in concentric circles, optical disc data are
typically stored along a single track that spirals outward from the center of the
disc to the outer edge. As illustrated in Figure 3-14, data are stored on the disc in
sectors, similar to the sectors on a hard disk.

Optical disc technologies are not necessarily compatible with one another, and
some require a different type of disc drive and disc. Within each category there

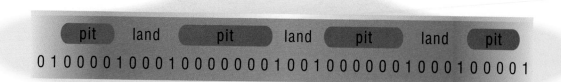

pit   land   pit   land   pit   land   pit

0 1 0 0 0 0 1 0 0 0 1 0 0 0 0 0 0 0 0 1 0 0 1 0 0 0 0 0 0 1 0 0 0 1 0 0 0 0 1

**Figure 3-12  What the Laser Reads**
The length of pits and lands indicates strings of binary 0s while a change
from a pit to a land or vice versa indicates a binary 1.

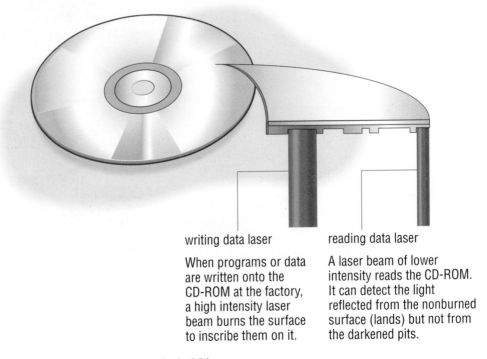

writing data laser

When programs or data
are written onto the
CD-ROM at the factory,
a high intensity laser
beam burns the surface
to inscribe them on it.

reading data laser

A laser beam of lower
intensity reads the CD-ROM.
It can detect the light
reflected from the nonburned
surface (lands) but not from
the darkened pits.

**Figure 3-13  Data Pattern on an Optical Disc**
An optical disc drive reads binary data stored on an optical disc.

are varying storage formats, although the **CD-ROM** is relatively standard for
computer data storage. Table 3-2 compares the storage capacities of various optical discs. Bit for bit, optical disc systems offer less expensive storage and greater
durability than hard disks and tape cartridges.

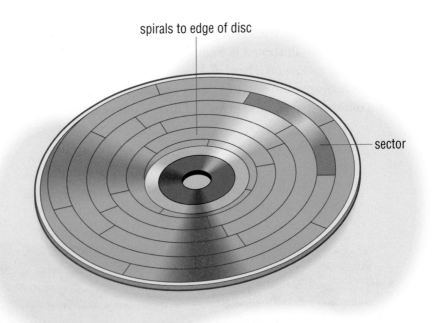

spirals to edge of disc

sector

**Figure 3-14  Compact Disc Sectors**
Information is stored on a series of sectors along a single track that spirals
outward from the center to the outer edge of the optical disc.

**Table 3-2  Types and Storage Capacities of Optical Discs**

| Optical Disc | Storage Capacity | Features |
|---|---|---|
| Compact Disc | 650 MB to 700 MB | |
| CD-ROM | | can be written to only once; used for distributing digital data such as computer software and for storing large data and graphics files |
| CD-R | | used mainly in small businesses for creating one-of-a-kind CDs |
| CD-RW | | allows rewriting; used mainly for backing up important files |
| Digital Versatile Disc | 4.7 GB to 17 GB | |
| DVD-ROM | | can be written to only once; typically used to create master copies of movies |
| DVD-R | | can be written to only once |
| DVD-RW | | recordable and rewritable |
| DVD+R | | recordable one time only |
| DVD+RW | | recordable, rewritable up to 1,000 times; cannot be read by set-top players and many computer DVD drives |
| DVD-RAM | | recordable and rewritable up to 100,000 times |
| DVD-Video | | used in the entertainment industry for recording movies that are sold or rented |
| Blu-ray | | high-definition video and data |

## CD-ROMs

Most optical disc systems are of the CD-ROM type. Like an audio CD found in the home or automobile, a CD-ROM comes with data already encoded. The data are permanent and can be read many times, but they cannot be changed. A CD-ROM drive is needed to access the stored data. Since CD-ROMs conform to a standard size and format, any CD-ROM can be used with any CD-ROM drive. Computer CD-ROM drives are also capable of playing audio CDs. CD-ROMs are well suited for storing large computer applications containing graphics, sound, and video. A typical CD-ROM can hold about 650–700 MB of information. An example of this capacity in real terms is the fact that the entire 32-volume set of the *Encyclopaedia Britannica 2004* plus the *Merriam-Webster's Collegiate Dictionary and Thesaurus*, an atlas, and timelines can be stored on just two CD-ROMs.

Data transfer rates vary among different CD-ROM drives—a factor that can be very important depending on the application being used. For example, a

# Printers Go Chic!

**IN THE WORLD OF TECH GADGETS**, printers are seen as more than a little boring. They don't have the sleek, modern looks of laptops or mobile phones, and they never get their own splashy, hip TV commercials. People expect them to work when they are needed, and beyond that, they're ignored. But a new kind of printer, with many of the same capabilities as the hugely popular iPhone, could do wonders to improve their lackluster reputation.

HP's Photosmart Premium, released in summer 2009, performs all the mundane functions of an all-in-one printer (printing, copying, scanning, and faxing) but it is also the first printer to allow users to make purchases and download content from the Internet. It cannot be used for Web browsing, but users can download applications (like those for the iPhone) that help them perform functions on their favorite sites. The printer is Bluetooth enabled, so users can print directly from mobile devices without being connected by a cable, and it sports the largest touch screen of any all-in-one inkjet printer on the market. It's also Energy Star qualified, and automatically prints on both sides of the paper to aid in environmental conservation.

This new device could mark a big change in the fiercely competitive printer market, and it may even steal some market share from Amazon's Kindle, once apps (applications) are created to allow users to download and print books and magazines. Not bad for a lowly printer.

---

slow transfer rate can result in poor image quality or garbled sounds. CD-ROM speeds are expressed as a multiple of the speed of the first CD-ROM drives (150 KB per second). For example, the data transfer rate of a 20X CD-ROM drive is 3,000 KB per second (150 KB × 20 = 3,000 KB) and a 40X CD-ROM drive is 6,000 KB per second (150 KB × 40 = 6,000 KB). The higher the number, the faster the data transfer rate of the CD-ROM drive. Faster speeds result in clearer images and better sounds. Newer CD-ROM drives have data transfer rates ranging from 40X to 75X.

## CD-Rs

A **CD-R drive** allows a PC user to record, or "burn," information on a **CD-R**. A CD-R drive is also referred to as a CD burner. This device writes once to the disc, and the resulting CD or CD-ROM can be read by a standard CD-ROM drive.

Most CD-R drives can read and write data at speeds up to 52X. In describing the speed of a CD-R, the device's writing speed is listed first. For example, a speed of 8 X 24 means the drive writes at a speed of 8X and reads at a speed of 24X. The main disadvantage of a CD-R is that it can be written on only one time. CD-RW technology overcomes this limitation.

## CD-RWs

A **CD-RW** (compact disc–rewritable) uses an erasable disc that can be rewritten multiple times, similar to a flash drive or hard disk. To use a CD-RW system, a CD-RW drive and special software are required. CD-RW discs are often used in the movie industry for making original copies of movies. Once perfected, the movie is copied to other optical discs that cannot be changed.

A typical CD-RW drive can read and write at speeds up to 32X. These speeds are usually shown on a CD-RW drive package as 12X/4X/32X. Rewrite speeds are typically slower than write speeds because the drive must first locate the file containing the information to be rewritten and then make the required changes.

With storage capacities of up to 700 MB or more, CD-RW discs are ideal for storing and backing up large or important files, such as the contents of a hard disk. In addition, they allow the creation of large files, such as those containing music, that can be shared with other users who have CD-ROM drives. Newer CD-RW burners can write an entire CD in 4 minutes and copy a 3-minute song to the user's hard drive in 5 seconds. Because of their flexibility, CD-RWs are rapidly replacing the more limited CD-Rs.

## DVD-ROMs

Many of today's complex applications demand huge amounts of storage capacity, often requiring several standard CD-ROMs. DVD-ROM technology was developed to overcome this limitation. A **DVD-ROM** is an extremely high-capacity disc capable of holding many gigabytes of data, currently ranging from 4.7 gigabytes (GB) to 17 gigabytes. In appearance, a DVD looks just like a CD. The basic technology for storing data on these two types of optical discs also is the same, although minor differences in DVD technology allow for higher storage capacities. For one, packing the pits more closely means a denser disc. Manufacturers can also create two layers of pits, approximately doubling the storage capacity, and they can create double-sided discs. These variations in techniques account for the range of storage capacities from 4.7 GB for a single-sided, single-layered disc to 17 GB for a double-sided, double-layered disc. A 17 GB disc can hold the entire contents (text and color images) of a large retailer's catalog.

CD-R discs offer an inexpensive way for individuals and businesses to create their own CDs.

A DVD disc looks like its relative, the compact disc, but can store five times more data.

DVD-ROM technology was initially developed to store full-size movies. However, a DVD can also store text, graphics, images, and sound. This technology requires the use of a DVD-ROM drive or player. Because DVD-ROM drives and DVD players are backward-compatible, most can also read CD-ROMs, CD-Rs, CD-RWs, and audio CDs. Newer DVD-ROM drives are capable of reading from the disc at speeds up to 40X. DVD-ROMs are available in a variety of versions, including versions that are both recordable and rewritable. Two of the more widely used formats are DVD-R and DVD-RW.

**DVD-Rs**   As with CD-R discs, a **DVD-R**, can be recorded on only one time. Once data, video, or sound is recorded on the disc, the information is permanently stored. DVD-R discs created by a DVD-R device can be read by most commercial DVD-ROM players.

DVD-R discs are used extensively by the music and movie industries for creating commercial copies of music and movies. Several thousand or even millions of copies can be made from the original DVD-R.

A typical DVD-R disc can hold up to 4.7 GB of data, enough capacity to hold a full-length movie or hundreds of music pieces. Using a two-layer standard, manufacturers can increase the storage volume to 8.5 GB, and adding a second side means boosting the total capacity to 17 GB. A new format called the Blu-ray Disc will store 27 GB, which represents more than 13 hours of movies compared to the standard DVD capacity of 133 minutes. Nine electronics companies, including Sony, have collaborated in developing the Blu-ray Disc, and industry observers predict that this disc may soon become the standard recording format. Manufacturers are continually researching new techniques for creating discs with even greater storage capacities.

**DVD-RWs**   Another type of digital versatile disc, called a **DVD-RW**, allows recorded data to be erased and recorded over numerous times without damaging the disc. The rewriting capability makes DVD-RW discs more versatile and therefore more popular among users needing inexpensive, reusable storage media with large storage capacities. A single-layered, single-sided DVD-RW disc can store up to 4.7 gigabytes of data.

DVD-RW players and discs are becoming increasing popular. They can be used for routine storage of programs, files, and data, for making a back-up copy of the contents of a hard disk, and for archiving important files. Like DVD-Rs, data recorded on a DVD-RW disc by a DVD-RW device can be read by most commercial DVD-ROM players.

## Caring for Optical Discs

Table 3-3 lists guidelines for the handling and care of compact discs and DVDs. Dirt or other foreign substances on optical discs can cause read errors and/or cause a disc to not work at all. However, an optical disc does not require routine cleaning and should be cleaned only when necessary. Using a commercially available cleaning kit is recommended, but other methods can be used, such as the procedure outlined in Table 3-4. Figure 3-15 shows the proper technique for wiping the data side of an optical disc.

Go to this title's Internet Resource Center and read the article titled "DVD Technology." www.emcp.net/CUT4e

**Table 3-3  Care Instructions for Optical Discs**

| Do |
|---|
| Store each disc in a jewel case or disc sleeve when not in use. |
| Use felt-tip, permanent marker to write on the nonshiny side of the disc. |
| Hold the disc only by its edges. |
| Use the recommended disc cleaning method to remove dirt or other substances. |

| Do Not |
|---|
| Allow anything to touch the shiny (data) side of the disc. |
| Stack disks that are not in a jewel case or disc sleeve. |
| Place objects on the disc. |
| Expose disc to direct sunlight or excessive heat. |
| Place food or beverages near a disc. |

# Large Computer System Storage Devices

Large computer systems, such as mainframe and server systems, typically use storage devices and media similar to those used with smaller computers. However, large computer storage devices provide much higher capacities than smaller computers because of the huge amounts of data they deal with. For example, a large business would need multiple hard disks for storing thousands of employee records. Similarly, imagine the capacities needed for storing all domestic airline flight schedules for a year.

## Magnetic Storage Devices for Large Computer Systems

Large computer systems typically use magnetic disk and magnetic tape secondary storage devices and media. For large computers, **magnetic disk storage** consists of a disk drive housing multiple hard disks contained in a rigid plastic container

**Table 3-4  Steps for Cleaning an Optical Disc**

| |
|---|
| 1. Blow on the shiny side of the disc to try to remove dirt or dust without touching the disc. |
| 2. If further cleaning is needed, wipe the disc from the center to the edges with a clean, lint-free, cotton cloth. |
| 3. If further cleaning is necessary, rinse the disc in plain water. Allow the disc to air dry or wipe the disc dry according to Step 2. |
| 4. If further cleaning is necessary, use a commercially available optical disc cleaning solution or use isopropyl (rubbing) alcohol. Apply the cleaning solution from the center to the edges of the disc. Allow the disc to air dry or wipe the disc dry according to Step 2. |

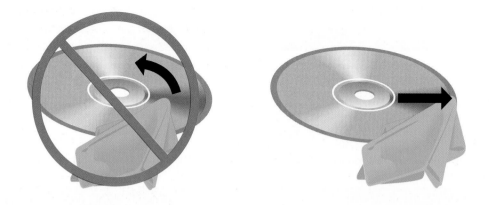

**Figure 3-15  Cleaning an Optical Disc**
Do not wipe a disc in a circular motion because wiping with the tracks may put scratches on the disc.

called a **disk pack**. A disk pack is mounted inside a disk drive. A metal shaft extends through the center of the vertically-aligned disks (Figure 3.16). When activated, electromagnetic read/write heads record information and/or read stored data by moving inward and outward between the disks.

Disk storage provides users with direct, or random, access to stored data. Disk storage is preferred when users need to access stored information quickly. For example, disk storage allows bank and utility company employees to quickly access and update thousands of customer accounts.

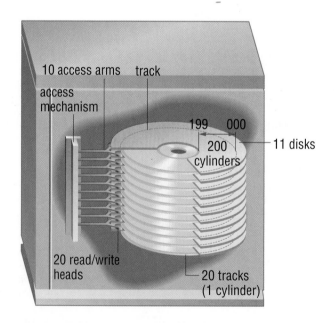

**Figure 3-16  Parts of a Disk Pack**
A disk pack houses multiple vertically aligned disks in a rigid plastic container placed inside a disk drive. When activated, read/write heads read or record on the disks by moving inward and outward between them.

Another type of secondary storage for large computer systems is **magnetic tape storage**, which uses removable reels of magnetic tape. The tape contains tracks that extend the full length of the tape. Each track contains metallic particles representing potential 0 and 1 bits. As is true of magnetic disks, combinations of bits are magnetized, or not magnetized, to represent bytes of data. The data is stored and accessed sequentially along the full length of the tape. Figure 3-17 shows how a tape drive reads and writes data.

Because magnetic tape is a sequential storage technology, information is accessed or updated in sequential order, that is, in numerical order. For example, if the user wants to access the twentieth record on the tape, the previous 19 records must first move past the read/write heads before the twentieth record can be accessed. Magnetic tape storage is typically used in situations where large amounts of information, such as all employee payroll records, are to be updated. In this case, all records are to be updated and the order in which individual records are processed is not important.

Magnetic tape storage may be used for other kinds of applications. Information stored on magnetic disk is often backed up onto tape and stored in a safe place in case it is needed. For example, a serious fire could damage or destroy a company's disk drives, tape drives, and other equipment. Having a backup copy of the data can eliminate the need to reconstruct important information.

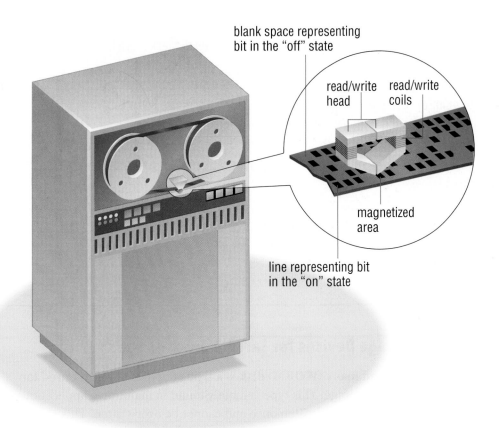

blank space representing
bit in the "off" state

read/write
head

read/write
coils

magnetized
area

line representing bit
in the "on" state

**Figure 3-17 How a Tape Drive Reads and Writes Data**
A magnetic tape contains tracks that extend the full length of the
tape. Each track contains metallic particles representing potential
0 and 1 bits.

# Freedom in the Desert

**FOR ALL THE MIRACLES COMPUTERS PERFORM, THE GREATEST FEAT** of the new technology may be liberating people enslaved by truly horrible jobs.

Take camel racing. It's a sport of royals in a number of Arab lands. The animals may cost hundreds of thousands of dollars, but the riders needed to goad them forward are dirt poor. Children, some as young as four, are recruited or virtually stolen from other countries such as Sudan or Pakistan.

The lives of the camel jockeys are bleak—they receive no schooling, they're kept on starvation diets to keep their weight down, and their injuries often go untreated. Their lives consist of obeying orders barked at them from walkie-talkies strapped to their chests while hurling down a racetrack on an enormous camel.

Qatar happens to be a superbly rich Arab country that, while still tied to past traditions, leans closer to the West than many of its neighbors. When the United Nations and the U.S. State Department started pressuring Qatar about this form of slavery, the current emir, Hamad Bin Khalifa Al-Thani, responded. There would be no more child jockeys in his country, he declared.

K-team, a Swiss company, was assigned the job of creating a replacement that could perform as well as a four-year-old and yet deal with the extreme temperature, dust, and shocks that camel racing entails. The K-team came up with a 2-foot, 35-pound robotic structure. The right "hand" bears the whip and the left manipulates the reins. Inside the jacket is a box containing microcontrollers, processor, soundboard, and GPS.

The trainers race alongside the track in SUVs, using joysticks to control the jockey and a remote screen to monitor camel heart rate and speed as well as the jockey's battery life.

The camels balked at being ridden by mere boxes, so a head was added to the jockey. The childlike head is empty and exists only to keep the skittish camel under the pretense that a human is on board. But after training, the faces are removed in deference to Islamic law forbidding human likenesses.

The Qatar government pays $10,000 per computer jockey, which is then leased to camel racers. For the camel jockeys who have been returned to their homelands, the value must be far more.

## Optical Storage Devices for Large Computer Systems

A **write once, read many (WORM) disk** is a type of optical laser disk used for very high-capacity storage. This type is mainly found in mainframe applications. WORM disks can only be written once and cannot be overwritten. This safety feature, combined with their high capacity, makes them ideal for storing archival-type material such as records or images. One of the drawbacks to WORM disks is that they are usually readable only by the drive on which they were written. The rapid advances in optical disk technology mean that newer optical disk formats such as CD-R are gradually supplanting WORM disks.

# OnThe**Horizon**

**SCIENTISTS, COMPUTER ENGINEERS, AND ENTREPRENEURS OF ALL KINDS** are working feverishly to develop new and improved hardware devices that will make information access faster and easier. After all, much is at stake—the millions and billions of dollars in revenue to be shared by successful individuals and companies. Inventors are also motivated by the great satisfaction that comes with creating something new and better. Several trends are worth watching.

## Increased Optical Disc Storage Capacity

Computer users needing huge storage capacities may be pleased with a new type of optical disc storage called High Definition Digital Multilayer Disc (HD-DMD). Manufactured by D Data Inc., an HD-DMD disc currently holds up to 32 gigabytes (GB) of data, a capacity to increase up to 100 GB. This amount is currently 45 times greater than a CD-ROM and 5 times greater than a DVD-ROM.

HD-DMD discs contain fluorescent materials embedded in the pits and grooves of all 10 or more layers. The fluorescent materials are stimulated to produce coherent and incoherent light when in contact with a laser. Data are stored in the incoherent light. Because the technology is not based on reflection, multiple layers are read at the same time.

Current plans are for HD-DMD discs to be used in a read-only format, which will require an HD-DMD drive. HD-DMD drives will likely be backward-compatible with DVD disc formats.

## Solid State Drives

Lower production and raw material costs are making solid state drives an increasingly attractive option for notebook computers and other mobile computing devices. Non-volatile flash memory forms the core of these drives. Because they contain no moving parts the drives are less vulnerable to damage from shock and impact than hard disk drives. Additional benefits include improved read access times, reduced power requirements of up to 50%, and quieter operation.

## Holographic Storage

IBM's Almaden Research Center has conducted pioneering research in computer storage since its founding in 1986, and has been responsible for a number of advances in hard disk drive technology. Anticipating future storage needs, researchers at Almaden are currently working on making holographic storage practical. The use of multidimensional holographic images will allow the layering of digitized information, vastly exceeding the storage capacity of today's magnetic and optical discs. IBM estimates that by 2010 we will see CD-size holographic storage media with a storage capacity of a terabyte of data (1,000 GB), the equivalent of 1,600 of today's CDs.

Holographic storage media may provide huge storage capacity for text and images, which would be displayed using a plastic-like material. Shown here is Plastic Logic's flexible display using E Ink Imaging Film.

## Wireless Power Supply

While wireless technologies can be used to communicate with output devices, supplying those devices with the electrical power they require involves dealing with a variety of different electrical sources and an often unruly tangle of power cords. Those headaches may soon be a thing of the past as MIT researchers are now working on a power delivery system that will wirelessly transmit electrical energy from one object to another. The basic principle employed is resonance, a phenomenon which causes objects to vibrate when subject to certain energy frequencies. Power would be transmitted through electromagnetic waves and absorbed by receiving devices. Once this technology is perfected, wireless equipment will be truly wireless in all respects, eliminating the need for power adaptors and rechargers and resulting in a much-simplified connection process.

# Chapter**Summary**

 *For an interactive version of this summary, go to this text's Internet Resource Center at www.emcp.net/CUT4e. A Spanish version is also available.*

## What is output?

**Output** is processed data, usually text, graphics, or sound that may be produced as hard copy or soft copy. An **output device** is a hardware device that makes information available to a user. An **output medium** is material on which information is recorded. Computer systems can produce four types of output: **text**, **graphics**, **audio**, and **video**.

## How do display devices work?

A **monitor** is the most common soft-copy output device. **Cathode ray tube (CRT) monitors** are being replaced by **flat-panel displays**. **Screen projectors** display the output from the monitor onto a much larger screen. Factors in monitor performance and quality include the **video card**, the monitor's **resolution**, and the **refresh rate**.

## What types of printers are available?

Considered the most common hard-copy output devices, **printers** are classified as **impact printers** that print by physically striking an inked ribbon against the paper or **nonimpact printers** that form characters and images using electricity, heat, laser technology, or photographic techniques to produce output. **Dot-matrix printers** and **line printers** are examples of impact printers. **Inkjet printers**, **laser printers**, **thermal printers**, and **plotters** are examples of nonimpact printers. **Postage printers**, **label printers**, and **photo printers** are special-purpose nonimpact printers.

A **multifunction device** is a single piece of equipment that provides multiple capabilities, including scanning, copying, printing, and sometimes faxing. A **facsimile (fax) machine** is a device that can send and receive copies or duplicates of documents through a telephone line.

## What is audio output?

Computer users want to be able to hear speech and music related to their computer activities. Most personal computers have built-in **speakers**, and newer models often include a **speaker headset**. **Voice output** is available with all new computers and is becoming increasingly popular.

## What are storage devices and storage media?

Also called auxiliary storage or secondary storage, permanent storage devices and media provide the capability of reentering and reusing stored information. A **storage device** is a component that houses a **storage medium** on which data are recorded (stored). Two main types of storage systems are magnetic and optical.

A **magnetic storage device** works by applying electrical charges to iron filings on revolving media, orienting each filing in one direction or another to represent a "0" or a "1." Data are stored and retrieved, or accessed, either sequentially (in linear order) or directly (in any order, randomly). Two main types of magnetic storage media are hard disks and tape cartridges. Data are stored along the **tracks** and in the **sectors** of a **hard disk**. A **hard drive** system consists of one or more rigid metal platters (disks) mounted on a metal shaft and sealed in a container that contains an access mechanism. **Tape cartridges**, consisting of a small plastic housing containing a magnetically coated ribbon of thin plastic, are used mainly for backing up the contents of a hard drive and for archiving large amounts of data.

Data or information created and saved using a computer is called a **file**. A file name is typically followed by a period (.) and a set of characters called a **file extension**, which identifies the type of file. Similar files are often stored in a directory, a special kind of file that allows other files to be grouped together logically. A file's extension is usually created by the software program.

## How do optical storage devices store data?

Optical disc systems are widely used on computer systems of all sizes. Most new PCs come equipped with an **optical disc drive** that can read data recorded on an **optical disc**, which is a flat, round, plastic disk. Data are stored as tiny indentations, called **pits**, and flat areas, called **lands**. Two lasers record and read the data. The main optical disc formats are **CD (compact disc)** and **DVD (digital versatile disc)**. Each disc type has various versions, including recordable one time only and both recordable and rewritable.

## What storage devices are used in large computer systems?

Mainframe systems typically use storage devices and media similar to those used with smaller computers. For large computers **magnetic disk storage** consists of a disk drive housing multiple hard disks contained in a rigid plastic container called a **disk pack**. Another type of secondary storage for large computer systems is **magnetic tape storage** using removable reels of magnetic tape. **WORM (write once, read many) disks** are a type of optical laser disc used for very high-capacity storage such as images.

# KeyTerms

*Numbers indicate the pages where terms are first cited in the chapter. An alphabetized list of key terms with definitions (in English and Spanish) can be found on the Encore CD that accompanies this book. In addition, these terms and definitions are included in the end-of-book glossary.*

# Chapter**Exercises**

 *The following chapter exercises, along with new activities and information, are also offered in the Internet Resource Center for this title at www.emcp.net/CUT4e.*

## *Tutorial >* **Exploring Windows**

Tutorial 3 teaches the four methods for running an application: from the Start menu, using the desktop icons, using the Run command, and from a file management window. You will learn to choose a method based on the situation.

## Expanding Your Knowledge > **Articles and Activities**

 *Visit the Internet Resource Center for this title at www.emcp.net/CUT4e, read the articles related to this chapter, and complete the corresponding activities. The article titles are as follows:*

- Topic 3-1: Storage Resource Management
- Topic 3-2: Data Protection
- Topic 3-3: Network Storage
- Topic 3-4: DVD Technology

## Terms Check > **Matching**

 *For additional practice, go to the Internet Resource Center for this title at www.emcp.net/CUT4e for a chapter crossword puzzle.*

Write the letter of the correct answer on the line before each numbered item.

a. plotter      f. sector
b. pixel      g. jump drive
c. optical disc      h. monitor
d. ergonomics      i. facsimile machine
e. laser printer      j. dot-matrix printer

_____ 1. A type of printer used for large-sized high-quality printing, including architectural drawings, charts, maps, diagrams, and other images.

_____ 2. A hard-copy output device that produces characters in a manner similar to the way in which numbers appear on a football scoreboard.

_____ 3. An electronic device that can send and receive documents through a telephone line.

_____ 4. A tiny single point in an alphabetic letter, number, graphic, or picture displayed on the screen.

_____ 5. A numbered section of a disk similar to a slice of pie.

_____ 6. A flat, round, plastic disc measuring approximately 4.75 inches in diameter on which data are stored in the form of pits and lands.

_____ 7. The study of the interaction between humans and the equipment they use.

_____ 8. The most common soft-copy output device.

_____ 9. A hardware device that produces high-quality hard-copy output using a technology similar to that of photocopy machines.

_____ 10. Another name for a flash drive.

## Technology Illustrated > **Identify the Process**

What process is this? Identify the process illustrated in the drawing below and write a paragraph explaining it.

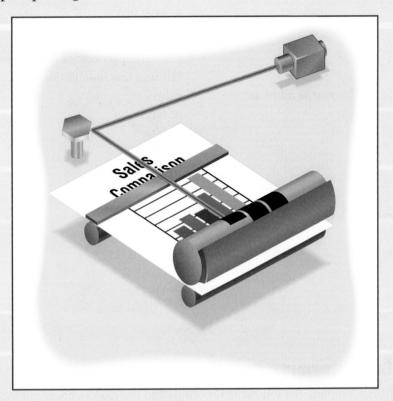

## Knowledge Check > **Multiple Choice**

 *Additional quiz questions are available on the Encore CD that accompanies this book, as well as on the Internet Resource Center for this title at www.emcp.net/CUT4e.*

Circle the letter of the best answer from those provided.

1. Processed data that can be used immediately or stored in computer-usable form for later use are called
   a. input.
   b. output.
   c. data retrieval.
   d. manipulated data.

2. A term that describes the number of pixels in the display, or the quality of the text and graphics being displayed, is
   a. resolution.
   b. density.
   c. coordination.
   d. element filtering.

3. The most common type of device for producing hard-copy output is the
   a. monitor.
   b. printer.
   c. plotter.
   d. speaker.

4. A type of printer that produces output of exceptional quality using a technology similar to that of a photocopy machine is the
   a. ink-jet printer.
   b. dot-matrix printer.
   c. impact printer.
   d. laser printer.

5. A piece of equipment that looks like a printer or copy machine, but which provides a variety of capabilities, including scanning and copying, is known as a
   a. scanner.
   b. duplicator.
   c. multifunction device.
   d. special-purpose device.

6. Permanent storage is also known as all of the following except
   a. secondary storage.
   b. auxiliary storage.
   c. primary storage.
   d. external storage.

7. The time a disk storage device spends locating a particular file is called
   a. data transfer rate.
   b. access time.
   c. file search time.
   d. disk spin rate.

8. The most common removable magnetic storage device is the
   a. CD-RW drive.
   b. DVD-ROM drive.
   c. tape drive.
   d. USB flash drive.

9. On a compact disc, a laser records data by burning tiny indentations onto the disc surface called
   a. lands.
   b. pits.
   c. tracks.
   d. sectors.

10. Which one of the following is not an optical disc format?
    a. hard disk
    b. CD-ROM
    c. CD-RW
    d. DVD

## *Things That Think >* **Brainstorming New Uses**

In groups or individually, contemplate the following questions and develop as many answers as you can.

1. Car washes and parking garages currently use digital license plate readers to identify customers' vehicles and to ensure that correct fees are paid for the companies' services. A camera in the license plate reader takes a picture of the front or rear of the vehicle. Optical character recognition software then converts the number in the photo to text, which is sent to a database of license numbers for verification. Although the digital license plate readers have some limitations, including problems reading curvy letters or unusual typefaces, security experts think this technology could be valuable in tracking the movement of vehicles around airports or other high-security areas. What other uses can you think of for digital license plate readers?

What kinds of problems might be associated with the technology?

2. Smart cards are plastic cards the size of credit cards with tiny chips embedded in them. They are growing in popularity with major U.S. corporations because of their ability to protect personal information, such as account numbers, during Internet business transactions. With a Web-enabled cell phone, a user could access a company Web site, order a product, and then pay for it by inserting a smart card into a slot in the phone. Can you think of other ways in which this intelligent plastic could be used? Brainstorm applications in business and beyond.

## Key Principles > Completion

Fill in the blanks with the appropriate words or phrases.

1. A(n) _____ is a computer-generated picture produced on a computer screen, paper, or film.

2. A(n) _____ display is used for portable computers and other applications where weight and space considerations are critical.

3. The distance between pixels on a display is called _____.

4. Processed data that can be used immediately or stored in computer-usable form for later use are called _____.

5. _____ is a term that refers to the permanent storage of computer programs, files, and data.

6. A(n) _____ system consists of one or more rigid metal platters (disks) mounted on a metal shaft and sealed in a container containing an access mechanism.

7. A(n) _____ is a secondary storage medium on which data are typically recorded by means of a high-intensity laser.

8. Printers that form characters and images using electricity, heat, laser technology, or photographic techniques to produce output are called _____ printers.

9. A file name is typically followed by a(n) _____, which identifies the type of file.

10. A flash drive plugs into a _____.

## Tech Architecture > Label the Drawing

In this illustration of an internal hard drive, identify and label the parts indicated and describe their use.

1. _____

2. _____

3. _____

4. _____

## Techno Literacy > Research and Writing

Develop appropriate written responses based on your research for each item.

1. What is inside the printer? Ask your instructor to allow you to open up a printer in the computer lab and look at the components inside. Using paper and pen, draw the components that you recognize and label each of them. At a minimum, include the printing mechanism, the ribbon, ink or toner container, and paper tray or container. Ask your instructor to explain other components you do not recognize. Write a brief summary of each component's function.

2. How many ways can a user output data? Page through a computer magazine such as *PC World*, or visit a computer store and select a personal computer that interests you. Research and describe all the different output devices that could be used with that particular computer system.

3. Which features should be considered when you purchase a printer? Hewlett-Packard is a major manufacturer of printers for personal computers. Visit the company's Web site at www.hp.com to learn about the various kinds of printers HP produces. Select one printer and write a brief report describing the following features of the printer:

   a. type of printer (ink-jet, laser, etc.)
   b. model number
   c. printing speed
   d. color printing capability
   e. amount (if any) of storage capacity inside the printer
   f. graphics printing capability

4. Which storage device meets my needs? Numerous secondary storage devices are available for personal computers. Research the major brands and models. Create a table that compares the various storage devices and media. Identify the one that would best meet your needs, and explain why. How would you use it?

## Technology Issues > Team Problem-Solving

In groups, brainstorm possible solutions to the issues presented.

1. Computers currently offer both visual and audio communication. Under development are devices and technologies that will incorporate olfactory communication, allowing users to smell various types of products while looking at them on the computer screen. What are some new applications of this technology for the food industry? Can you think of other industries that could use this capability?

2. Picture yourself working in the Information Technology department of a mid-sized company. Your responsibilities include evaluating employees' computer system needs and recommending equipment purchases. Recently, the company president hired a new employee and you must evaluate her computer system needs.

The new employee is Marsha Wellington, a graphics designer, who will be responsible for designing sales and promotional pieces for the company.

Considering you have a budget of $8,500 for equipping the computer system (or systems) she needs, research possible configurations and prepare a report outlining your recommendations, including costs. Assume that she needs a complete computer system, including graphics software, high-resolution color monitor, and high-resolution printing capability. (*Hint: Check computer magazines, retail stores, and Internet sites such as* www.gateway.com, www.dell.com, *and* www.apple.com.)

## *Mining Data >* **Internet Research and Reporting**

Conduct Internet searches to find the information described in the activities below. Write a brief report that summarizes your research results. Be sure to document your sources, using the MLA format (see Chapter 1, page 42, to review MLA style guidelines).

1. Renting data storage is becoming widely used among large companies that generate huge amounts of data. Using the Internet, locate information that explains data storage hosting and discusses the benefits, costs, and potential growth rate for this service.

2. Using an Internet search engine, find out how "geographic information systems" (also called GIS) are used. Find three companies or government agencies that use GIS and summarize how they use this technology.

## *Technology Timeline >* **Predicting Next Steps**

Look at the timeline below that outlines the major milestones in the development of storage devices and media. Research this topic and think of what the next steps will be. Complete the timeline through the year 2010 or later, if the research warrants it.

**1956** IBM unveils the 350 Disk Storage Unit, the first random access (direct access) hard disk.

**1973** IBM releases the 3340, the first Winchester hard disk with a capacity of 70 megabytes (MB) spread over four disk platters.

**1985** The first CD-ROM drives make their debut on personal computers.

**1998** The DVD-ROM drive debuts with 5.2 gigabytes (GB) of rewritable capacity on a double-sided cartridge—enough to hold a two-hour movie.

**2001** Constellation 3D Inc. introduces a new type of optical disc storage called FMD-ROM, which holds up to 140 GB of data.

**2003** USB flash drives hit the consumer market.

**2003** D Data, Inc., acquires FMD-ROM patents and begins manufacturing multi-layer optical disk storage technology called HD-DMD.

**2009** Photofast announces the G-Monster PROMISE solid state drive with capacities up to 1 terabyte (TB) and read/write speeds of 1000 MB/sec.

## *Ethical Dilemmas >* **Group Discussion and Debate**

As a class or within an assigned group, discuss the following ethical dilemma.

Many companies today have the ability to monitor employees' Internet usage as well as their inbound and outbound e-mail messages. Employees may consider this an invasion of privacy, but employers contend that they have the right to track usage of company property and ensure employees are doing their jobs efficiently. Is it legal for companies to monitor employee Internet and e-mail usage? Is it ethical for them to do so? Should employers be required to tell employees when they are being monitored? How much personal use of workplace computers should employees be allowed?

# CHAPTER 4

# System Software

## Learning Objectives

> Define software and identify the three principal types of system software

> Explain the concept of an operating system and identify its main functions

> Identify the differences between command-line interfaces and graphical user interfaces (GUIs)

> Differentiate PC, server, and handheld device operating systems

> Describe the different types of utility programs and their functions

> Explain language translators and describe the primary difference between compilers and interpreters

# CyberScenario

**SHORTLY AFTER SUNRISE,** Vincente Chamarro boards the high-speed train that will take him to his biweekly staff meeting at InterMed. The company designs and manufactures pacemakers and other medical devices that can be monitored over the Internet. Vincente is a product manager for InterMed's Cardiac Devices division. For more than three years he has worked from his mountain home and communicated with the InterMed office by computer and telephone (telecommuting), but he meets face to face with the marketing team every two weeks to maintain personal contact and to resolve any issues that cannot be handled well through remote communication.

Arriving in the city at 7:30 a.m., Vincente gets off the train and heads for the company headquarters two blocks away. As he walks to work he pulls a cell phone from his pocket and says a Web address, "www.ananova.com," into the mouthpiece. In a few seconds the face of a virtual newsreader named Ananova appears on the high-resolution screen of the cell phone. Vincente says, "Latest business news," and Ananova begins reading the latest business headlines from around the world.

As he walks into his office on the ninth floor of the InterMed building, Vincente remembers that he needs to check his bank balance. He issues a command to his computer with the words, "Turn on and go to the Web site for Fidelity National Bank." He continues with, "This is Vincente Chamarro. What's the balance in my checking account?" The bank's automated teller system recognizes his voice and promptly reports that he has $1,956 in his account. "Good," he thinks, "no need to transfer any funds from savings."

The marketing team will meet to discuss plans for exhibiting at an upcoming international trade show for cardiac surgeons to be held in Zurich, Switzerland. Reflecting on his communication needs for the show, Vincente decides to buy a new handheld device that will let him track all the materials his company ships to Zurich. A handheld would also provide access to current cultural events as well as maps and directions for Zurich and other European cities.

Vincente accesses a Web site where he can purchase the most powerful handheld on the market. A webcam enabled with advanced pattern recognition software captures his image and quickly compares it with others in a database of images. "Hello, Vincente," says a human-sounding voice. "What can I help you with today?" Vincente tells the automated system that he is looking for a new handheld device. The voice asks whether he is interested in upgrading his smartphone at the same time. Vincente agrees with the system's recommendation and is presented with two options. He tells the automated ordering system which one he wants. The order is repeated for confirmation and the purchase is deducted from his bank account. He can expect to receive his new "toy" in two days.

Vincente's meeting with his marketing manager and team members proceeds without a hitch. They approve his plan to use the company's Ananova-like synthetic character, Jillian, to pitch their new devices over computer monitors at the international trade show. Vincente stays late to finish a rough draft of the script for Jillian, dictating to his computer until 8 p.m. He sets the presentation up to be multilingual, rotating between English, German, and French to appeal to the international audience. He then directs the computer to send copies to team members and leaves to catch the 8:50 train home.

Vincente Chamarro's job is made easier through advances in speech recognition, natural language processing, language translation, and artificial intelligence technologies. Driving these changes is an intricate interaction among computer hardware manufacturers, scientists, and software developers.

# The Function of System Software

**Software** is the term for the programs that tell a computer what to do and how to do it. Software manages the computer's resources, including all hardware devices. Software programs work by issuing instructions to computers to perform actions in a certain order, allowing them to process data into information. **Hardware** is the term for the physical components of any computer system, such as the motherboard, circuitry, and peripheral devices. A popular expression in computer circles is that "software drives hardware," meaning that without software a computer can do little more than search for essential program files that direct the computer to load additional software. It is the software that launches information processing and puts the hardware to work.

Software is divided into two main categories: application software and system software. **Application software** includes programs that perform a single task such as word processing, spreadsheet analysis, or database management. (Application software will be discussed in Chapter 5.) **System software** includes those programs that control the operations of a computer system, meaning the system unit as well as all components and devices that make up the computer system.

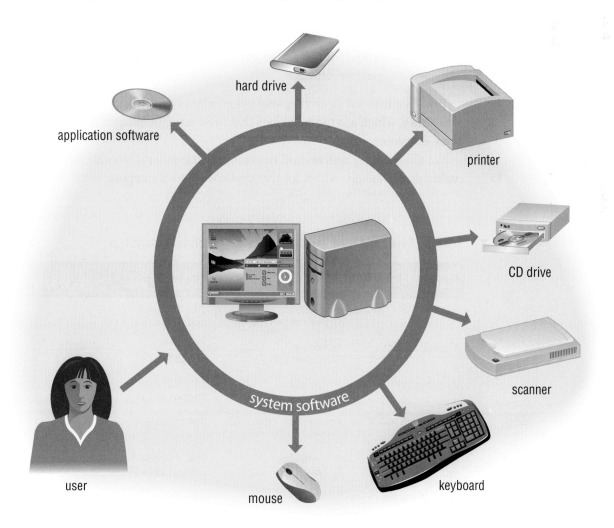

**Figure 4-1 The System Software as a Gateway**
System software serves as the gateway (interface) between the user, the user's application software, and the computer's hardware.

System software performs a number of essential functions, including starting the computer, formatting disks, copying files, and enabling applications to work smoothly with a computer. It thus serves as the gateway between the user, the user's application software, and the user's computer hardware (see Figure 4-1). The three major categories of system software are operating systems, utility programs, and language translators.

# The Function of the Operating System

An **operating system (OS)** is the most important piece of software on a personal computer. The location of the operating system identifies the **boot drive** for the personal computer. Typically, this is the hard drive. When the computer is started (or booted), the operating system is loaded into random access memory (RAM) from the boot drive. Once started, the operating system manages the computer system and performs a variety of interdependent functions related to the input, processing, output, and storage of information, including:

- managing main memory, or RAM
- configuring and controlling peripheral devices
- managing essential file operations, including formatting or copying disks, and renaming or deleting files
- monitoring system performance
- providing a user interface

Table 4-1 lists the operating systems commonly found on today's personal computers, which are the machines that predominate in the workplace and home environments.

Not all operating systems will run on every computer. For example, an operating system designed and written for the Apple Macintosh computer usually will not run

**Table 4-1 Commonly Used Operating Systems for Personal Computers**

| Operating System | Developer | Computer Designed for | Year Introduced |
|---|---|---|---|
| Windows 7 | Microsoft Corporation | IBM PC and compatibles | 2009 |
| Windows Vista | Microsoft Corporation | IBM PC and compatibles | 2007 |
| Windows XP | Microsoft Corporation | IBM PC and compatibles | 2001 |
| Macintosh OS X | Apple Computer | Macintosh | 2001 |
| Windows 2000 | Microsoft Corporation | IBM PC and compatibles | 2000 |
| OS/2 Warp | IBM | IBM PC and compatibles | 1994 |
| Linux | various, including Red Hat, Novell, SUSE, and Ubuntu | various | various |

# Booting Up Bhutan

**BHUTAN IS A TINY BUDDHIST NATION** nestled in the snow-capped mountains between India and China. The Himalayan kingdom has managed to stay isolated by virtue of both geography and choice.

Aversion to contact with the outside world stemmed from the King's philosophy that happiness takes precedence over prosperity, and that happiness is rooted in a strong national identity. Television and the Internet were kept out until 1999, and recent laws enforce the use of Dzongkha, Bhutan's national language.

The gap between Western modernity and traditional Bhutanese culture was bridged in 2006, when Bhutan's Department of Information Technology completed a computer system that operates in Dzongkha. Among other benefits, Buddhist monks in Bhutan's monasteries will now be able to work on their sacred texts on computers instead of copying them by hand.

Credit for the Bhutan-customized software goes to Debian, a collaboration of global volunteers who work together to develop and distribute free software in local languages. The moniker Debian is a mix from the names of the founder, Ian Murdock, and his wife, Debra.

Debian has a long history of "localizing" computers. The first Debian installation program produced in 2002 supported 16 languages. The current version supports 65, with 82 languages already slated for support in the next release.

on an IBM-compatible computer. The computers are said to have different platforms. A **platform** is a foundation or standard around which software is developed.

The two determinants of a platform are the operating system and the processor type. For example, early versions of Windows were called 16-bit operating systems because they supported microprocessors that could process 16 bits of data at a time. Later Windows versions, including Windows 95 and 98, supported 32-bit processors, and Windows XP, Vista, and 7 have both 32- and 64-bit versions.

Operating systems and other software that run on a specific personal computer platform are referred to as native to that platform. Thus there is software native to the PC platform and to the Macintosh platform. Recently, Microsoft and Apple have released their operating systems for use on alternate platforms.

## Booting (Starting) the Computer

The procedure for starting or restarting a computer is called **booting**, because the operating system is housed in the boot drive. Starting a computer after power has been turned off is referred to as a **cold boot**. Restarting a computer while the power is still on is called a **warm boot**. Most computer systems allow users to perform a warm boot by pressing a combination of keyboard keys.

When a computer is booted, an electrical current from the power supply sends signals to the motherboard and its components, including the processor chip. The electrical current resets the processor, which then looks for the read-only memory (ROM) chip containing the basic input/output system (BIOS).

The BIOS chip contains instructions that start the computer. The BIOS chip(s) also performs a series of tests, called power-on self test (POST). POST instructions check the computer's components and peripheral devices, including RAM, the system clock, keyboard, mouse, and disk drives. The POST checks determine whether the components and devices are connected and functioning properly. If problems are identified, many operating systems will notify the user to take corrective action. If components and devices are working properly, the BIOS searches the boot drive for operating system files.

The operating system then takes control of the computer and loads the system configuration and other necessary operating system files into memory. Portions of the operating system are automatically loaded from the hard disk into the computer's main memory, including the kernel and frequently used operating system instructions. The **kernel** is an operating system program that manages computer components, peripheral devices, and memory. It also maintains the system clock and loads other operating system and application programs as they are required. The kernel is **memory resident**, remaining in memory while the computer is in operation. Other operating system parts are **nonresident** and remain on the hard disk until they are needed. The loaded portion (memory resident) contains the most essential instructions for operating the computer, controlling the monitor display, and managing RAM efficiently to increase the computer's overall performance.

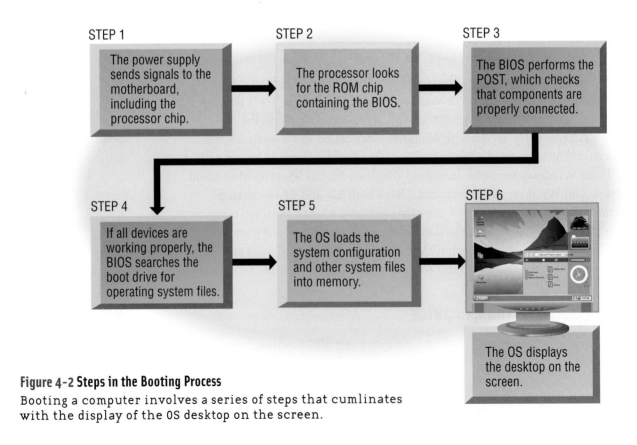

**Figure 4-2 Steps in the Booting Process**
Booting a computer involves a series of steps that cumlinates with the display of the OS desktop on the screen.

# Coming Soon—Transistors on Steroids!

**WHAT'S IN A CHIP?** Millions of microscopic transistors, those tiny pieces of semiconductor material, usually silicon, that amplify a signal or open and close a circuit. So what happens when you lace silicon with the chemical element geranium and plunge it to a temperature of absolute zero? You get a supersonic transistor, the building blocks of supersonic chips. That's what IBM has done, creating a super-fast transistor that will lead to ever-faster computers and wireless networks.

IBM's super-speedy transistors run 100 times faster than those currently available, reaching speeds of 500 gigahertz (GHz). For comparison, cell phone chips dawdle along at a mere 2 GHz, digital music players around 5 GHz.

In initial tests, the IBM transistor attained its highest speed at a temperature near absolute zero (that's minus 451 degrees Fahrenheit), but was still running at 300 GHz at room temperature. While mass-produced prototypes would probably not match the racecar speed of the prototypes, mere much-faster-than-today transistors would be economical to produce.

Super-fast transistors may soon lead to wireless networks that can download a DVD in five seconds, buildings outfitted with 60 GHz wireless connections, and cars equipped with radar that would automatically adjust speed according to traffic or swerve to avoid an oncoming car.

---

With Microsoft Windows Vista, the operating system displays the Windows desktop and executes programs in the StartUp folder once loading is complete. Users can then click on the Office Start button, point to *Programs*, point to *Microsoft Office*, and then activate an application program such as Microsoft Word or Excel. The process of booting a computer is illustrated in Figure 4-2.

## Managing Memory

An important operating system function is optimizing RAM so that processing occurs more quickly, an activity referred to as throughput. **Throughput** is a measure of the computer's overall performance. Loading programs and data from secondary storage into RAM speeds up processing because it takes significantly less time for the processor to access the programs from RAM than from secondary storage. Processing cannot occur until the programs and data are moved from RAM to the processor. Users can add RAM chips or upgrade the processor if programs, such as downloads from e-mail or Web pages, execute slowly.

To speed up the transfer of programs and data to the processor even further, some computers contain cache memory. Recall from Chapter 2 that cache memory may be contained on the CPU in the form of memory chips hardwired onto the motherboard or as reserved space on a storage device such as a hard disk. Some operating systems also allow users to set aside a portion of RAM to be used as cache memory.

As information is being processed, the operating system assigns application programs and data to selected areas of RAM called buffers. A **buffer** holds information and data waiting to be transferred to or from an input or output device. When the information or data residing in the buffers is no longer needed, it is erased (cleared) by the operating system. When a document is placed in a buffer, the CPU is free to begin executing the next computer instruction or carry out the user's next command.

Some output devices, such as printers, may contain their own buffer memory chips. A computer typically sends a document to a printer much faster than the printer can print it. With **print spooling**, a document is held in a buffer until the printer is ready. Once printed, the buffer is cleared and ready to accept other printing jobs.

An important part of managing RAM is allowing an individual user to work on two or more applications at the same time. This capability is called **multitasking**. When using a multitasking operating system, such as Microsoft Windows, it is not necessary to quit one application before working in another. For example, if a Microsoft Word document and a Microsoft Excel spreadsheet are both loaded into RAM, users can switch back and forth between the two applications as often as they wish.

## Configuring and Controlling Devices

Configuring and controlling computer components and attached devices is a major function of the operating system. Included with a computer's operating

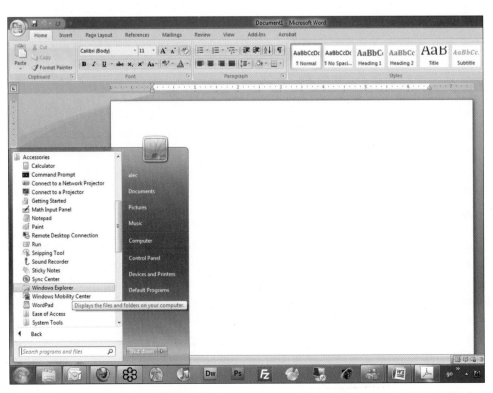

A user can access Windows Explorer in Microsoft Windows Vista through the Programs/Accessories submenu. Windows Explorer allows users to view, copy, delete, and move files.

system are small programs called drivers. A **driver** enables the operating system to communicate with peripheral devices, including the keyboard, monitor, mouse, modem, printer, and disk drives. A keyboard driver recognizes input, while a monitor driver directs the display of text and images. If a user decides to add other devices, a driver will need to be installed for each new device. A driver program usually accompanies the device, and is contained on a disk with easy-to-follow instructions to guide users through the installation process. Many driver programs are also available on the device manufacturer's Web site.

Tech Demo 4-1
Device Driver
Path

## Managing Essential File Operations

An operating system contains a program called a **file manager** to maintain a record of all stored files and their locations, allowing users to quickly locate and retrieve files. File managers also perform basic file management functions, such as keeping track of disk storage space; formatting and copying disks; and renaming, deleting, sorting, or viewing stored files. For example, users can copy, delete, and move files using Windows Explorer.

## Monitoring System Performance

An operating system typically includes a **performance monitor** for checking the computer system's speed and efficiency, as well as the performance of the CPU, memory, and storage disks. In Microsoft Windows Vista, clicking the command sequence of Office Start button, Control Panel, System, and Performance opens a window from which system performance can be evaluated and improved.

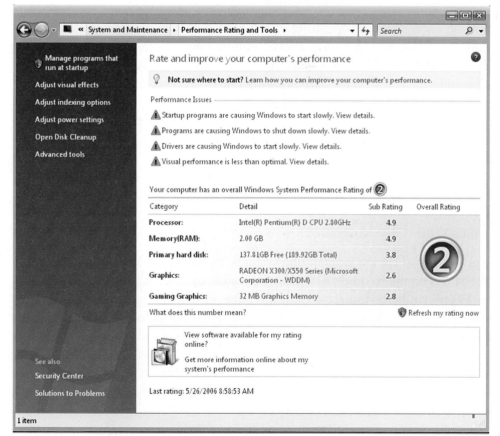

The Performance Information and Tools window allows a user to evaluate the computer's performance and make improvements if needed.

A system's performance rating depends not only on the installed hardware but also on settings configured in the operating system such as video display mode and drivers set to load automatically at system startup.

## Providing Basic Security Functions

An operating system can protect against unauthorized users gaining access to the computer and stored information. Many operating systems require users to enter a valid name and password before they can access a computer or network. A **user name**, also called a user ID, is a unique combination of characters (letters and numbers) identifying an individual user.

A **password** is a unique combination of characters that allows a user to gain access to computer resources, such as data and files. When a password is typed, most operating systems display a series of characters (such as asterisks) that differ from those entered. This is to prevent other people from seeing the entered characters. The user ID and password combinations are compared with a list of authorized users. If the combination of user ID and password is on the list, the operating system allows access. The operating system denies access if the user ID and password combination does not match any of those on the list.

Computer network operating systems provide additional security measures, such as maintaining a record of attempts to access the network and its resources. The network administrator can determine which computer made the attempt and the time the attempt was made, allowing suspicious activity to be traced.

# Software User Interfaces

All software, including operating systems, contains a **user interface** that allows communication between the software and the user. The interface controls the manner in which data and commands are entered, as well as the way information and processing options are presented on the screen. Application programs are written for use with specific operating systems. The operating system and application software user interfaces must be able to work together (be compatible). Two types of user interfaces have been developed for personal computers:

- command-line interfaces
- graphical user interfaces (GUIs)

## Command-Line Interfaces

Early personal computer operating systems, including CP/M (Control Program for Microcomputers) and DOS (Disk Operating System), used what is known as a **command-line interface**. This interface presents the user with a symbol called a **prompt** (for example, C:\>), indicating the computer is ready to receive a command. Users would respond by typing in a line of code telling the computer what to do. For example, the command COPY A:\INCOME.STM C:\ instructs the computer to copy the file named INCOME.STM, located on drive A, to drive C. Command-line interfaces were ideal for early personal computers, which had limited graphical display capabilities. They could also be complicated

```
MS-DOS Prompt                                                    _ □ ✕
T  8 x 14 ▾   □  🗐 🗐  🔲  🗐🗐  A
HEALTH   EXE      405,952  06-03-96 11:55a HEALTH.EXE
HEALTH   ICO          766  08-15-95  9:34a HEALTH.ICO
HEALTH   Z      2,266,038  06-03-96  2:34p HEALTH.Z
HEALTH96        <DIR>      03-13-96  7:47p HEALTH96
INTRO    BMP      153,516  08-18-95  2:58p INTRO.BMP
IVI      BMP      308,280  08-04-95  2:26p IVI.BMP
IVIPBW32 DLL      459,776  02-05-96 12:50p IVIPBW32.DLL
IVIPUBW  DLL      280,123  05-16-96  2:43p IVIPUBW.DLL
QTW             <DIR>      03-22-96 11:58a QTW
README   DOC       29,696  03-01-96  2:59p README.DOC
REVLOG   TXT          393  06-03-96 11:46a REVLOG.TXT
SETUP    BMP      158,382  08-17-94  4:48p SETUP.BMP
SETUP    EXE       44,064  05-15-96 10:15a SETUP.EXE
SETUP    INI           65  04-22-96  4:33p SETUP.INI
SETUP    INS       69,227  06-03-96  2:30p SETUP.INS
SETUP    PKG          406  06-03-96  2:34p SETUP.PKG
UNINST   EXE      269,312  09-02-95  3:57p UNINST.EXE
_INST32I EX_      312,294  05-15-96  5:03p _INST32I.EX_
_ISDEL   EXE        8,192  09-08-95  1:22a _ISDEL.EXE
_SETUP   DLL        5,984  04-29-96  8:25a _SETUP.DLL
_SETUP   LIB      603,899  06-03-96  2:36p _SETUP.LIB
        21 file(s)      5,383,575 bytes
         2 dir(s)               0 bytes free

E:\>DIR_
◀                                                               ▶
```

This DOS command DIR shows a directory, or list of files, stored on a medium such as a hard disk.

and difficult to learn, because the commands often involved long sequences of code. A mistyped letter would lead to an error message, forcing the user to type the command again.

## Graphical User Interfaces

In 1983, Apple Computer introduced its Lisa computer. Lisa featured an entirely new kind of operating system with a screen display known as a **graphical user interface (GUI)**. Based on the Alto computer operating system developed at the Xerox Corporation's Palo Alto Research Center, this new type of interface was graphics-based rather than command-based, making it more intuitive and user-friendly. Unfortunately, the Apple Lisa was a commercial failure because of its high price and the limited availability of software applications. The following year Apple introduced the Macintosh, another computer incorporating a GUI. This time Apple scored a success. The Macintosh operating system revolutionized personal computing.

GUIs are now the most popular type of personal computer interface. They are easier to use than command-line interfaces because they enable users to interact with on-screen simulations of familiar objects. Remembering long strings of commands is no longer necessary, since the screen itself becomes a virtual desktop on which the user's work (programs and documents) is spread out. An **icon**, or thumbnail picture, appears on the screen and represents such familiar items as a trash can or recycle bin (for deleting or throwing away files) and file folders (for storing groups of files).

In addition to representing common commands, icons are used to symbolize programs and files. For example, a calculating program may be represented by a tiny calculator on the screen, or a time management program might be represented by a

Apple's Macintosh, introduced in 1984, quickly became popular because of its innovative operating system.

clock. To use an analogy, GUIs are to operating systems what special keyboards are to cash registers in fast-food restaurants. Both use pictures or text symbols to stand for complex commands, simplifying and streamlining actions for the user.

GUIs were made possible with the development of mouse technology and the introduction of more powerful computers and high-resolution monitors. Almost all PCs arrive from the factory with a GUI operating system preinstalled, and most application software is designed to work with them smoothly. Once a user knows the features of a GUI such as Windows, the fundamental operations of any Windows-based application are easy to execute because both the operating system and the application use the same icons and commands. A typical GUI offers many features to make tasks easier, including:

- on-screen desktop
- display windows
- key feature option menus
- common command icons
- dialog boxes
- online help

**On-Screen Desktop** GUIs for personal computers incorporate the concept of an on-screen **desktop**. A desktop is a screen on which graphical elements such as icons, buttons, windows, links, and dialog boxes are displayed, much as manila folders, pens, scissors, and paper might be arranged on a desk. Using a desktop containing these elements is easier for many users because it allows them to interact quickly and accurately with the computer. During the installation of a software application, an icon representing the program may be automatically added to the desktop.

A **button** is a graphical element that causes a particular action to occur when selected. For example, clicking the Office Start button in the lower left corner of the screen displays a list of options related to starting and operating the computer.

The Windows 7 GUI desktop is a work area displaying graphical elements such as icons, windows, and buttons. Graphical elements allow faster, easier access to programs and commands.

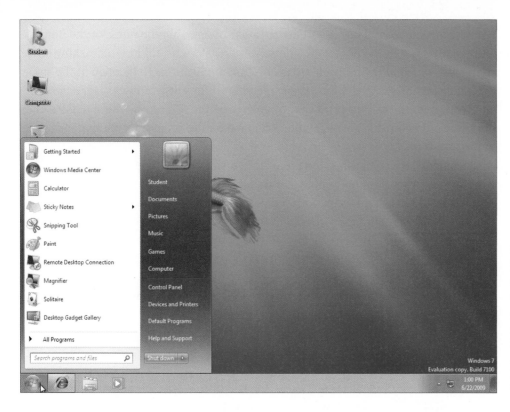

Clicking the Start button in Windows 7 displays a menu of options, including programs to run such as Internet Explorer, folders to display such as Documents and Pictures, and utilities to use such as Search.

In many GUIs, when a button is selected, the button changes color or appears in depressed form, as though a user's finger has pressed it.

**Display Windows** The main feature of a graphical user interface is the **display window**. A display window is a rectangular area of the screen used to display a program or various kinds of data, such as text and numbers. At the top of each

Most GUIs allow users to work with multiple applications at the same time. Each application appears in its own window. A user can switch back and forth among applications by clicking on a window's title bar.

window is a horizontal bar called the **title bar**, displaying the name of the item and the program in the display window. Windows are useful in multitasking environments, which allow multiple programs and applications to be open at the same time (concurrently). By dividing the screen into different windows, users can see and work with the output produced by each program. To work within a particular program—to enter data, for example—clicking on the program's window brings it to the forefront.

Documents are sometimes too large to be displayed in their entirety in a window. To overcome this problem, a **scroll bar** at a window's side or bottom enables users to see and work with the portions of a document that are beyond the edge of the screen. Small arrows at the tips of a scroll bar can be used to move documents horizontally or vertically. A small box between the two arrows can also be used to scroll through a document page by page.

**Key Feature Option Menus** A **menu** provides a set of options. Users can select options they want by highlighting the option and clicking on it with the mouse, or by typing one or more keystrokes. Making a selection launches an action, such as saving a document.

When activated, many software programs display a horizontal or vertical bar at the top or side of the screen. This **menu bar** (also called a main menu) lists the highest-level command options by name, usually composed of one or two words. Each high-level option may be accompanied by another menu, called a **drop-down menu** (or pull-down menu), containing various lower-level options. These menus may in turn include submenus offering more precise choices.

In Microsoft Office 2007 programs, sets of commands on a tabbed **ribbon** are used instead of a menu bar. The tabs are like menu names, and the commands on the tabs are like menu commands.

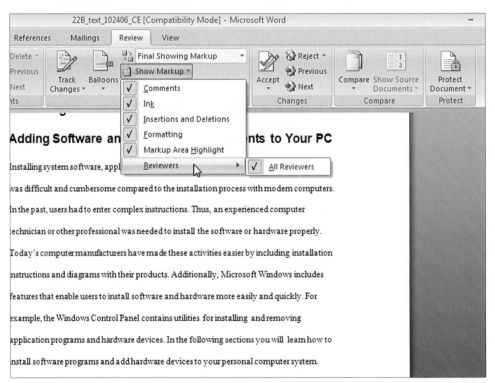

Most programs provide a menu bar. For example, when users select a menu item, a drop-down menu is displayed, providing additional choices.

The ribbon was introduced in Microsoft Office 2007 programs. This design reduces the use of menus, allowing users quicker access to basic features and options.

Software programs usually contain predetermined default options. A **default option** is a setting that the software publisher has preprogrammed under the assumption that this option is the choice favored by most users. For example, WordPad (the word processor that comes with Windows) uses 10-point Arial as the default font. Users can choose a different font by clicking the *Format* option on the menu bar, and then the *Font* option from the drop-down menu that appears.

Depending on the action being taken, some drop-down menu options may be unavailable to users at certain times. Options that are available typically appear in darker type. Unavailable options usually appear grayed out, or dimmed, letting the user know the option cannot be chosen. Figure 4-3 shows a drop-down menu containing choices that are available and one that is not.

On some menus, a small triangular pointer to the right of an option indicates that additional options are available. Clicking on the pointer displays the associated menu. A check mark at the left of an option indicates the option has been

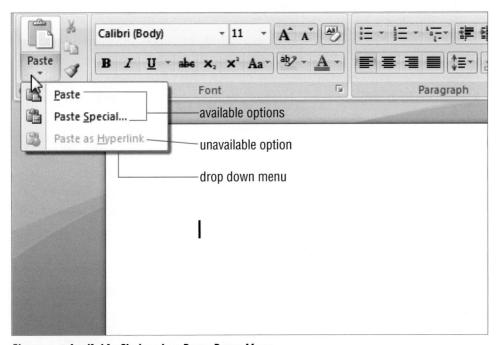

**Figure 4-3 Available Choices in a Drop-Down Menu**
Options available on a menu appear in darker print. Options that are unavailable appear in grayed-out print.

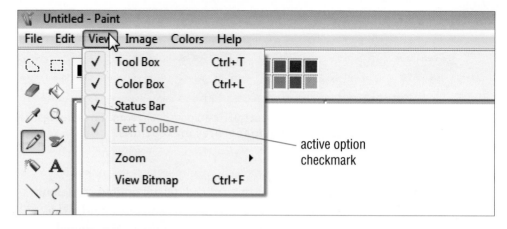

Figure 4-4 **Active Check Mark**
A check mark to the left of an option such as the Tool Box option on the View drop-down menu in Microsoft Paint indicates that the option has been selected and is therefore active.

selected and is therefore active. Figure 4-4 shows a drop-down menu associated with the *View* option in Microsoft Paint.

**Common Command Icons**  Because clicking on an icon is easier than having to remember and enter a series of keystrokes, GUIs use icons to represent common actions such as opening, saving, or printing files. These icons may be displayed in a row near the top of the screen, called a **toolbar**. To reinforce the meaning of the icons, when the mouse pointer is positioned on an icon, a one- or two-word identification label (often called a Screen Tip) displays immediately below it. Clicking the icon launches the associated action.

As with menus, some icons may be unavailable and appear in grayed-out or dimmed form. These icons usually represent actions that depend on a related, previous action. For example, users cannot select the scissors icon (for "cutting" or removing text) until some text or an object to be deleted has been highlighted (selected) with the mouse.

**Dialog Boxes**  A **dialog box** is a window that displays temporarily and disappears once the user has entered requested information. GUIs use dialog boxes to provide information and to prompt responses. Interactions between the user and the software are carried out through various elements that allow choices. Some of the more common elements are tabs, option buttons, check boxes, and text boxes.

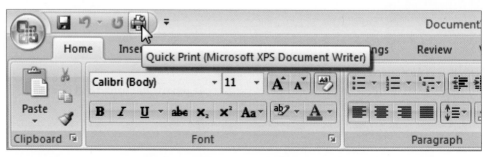

Screen Tips were used extensively in Microsoft Word 2007.

- **Tabs** Many dialog boxes offer several option subsets, each labeled as if it were a manila folder within a file drawer. The name of a subset of options is displayed in a **tab** at the top of the folder. Clicking the tab brings the selected group of options to the front of the dialog box (the file drawer).

- **Option Buttons** Another standard dialog box element is an outlined box containing a set of buttons, each one called an **option button** (or a radio button). Named for their resemblance to old-fashioned push buttons on car radios, these buttons offer different choices. Only one button can be activated at a time. For example, in the Microsoft Word Print dialog box there are option buttons in the *Page Range* section directing Word to print *All, Current Page,* or specific pages. Only one of these options can be selected at a time.

- **Check Boxes** A **check box** allows users to select an option that can be turned on or off. An option in the box can be turned on by clicking it. When an option is activated, a check mark appears in the check box. Unlike option buttons that limit users to selecting a single option, check boxes allow users to choose multiple options at one time.

- **Text Boxes** Information is entered into a **text box** to allow the computer to continue or complete a task. For example, to save a document in Microsoft Word, users must click on the *Save* button to display the Save As dialog box. Once the dialog box appears, a drive where the document will be saved needs to be indicated, and a file name for the document keyed in a text box . Most dialog boxes also contain command buttons such as Save (or OK) and Cancel that enable users to submit or re-enter the information entered into a text box or a check box.

**Online Help** Computer users will occasionally encounter problems or think of questions while they are working with an operating system or application. Answers can be found by clicking the Help option or by pressing a designated

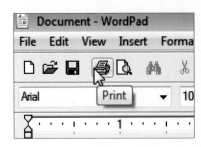

Picture icons are reinforced with Screen Tips to explain the function of the icon, such as this Print button in WordPad.

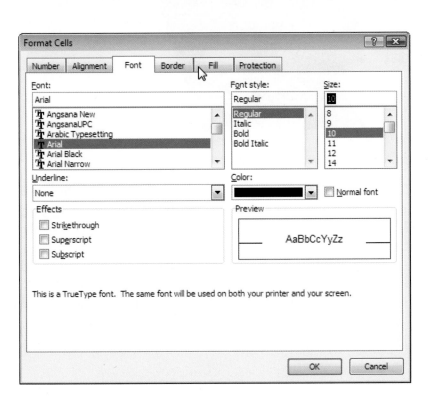

Dialog boxes provide information to a user and also offer choices or prompt responses so commands can be executed. The Format Cells dialog box in Excel is an example of such an interface.

## CHAIRMAN, MICROSOFT CORPORATION

# Bill Gates

**WILLIAM H. (BILL) GATES III** is a cofounder and, at present, chairman of the board of directors of Microsoft Corporation, the world's leading provider of software for personal computers. Born on October 28, 1955, Gates grew up in Seattle, Washington, where he attended public elementary school before moving on to the private Lakeside School in North Seattle. He began programming computers at the early age of 13.

In 1973, Gates entered Harvard University. While at Harvard, he developed a version of the BASIC programming language for the first microcomputer, called the MITS Altair. He dropped out of Harvard in his junior year to devote his full time to building Microsoft Corporation, a company he had started in 1975 with his boyhood friend Paul Allen. Guided by a belief that the personal computer would be a valuable tool on every office desktop and in every home, Gates and Allen began developing software for personal computers.

Twenty-five years later, Microsoft and Bill Gates (along with Allen and other early players) are worth billions. Under Gates's leadership, Microsoft has forged a mission to advance and improve software technology to make it easier, more cost-effective, and more enjoyable for people to use computers. The company is committed to a long-term view, which is reflected in its annual investments of millions of dollars for research and development. Gates and his wife, Melinda, have endowed a foundation with more than $21 billion to support philanthropic causes dedicated to worldwide health and education, such as providing vaccines for children in developing countries and scholarship programs for low-income high-achievers.

Microsoft has been quick to take advantage of opportunities created by the Internet. Gates has a substantial investment, along with cellular telephone pioneer Craig McCaw, in the Teledesic project, an ambitious plan to launch low-orbit satellites around the earth to provide a worldwide two-way broadband telecommunications service.

key. Clicking the Help option causes a dialog box to appear that offers topics to browse and a Search box in which to type keywords. When you enter a keyword and press *Enter* or click on one of the topics, the program searches its online documentation and displays articles that match that specification.

Some programs display a **context-sensitive Help message** based on either the user's location in the program or the activity the user is performing. This kind of Help system can suggest Help topics that are relevant to what the user is doing.

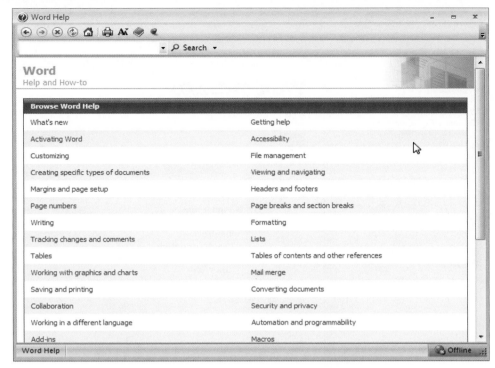

Clicking on the Help option displays a list of topics from which a selection can be made.

# Personal Computer Operating Systems

Microsoft Windows is currently the dominant operating system for personal computers. Over a period of about 19 years, Windows has evolved from a GUI/DOS combination (Windows 3.0 through 3.11) to a true GUI with versions for all types of personal computers (Windows Vista and Windows 7). The newer versions of Windows provide numerous useful features users prefer. According to some estimates, Windows is used on about 90 percent of all PCs. The remaining 10 percent are primarily Apple Macintosh personal computers using the Apple Mac OS operating system. The following sections explain some versions that have been developed during more recent years.

## Windows

Microsoft embraced the term "windows" to describe the graphical user interface it developed for use on PCs. The first versions of Windows, referred to as Windows 3.x, were not actually operating systems. Each was an **operating environment**, meaning they were graphical user interfaces on top of an underlying DOS kernel. Windows 95 offered Internet access, and it still included some DOS programs and could run DOS-based applications. Windows 95 enjoyed immediate acceptance by users with its improved GUI, increased speed, and ease of use.

Upgraded from earlier versions of Windows, Windows 98 contained several new and improved features. Windows 98 offered improved access to the Internet and World Wide Web through its Web browser, Internet Explorer. Equally important, Windows 98 provided support for multimedia peripherals, including DVD-ROM drives and USB devices. Windows NT Workstation was a power-

Tech Demo 4-2
History of
Windows

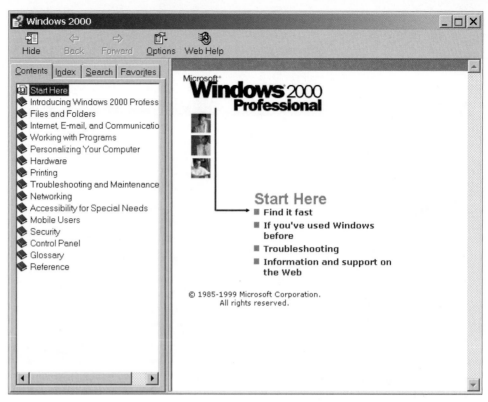

Windows 2000 was intended for networked environments.

ful GUI operating system designed for executing large applications in networked environments. This idea was reinforced by abbreviating "new technology" as NT in the operating system name.

**Windows 2000** **Windows 2000**, which was introduced in late 1999, was designed for use with business computers and was the successor to Windows 98 for office environments. Incorporating the power of Windows NT, Windows 2000 was used to link computers in a network environment. Its more-advanced operating system was particularly well suited for newer, faster, and more powerful PCs. Because it required more disk space for storage, it ran better on computers equipped with newer microprocessors. Minimum system requirements for Windows 2000 were:

- 133 MHz or higher Pentium-compatible processor
- 64 MB of RAM
- 2 GB hard disk with a minimum of 650 MB of available space
- CD-ROM, CD-R, CD-RW, or DVD-ROM drive
- VGA or higher-resolution monitor
- Microsoft mouse or compatible pointing device

**Windows XP** Microsoft's **Windows XP** was designed for computers that were fast, powerful, and had lots of memory and hard disk space. The XP operating system combined the more powerful features of Windows 2000 and Windows NT. Microsoft Corporation touted XP as virtually crash-proof, offering greater stability and reduced computer downtimes for large corporate users.

The Windows XP desktop sported a refreshingly clean look.

XP was designed to work smoothly with more than 12,000 hardware devices and keep files and settings separate for every PC user. Users logged on with a name and password so the operating system would know which desktop to bring up.

Windows XP was extremely user-friendly. For example, a new CD could be burned simply by dragging folders and files onto the CD burner icon. A new "E-mail this file" button shrank digital photos to a usable size as they were sent, to avoid tying up a recipient's phone line for long periods. Built-in automatic firewall software helped block hacker invasions from the Internet. A new Windows Messenger program allowed the exchange of instant messages over the Internet with other users on MSN, Hotmail, or Windows Messenger "Buddy Lists."

Many older PCs did not support Windows XP's increased needs. Minimum system requirements for installing and effectively using Windows XP included a 300 MHz or faster Pentium-compatible or Celeron-compatible processor, 2 GB of hard disk space for installation, a minimum of 64 MB of memory (128 MB was recommended), CD-ROM or DVD drive, and a Microsoft mouse or compatible pointing device.

**Windows Vista** Released in 2007, **Windows Vista** improved and expanded upon Windows XP's capabilities in several key areas—with a focus on security and visual aesthetics. Because of the increasing threat of viruses and other attacks from the Internet, Windows Vista included much more robust security features than any earlier version. The centerpiece of this security system was **User Access Control (UAC)**, a protection system that prompted the user for administrator-level credentials whenever an operation was attempted that might affect system stability or security in some way, such as moving or deleting an important system file.

**Windows Defender**, which monitors for and defends against spyware and adware, and **Windows Firewall**, which blocks other computers, were also introduced.

The new graphical user interface, called Aero, offered many visual improvements including translucent windows, Windows Flip and Windows Flip 3D, Aero glass, and Live Preview for taskbar thumbnails. The Start menu in Windows Vista had a new look. Rather than opening fly-out submenus for each menu level, it collapsed and expanded folders within the main pane of the menu system. The Windows Vista menu system provided a new way to present files and programs. This kept the Start menu at a manageable size no matter how much it contained and made it easier to access commonly used shortcuts and locations.

Windows Vista also came with new and improved versions of its most popular utilities and productivity applications, including Internet Explorer and Windows Media Player. The aging Outlook Express from earlier Windows versions was replaced by a new, more powerful e-mail client called Windows Mail.

While all the visual enhancements sought to improve the user experience, they came at a price—performance was notably lessened when compared to Windows XP.

**Windows 7** **Windows 7**, released in late 2009, includes many usability and performance updates. The Aero interface includes the following new features:

- Aero Peek—point to a taskbar button to show a thumbnail of that window, then point to the thumbnail to preview that program in full view. Point to the new Show Desktop button in the lower right corner of the screen to temporarily hide all open windows.

The Windows 7 menu system provides a new way to present files and programs.

- Aero Shake—quickly drag back and forth on a window's title bar to minimize all other windows, and then shake the title bar again to bring the minimized windows back.
- Aero Snap—drag any window to the top edge of the screen to maximize, or drag a window to the right or left edge of the screen to fill that half of the screen. This makes it easy to compare the windows side by side.

The Quick Launch toolbar has been replaced with an improved taskbar at the bottom of the screen which allows you to permanently pin a program icon to it—and icons on the taskbar can now be rearranged. Right-click any taskbar icon to view a Jump List of that program's recent documents.

Windows 7 also comes with Internet Explorer 8, the newest version of Microsoft's Web browser. Windows Touch supports touch-screen monitors for a more interactive and natural way to work by using your fingers to scroll, resize windows, play media, pan, and zoom. Hundreds of other usability improvements are included with Windows 7, making it the most intuitive and interactive Windows operating system to date.

Windows 7 improves upon Windows Vista's performance by booting and shutting down faster. Many extraneous utilities formerly included with Windows Vista, such as Windows Mail, Windows Movie Maker, and Windows Photo Gallery are not included with Windows 7 but are available as a free download from the Microsoft Web site.

Powerful hardware is required to run Windows 7, including a 1 GHz or faster processor, 1 GB of RAM for 32-bit systems (2 GB of RAM for 64-bit systems), 16 GB free hard drive space, and a graphics device that supports DirectX 9 with WDDM 1.0 or higher.

## Macintosh Operating System

The **Macintosh OS** was the first commercial GUI, released in 1984 and updated many times since the initial release. It included a virtual desktop, drop-down menus, dialog boxes, and icons representing common commands and programs. With its impressive graphics and ease of use, it quickly became the model for other GUIs. Soon after its introduction, manufacturers and users of IBM-PCs and compatibles wanted a comparable GUI for their computers. Within a short time Microsoft introduced its first Windows product for IBM-PCs and compatibles.

Until recently, the Mac OS ran only on Apple Macintosh computers. The Tiger release of Mac OS X can also be installed on Intel-based personal computers. The Mac OS contains many impressive and useful features, including both the Netscape Navigator and Internet Explorer Web browsers. Its extraordinary graphics capabilities help make the Apple Macintosh the computer of choice among graphic designers, desktop production specialists, printing companies, and publishers.

Mac OS 9, the version widely available in 2000, contained several new and improved features. It offered better speech recognition, supported files up to 2 terabytes (2 trillion bytes), provided for multiple users, allowed for file encryption, and supported voice-entered passwords.

The Mac OS X Interface, called Aqua, is interactive and easy to use.

Mac OS X was introduced in spring 2001. Particularly noteworthy was the new interface, called Aqua, and its UNIX operating system foundation, widely considered a stable and powerful system. With the debut of Mac OS X, more than 200 developers, including Microsoft, Adobe, IBM, Sun Microsystems, and Hewlett-Packard, agreed to create software for the new system. Mac OS X provided greater stability and true multitasking capability.

The bottom of the startup screen is similar to the Windows taskbar. Mac OS X also provides a terminal window that reveals the file system tree, enabling users to quickly locate programs and files. Mac OS X includes versions of popular programs, including the QuickTime player and Stuffit, a file compression program. It comes with Apple's Safari web browser and FTP capability, allowing users to easily send and receive large files. Its backward compatibility supports applications from previous versions, such as OS 9.

## OS/2

IBM's **OS/2** GUI operating system was the company's response to the popularity of Microsoft Windows and the Apple Mac OS. The latest version of OS/2 is called OS/2 Warp. In addition to running native application programs, OS/2 can run programs written for DOS and Windows systems. The OS/2 operating system is designed mainly for business PC users running business applications. IBM announced that they are ending support for OS/2 on December 31, 2006, but there are still several companies that have applications running on this platform.

## Linux

Tech Demo 4-3
Linux Timeline

**Linux** (pronounced LIN-UKS) is a UNIX-based operating system that runs on a number of computer platforms, including PCs, servers, and handheld devices. The Linux kernel (the central module or basic part) was developed mainly by

Linus Torvalds. Torvalds designed Linux as an **open-source software program**, which means that the developer retains ownership of the original programming code but makes the programming code available free to the general public, who is encouraged to experiment with the software, make improvements, and share the improvements with the entire user community.

Open-source software contrasts with another category called proprietary software, which includes the majority of programs in widespread use. **Proprietary software** is software that does not adhere to open standards but instead uses algorithms, protocols, file formats, and so on that were exclusively for this software by its developers to fulfill a certain purpose. A company or an individual owns proprietary software programs and requires a fee for using the software.

Fans of Linux praise its stability, flexibility, security, and generally low cost (vendors usually package it with various tools; hence there is a charge). Red Hat Linux, Novell Linux Desktop, SUSE Linux, and Ubuntu Linux are commercially available Linux software packages for personal and business computers.

The popularity of Linux on personal computers is growing, especially as the number of software programs available on the Linux platform increases. Word processing, spreadsheet, and presentation programs are available in an open source format called Open Office. Software companies are also developing software programs that will allow Windows-based programs to run on Linux-based computers.

## Server Operating Systems

Some operating systems are designed specifically for use with local area networks, allowing multiple users to connect to the server and to share network

Linux is one of the fastest-growing server operating systems. Red Hat produces a version of Linux, called Red Hat Linux, that is gaining popularity among businesses and government agencies including the Federal Aviation Administration.

TechVisionary

CREATOR OF THE LINUX OPERATING SYSTEM

# Linus Torvalds

**LINUS TORVALDS IS THE CULT HERO** of computer nerds worldwide. This is because, as a student, he challenged Big Business by writing the Linux operating system. He was upset with how many flaws there were in MS-DOS, the software he was using, so he wrote a new program and stuck his penguin mascot named Tux to it. By putting his new software on the Web for other computer users to retool and refine, he created a movement of support for his new, independent program. That program would eventually become a viable substitute for the industry standard.

Born December 28, 1969, in Helsinki, Finland, he was named after Linus Pauling, the American Nobel Prize–winning chemist. Torvalds's first experience with a computer was at the age of 10, using his grandfather's Commodore VIC-20. Once enrolled in college, he already felt capable of writing his own operating system. His goal was to write a PC-based version of UNIX, a different operating system. When he finished, he

posted the software for free downloading from the Internet and made the source codes available, as was customary for software developers at the time. The availability of source codes meant that anyone with proper know-how could add their own modifications to Linux and warp it to their personal needs. Over the years, Linux has been changed constantly by its adoring fans, while Torvalds chose which alterations to include in the newest versions.

He wrote a master's thesis titled *Linux: A Portable Operating System*, and graduated in 1996 from the University of Helsinki with a master's degree in computer science.

Linux and Torvalds shot into stardom when the competitors of Microsoft Corporation began taking the free operating system seriously. Netscape Communications Corp., Corel Corp., Oracle Corp., Intel Corp., and other companies announced their plans to support the Microsoft Windows alternative.

While roughly 2 percent of the Linux program can be credited to Torvalds directly, he still has the right to monitor the use of it through the nonprofit organization Linux International. About 7 million computers operated on Linux in 1999, and his wide fan base makes it difficult for people to abuse the program because it is nearly constantly checked by other users.

Throughout the years Torvalds has kept a relatively low profile. He remains neutral in most debates among program writers, unless the subject is open-source and free software, which he staunchly defends.

In 1997 he began working with Transmeta Corporation, a company spearheaded by Paul Allen, who codeveloped Microsoft Corporation with Bill Gates. He received some criticism for allegedly joining the enemy, but he didn't seem to mind. Torvalds left Transmeta in 2003 and now works at Open Source Development Labs, a software corporation based in Beaverton, Oregon.

His status as a cult-hero has caused people to praise him, both formally and informally. In 1996 "Asteroid 9793 Torvalds" was named after him. In 1998 he received the EFF Pioneer Award. In the 2001 film *Swordfish*, a character named Axl Torvalds is the number one computer hacker in the world. In 1999 he was voted to number 17 in *TIME* magazine's Person of the Century poll, and in 2004 he was named one of the most influential people in the world by *TIME* magazine.

resources such as files and peripheral devices such as printers. The kind of operating system selected for use with a network depends on network architecture and processing requirements. Some server operating systems that became widely used are explained in the following sections.

## Novell NetWare and Open Enterprise Server

**NetWare**, developed by Novell, Inc. during the 1980s, was a popular and widely used operating system for microcomputer-based local area networks. Network users had the option of working with or without network resources. When a user logged on to a NetWare-equipped network, NetWare provided a shell around the user's personal desktop operating system (such as Windows), allowing the retrieval or saving of files on the server's shared hard disk. Users could also print using the network's shared printer. The NetWare operating system resided on the network's shared hard disk, allowing network users to communicate with the operating system.

NetWare was replaced by Novell's **Open Enterprise Server (OES)** in 2005. OES offers the same basic functionality as Novell, but it integrates closely with Linux.

Go to this title's Internet Resource Center and read the articles titled "Network Operating Systems" and "Setting Up a Home Network." www.emcp.net/CUT4e

## Windows

Microsoft's **Windows NT Server** was one of Microsoft's earlier entries into the client/server market. It supported the connection of various peripheral devices (including hard drives and printers) and multitasking operations in which networked computers could process applications at the same time. It was quickly adopted for many local area networks immediately after it was introduced. Windows NT Server was replaced by Windows 2000 Server.

**Windows 2000 Server**  Microsoft's **Windows 2000 Server** was designed for network servers. It supported multitasking operations and allowed for the connection of various peripheral devices. Installed on a properly equipped server computer, Windows 2000 Server provided for Internet access and the development of Web pages. Windows 2000 Advanced Server and Datacenter Server were editions created for the largest network environments. Advanced Server supported up to nine processors and could handle up to 8 gigabytes of data, while Datacenter Server could support up to 32 processors and 64 gigabytes of data.

**Windows Server 2003**  Microsoft offered **Windows Server 2003** in four editions: Standard Edition, Enterprise Edition, Datacenter Edition, and Web Edition. The Standard Edition was intended to support small-to-medium sized businesses. The Enterprise Edition supported large businesses that clustered multiple servers together for increased power. The Datacenter Edition was also meant for large organizations, as it offered the ability to cluster even more servers together for mission-critical application support. The Web Edition was a scaled-down version of the software that allowed companies to choose a more economical solution for servers that hosted only Web applications.

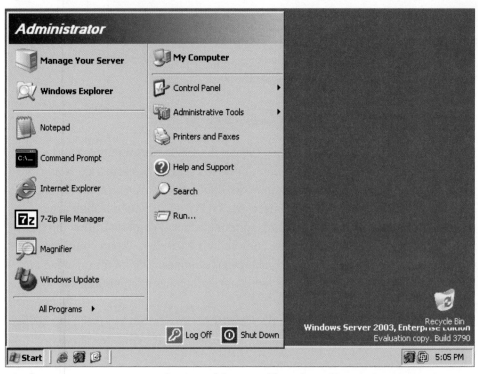

Windows Server 2003 was designed for small and medium-size LANs. Many small and medium-size businesses found this server software ideally suited for their needs.

**Windows Server 2008** **Windows Server 2008** is the server version released following Windows Vista. This new server was referred to by its code name, Longhorn, during development. It shares the many benefits described earlier of the Windows Vista platform over earlier versions, and also offers server-specific tools, protocols, and utilities for network management. For example, Windows Server 2008 contains a Network Access Protection tool that enables an IT administrator to define health requirements for the network, such as the presence of updated antivirus software, and to restrict computers that do not meet these requirements from using the network. Windows Server 2008 also makes it easier for administrators to deploy installations and patches remotely and to use and configure services. It has a new and greatly improved version of Internet Information Services (IIS), Microsoft's Web server technology, and Windows SharePoint Services, used for team collaboration and document sharing.

## UNIX

Developed in the early 1970s by programmers at Bell Laboratories, the **UNIX** (pronounced YOO-NIKS) operating system was originally designed for servers and large computer systems. It uses a complex command-line interface and offers some superb capabilities, including simultaneous access by many users to a single powerful computer. There are several variations of UNIX, including Linux and Solaris.

From its inception, UNIX has been a **multi-user operating system**, an operating system that allows many people to use one CPU from remote stations. It is also a **cross-platform operating system**, one that runs on computers of all kinds, from PCs to supercomputers. UNIX was the first language of the Internet because of its dominance in universities and laboratories, and many Internet service providers continue to use it to maintain their networks.

# Sharing Code through Krugle

**OPEN SOURCE MEANS SHARING CODE**—using software that others have created before to develop new and improved software. It's a nice idea, but in actuality the majority of programmers simply write their own code from scratch. It's just too darn hard to find the relevant bits of code they need.

Fortunately, one company is dedicated to solving this problem. Krugle started out as a search engine designed to make it easier for programmers to find and share code. Its creators hoped that by creating an orderly, accessible library of freely available code, Krugle could increase the efficiency of programmers. The search engine stands out from other source-code search engines because it lets programmers search by programming language, as well as annotate code and documentation, create bookmarks, and save search results in a tabbed workspace.

Now Krugle has taken their desire to help programmers one step further. In 2007, they released Krugle Enterprise, an internal-network appliance that helps software-development companies to keep their own comprehensive, searchable libraries of all the source code they use or have used. This appliance, which continues to grow and develop, has helped programmers to be more efficient, saving companies time and money and proving that open source, when combined with the right tools, can be more than just a nice idea—it can be a profitable one.

**Linux** Linux is one of the fastest-growing server operating systems. As discussed in the previous section on personal computer operating systems, Linux is an open-source software program based on the UNIX operating system.

Like UNIX, Linux was originally designed for use with servers and large computer systems, including midrange servers and mainframes. Linux can be downloaded via the Internet for free, and numerous utilities are also available. In addition to downloading Linux from the Internet, there are other ways Linux can be obtained. Some vendors will install Linux on new computers, or provide a CD-ROM containing the software. Some books about the software include a CD-ROM that can be used to install it. A copy of the software may also be obtained from other users. Various versions of Linux are available, including command-line versions and GUI versions. Two popular GUI versions are called GNOME and KDE.

Linux software has quickly gained widespread acceptance and usage because of its low cost (in many cases, free) and its cross-platform nature. Most UNIX software programs can run on the Linux platform. Some companies market their own versions of the software, such as Red Hat and Novell. Many computer professionals believe Linux is a strong competitor with other, more established operating systems. IBM and Hewlett-Packard have created internal Linux business units to support their customers' ventures into the Linux environment.

The future for Linux is promising. Its popularity as a general-purpose operating system is growing, and several companies are testing and refining Linux for use with the embedded chips found in a variety of mobile devices, including Internet appliances and handheld devices.

**Solaris** **Solaris** is a UNIX-based operating environment developed by Sun Microsystems. It was originally developed to run on Sun's SPARC workstations, but, the software now runs on many workstations from other manufacturers.

Solaris includes the SunOS operating system and a windowing system. It currently supports multithreading, multiprocessing, networking, and centralized network management. An add-on program, called Wabi emulator, is available that allows Solaris to run numerous Windows applications.

## Operating Systems for Handheld Devices

In recent years, two operating systems have solidified their place in the handheld device market. Palm OS and Windows Mobile have become standard choices for the multitude of PDAs, smartphones, and other handheld computing devices.

The Palm Treo Pro handheld computer uses the Palm OS.

### Palm OS

Palm Inc., manufacturer of one of the earliest calendar and time management devices on the market, has developed its own operating system for its handheld personal digital assistants (PDAs). Called **Palm OS**, this system provides a simple graphical user interface that is used in the various versions of the Palm PDAs, Sony PDAs, and several smartphones, including the Treo. The Palm OS is the most common operating system for handheld PDAs in the corporate environment.

### Windows Mobile

The **Windows Mobile** operating system is used in wireless devices and other systems with embedded processors, such as smartphones, PocketPC PDAs, and other handheld devices. Replacing a previous operating system called Windows CE, Windows Mobile is a 32-bit, multitasking, GUI operating system with special built-in power management, Internet, and e-mail capabilities. A user can easily set up a Wi-Fi (wireless) connection for connecting to the Internet. On handheld LCD screens, data and images appear clearly. Windows Mobile allows the interchange of information with desktop and networked Windows-based PCs.

Windows Mobile enables a user to check Outlook e-mail and attachments, schedule meetings, browse the Internet, and even listen to music. For a business user, Windows Mobile allows the user to access e-mail and the Internet and to perform various business tasks.

## Utility Programs and Translators

System software may contain other special software, or allow for the use of specialized programs. Two important examples of this kind of system software are utility programs and translators.

Windows Mobile is used in a variety of handheld devices, including PocketPC PDAs and smartphones.

## Utility Programs

A **utility program** performs a single maintenance or repair task, such as checking for viruses, uninstalling programs, or deleting data no longer needed. An operating system typically includes several utility programs that are preinstalled at the factory. Several companies, including Symantec and McAfee, produce software suites containing a variety of utility programs. Symantec's Norton SystemWorks includes programs that allow users to check for and erase viruses, diagnose and

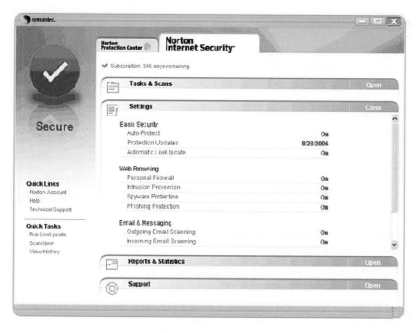

Symantec's Norton SystemWorks can perform a variety of maintenance and repair tasks, including defragmenting a disk and checking for viruses and quarantining them.

**Table 4-2** Utility Programs and Their Functions

| Utility Program | Function |
|---|---|
| antivirus software | protects the computer system from a virus attack |
| anti-spyware | protects the computer system from software that tracks the activity of Internet users |
| backup utility | makes a backup copy of files on a separate disk |
| device driver | allows hardware devices, such as disk drives and printers, to work with the computer system |
| diagnostic utility | examines the computer system and corrects problems that are identified |
| disk optimizer | identifies disk problems, such as separated files, and rearranges files so they run faster (includes disk scanners and disk defragmenters) |
| disk toolkit | recovers lost files and repairs any that may be damaged |
| extender utility | adds new programs and fonts to the computer system |
| file compression utility | reduces the size of files so they take up less disk space |
| file viewer | displays quickly the contents of a file |
| firewall | protects a personal computer or network from access by unauthorized users such as hackers |
| screen capture program | captures as a file the contents shown on the monitor |
| spam blocker | filters incoming spam messages |
| uninstaller utility | removes programs, along with related system files |

Go to this title's Internet Resource Center and read the article titled "Utility Software." www.emcp.net/CUT4e

Tech Demo 4-4 Antivirus Software

repair hard disk problems, optimize hard drive performance, restore deleted files, erase deleted files permanently, perform file management, and rescue and restore files from a crashed hard drive. Users can also purchase and install additional utility programs of their choice. Table 4-2 lists some popular kinds of utility programs. Utility programs are usually stored on a hard disk along with the basic operating system and activated when needed by the user.

Utility programs are useful for correcting many of the problems that computer users are likely to encounter. Some of the most popular kinds of utility software are antivirus software, firewalls, diagnostic utilities, uninstallers, disk scanners, disk defragmenters, file compression utilities, backup utilities, disk toolkits, spam blockers, and anti-spyware.

**Antivirus Software** **Antivirus software** (also called a virus checker) is one of the most important types of utility programs. Examples include Norton AntiVirus and McAfee VirusScan. A **virus** is programming code buried within a computer program, data, or e-mail message and transferred to a computer system without the user's knowledge. Virus contamination of a computer system can have consequences varying in severity from the mildly annoying to the disastrous. Antivirus utilities perform many functions to keep a computer's software healthy. They scan new disks or downloaded material for known viruses, and diagnose storage media for viral infection. They can also monitor system operations for suspicious activities, such as the rewriting of system resource files, and alert users when such activities are occurring. Most businesses use antivirus utilities as a daily startup routine. Home users find them valuable as well, as their computer systems are no less vulnerable to damaging viruses. The spread of viruses across the Internet represents the major source of virus transmission, principally through attachments to e-mail messages.

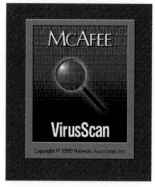

McAfee VirusScan is a popular virus-checking utility.

**Firewalls** A **firewall** is a security system that acts as a boundary to protect a computer or network from unauthorized access. Firewalls may consist of hardware, software, or a combination of both. A main use is to prevent unauthorized Internet users from accessing a personal computer or a network connected to the Internet. Incoming and outgoing messages pass through the firewall, which examines each message and blocks those that do not meet specified security criteria. Firewalls are designed to work in a manner similar to the way firewalls between individual housing units in an apartment building are designed to prevent fire from spreading from one apartment to other apartments.

A **personal firewall** such as McAfee Internet Security or Norton Internet Security is a software-based system designed to protect a personal computer from unauthorized users, called hackers, attempting to access other computers through an Internet connection. Hackers who gain access to other PCs can access the information on them, such as passwords, personal data, and possibly use those computers for a variety of illegal activities. Windows XP Service Pack 2, Windows Vista, and Windows 7 also include a personal firewall called Windows Firewall that is enabled by default and is adequate for most PCs.

A **network firewall** typically consists of a combination of hardware and software. In addition to installing firewall software, a company may add a hardware device, such as a dedicated firewall device or proxy server, that screens all communications entering and leaving networked computers to prevent unauthorized access (see Figure 4-5). For example, the device or server may check an incoming message to determine whether the message is from an authorized user. If not, the message is blocked from entering the network.

Firewalls provide a first line of defense against unauthorized access and intrusion. Although most firewall systems are effective, users should practice other security measures, such as safeguarding passwords.

**Diagnostic Utilities** A **diagnostic utility** diagnoses a computer's components and system software programs and creates a report identifying problems. The utility provides suggestions to correct any problems encountered, and in some situations can repair problems automatically. The Windows operating system contains a diagnostic utility. More advanced diagnostic utility software can be purchased separately from software vendors.

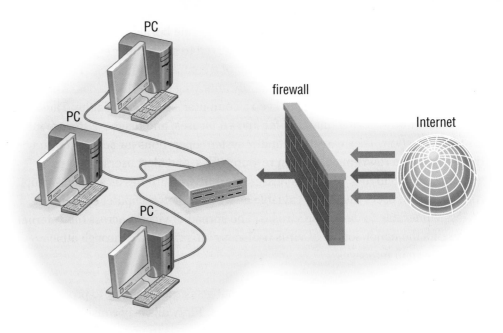

**Figure 4-5 A Firewall**
Firewalls are designed to prevent unauthorized Internet users from accessing a personal computer or a network connected to the Internet.

**Uninstallers** An **uninstaller** is a utility program for removing (deleting) software programs and any associated entries in the system files. When an application program is installed, the operating system stores additional files related to the program. Associated files may remain on the hard disk and waste valuable space if a user attempts to remove a program without using an uninstaller utility. An uninstaller utility solves this problem and frees up disk space by automatically removing both programs and related files.

**Disk Scanners** A **disk scanner** examines hard disks and their contents to identify potential problems, such as bad sectors. During the scanning process a disk scanner program checks for both physical and logical problems. For example, it detects and notifies users if a disk contains clusters or sectors that are damaged and therefore unusable. Scan Disk is the disk scanner utility included with the Microsoft Windows operating system.

**Disk Defragmenters** A **disk defragmenter** utility scans hard disks and reorganizes files and unused space, allowing operating systems to locate and access files and data more quickly. Operating systems store a file in the first available sector on a disk. However, there may not be enough space in one sector to store the entire file. If a portion of the sector already contains data, the remaining portions of the file are stored in other available sectors. This may result in files stored in noncontiguous (separated) sectors, known as fragmented files. This causes operating systems to take more time locating and retrieving all segments of a particular file.

This problem can be solved by **defragmenting** the disk so files are stored in contiguous sectors. Microsoft's Windows operating system includes a disk defrag-

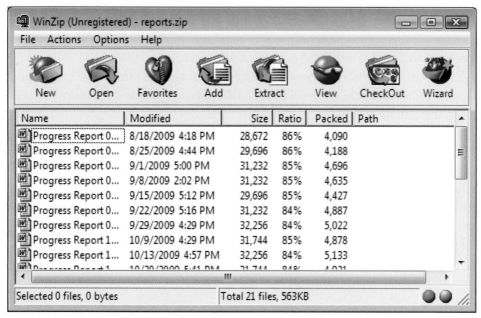

WinZip allows users to compress and decompress files for sharing and storage.

menting utility called Disk Defragmenter. If a system does not come equipped with a disk defragmenter, utilities packages containing one can be purchased.

**File Compression Utilities** A **file compression** utility compresses (shrinks) the size of a file so it occupies less disk space. Examples of compression utilities are WinZip, PKZIP, and StuffIt. Files are compressed by reducing redundancies, such as the binary descriptions of rows of identically colored pixels in graphics files. The ability to compress and decompress files is especially helpful when sending or receiving large files on network systems or over the Internet.

Compressed files, often called zipped files, typically have a .zip file extension. Users must compress (zip) the file. When a compressed (zipped) file is received, it must be uncompressed (unzipped) to restore its original form. Both senders and recipients of compressed files must have compression software installed on their computers.

**Backup Utilities** A **backup utility** allows users to make copies of the contents of disks or tapes. The utility can be directed to back up the entire contents or only selected files. Some backup utilities will compress files so they take up less space than the original files. Because compressed files are unusable until they are uncompressed, many backup utilities include a restore program for uncompressing files.

**Disk Toolkits** A **disk toolkit**, such as Norton Utilities Disk Doctor, contains utility programs that let users identify and correct a variety of problems they may have with a hard disk. Disk toolkits can diagnose and repair problems with files on the disk as well as physical damage to the disk.

**Spam Blockers** The proliferation of unwanted e-mail messages, called spam, is a serious concern among Internet users. According to Brightmail, a company that blocks spam for some of the nation's top Internet service providers, spam messages that advertise products and services ranging from automobiles to dating services now account for nearly 80 percent of all Internet e-mail traffic.

A utility program called a **spam blocker** is often used to filter incoming spam messages. Popular spam blockers include iHateSpam, Matador, SpamCatcher, and SpamSubtract PRO.

**Anti-Spyware** **Spyware** is a form of **malware** (malicious software) that tracks the activities of Internet users for the benefit of a third party. Spyware is unknowingly downloaded to an Internet user's computer to collect keystrokes or Web site activity for malicious purposes such as password interception, fraudulent credit card usage, or identity theft. One particular type of spyware, called **adware**, is more annoying than harmful. Adware tracks the Web sites that a user visits in order to collect information for marketing or advertising. Some adware presents users with pop-up advertisements that contain contests, games, or links to unrelated Web sites.

Not all antivirus software protects Internet users from spyware, but separate anti-spyware and adware protection software is available. Windows Vista and Windows 7 contain anti-spyware software called Windows Defender. Other popular anti-spyware software includes Webroot Spy Sweeper, Lavasoft's Ad Aware, and Bayden Systems' Popup Blocker.

## Translators

A computer cannot understand programming code written in a human language, such as English or Spanish. Instead, it can only understand machine language: binary code written in zeros (0s) and ones (1s). (The concept of machine language was explained in Chapter 2.) Operating systems and other programs may be written using machine language, which enables them to execute very quickly.

Machine language is difficult to learn and programmers find that writing machine language programs is time-consuming. To avoid this, application programs are usually written using an English-like programming language, called a **high-level language**. Examples of high-level languages are COBOL, Java, and BASIC, which has several versions. Figure 4-6 shows a sample of programming code in DOS BASIC.

High-level languages must be translated into machine-language format before the CPU can execute them. To accomplish this task, a special program called a **language translator** is used to translate (convert) high-level language into machine language so it can be run by the computer. Microsoft Windows includes a version of BASIC.

The two major types of language-translating software are interpreters and compilers. Each programming language generates code that needs to be either compiled or interpreted for execution. A **compiler** translates an entire program into machine language before the program will run. Each language has its own unique compiler. After reading and translating the program, the compiler displays a list of program errors that may be present. Once the errors are corrected, a compiled program will usually execute more quickly than an interpreted program.

```
10 REM ***SIMPLIFIED PAYROLL PROGRAM***
20 PRINT "ENTER HOURS WORKED";
30 INPUT H
40 PRINT "ENTER HOURLY PAY RATE";
50 INPUT R
60 REM *** COMPUTE WAGE***
70 LET W=H*R
80 PRINT "WEEKLY WAGE IS $";W
90 END
RUN

OUTPUT

ENTER HOURS WORKED? 40
ENTER HOURLY PAY RATE? 8
WEEKLY WAGE IS $ 320
```

By typing the RUN command, the program executes and these messages appear on screen.

User enters the hours worked and the hourly pay rate.

When the program is executed (RUN), the computer multiplies the hours worked (40) by the hourly pay rate (6) and automatically displays the weekly wage (240) on the screen.

**Program Explanation**
Every instruction begins with a line (instruction) number. A **REM** (short for remark) is a statement that describes what the program does but has no effect on the program itself. A PRINT statement displays on the screen the text within quotes. An **INPUT** instruction requires the programmer to enter specific data when prompted. A **LET** statement processes the data according to the formula identified. An **END** statement indicates the end of the program.

**Figure 4-6 DOS BASIC Payroll Program**
Shown is a simple payroll program written in DOS BASIC.

An **interpreter** differs from a compiler by reading, translating, and executing one instruction at a time. Since an interpreter acts on just one line of instruction at a time, it identifies errors as they are encountered, including the line containing the error, making it somewhat more user-friendly.

# OnThe**Horizon**

**INSPIRED BY BREAKTHROUGHS IN PROCESSING TECHNOLOGY** as well as changing market needs, developers of system and utilities software are continually brainstorming new programs and improvements to existing software. Although trying to divine the path of software development is risky, some of today's leading-edge technologies provide clues to the future.

## Linux Gets a Boost

The open source Linux operating system will get a big push if the One Laptop per Child project succeeds as planned. The project aims to produce laptops for every child in developing nations, at a price of around $100 per machine once production is in full swing. Project engineers needed a scaled-down operating system that used little power, and decided that Linux was the best match for those requirements. Production is planned in the tens of millions, and Project Head Nicholas Negroponte feels that this choice will one day make Linux as popular on desktop computers as it is currently on servers.

## Software Streaming

Software streaming is a promising alternative to installed software, involving the distribution of operating system and applications software to networked computers from centrally managed servers. When networked computers are switched on they send a request for operating system and applications software. The advantages of this type of software platform include lower maintenance costs, ease of software upgrades, and improved security because no software remains on individual machines when they are switched off. Results of this method of software distribution are promising, and some think it may one day become a leading method of software distribution.

## Web-Based Operating Systems

Desktoptwo is an innovative new operating system that lets users run applications located on a desktop resident on a remote Web server. Desktoptwo uses a combination of scripting and markup languages known as Ajax (Asynchronous JavaScript and XML) to create a remote desktop with speed and interactivity comparable to that offered by desktop programs. Currently available in beta version, Desktoptwo and other similar projects may develop into popular alternatives to computer-based operating systems.

# Chapter**Summary**

 *For an interactive version of this summary, go to this text's Internet Resource Center at www.emcp.net/CUT4e. A Spanish version is also available.*

## What is the function of system software?

**Software** is the broad term for the programs that tell a computer what to do and how to do it. Programs are sets of instructions telling computers to perform actions in a certain order. The two main categories of software are **application software** and **system software**. Application software includes programs that perform a single task such as spreadsheet analysis. System software includes programs that manage the basic operations of a computer such as starting up and saving and printing files.

## What is the function of the operating system?

The **operating system** is the most important piece of software on a personal computer. It manages main memory, or RAM; controls and configures peripheral devices; formats and copies disks; manages essential file operations; monitors system performance; and provides a user interface. Operating systems are designed for a particular **platform**, which is determined by the type of computer and processor.

## What are the two types of software user interfaces and how do they work?

All software, including operating systems, must have a **user interface** to allow communication between the software and the user. The interface controls the manner in which data and commands are entered and the way information and processing options are presented on the screen. Two types of user interfaces have been developed for personal computers: command-line interfaces and graphical user interfaces (GUIs). **Command-line interfaces** are, as the name suggests, designed to accept commands from the user in the form of lines of text code. The DOS operating system has a command-line interface. **Graphical user interfaces (GUIs)** accept user commands in the form of mouse clicks on icons or menu items. Windows is the most commonly used GUI for personal computers, and it uses the same icons and basic file commands as Windows-based applications, which makes learning the new applications much easier. The major GUI features with which users interact include an on-screen desktop, display windows, key feature menus, common command **icons**, **dialog boxes**, and **context-sensitive help**.

## What are the popular operating systems in use on personal computers?

Since its development in 1985, the Windows operating system has dominated the PC market, from Windows 3.1 through **Windows 2000**, **Windows XP**, **Windows Vista**, and **Windows 7**. Besides adding features with each version, the Windows releases have required increasingly more powerful microprocessors and more disk space for installation. The **Mac OS** was the first commercial GUI, serving as a model for the Windows GUI that followed. Long a favorite of graphic artists and designers, the Mac OS now runs on both Apple Macintosh and Intel-based personal computers. Its newest version, Mac OS X, includes a new interface called Aqua and is based on the UNIX operating system. IBM's **OS/2** GUI operating system was developed to compete with Microsoft Windows and the Apple Mac OS. The latest version, OS/2 Warp, can run programs written for both DOS and Windows systems. **Linux**, an open-source operating system based on UNIX, is emerging as the next competitor in the personal computer operating system market.

## What are the popular operating systems used on servers?

Server operating systems are designed for local area networks, allowing multiple users to connect to the server computer and to share data files, programs, and peripheral devices. **Open Enterprise Server (OES)** replaced NetWare as a popular and widely used operating system for microcomputer-based local area networks. Other major server operating systems include Windows (including **Windows Server 2003** and **Windows Server 2008**) and **UNIX** (including Linux and **Solaris**).

## What are the operating systems used for handheld devices?

The development of handheld devices has created a need for operating systems designed exclusively for these mobile computers with smaller screens. The two operating systems for handheld devices are **Palm OS** and **Windows Mobile**.

## How are the functions of utility programs different from translators?

A **utility program** performs a single maintenance or repair task. Common utility programs include **antivirus software**, **firewalls**, **diagnostic utilities**, **uninstallers**, **disk scanners**, **disk defragmenter**s, **file compression** utilities, **backup utilities**, **disk toolkits**, **spam blockers**, and anti-spyware.

A **language translator** is a special program that converts a high-level program language into machine language so the computer can run the program. Two major types of language translators are **compilers** and **interpreters**. Compilers translate an entire program at once, whereas interpreters act on just one line of instruction at a time.

# KeyTerms

*Numbers indicate the pages where terms are first cited in the chapter. An alphabetized list of key terms with definitions (in English and Spanish) can be found on the Encore CD that accompanies this book. In addition, these terms and definitions are included in the end-of-book glossary.*

# Chapter**Exercises**

*The following chapter exercises, along with new activities and information, are also offered in the Internet Resource Center for this title at www.emcp.net/CUT4e.*

## *Tutorial >* **Exploring Windows**

Tutorial 4 focuses on maximizing, minimizing, and restoring application and file management windows. You also will learn how to move and resize a window.

## Expanding Your Knowledge > **Articles and Activities**

 *Visit the Internet Resource Center for this title at www.emcp.net/CUT4e, read the articles related to this chapter, and complete the corresponding activities. The article titles include:*

- Topic 4-1: Open Source Software
- Topic 4-2: Network Operating Systems
- Topic 4-3: Setting Up a Home Network
- Topic 4-4: Utility Software

## Terms Check > **Matching**

 *For additional practice, go to the Internet Resource Center for this title at www.emcp.net/CUT4e for a chapter crossword puzzle.*

Write the letter of the correct answer on the line before each numbered item.

|   |   |   |   |
|---|---|---|---|
| a. | on-screen desktop | f. | system software |
| b. | window | g. | graphical user interface (GUI) |
| c. | interpreter | h. | icon |
| d. | utility | i. | menu bar |
| e. | software | j. | platform |

_____ 1. Programs that tell a computer what to do and how to do it.

_____ 2. An interface that uses menus, buttons, and symbols, making it easier to work with text, graphics, and other elements.

_____ 3. A horizontal or vertical row display that shows the highest-level command options.

_____ 4. An on-screen work area displaying graphical elements such as icons, buttons, windows, links, and dialog boxes.

_____ 5. A picture or symbol representing an action such as opening, saving, or printing a file.

_____ 6. A rectangular area of the screen used to display a program, data, or information.

_____ 7. Translation software that reads and executes one program line at a time.

_____ 8. A type of program that performs a maintenance or repair task, such as formatting a disk.

_____ 9. The foundation or standard around which software is developed.

_____ 10. A set of programs controlling the operation of a computer system, including all components and devices connected to it.

## Technology Illustrated > **Identify the Process**

What features are illustrated in this screen capture? Identify the features and write a paragraph describing them.

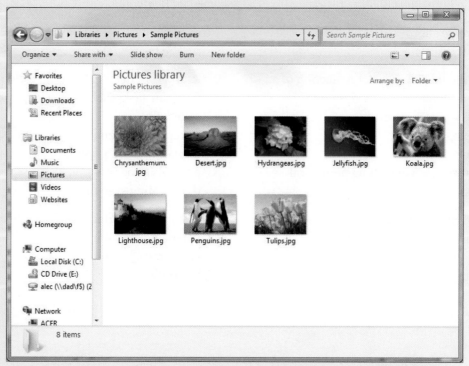

## Knowledge Check > **Multiple Choice**

Circle the letter of the best answer from those provided.

1. An option that has been built into a software program under the assumption that it is the one most likely to be chosen is called a(n)
   a. default.
   b. driver.
   c. buffer.
   d. algorithm.

2. A rectangular area of the screen used to display a program, data, or information is a
   a. pane.
   b. menu.
   c. toolbar.
   d. window.

3. A box that provides information or requests a response is called a(n)
   a. query box.
   b. dialog box.
   c. answer box.
   d. data box.

4. A small program that enables a computer to communicate with devices such as printers and monitors is a
   a. driver.
   b. graphical user interface (GUI).
   c. speaker.
   d. compiler.

5. A program that converts a high-level programming language into machine language is called a(n)
   a. coprocessor.
   b. binary operator.
   c. utility program.
   d. language translator.

6. Which of the following is not a function of an operating system?
   a. providing a user interface
   b. processing data
   c. managing RAM
   d. configuring and controlling peripheral devices

7. A foundation or standard around which software is developed is called a(n)
   a. system program.
   b. platform.
   c. utility.
   d. PC model.

8. A screen on which graphical elements such as icons, buttons, windows, links, and dialog boxes are displayed is called the
   a. desktop.
   b. menu bar.
   c. icon interface.
   d. title bar.

9. A program that performs a single maintenance or repair task, such as checking for viruses, is called a(n)
   a. repair program.
   b. maintenance program.
   c. utility program.
   d. operating system.

10. The most important piece of software on a personal computer is the
    a. operating system.
    b. utility program.
    c. application program.
    d. defragmenting program.

## *Things That Think >* Brainstorming New Uses

In groups or individually, contemplate the following questions and develop as many answers as you can.

1. One of the features introduced in Windows XP is the "remote assistance" feature. This allows someone with Windows XP to access (via the Internet) another user's Windows XP computer as if he/she were there in person. The primary intent is for software vendors or ISPs to provide technical support to their customers from distant locations. What other uses of this remote assistance technology can you imagine? What problems can you see this technology causing?

2. One of the features introduced in Windows XP is a copy-protection feature called "product activation" that Microsoft included to reduce software piracy. When Windows XP is installed on a PC, the installer must use an activation wizard to register the product key. This product key is then permanently tied to the internal address of that computer. If someone tries to install the same copy of Windows XP on another computer, the activation process will not work. Can

you think of legitimate needs that consumers might have to reinstall or copy the software that would not be considered piracy? Can you think of any nonsoftware industries that might have a use for this copy-protection technology?

3. Many antivirus utility programs use "heuristics" to discover new viruses. The use of heuristics means that the antivirus program assesses programming code against a set of rules to determine if the programming code exhibits any suspicious behavior. For example, if the programming logic appears to modify system files, send out hundreds of e-mails at a time, or performs an action that could be dangerous to a computer system, the file (or e-mail) message will be quarantined for the user's protection. This behavior-based approach to identifying viruses has proved to be more effective than traditional virus discovery techniques. Can you think of other uses for behavior-based problem-solving software?

## Key Principles > Completion

Fill in the blanks with the appropriate words or phrases.

1. A collection of programs that manage basic operations such as starting and shutting down the computer and saving and printing files is known as _____.

2. A foundation or standard around which software is developed is called a(n) _____.

3. An operating system program that manages computer components, peripheral devices, and memory is the _____.

4. A _____ is a unique combination of characters that allows a user to gain access to computer resources such as programs, data, and files.

5. A _____ is a graphical element that causes a particular action to occur when selected.

6. GUIs use _____ boxes to provide information and prompt responses to the user.

7. The _____ was the first commercial GUI, released in 1984 and updated many times since the initial release.

8. One of the fastest growing operating systems, called _____, was developed by Linus Torvalds, and is based on the UNIX operating system.

9. A _____ is programming code buried within a computer program or an electronic mail message and transferred to a computer system without the user's knowledge.

10. A utility program that scans hard disks and reorganizes files and unused space, allowing operating systems to locate and access files and data more quickly is called a disk _____.

## Tech Architecture > Label the Drawing

In this illustration of an application window, label the four graphical elements called out with arrows.

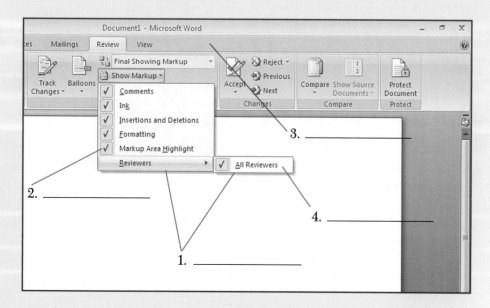

## *Techno Literacy* > **Research and Writing**

Develop appropriate written responses based on your research for each item.

1. How does open-source productivity software stack up against Microsoft Office? Research Linux-based Open Office productivity software and compare it with that found in Microsoft Office. Are the same types of applications in Microsoft Office available in Open Office? Are there any unique features of Open Office that are not available in Microsoft Office? Can files created in one product be viewed and edited in the other product? How do the prices compare? Are the same support resources available for both products (e.g., manuals, books, online help)? Which would you prefer, and why?

2. Is there a vaccine for this virus? With team members assigned by your instructor, investigate a computer virus that has infected large numbers of computers in recent years. Discuss and answer these questions:

   - What does the virus do?
   - Where did it originate, and how does it spread?
   - What were the costs of the damage?
   - How widespread was the outbreak?
   - How was the virus stopped?

## *Technology Issues* > **Team Problem-Solving**

In groups, brainstorm possible solutions to the issues presented.

1. User expectations for operating systems are complex. Some users want more robust technical features and programming utilities, and others want them to become more user-friendly and "intelligent," so the OS can predict what the user wants or needs to do. Brainstorm ways developers of operating systems can resolve, address, or reconcile these conflicting expectations.

2. Researchers and developers claim that one of the most important goals for operating systems is to become self-healing. Discuss what this characteristic means and list the types of problems "self-healing" computers will be designed to solve.

3. Microsoft claims it will soon break the mold and create a new generation OS interface that is touch- and voice-driven. If the company is right, what adaptors or utilities will be required to accommodate physically disabled customers and others with special needs?

## *Mining Data* > **Internet Research and Reporting**

Conduct Internet searches to find the information described in the activities below. Write a brief report summarizing your research results. Be sure to document your sources, using the MLA format (See Chapter 1, page 42, to review MLA style guidelines).

1. Research the advantages and disadvantages of open-source software programs such as Linux. Is there evidence to suggest that providing source code to developers results in better programs over a shorter development time?

2. Several companies are dreaming up designs for the PC of the future. Research the design ideas of companies such as Lenovo, Microsoft, Asus Design, Personal Computer Environments, and Dell. Discuss these questions as you study their computer designs for the future:

- What design objectives are guiding the design decisions?
- What markets are being targeted?
- How might the market respond?
- Will these products win acceptance?
- What advice could you offer designers to ensure a positive market response?

3. A variety of utility programs are currently available, and new ones are being developed on an ongoing basis. Research the topic of utility programs to answer the following questions:

- What are the most popular utilities? (Which are used most often, according to industry research?)
- What utilities are included in Windows XP and Windows Vista?
- What are some new utilities now under development?
- What is the most effective way to "package" utilities for consumers? Individually? In groups of those most commonly used? What are other options?

## Technology Timeline > Predicting Next Steps

Many improvements have been made to the Windows operating system since Microsoft first introduced it. Below is a timeline showing versions of Microsoft Windows for the personal computer and the year each was introduced. Visit Microsoft's Web site at www.microsoft.com and other sites to learn more about Windows and its features. Predict when the next version is likely to be introduced, and prepare a list of features you believe the next version will, or should, include.

| | | |
|---|---|---|
| **1985** Windows 1.0 | **1998** Windows 98 | **2001** Windows XP |
| **1992** Windows 3.1 | **2000** Windows 2000 | **2007** Windows Vista |
| **1995** Windows 95 | **2000** Windows Millennium Edition | **2009** Windows 7 |

## Ethical Dilemmas > Group Discussion and Debate

As a class or within an assigned group, discuss the following ethical dilemma.

The illegal copying of commercial software is a major concern among software publishers, including Microsoft and Corel. According to publishers, thousands of copies are made and distributed to other users in violation of copyright laws.

Software publishers may spend thousands and even millions of dollars developing new software products. Illegal copies distributed to other users rob publishers of profits they would have gained from the sale of these products. Additionally, publishers say they must charge legitimate customers higher prices to make up for lost sales.

Many users believe that purchasing a legal copy makes the buyer the product's owner, which should entitle them to make extra copies. Additionally, they point out that because software publishers have the option of making their products "copy protected," publishers must not consider copying a serious problem.

What is your position on this issue? Are there situations that justify copying copyrighted software? Why or why not? What are your ethical obligations, if any, concerning this matter?

# CHAPTER 5

# Application Software

## Learning Objectives

> Define application software and provide examples of the different kinds of tasks it can be used for

> Differentiate between the four major types of application software

> Describe the activities that productivity software supports

> Identify examples of software that are used in the household

> Describe the different types of graphics and multimedia software

> Explain how communications software is used

# CyberScenario

**ERIK TOWNSEND LIVES IN WASHINGTON,** North Carolina, and grooms dogs and cats for a living. He has always wanted to complete his college degree, but his work schedule and family obligations made it difficult to enroll in local colleges or universities. After researching online degree programs, Erik decided to enroll at the University of Phoenix to complete a B.S. in Business Management.

Using his high-speed Internet connection, Erik walks through the tutorial for succeeding in University of Phoenix's online programs. He learns that an important task in his first class will be to share an autobiography so other class members can get to know him. Erik opens up his word processing software program and begins typing his student profile, which includes facts and goals about his work, family, and personal experiences. Thinking that he should include a photo, he digs through his online photo album. After finding a good picture, he adjusts the size in his image-editing software, pastes it into his profile, and saves the document.

Erik clicks on a link in his registration e-mail and logs into the school's Web site to enter his first class, Introduction to Management. Just as he expects, there is an assignment from his instructor asking everyone to upload their profile with a picture so that the students in the class can get to know each other. He also sees the breakout of groups for the course and notes that his group is having a webconference the next evening to discuss how to tackle their first project.

After checking the first week's assignments for the course, Erik starts the research for his first paper on teambuilding exercises. He knows he will need to use research databases and other reference sources in the school's online library as well as Internet search engines to find the information he needs.

After additional research and planning, Erik is ready to write a draft of his paper. He uses a word processing program for the text and creates supporting illustrations and charts using presentation graphics software and spreadsheet software. After this week's lecture and discussions, Erik will need only to edit the text and lay out the diagrams and figures using a desktop publishing program.

Different software programs help Erik Townsend make effective use of his most valuable resource—time. He is able to schedule his class work at his convenience, work with members of a group online, edit digital photos, access the resources of a full business school library from his home computer, and prepare documents that look as though a commercial publisher created them. Erik is using software programs to greatly improve his productivity, which is the major purpose of application software for individual use.

Millions of individuals use application software programs in their daily activities, as do companies, organizations, and government agencies.

# Types of Application Software

**Application software** enables users to perform the types of activities and work that computers were designed for. The specific type of application used depends on the intended purpose, and there are application programs available for almost every need.

Three broad types of application software are available for business users: individual, collaboration, and vertical programs. Table 5-1 displays the different application software categories and their uses.

**Individual application software** refers to programs individuals use at work or at home. Examples include word processing, spreadsheet, database management, and desktop publishing programs.

**Table 5-1 Types of Application Software for Business Users**

| Business Software Type | Uses |
|---|---|
| individual application software | create letters, spreadsheets, slide shows, and database reports<br>design and develop publications<br>design Web pages |
| collaboration software (also called groupware) | collaborate on the development of documents<br>communicate online through instant messaging and e-mail<br>conduct virtual meetings<br>share calendars, image banks, and databases of information<br>track and manage projects<br>generate Web pages |
| vertical application software | perform core business processes for a particular type of industry<br>software is typically custom-designed |

**Collaboration software** (also called groupware) enables people at separate PC workstations to work together on a single document or project, such as designing a new automobile engine.

**Vertical application software** is a complete package of programs that work together to perform core business functions for a large organization. For example, a bank might have a mainframe computer at its corporate headquarters connected to conventional terminals in branch offices, where they are used by managers, tellers, loan officers, and other employees. All financial transactions are fed to the central computer for processing. The system then generates managers' reports, account statements, and other essential documents. This type of software is usually custom-built and is frequently found in the banking, insurance, and retailing industries.

## Commercial Application Software

Application software is also categorized by its market availability. **Commercial software** is intended for businesses or other organizations with multiple users. Packaged application software is available in the mass market for purchase or lease, whereas customized software is usually developed to meet the special needs of a single company. Because packaged programs have a huge market, they cost much less than a custom program built for one customer.

**Packaged Software**  **Packaged software** includes programs created and sold to the public on a retail basis by software development companies such as Microsoft, Adobe, and Corel. Both individuals and companies buy commercial software, although businesses typically purchase network versions that can be installed on servers for access by more than one employee.

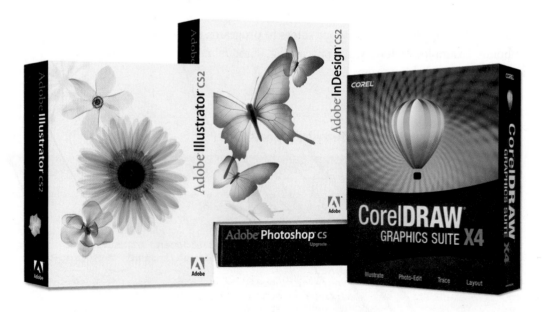

Many packaged software programs are available from software developers such as Adobe and Corel.

Warning: This computer program is protected by copyright law and international treaties. Unauthorized reproduction or distribution of this program, or any portion of it, may result in severe civil and criminal penalties, and will be prosecuted to the maximum extent possible under the law.

[ OK ]

[ System Info... ]

[ Tech Support... ]

[ Disabled Items... ]

Software manufacturers usually obtain a copyright that prohibits the illegal copying and distribution of software. Warnings such as this one are designed to remind users of the copyright law.

These products are considered **proprietary software**, meaning that a company or an individual owns the copyright. A license packaged with the software grants the customer or user permission to make a backup copy, but prohibits the distributing of copies to other people. The illegal copying or unauthorized use of copyrighted software is called **software piracy**. By completing and submitting the product registration information, purchasers receive a license from the manufacturer granting them the right to use, but not own, the software. In a network environment, a **site license** provides multiple-user rights. Registering the software provides the benefits of technical assistance and notification of software upgrades.

Packaged software can be obtained from many sources, including manufacturers, computer stores, bookstores, mail-order houses, and the Internet. Programs purchased through a retail source are usually contained on one or more CD- or DVD-ROMs and come in a box with documentation and a registration card. Programs purchased and downloaded from a Web site typically include online documentation and an electronic registration form that can be e-mailed to the vendor. Many application programs are commercially successful and are periodically upgraded, while others enjoy only brief marketplace popularity and soon disappear.

**Customized Software** Businesses often have needs that commercial software cannot meet. For example, since payroll data and processing requirements vary among companies, commercial payroll programs may lack certain specialized features. The alternative to purchasing commercial software is to hire programmers to develop software to meet the company's requirements. The resulting software is called **customized software** or a custom program, and is usually owned by the customer. Because of their unique processing requirements, large businesses often maintain a substantial inventory of customized application software programs.

## Other Application Software Models

Relatively few software programs were available for purchase when PCs were still in their infancy in the early 1980s. Some programmers began writing software to meet their own needs and made the programs available for free, or for a small fee, usually over the Internet. Others wanted computer users to test their programs and offer suggestions for improvement. This type of software program distribution can be divided into two categories: shareware and freeware.

Tech Demo 5-1
Applications on the Web

Go to this title's Internet Resource Center and read the article titled "Software Licensing Arrangements." www.emcp.net/CUT4e

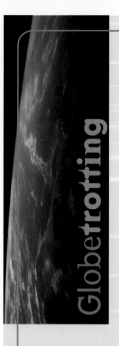

# To Stop a Moving Target

**HEART SURGERY IS ALWAYS RISKY BUSINESS**. It involves opening the chest, stopping the heart, and using an artificial pump to keep the blood flowing throughout the body while the operation proceeds. Another option is to slow down the heart by cooling it, but even the movements of a slowly beating heart can be a steep challenge for a surgeon. Either route is traumatic for the body.

An Englishman has found a way to let the heart keep beating while making it look like it is perfectly still. George Mylonas of Imperial College London has developed motion compensation software that enables a surgeon to operate on a beating heart without even opening the chest cavity.

The software is designed for use with a miniature surgical robot inserted into the patient's chest. The robot's endoscope records real-time images of the heart with its two infrared cameras. The software calculates the changes in focal point as the heart beats, and then synchronizes the endoscope to move exactly with the heartbeats. This creates a 3-D image that appears stationary for the surgeon. The software also moves the robot's instruments back and forth in exact time with the heartbeats to make the needed incisions.

So far the software has been tested only on an artificial heart using a robotic arm, but the future for a heart procedure that is less invasive and easier on the patient looks bright.

**Shareware** **Shareware** is software developed by an individual or software publisher who retains ownership of the product and makes it available for a small "contribution" fee. The fee is typically $5 to $50, and is payable only after a user has tried the product and decided to continue using it. The voluntary fee normally entitles users to receive online or written product documentation, new software updates, and technical help. Most shareware developers even encourage users to share the product with others in the hope that they will end up paying for product support, which is how the developers make their money.

Tech Demo 5-2
Shareware and
Freeware

**Freeware** **Freeware** is software that is provided free of charge to anyone wanting to use it. Hundreds of freeware programs are available, many written by college students and professors who create programs as class projects or as part of their research. Their motive is altruistic—they want to share their creation with others and are not interested in making a profit. Some freeware programs have become quite widely used, including 123 Free Solitaire, a popular entertainment site, and Ad-Aware, a popular spyware prevention program. Some freeware programs—for example, WebCT—begin as free software but eventually become viable commercial products. WebCT has recently been acquired by Blackboard, another educational and communications software program.

Freeware does have some drawbacks compared with commercial software. Because freeware developers do not charge for their products, they are not obligated to guarantee that the products are error-free. They also may not provide users with documentation or technical help.

Early freeware programs were distributed over electronic bulletin boards and at computer users' club meetings. Now, the Internet provides an almost unlimited market for both shareware and freeware.

**Open-Source Software**  As discussed in Chapter 4, an open-source software program is software whose programming code is owned by the original developer but made available free to the general public, who is encouraged to experiment with the software, make improvements, and share the improvements with the user community. A software company or individuals may develop open-source software. Other programmers can copy, modify, and redistribute the programming code without paying license fees to the developers. Often, developers and users work together in a cooperative manner to improve the software. Linux, Eclipse, Apache, and Mozilla are some examples of open-source initiatives.

Tech Demo 5-3
Installing
Applications

## Application Software for Individual Use

The thousands of application programs that individuals use to perform computing tasks at work and at home can be grouped into four types:

- productivity software
- software for household use
- graphics and multimedia software
- communications software

The rest of this chapter will focus on each of these types of application software in more depth.

The Jumbo! Web site is one of several Web sites with freeware programs for downloading.

# Productivity Software

**Productivity software** is designed to improve efficiency and performance on the job and at home, and is the largest category of application software for individual use. Employment notices appearing in newspapers and magazines often identify required computer skills, such as word processing or spreadsheet expertise. Some employment notices even specify that an applicant must be certified in a particular application, such as Word, Excel, or WordPerfect. Certified applicants often receive priority consideration over those without such qualifications.

In-depth knowledge and skill in using productivity software applications can make a potential employee more valuable to a business, organization, or agency. Table 5-2 lists productivity software categories and examples and common uses of each group.

## Word Processing

**Word processing software** can be used to create almost any kind of printed document. Word processors are the most widely used of all software applications because they are central to communication. Communicating is a skill essential to nearly every business endeavor. At one time computers appealed only to scientists and programmers. Their utility for everyone became evident when they advanced enough to allow the easy creation, editing, saving, and printing of documents. Computers would not play the central role that they do in our society today without their word processing capabilities.

Almost all computers can run word processing software applications, and word processing is probably the easiest application to learn and use. Word processing programs are often available for more than one platform. For example,

**Table 5-2 Examples of Productivity Software**

| Category | Software Example | Common Uses |
|---|---|---|
| word processing | Microsoft Word, Corel WordPerfect | write, format, and print letters, memos, reports, and other documents |
| desktop publishing | Microsoft Publisher, QuarkXPress, Adobe InDesign | produce newsletters, advertisements, and other high-quality documents |
| spreadsheet | Microsoft Excel, Lotus 1-2-3, Corel Quattro Pro | produce spreadsheets and manipulate financial and other numerical data |
| database management | Microsoft Access, Corel Paradox, Lotus Approach | organize and manipulate textual, financial, and statistical records and data |
| presentation graphics | Microsoft PowerPoint, Corel Presentations, Lotus Freelance | create and display slide shows |
| software suite | Microsoft Office | link data or share information between individual programs |
| personal information manager (PIM) | Microsoft Outlook, Palm Desktop | organize calendar, address book, task lists, and notes |
| project management | Microsoft Project | schedule and manage projects |

Microsoft Word is available for Windows and Macintosh computers. Another popular word processor is Lotus Software's Word Pro.

Whatever the type of document created with a word processing program, the essential parts of the procedure remain the same:

- create (enter) text
- edit the text
- format the document
- save and print the file

**Creating Text** Creating text refers to the development of a document by entering text, numbers, and graphics using one or more input devices, such as a keyboard or mouse. Documents can be created starting from a blank page, or by using a previously created and stored form called a **template**. A feature called a **wizard** guides a user through a series of steps that allow the user to select content, format, and layout options. For example, with a wizard a user creates template-type documents incorporating specific information about the user, such as company name and address. Both templates and wizards are used extensively in the Microsoft Office and Corel WordPerfect suites.

Word processing is a popular and widely used productivity software application.

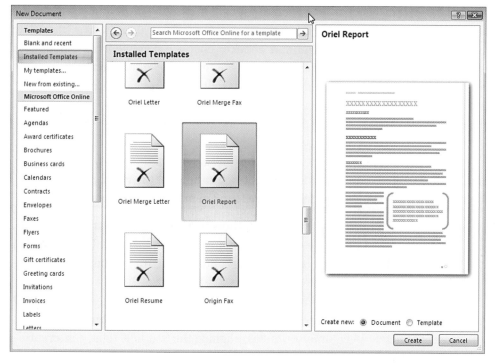

Microsoft Word 2007 and 2010 contain preformatted templates with specialized formatting that can be adapted to help create professional-looking documents. These templates are accessible through the New Document dialog box. With an active Internet connection, a user can access additional templates through the Microsoft Office Online section of this dialog box.

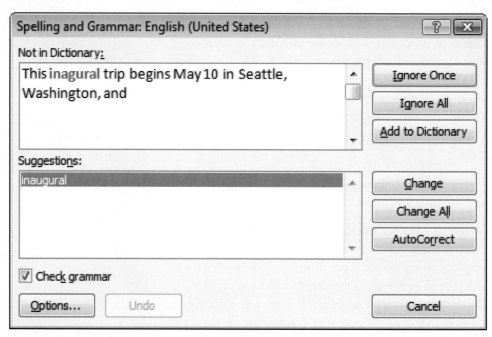

Microsoft Word, like many word processors, includes a proofing feature that helps to catch misspelled words. Proofreading is still important because the spelling checker is not context-sensitive.

**Editing Text** The process of altering the content of an existing document is called editing. Editing occurs anytime something is inserted, deleted, or modified within a document. Editing features allow users to make changes until they are satisfied with the content. Perhaps the most valued word processor editing feature is a **spelling checker**, which matches each word in a document to a word list or dictionary. A spelling checker is not context-sensitive. It will not flag words that have been spelled correctly, but used incorrectly—for example, "their" when "there" would have been correct. A **grammar checker** checks a document for common errors in grammar, usage, and mechanics. Grammar checkers are no substitute for careful review by a knowledgeable editor, but they can be useful for identifying such problems as run-on sentences, sentence fragments, double negatives, and misused apostrophes.

**Formatting Text** Word processing software allows many different types of formatting, or the manipulation of text to change its appearance at the word, paragraph, or document level. The following features are found in many word processors:

- **Text formatting.** Text formatting features include the ability to change font type, size, color, and style (such as bold, italic, or underlined). Users can also adjust leading (the space between lines) and kerning (the amount of space that appears between letters).
- **Paragraph formatting.** Paragraph formatting changes the way a body of text flows on the page. Features related to the appearance of a paragraph include placing the text in columns or tables; aligning the text left, right, center, or justified within the margins; and double- or single-spacing lines.

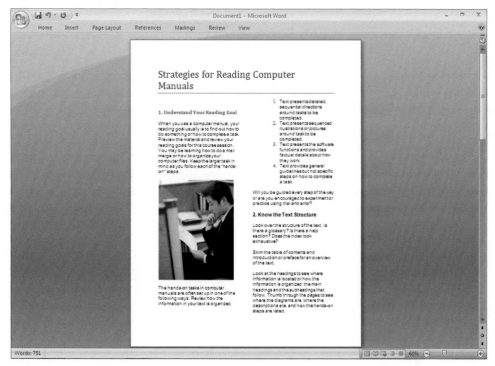

Word processing software include several formatting features that can be applied to words, lines, paragraphs, pages, or entire documents.

- **Document formatting.** Document formatting lets users specify the form of a document as a whole, defining page numbers, headers, footers, paper size, and margin width. A **style** is a special shortcut feature that allows text to be formatted in a single step. Styles allow users to apply text and paragraph formatting to a page, and then automatically apply those same attributes to other sections of text.

**Saving and Printing** Storing a copy of the displayed document to a secondary storage medium such as a flash drive or CD is called saving. A saved document (or portion of a document) can be retrieved and reused. Saving a document requires specifying the drive and assigning a file name to the document. The application generally automatically adds an extension following the file name. The extension identifies the type of file.

Printing means producing a hard copy of a document on another physical medium, such as paper or transparency film. Although most documents are eventually printed, a document may first be sent electronically over a network to another computer, where the receiver may choose to print the document.

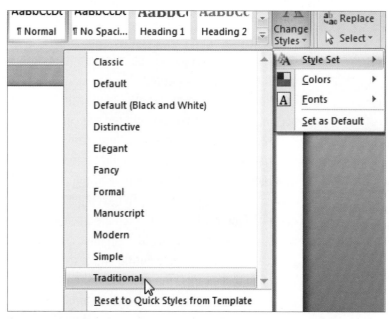

Microsoft Word documents contain style sets called Quick Styles. Using this feature, it is possible to apply paragraph and character styles to specific text.

## MACPAINT AND HYPERCARD
# Bill Atkinson

**RARELY DOES A COMPUTER PROGRAMMER** achieve the status of a hero, but many computer users have reason to grant heroic status to Bill Atkinson, the legendary programmer who created the first painting program for personal computers, MacPaint. Atkinson's concept for the program, which helped to popularize the first personal computer graphical user interface, was simple and clever: The user was presented with a white screen (a sketchpad) and a set of painting tools, including a paintbrush and a paint bucket. Selecting the paintbrush with the mouse cursor changed the cursor into a brush tip. When the brush tip was moved across the white screen with the mouse button depressed, it turned the pixels beneath it from white to black. By this means, shapes were formed on the screen. Selecting the paint bucket enabled the user to fill an area with a predefined pattern. Later, Atkinson and others developed color versions of painting programs based on the same concept.

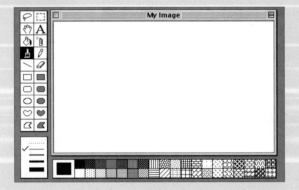

MacPaint was the first painting program.

Not content to rest with this significant accomplishment, Atkinson initiated a second software revolution by creating Hypercard, a program that enabled users to build customized programs, called stacks, without learning a complex programming language. To develop a program in Hypercard, a user first created a stack of cards, like the cards in an old-fashioned library card catalog, employing painting and text tools to design these cards. The user could then add buttons, icons, and text fields to the cards. The user could apply simple scripts in the HyperTalk scripting language to these objects. These scripts caused the buttons, icons, and text fields to perform such tasks as moving to another card, making mathematical calculations, importing text, animating graphics, and bringing up dialog boxes. Using Hypercard, nonprogrammers were able to create their own programs. Hundreds of thousands of Hypercard programs were created, including tutorials, grade books, statistical analysis applications, and slide shows.

Hypercard is not widely used today, but it was the program that first introduced many personal computer users to the concept of hypertext—pages containing text and graphics that are linked to one another in an associative rather than linear fashion. The same concept is today the basis of the World Wide Web. Hypercard was also ahead of its time because it gave ordinary computer users—people who were not programmers—the ability to assemble their own programs using object-oriented programming, in which user-definable objects, containing both instructions and data, were combined in erector set fashion to produce full-scale applications. In the future, it is likely that successors to Hypercard—programs that enable users to create individualized applications—will be widely used on corporate intranets, on the Internet, and on the network user interfaces that will replace older operating systems. For these reasons, many people consider Atkinson a visionary, one of those rare programmers whose work takes a quantum leap into the future.

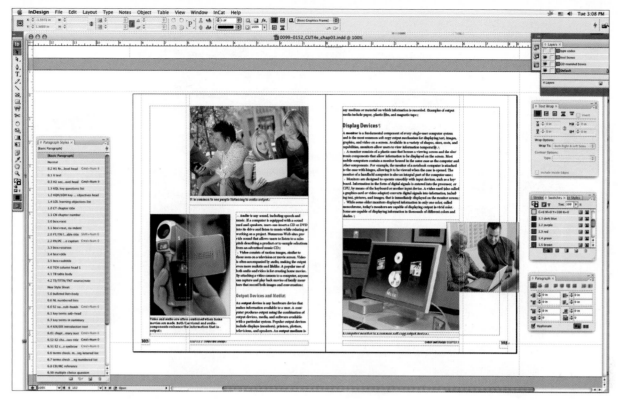

Desktop publishing software, such as Adobe InDesign, is used to produce visually appealing newsletters, magazines, and other print products—even this textbook.

## Desktop Publishing

**Desktop publishing (DTP) software** allows users to create impressive documents that include text, drawings, photographs, and various graphics elements in full color. Professional-quality publications can be produced with DTP software. Textbooks such as this one may be designed and laid out with a desktop publishing application such as QuarkXPress or Adobe InDesign. The completed files are sent to a commercial printer for printing on high-quality paper. The pages are then collated and bound into finished books. Using a page layout program requires extensive training and a background in graphic design.

Major word processors such as Microsoft Word offer a growing selection of desktop publishing features, including the capability of drawing graphics, importing images, formatting text in special fonts and sizes, and laying out text in columns and tables. These features are sufficient for creating simple newsletters, fliers, and brochures. Microsoft Publisher, included in some editions of the Microsoft Office suite, provides more sophisticated desktop publishing elements, including predefined layouts, pull quotes, picture captions, and picture frames.

InDesign, a feature-rich program from Adobe Systems, Inc., allows users to create a master page that establishes the format of repeating elements on all pages of a publication, such as page numbers and the chapter number and title. The program includes page description features that allow users to determine how each page will look. Graphics can be cropped and placed precisely where they are wanted. When an image is inserted into a publication, InDesign inserts tiny rectangles at the edges, allowing it to be resized by dragging the rectangles to the desired position.

High-quality color documents like these can be produced using desktop publishing software.

## Spreadsheets

**Spreadsheet software** is an electronic version of the ruled worksheets accountants used in the past. Spreadsheet software provides a means of organizing, calculating, and presenting financial, statistical, and other numerical information. For example, an instructor may use Microsoft Excel to calculate student grades. Other well-known spreadsheet programs include Lotus 1-2-3 and Corel Quattro Pro.

Businesses find spreadsheets particularly useful for evaluating alternative scenarios when making financial decisions. The spreadsheet uses "what if" calculations to evaluate possibilities. For example, company management might ask, "What happens to our profit if our sales increase by 50 percent, or our labor costs decrease by 10 percent?" These types of questions can be answered quickly and accurately by entering a **value** (such as a number) and a mathematical **formula** into a spreadsheet. Calculations are made immediately.

"What if" calculations are used in school and home scenarios as well. A college instructor could show a worried student the test score needed in order to achieve a certain grade. Or, a young couple could determine the effects of various income and savings strategies on their retirement plans. Since the computer does all of the tedious calculations, users can experiment with many different data combinations.

Other common business uses of the spreadsheet include calculating the present value of future assets, analyzing market trends, making projections, and manipulating customer and company statistics.

## The Waterfront Bistro
### Quarterly Sales Report

| | October | November | December | Quarter Total |
|---|---|---|---|---|
| Food - Dining Room | $ 42,155 | $ 45,876 | $ 52,144 | $ 140,175 |
| Food - Patio | $ 1,588 | $ - | $ - | $ 1,588 |
| Food - Catering | $ 28,653 | $ 31,455 | $ 60,488 | $ 120,596 |
| **Total Food** | $ 72,396 | $ 77,331 | $ 112,632 | $ 262,359 |
| Beverage - Dining Room | $ 39,658 | $ 4,477 | $ 5,103 | $ 49,238 |
| Beverage - Patio | $ 144 | $ - | $ - | $ 144 |
| Beverage - Catering | $ 2,963 | $ 2,966 | $ 5,843 | $ 11,772 |
| **Total Beverage** | $ 42,765 | $ 7,443 | $ 10,946 | $ 61,154 |
| Beer & Liquor - Dining Room | $ 3,647 | $ 4,655 | $ 4,761 | $ 13,063 |
| Beer & Liquor - Patio | $ 106 | $ - | $ - | $ 106 |
| Beer & Liquor - Catering | $ 2,844 | $ 3,264 | $ 6,149 | $ 12,257 |
| **Total Beer & Liquor** | $ 6,597 | $ 7,919 | $ 10,910 | $ 25,426 |
| | | | | |
| **TOTAL SALES** | $ 121,758 | $ 92,693 | $ 134,488 | $ 348,939 |

Many businesses use spreadsheets such as Excel to record and calculate financial reports.

For the individual user, spreadsheets fulfill many purposes, including:

- preparing and analyzing personal or business budgets
- reconciling checkbooks
- analyzing financial situations
- tracking and analyzing investments
- preparing personal financial statements
- estimating taxes

C3    $f_x$  =B3*$B$14

| | A | B | C | D | E |
|---|---|---|---|---|---|
| 1 | | CORPORATE SALES QUOTAS | | | |
| 2 | **Salesperson** | **Current Quota** | **Projected Quota** | | |
| 3 | Allejandro | $ 95,500.00 | $ 114,600.00 | | |
| 4 | Crispin | $ 137,000.00 | $ 164,400.00 | | |
| 5 | Frankel | $ 124,000.00 | $ 148,800.00 | | |
| 6 | Hiesmann | $ 85,500.00 | $ 102,600.00 | | |
| 7 | Jarvis | $ 159,000.00 | $ 190,800.00 | | |
| 8 | Littleman | $ 110,500.00 | $ 132,600.00 | | |
| 9 | Massey | $ 90,000.00 | $ 108,000.00 | | |
| 10 | Silverstein | $ 140,500.00 | $ 168,600.00 | | |
| 11 | Ting | $ 100,000.00 | $ 120,000.00 | | |
| 12 | Zimmerman | $ 115,500.00 | $ 138,600.00 | | |
| 13 | | | | | |
| 14 | 20% Increase | 1.2 | | | |
| 15 | | | | | |
| 16 | | | | | |

"What if" calculations can be used to evaluate different possibilities. For example, if salesperson Allejandro increases sales by 20 percent, the new quota becomes $114,600. To calculate what happens if Allejandro increases sales by 40 percent, one could simply change the value of field B14 to 1.4.

| | A | B | C | D | E | F |
|---|---|---|---|---|---|---|
| 1 | | **THE WATERFRONT BISTRO** | | | | |
| 2 | | **OPERATING EXPENSES** | | | | |
| 3 | | Qtr1 | Qtr2 | Qtr3 | Qtr4 | Total |
| 4 | Advertising | $ 2,200.00 | $ 1,850.00 | $ 2,347.00 | $ 1,777.00 | $ 8,174.00 |
| 5 | Bank Charges | 329.00 | 541.00 | 624.00 | 7?0.00 | 2204.00 |
| 6 | Cleaning | 650.00 | | | | |
| 7 | Linens | 985.00 | | | | |
| 8 | Office supplies | 143.00 | | | | |
| 9 | Telephone | 256.00 | | | | |
| 10 | Utilities | 1142.00 | | | | |
| 11 | | | | | | |
| 12 | Total | $ 5,705.00 | $ | | | |
| 13 | | | | | | |
| 14 | Proof Total: | $24,406 | | | | |

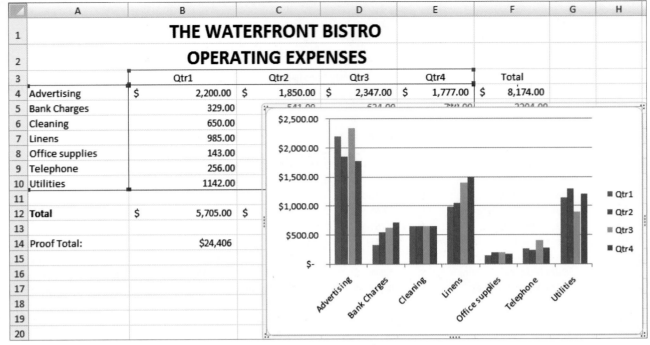

Microsoft Excel includes several charting options. These features allow users to present numerical values visually. This 3-D column chart is just one of the chart types Excel supports.

Although spreadsheet programs differ, most offer the following features:

- **Grid.** Spreadsheets display numbers and text in a matrix, or **grid**, formed of columns and rows. Each intersection, or **cell**, has a unique address consisting of the column and row designations. Columns are usually identified alphabetically, while rows are numbered. For example, cell address A1 refers to the cell located at the intersection of column A and row number 1.
- **Number formatting.** Numbers may be formatted in a variety of ways, including decimal point placement (1.00, 0.001), currency value ($, £, ¥), or positive or negative quanity (1.00, -1.00).
- **Formulas.** Mathematical formulas ranging from addition to standard deviation can be entered into cells, and they can process information derived from other cells. Formulas use cell addresses, not their contents. For example, a formula might direct a program to multiply cell F1 by cell A4. The formula would then multiply the numerical contents of the two cells. The use of cell addresses means that a spreadsheet can automatically update the result if the value in a cell changes.
- **Macros.** Most spreadsheets allow users to create a **macro**, a set of commands that automates complex or repetitive actions. For example, a macro could check sales figures to see if they meet quotas, and then compile a separate chart for those figures that do not. The macro would automatically perform all the steps required.
- **Charting.** A **chart** is a visual representation of data that often makes the data easier to read and understand. Spreadsheet programs allow users to display selected data in line, bar, pie, or other chart forms.

# Database Management

Prior to computers, employee, voter, or customer records were typically placed in file folders and stored in metal cabinets, along with thousands of other folders. Locating a particular folder could prove time-consuming and frustrating, even if the records were stored in an organized manner.

Electronic databases that use appropriate software to manage data more efficiently have replaced many of these manual systems. Although the first electronic databases were developed for large computer systems, today's database software is also available for PCs. Microsoft Access, Lotus Approach, Corel Paradox, and FileMaker Pro are among the more popular and best-selling database programs for personal computers.

In a computerized database system, data are stored in electronic form on a storage medium, such as flash drives or CDs. A **database** is a collection of data organized in one or more tables consisting of individual pieces of information, each located in a **field**, and a collection of related fields, each collection making up one **record**. Figure 5-1 shows an example of a table created in a database program. A commercial database program typically allows users to create a form for entering data. A user can design an electronic form to make entering information into the database easier. The information entered using such a form will become a record in a table. Users can add, remove, or change the stored data.

A **database management system (DBMS)** allows users to create and manage a computerized database and to produce reports from stored data. Almost all businesses and organizations use database management systems to manage inventory

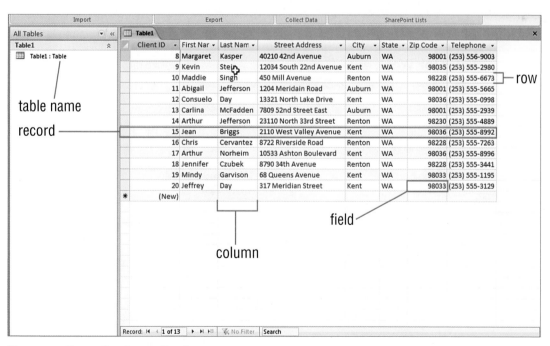

**Figure 5-1 Parts of an Access Database**

Within a database program, data are organized into one or more tables, each with its own name. A table consists of columns and rows. A complete row of information is called a record.

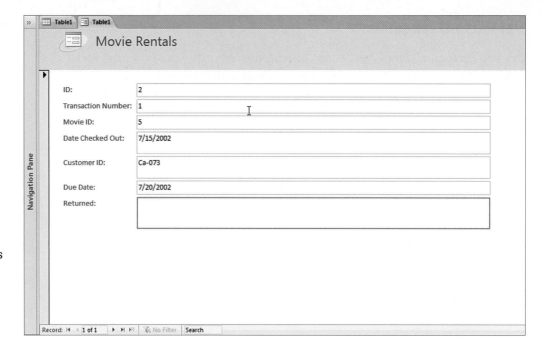

Forms such as this one created in Access provide an efficient way to enter data into a table.

records, scientific or marketing research data, and customer information. For example, a university collects the data students supply during the course registration process and stores those data in a database. To produce a roll for each class, the DBMS is instructed to locate and retrieve the names of students registered for each course and to insert (in a specified order) the names in a report. The printed report is sent to the instructor.

A report is a selection of data in a database. The user chooses which types of information should be included in the report, and the database automatically finds and organizes the corresponding data.

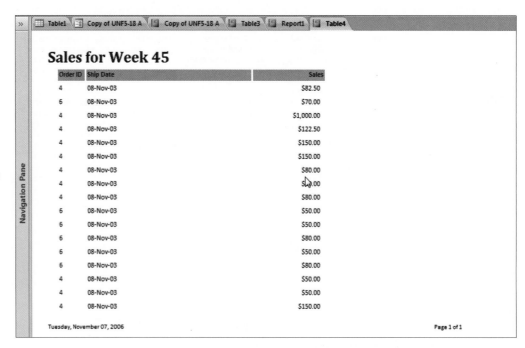

Businesses use database software in much the same way. For example, a business storing customer data in a database can use a DBMS to create and print reports containing the names of customers in specific areas or territories. Sales representatives can use the reports to contact the listed customers.

Although various DBMS programs are available, the most popular type is the **relational database** model. In a relational database, tables can be linked (or related) in a way that allows data to be retrieved from more than one table. Tables are linked through a common data field, such as a product number. Accessing a product number lets users retrieve different kinds of information associated with that number, even though the information may be stored in several different tables in the database.

For example, suppose a potential customer visits an automobile dealer and expresses an interest in buying a blue Chevrolet Corsica. The dealer may have several Chevrolets in stock, but may not know if there is a blue Corsica among them. Using a computerized relational database, the dealer can quickly find the answer by querying (asking) the database, which would then search all linked tables for blue Corsicas. Figure 5-2 illustrates the manner in which separate tables are linked to provide a response to a query.

Database programs typically include the following features:

- **Sort.** Records can be sorted (arranged) in many different ways by using a **sort** feature. For example, records included in a table consisting of cities and ZIP codes for each customer can be sorted alphabetically by the record's city name or numerically by the ZIP code.
- **Find.** Information in a table can be located by using **Find** to look up a number or a particular type of text, such as a name or an address.
- **Query.** Searches too advanced for the Find command to handle can be made by using a **query**, or method of asking the database for results. The

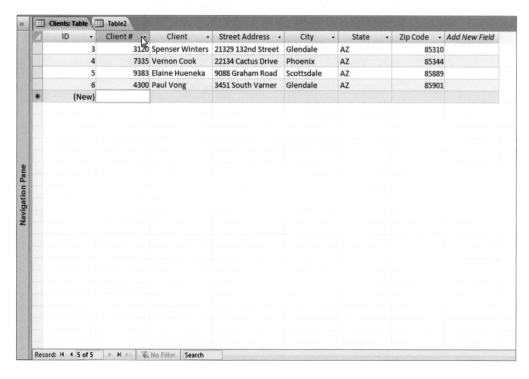

Records in a Clients table created in Microsoft Access can be sorted in different ways and used to create a report that answers a specific query, or question.

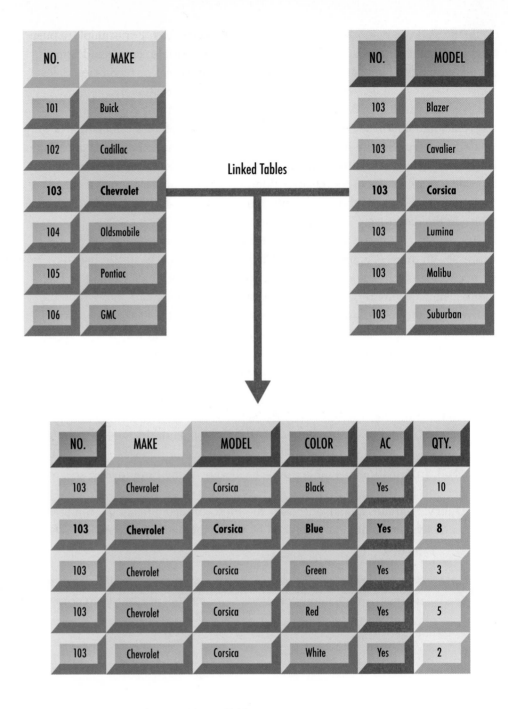

| NO. | MAKE |
|---|---|
| 101 | Buick |
| 102 | Cadillac |
| **103** | **Chevrolet** |
| 104 | Oldsmobile |
| 105 | Pontiac |
| 106 | GMC |

Linked Tables

| NO. | MODEL |
|---|---|
| 103 | Blazer |
| 103 | Cavalier |
| **103** | **Corsica** |
| 103 | Lumina |
| 103 | Malibu |
| 103 | Suburban |

| NO. | MAKE | MODEL | COLOR | AC | QTY. |
|---|---|---|---|---|---|
| 103 | Chevrolet | Corsica | Black | Yes | 10 |
| **103** | **Chevrolet** | **Corsica** | **Blue** | **Yes** | **8** |
| 103 | Chevrolet | Corsica | Green | Yes | 3 |
| 103 | Chevrolet | Corsica | Red | Yes | 5 |
| 103 | Chevrolet | Corsica | White | Yes | 2 |

**Figure 5-2 Results of a Query to Linked Tables**
A relational database allows multiple tables to be linked so that users can retrieve related data from more than one table.

database can be queried using **Structured Query Language (SQL)** or **Query by Example (QBE)**. For example, in a table containing many customers in several ZIP codes, a query can be to locate all of the contacts with a specific ZIP code. One of these query methods could be used to search a table for contacts in ZIP code 85889.

- **Links.** Tables can be linked in meaningful ways that make sense for a particular business. For example, for an insurance company, the Clients table could be linked to Claims and Policy List tables.
- **Reports.** Tables can be linked in order to create a **report** of combined information from the linked tables. For example, Client and Policy List tables could be combined to produce invoices for clients.

## Presentation Graphics

Anyone who has attended group lectures or presentations knows how boring they can be. One way to make a presentation more interesting is to use presentation graphics software. **Presentation graphics software** allows users to create computerized slide shows that combine text, numbers, animation, graphics, sounds, and videos. A **slide** is an individual document that is created in presentation graphics software. A **slide show** may consist of any number of individual slides. For example, a sales representative may use a slide show to promote products to customers, using the electronic format to feature key components of the product. An instructor may use a slide show to accompany a lecture to make it more engaging and informative. A businessperson may use a slide show to deliver information and present strategies at a meeting. Microsoft PowerPoint and Apple Keynote are two popular presentation software programs.

With presentation graphics software, you can create dramatic slide shows that combine text, graphics, sound, and video.

Another advantage of presentation software is that it allows users to easily repurpose information, meaning that the information can be modified to suit different audiences. Other capabilities include being able to import files created in other programs, such as word processors or spreadsheets. This material can then be incorporated within one presentation.

In addition to presenting a slide show via computer, users can also output the presentation as 35 mm slides, transparencies, or hard-copy handouts. A presentation run on a portable computer can be projected onto a screen using a multimedia projector (a self-contained projection unit with a plug-in for a computer) or an LCD panel (a semitransparent projection device that attaches to the computer and sits on top of an overhead projector).

Presentation applications typically include the following features:

- **Wizards.** Most presentation programs offer users a choice of presentation types. After a particular type is chosen, the program provides a wizard to guide the user step by step through the creation of the slide show.
- **Templates.** A predesigned style format, called a template, saves time because the file contains background colors, patterns, and other elements that work well together. Users can also create their own personalized templates.
- **Handouts.** Creating handouts with Microsoft PowerPoint is as easy as selecting an option from the Print dialog box. Handouts can be in outline or note format. It is also possible to create handouts containing graphic reproductions of the slides.

## Employee Benefits

- Health/Dental
- Disability Insurance
- Life Insurance
- Retirement

## Costuming Process

- Internet
- Archive
- Library

**Research**

- Preliminary
- Sketches
- Sketch
- Approval

**Design**

- Pattern Design
- First Fitting
- Final Fitting

**Sewing**

Microsoft PowerPoint includes many clip art images and charting features that can be integrated into presentations to help make them more interesting.

- **Clip art.** Powerful, attention-grabbing graphics enliven presentations and can sometimes convey messages more effectively than text alone. Presentation programs generally include collections of **clip art** (simple line drawings) that can be inserted into slides. Additional images can be located and imported from other sources, including the Internet and clip art software packages.

## Software Suites

Some software vendors bundle and sell a group of software programs as a single package called a **software suite**. Software suites consist of **integrated software programs**. In other words, the individual programs are designed to work well together, with similar interface design and features. Software suites typically include the four most widely used applications: word processing, database management, spreadsheet, and presentation programs. Some, such as Microsoft Office, also include Web page authoring programs since the development of personal Web sites is becoming increasingly important to consumers. Suites are popular because buying one is cheaper than purchasing the component programs separately.

Software suites offer other advantages. Because the programs were developed using the same user interface, all programs in the suite work in a similar manner. Once someone has become familiar with one program, learning to use the others is easier because of the similarity of screen layouts, menus, buttons, icons, and toolbars.

Another strong feature of suites is their ability to seamlessly integrate files from other programs. For example, information produced using a spreadsheet can be placed into a word processing document, or a database table can be imported into a slide show presentation.

One method of moving information from one suite program to another is by copying and pasting. Although quite easy, this method has some disadvantages. For example, if a user created a PowerPoint slide show containing a copied Excel spreadsheet file, the Excel file would need to be recopied each time it is updated with new calculations.

A second method called **object linking and embedding (OLE)** addresses the problem of changing or updating information. It involves creating an object (a table, chart, picture, or text) in one program and then sharing it with another program. Two types of sharing are possible: embedding and linking. Embedding is a type of copying, allowing the embedded file to be changed using the original program's editing features. However, the changes are not reflected in the original file. Using the example in the previous paragraph, a spreadsheet file embedded in the PowerPoint presentation could be edited, but the changes would appear only in the PowerPoint presentation. However, linking the file ensures that any changes made in the original spreadsheet will also be reflected in the PowerPoint presentation.

## Personal Information Manager (PIM)

Many PDAs have application software called a **personal information manager (PIM)**. This software helps organize contact information, appointments, tasks, and notes. An increasing number of smartphones also have a PIM. Typically, the PIM also allows this organized information to be synchronized with similar software on a desktop or laptop. This allows users to view and modify the information on a full-size screen. The most common PIMs are Microsoft Outlook and Palm Desktop.

Project management software is widely used to plan construction projects and to track schedules and budgets.

## Project Management

Many businesses regularly engage in planning and designing projects, as well as scheduling and controlling the various activities that occur throughout the life of the project. For example, before a construction firm begins erecting a building, it needs to develop a comprehensive plan for completing the structure. During planning, an architect prepares a detailed building design, or set of blueprints. Schedules are then prepared so that workers, building materials, and other resources are available when needed. Once construction begins, all activities are monitored and controlled to ensure that they are initiated and completed on schedule.

Prior to computers, projects like this were planned, designed, scheduled, and controlled manually. Today these tasks are performed using **project management software**. This type of software facilitates the effective and efficient management of complex projects. It can be used for just about any project, including those involving construction, software development, and manufacturing. Microsoft Project is the most prevalent project management software today, helping to optimize the planning of projects and to track schedules and budgets.

Go to this title's Internet Resource Center and read the article titled "Project Management Software." www.emcp.net/CUT4e

# Software for Household Use

When browsing computer stores, shoppers are likely to see numerous software applications designed for use in the household. Among the many products available are applications for writing letters, making out wills, designing a new home, landscaping a lawn, preparing and filing tax returns, and managing finances. Software suites are also available for home and personal use, although sometimes the suites available for home use do not contain all the features found in business versions.

More than one-half of U.S. homes now include a personal computer on which a variety of software applications has been installed. Most application software programs are relatively inexpensive. Some vendors advertise popular word processing software for as little as $99, and more organizations are offering open source software versions of popular software titles.

## Personal Finance

**Personal finance software** assists users with paying bills, balancing checkbooks, keeping track of income and expenses, maintaining investment records, and other financial activities. The software also enables users to readily view how their money is being spent.

Some personal finance software provides online services available over the Internet and Web. These services allow users to go online to learn the status of their investments and insurance coverage. They can also conduct normal banking transactions, including accessing and printing bank statements showing monthly transaction summaries. These programs can perform most of the financial activities previously requiring mail or telephone contact.

Personal finance software enables users to manage their money by helping them pay bills, balance checkbooks, keep track of income and expenses, maintain investment records, and other financial activities.

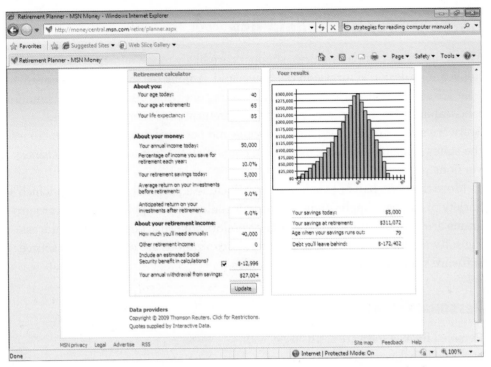

Many personal finance Web sites offer retirement calculators to help individuals determine how much to save to meet their retirement goals.

## Tax Preparation

**Tax preparation software** is designed to aid in analyzing federal and state tax status, as well as to prepare and transmit tax returns. Most of the programs provide tips for preparing tax documents that can help identify deductions, possibly

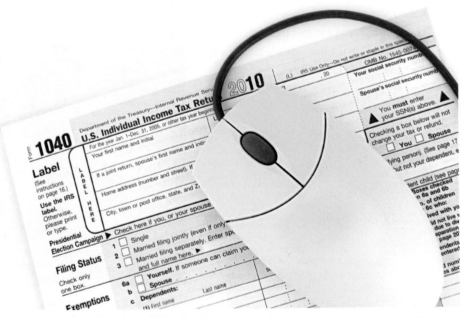

Tax preparation software allows users to efficiently fill out state and federal tax forms and submit them electronically.

resulting in great savings. Some programs include actual state and federal tax forms for entering tax data. Programs that do not include forms provide instructions for downloading them from the software publisher's Web site. Finished tax returns can be printed for mailing or filed electronically. Because federal and state tax laws change frequently, as do tax forms, users will probably need to obtain the software version for the appropriate taxable years or period.

## Legal Documents

**Legal software** is designed to help analyze, plan, and prepare a variety of legal documents, including wills and trusts. It can also be used to prepare other legal documents, such as the forms required for real estate purchases or sales, rental contracts, and estate planning. Included in most packages are standard templates for various legal documents, along with suggestions for preparing them.

The program begins by asking users to select the type of document they want to prepare. In order to complete a document, users may need to answer a series of questions or enter needed information on a form. Once this activity is complete, the software adapts the final document to meet individual needs.

After a document is prepared, it can be sent to the appropriate department, agency, or court for processing and registration. It is always a

Home legal software can assist in the creation of documents such as wills and contracts.

Entertainment software allows users to enjoy a variety of entertainment experiences, including music and games.

good idea to have an attorney review documents to make certain they are correct and legal in the intended state or local jurisdiction.

## Games and Entertainment

**Entertainment software** refers to programs that provide fun as well as challenges. Included in this group are interactive computer games, videos, and music. Versions of Microsoft's Windows operating system come with several popular entertainment programs, including Hearts, Pinball, Solitaire, and Minesweeper.

If a PC is equipped with a CD-ROM drive, users can play music CDs just as they would on a stereo CD player. Music can also be downloaded from commercial and personal Web sites. If a PC is equipped with a DVD drive, users can purchase or rent movies and play them on their computers.

Reference material is available online, such as from www.reference.com.

## Educational and Reference Software

The widespread use of home computers has brought about an increase in the availability of educational and reference software, making computers a popular learning and reference tool. Examples of **educational and reference software** include encyclopedias, dictionaries, and tutorials.

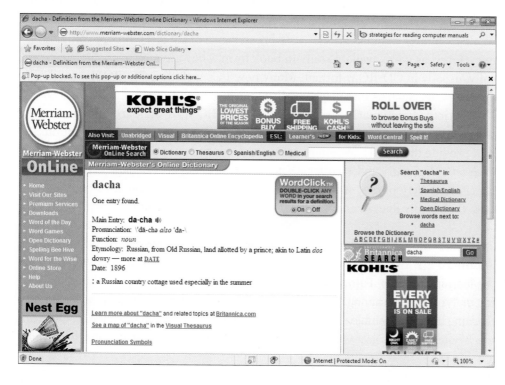

The Merriam-Webster Collegiate Dictionary in online form gives users access to terms and definitions in an easy-to-access format.

# To Catch a Plagiarist

**WARNING TO COLLEGE KIDS:** Think twice about using the essay-writing Web sites and online databases for term papers. Antiplagiarism software can fish you out in a nanosecond.

Plagiarism has become an epidemic on college campuses. According to one study, 36 percent of students admit to having plagiarized a written paper at some point in their college career. The causes for this growth of copycat behavior may be varied. Some college students left high school without getting a proper education in using citation for research papers. Today's kids, who file-swap music without a care, have a foggier definition of property ownership. And the Internet, of course, makes finding information and patching it together all too easy.

To combat the misappropriation of the written word, more colleges are turning to software such as Turnitin and SafeAssign.com.

These antiplagiarism software programs generate a "digital fingerprint" of a document that has been electronically submitted. The paper's verbal patterns are cross-checked against a huge database of Internet, newspaper, and encyclopedia archives, as well as previously submitted student work. Suspicious sentences or paragraphs are highlighted, and source matches annotated. The thieving writer is—in seconds—busted.

Students can also use the software as a self-screening tool. And even for classes whose professors do not use this plagiarism-detection software, its very existence acts as a deterrent to students prone to copycat writing.

Antiplagiarism software is also catching the attention of newspaper editors and publishing houses alarmed by recent scandals.

Go to this title's Internet Resource Center and read the article titled "Computer-Based Learning." www.emcp.net/CUT4e

**Encyclopedias and Dictionaries** Almost everyone has used an encyclopedia or dictionary at one time or another. An encyclopedia is a comprehensive reference work containing detailed articles on a broad range of subjects. Before computers, encyclopedias were available only in book form. They are now available electronically, usually in CD-ROM format. Many new PCs include a CD-ROM–based encyclopedia, such as *Encyclopaedia Britannica*.

A variety of dictionaries are available on CD-ROM. A standard dictionary is a reference work containing an alphabetical listing of words, with definitions that provide the word's meaning, pronunciation, and usage. Examples include *Webster's Dictionary* and *Webster's New World Dictionary of Computer Terms*. Other specialized dictionaries, such as multilanguage dictionaries, contain words along with their equivalent in another language for use in translation.

**Tutorials** Many people learn new skills by using CD- or Internet-based tutorials. A **tutorial** is a form of instruction in which students are guided step by step through the learning process. Tutorials are sometimes referred to as computer-based training or Web-based training. Tutorials are available for almost any subject, including learning how to assemble a bicycle, use a word processor, or write a letter. Once an electronic tutorial is accessed, students need only follow the instructions displayed

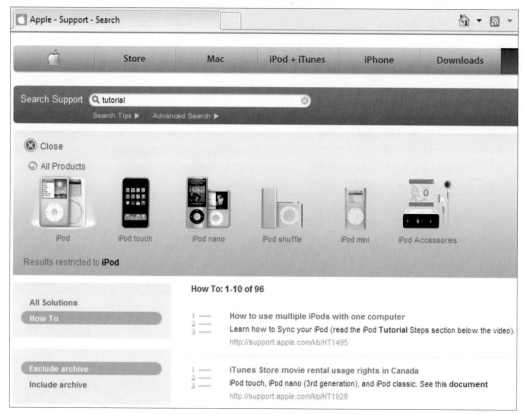

Tutorials guide users step by step through the learning process using graphics, text, and audio media, such as the online tutorials that provide instructions on using an iPod.

on the screen. Many tutorials include graphics to help guide students during the learning process. Software manufacturers often provide tutorials for training users in the application of software products, such as their word processors, spreadsheets, and databases. The goal is to help users acquire skill in using the manufacturer's product, in the hope that this will entice users to make a purchase.

# Graphics and Multimedia Software

**Graphics and multimedia software** allows both professional and home users to work with graphics, video, and audio. A variety of application software is focused in this area, including painting and drawing software, image-editing software, video and audio editing software, Web authoring software, and computer-aided design (CAD) software.

## Painting and Drawing Software

Painting and drawing programs are available for both professional and home users. The more expensive professional versions typically include more features and greater capabilities than do the less expensive personal versions.

With a **painting program**, a user can create images in bit-map form and also color and edit an image one bit at a time. Microsoft Paint is an example of a popular painting program. A **drawing program** enables a user to create images that

**CODEVELOPER OF VISICALC**

# Dan Bricklin

**HAVING WORKED ON PROGRAMMING** for an online calculator and a word processing program for DEC, Bricklin understood how useful computers could be in business, but his classroom experience also showed him their limitations and inefficiencies. Students had to learn to perform calculations for business spreadsheets manually, inserting new figures for everything from labor costs to shipping, then recalculating the effect of each change on the bottom line. The process was tedious and every new calculation was an opportunity for mistakes that could lead to serious business errors.

Out of his frustration with the tasks and his certainty that there must be a better way to do it, Bricklin began to develop a software program that would do for numbers what word processing did for words—enable the user to insert and delete data and to see an immediate change in the results.

Bricklin joined up with Bob Frankston, his friend from MIT, and together they began to turn Bricklin's basic ideas into a commercially viable product. Founding a company called Software Arts in 1978, Bricklin worked on the functional design and documentation of the new software while Frankston wrote the programming. By the fall of 1979 a version of their program was ready. The program was called VisiCalc, short for Visual Calculation. Almost immediately, VisiCalc became a huge commercial success and the foundation for the development of a long line of spreadsheet programs that followed.

VisiCalc had a major impact in two ways. First, it allowed businesses to redistribute costs and revenues on a trial basis to see immediately how the changes would affect the bottom line. The second impact was on the computer industry itself. For the fledgling Apple Computer Company, VisiCalc was a tremendous boost because the first version was written to run on the Apple II, and people bought the computer just so they could run VisiCalc. The reputation of VisiCalc as a serious business application did much to establish the PC as a legitimate business computer. In 1985, Lotus Software purchased Software Arts.

Bricklin continues making contributions in the computing field. With his present venture, called Trelix, Bricklin helps individuals and businesses create and edit Internet projects.

can be easily modified. The size of a drawn image can be decreased without a reduction in image resolution. However, increasing the size may result in a loss of resolution quality. Popular drawing programs used in professional environments include CorelDRAW and Adobe Illustrator.

Both painting programs and drawing programs provide an intuitive interface through which users can draw pictures, make sketches, create various shapes, and edit images. Programs typically include a variety of templates that simplify painting or drawing procedures. Once finished, a painting or drawing can be imported into other documents, such as personal letters, signs, business cards, greeting cards, and calendars.

A painting program allows a user to create images and to color and edit an image one bit at a time. Once finished, a painting or drawing can be imported into other documents.

## Image-Editing Software

The market demand for image-editing programs has increased concurrently with the popularity of digital cameras. An **image-editing program** allows a user to touch up, modify, and enhance image quality. Editing features include changing color, cropping, resizing, applying special features, and eliminating red-eye effects from photographs. Once edited, images can be stored in a variety of formats and inserted into other files, such as letters, advertisements, and electronic scrapbooks. Microsoft Windows Live Photo Gallery is a free program available for download and is targeted at home users. Adobe, maker of the industry standard professional image editing software Photoshop, has two image editors targeted at home users: Photoshop Elements (available for purchase) and Photoshop.com (a free online tool).

## Video and Audio Editing Software

As digital video cameras and other portable technologies have become more common, users have desired the ability to create and modify recorded video and audio clips using **video and audio editing software**. To create DVDs, CDs, or digital video or audio files, home users can often use basic video and audio editing software contained within their computer's operating system. Some users prefer the additional features of an application software package such as Pinnacle Studio MovieBox. Professionals use more expensive, feature-rich software such as Sony's Vegas or Sound Forge for editing audio and video.

Adobe Photoshop is a popular image-editing program that provides numerous tools for editing an image.

## Web Authoring Software

**Web authoring software** helps users develop Web pages without learning Web programming. Software packages such as Adobe DreamWeaver and Microsoft Expression Web use a **WYSIWYG** (what you see is what you get) approach to Web page development. This means that during the development process, the layout and content of the actual Web page can be seen within the Web authoring software. Software such as Adobe Flash and Adobe Fireworks allows users to add interactive graphics and animation to Web pages.

Web authoring software allows a user to create Web pages without learning Web programming. A user can add and edit text, photographs, sound, and video for Web pages.

## Computer-aided Design Software

**Computer-aided design (CAD) software** is a sophisticated kind of drawing software, providing tools that enable professionals to create architectural, engineering, product, and scientific designs. Engineers can use the software to design buildings or bridges, and scientists can create graphical designs of plant, animal, and chemical structures. Some software programs display designs in three-dimensional form so they can be viewed from various angles. Once a design has been created, changes can easily be made until it is finalized.

An aircraft engineer designing a new type of aircraft can use CAD software to test many design versions before the first prototype is built. This process can save companies considerable time and money by eliminating defective designs before beginning production.

Full-feature CAD programs are very expensive. Some producers of CAD software offer scaled-down versions of their more expensive software for use by small businesses, and for individual and home use.

Computer-aided design software is used to create designs for buildings, bridges, and commercial products.

# Communications Software

One of the major reasons people use computers is to communicate with others and to share information. Software that enables communication over the Internet and the Web is available for individual, home, and business use. This software allows users to send and receive e-mail, browse and search the Web, engage in group communications and discussions, and participate in webconferencing activities.

## Electronic Mail

Electronic mail (e-mail) is rapidly becoming the main method of communication for many individual, home, and business users. **E-mail** is the transmission and receipt of electronic messages over a worldwide system of communications networks. The real value of e-mail lies in its speed and low cost. Messages can be sent and received within seconds or minutes, and transmission costs are minimal.

Sending and receiving e-mail requires the use of special software called an e-mail client or simply a Web browser. Some of the more common e-mail clients are Microsoft Windows Mail, Mozilla Thunderbird, and Eudora. Web-based e-mail services such as Yahoo! Mail, MSN Hotmail, and GMail require a Web browser pointed at a Web address (or URL).

Preparing an e-mail message is similar to preparing a word processing document. Users can create, edit, spell-check, print, and store messages. In addition, the software allows users to send, receive, and delete messages and maintain contact address information within the program. Most e-mail software will notify users when a message has been received.

Go to this title's Internet Resource Center and read the article titled "Collaboration Software Trends." www.emcp.net/CUT4e

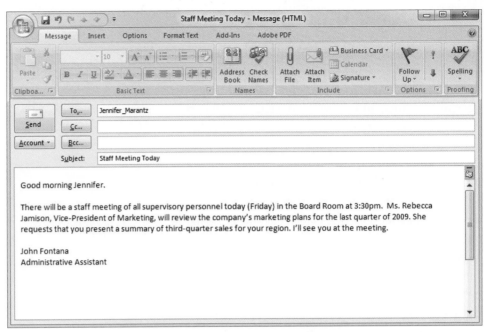

E-mail is a fast and efficient way of communicating with other computer users.

## Web Browsers and Search Engines

Recall that Web browsers, also called browsers, allow users to move from one location to another on the Web, and to access and retrieve Web pages. Web browsers use a GUI that can retrieve and display Web pages containing graphics, pictures, and other high-resolution text and images.

Text messaging allows people to send quick, short messages via cell phones.

Most browsers provide for sending and receiving e-mail messages, participating in chat groups, and maintaining a listing of favorite Web sites and pages. The two most popular browsers are Microsoft's Internet Explorer and Mozilla's Firefox.

A **search engine** is used to search, locate, and retrieve information from various Web sites. Among the more popular search engines are Yahoo!, WebCrawler, Google, and AltaVista. Users can access these programs by typing the search engine Internet address in the browser address box.

## Instant Messaging Software

**Instant messaging (IM) software** is a technology that enables people to communicate with other users over the Internet in real time. Several IM services are available, including AIM, MSN, and Yahoo!. Although the industry is working on IM standards, not all IM software is compatible with other IM services. Instant messaging can be used on all types of devices, including PCs, handheld computers, notebook computers, and Web-enabled cell phones

Instant messaging software allows users to communicate in real time using text, audio, and video.

or smartphones. PCs, handheld computers, and notebook computers require the instant messaging software to be installed, whereas cell phones and smartphones typically have built-in messaging capabilities. Subscribers to instant messaging services must have instant messaging software installed on their computers.

Tech Demo 5-4
PDA Applications

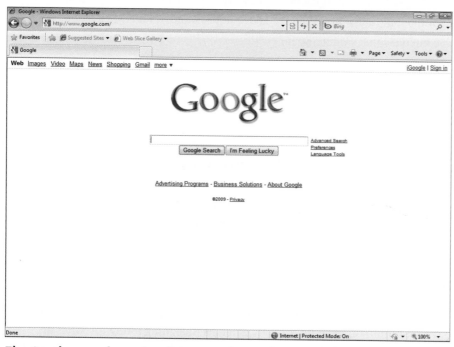

The Google search engine (www.google.com) is a popular tool for finding information on a specific topic on the Internet.

# Can You Meet Me Now?

**FOR THE COLLEGE KID WHO IS HUNGRY—** right here, right now—and doesn't want to eat alone, MoSoSo can make it happen.

MoSoSo stands for Mobile Social Software, and it's the logical extension of social networking services on the Web. Accessible from either a mobile phone or a laptop, MoSoSo weaves time and location into digital networking. MoSoSos typically cater to the tech-savvy, in-the-moment youth market.

For example, the MoSoSo software at brightkite.com lets people share their location with friends, post photos and notes to locations, and meet others nearby depending on their personal privacy settings.

Similarly, Playtxt is a cell-phone service using MoSoSo that connects users with similar music and sports interests within their ZIP code.

The hitch with MoSoSo applications is that they require critical mass to catch on. If users log on repeatedly without getting any results, they'll quickly lose interest. That's where Roger Desai is ahead of the game. His start-up, Rave Wireless, has made the campus connection. He's found the perfect market—thousands of students condensed in one area, all with cell phones and computers, all needing to know the location of tonight's kegger.

Students can get updates on what's happening through both text messaging and mobile Internet browsing combined with a GPS system. They simply type in "moods" such as *hungry*, *bored*, or *studying*, and will immediately connect with other like-minded students.

Rave Wireless features also allow students to track in real time more pragmatic college-life information such as bus schedules, library resources, or schedule changes. The service also can act as a personal alarm, alerting 911 to the location of a student in distress. In fact, the software is so appealing to administrators on campuses that one in five universities using Rave Wireless actually require students to have the software on their cell phones.

Once members are signed up with an instant messaging service, they can exchange messages or files and use the service to participate in chat groups. Some IM services will notify members of an incoming message and also provide financial news, stock quotes, appointments, weather updates, and other practical information.

## Groupware

**Groupware**, also called collaboration software, allows people to share information and collaborate on various projects, such as designing a new product or preparing employee manuals. Groupware can be used over a local area network

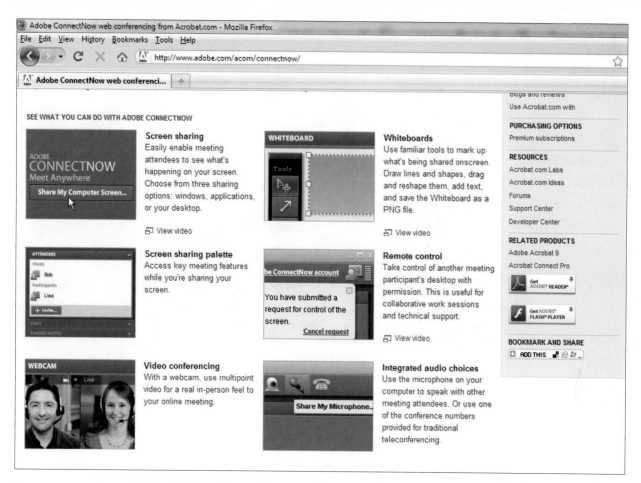

Groupware, also called collaboration software, allows people to share information and collaborate on various projects, such as designing a new product or preparing an employee manual.

(LAN), wide area network (WAN), or the Internet. All group members must be using the same groupware programs to collaborate on projects.

Most groupware includes an address book of members' contact information and an appointment calendar. One of the most desirable features of groupware is a scheduling calendar that allows each member to track the schedules of the other members. This makes it possible to coordinate activities and to arrange meetings to discuss project activities and other matters.

## Webconferencing

A **webconference** is an online meeting between two or more participants at different locations using computer networks and **webconferencing software** to transmit electronic information. Participants share presentations, diagrams, documents, and spreadsheets within webconferencing software. They may also use special features in the software such as an electronic whiteboard and marker, highlighting, and instant messaging. For audio, participants will use either Internet voice capabilities or a phone line.

Because it saves time and travel expenses, many businesses are promoting the use of webconferencing software over face-to-face meetings. Most webconferencing software

Webconferencing software enables meeting participants to communicate and share information over long distances as though everyone is in the same room.

is Web-based and just requires a browser on each participant's computer. WebEx, Centra, MeetingPlace, and Microsoft Office Live Meeting are some examples of webconferencing software currently in use.

# OnThe**Horizon**

**INSPIRED BY BREAKTHROUGHS** in processing technology and changing market needs, software developers are continually brainstorming new programs or improvements to existing software. Some of today's leading-edge technologies allow us to make educated guesses about digital applications that soon may be standard-issue.

## Automatic Multimedia Tagging Software

Tags are keyword descriptions that can be attached to multimedia files in order to assist in identifying and retrieving the files at a later date. For example, an image of a lakeside cabin with people standing in front of it might be tagged with "cabin," "people," and "lake." Tag creation is currently a time-consuming manual process, but an EU-supported project is working on automating this task. The proposed system would use a combination of imaging technology and analytical tools to scan through files in order to identify content and automatically create the appropriate tags, and will work with both still and moving images. The concept has proved viable, and efforts to expand system capabilities are ongoing.

## Advances in Speech Recognition Software

Several hardware devices and productivity applications currently incorporate speech recognition software. Although much improved compared with earlier attempts, the present speech recognition technologies have yet to meet the high accuracy transcription demanded by industries such as medicine. The proliferation of Web-enabled handheld computers indicates a trend of continuing improvements in speech recognition, simply because of rising market demand.

IBM has pioneered a technology called speech biometrics, which may provide one of the significant advances. The goal of IBM's Super Human Speech Recognition Initiative is to perform better than a human in transcribing speech in memos, customer service calls, and meeting minutes.

This type of technology is also suited for identification and verification needs, such as those required during Internet purchases. The technology works by comparing voices with a database of voices of known speakers. The software is able to recognize voices even though the database may not include the exact words spoken.

A related technology called natural-language processing (NLP) has advanced to the stage where systems can understand the conversations of a five-year-old child. A number of challenges remain, but if NLP software can live up to its potential and accurately recognize adult speech, it will revolutionize personal and business communications.

## Pattern Recognition Software

Pattern recognition is a branch of artificial intelligence (AI) that compares data with previous information or extracts statistical data to form a new model for information. The security implications of pattern recognition have focused interest on this technology in the wake of 9/11, and it is employed in a number of different fingerprint and facial identification systems currently in use. Pattern recognition also forms the basis for spam filters used to differentiate legitimate e-mail messages from spam.

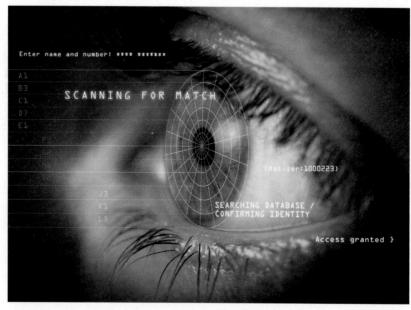

Retinal scanning can be used with pattern recognition software to confirm a person's identity.

## Distributed Computing

Software designers are picturing a future in which software programs consist of groups of services available through the Internet, rather than from CD-ROMs. The first generation of companies offering these programs were called application service providers (ASPs), and though their vision held great promise, market enthusiasm for the idea cooled in 2000.

The next generation of software as services will be offered in the distributed computing model; computer industry giants IBM, Microsoft, and Sun Microsystems are leading the quest. Based on an open set of standards and protocols, the distributed computing model combines the power of an almost limitless number of computers over the Internet. Distributed computing is often called grid computing, as well, particularly in reference to some of the huge, scientific research projects that have been launched in recent years. SETI@Home, for example, is a project in which home computer users donate overnight usage of their systems to search for signs of intelligent life beyond our planet. Special software recognizes times when the computer is idle and uses that time toward the project. Industry experts estimate that the SETI@Home project has amassed the effect of thousands of years of computing power, simply by harnessing idle PC processing time.

Recently, computer industry leaders have adapted the distributed computing technology for the business world by developing distributed computing software that allows the pooling and sharing of resources over the Net. Possible applications are limitless, but the more pragmatic ones include actuarial analysis, processing of financial market trades, generation of extremely detailed engineering drawings, and scientific simulations. In effect, companies create virtual organizations to share data and computing, as well as human brainpower and resources. The end result is enormous cost savings and skyrocketing productivity.

# Chapter**Summary**

 *For an interactive version of this summary, go to this text's Internet Resource Center at www.emcp.net/CUT4e. A Spanish version is also available.*

## What is application software?

**Application software** performs the types of activities and work that computers were designed for. **Individual application software** refers to programs used by individuals. **Collaboration software** enables people at separate PC workstations to work together. **Vertical application software** is a complete package of programs for performing core business functions.

**Commercial software** refers to programs intended for businesses or other organizations with multiple users. **Packaged software** includes programs created and sold to the public on a retail basis by software development companies. **Proprietary software** is copyrighted software owned by a company or an individual. Software developed to meet special business needs is called **customized software**. **Software piracy** involves the illegal copying or unauthorized use of copyrighted software. **Shareware** is software available for a small "contribution" fee. **Freeware** is software provided for free. Open source software is software whose programming code is owned by the original developer but made available free to the general public, who is encouraged to experiment with the software, make improvements, and share the improvements with the user community.

## How is productivity software used?

**Productivity software** is designed to improve efficiency and performance on the job. **Word processing software** can be used to create almost any kind of printed document. **Desktop publishing (DTP) software** allows the creation of professional-looking printed documents. **Spreadsheet software** provides a means of organizing, calculating, and presenting financial, statistical, and other numeric information. A **database** is a collection of data organized in one or more tables containing records. A commercial database program usually allows users to create forms for entering data into a database. A **database management system (DBMS)** allows users to create and manage a computerized database and to create reports. A **relational database** allows tables to be linked in a way that allows data to be retrieved from more than one table. **Presentation graphics software** lets users create computerized **slide shows**. **Software suites** are software programs bundled and sold as a single package. A personal information manager (PIM) is software that helps users organize contact information, appointments, tasks, and notes. **Project management software** assists with the management of various kinds of complex projects.

## What types of application software are used in the household?

Many of the productivity programs used on the job are also used by individuals on their home computers. **Personal finance software** can help users manage their money. **Tax preparation software** helps users prepare and transmit tax returns. **Legal software** is designed to analyze, plan, and prepare a variety of legal documents. **Entertain-ment software** refers to a large group of software programs that provide fun and often challenge users' thinking abilities as well. The widespread use of home computers has brought about an increase in the availability of **educational and reference software** such as encyclopedias, dictionaries, and tutorials. A **tutorial** is a form of computerized instruction in which the student is guided step by step through the learning process.

## What are examples of graphics and multimedia software?

**Graphics and multimedia software** allows users to work with graphics, video, and audio files. **Painting programs** allow users to create images in bit-map form and also to color and edit an image one bit at a time. **Image-editing programs** allow a user to touch up, modify, and enhance image quality. **Video and audio editing software** allows users to create and modify recorded video and audio clips. **Web authoring software** helps users develop

Web pages without learning Web programming. **Computer-aided design (CAD) software** provides tools that enable professionals to create architectural, engineering, product, and scientific designs.

### How can application software make communicating easier?

One of the main purposes for which people use computers is to communicate with others and to retrieve and share information. **E-mail** is the transmission and receipt of messages over a worldwide system of communications networks. Web browsers allow users to move from one location to another on the Web, and to access and retrieve Web pages. **Search engines** find information located on Web sites. **Instant messaging (IM) software** allows users to communicate with each other in real time. **Groupware** allows people to share information and collaborate on various projects. A **webconference** is an online conference between two or more participants at different sites, using computer networks and **webconferencing software**.

# Key Terms

*Numbers indicate the pages where terms are first cited in the chapter. An alphabetized list of key terms with definitions (in English and Spanish) can be found on the Encore CD that accompanies this book. In addition, these terms and definitions are included in the end-of-book glossary.*

# Chapter**Exercises**

 *The following chapter exercises, along with new activities and information, are also offered in the Internet Resource Center for this title at www.emcp.net/CUT4e.*

## *Tutorial >* **Exploring Windows**

In Tutorial 5, you will learn to use the computer window to browse the contents of your computer's hard drive.

## *Expanding Your Knowledge >* **Articles and Activities**

 *Visit the Internet Resource Center for this title at www.emcp.net/CUT4e, read the articles related to this chapter, and complete the corresponding activities. The article titles include:*

- Topic 5-1: Software Licensing Arrangements
- Topic 5-2: Project Management Software
- Topic 5-3: Computer-Based Learning
- Topic 5-4: Collaboration Software Trends

## *Terms Check >* **Matching**

 *For additional practice, go to the Internet Resource Center for this title at www.emcp.net/CUT4e for a chapter crossword puzzle.*

On the next page, write the letter of the correct answer on the line before each numbered item.

a. software piracy
b. database
c. software suite
d. legal software
e. word processing software
f. proprietary software
g. presentation graphics software
h. productivity software
i. tutorial
j. application software

1. A collection of data organized in one or more tables consisting of fields and records.

2. Software produced and owned by a business and offered for purchase or lease.

3. A form of instruction in which students are guided step by step through the learning process.

4. Software designed to enhance efficiency and performance in the workplace.

5. The illegal copying or unauthorized use of copyrighted software.

6. Software used to create documents such as wills, trusts, or rental contracts.

7. A software program used to create slide shows.

8. A broad category of software that allows users to perform tasks such as creating documents or preparing income tax returns.

9. The most widely used of all software applications.

10. A group of productivity programs bundled and sold as a single package.

## *Technology Illustrated* > **Identify the Process**

What process is illustrated in this drawing? Identify the process and write a paragraph describing it.

| No. | Make | No. | Model | No. | Color |
|-----|------|-----|-------|-----|-------|
| 101 | Chevrolet | 102 | Taurus | 102 | Beige |
| 102 | Ford | 102 | Mustang | 102 | Red |
| 103 | Buick | 102 | Thunderbird | 102 | Green |
| 104 | Chrysler | 102 | F-150 | 102 | Silver |

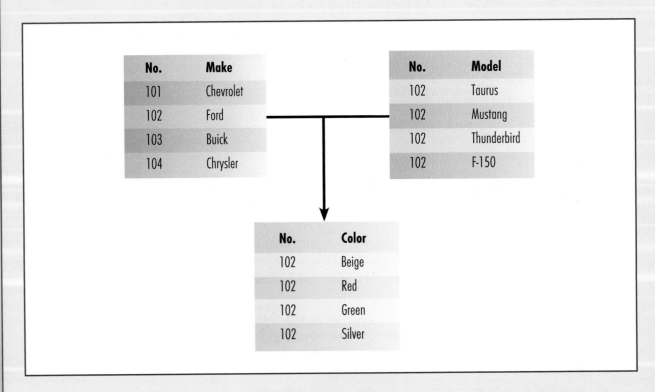

# Knowledge Check > **Multiple Choice**

 *Additional quiz questions are available on the Encore CD that accompanies this book as well as on the Internet Resource Center for this title at www.emcp.net/CUT4e.*

Circle the letter of the best answer from those provided.

1. Software that enables users to perform the types of activities and work computers were designed for is called
   a. working software.
   b. tutorial.
   c. system software.
   d. application software.

2. Software used to create professional-quality publications is called
   a. a desktop publishing (DTP) software.
   b. a word processor.
   c. application software.
   d. print software.

3. A previously created and stored form is called a(n)
   a. user form.
   b. program form.
   c. electronic form.
   d. template.

4. A word processor editing feature that checks a document for common errors in grammar, usage, and mechanics is called a(n)
   a. spelling checker.
   b. grammar checker.
   c. English checker.
   d. syntax checker.

5. The transmission and receipt of messages over a worldwide system of communications networks is called
   a. e-mail (electronic mail).
   b. file transfer.
   c. telnet.
   d. electronic communication.

6. Software versions of the ruled worksheets accountants used in the past are called
   a. accounting software.
   b. worksheet software.
   c. electronic spreadsheets.
   d. financial software.

7. A collection of data organized in one or more tables consisting of fields and records is known as a(n)
   a. electronic spreadsheet.
   b. raw data.
   c. composite information.
   d. database.

8. A group of software programs bundled into a single package is called
   a. combination software.
   b. a software suite.
   c. a special package.
   d. a software collection.

9. A communication method that enables people to communicate over the Internet with other users in real time is called
   a. real-time processing.
   b. electronic telephoning.
   c. instant messaging.
   d. electronic messaging.

10. Software that allows people to share information and collaborate on various projects, such as developing a new product, is called
    a. collaboration software.
    b. groupware.
    c. shareware.
    d. developmental software.

## *Things That Think >* **Brainstorming New Uses**

In groups or individually, contemplate the following questions and develop as many answers as you can.

1. Many application software programs feature wizards. Wizards assist with tasks by prompting users to enter data and then automatically performing the needed functions. Microsoft PowerPoint is one example of a program featuring wizards that guide users through the process of creating a slide show. Discuss some of the software programs you are familiar with and come up with ideas for wizards that might make the software even more user-friendly. Are there any types of situations where you would not want a wizard to assist you? If so, describe them.

2. Encyclopedias have moved from the printed page to the electronic age in the space of less than 10 years. Electronic encyclopedias offer extra features that the printed versions could not. Users can learn about subjects by watching videos, by viewing three-dimensional images, or by listening to sound or music. Another convenience is the ability to instantly view related material using hyperlinks. The same features can and are being used to develop electronic textbooks, and some industry observers predict that these features could someday make textbooks such as the one you are reading obsolete. Do you agree, or do you feel that textbooks still offer advantages that an electronic version might not? Support your answer with examples.

## *Key Principles >* **Completion**

Fill in the blanks with the appropriate words or phrases.

1. The process of altering content of an existing document is called _____.

2. A set of commands that automates complex or repetitive actions is known as a(n) _____.

3. A program that allows the user to create and manage a computerized database, and to produce reports from stored data is a(n) _____.

4. _____ software makes it possible to create slide shows that combine text, numbers, graphics, sounds, and video.

5. _____ software is a sophisticated kind of software providing tools that enable professionals to create architectural, engineering, product, and scientific designs.

6. A(n) _____ is a form of instruction in which students are guided step by step through the learning process.

7. Spreadsheets display numbers and text in columns and rows known as a matrix or _____.

8. _____ software enables users to readily view how their money is being spent.

9. A(n) _____ database allows tables to be linked in a way that allows data to be retrieved from more than one table.

10. Software provided without charge to anyone wanting to use it is called _____.

## Tech Architecture > **Label the Drawing**

The figure below is a spreadsheet into which text and numerical data have been entered and calculations performed. Label each of the spreadsheet components as indicated.

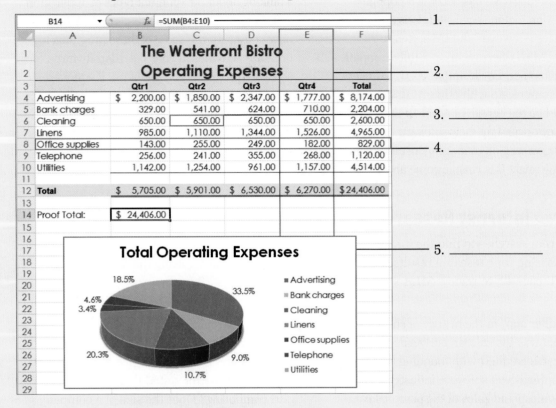

1. _____

2. _____

3. _____

4. _____

5. _____

## Techno Literacy > **Research and Writing**

Develop appropriate written responses based on your research for each item.

1. Which program can improve my productivity? Visit a computer store in your area. Select a particular productivity program on display and read the product description on the package. What platform is the program written for? What is the price? Will the program run on your computer? For what purpose(s) might you be able to use the program?

2. What's hot in application software? Visit your school library and look through computer magazines to find an article describing a new and innovative productivity software program. Write a summary describing the program's purpose, main features, and specifications. Include information about the user interface, the amount of internal memory needed to run the program, and the amount of disk space required to store the program. Why do you think this program is innovative? What needs does this product fulfill? Are there competing products on the market? Do you think the product will be a commercial success? Why or why not?

3. Is a picture worth a thousand words? Ask your instructor (or another person) for the name of a business or organization in your area that regularly uses presentation graphics software to train sales representatives or to provide information. Find out if you can obtain a copy of a presentation. Watch the slide show and then write an evaluation of its effectiveness. List the technologies used (hardware and software), and describe the features that impressed you most.

## Technology Issues > Team Problem-Solving

In groups, brainstorm possible solutions to the issues presented.

1. Instant messaging (IM) has become a popular communication tool in social situations and in the workplace. However, the IM software AOL, Yahoo!, and MSN offerings are not fully compatible with each other. For example, AOL IM users can only communicate with other AOL IM users. What would be the benefits to each of these companies if they opened up their software to allow communication with anyone using instant messaging? How might this change come about?

2. Thinking about the different types of application software discussed in this chapter, determine how you might use some of these programs to organize activities in your life. Identify three software programs you might use if you were planning a vacation. Why did you pick these programs? What aspects of vacation planning do each of the three application software programs support?

## Mining Data > Internet Research and Reporting

Conduct Internet searches to find the information described in the activities below. Write a brief report summarizing your research results. Be sure to document your sources using the MLA format (see Chapter 1, page 42, to review MLA style guidelines).

1. The first "killer app" in the history of software development was Visicalc, an early calculation program that is credited with founding the electronic spreadsheet software industry and launching widespread sales of the personal computer. Research the meaning of the term "killer app" and propose some possibilities for the next one. Explain the reasons for your choice.

2. Explore the topic of grid computing. What kinds of applications are IBM, Microsoft, and Sun Microsystems planning? Are some types of industries better suited than others for using grid computing? Does the size of a company make a difference?

## Technology Timeline > Predicting Next Steps

Look at the timeline below outlining the key milestones in the evolution of encyclopedias from printed books to digital content. Thinking about the increase in information available and the rapid growth in computing technologies, predict two additional milestones in the encyclopedia marketplace that are likely to occur within the next 20 years.

**1771** The first Encyclopaedia Britannica is printed.

**1917** The first World Book Encyclopedia is published.

**1981** The first digital version of Encyclopaedia Britannica is created for the Lexis-Nexis service.

**1993** Microsoft announces the availability of the first release of Encarta, an online encyclopedia on CD-ROM.

**1994** Encyclopaedia Britannica is made available on the Internet and on CD-ROM.

**1998** The complete World Book Online Web site is launched.

**2001** A multilingual encyclopedia called Wikipedia is launched and supported in an "open source" model.

**2006** Wikipedia announces that the one-thousandth user-written article has been published.

## *Ethical Dilemmas >* Group Discussion and Debate

As a class or within an assigned group, discuss the following ethical dilemma.

When software is downloaded from the Internet and installed on a personal computer, there is a possibility that it contains spyware. Spyware is software that gathers information through an Internet connection without a user's knowledge. Some of the information commonly gathered includes a user's keystrokes, hardware configuration, Internet configuration, data from the user's hard drive, and data from cookies. Typically, this information is gathered and sent to the spyware author, who then uses it for advertising purposes or sells the information to another party.

Do you consider this to be an invasion of privacy? Should it be illegal to include spyware inside another software program? What if the software license agreement includes a disclaimer that says that spyware may be installed? Is it harmless if the information is just being gathered for market research? What other problems do you see with this technology? Can you think of any ways to protect Internet users from spyware?

# CHAPTER 6

# Telecommunications and Networks

## Learning Objectives

> Explain the role of telecommunications in the operations of networks and the Internet

> Describe the characteristics of data transmission

> Identify the types of wired and wireless media and explain how they are used

> Compare the major network classifications and discuss their functions

> Define network topology and discuss the four principal types

> Describe communications protocols and explain their functions in data communications

# CyberScenario

**STANDING IN FRONT OF HIS PARTIALLY COMPLETED** new home, Steve Rodriguez pictures the day it is finished and imagines the excitement of moving in. His dream house is halfway to becoming a reality—on time, and better yet, at a cost nearly 30 percent less than he originally estimated. What accounts for the extraordinary savings?

The remarkable cost savings in constructing Steve's new home are a direct result of using a collaborative project management software application accessed over the Internet. This Web tool links the builder, the contractors, the materials manufacturers, and all vendors—plus the customer—at a central information site where the progress and vision of the project are apparent at all times.

Significant savings are achieved using collaborative project management software because builders can order materials online directly from manufacturers, a fac-

tor further lowering expenses. A builder can request an order to be delivered on the day it is needed, a concept called "just in time." Builders also can assign contractors to jobs in the most time-effective manner, as related phases of the work are completed. For example, the heating and air conditioning systems installer is scheduled and called immediately after the carpenter finishes framing the house—not too soon, and not a day too late. Since time lost is money lost, collaborative project management software can help reduce backlogs, delays, and scheduling errors.

Collaborative project management software also allows builders to customize access to project details for different subcontractors. When a plumbing contractor logs into the project management Web site, he or she will see all the information relevant to the plumbing jobs to be done. This would be slightly different than the view that a roofing firm would see. The builder would have access to all information, including updates the different subcontractors provide. This makes key information easier to access, saving time for all parties involved. Even vendors not officially part of the project can be granted access to the site on an as-needed basis.

Web-based access means that all parties can access information and communicate anytime, anywhere. Team members confer with each other using a variety of Web-enabled hardware, including desktop PCs, cell phones, and handheld pocket PC or palm devices. This allows problems to be resolved in real time and communicated to all interested parties consistently. Collaborative project management software can help streamline the entire construction process for efficiency and cost-effectiveness.

## The Evolution of Networking

In Chapter 1 you learned that sharing information among computers is made possible by linking computers together in a network, and that the Internet is a worldwide network of networks. Additionally, you learned that the World Wide Web is a global system of computer networks that allows users to move (jump) from one Web site to another Web site. This worldwide linkage of computers enables users to communicate and work together efficiently and effectively.

Working together over the Web highlights the value of networks, especially the power and promise of the largest network in the world—the Internet. For years companies have managed projects by communicating over their internal networks. Expanding the process to include all of the companies involved in a project is a major new direction, prompted by the increased outsourcing of projects and enabled by the growth of the Internet.

Different types of online collaborative project management software offering many of the features mentioned above are available, such as eRoom by EMC Documentum. A more futuristic version of the technology is called CAVE (computer automatic virtual environment), a product that lets participants at different locations inhabit the same virtual space on the Internet. Rather than requiring user input, the software tracks each participant's actions and automatically and continually updates them on-screen. Moving this networking technology from leading-edge to mainstream status will require continuing improvements in hardware, in software, and in the speed of today's telecommunications systems.

Computers were originally stand-alone devices, incapable of communicating with other computers. This situation changed with the development of special telecommunications hardware and software in the 1970s and 1980s that led to the creation of the first private networks, allowing connected computers to exchange data. Data could take the form of a request for information, a reply to a request from another computer, or an instruction to run a program stored on the network.

**Telecommunications** originally referred to the sending and receiving of information over telephone lines. As telecommunications systems evolved, the term was broadened to include other types of media used to transmit data, including satellite systems, microwave towers, and wireless devices such as cell phones. Figure 6-1 illustrates the basic concept of telecommunications.

Recall that a network consists of two or more computers, devices, and software connected by means of one or more communications media, such as wires, telephone lines, or wireless signals. These media form the fundamental part of a network—the channel or medium through which data bits and bytes are transmitted. Because communications media are basic to networking, it is helpful to begin the study of networks by exploring the process of data transmission and the different types of media used to send data across networks.

# Data Transmission Characteristics

The transmission of data over computer networks is characterized by the:

- rate of transmission (bandwidth)
- type of signal (analog or digital)
- order of bits (parallel or serial)

## Bandwidth

Data is transferred from one computer to another in digital form (1s and 0s), known as bits. In a network, the number of bits that can be transferred per second over a given medium is known as **bandwidth**. The basic measurement of bandwidth is **bits per second (bps)**. Table 6-1 lists common incremental measurements of bandwidth.

Bandwidth varies among different types of communications media. To understand bandwidth, consider the difference in the amount of traffic that can be

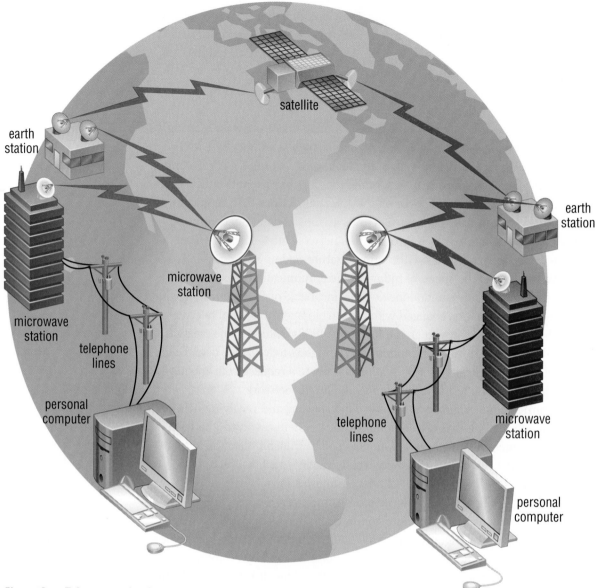

**Figure 6-1 Telecommunications**

Telecommunications, the combined use of computer hardware and communications software for sending and receiving information over communications media, makes it possible for computer users throughout the world to communicate.

handled per hour by a two-lane highway compared with a four-lane highway. The broader, four-lane highway can handle more traffic than a two-lane highway, just as broader bandwidth media can handle greater volumes of data than narrower bandwidths. A communications medium capable of carrying a large amount of data at faster speeds is referred to as a **broadband medium**, whereas one carrying a smaller amount of data at slower speeds is referred to as a **narrowband medium**. Fiber-optic cable is an example of a broadband medium; twisted-pair cable, commonly used in telephone lines, is an example of a narrowband medium.

Bandwidth can be an important factor in choosing a communications medium. Broadband media are more suitable when large amounts of data need to be transmitted quickly, such as with high-quality sound and video transmission. When only small amounts of data need to be transmitted and transmission time is less

**Table 6-1  Terms for Measuring Bandwidth**

| Term | Abbreviation | Meaning |
|------|--------------|---------|
| 1 kilobit per second | 1 Kbps | 1 thousand bits per second |
| 1 megabit per second | 1 Mbps | 1 million bits per second |
| 1 gigabit per second | 1 Gbps | 1 billion bits per second |
| 1 terabit per second | 1 Tbps | 1 trillion bits per second |
| 1 petabit per second | 1 Pbps | 1 quadrillion bits per second |

important, such as for simple text transmission, narrowband media may be suitable. Price is always a consideration, as more bandwidth is costly.

## Analog and Digital Transmission

Telephone systems were established to carry voice transmissions using analog signals. An **analog signal** is composed of continuous waves transmitted over a medium at a certain **frequency range**, which is the number of complete fluctuations in energy per sound wave. Changes in the wave transmissions reflect changes in voice and sound **pitch**, or tone. In addition to using telephone lines, some cellular networks, cable television systems, and satellite dishes use analog communications media for carrying voice and sound transmissions.

Computers cannot understand data in analog form. Instead, computers use the binary number system to transform data into digital signals. Newer communications technologies generally employ digital signals.

Whenever digital data is sent from one computing device to another over an analog communications medium, such as a telephone line, both the sending and receiving devices must be equipped with a modem (Figure 6-2). A **modem**

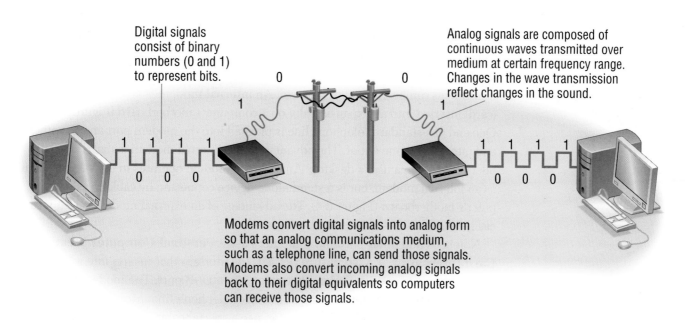

Digital signals consist of binary numbers (0 and 1) to represent bits.

Analog signals are composed of continuous waves transmitted over medium at certain frequency range. Changes in the wave transmission reflect changes in the sound.

Modems convert digital signals into analog form so that an analog communications medium, such as a telephone line, can send those signals. Modems also convert incoming analog signals back to their digital equivalents so computers can receive those signals.

**Figure 6-2  Translating Digital Signals to Analog Signals**

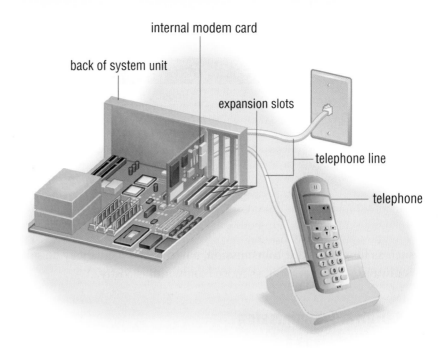

internal modem card

back of system unit

expansion slots

telephone line

telephone

**Figure 6-3  An Internal Modem**

An internal modem is an electronic board plugged into a slot on a computer's motherboard.

Tech Demo 6-1
Cable Type
Specification

Tech Demo 6-2
Modems

converts digital signals into analog form so an analog communications medium can send those signals. Modems also convert incoming analog signals back to their digital equivalents so computers can receive those signals. Some newer modems are able to transmit and receive digital data without analog conversion, provided they are connected to the right communications media.

The term *modem* is derived from the words **mo**dulate and **dem**odulate. **Modulation** refers to the process of changing a digital signal into an analog signal, while **demodulation** refers to the process of changing an analog signal into a digital signal. Originally, personal computers used a type of modem called a **dial-up modem**, which can dial a telephone number, establish a connection, and close the connection when it is no longer needed. Many personal computers today use a cable modem or a DSL modem that uses a broadband connection to the Internet.

Modems can be internal or external. An **internal modem** is an electronic board (card) inserted into an expansion slot on a computer's motherboard (Figure 6-3). One end of a standard telephone line is plugged into the modem port and the other end into a telephone outlet. The advantage of an internal modem is that it does not take up space on a user's desktop. An **external modem** operates in the same fashion as an internal modem, but is a stand-alone device connected by cable to a computer's motherboard (Figure 6-4). The advantage of an external modem is that it can easily be moved from one computer to another.

Notebook and other portable computers use a **Personal Computer Memory Card International Association (PCMCIA) modem** that inserts into a PCMCIA slot or a USB modem that plugs into a USB port. The modem is connected to a telephone outlet using a standard telephone line. Mobile users without access to standard telephone outlets can use a special cable to connect the modem to a cellular phone.

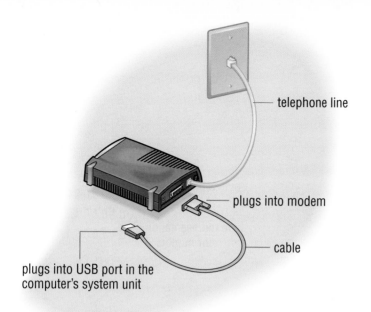

telephone line

plugs into modem

cable

plugs into USB port in the
computer's system unit

**Figure 6-4  An External Modem**
An external modem is a stand-alone device connected by cable to a computer.

## Parallel and Serial Transmission

Recall that peripheral devices typically are connected to the system unit of a personal computer by means of a cable, one end of which is plugged into the device and the other end plugged into a port, or interface, on the system unit. Also, recall that an add-on board, such as an internal modem, contains a port that allows a computer to be connected to a medium, such as a telephone line.

Older computers are equipped with two types of ports: parallel and serial. A parallel cable is needed to connect a device to a parallel port, whereas a serial cable is needed to connect a device to a serial port. Many older peripheral devices, including printers and mice, may be either parallel or serial. Universal Serial Bus (USB) is a type of high-speed serial transmission that has replaced serial and parallel ports on newer computers.

Data travels within a computer system and over long distances in either parallel or serial form. During transmission, 8 bits (representing a single byte) plus 1 bit called a **parity bit** are transmitted. A parity bit is an extra bit added to a byte, character, or word to ensure there is always either a predetermined even or odd number of bits and therefore an accurate transmission. The parity bit also indicates the end of the 8-bit byte. In **serial transmission**, the byte plus the parity bit are transmitted one bit after another in a continuous line (Figure 6-5). In **parallel transmission**, 8 bits (a byte) plus a parity bit are transmitted at the same time over nine separate paths (Figure 6-6). Thus, parallel transmission is generally faster than serial transmission. A modem that connects the system unit to a telephone line contains a serial port because the telephone line expects the data being transmitted to be in serial form. Serial ports are designed and built according to either the RS-232 or RS-422 standard, which specifies the number of pins required for the port's connector. Two common connectors for serial ports are a 9-pin connector and a 25-pin connector.

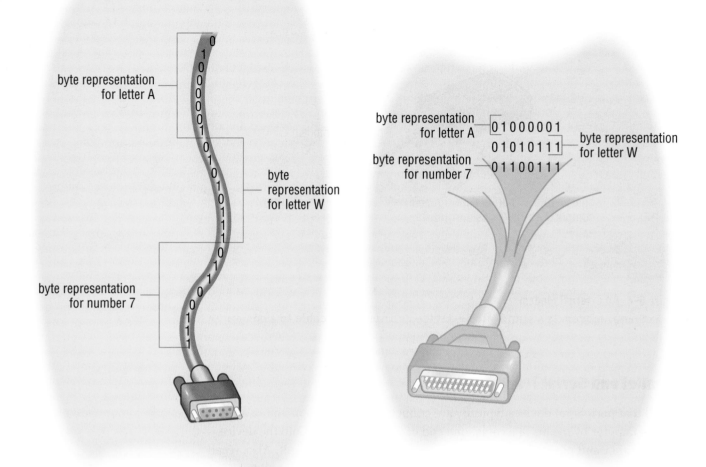

**Figure 6-5  Serial Transmission**
In serial transmission, all the data bits are transmitted one bit after another in a continuous line.

**Figure 6-6  Parallel Transmission**
In parallel transmission, a group of 8 bits (1 byte) plus a parity bit are transmitted at the same time over nine separate paths, resulting in a transmission that is faster than a serial transmission.

## Communications Media

Go to this title's Internet Resource Center and read the article titled "High-Speed Internet." www.emcp.net/CUT4e

Users must have access to communications media to communicate between computing devices. A **communications medium** is a link (a connection) that allows computers in different locations to be connected. When communications take place between distant computers, a combination of media may be used, some of which the user may never see. Communications media are broadly classified as either wired or wireless.

### Wired Communications Media

While many computers, devices, and networks now use wireless technologies, many others continue to use wired technologies as a means of communicating.

The medium chosen depends mainly on user requirements relating to availability, cost, speed, and other factors.

**Twisted-Pair Cable** **Twisted-pair cable**, one of the older types of communications media, was originally developed for telephone networks. Early versions consisted of wires wrapped (twisted) around one another to reduce noise. Today such cables used with computer networks typically consist of two parallel copper wires, each individually wrapped in plastic and bound together by another plastic casing (see Figure 6-7). The pairs are often bundled in packs of hundreds or thousands, buried in underground electrical conduits (pipes), and run to various locations, such as buildings and rooms, where they can be connected to standard phone jacks.

Twisted-pair cable can be used to connect computers in networks for transmitting data over relatively short distances. Millions of home computer owners use this medium with a modem because the cable is already in place. The advantages of twisted-pair cable are its availability and low price. To ensure more accurate transmissions over long distances, repeater stations may be positioned along the way to refresh (strengthen) the communication signals.

**Coaxial Cable** **Coaxial cable** is commonly used for cable television connections, in telephone networks, and in some computer networks. The cable consists of an insulated center wire grounded by a shield of braided wire (Figure 6-8). Coaxial cable is more expensive than twisted-pair, but is less susceptible to interference and can carry much more data. Baseband coaxial cable, often used in computer networks, is about $^3/_8$ inch thick and has a single channel for transmitting digital signals at about 10 Mbps. Broadband coaxial cable has several channels, each of which can carry about 10 Mbps. Broadband is used for cable television transmissions.

Millions of cable television subscribers already have cable installed in their homes and offices. By adding a **cable modem**, television subscribers can take

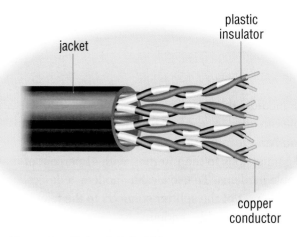

**Figure 6-7 Twisted-Pair Cable**
One of the older types of communications media, twisted-pair cable can be used to connect computers in networks for transmitting data over relatively short distances.

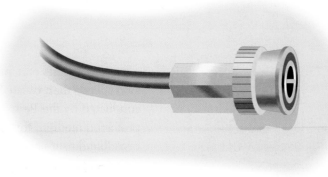

**Figure 6-8 Coaxial Cable**
Coaxial cable can be used for connecting computers in a local computer network, such as a network located on a college campus.

## INVENTOR OF ETHERNET
# Robert Metcalfe

**BORN IN BROOKLYN, RAISED ON LONG ISLAND,** and educated at MIT and at Harvard (where he received a Ph.D. in computer science), Robert M. Metcalfe earned fame and fortune as the inventor of the world's most widely used LAN communication protocol, Ethernet. More than one hundred million computers are linked with Ethernet LANs, and many of them are connected to the Internet.

Metcalfe conceived of Ethernet in 1973 while working at the Xerox Palo Alto Research Center (Xerox PARC), which was also the birthplace of the graphical user interface, of WYSIWYG computing, and of the pointing device known as the mouse. For a while, Metcalfe taught at Stanford University, but in 1979 he left to found 3Com Corporation, of Santa Clara, California, the leading manufacturer of Ethernet adapter cards and other equipment. Metcalfe's invention has made him a billionaire.

In the 1980s Metcalfe taught at Stanford University and in the early 1990s he was a visiting fellow at the University of Cambridge, England. During this time he became known for his writing in addition to his previous technical and business accomplishments. Metcalfe became CEO of InfoWorld Publishing in 1992, and vice president

of IDG Technology in 1993. In one of his "From the Ethernet" columns for *InfoWorld* magazine, he predicted a collapse of the Internet due to excessive traffic. While such a collapse has not yet occurred, many people do experience excessive delays when using the Internet, and most observers agree that network backbone upgrades are necessary. Metcalf is also widely known for what is called Metcalfe's Law, which states that the value of a network increases exponentially with the number of machines (and users) connected to it.

advantage of this communications medium to receive much faster data transmission speeds than twisted-pair cable can offer. According to a June 2009 survey conducted by the Pew Internet and American Life Project, cable modems are a preferred medium for broadband connections to the Internet, with 41 percent of broadband users connecting via cable modems. To use a cable modem, a device called a splitter must be installed. One part of the splitter connects to the television cable, and the other part connects to the cable modem.

**Fiber-Optic Cable** A twisted-pair cable and a coaxial cable both contain copper conductors and transmit electrical signals—streams of electrons. Instead of copper, a **fiber-optic cable** uses a string of glass to transmit photons—beams of light. Figure 6-9 shows the construction of a single fiber-optic cable. However, a fiber-optic cable typically consists of hundreds of clear fiberglass or plastic

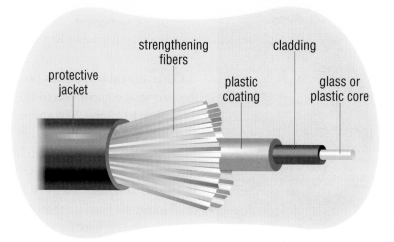

**Figure 6-9 Fiber-Optic Cable**
Fiber-optic cable transmits beams of light through a glass or plastic core.

fibers (threads), each approximately the same thickness as a human hair. Data is converted into beams of light by a laser device and transmitted as light pulses. Billions of bits can be transmitted per second. At the receiving end, optical detectors convert the transmitted light pulses into electrical pulses that computing devices can read. The advantages of using fiber-optic cables include:

- faster transmission speeds (up to 1 trillion bits per second)
- higher data transmission volumes
- minimal interference
- greater security
- longer cable life

Fiber-optic cable is expensive and difficult to work with, but the advantages of using the technology outweigh the disadvantages. The most important advantage of fiber-optic cables is that they are a very high bandwidth (broadband) medium, and therefore they have become the medium of choice for many local area networks. However, when data must be sent to distant computers or to networks using analog media, the sending computer or the network's host computer uses a modem to convert the data into analog form.

**Integrated Services Digital Network (ISDN) Lines** In some locations a special digital telephone line, called **Integrated Services Digital Network (ISDN) line**, is available. This type of line can be used to dial into the Internet and transmit and receive information at very high speeds, ranging from 64 Kbps to 128 Kbps. Using an ISDN line requires a special ISDN modem. Monthly fees for ISDN lines are higher than for regular phone lines, adding to a user's communications costs. With the widespread adoption of high-speed cable modems and DSL lines at a relatively low cost, the growth of ISDN line usage remains flat.

**Digital Subscriber Line (DSL)** **Digital Subscriber Line (DSL)** technology uses existing copper phone lines and new optimized switched connections to achieve faster telecommunications speeds than traditional dial-up phone access. DSL separates voice and data into discrete channels so that users can still make phone calls while connected to the Internet via a DSL modem. DSL is considered a

Tech Demo 6-3
DSL vs. Cable
Modems

A fiber-optic cable typically consists of hundreds or thousands of clear glass or plastic fibers, each about the same thickness as a human hair.

broadband technology, as connection speeds range from 144 Kbps to 1.56 Mbps.

Currently cable modems provide the strongest competition to DSL lines. According to a June 2009 survey by the Pew Internet and American Life Project, 33 percent of households with broadband connections to the Internet used DSL. However, DSL technology is not available in all locations because there is a physical limitation on how far away from a telephone company office a DSL line can reach.

**T Lines** The generic term **T line** refers to any of several types of digital high-speed long-distance telephone lines developed by Bell Labs that are capable of carrying multiple types of signals across the line, including both voice and data. T lines can carry data at very high speeds, but they are expensive. Their high cost typically limits their use to large companies and organizations.

Unlike a standard dial-up telephone line that can carry only a single signal, T lines use multiplexing, thereby making it possible for multiple signals to share a single telephone line. Two popular types of digital T lines are T1 lines and T3 lines, both of which can carry voice and data. There are no T2 lines.

A **T1 line** is a popular leased line option for businesses connecting to the Internet and for Internet service providers (ISPs) connecting to the Internet backbone. A T1 line can carry data at a speed of 1.54 Mbps. A T1 line actually consists of 24 individual channels, each of which supports 64 Kbits per second. Each 64 Kbit per second channel can be configured to carry voice or data traffic. Most telephone companies allow a customer to buy just some of these individual channels, known as fractional T1 access.

A **T3 line** is much faster and more expensive than a T1 line. A dedicated T3 line provides a data transfer rate of about 43 Mbps, making a T3 line much faster than a T1 line. A T3 line actually consists of 672 individual channels, each of which supports 64 Kbps. T3 lines are used mainly by ISPs connecting to the Internet backbone and for the backbone itself.

# Wireless Communications Media

Wireless media transmit information as electromagnetic signals through the air in much the same way as a battery-operated radio sends radio waves. Individual users, businesses, and organizations are rapidly embracing wireless technologies as workers become more mobile and wireless devices become more powerful. Wireless technologies include:

- microwave systems
- satellite systems
- infrared technology
- cellular technology
- Wi-Fi technology
- Bluetooth technology

Go to this title's Internet Resource Center and read the article titled "Certified Wireless USB." www.emcp.net/CUT4e

**Microwave Systems** Microwave transmission involves the sending and receiving of information in the form of high-frequency radio signals. A **microwave system** transmits data through the atmosphere from one microwave station to another, or from a microwave station to a satellite and then back to earth to another microwave station, as shown in Figure 6-10. When data is sent between microwave stations, the stations must be positioned at relatively short line-of-sight intervals because radio signals cannot bend around mountains and other obstacles. Therefore, there must be no visible obstructions between the sending and receiving microwave stations. The terrain determines the distance between microwave stations; it is rarely more than 25 miles. Microwave stations are often placed on top of hills, mountains, or buildings to ensure unobstructed transmission routes.

Tech Demo 6-4
Wireless Media

**Satellite Systems** A **communications satellite** is a solar-powered electronic device containing several small, specialized radios called transponders. A **transponder** receives signals from a transmission station on the ground, called an

Tech Demo 6-5
Satellite Internet Service

**Figure 6-10  A Microwave System Transmitting Radio Signals**
In this microwave system, data is sent as radio signals through the atmosphere from one microwave station to another. The stations must be positioned at relatively short line-of-sight intervals because radio signals cannot bend around objects such as mountains.

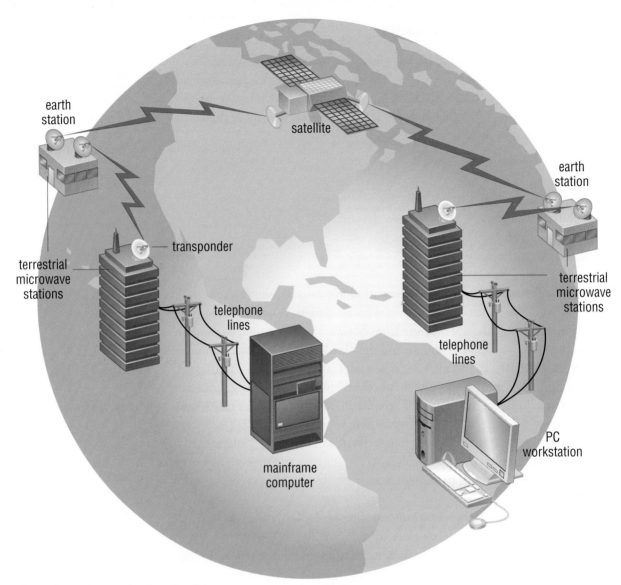

**Figure 6-11 Communications Satellite**

A communications satellite is a solar-powered electronic device containing small, specialized radios called transponders for receiving signals from transmission stations on the ground. A satellite receives the transmitted signals, amplifies them, and then retransmits them to the appropriate locations on earth.

**earth station**. Communications satellites are positioned thousands of miles above the earth. A satellite receives transmitted signals, amplifies them, and then retransmits them to the appropriate locations on earth (see Figure 6-11). Satellites orbit the earth at the same speed as the earth's rotation, making them appear stationary when viewed from the ground. This is called a **geosynchronous orbit**. One of the benefits of satellite systems is the small number of satellites needed to transmit data over long distances. In fact, a small number of satellites properly positioned can receive and transmit information to any location on earth.

Communications satellites are capable of transmitting billions of bits per second, making them ideal for transmitting very large amounts of data. Because of the time it takes to send and receive data across such long distances, satellites are more appropriate for one-way communications such as television and radio applications, rather than for interactive applications such as telephone conversations or computer conferencing. The expense involved in building a satellite, sending it into orbit, and maintaining it is very high. Because of this, companies often share satellite technology as they are unable to bear the full cost of operating their own system.

Several satellites now in orbit handle domestic and international data, video, and voice communications for owners and subscribers. For instance, banks use satellites to transmit thousands of customer transactions to other banks. Money can be transferred from an account in New York to an account in London within seconds.

**Infrared Technology** In recent years infrared technology has become increasingly popular for providing wireless communication links between computers and peripheral devices. **Infrared technology** transmits data as light waves instead of radio waves (Figure 6-12). Television remote control units use the same technology. One drawback to infrared technology is that objects placed between sending and receiving devices can interrupt transmissions because the light waves must follow a line-of-sight path.

Wireless keyboards, also called cordless keyboards, are a recent application of infrared technology. The battery-powered keyboards communicate with computers by transmitting data to a receiver connected to a port on the computer's system unit. A wireless mouse is another popular infrared device that works in the same way as a wireless keyboard, requiring less desktop space because there is no need for a cable.

**Cellular Technology** People can communicate wirelessly to and from nearly anywhere in the world using **cellular technology**. Cellular phones and devices work by maintaining contact with cellular antennae that resemble metal telephone poles positioned throughout a cellular calling area. Each area, called a **cell**, has its own

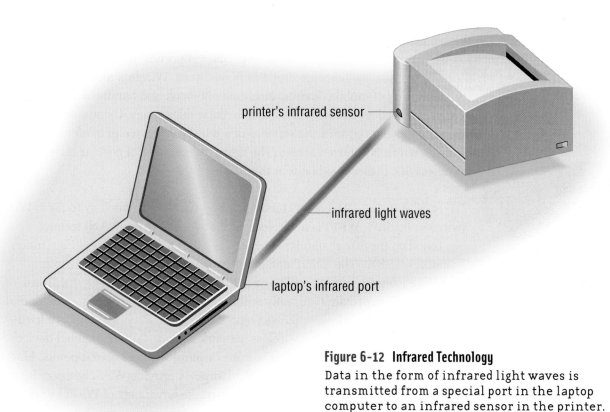

printer's infrared sensor

infrared light waves

laptop's infrared port

**Figure 6-12 Infrared Technology**
Data in the form of infrared light waves is transmitted from a special port in the laptop computer to an infrared sensor in the printer.

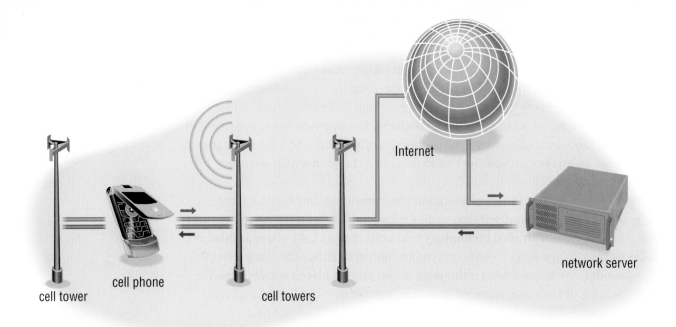

cell tower     cell phone     cell towers     Internet     network server

**Figure 6-13 Cellular Technology**
Signals sent by cell phones are transmitted and received from cell to cell until they reach their intended destination.

antenna encompassing an area approximately 10 to 12 square miles in diameter. As users move from cell to cell, the closest antenna picks up the signal and relays it to the appropriate destination, as shown in Figure 6-13.

Communications networks that support cellular communications also work well for handling business data. Using a portable computer with a cellular modem, a person can access both Internet resources and information stored on a company's intranet databases. This can be especially important for users in areas where communications facilities are crude or nonexistent. Wireless modems may be used with a variety of mobile devices, including notebook and handheld computers, personal digital assistants (PDAs), and cellular telephones. Using a device with a wireless modem requires the services of a **wireless service provider (WSP)** to provide wireless Internet access. The newest generation of cellular technology, Wireless 3G, is discussed later in this chapter.

A wireless access point is a device that connects Wi-Fi-enabled devices to a local area network.

**Wi-Fi Technology** The most commonly used wireless technology today is Wi-Fi (wireless fidelity). **Wi-Fi** is a wireless local area network (WLAN) technology based on the 802.11 standards of the Insititute of Electrical and Electronics Engineers (IEEE). The 802.11 standards are discussed later in this chapter.

A Wi-Fi device, such as a PDA or a notebook computer with a Wi-Fi card, must be in close proximity (usually within 150 feet indoors or 300 feet outdoors) to a device called a wireless access point. The **wireless access point** is a hardware device that transmits a wireless network signal to Wi-Fi–enabled devices. A Wi-Fi **hotspot** is a location that has one or more wireless access points. Many restaurants, hotels, school campuses, and airports provide Wi-Fi hotspots for a fee or at no charge. Home networks can also take advantage of Wi-Fi by adding a wireless access point to a broadband modem or router (Figure 6-14).

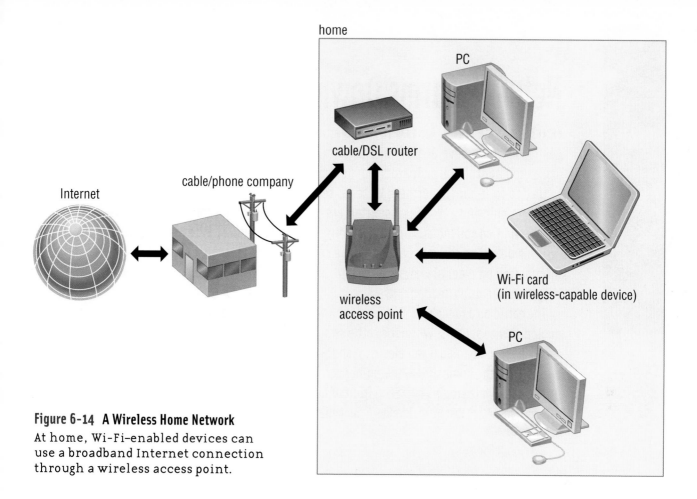

home

PC

cable/DSL router

cable/phone company

Internet

wireless
access point

Wi-Fi card
(in wireless-capable device)

PC

**Figure 6-14  A Wireless Home Network**
At home, Wi-Fi-enabled devices can
use a broadband Internet connection
through a wireless access point.

**Bluetooth Technology**  **Bluetooth** wireless connectivity is becoming increasingly common. Most PDAs, cell phones, and notebook computers have built-in Bluetooth capabilities. This technology offers short-range (usually 15 to 20 feet) connectivity with other Bluetooth devices. Devices connected with Bluetooth essentially form their own small, temporary network that can transmit both voice and data. Common uses of Bluetooth include connecting mobile headsets to cell phones and synchronizing PDA information with notebook computer or cell phone information.

# Network Classifications

Networks vary enormously, from simple interoffice systems connecting a few personal computers and a printer, to complex global systems connecting thousands of computers and computer devices. Networks can be classified by their architecture, by the relative distances they cover, and by the users they are designed to support.

Cell phone users can
talk on a hands-free
Bluetooth headset
while their phone is in
a bag or jacket pocket.

## Networks Classified by Architecture

The term **network architecture** refers to the way a network is designed and built, just as the architecture of a building refers to its design and construction. Client/server and peer-to-peer are the two major architectural designs for networks.

# Network Farms Down Under

**FENCES, CATTLE DOGS, AND LONG RIDES** around the property may soon become obsolete on Australian farms. Several experimental farms in Australia are using sensor network technology to make their agricultural endeavors more efficient.

On one fruit farm in northern Victoria, several hundred wireless sensors, each containing a computer chip and a Wi-Fi transmitter, are located throughout the farm. The sensors gather information on soil moisture, water quality, leaf temperature, evaporation rates, and salinity. This data is continuously relayed to a central server. The farmer-scientists overlay the information onto aerial views of the farm obtained using Google Earth and adjust the wireless irrigation pumps as needed.

The cattle on a ranch near Brisbane chew their cud while wearing solar-powered collars equipped with sensors. When the cattle stray from their virtual borders, the collars emit an audio warning, accompanied by an electrical shock. The cattle quickly learn to pick up on the first audio cue. Back at the home office, the farmer can monitor cattle movement or move virtual paddock boundaries while sipping coffee in front of his computer screen.

These farms are just in "field trials," but commercial applications should be ready within two years.

**Client/Server Architecture** In **client/server architecture**, a **client** (such as a networked personal computer, workstation, or terminal) can send requests to, and receive services from, another typically more powerful computer called a **server** (see Figure 6-15). The server can store programs, files, and data that are available to authorized users. For example, suppose that someone wants to use a PC in the school's computer lab to write a letter to a friend. After starting the client computer, the user issues a request to use Microsoft Word, perhaps by simply clicking the Word icon displayed on the computer screen. The request goes to the network's server, where Microsoft Word is stored. The server prepares a copy of Microsoft Word and sends it to the client computer. Once the software is loaded, it can be used to type and print the letter.

A major advantage of the client/server model is that application programs, such as Microsoft Office, can be stored on the server and accessed by multiple users. This eliminates the need to install individual copies of programs on each computer within the network.

Tech Demo 6-6
Peer-to-Peer
Network

**Peer-to-Peer Architecture** **Peer-to-peer architecture** is a network design in which computers comprising the network have equivalent capabilities and responsibilities, each acting as both client and server (see Figure 6-16). Peer-to-peer networks are usually simpler to install and maintain and are less expensive. However, they may not perform as well as client/server networks when operating under

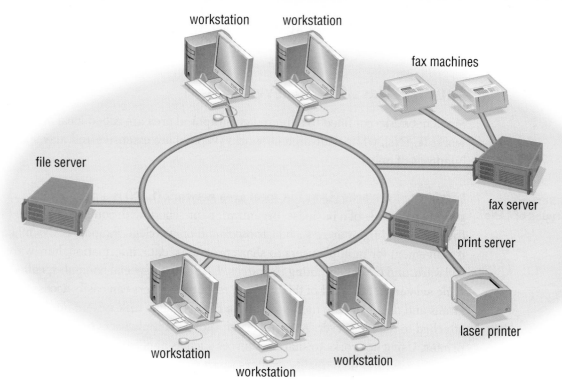

## Figure 6-15 Client/Server Architecture

In this type of network architecture structure, the networking paths allow a networked client computer to send information to a server, which then can relay the information back to the client computer, or to another client on the same network. In this network, the two fax machines and the laser printer are shared resources, available through their respective servers. In addition, the file server provides access to a shared hard disk.

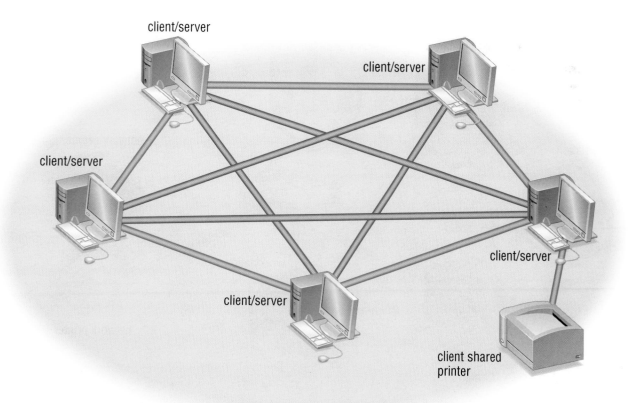

## Figure 6-16 Peer-to-Peer Architecture

In this network architecture, computers act as both client and server.

heavy workloads. Windows XP Professional, Windows Vista, and Windows 7 contain software to set up a peer-to-peer network.

## Networks Classified by Coverage

Small networks confined to a limited geographical area are called local area networks (LANs), while wide area networks (WANs) are extensive and may span hundreds of miles.

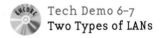
Tech Demo 6-7
Two Types of LANs

**Local Area Networks (LANs)** A **local area network (LAN)** is a private network serving the needs of a business, organization, or school with computers located in the same building or area, such as those found on a college campus. LANs make it convenient for multiple users to share programs, data, information, hardware, software, and other computing resources. LANs use a special computer, called a **file server**, to house all of the network resources. Users can easily access programs and data from the file server and a high-capacity disk system internal to or attached to the file server. A **print server** allows multiple users to share the same printer. Using networks to share resources such as applications programs, hard disk capacity, and high-quality printers saves companies money in hardware, software, and related costs. Figure 6-17 shows the arrangement of a LAN.

Tech Demo 6-8
Wide Area
Networks

**Wide Area Networks (WANs)** A **wide area network (WAN)** spans a large geographical area, connecting two or more LANs (see Figure 6-18). A business might use a WAN to communicate between a manufacturing facility in one state and corporate headquarters in another. Governments, universities, and large corpora-

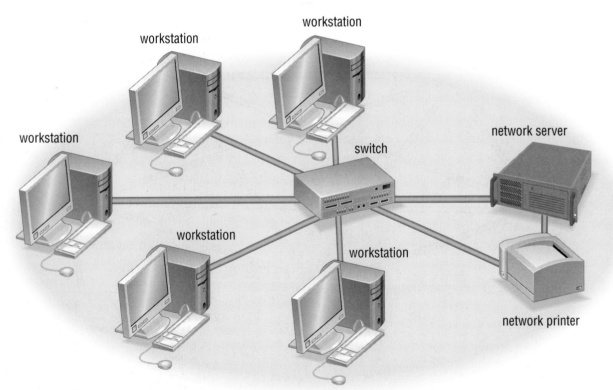

**Figure 6-17  A Local Area Network (LAN)**
In a LAN, workstations are connected to network resources such as printers and servers via a hub.

**CHAPTER 6** Telecommunications and Networks

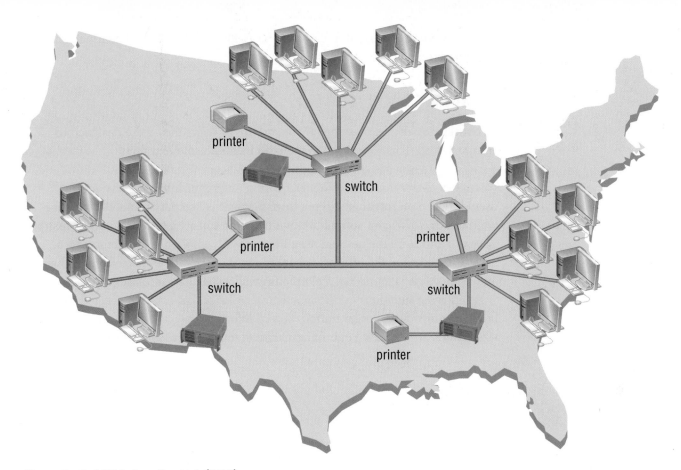

**Figure 6-18  A Wide Area Network (WAN)**
In this WAN, three offices, each with an individual LAN, are able to share resources
through the network connection.

tions use WANs to share data among separate networks. WANs typically make
use of high-speed leased telephone lines, wireless satellite connections, or both.

There are several types of wide area networks. A **metropolitan area network
(MAN)** is a wide area network limited to a specific site, such as a city or town. A
**public access network (PAN)** is a wide area network operated and maintained
by a large company, such as AT&T, MCI, or Sprint, which provides voice and
data communications capabilities to customers for a fee. Businesses that use the
facilities of large communications companies to provide subscribers with additional services are called a **value added network (VAN)**. Typical services offered
include access to various network databases, electronic mail, and online advertising and shopping. America Online is a well known VAN.

In recent years a special type of Internet-based WAN has become increasingly
popular among large businesses that need a cost-effective way to expand their networking options. This specialized WAN is called a **virtual private network (VPN)**.
Instead of leasing T1 lines to connect distant offices across the country, a company
establishes a VPN by having each branch office set up a local Internet connection.
Additional software and security procedures overlay these public Internet connections to create a secure private network that allows offices to communicate as
if they were within the same corporate network—even though they are actually
using the Internet. Factors that make a VPN an attractive option are the cost savings (about $200 to $300 per month for an Internet connection versus $500 or more

per month for a T1 line), and the reliability, wide availability, and nearly unlimited bandwidth capacity of the Internet.

## Networks Classified by Users

Networks can also be classified by the groups of users they were designed to accommodate. This classification includes intranets and extranets.

**Intranets**  A network that is housed within an organization to serve internal users is called an **intranet**. Access to an intranet is typically protected by a **firewall**, which consists of special hardware and/or software that prevents or restricts access to and from the network (see Figure 6-19). All inquiries and messages entering or leaving the intranet pass through the firewall, which examines them and blocks those that do not meet the firewall's specified security criteria.

An intranet functions in the same way as a LAN that is not connected to other networks outside the organization. Stored information is available only to authorized users, and certain kinds of information may be available only to specific

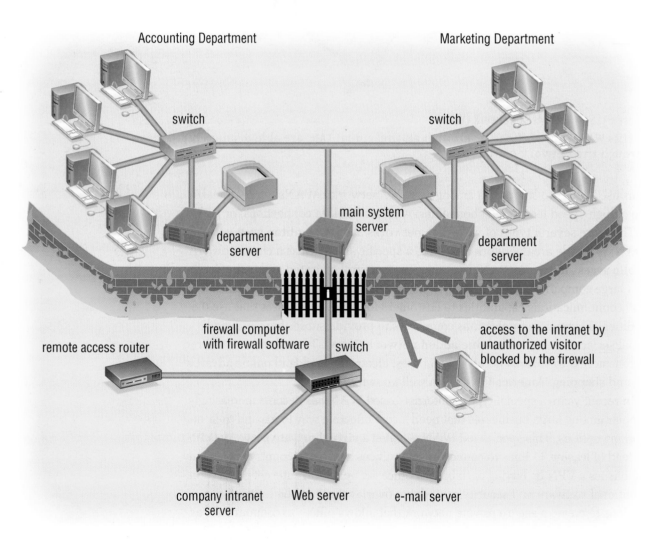

**Figure 6-19  An Intranet with a Firewall**
Access to an intranet is typically protected by a firewall consisting of special hardware and/or software that limits usage to authorized users.

persons, groups, or departments within the organization. For example, access to a company's new product designs may be restricted to employees in the research and design department who have special passwords.

**Extranets** An **extranet** is an extension of an intranet that allows specified external users, including customers and business partners, access to internal applications and data via the Internet. An extranet allows external users with a valid user ID and password to pass through the firewall and access certain resources in the organization's network. Use of network resources is restricted by what the external user is authorized to access. Figure 6-20 illustrates an extranet as well as the process by which an authorized user can access systems behind the organization's firewall.

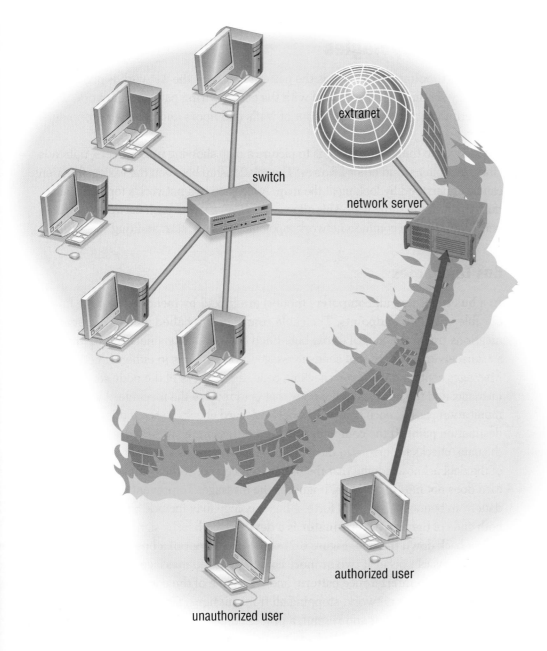

**Figure 6-20  An Extranet with a Firewall**
An extranet allows authorized users (for example, customers, business partners, employees) to access a company's internal systems via the Internet but prevents unauthorized users from doing so.

A properly designed and implemented extranet can provide many useful services. Many companies use extranets to allow workers to access systems from non-work locations. Mobile workers can connect their notebooks or handheld computers to a company extranet via a communications medium such as a telephone line. Once connected, workers can send and receive e-mail messages. Managers can contact mobile workers carrying small pagers. Some newer pagers allow users to exchange e-mail messages. Extranets may also allow fax transmission.

Like intranets, extranets can be used for a variety of business activities. For example, an automobile manufacturer can post a request for bids for raw materials, such as engine parts, seat covers, and tires. An accompanying electronic bid form allows potential suppliers to submit a bid to supply these materials.

## Network Topologies

Tech Demo 6-9
Network
Topologies

**Network topology**, or layout, is the pattern by which the network is organized. Topology should not be confused with the actual wiring path of a network, which is determined by the physical layout of walls and floors and other environmental factors.

One way to think of topology is to picture a map showing roads, rivers, railroads, cities, mountains, and other features. The relationship between the various locations can be understood by looking at the map. A diagram of a network's topology functions in much the same way. This allows a viewer to locate each network component, or **node**. The common network topologies are bus, star, and ring.

### Bus Topologies

In a **bus topology**, all computers (nodes) are linked by means of a single line of cable with two endpoints. The cable connection is called a **bus**. All communications travel the length of the bus. Each computer has a network card with a **transceiver**, a device that sends messages along the bus in either direction. Messages contain data, error-checking code, the address of the node sending the message, and the address of the node that is to receive the message. As the communication passes, each computer's network card checks to see if it is the assigned destination point. If the computer finds its address in the message, it then reads the data, checks for errors in the transmission, and sends a message to the sender of the data acknowledging that the data was received. If the computer's network card does not find its address, it ignores the message. To prevent transmitted data from bouncing back and forth, a bus topology may include a terminator at both ends of the line. A **terminator** is a device that absorbs signals so they do not reflect back down the line. Figure 6-21 shows the layout of a bus topology.

Problems can occur if two or more computers send messages at the same time. This creates an interference pattern, and when one of the computers detects this pattern it jams the network, stopping all transmissions. Computers that are sending messages then wait and resend, a process that is repeated until a message gets through without being blocked. Another problem with linear bus topology is that a broken connection along the bus can bring down the whole network. Bus topologies commonly use coaxial or fiber-optic cables. They are less expensive than some other network layouts, but may be less efficient.

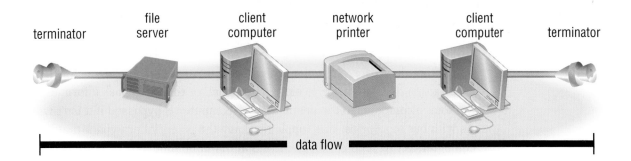

**Figure 6-21  Bus Topology**
In a bus topology, all communications travel the full length of the bus, with each computer's networking transceiver checking the message for its intended destination.

## Star Topologies

In a **star topology** (also referred to as a hub-and-spoke topology), multiple computers and peripheral devices are linked to a central hub, in a point-to-point configuration resembling a star (Figure 6-22). The hub acts as a switching station, reading message addresses the nodes send and routing the messages accordingly. Companies with multiple departments needing centralized access to databases and files often prefer this topology.

The chief disadvantage of star topology is its dependence on the host computer. Because all communications must go through the hub, the network becomes inoperable if it fails to function properly. On the other hand, the hub can prevent the data collisions that may occur with bus topologies, and the rest of the network can remain operational if a node's connection is broken.

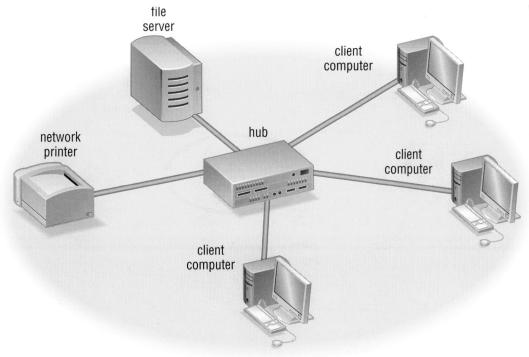

**Figure 6-22  A Star Topology**
In a star topology, all computers are linked to a central host computer, through which all communications travel.

## Ring Topologies

In a **ring topology** there is no hub, and each computer is connected to two or more other devices in a circular path (Figure 6-23). A type of ring technology called token ring uses a single electronic signal, or **token**, to pass information from the source computer to the destination. A computer is bypassed if it isn't working. As with bus topologies, ring topologies have the potential drawback that if two computers try to send communications at the same time, one or both messages may become garbled.

## Hybrid Topologies

Some businesses prefer using one kind of topology throughout the organization, while others prefer to use several different kinds. Indeed, the more common practice is for companies to combine network layout types to suit their particular situation. A system that mixes topologies in a network is called a **hybrid topology**. For example, a company's plant in Ohio may use a ring topology, while another plant in North Carolina may set up a bus topology. When the company's two plants are connected, they form a hybrid topology.

## Physical versus Logical Topologies

One of the elements that makes networking potentially confusing to beginners is that the term *topology* has two levels of meaning. On the one hand, it refers to the physical arrangement of LAN components, including PCs, peripherals, and cables as discussed in the preceding section. On the other hand, it refers to the way the data travels through the physical connections, which is called its logical arrangement. For example, workstations might be physically connected to a central hub,

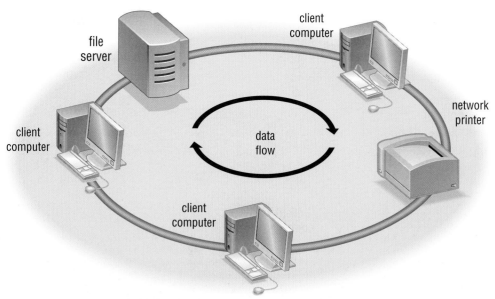

**Figure 6-23 Ring Topology**
In a ring topology, each computer is connected to two or more other devices in a circular path.

# Network-in-a-Box

**AFTER A DISASTER SUCH AS A HURRICANE,** a terrorist attack, or earthquake, the first task of relief workers is to assess damage and coordinate resources and equipment. But in situations where electricity has been cut off and phone lines are down, their ability to respond rapidly and effectively is severely hampered. NetHope is a consortium of 26 large nonprofits that focuses on exactly this issue—the need to deliver information and communication technology to the relief worker. With the help of Cisco System engineers, NetHope has developed a network-in-a-box that can provide instant, durable communications in the most extreme conditions.

The box is called the NetHope Relief Kit (NRK) and consists of off-the-shelf components crammed into a small suitcase-size box with a handle. It sets up in twenty minutes, runs off a car battery, and is cooled by fans. One NRK can support up to 50 laptops and multiple wireless phones. A half-dozen NRKs working with an RV equipped with networking technology and a satellite broadband connection can cover 350 square miles.

Cisco engineers designed the NRK in response to the September 11, 2001, attacks and were planning field tests in Africa when the 2004 tsunami in Southeast Asia suddenly demanded a live run. Thanks to the NRKs used in Indonesia and Thailand, relief workers hours or miles away from the central field office could immediately focus on food distributions, medical programs, psychological crisis intervention, and relocation without waiting for electricity and phone lines to be restored.

forming a star, but might pass data from PC to PC in a circular fashion, forming a logical ring.

There are two primary logical topologies: bus and ring. The main difference between them is in the way they avoid collisions in network traffic. In a logical bus topology, the network is like a telephone party line. A computer that wants to send some data listens to make sure no other PC is sending data, and then it sends. In a logical ring topology, the token system is used to prevent collisions. There is only one token in the ring, and only the PC in possession of it may send data. PCs do not monitor the network to see whether the line is free; instead they wait until they receive the token.

## Network Hardware

Setting up a computer network generally requires special hardware to link all of the computers and to facilitate communications. LANs and WANs may require different hardware devices.

## Hubs

A **hub** is an electronic device used in older LAN topologies to link computers and allow them to communicate with one another. The hub is usually a separate hardware device, but it can also be a server that can function as a hub. The hub coordinates the message traffic computers connected to the network send and receive. Most manufacturers have ceased production of hubs, focusing instead on switches and other more powerful networking hardware.

## Switches

A **switch** is a hardware device that joins multiple computers together within one LAN. Physically, network switches appear to be nearly identical to network hubs but, unlike hubs, are capable of inspecting data packets as they are received, determining the source and destination device of that packet, and forwarding it to the appropriate destination. In general, this capability renders a network switch a higher-performance alternative to a hub.

## Repeaters

Information often travels long distances. However, the wires and cables used may not be designed to carry messages the full distance. A **repeater**, also called an amplifier, is a specially designed electronic device that receives signals along a network, increases the strength of the signals, and then sends the amplified signals along the network's communications path. Thus, a repeater helps rectify the problem of information not being able to go the full distance of that path. They function much like an amplifier in a home stereo system. A network spread over wide distances may use several repeaters along the way.

A network repeater is designed to increase signal strength for longer distances.

## Routers

A **router** is an electronic device usually found in large networks, including the Internet. Routers connect different networks to each other to carry messages to their intended destinations. When a router receives a message, it sends (routes) it along the path to the next router, and so on, until the message reaches its final destination. Routers are designed and programmed to work together. If a part of the network is not working properly, a router can choose an alternate path so the message will still arrive at its final destination.

With the growth of home networks and broadband Internet access, special devices called cable/DSL routers are used to connect a home network to a cable Internet service provider or a DSL Internet service provider. These devices act as both a modem and a router.

A router connects a home network to an Internet service provider.

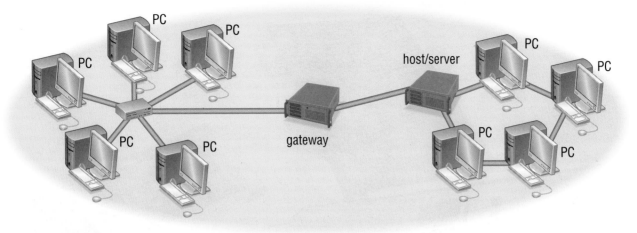

**Figure 6-24 A Gateway**
A gateway is a combination of hardware and software that allows dissimilar networks to communicate. This gateway is a server connecting a star network to a ring network.

## Gateways

A **gateway** is hardware and/or software that allows communication between dissimilar networks. For example, a gateway is needed if an investment broker using a ring topology network wants to retrieve information stored on a star topology network, as shown in Figure 6-24.

## Bridges

A **bridge** consists of hardware and/or software allowing communication between two similar networks. If the investment broker in the previous example wants to retrieve information stored on the same kind of network another broker is using, a bridge between the two networks allows mutual communication, as shown in Figure 6-25.

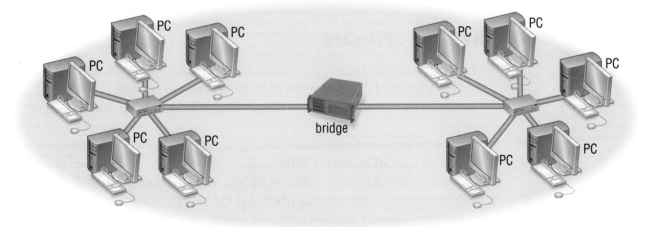

**Figure 6-25 A Bridge**
A bridge is a combination of hardware and software that enables devices on similarly structured networks to communicate. This bridge connects two star networks.

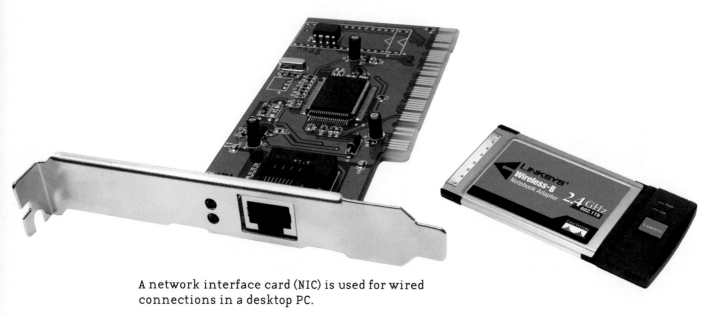

A network interface card (NIC) is used for wired connections in a desktop PC.

A wireless PC card allows notebook computers to use Wi-Fi hotspots.

### Network Interface Cards

The most common LAN architecture is the client/server model, although a variety of LAN architectures is used. Recall that in a client/server LAN a personal computer, workstation, or terminal (a client) is used to send information or a request to another computer (a server). This computer then relays the information back to the original client computer, or to another client computer. In order for a client computer to communicate with a server or another computer it must be connected to a network. Each networked client computer must contain a **network interface card (NIC)**. Most NICs are designed for a particular kind of network, protocol, and media, although some can work with more than one type of network.

## Network Software

Many different kinds of software are required to make a network operational. A network's architecture determines the kind of software needed. For example, a client/server network requires a different kind of software than a peer-to-peer network.

The most important type of networking software is a network operating system. A **network operating system (NOS)** controls the flow of messages from client computers and also provides services such as file access and printing. Some network operating systems, such as UNIX and the Mac OS, have networking functions built in. Popular network operating systems for Windows systems include Microsoft's Windows 2000 Server, Windows Server 2003, and Windows Server 2008, each of which is designed to enhance a system's basic operating system by adding networking features.

# Mesh Networking

**IT IS ARDUOUS, DANGEROUS WORK** collecting seismic data from an active volcano. The seismologist and a mule trudge up the mountainside carrying heavy sensors, each attached to two car batteries for power, along with cables and data logging and storage equipment. After planting the sensors, the seismologist must return every few days to physically retrieve the data—not a welcome task when snowball-size balls of molten rocks spew from the top. So in 2005 when Matt Welsh, an assistant professor of computer science at Harvard University, was preparing to collect data from Reventador, a feisty 12,000-foot volcano in northern Ecuador, he decided to blanket a side of the mountain with a wireless mesh network.

A mesh network is a decentralized method of moving data that uses a series of interconnected nodes. Since information hops from node to node, it can reroute itself and continue if one node breaks down. Mesh networking is relatively inexpensive and offers a reliable connection that can span large distances. For that reason, mesh networks are becoming increasingly popular as a method for collecting and sharing data on the battlefield, on oil rigs, and at large-scale disaster scenes.

Welsh's wireless mesh network for Reventador consisted of 16 small, low-power sensor stations that run on D-cell batteries, each the size of a lunchbox. He and a team of seismologists deployed the sensors in an ad hoc mesh network that covered two miles of one side of Reventador. Then they returned to base to monitor the mountain's nonstop volcanic activity.

Welsh's project, the first to use a wireless mesh network on a volcano, didn't flow as smoothly as lava. Because Welsh's hotel only ran electricity during the day, Welsh hired someone to monitor the generator throughout the night. Alas, the keeper fell asleep, the generator ran out of electricity, and the laptop collecting data died. A system crash in the midst of the three-week run also caused an interruption. But in the end, the experiment was a success. Welsh's team collected—from the safety of the base station— information on 230 seismic events. Welsh is counting on using enough sensors in his next seismic assignment to create a 3-D image of the volcano.

Open Enterprise Server (OES) is a popular LAN operating system developed by Novell Corporation. OES runs on a variety of different types of LANs. OES provides users with a consistent interface that is independent of the actual hardware used to transmit and receive messages. Novell's newest version, called Open Enterprise Server 2, includes new functions that make it even more versatile than previous versions. The software works smoothly with the network operating system, making it into a vehicle for accessing services over the Internet. Users can access OES software from any browser via a single URL. OES provides for the transfer of information in virtually any file format, and can be installed on networks of all sizes and complexities.

# Communications Software and Protocols

Go to this title's Internet Resource Center and read the article titled "Protocols and Transmission Standards."
www.emcp.net/CUT4e

Recall from Chapter 5 that communications software is a type of utility software that allows computers to "talk" with each other. Combined with the appropriate hardware, communications utilities allow users to connect their computers to other computers, such as network servers, and to access and use resources on a LAN or WAN. Communications software also allows modem dial-up for sending e-mail messages, accessing the Internet, surfing the Web, and more. The software must adhere to a particular network protocol for network communications.

Newer PCs containing a modem often come equipped with communications software. If not, it can be purchased from a variety of sources. Users who subscribe to an Internet service provider are typically provided with communications software that can be installed.

## Communications Utilities Features

Communications software programs contain many useful features. Most programs can be used to:

- access and use the services of an Internet service provider (ISP), such as e-mail and use of Web browsers
- send and receive information to and from other computers through LAN and WAN networks
- send and receive faxes

## Communications Protocols

A **protocol** is a set of rules and procedures for exchanging information among computers on a network. To avoid transmission errors, the computers involved must have the same settings and follow the same standards. Numerous protocols have been developed over the years. Table 6-2 shows a sample of communications protocols now being used.

Table 6-2 **Examples of Communications Protocols**

| Type of Protocol | Purpose/Use |
|---|---|
| Hypertext Transfer Protocol (HTTP) | defines how Web pages are transmitted |
| Simple Mail Transfer Protocol (SMTP) | sends e-mail between servers |
| Post Office Protocol (POP) | retrieves e-mail from a mail server; newest version is POP3 |
| Internet Message Access Protocol (IMAP) | retrieves e-mail from a mail server; newer than POP; has replaced POP on some e-mail servers; newest version is IMAP4 |
| Transmission Control Protocol/ Internet Protocol (TCP/IP) | connects host computers on the Internet |
| File Transfer Protocol (FTP) | allows large files to be transmitted and received over the Internet |

Efforts are currently under way to simplify protocols by establishing standards that all computer and communications equipment manufacturers will adopt and follow. The International Organization for Standardization, based in Geneva, Switzerland, has defined a set of communications protocols called the **Open Systems Interconnection (OSI) Reference Model** (or simply OSI model). The United Nations has adopted the OSI model. However, a variety of protocols likely will remain in use unless users universally accept the OSI model.

**Directional Protocols** Almost all communications use directional protocols to determine the flow of transmissions among devices. The three possible directions are simplex, half-duplex, and full-duplex transmissions.

- **Simplex Transmission.** Communications flow in only one direction with **simplex transmission** (Figure 6-26). This can be compared with a public announcement system at a football game. The announcer can speak to the audience, but cannot receive messages from the audience. Likewise, a computer that transmits data via a simplex channel can either send or receive data, but cannot do both.
- **Half-Duplex Transmission.** With **half-duplex transmission** communications can flow in both directions, but not at the same time (Figure 6-27). A walkie-talkie system is an example of half-duplex transmission. Two-way communication is possible, but only one person can speak at a time. When used over long distances, half-duplex transmission often results in delays. Thus, half-duplex transmission is typically used with a central computer system and the terminals connected to it. Users usually need to wait for a response from the main computer before continuing.
- **Full-Duplex Transmission.** Simultaneous transmission in both directions is achieved through **full-duplex transmission** (Figure 6-28), which is similar to two people communicating via telephone. Both can speak and hear at the same time. Full-duplex transmission eliminates delays due to response time, which can be an important advantage when large amounts of data are transmitted between mid-size servers, mainframe computers, and supercomputers.

**Figure 6-26**
**Simplex Data Transmission**
In this type of directional protocol, data flows in only one direction.

**Figure 6-27**
**Half-Duplex Data Transmission**
In this type of directional protocol, data flows in both directions, but only one direction at a time.

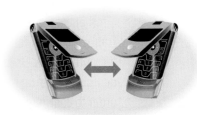

**Figure 6-28**
**Full-Duplex Data Transmission**
In this type of directional protocol, data flows in both directions at the same time.

**CEO, CISCO SYSTEMS INCORPORATED**

# John T. Chambers

**JOHN T. CHAMBERS IS HAILED** as being one of the top chief executive officers (CEOs) in business today. Since he became CEO for Cisco Systems Incorporated in 1995 the company's annual revenues have increased from $1.2 billion to $23.8 billion a year. His work has helped lead the computer networking equipment firm to more than a 10-fold increase in revenue—otherwise known as a growth of 1,700 percent! Cisco Systems Inc. was considered the third-largest company in the world in 2000, falling behind such juggernauts as General Electric Co. and Microsoft Corp.

Chambers was born August 23, 1949, in Cleveland, Ohio. He went to college at West Virginia University to receive a bachelor's degree in business and a law degree. He also received an M.B.A. in finance and management from Indiana University at Bloomington.

His first job began at IBM Corp. in 1976. After six years he started working for Wang Laboratories, and eventually rose to senior vice president of U.S. Operations. In 1991 he joined Cisco Systems Inc. as senior vice president of Worldwide Operations. He joined the board of directors in 1993 before elevating to CEO.

He set a quick pace for Cisco when he started, fully realizing that the competition of business over the Internet left no room for late arrivals to succeed. Even when the company became bigger than its competitors, Chambers set a nearly frantic schedule for advancing the technology of its routers. Now Cisco's networking and routing equipment define what the Internet can do. In order to continue advancing their technologies, Chambers arranged the acquisition of more than 60 companies since 1994. In 1997, Cisco did one-third of the world's electronic commerce.

Chambers' success has led him to serve two American Presidents. He was on President Clinton's Trade Policy Committee and has served President Bush as vice-chairman of the President George Bush National Infrastructure Advisory Council (NIAC). The council's goal is to protect the critical infrastructure of the United States by offering industry advice and leadership.

Cisco Systems Inc. conquered the networking industry, due in large part to Chambers' vision, but has great plans for the future. Chambers has a strong belief that Cisco's future lies in the telecommunications business. Chambers always sets his goals high, and throughout his tenure has created one of the largest businesses in the world.

Chambers is admired for not only his business acumen, but also his abilities as a leader. He gives himself the same treatment his employees receive. His office is the same size as an entry-level employee at Cisco. He and the other top executives of the company fly coach class and have no reserved parking places at their business headquarters. For actions like these, he has been described as the "best boss in America" by the television program *20/20*.

For all his achievements he has received many awards. Most notably he received the Woodrow Wilson Award for Corporate Citizenship, the Smithsonian Lifetime Achievement Award, and the Presidential Award. He also has a plethora of magazine awards, including "Most Influential CEO" and "Best CEO of the Year," and has been ranked in the top 25 CEOs worldwide.

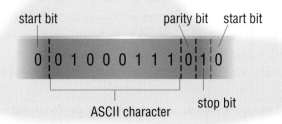

**Figure 6-29  Asynchronous Transmission**
In this type of transmission, control bits surround each byte of data. An
extra bit is added at the beginning and end of each character to signal its
beginning (start) and ending (stop). A parity bit checks for errors.

**Asynchronous and Synchronous Transmission Protocols**  Earlier you learned
that data is sent over communications media in serial form, that is, one bit after
another bit until the complete message is transmitted. Since the bits in serial
transmission are sent out one at a time, transmission protocols have been developed to alert the receiving device as to where characters (bytes) begin and end.
These protocols are called asynchronous and synchronous transmission.

When communications are sent by **asynchronous transmission**, each byte of
data is surrounded by control bits (Figure 6-29). The front bit, called a **start bit**,
signals the beginning of a character. The bit at the end, called a **stop bit**, signals
the end of that character. As explained earlier, there is also an error-checking
bit called a parity bit. Data sent by asynchronous transmission is transmitted at
irregular intervals, and a modem is usually involved.

Synchronous transmission provides a faster and more efficient way of sending data.
With **synchronous transmission**, blocks of bytes are wrapped in start and stop bytes
called **synch bytes** (Figure 6-30). Large computer systems often use synchronous transmission due to the faster transmission speed. PC users wanting to retrieve data from
large computer systems can buy add-in boards that provide synchronous transmission.

Computers communicating with each other must use the same transmission
method. If a computer uses the asynchronous method to send data, a computer
using the synchronous method will not be able to receive the data.

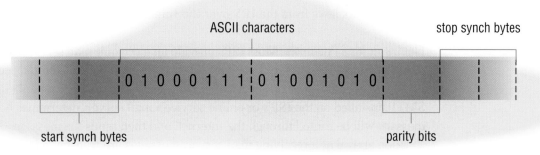

**Figure 6-30  Synchronous Transmission**
This model of transmission provides a fast and efficient way of sending data. Blocks of bytes are
wrapped in start and stop bytes called synch bytes.

**Local Area Network (LAN) Protocols** Protocols that govern data transmissions vary among LANs using different topologies or different PCs and workstations. Most LANs of the bus topology type are set up using an **Ethernet protocol**. These protocols specify how the network is to be set up, how network devices communicate with each other, how problems are identified and corrected, and how components are connected. Ethernet provides for fast and efficient communications.

Ring and star topology networks use a **token ring protocol** that sends an electronic signal (token) around the ring quickly. The token is capable of carrying both an address and a message. As a token passes by a workstation, the workstation checks to see if the token is addressed. If the token has no address, the workstation can latch onto the token, thereby changing the token's status from free to busy. The workstation then adds an address and message to the token. The receiving station receives the message and changes the token status back to free. The token then continues around the ring.

**Wide Area Network (WAN) Protocols** Protocols have been developed for use with WANs. A widely used networking program called **Systems Network Architecture (SNA)** uses a **polling protocol** for transmitting data. Workstations are individually asked if they have a message to transmit. If a polled workstation replies "yes," the protocol transmits the message and then questions (polls) the next device.

A newer type of network software for ring networks dispersed over a large area and connected by fiber-optic cables is called **Fiber Distributed Data Interface (FDDI)**. The software links the dispersed networks together using a protocol that passes a token over long distances. FDDI may be used to connect various university campuses wanting to share information.

Go to this title's Internet Resource Center and read the article titled "Packet Switching."
www.emcp.net/CUT4e

**Internet and Web Protocols** The Internet and the Web require specific protocols to communicate with computers around the world. The Internet uses a transmission technique called packet switching, in which data is divided into small blocks, or packets, which are sent along the Internet to their destinations. A protocol called **Transmission Control Protocol/Internet Protocol (TCP/IP)** governs how packets are constructed and sent to their destinations.

The World Wide Web uses the **Hypertext Transfer Protocol (HTTP)** to transfer Web pages to computers. Most Web addresses, or URLs, begin with the letters "http" to indicate the protocol is being used. Millions of files are available to Web users. Large files can be transmitted and received using **File Transfer Protocol (FTP)**. For example, a company accountant can send a multipage employee report to the U.S. Department of Labor, or receive a complete copy of the newest tax laws from the IRS over the Internet.

**Electronic Mail Protocols** Most ISPs provide an electronic mail service to facilitate the sending and receiving of e-mail messages. Messages are transmitted according to a communications protocol called **Simple Mail Transfer Protocol (SMTP)**. SMTP, installed on the ISP's or online service's **mail server**, determines how each message will be routed through the Internet, and then sends the message.

Upon arrival at a receiving mail server, messages are transferred to another server, called a **Post Office Protocol (POP) server**. POP allows the recipient to retrieve the message. Figure 6-31 illustrates how electronic mail is sent and received with SMTP and POP.

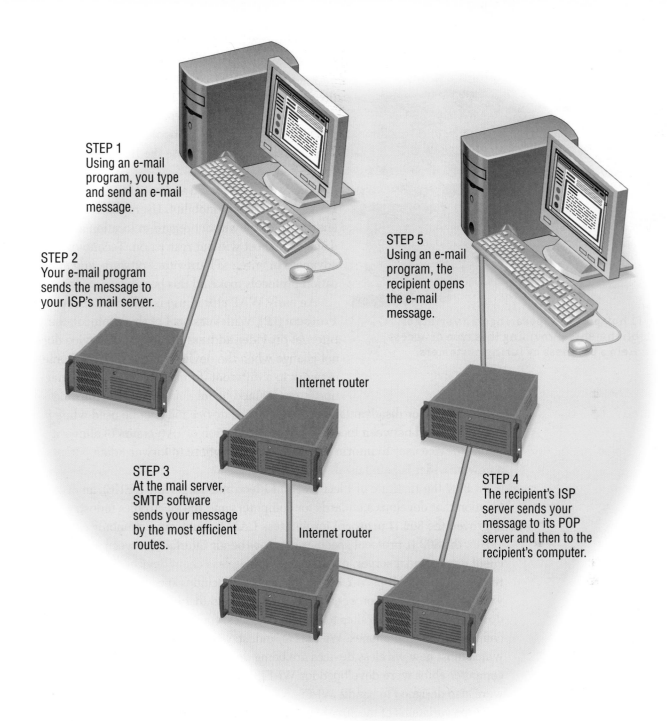

**STEP 1**
Using an e-mail program, you type and send an e-mail message.

**STEP 2**
Your e-mail program sends the message to your ISP's mail server.

**STEP 5**
Using an e-mail program, the recipient opens the e-mail message.

Internet router

**STEP 3**
At the mail server, SMTP software sends your message by the most efficient routes.

Internet router

**STEP 4**
The recipient's ISP server sends your message to its POP server and then to the recipient's computer.

**Figure 6-31 The Process for Sending Electronic Mail with SMTP and a POP Server**
Most electronic mail systems use a mail server to receive incoming e-mail messages. The messages are then sent to, and stored on, the ISP's POP server, from which the recipient can retrieve the messages.

**Wireless Application Protocols** The market for wireless communications has enjoyed tremendous growth, with wireless technology now available in virtually every location on earth. Every day, millions of users exchange information using a variety of devices, including notebook computers, cellular telephones, pagers, messaging services, and other wireless communications products.

Wi-Fi hotspots are appearing in a variety of establishments. Providing this type of access can help a business by luring customers.

Until recently, LANs were limited to the physical hard-wired infrastructure of the building in which they were located. Wireless technologies break down these physical communications barriers by eliminating the need for the expensive hard wiring. The **Wireless Application Protocol (WAP)** enables wireless devices to access and use the Internet using a client/server network.

The major motivation and benefit of wireless LANs are increased mobility. Users can access LANs and the Internet without regard to location and distance, almost without restriction. Technological advances in wireless hardware, software, and application protocols make all this possible.

An early WAP still in use is called **Internet Protocol (IP)**. With version 4 of this protocol, the Internet provider address of the mobile device does not change when the device is moved from a home network to a different (foreign) network. A connection is maintained by implementing a forwarding routine. A major disadvantage of IP is that the device may not be used while it is being moved between locations. A newer version of IP (version 6) allows a mobile device user to inform the local provider where to forward data packets if a new provider is being used.

In 1997 the Institute of Electrical and Electronic Engineers (IEEE), an organization that develops standards for computers and the electronics industry, approved the **802.11 protocol** for wireless LAN technology. Commonly called Wi-Fi, the 802.11 protocol specifies an over-the-air interface between a wireless client device and a server, or between two wireless client devices. Based on a transfer rate of 1 Mbps to 2 Mbps, the protocol includes specifications that provide for the transmission of data and graphics, and that allow information to be downloaded from Web sites to wireless devices, such as Web-enabled notebook computers and cell phones. Wi-Fi is an industry standard and is the basis on which most new wireless devices are being designed and built. Intel's Centrino computer chips were developed for Wi-Fi, and Windows XP and Windows Vista were also designed to handle Wi-Fi.

Three variations of the 802.11 protocol are widely used, with a fourth already gaining ground (see Table 6-3). The first major revision, the **802.11b** protocol, was

**Table 6-3 Variations of the 802.11 Protocol**

| Standard | Year Introduced | Frequency Range | Data Transfer Rate |
|---|---|---|---|
| 802.11n | 2009 | 5 GHz and/or 2.4 GHz | Up to 60 Mbps |
| 802.11g | 2003 | 2.4 GHz | Up to 54 Mbps |
| 802.11a | 2001 | 2.4 GHz | Up to 54 Mbps |
| 802.11b | 1999 | 5 GHz | 5.5 Mbps to 11 Mbps |

approved in 1999 by IEEE. Offering a relatively low cost and a faster transfer rate of 5.5 Mbps to 11 Mbps at a range of up to 250 feet (76 meters), 802.11b is popular in home and small office wireless networks.

In 2001, IEEE approved the **802.11a** protocol standard, which offers transfer rates of up to 54 Mbps when devices are at a range within 60 feet of the primary access point, or hub. Transfer rates are approximately 22 Mbps at longer distances. The 802.11a standard operates in a different frequency range, which results in less interference from other devices. One potential drawback is that 802.11a networks are costly to implement in comparison with 802.11b networks. In June 2003, IEEE approved the **802.11g** protocol standard, which operates in the same frequency range as 802.11b but offers transfer rates similar to 802.11a—up to 54 Mbps. **802.11n**, published in late 2009, increases transfer rates to a theoretical 600 Mbps and can operate at 2.4 GHz (like 802.11g) and/or 5 GHz (like 802.11a).

Wireless data transmission technologies have been popular with some businesses that need to contact agents or representatives in the field, such as the insurance industry. However, some businesses have found wireless transmission technologies unattractive, because they require too much bandwidth. **3G** is a third-generation cellular technology offering exceptional transfer speeds for both voice and non-voice data. The bandwidth for devices using 3G ranges from 384 Kbps for mobile device users up to 2 Mbps for stationary users. Financial institutions will likely be among the principal beneficiaries of wireless 3G technologies.

# OnThe**Horizon**

**THE FUTURE HOLDS TREMENDOUS PROMISE** for computer network users. New hardware, software, and media are appearing that will make telecommunications and networks more efficient, reliable, and useful. Some of these technologies already exist, and are in the process of further development to unleash their full potential. New developments in fiber-optic technology and infrared transmission hold promise in solving existing obstacles to high-speed communication over networks, including the Internet.

## Free-Space Optics

Some small businesses and organizations are unable to obtain access to the fiber-optic communications medium since carriers and service providers are often unwilling to extend connectivity to areas that do not offer a sufficient customer base. Restrictions or prohibitions on underground installations in some areas pose another obstacle to fiber-optic networks. One possible solution is free-space optics, a nascent technology that uses lasers to send optical signals through the air. San Diego-based LightPointe Communications has installed a number of free-space optics outdoor wireless systems around the world, capable of supporting a bandwidth of 1.25 Gbps.

## The Future of Optical Fiber

The backbone of modern networks is fiber-optic–based, but expanding the optical medium nationwide—and eventually worldwide—will increase transmission speed and capacity by what will seem like light-years compared with today's capabilities. A number of developments in optical fiber technology promise to further expand the potential for optical fiber networks.

Dense wave division multiplexing (DWDM) is a technology that uses different wavelengths of laser light to enable multiple data streams to be transmitted over a single optical fiber. The prohibitive cost of constructing new fiber optic networks makes DWDM an attractive option for dealing with the increasing demand for high-speed Internet access.

Current optical fiber utilizes a glass core to transmit light waves, but in a new twist hollow-core optical fibers guide light through hollow corridors filled with air. This results in much lower light dispersion, allowing signals to travel two to five times farther than in conventional fibers. This capability has the potential of reducing or even eliminating the need for costly optical repeaters needed for long-distance transmission, thus reducing the overall cost of installing and operating fiber optic networks.

The current generation of fiber optic networks requires the assistance of external electronic devices to handle the flow of data, devices that consume power and reduce overall network bandwidth. Researchers in the United States and United Kingdom are now working on incorporating semiconductors inside the optical fibers. Although a number of years away from realization, perfection of this technology would further reduce the cost of operating fiber optic networks and increase bandwidth.

## Beaming Data

Drs. Moshen Kavehrad and Svetla Jivkova, researchers at Pennsylvania State University, are now working to develop faster infrared transmission technologies over networks, replacing the radio waves now used with some networking systems, including Apple's AirPort system. Infrared transmission represents tremendous potential for the future. Data traveling through space in the form of infrared light can move faster than radio waves, and with potentially less interruption. The goal of the research is a technology that would allow the transmission of data using beams of infrared light that would connect computers to one another, and to a central transmitter and receiver connected to a larger network. Using infrared light would allow computing devices to be pointed in any direction.

This infrared technology could transmit 2 GB a second, approximately a thousand times as much data as a cable modem, and with few transmission errors. Infrared offers an advantage for activities that require huge bandwidths for transmitting graphic and voice data, such as videoconferencing.

# Chapter**Summary**

*For an interactive version of this summary, go to this text's Internet Resource Center at www.emcp.net/CUT4e. A Spanish version is also available.*

### How has networking evolved?

**Telecommunications** refers to the use of computer hardware and software for sending and receiving information over communications media, making it possible for computer users throughout the world to communicate with each other. This technology of connecting individuals through shared hardware and software has evolved from being telephone-based to being wireless-based. These connections allow data to be shared across networks.

### What are the characteristics of data transmission?

The number of bits that can be transferred per second over a given medium is known as **bandwidth**. **Analog signals** take the form of continuous waves transmitted over a medium at a certain **frequency range**. Digital signals send data in the form of bits. In **serial transmission**, all of the data bits are transmitted one bit after another in a continuous line. In **parallel transmission**, the data bits are sent at the same time along multiple paths.

### What types of communications media allow computers to connect?

A **communications medium** is a physical link that allows computers to be connected to other computers in different locations. Communications media are broadly classified as either wired or wireless. **Twisted-pair cable** consists of two independently insulated wires twisted around each other. **Coaxial cable** consists of an insulated center wire grounded by a shield of braided wire. A **fiber-optic cable** contains hundreds of clear fiberglass or plastic fibers (threads). An **ISDN line** is a special digital telephone line that transmits and receives information at very high speeds. **T lines** are extremely high-speed dedicated connections between two points.

A **microwave system** transmits data via high-frequency radio signals through the atmosphere. **Satellite** systems receive transmitted signals, amplify them, and then transmit the signals to the appropriate locations. **Infrared technology** transmits data as infrared light waves from one device to another, providing wireless links between PCs and peripherals. **Cellular technology** uses antennae resembling telephone towers to pick up signals within a specific area (cell).

**Wi-Fi** (also called 802.11 protocol) specifies the way in which a client can connect to a server or another wireless device using a **wireless access point**. **Bluetooth** is a wireless technology that offers short-range connectivity with other Bluetooth devices through a small, temporary network that can transmit both voice and data.

### How are networks classified?

**Network architecture** refers to the way a network is designed and built. **Client/server architecture** sends information from a client computer to a server, which then relays the information back to the client computer, or to other computers on the network. In **peer-to-peer architecture**, each PC or workstation has equivalent capabilities and responsibilities.

**Local Area Networks (LANs)** are private networks that connect PCs or workstations located in close proximity, storing software applications and other resources on a special computer called a **file server**. A **print server** allows multiple users to share the same printer. A **wide area network (WAN)** spans a large geographical area. There are various types, including **metropolitan area networks (MANs)**, **public access networks (PANs)**, **value added networks (VANs)**, and **virtual private networks (VPNs)**. An **intranet** is a network that is accessible only by a business or organization's members, employees, or other authorized users. Access to an intranet's Web site is restricted by a **firewall**. An **extranet** is a network that makes certain kinds of information available to users within the organization, and other kinds of information available to outsiders, such as companies doing business with the organization.

### What are the common network topologies?

**Network topology**, or layout, refers to the way computers and peripherals are configured to form networks. In a **bus topology**, all computers are linked by a single line of cable. In a **star topology**, multiple computers and peripheral devices are linked to a central computer, called a host. In a **ring topology**, each computer or workstation is connected to two other computers, with the entire network forming a circle. **Hybrid topologies** combine different kinds of network layouts into one.

### What network and communications hardware is needed to link computers and facilitate communication?

A **hub** is an electronic device used in a LAN to link groups of computers. A **switch** is a small hardware device that joins multiple computers together within one LAN. **Repeaters**, also called **amplifiers**, are electronic devices that receive signals and amplify and send them along the network. **Routers** are electronic devices that connect two or more networks. A **gateway** consists of hardware and/or software that allows communication between dissimilar networks. A **bridge** consists of hardware and/or software that allows communication between two similar networks.

### What network software is required to make a network operational?

The most important type of networking software is a network operating system. A **network operating system (NOS)** controls the flow of messages from client computers and also provides services such as file access and printing. Common network operating systems include Novell's NetWare, UNIX, and Windows Servers.

### What communications software and protocols are required to allow computers to share information?

Communications software allows computers to connect to other computers and to access and use network resources. A **protocol** is a set of rules and procedures for exchanging information between network devices and computers. Directional protocols determine the directional flow of transmissions among devices. Three possible directions are **simplex**, **half-duplex**, and **full-duplex**. Data sent by **asynchronous transmission** protocols is transmitted at irregular intervals. With **synchronous transmission**, blocks of bytes are wrapped in start and stop bytes called **synch bytes**. On the Internet, **Transmission Control Protocol/Internet Protocol (TCP/IP)** governs how packets are constructed and sent to their destinations. The World Wide Web uses the **Hypertext Transfer Protocol (HTTP)** to transfer Web pages to computers. Large files can be transmitted and received using **File Transfer Protocol (FTP)**. Messages are transmitted using **Simple Mail Transfer Protocol (SMTP)**. **Post Office Protocol (POP)** allows the recipient to retrieve messages. **Wireless Application Protocol (WAP)** enables wireless devices to access and use the Internet using a client/server network. In 1997, the Institute of Electrical and Electronic Engineers (IEEE) approved a new protocol for wireless LAN technology, called **802.11**. Since then, four versions have been approved: **802.11b**, **802.11a**, **802.11g**, and **802.11n**. **3G** is a third-generation cellular technology offering exceptional transfer speeds for both voice and non-voice data.

# KeyTerms

*Numbers indicate the pages where terms are first cited in the chapter. An alphabetized list of key terms with definitions (in English and Spanish) can be found on the Encore CD that accompanies this book. In addition, these terms and definitions are included in the end-of-book glossary.*

# Chapter**Exercises**

*The following chapter exercises, along with new activities and information,
are also offered in the Internet Resource Center for this title at www.emcp.net/CUT4e.*

## *Tutorial >* **Exploring Windows**

Tutorial 6 focuses on the steps and strategies for creating and renaming folders on your hard drive.

## *Expanding Your Knowledge >* **Articles and Activities**

*Visit the Internet Resource Center for this title at www.emcp.net/CUT4e, read the articles related
to this chapter, and complete the corresponding activities. The article titles include:*

- Topic 6-1: High-Speed Internet
- Topic 6-2: Certified Wireless USB
- Topic 6-3: Protocols and Transmission Standards
- Topic 6-4: Packet Switching

## Terms Check > Matching

*For additional practice, go to the Internet Resource Center for this title at www.emcp.net/CUT4e for a chapter crossword puzzle.*

Write the letter of the correct answer on the line before each numbered item.

a. protocol
b. broadband medium
c. star network
d. simplex
e. intranet

f. gateway
g. LAN
h. communications satellite
i. telecommunications
j. network topology

_____ 1. A solar-powered electronic device containing a number of small, specialized radios, called transponders, that receives signals from transmission stations on the ground.

_____ 2. A communications medium capable of carrying a large amount of data at fast speeds.

_____ 3. The way computers and peripherals are configured to form networks.

_____ 4. A set of rules and procedures for exchanging information between network devices and computers.

_____ 5. Hardware and/or software that allows communication between two dissimilar networks.

_____ 6. A transmission method in which information can flow in only one direction.

_____ 7. A private network that serves the needs of an organization with computers located in close proximity.

_____ 8. An internal network that is accessible only by a business's employees.

_____ 9. The combined use of computer hardware and communications software for sending and receiving information over communications media.

_____ 10. A network in which multiple computers and peripheral devices are linked to a central, or host, computer.

## Technology Illustrated > Identify the Process

What process is illustrated in this drawing? Identify the three types shown and explain the main difference among them.

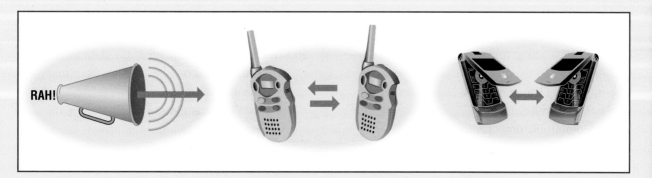

## Knowledge Check > Multiple Choice

  *Additional quiz questions are available on the Encore CD that accompanies this book as well as on the Internet Resource Center for this title at www.emcp.net/CUT4e.*

Circle the letter of the best answer from those provided.

1. A(n) _____ signal is a transmission signal in which information is sent in the form of continuous waves over a medium at a certain frequency range.
   a. analog
   b. digital
   c. serial
   d. bandwidth

2. The term _____ refers to the amount of data that can travel over an analog medium.
   a. synchronous
   b. digital
   c. serial
   d. bandwidth

3. _____ is an increasingly popular communications medium that requires no phone lines or cables.
   a. Coaxial cable
   b. Cellular technology
   c. Twisted-pair cable
   d. Fiber-optic cable

4. A _____ is an electronic device used in a local area network that links computers and allows them to communicate.
   a. gateway
   b. router
   c. repeater
   d. hub

5. Standards (rules) that govern the transfer of information among computers on a network and those using telecommunications are called
   a. parallel transmissions.
   b. serial transmissions.
   c. communications protocols.
   d. Web languages.

6. A network architecture that uses a central, or host, computer through which all transmissions pass is called
   a. client/server architecture.
   b. peer-to-peer architecture.
   c. computer architecture.
   d. layout architecture.

7. A _____ consists of hardware and/or software that allows communication between dissimilar networks.
   a. bridge
   b. repeater
   c. multiplexer
   d. gateway

8. A _____ is a private network that connects PCs and workstations located in close proximity, storing software applications and other resources on a special computer called a file server.
   a. local area network
   b. wide area network
   c. value added network
   d. metropolitan area network

9. In a _____ topology, multiple computers and devices are linked to a central computer, called a host.
   a. bus
   b. ring
   c. star
   d. hybrid

10. In _____ , all of the data bits are transmitted one bit after another in a continuous line.
   a. parallel transmission
   b. serial transmission
   c. unilateral transmission
   d. digital transmission

## Things That Think > Brainstorming New Uses

In groups or individually, contemplate the following questions and develop as many answers as you can.

1. Currently, connectivity to the Internet is achieved through utility providers such as telephone, cable, and wireless providers. What other utilities or service providers do you think might be used to provide additional ways to access the Internet? What benefits do these alternatives provide as compared with today's alternatives? What obstacles need to be overcome in order to make these alternatives appealing to the market?

2. Home builders often install sophisticated networks in new homes. Additional features above and beyond standard home wiring include high-speed Internet access; integrated security systems; appliance automation; and home theater wiring with Surround Sound.

How could this type of network wiring benefit institutions such as schools, libraries, and hospitals?

3. Infrared technology has been implemented in computer peripherals such as the keyboard and the mouse, and it can also be used to synchronize data between handheld computers and desktop computers. Because infrared signals are easily interrupted, this technology is most useful for devices that will be in close proximity to the desktop computer. Keeping that in mind, what other peripheral devices could take advantage of infrared technology? What devices should probably remain connected in other ways to maintain a constant connection?

## Key Principles > Completion

Fill in the blanks with the appropriate words or phrases.

1. _____ refers to the use of computer hardware and software for sending and receiving information over communications media, making it possible for computer users throughout the world to communicate with each other.

2. A physical link that allows computers to be connected to other computers in different locations is called a _____.

3. _____ refers to the way a network is designed and built.

4. A _____ topology combines different kinds of network layouts into one.

5. In a _____ topology, all computers are linked by a single line of cable.

6. In a _____ topology, each computer is connected to two other computers, with the entire network forming a circle.

7. Hardware and/or software that allows communication between two similar networks is called a _____.

8. Notebook and other portable computers use _____ modems.

9. Three possible directional protocols that determine the directional flow of transmissions among devices are _____, _____, and _____.

10. The World Wide Web uses the _____ to transfer Web pages to computers.

## *Tech Architecture >* **Label the Drawing**

In this illustration of a network, identify the type of topology. Then label each component and use arrows to show the path of communication on the network.

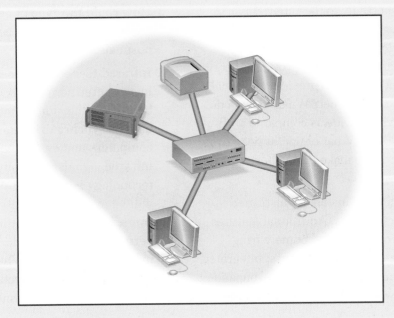

## *Techno Literacy >* **Research and Writing**

Develop appropriate written responses based on your research for each item.

1. What kinds of networks are used in your local area? Investigate the types of networks that local organizations are using. Begin your research with your school, then call or visit three businesses. Ask all parties for the same information: type of network, network topology, number of computers on the network, and the communications media used, including whether wired or wireless. Write a summary explaining why each organization established its particular setup. What were their primary needs, and how does the network meet those needs?

2. What are the benefits to businesses of providing free Wi-Fi access for customers in their establishments? Choose two or three businesses (near you, if possible) that provide Wi-Fi access to their customers. Possibilities include restaurants, cafes, and shopping malls. Determine whether they are providing free access to the public or whether they charge a fee for Wi-Fi usage. Summarize why you think the businesses do or do not provide free Wi-Fi access. Then describe what benefits businesses can realize by providing this access at no charge to customers.

## *Technology Issues >* **Team Problem-Solving**

In groups, brainstorm possible solutions to the issues presented.

1. Intranets typically provide individuals within an organization with access to relevant information, applications, and other resources, and an extranet typically extends access to a subset of these items that are relevant to specified external users. Prepare a list of subjects or areas that your school's intranet contains (or should contain). Now identify which of these areas might be relevant to provide to your family via an extranet.

2. Some companies and individuals find it difficult to obtain high-speed Internet access because they are located in remote areas, or in places with a customer base too small to interest an ISP. What do you think can be done to help these businesses and individuals? Do you think people have a right to high-speed Internet access? Should the government play a role in solving this problem?

## *Mining Data >* **Internet Research and Reporting**

Conduct Internet searches to find the information described in the activities below. Write a brief report summarizing your research results. Be sure to document your sources, using the MLA format (see Chapter 1, page 42, to review MLA style guidelines).

1. Data mining is a technology that businesses use to glean new information from the data stored in their databases. The technology uses relational tables similar to the way they are used in relational databases. For example, an auto dealership could use data mining to identify past customers who paid their car loans on time and then send those customers new product offerings. Large companies such as IBM and SAS are developing a comparable tool called text mining. Text mining will facilitate the analysis of thousands of textual documents that may be stored on a company's file server. Locate information explaining text mining; then write a summary of what it is and how it could be used. Try IBM's Web site as a first source: www.ibm.com.

2. Some cities and counties are building infrastructures to allow broadband wireless Internet access from any point within the jurisdiction, but many telecommunications and cable companies are opposed. Locate some examples of cities or counties that are implementing municipal wireless, and research the positions of both the government and the telecommunications and cable companies.

## *Technology Timeline >* **Predicting Next Steps**

Look at the timeline below summarizing major benchmarks in the development of the Internet. On the basis of your knowledge and any research you might conduct, think of three changes that may occur over the next 10 years and add them to the timeline.

**1957** With the Soviet Union's launch of Sputnik, the United States forms the Advanced Research Projects Agency (ARPA).

**1966** ARPA introduces its plan for a national network.

**1973** First international connections are made to the ARPAnet.

**1986** NSFNET is created.

**1991** World Wide Web is launched.

**1999** First full-service, Internet-only bank is opened.

**2000** The Department of Justice, FBI, and National White Collar Crime Center launch the Internet Fraud and Complaint Center (IFCC).

**2002** U.S. online retail sales reach $45 billion.

**2003** Nielsen NetRatings estimates there are 580 million Internet users worldwide.

**2005** The number of worldwide Internet users tops 1 billion.

**2009** 63% of American adults have broadband Internet connections at home.

## *Ethical Dilemmas* > **Group Discussion and Debate**

As a class or within an assigned group, discuss the following ethical dilemma.

As companies realize the consequences of security breaches in their systems, they are looking for experienced computer security specialists to help protect their systems from intrusions. Some companies hire former hackers, many of whom are convicted criminals, because they believe that their experience finding security holes is extremely valuable. Other companies would not even consider hiring them because of the security threats they pose to their employers.

If you were responsible for the security of a large company's network and systems, would you hire a consultant who was an experienced hacker or stick to a security consultant without a record of hacking? How would you convince management that you made the right decision? What safeguards would you put in place with the consultant to make sure that he or she was being thorough in the security assessment without taking advantage of his or her position?

# The Internet and the World Wide Web

# Cyber**Scenario**

**LYNETTE MENDOZA SPENDS HER LUNCH HOUR** planning the menu for a dinner party with friends later in the week. Using her desktop computer, she searches several recipe Web sites to find the right appetizer, soup, salad, main course, and dessert. After narrowing down her choices, she begins jotting down a grocery list.

Not remembering exactly which ingredients she already has at home, Lynette checks her refrigerator and pantry over the Internet. After logging into her family's Web site, Lynette selects a live video feed, and from miles away a webcam begins transmitting images of the refrigerator contents. She smiles, recalling the day she purchased the refrigerator with all its ultramodern connectivity features. Lynette remembers telling her husband that the options were great, but that she could

not picture herself ever using them. But here she is, viewing a full-color display of the inside of her refrigerator.

Lynette notes milk, eggs, cream, and several produce items that she needs. Scrolling back through the menu, she selects the pantry video feed to check her supply of pasta and baking staples. Once she finalizes her shopping list, she logs into her favorite online grocer's Web site. After clicking to add each item from the list into her virtual shopping cart, Lynette selects delivery for the following day and confirms her usual payment method.

In only thirty minutes, Lynette has planned a menu, determined which grocery items she needs to purchase, and placed an order for those items. A refrigerated delivery truck will deliver the groceries to her door at about the time she gets home the next day. With the time Lynette saved in each of these steps, she has much more time to spend preparing the meal in her kitchen.

As people with busy lives become more comfortable with the Internet, the usage of online grocery stores continues to rise. Industry studies projected online grocery sales to reach $6.2 billion in 2006, a 17 percent increase over 2005.

# The Internet: A Global Network

The Internet is the largest computer network in the world. Its design closely resembles a client/server model, with network groups acting as clients and Internet service providers acting as servers. An **Internet service provider (ISP)** is an organization that provides user access to the Internet, usually charging a subscription fee. Since the inception of the Internet in the early 1970s, this enormous invisible structure has expanded to connect more than 1 billion users worldwide. Many knowledgeable observers consider this vast system of networked computers and telecommunications systems the most significant technical development of the twentieth century, potentially connecting every person on Earth to vast resources of information and services.

Individuals, organizations, businesses, and governments use the Internet to accomplish a number of different activities, which can be subdivided into categories:

- communications
- entertainment
- electronic commerce
- research
- distance learning

## Communications

One of the chief functions of the Internet is its ability to allow people to quickly and easily communicate with one another. Internet users have a number of different communications applications that they can take advantage of, including e-mail, chat rooms, instant messaging, blogs, social networking services, electronic message boards, streaming video sites, telecommuting, and file transfer.

**Electronic Mail**   **Electronic mail (e-mail)** is the most widely used Internet application. It allows users to create, send, receive, save, and forward messages in electronic form. It is a fast, convenient, and inexpensive way to communicate. Computer industry research firms estimate that the number of e-mail mailboxes worldwide reached 1.3 billion in 2008. Further, IDC estimates that the number of e-mails sent on an average day now exceeds 36 billion. Unfortunately, about 80 percent of these messages are unwanted advertisements known as spam.

Each e-mail user has a unique electronic address, which is supplied by the user's ISP. Sending an e-mail message is simple. A message writer only has to specify the recipient's e-mail address, type a subject in the subject bar, create a message, and click the *Send* button. Figure 7-1 shows the Microsoft Outlook New Mail Message window.

In addition to sending messages, users can attach files to their e-mail messages. In Microsoft Outlook and Windows Mail, the attachment feature is called Insert File, and this button is marked with a paper clip. Virtually any kind of electronic document can be attached and sent with an e-mail message, including reports, spreadsheets, photos, and video files. Recipients can then open the attached files for viewing or storing on their computer.

Large file attachments are often compressed as zip files. A **zipped file** is usually half the size of the original file, meaning that it takes half the time to

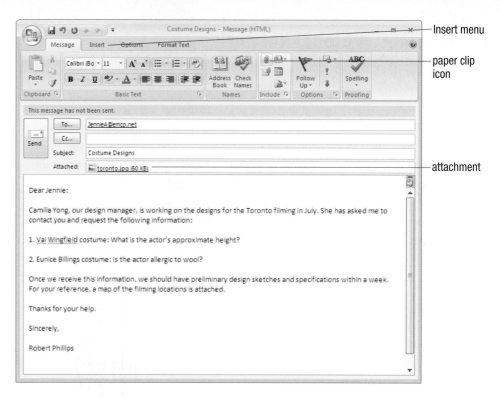

Figure 7-1 **Microsoft Outlook New Mail Message Window**
In Microsoft Outlook, users attach files to e-mail messages by clicking the paper clip icon, or by clicking Insert on the Menu bar.

**download** (copy from the host computer). Before a zipped file can be viewed it must be unzipped, a process that reverses the compression process and creates a new file that is full sized again.

Several free e-mail services are available, including Hotmail, Gmail, and Yahoo! Mail. Free e-mail services work by using a Web browser as an e-mail interface. After logging on to a free e-mail Web site, a computer user can send and receive e-mail messages. Providers can offer this service for free because their income is derived from the advertising that users must endure as they use a free e-mail account.

These services have several advantages over the mail service an ISP provides. The chief advantage, of course, is that they are free. Another advantage is that they can be accessed from any Internet connection because users are not tied to the connections their ISP offers. Users can also establish several free e-mail accounts to use for different purposes. Another convenience of free e-mail is that if users ever experience a problem, such as harassment, they can shut down their old free e-mail account and open a new one.

**Chat Rooms**   A **chat room** is an application that allows users to engage in **real-time dialog**, or live, instantaneous conversations with one or more participants. Most online services provide chat rooms. Users can sign up to participate in a chat room on almost any topic. For example, an environmentally conscious user can participate in a chat room discussing global warming. User comments and opinions can be exchanged freely and anonymously with other online participants, and are often frank and uncensored.

Go to this title's Internet Resource Center and read the article titled "Internet Social Networks." www.emcp.net/CUT4e

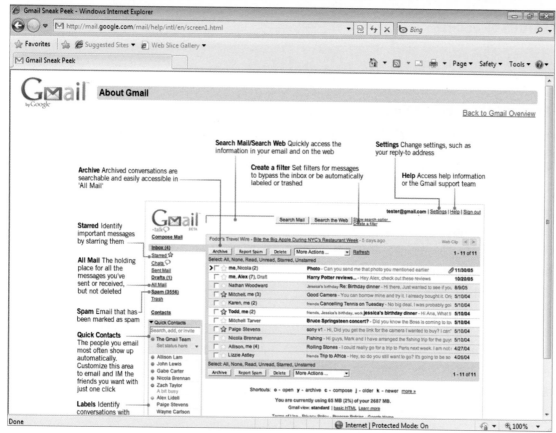

Google's Gmail is a free e-mail service that includes many valuable features.

**Instant Messaging**   **Instant messaging (IM)** works like a chat room, but usually with only two participants in a connection. IM also allows for conversations to take place in real time, using a chat-room-like environment. The process is similar to a telephone conversation, but all the communication is done via typing. People who know one another's handle (user name) can open connections and engage in one-on-one conversations. What makes this system different from normal chatting is that it constantly runs in the background while users are working on their PCs. The program automatically notifies users when someone wants to contact them for a chat. Because of this feature, IM systems demand a person's attention, making them more interruptive than e-mail.

Signing up for an instant messaging service is similar to signing up for a free e-mail account, such as is offered by hotmail.com. Usually, there is no fee for the service. AOL Instant Messenger, Yahoo! Messenger, and IRC (Internet relay chat) are popular IM systems. It is important for users to remember when talking to strangers through any form of chat that the system is essentially anonymous, and it can be difficult to determine with whom one is really communicating—and whether or not that person can be trusted.

The main use of IM has been social, but the corporate world has gradually accepted it as a business communications tool. Some corporate Web sites offer users the option of having interactive conversations with customer service representatives via instant messaging. Employees accustomed to instant messaging in their personal lives also find it convenient to communicate with coworkers and

**CREATORS OF GOOGLE**

# Larry Page and Sergey Brin

**LARRY PAGE AND SERGEY BRIN** succeeded in the market of online search engines and Internet directories at a time when it was already over-saturated with them. As the creators of Google Inc., they built the Internet's largest database of searchable content from the ground up by using new technology and continuous innovation.

Page and Brin met as graduate students at Stanford University. It took them a while to find a topic that they agreed on, but eventually they began working together to create a new type of search engine. Search engines operated on the basis of analyzing words and their location within Web sites. Brin and Page believed search results would be more relevant if they prioritized the Web sites whose links were posted most often.

They didn't originate this idea, but in 1998 they were the first people to build a program that could do it. The result: The most popular Web pages were the easiest to find.

Arriving several years after competitors such as Yahoo! Inc. took over the market, they had difficulty finding investors for their product.

Page and Brin first operated out of a dorm room at Stanford, and later moved to a friend's garage after raising almost $1 million. Google.com was answering 10,000 searches a day when *USA Today* wrote an article about the search engine with relevant results.

Brin and Page moved in early 1999 at a time when Google Inc. answered half a million queries per day, and they had a total of eight employees. Advertisers started paying attention to them and eventually some venture capital firms in Silicon Valley invested $25 million into Google. They quickly started hiring professionals from other companies and moved to the Googleplex, their headquarters in Mountain View, California.

After AOL/Netscape decided to use Google's search engine on its browser, Google jumped to 3 million searches every day. The site was named to the Top Ten Best Cypertech list in *TIME* magazine in 1999. In 2000, it became the largest search engine with over a billion page index. Page and Brin also pioneered a new type of advertising that used key-word targeting. The program, called Adwords, advertises products to the people most likely to be interested in them. This service opened another source of revenue for the company and as 2000 ended, Google was handling more than 100 million search queries a day.

Since going public in 2004, Google has been rolling out new features. The features, like the popular Google Toolbar, have helped the company survive in a market already heavily contested by Yahoo!, MSN, and AOL. Brin and Page have integrated more types of files into their database than any other search engine, and are now an internationally recognizable name.

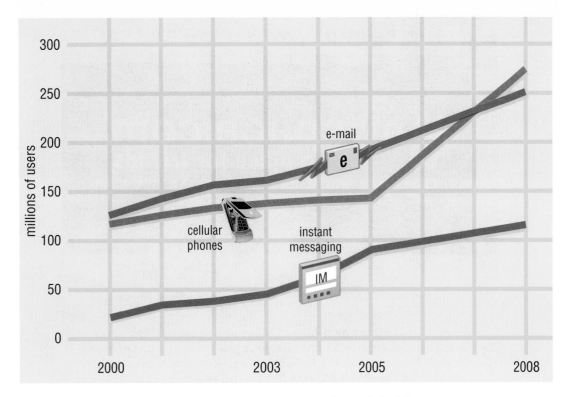

**Figure 7-2  Comparison of E-mail, Cell Phone, and IM Usage in the United States**

clients using this medium. As more organizations have realized the benefits of instant messaging, the vendors of instant messaging software have added business features and robust security to support this growing trend. Figure 7-2 shows a comparison of user numbers for e-mail, cell phones, and instant messaging based on statistics from Pew Research.

**Blogs**  Originally called a weblog (a combination of the words *Web* and *log*), a **blog** is a frequently updated journal or log containing chronological entries of personal thoughts and Web links posted on a Web page. The content and style of blogs vary as widely as the people who maintain them (called "bloggers"), but in general they function as a personal diary or guide to others with similar interests. Myspace.com and Blogger.com are Web sites specifically dedicated to supporting blogs. Collectively, the world of blogs is known as the **blogosphere**.

In the corporate world, blogs provide a unique opportunity for businesses to communicate with their employees, customers, and partners.

Blogging has become very popular among young adults and many campuses now ban access to blogs using school computers.

The largest and best-known host of blogs and personal Web pages is MySpace.com. Especially among the young, a great amount of Internet usage is being devoted to MySpace blogs. Many colleges and high schools around the United States have banned access to MySpace or are considering doing so.

Bloggers add a personal, informal tone to company communications, achieving a realism that sometimes is absent from the traditional glossy marketing brochures. This growing trend is under the careful watch of company attorneys, who are responsible for the company's image and disclosure of sensitive information.

**Social Networking Services**   Several very successful Web sites have arisen in recent years that allow people to create their own personal Web space and interact socially. These **social networking services**, such as Facebook, MySpace, and Twitter, have become a second home for millions of users. These sites are free and open to anyone to open an account and create their own content. Similar to personal blogs, but with less focus on essays and commentary, Facebook and MySpace pages are usually personalized with photos, message boards, and music. Twitter operates differently, allowing people to share text messages called *tweets* with anyone who cares to read their messages. Celebrities and journalists have their own Twitter accounts, so anything they transmit is relayed to thousands of followers.

**Message Boards**   A **message board**, often called simply a forum, is an electronically stored list of messages that anyone with access to the board can read. As with a classroom or dormitory bulletin board, users can post messages, read existing messages, or delete messages. The Internet provides access to thousands of boards around the world.

Like chat rooms, most message boards are centered on topics. Some people prefer them to social networking services because they are less intrusive. Instead of receiving e-mail messages that can fill up their mailboxes, users have the option of checking the boards at their convenience. Forums soon build up a body of information that users can access for future reference or research.

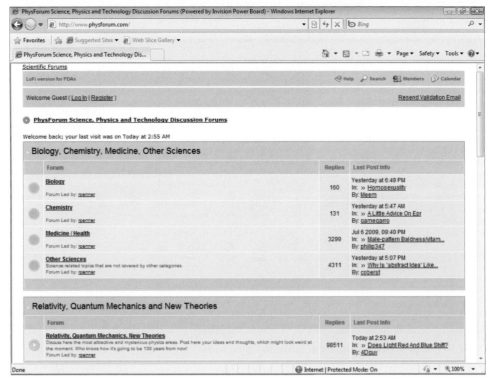

A message board provides access to posted messages related to a specific topic.

### Streaming Video Sites
Sites such as YouTube have become the Internet standard in **video streaming**. These Web sites offer free (except for the commercials) access to any videos that people care to upload. The videos range from political commentary to product reviews to random silliness. In order to be viewable without long wait times, the clips are often smaller and of lower visual quality than those watched on television.

### Telecommuting
Millions of workers are now performing their work activities at home by using a computer, a modem, and a telephone line. This activity is known as **telecommuting** (also called teleworking). Some employers have discovered that allowing employees to telecommute offers important advantages, including increased employee productivity, an opportunity to employ highly productive but disabled workers, and savings on travel costs to and from the workplace. Currently, about 15 percent of workers in the United States telecommute on a regular basis as part of their jobs.

Tech Demo 7-1
Real-Time
Meetings

### File Transfer Protocol
**File Transfer Protocol (FTP)** allows users to communicate by transferring files to and from remote computer systems. FTP was the original method used for transferring files on the Internet. Although Hypertext Transfer Protocol (HTTP) is now the standard means for accomplishing file transfers, FTP is still extensively used. Users often need authorization before they can access any files available on the remote system (FTP site), but some site operators allow users to log on anonymously. An FTP site displays files that users can click on to download to their computers. FTP allows any kind of file to be retrieved. For example, students can download lecture outlines made available on their school's FTP site, or an engineer can download and view blueprints placed on an architect's FTP site.

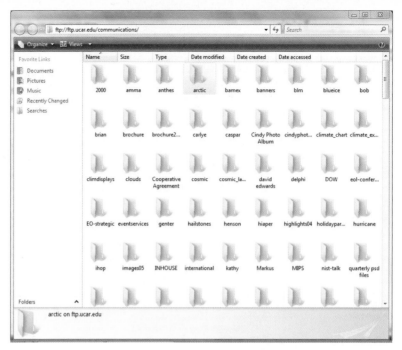

This FTP site shows files available for downloading.

## Entertainment

Using computers for entertainment purposes is a common activity among Internet users of all ages. Computers are capable of emulating almost all entertainment devices, and they can be used to play games, gamble, listen to music, or even to watch movies or video programs.

**Online Games**  The number of free games available online—including traditional games such as backgammon, checkers, and bridge—is enormous. Figure 7-3 illustrates the dramatic increase in Internet gaming revenue growth since 2000. Some

The online game *World of Warcraft* is the most popular online game in the world.

## FATHER OF THE WORLD WIDE WEB
# Tim Berners-Lee

**TIM BERNERS-LEE,** the father of the World Wide Web, graduated from Queen's College, Oxford, in 1976. While working as an independent consultant for the Centre Européen pour la Recherche Nucléaire (CERN) in Geneva, Switzerland, he conceived of a program for storing information based on the associations between ideas. This program, which Berners-Lee called Enquire, later became the basis for the World Wide Web. In 1984, Berners-Lee began a fellowship at CERN, where he worked on computer systems for scientific data acquisition. While a fellow at CERN, he proposed a hypertext system, based on his Enquire program, to be known as the World Wide Web. This system would allow computer users around the world to exchange information using linked hypertext documents. Berners-Lee introduced URLs, HTTP, and HTML; wrote the first World Wide Web server-and-client software; and created a WYSIWYG ("what you see is what you get") hypertext browser for the NeXT Step operating system.

The World Wide Web made its debut on the Internet in the summer of 1991. Since then, the Web has grown to become one of the primary modes of communication in the contemporary world. In 1994, Berners-Lee took a staff position at the Laboratory for Computer Science at the Massachusetts Institute of Technology, where he works as director of the W3 Consortium, an organization that sets standards and helps to bring coherence to global Web development.

Berners-Lee's efforts have earned him numerous awards. In 1995, he received the Kilby Foundation's Young Innovator of the Year award and was corecipient of the ACM Software Systems award. He has honorary degrees from the Parsons School of Design, New York, and Southampton University and is a Distinguished Fellow of the British Computer Society.

---

retail games, for example, *EVE Online* and *World of Warcraft,* require users to buy the software. Users can play by themselves or compete with other players. Virtual reality games are also on the rise. **Virtual reality (VR)** involves a computer simulation of an environment or set of surroundings that does not exist, but is reasonably convincing to the user. Games attempt to create a virtual reality by giving people a virtual body, called an **avatar**, which serves as their point of view in the game world. More than 11.5 million players pay monthly fees of approximately $15 to play *World of Warcraft*, the most popular online game in the world.

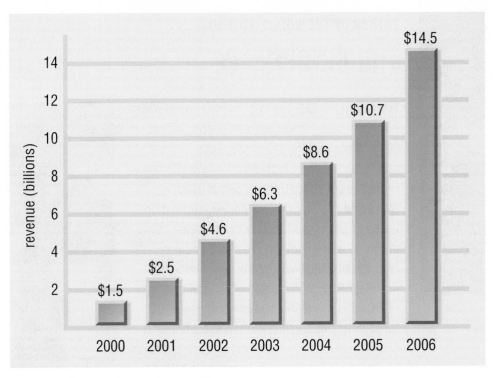

**Figure 7-3  Internet Gaming Revenue Growth**

**Online Gambling**  Online casinos are a novel and controversial entertainment feature. Users can log on and gamble in a virtual casino online. Although they may be prohibited by law in many areas, online casinos are difficult to police as they may be located in any part of the world. It may seem like playing a game, but any losses are real and will be billed to the user's credit card.

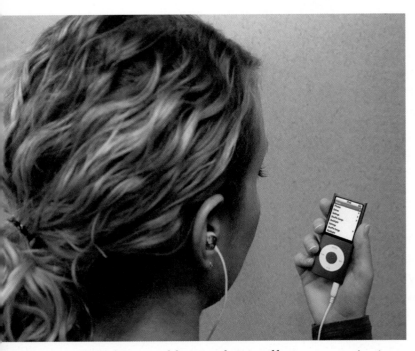

An iPod, a portable MP3 player, offers a convenient way to listen to music downloaded from the Internet.

**Music and Video**  Music from various Internet sources can be downloaded and played on computers. The most popular of the music download services is iTunes from Apple. Most music download Web sites charge service fees. Copyright considerations have placed some companies in legal jeopardy, with lawsuits and criminal liability, so downloading free music is not as easy as it once was. The section on peer-to-peer file sharing later in this chapter covers this issue in more depth.

Moving Pictures Expert Group Layer III (MP3) is the most widely used music file format. **MP3** is a compression format capable of reducing the size of CD music files by a factor of 10 to 14. This is done by removing recorded sound that the human ear cannot perceive. Because the MP3 format results in much smaller files, they are easily downloaded. Once a file is on a computer's hard disk, it can be transferred to a portable MP3 player, where it resides on the player's hard drive.

It is also possible to view video over the Internet, including television shows, music videos, and even movies. Many news networks and newspapers offer video on their Web sites. Users can click on a story and then view a short video newscast filling them in on all the details.

Internet users can view video files using an application such as Microsoft Windows' Media Player. There are many formats used for digital movies, such as MPEG, or the newer MP4 and WMV formats. There is no single standard that dominates digital movies the way MP3 files dominate music. Because video files are very large, downloading movies or long clips is a slow process unless a user has a high-speed Internet connection.

Obtaining and viewing illegal digital copies of movies is a common occurrence on many college and university campuses because these institutions are often equipped with the high-speed Internet connections that speed up the downloading process. As is the case with many music files, some video files are placed on the Internet in violation of their copyright terms, and are the subject of law enforcement efforts.

Go to this title's Internet Resource Center and read the article titled "Streaming Media." www.emcp.net/CUT4e

It is possible to download and play movies on tiny screen systems such as video iPods.

## Electronic Commerce

**Electronic commerce (e-commerce)** refers to the Internet exchange of business information, products, services, and payments. E-commerce is commonly divided into two categories defined by target audience: business-to-consumer (B2C) and business-to-business (B2B).

Online shopping expenditures make up the bulk of B2C e-commerce, with the top category being apparel, followed by books, music, videos, auction items, toys, and computer hardware. Each year, retail e-commerce sales continue to grow about 15 percent per year as a segment of overall spending. According to the U.S. Commerce Department, for example, retail e-commerce sales for the year 2008 were $134 billion and will grow to $329 billion by 2010. Online purchasing represents only about 2 percent of total retail sales, but the percentage has grown steadily for years (see Table 7-1).

Many retailers post online catalogs that potential buyers can browse before making a purchase. Selected items are added to a virtual "shopping cart." The shopping cart functions just like a real shopping cart, allowing customers to place purchases in the cart or remove them later if they change their mind. Once shop-

**Table 7-1  Retail Sales: Total and Online in 2008**

| 2008 Period | Total Retail Sales (millions) | E-Commerce Retail Sales (millions) | E-Commerce Percent of Total Sales |
|---|---|---|---|
| 4th quarter | $938 | $32 | 3.4% |
| 3rd quarter | $1,018 | $34 | 3.3% |
| 2nd quarter | $1,034 | $34 | 3.3% |
| 1st quarter | $1,027 | $34 | 3.3% |

Note: Figures do not include online travel services and ticket sales.
Source: http://www.census.gov/mrts/www/data/html/08Q4.html

ping is finished, the next stop is a virtual "checkout counter," where the customer pays for the purchase by entering a credit card number or by another electronic payment method. Within a few days, the items will arrive at the purchaser's address.

In addition to selling products and services, businesses are using the Internet to advertise products, order inventories from manufacturers and wholesalers, order raw materials, recruit employees, file government reports, and many other activities. These categories constitute the B2B segment of e-commerce. New business uses for the Internet are being discovered every day, and current uses are continually being improved to make them even more successful.

## Research

The Web has opened up thousands of opportunities for people interested in research. Aided by increasingly sophisticated software, users can explore any topic, from anacondas to Zen Buddhism. Information retrieval has become an important application for students, writers, historians, scientists, and the curious.

In addition to the information available on millions of Web sites, material from libraries and databases around the world also is available for viewing at the touch of a keyboard. Researchers can access books, periodicals, photos, videos, and sound files from the comfort of their own homes. Information can be read online or downloaded for later use.

A search engine is a good starting place to find practically anything on the Internet. Search engines are software programs available at Web sites that store searchable snapshots of the information found on millions of other Web sites. Most college research projects today begin on the Web rather than in the library, and the first tool used is the student's favorite search engine. Searching for information on the Internet will be discussed later in this chapter.

## Distance Learning

Many colleges offer online courses and study programs over the Internet. This relatively new Internet application is referred to as distance learning. **Distance learning** may be defined as the back and forth electronic transfer of information and course materials between learning institutions and students. A course presented in this manner is called an online course.

CREATORS OF YAHOO!
# David Filo and Jerry Yang

**DAVID FILO AND JERRY YANG** could be considered dinosaurs even though they are in their 30s. That's because they represent two of the few entrepreneurs to survive the dot-com meltdown. They were pioneers in the mid-nineties when they started classifying Web sites into categories and making the list accessible online in http format. The Internet directory they created would grow from *David and Jerry's Guide to the World Wide Web*, into Yahoo! Inc., the world's best-known Internet brand name, in a matter of years.

Yahoo! started developing as a business in 1995 after their pet Web site started getting more than 100,000 visitors daily. At the time it was run on a Stanford University server, but Yang and 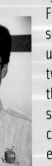 Filo's site was crashing the server because it was taking up too much space. The two were quick to realize the potential of the Web site and found a venture capitalist who was interested in supporting Yahoo! Meanwhile, they dropped out of Stanford and started making a business out of the site. They had to start hiring employees to deal with the workload, and the company soon started receiving take-over offers from bigger corporations.

America Online and Netscape Communications offered generous amounts of cash, but Yang and Filo refused. Their goal wasn't to become millionaires. They wanted to be in the business, to be the next Bill Gates. History shows that Yahoo! helped turn the Internet into what it is today.

In the following months they had plenty of challenges. The popular Web browser Netscape Navigator dropped the Yahoo! link after selling the top slot to a competing Internet Directory. However, Yahoo! quickly recovered from the blow and soon regained its growth rate. Eventually, the executives at Netscape changed their minds. They started carrying more than one Web directory link and charged an equal fee that was more reasonable to the companies. In this way many companies benefited and competition led to the further refinement of the directories.

By this time, Yang and Filo had decided not to sign onto any particular company because the market had not yet sorted out the winners from the losers. If they allied with a browser that failed, then they would have been out of business too. In 1996 Yahoo! went public and the business took off. The new billionaires Yang and Filo were granted reprieve from the business side of operating a company when the company hired CEO and President Terry Semel.

In today's market, Yahoo! is the best-known brand on the Internet and has more than 345 million users each month. They are also number one in advertising revenue, in large part due to the wide popularity of the site. In 10 years, Yahoo! became just another success story about a couple of kids from Silicon Valley. The site now offers news, e-mail, finance, personals, music, and shopping. The company has 7,600 employees in offices around the world.

Competitors such as Microsoft's MSN, AOL, and Google have begun to challenge Yahoo! Partly for this reason, the company is now turning more to entertainment under Semel's lead. Yahoo! and its creators still feel strongly about giving their users the services they want, and that philosophy should continue to help Yahoo! influence Web browsing in the future.

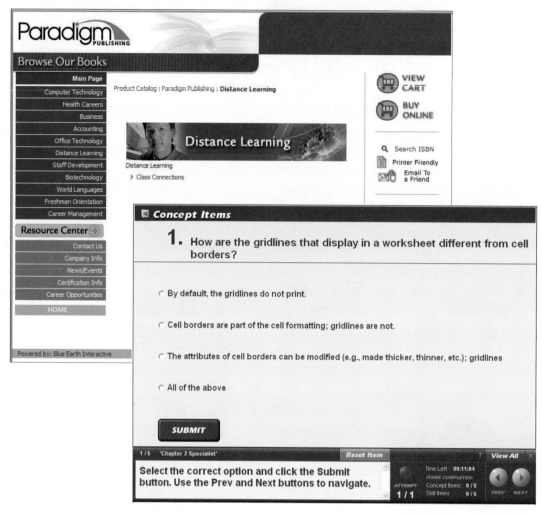

Online Learning Management Systems provide course resources to help both instructors and students with online course materials.

Preformatted platforms are available, and these platforms include pages to provide information about the course, communication tools such as online chat and e-mail, the ability to post and grade tests online, as well as provide learning resources to support course content. The top two online course platforms, WebCT and Blackboard, merged in 2006. The platform will remain under the Blackboard name, incorporating the best of both products. With Blackboard, instructors can provide their own content or take advantage of Blackboard-ready course content developed by textbook publishers.

Distance learning is becoming increasingly popular with students of all ages, and with people whose interests may not be included in a standard college curriculum or at a nearby school. It has also proved an attractive learning alternative for students whose schedules or careers make it difficult for them to attend regular classes. Distance learning offers them an opportunity to pursue or continue their education while maintaining their jobs.

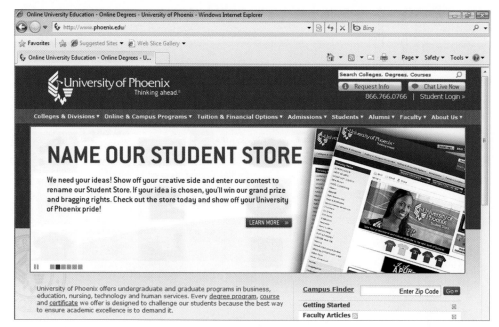

The University of Phoenix was one of the first providers of online college courses, and it remains a well-known provider of online learning opportunities.

# Connecting to the Internet

Millions of people throughout the world are able to connect to the Internet. Although China has the largest number of Internet users, some areas in Europe are showing strong growth. Figure 7-4 shows the top 15 countries in Internet usage as of the end of 2008, according to the Miniwatts Marketing Group. The organization estimates that by March 2009, the worldwide number of Internet users reached almost 1.6 billion.

## Hardware and Software Requirements

The following equipment and software are required to connect to the Internet:

- computer, personal digital assistant (PDA), or smartphone
- wireless network card, local area network card, digital subscriber line (DSL) modem, cable modem, or dial-up modem
- wireless network, local area network, telephone line, or cable connection
- Web browser
- an account with an Internet service provider (ISP) or value added network (VAN)

As previously defined, an ISP is a company that provides Internet access for a fee, or sometimes for free. Firms that provide free access usually require subscribers to view advertisements when viewing Web pages. A **value added network (VAN)** is a large ISP company that provides a connection to the Internet as well as additional content such as online news, weather forecasts, financial reports, and sports news. Some popular VANs are America Online (AOL) and the Microsoft Network (MSN). It should be noted that all ISPs and online services are equal in terms of the number of e-mail users and Web sites they can reach.

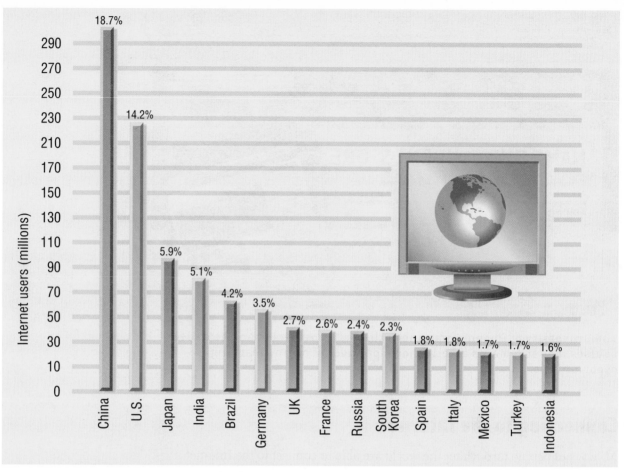

**Figure 7-4  Top 15 Countries in Internet Use in 2008**
The percentages indicate the percentage of total Internet use for each country.
Source: Miniwatts Marketing Group

ISPs are available on the local, regional, and national level. In the United States, local ISPs typically operate within a state, regional ISPs serve one or more states, and national ISPs provide connections from anywhere in the country. Larger ISPs provide local telephone numbers in several cities so that connections can be made without paying for long-distance calls. National ISPs are convenient for people who travel a great deal, but their monthly charges are usually considerably higher than local ISPs.

Many users opt for free ISP connections. These connections work well, but are always dial-up only. They also come with banner ads that take up a significant portion of the screen and are nearly impossible to avoid. Free services may insist that users occasionally click on ads or they will be disconnected. Anyone willing to put up with this inconvenience can surf for free.

## Types of Internet Connections

There are several different ways for users to connect to the Internet: dial-up, local area network (LAN), cable modem, digital subscriber line (DSL), wireless network, and satellite. Table 7-2 compares the connection speeds for each. Pew Internet and American Life Project reported that in 2008 nearly 85% of all connected households in the U.S. had DSL, digital cable, or satellite service.

**Table 7-2  Comparison of Internet Connection Speeds**

| Hardware | Download Speed* | Upload Speed* |
|---|---|---|
| 56 Kbps dial-up modem | 28 Kbps | 28 Kbps |
| LAN connection | 1 Mbps | 1 Mbps |
| cable modem | 1 Mbps | 500 Kbps |
| DSL | 1 Mbps | 500 Kbps |
| wireless | varies widely | varies widely |
| satellite | 500 Kbps | 56 Kbps |

*Upload speed means how fast you can send a file from your computer to another computer on the Internet. Download speed measures how fast you can receive a file from another computer. In most cases, download speed is more important.
Note: The speeds actually attained may vary greatly depending on quality of service and equipment.

**Dial-up Access**   **Dial-up access** allows access to the Internet over a standard telephone line by using a computer and a modem to dial into an ISP or VAN connection. Dial-up access is a feature typically included with the software an ISP or VAN provides. Once the software is installed, a dial-up access icon can be placed on the user's computer desktop (see Figure 7-5). Clicking on the ISP or VAN icon initiates a connection to the Internet. Advanced computer users can also configure dial-up connections from within a Windows operating system.

**Local Area Network (LAN) Connection**   A **local area network (LAN) Internet connection** provides faster and more direct Internet access by connecting users to an ISP on a direct wire at speeds 20 or more times faster than can be achieved through a dial-up modem. Because they are more expensive than dial-up access,

**Figure 7-5  Windows Vista Desktop with ISP Setup Icons**
Clicking one of the ISP or VAN icons provides a connection to the Internet.

# Surf 'n' Fly

**HAVE YOU EVER WANTED TO CHECK E-MAIL** or browse the Internet during an airline flight? Broadband service in flight is a reality.

For a short time, Boeing's Connexion wireless service was offered on commercial airlines but was phased out at the end of 2006. In 2008, Aircell began offering Gogo Inflight Service on American Airlines and it is now offered on several other airlines. Passengers can connect with any Wi-Fi-enabled device, including Macintosh and Windows laptops, certain BlackBerry and Palm devices, and Apple iPhone and iPod Touch. Usage plans range from about $8 to $50, and free content such as travel guides and access to the Wall Street Journal Online is offered with the service. Currently over 5,000 Aircell systems are installed and in the air, with about 410 of those systems on commercial airlines. Tests gauge the connection speeds at about 600 Kbits for downloads and 300 Kbits for uploads.

Panasonic plans on releasing a competing service in mid-2009 called eXconnect with rates starting at $11.95. With download speeds of 30-50 Mbit and upload speeds of 1.5 Mbit, eXconnect will offer much faster connection speeds than Aircell.

Both systems rely on satellite Internet connections but use different hardware infrastructures. Boeing's Connexion service failed largely due to a lack of popularity among passengers. But as broadband adoption in the home continues to grow, it is likely the population's reliance on a constant Internet connection will translate to more demand for the service on flights—which could mean huge success for Aircell and Panasonic.

LAN connections are more commonly found in the workplace. Despite the increased cost ($20 to $50 per month), by the end of 2008 more than 66 million (up from 42 million in 2005) LAN users in the United States were using cable and DSL connections to connect from their homes.

**Cable Modem**   The same coaxial cable that provides cable television service can also provide Internet access to a household. Cable TV companies provide a special modem and software for **broadband** (high-speed) Internet access. This method allows simultaneous television viewing and Internet usage, but the service is not available everywhere. In addition, the service slows down as more subscribers sign up in a neighborhood or location. Nationwide, as of 2008, there were more subscribers to DSL than to cable modem service, with about 46% of home broadband users on DSL and 39% on cable. The cost of basic cable modem service is about $30 to $60 monthly, plus a possible installation fee.

**Digital Subscriber Line** **Digital subscriber line (DSL) Internet service** is also broadband Internet access. It is as fast as a cable modem and provides simultaneous Web access and telephone use, but the service is usually available only to users within three miles of the telephone carrier's central switching office. The line is dedicated to one household, and is not shared with neighbors. A DSL provides access to the Internet through the user's existing phone lines, with the phone carrier or Internet service provider providing the DSL modem and the network card. DSL service costs about $20 to $50 monthly, plus an installation fee. Some carriers include the Internet service account in the monthly fee for the line.

**Wireless** The fastest growing segment of Internet service involves wireless connections to the Internet. Thousands of wireless or Wi-Fi hot-spots are springing up, allowing access in public places and even aboard airplanes with a wireless network card. Wi-Fi supports the IEEE standard for radio-wave connections to the Internet. Wireless connections to the Internet are often slower than wired connections, but they provide a great deal of portability. Many Wi-Fi hot-spots are free for users, and wireless service providers also provide broader access for a fee.

**Satellite** Downloading Web files is quick via satellite, but uploading is not as fast. To use a satellite connection, a person needs a satellite dish, a modem built into the PC or handheld, and an Internet account. Costs are about $50 per month for the service, plus about $350 for the dish, modem, and installation charges.

Users can access the Internet if they have a wireless network card in their computer and there is a wireless router in range.

# Navigating the Internet

Once they are connected and online, the next step for users is to start up a Web browser to begin surfing the Web. To access and move about the Web they need to know how to navigate using a browser, an activity called **surfing**. It is also helpful to know something about Internet protocol (IP) addresses and Uniform (or Universal) Resource Locators (URLs), and to know how these are used to identify and locate all the resources available on the Internet.

Tech Demo 7-2
Wireless Access Point

## Web Browsers

A Web browser is an application that finds Web pages and displays them on the computer screen. The two most popular browsers are Microsoft's Internet Explorer and Mozilla's Firefox. Internet Explorer currently holds about 70 percent of the browser market. Both offer the following capabilities:

- automatic identification and connection to any local port providing a connection to the Internet
- HTML code viewing (the language of Web pages)
- Java applet support (special programs written for the Web)
- easy-to-use interfaces that allow for control commands such as a favorites list, a stop access button, and a go-back button

Go to this title's Internet Resource Center and read the article titled "Browser Evolution." www.emcp.net/CUT4e

## Internet Protocol Addresses and Universal Resource Locators

Tech Demo 7-3
URL Structure

Web browsers locate material on the Internet using **Internet Protocol (IP) addresses**. An IP address works like an Internet phone number. It is a four-group series of numbers separated by periods, such as 207.171.181.16, representing a server on the Internet. Every server connected to the Web can be located using its IP address.

Since remembering IP numbers would be difficult, every computer also has a corresponding Web address called a **Uniform** (or **Universal**) **Resource Locator (URL)**. For example, the IP address above is represented by the URL http://www.amazon.com, home page of the pioneering online bookseller Amazon.com.

A URL constitutes a **pathname** describing where the information can be found on the Internet. It contains several parts separated by a colon (:), slashes (/), and dots (.). The first part of a URL identifies the communications protocol to be used. In the case of the Amazon home page above, it is hypertext transfer protocol (HTTP). The material immediately following the protocol is format information, such as *www* for World Wide Web pages. Following the format information is the **domain name**, identifying the person, organization, server, or topic (such as Amazon) responsible for the Web page. The **domain suffix** comes last, identifying the type of organization.

In the Amazon example, *com* stands for company. A Web-based enterprise is often referred to as a **dot-com company** because the company's domain name ends with ".com". Table 7-3 lists other domain suffixes in common use. Table 7-4 lists the country abbreviations.

In 1998, the U.S. Commerce Department created the Internet Corporation for Assigned Names and Numbers (ICANN) and assigned it the task of expanding the list of existing domain suffixes. In late 2000, ICANN acted on this authority to approve a number of new suffixes (see Table 7-5).

Experienced Web surfers may notice that some URLs include a forward slash (/) and a name after the domain suffix, such as http://www.nasa.gov/mars. This

### Table 7-3  Common Domain Suffixes Used in URLs

| Suffix | Institution or Organization | Example |
|---|---|---|
| .com | company or commercial institution | Ford, Intel |
| .edu | educational institution | Harvard, Washington University |
| .gov | governmental site | NASA, IRS |
| .int | international treaty organization, Internet database | NATO |
| .mil | military site | U.S. Department of Defense |
| .net | administrative site for the Internet or ISPs | EarthLink, Qwest |
| .org | nonprofit or private organization or society | Red Cross |

### Table 7-4  Country Name Abbreviations in URLs

| | | | | | | | |
|---|---|---|---|---|---|---|---|
| **af** | Afghanistan | **fr** | France | **nz** | New Zealand | **ch** | Switzerland |
| **au** | Australia | **de** | Germany | **no** | Norway | **tw** | Taiwan |
| **at** | Austria | **il** | Israel | **pl** | Poland | **uk** | United Kingdom |
| **be** | Belgium | **it** | Italy | **pt** | Portugal | **us** | United States |
| **br** | Brazil | **jp** | Japan | **ru** | Russia | **yu** | Yugoslavia |
| **ca** | Canada | **kr** | Korea | **za** | South Africa | **zw** | Zimbabwe |
| **dk** | Denmark | **mx** | Mexico | **es** | Spain | | |
| **fi** | Finland | **nl** | Netherlands | **se** | Sweden | | |

element is an optional addition called a **file specification**, and indicates the name of a file or file folder. At some Web sites a vast amount of information is available on the server. Typing the file specification after the domain suffix will allow easier and faster access to the information, if a user knows the name of the file, page, or folder she is seeking.

## The Path of a URL

After a URL is typed into a browser window, it is sent to the Internet (see Figure 7-6). Routers then identify it and forward the request to the appropriate Web server. The Web server uses the HTTP communications protocol to determine which page, file, or object is being requested. Upon finding the item, the server sends it back to the originating computer, where it is displayed on the screen.

## Packets

A file sent over the Internet is not sent as a single file. Instead, messaging software breaks each file into packets and sends them over separate routes. The path a packet takes depends on which servers are available. This process is called

### Table 7-5  New Domain Suffixes

| Suffix | Category |
|---|---|
| .aero | airline groups |
| .biz | business use |
| .coop | business cooperatives |
| .info | general use |
| .museum | museums |
| .name | personal Web sites |
| .pro | professionals |

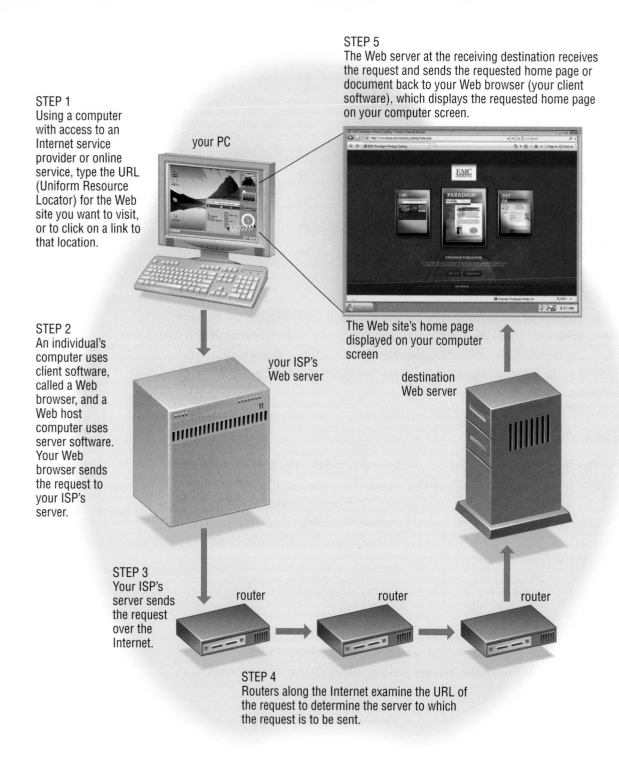

**STEP 5**
The Web server at the receiving destination receives the request and sends the requested home page or document back to your Web browser (your client software), which displays the requested home page on your computer screen.

**STEP 1**
Using a computer with access to an Internet service provider or online service, type the URL (Uniform Resource Locator) for the Web site you want to visit, or to click on a link to that location.

your PC

The Web site's home page displayed on your computer screen

**STEP 2**
An individual's computer uses client software, called a Web browser, and a Web host computer uses server software. Your Web browser sends the request to your ISP's server.

your ISP's Web server

destination Web server

**STEP 3**
Your ISP's server sends the request over the Internet.

router          router          router

**STEP 4**
Routers along the Internet examine the URL of the request to determine the server to which the request is to be sent.

**Figure 7-6  Connecting to the Internet**
A URL directs routers and servers to display the specific Web page identified by the URL.

**packet switching**. Figure 7-7 shows the journey an Internet message sent from Seattle might be broken down into packets, each taking a different route to the final destination of Miami. At the destination, a computer receives the data and reassembles the file. If any pieces are missing, the receiving computer requests that they be sent again. This is why Web pages sometimes appear incomplete, and some portions may take longer than others to fully load. The path a single packet takes is detailed in Figure 7-8.

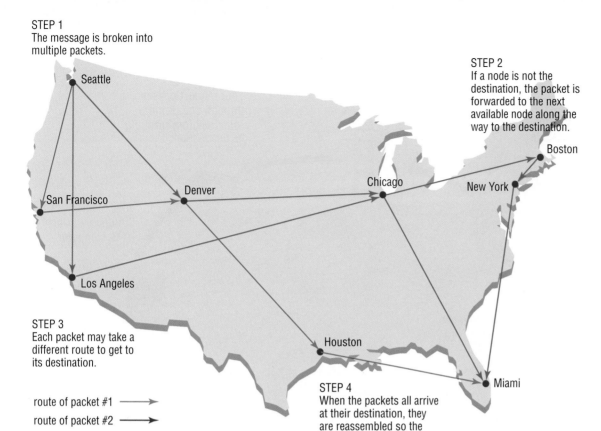

STEP 1
The message is broken into multiple packets.

STEP 2
If a node is not the destination, the packet is forwarded to the next available node along the way to the destination.

STEP 3
Each packet may take a different route to get to its destination.

route of packet #1 ⟶
route of packet #2 ⟶
route of packet #3 ⟶

STEP 4
When the packets all arrive at their destination, they are reassembled so the message can be read.

**Figure 7-7 Packet Switching**
Messages sent over the Internet are broken into separate files, or packets, and then are reassembled at the destination.

The concept of dividing files into packets has its origins in the Cold War, when the Internet was originally conceived as a system to maintain communication among the military and other government agencies in the event of a nuclear war. To prevent breakdowns, the system is designed to keep working even if part of it is destroyed or inoperable. A packet sent from New York to Los Angeles, for example, might travel through Denver or Dallas, but if those systems are busy (or destroyed) the packet could go up to Toronto before returning to Los Angeles. This design feature, called **dynamic routing**, is part of what makes the Internet work so well even with heavy traffic loads.

# Viewing Web Pages

A **Web page** is the term for a single document viewable on the World Wide Web. A **Web site** comprises all of the Web pages composing the site. The first Web page displayed when a Web site is accessed is usually the site's home page. Like the table of contents in a book, the **home page** is an overview of the information and features contained within the site.

A special type of Web site is called a **portal**, or a site that acts as a gateway to access a variety of information. A portal serves as a "launching pad" for users to navigate through categorized Web pages within the same Web site or across multiple Web sites. The U.S. government's FirstGov Web site (http://www.firstgov. gov) is an example of a portal. The majority of the material on the FirstGov site

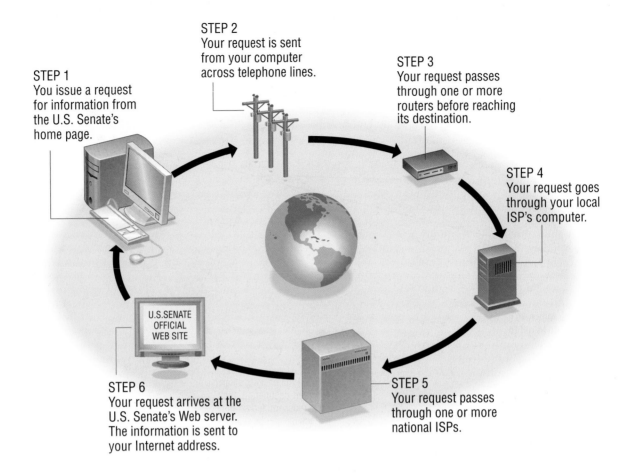

**STEP 1**
You issue a request for information from the U.S. Senate's home page.

**STEP 2**
Your request is sent from your computer across telephone lines.

**STEP 3**
Your request passes through one or more routers before reaching its destination.

**STEP 4**
Your request goes through your local ISP's computer.

**STEP 5**
Your request passes through one or more national ISPs.

**STEP 6**
Your request arrives at the U.S. Senate's Web server. The information is sent to your Internet address.

U.S.SENATE OFFICIAL WEB SITE

Figure 7-8 **The Path of a Single Packet across the Internet**

is located on the FirstGov servers, but there are also links to individual federal, state, and local government agency Web sites. The home page for FirstGov contains an overview of the information contained within the site.

## HTML

Web pages are created using **Hypertext Markup Language (HTML)**. HTML is the programming language used to create Web pages. A **markup language** is a set of specifications describing the characteristics of elements that appear on a page, including headings, paragraphs, backgrounds, and lists. A **hypertext document** presents information enhanced with links to other documents. This presentation method allows users to read only the basic information or click the links to access additional information on another Web page. Technically called a **hyperlink**, a Web link is any element on the screen that is coded in HTML to transport viewers to another page or site. Links are often underlined text. However, they can also take the form of buttons, photos, or drawings. HTML gives developers wide latitude in determining the appearance and design of Web pages. Most Web browsers, including Microsoft's Internet Explorer and Mozilla's Firefox, can display Web pages in HTML format.

The U.S. government's official Web site, called USA.gov (at http://www.usa.gov) is a portal, providing access to information about all aspects of government. This home page contains links to information on millions of government Web pages.

## XML

A new and improved Web language called **Extensible Markup Language (XML)** is becoming increasingly popular. Whereas HTML defines only the format of a Web page, XML organizes and standardizes the structure of data so that computers can communicate with each other directly. XML is more flexible than HTML,

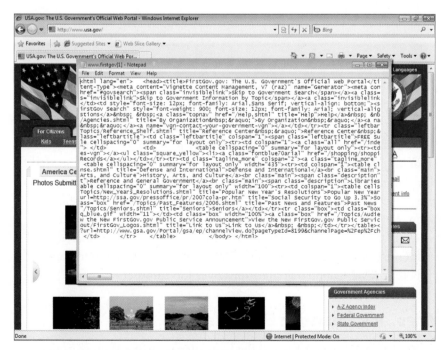

HTML tags are located within angle brackets (< >). The text in between the tags is the content that a visitor using a Web browser will view.

# The Web Squared World

**YOU'VE PROBABLY HEARD OF WEB 2.0.** The term, coined by O'Reilly Media founder Tim O'Reilly at a conference sponsored by his company in 2004, refers to the interactive and collaborative aspects of Internet content that was beginning to emerge at that time, most notably through Web sites like Facebook and Twitter. In 2004, Web 2.0 was the "future" of the Internet. But now that the future is the present, O'Reilly has come up with a new term to describe where the Internet is headed: Web Squared, or "Web meets world."

Web Squared describes the way the collaborative Internet content created in Web 2.0 is becoming increasingly integrated with the real world, particularly through the use of smartphones like the iPhone. These devices are called "smart" for a reason—they have their own senses, in the form of cameras, microphones, and motion and location sensors, which they put to use through the phone's various applications. According to O'Reilly, the "applications use all the senses, coordinating them much like the human brain." Current examples include GPS applications that track your progress as you travel toward a destination and update your arrival time based on traffic conditions, and the popular iPhone application that can identify a song's title and artist just by hearing a few seconds of it. In this way, Web Squared means the emergence of an enhanced reality, where the content of the Internet and the sensors on our smartphones combine with our own five senses to help us to instantly draw conclusions about the world that would not otherwise be apparent.

Web Squared is still growing, and new, often surprising, possibilities continue to be discovered. The Web has met the world—but what exactly will come of their relationship remains to be seen.

---

as it is really a **metalanguage** (a language for describing other languages). It allows developers to design their own custom languages that work with limitless types of documents and file formats. Using an XML application, for example, suppliers and manufacturers could turn their computers loose in the Internet market, letting them find, purchase, and sell products and services through XML-coded sites. Medical researchers could allow their computers to search the databases of other research centers to identify possible treatments based on new scientific breakthroughs. Several software producers, including Microsoft, are now using XML in developing some of their applications. Microsoft's .NET technology and the Microsoft Office suite both incorporate XML to manage data and to connect directly with other XML-enabled applications over the Internet.

## Audio, Video, and Animation Elements

Most computer users are accustomed to the basic elements of a Web page that attract and hold the interest of those viewing the page, such as text, photos, and links. As the Web grows more sophisticated, elements such as sounds and movies are being incorporated into pages to increase attention and expand the range of activities a Web page can perform. Various miniprograms make these additions possible, including Java applets, and plug-ins such as Shockwave, Apple QuickTime, Adobe Acrobat Reader, and Macromedia Flash Player.

**Java Applets**   **Java** is a programming language Web site designers frequently use. It was created for use on the Internet, and is similar in nature to the C or C++ programming languages. Java applets are small Java programs Web browsers run. (An *applet* is the term for a miniature program.) Like macros, Java applets provide the ability to program online games and highly interactive interfaces.

**Cookies**   A **cookie** is a very small file a Web site stores on a user's hard drive when the user visits the site. Often, these files are harmless and are used to store preference information, such as your user ID and password at a chat site. Sometimes, however, these files can be used to track the surfing habits of users without their knowledge. By placing a file on your computer that indicates what sites you have visited, other related sites can read this information and track your actions. Security settings on your browser can be adjusted to warn you when cookie files are being accessed or to prevent their operation altogether.

**Plug-Ins**   Sometimes a Web site will ask for approval to add a plug-in to the viewer's Web browser. A **plug-in** is a miniprogram that extends the capabilities of Web browsers in a variety of ways, usually by improving graphic, sound, and video elements. Most plug-ins are harmless, without any hidden features that may cause problems. However, as a general rule it is a good idea to view a site before giving permission to load any plug-ins. If there are viewing errors, they are probably caused by missing plug-ins. If users think the site is trustworthy, they can hit the *Refresh* button on the browser, which automatically reloads the site and causes the plug-in dialog box to reappear. The "Yes" box granting permission to install plug-ins can be selected, allowing improved Web page performance.

One of the most widely known plug-ins is Shockwave by Macromedia. Sites using Shockwave normally take longer to load, but are graphically superior, with higher-resolution graphics, interactive features, and streaming audio. Flash Player and Apple's QuickTime are two other popular plug-ins that let users experience animation, audio, and video.

Go to this title's Internet Resource Center and read the article titled "Plug-ins, Applets, and ActiveX Controls."
www.emcp.net/CUT4e

## Advertisements

Advertising is a necessary commercial Web page element, producing income for the companies that own and maintain Web sites. With the economic downturn the technology industry experienced in 2001, dot-coms came under increasing pressure from investors to earn more revenue from hits (visits) at their Web sites. As a result, many of these companies have experimented with forms of advertising that vary from being interesting to downright annoying.

**Banners**   A **banner** is a graphic that invites viewers to click it so that they will be directed to a new Web site selling a product or service. Banners are usually rectangular shapes appearing across the top or bottom of a Web page. This is a

Web sites sell advertising space in the form of pop-ups. Although this provides a source of revenue, it can result in visitors leaving the site.

common ad form that can provide helpful information for those interested in the product being advertised. However, some Web masters place so many banners on their Web pages that visitors find them annoying; sometimes to the point that they will leave a site and go elsewhere.

**Pop-Up Windows**   Another common and only slightly less intrusive form of advertisement is the **pop-up window**. Named for their tendency to "pop" unexpectedly into the middle of the screen, these windows can be closed or minimized so the viewer can see the Web page. Minimizing a pop-up will sometimes cause it to cease functioning, while closing it may make it pop up again later. In extreme cases, pop-ups may be designed to resist any attempt to remove them. They may have no readily apparent closing "X" in the upper corner, or they might just fire back onto the screen as fast as they can be clicked off. On Windows machines, pop-ups without *Close* buttons can often be removed by pressing Alt-F4. Most Web browser software has **pop-up blocker** features that can be turned on to avoid this sort of nuisance.

**Blind Links**   Some links misrepresent their true function. A frequently encountered example is a link with wording such as "Next Page," that actually directs viewers to an advertising Web page. This deception is called a **blind link**, and reputable Web page designers consider it bad form. Blind links are often encountered on free-host Web sites. These sites do not charge a fee for hosting Web pages, but do require that the pages display banners and other forms of advertising chosen by the company hosting the Web pages.

A blind link is designed to look like a Microsoft dialog box. If viewers click it, they will be directed to a Web page selling a product or service.

**Hi-Jacker**   Another common form of Web access trouble is the Web hi-jacker. A **hi-jacker** is an extension to your Web browser that causes your efforts to reach a certain page to be redirected to another page—generally one that is filled with advertisements. Sometimes these hi-jackers attempt to demand a fee to remove them. Often if you work with the security settings in your Web browser and delete and/or uninstall any Web browser extensions, you can get rid of the unwanted hi-jacker. In extreme cases, reinstalling windows always works, but is usually not necessary.

## Elements that Track Surfing

Many Web sites are connected to databases that allow retailers and other types of companies to gather information on visitors. Such Web pages implement a program, called a **Common Gateway Interface (CGI) script**, that automatically sends information to the Web page's database. Typically, the script is programmed to run when users perform a specific task on a Web site, such as click a *Purchase* button or an advertisement. Users will know that they are being tracked if they move their mouse over a possible advertisement and notice that a long URL appears on the browser status bar at the bottom of the screen. These URLs usually end with a string of letters and numbers. The issue of tracking Web site visitors is a hot topic among people concerned about protecting individual privacy.

## Escaping Web Page Traps

Some Web sites can actually change browser settings permanently, or may attempt to prevent viewers from leaving by continually popping up more windows and disabling the *Back* button. This is called a **Web page trap**. Viewers can avoid these traps by altering Web browser settings to increase the level of security. This will cause the browser to prompt users whenever it encounters suspicious behavior.

When the visitor's cursor is over the banner (red circle), the status bar (yellow highlight) reveals a URL with an address indicating the banner contains a CGI script designed to track visitors.

# Wireless, USA

**THE MOVE TO GO WIRELESS** is sweeping across the country. More than 250 municipalities have either already set up citywide Wi-Fi or have projects in the works. While some cities offer a high-speed Internet connection for a minimal rate, other municipal networks provide completely free access that relies on income from an advertising banner on the browser.

A wireless network is a boon for any city. Government workers on the road can stay connected to the home office. Schools and students will have unlimited access to educational resources. Local business has a new, high-tech venue to offer products and services. Most important, citizens previously unable to afford an Internet connection will get a chance to join the digital world.

Not everyone is pleased with the trend for government wireless. The telecomm companies that have already invested millions for existing services are understandably furious and are lobbying in a number of states for a ban on municipal broadband.

Critics also warn that cities committing to wireless may find themselves trapped by quickly outdated technology. Each hot spot can cover only so much ground, so a city-wide wireless system depends on a mesh network that extends transmission distance by relaying signals from one antenna to another. Yet there are no current standards for mesh systems, and many of the providers are relatively new and unproven. If a vendor goes under, it may be impossible for a city to update or connect with a new company.

Despite these concerns, cities are moving forward with their wireless plans. In a world where high-speed Internet connection is seen as not just a luxury but as an economic necessity, the desire to get everyone online is a major priority for city governments.

Unfortunately, these higher security settings may cause the browser to prompt users constantly, even when they are visiting legitimate sites. If users do fall into one of these traps, they can press the Control-Alt-Delete key sequence, which will open the Task Manager. The computer can be rebooted, or the affected program can be selected and closed.

## WebRings

One relatively safe way to move from site to site on the Internet is by using a WebRing. Each site on a **WebRing** maintains a link to the next site, forming a ring, hence the name WebRing. WebRings link sites devoted to a similar theme or topic. Sites dedicated to hobbies or special interests typically include this navigation feature. WebRings are generally moderated by someone who wants to help people find Web sites that would not otherwise be easily accessible. WebRings are an excellent way for hobbyists to find soul mates who share their passion for falconry, old cars, nineteenth-century tea sets, or hundreds of other interests.

The Yahoo! WebRing home page at http://dir.webring.com/rw has listings for hundreds of different WebRings organized around different topics.

# Searching for Information on the Internet

One of the most useful capacities of the Internet is its ability to act like a global library of limitless data on practically any topic. Better still, it doesn't even require a library card or a trip to a university to use it. At present, more than a billion pages of information are available on the Web.

Users can search for and retrieve information from Web pages by using a search engine. Recall that a search engine is a software program that can find and retrieve information located on the World Wide Web. Unlike a browser, in which an address is entered to access a Web site, a search engine allows users to locate information by entering search criteria in the engine's search box. For example, suppose a student wants to find information about the Battle of Vicksburg for a history class report. Typing the search criteria—in this case the words "Battle of Vicksburg"—in the search box, and clicking the *Search* button causes a list of articles, hyperlinked to their respective Web sites, to appear on the student's screen. They can be selected and read by clicking the article title. Figure 7-9 shows the basic search pages for two of the most frequently used search engines. Each of these pages contains a search text box as well as a search command button.

## Picking the Right Search Engine

Beginning Web users quickly discover that finding the information they need is not always easy. The first task is to locate a good search engine. Not all search engines offer the same features, and some perform certain types of searches better than others. Differences in capabilities are related to the number of Web pages an

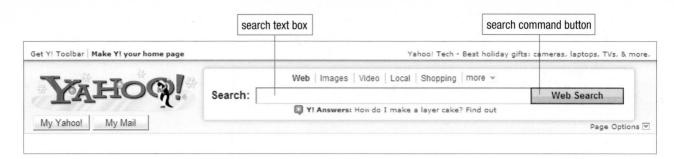

**Figure 7-9  Search Engine Text Boxes and Search Command Buttons**

engine catalogs, the search methodology used, and the number of different search tools available to refine searches.

Another factor to consider in selecting a search engine is that some now accept fees from Web sites so that they will be placed at the top of a search results list. This means that the first few entries on a search results list from that type of search engine may not necessarily contain information most relevant to the search criteria.

## Search Techniques

One of the primary considerations in any Internet search is placing the right **keywords** (also called search terms) in a search engine's search text box. Using too many keywords will result in users having to wade through hundreds or even thousands of search results to find what they are looking for. Using vague, obsolete, or incorrectly spelled terms further reduces the chances of a successful search. Users need to think of what combinations of words are likely to be found in the material they are looking for. To get the most out of a search, a user needs to know how a search engine's advanced search options work.

Advanced searching employs logic statements known as **search operators** to refine searches. Three of the most common search operators are AND, OR, and NOT. AND connects search terms and returns search results containing references to all the terms used. For example, asking the search engine to search for dogs AND cats would return only those sites containing references to both dogs and cats. Using OR returns results containing references to any of the search terms. Asking a search engine for dogs OR cats would result in sites that have references to either dogs or cats, or both. OR is usually the default logic option on search engines. NOT is used to exclude a keyword. Asking for

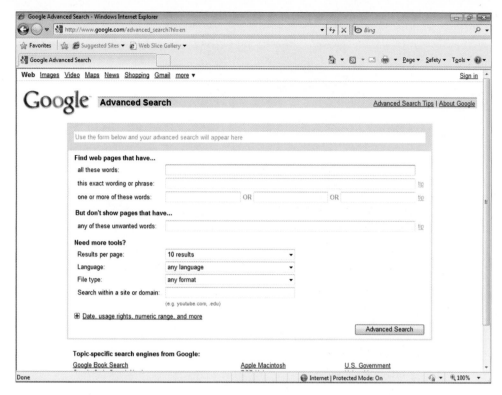

The Google Advanced Search page allows visitors to use advanced search functions in order to find more specific information.

dogs NOT cats would result in only sites that referred to dogs, but had no mention of cats.

Using logical statements and other advanced search features will greatly speed up the search process and increase the likelihood of success. There are almost a billion documents available on the Web, and as their numbers increase the likelihood of finding an individual document diminishes.

# Using Newer Internet Applications

The Internet is far from static. Not only does the content change daily, but the very way in which the Internet is used and understood as a communication medium is constantly evolving. Thousands of innovative applications are introduced each year, but only a few survive the tough demands of the marketplace.

## Peer-to-Peer File Sharing

**Peer-to-peer (P2P) file sharing** is a relatively recent player among popular ways to use the Internet. P2P allows people to download material directly from other users' hard drives, rather than from files located on Web servers. Napster, the famous pioneer of peer-to-peer file sharing, functioned by maintaining a list of files made available for sharing by subscribers to the system. For example, someone would let Napster know that he had 50 music files on his hard disk that he would be willing to share. Other users could then use Napster to locate these files and request that they be sent to their computers. Newer systems remove the central server entirely and allow user computers with the fastest connections to provide the search function and keep track of which computers have shared a file. Peer-to-peer is a power-

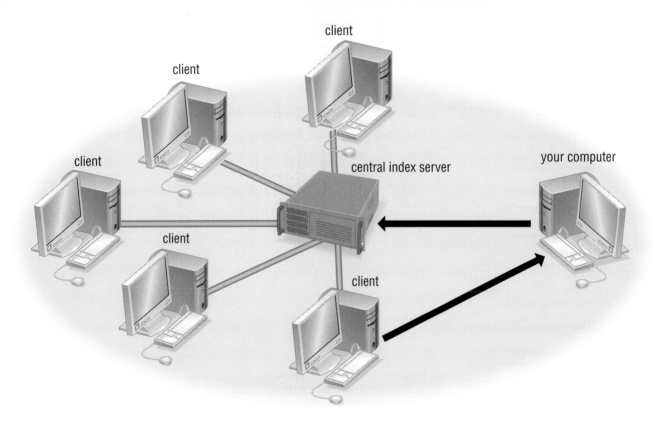

**Figure 7-10  Single File Download on a Peer-to-Peer System**

ful idea that allows every computer to function as a server as well as a client. Figure 7-10 shows the process of downloading a single file using a peer-to-peer system.

At its peak, Napster was being used to download music files by almost 70 percent of U.S. college students and had more than 70 million users worldwide. Unfortunately, many of the files being shared in this way were copyrighted material. Napster eventually lost a series of lawsuits copyright holders filed and was forced to shut down. After filing for bankruptcy and being acquired by Roxio, Inc., Napster was relaunched as a music download service in 2003. Currently, Napster is one of many services chasing market leader iTunes.

Today's peer-to-peer technologies allow the sharing of any type of file, including games, movies, and software programs. Since Napster, the biggest file-sharing technology has been BitTorrent. Industry research firms estimate that BitTorrent usage accounts for 35 percent of all Internet traffic. Although illegal files may be found and downloaded using BitTorrent, software companies and media companies such as TimeWarner are also embracing the distribution technology as another sales channel.

Using peer-to-peer technologies to harness the individual efforts of millions of computers around the world represents a vast potential for communications. However, with additional access comes increases in security risks.

### Internet Telephony

**Internet telephony** is another increasingly popular way to use the Internet. Through this technology, also called **Voice over IP (VoIP)**, two or more people with sufficiently good connections can use the Internet to make telephone-style

iTunes is the most popular music downloading service in the world.

calls around the world. Once the voices are digitized and broken down into packets, they can be transmitted anywhere, just like any other form of data.

There are three different methods of using VoIP: computer-to-computer, Internet-ready phones, and analog telephone adapter (ATA). Through computer-to-computer telephony, users at each end of the connection download and install a shareware program that uses the computer's sound card and Internet connection to translate the words spoken through a microphone by the sender into sounds that can be heard through speakers by the recipient. Internet-ready phones plug directly into an Internet connection and perform the same translation without separate software. ATA devices take the analog signal from a traditional phone and convert it into digital data that can be transmitted over the Internet. ATA is currently the most popular method in use.

The primary benefit of VoIP service is the elimination of long-distance telephone charges, and some customers are eliminating traditional telephone lines from their homes and making all calls using their VoIP service. In early 2006, there were more than 1,000 providers of VoIP services in the United States. The market leaders include pioneer Vonage as well as high-speed Internet service providers TimeWarner Cable and SBC Communications. The Yankee Group reported that the number of VoIP users likely reached 28.5 million by 2009, up from 150,000 users in 2003.

## Streaming Audio and Video

An alternative to downloading a piece of music or a video is to access it using a technique called **streaming** (also known as webcasting). Streaming sends a continuous stream of data to the receiving computer where it is immediately played as audio or video. Old data is erased as new data arrives. This protects the owner of copyrighted material to some degree, as a complete copy of the material is not downloaded, and therefore cannot be copied and shared. High-quality video streaming normally requires a broadband connection such as a cable modem, DSL, or LAN.

## Webcams

A tiny video camera called a **webcam** allows conversations over the Web through live video transmission. Often mounted on top of a computer monitor, the cameras automatically create and transmit video to the PC. Despite the fact that the images are a bit grainy and jerky, millions are in use. As the technology improves, their popularity is sure to increase even further.

## Audio Mail

**Audio mail** is a fledgling type of electronic mail that allows people to transmit messages by voice. As with e-mail, attachments can be included. The technology can be compared to voice mail, without telephone charges.

A webcam can be a fun way to stay connected through the Internet.

# Respecting the Internet Community

Internet users around the world form a community and, like any social organization, the community exhibits the entire range of behavior, from considerate and creative to insulting and damaging. Unfortunately, the anonymous nature of Internet interaction tends to bring out the worst in some people. The fear of embarrassment or shame that governs behavior in face-to-face encounters is lessened when people meet on the Internet. This means that some individuals act very differently than they would if they were in a public forum, ruining the Internet experience for many people. The problem is exacerbated by the fact that there are few repercussions for those behaving badly.

Guidelines for good Net behavior, called netiquette, have been developed to encourage people to interact productively. Moderated environments are another solution to inappropriate behavior. They allow a moderator to police behavior in certain settings such as chat rooms, social networking services, and message boards.

In addition to general guidelines, a number of technical and legal issues influence the direction and development of the Internet. Companies and individuals are clamoring for standard protocols and increased transmission bandwidths, consumers worry about the privacy and security of their Internet communications and transactions, and copyright holders are looking for stronger protection for their intellectual property.

## Netiquette

**Netiquette** is a collection of rules and guidelines that define good Net behavior. It is based on the Golden Rule, which stipulates that people should treat others as they would like others to treat them. The term netiquette is a result of combining the words *Net* and *etiquette*. Some netiquette exists to address behavior problems such as **flaming**, which is the Internet equivalent of insulting someone in a face-

**Table 7-6  Core Rules of Netiquette**

| | |
|---|---|
| **Rule 1** | Remember the human. |
| **Rule 2** | Adhere to the same standards of behavior online that you follow in real life. |
| **Rule 3** | Know where you are in cyberspace. |
| **Rule 4** | Respect other people's time and bandwidth. |
| **Rule 5** | Make yourself look good online. |
| **Rule 6** | Share expert knowledge. |
| **Rule 7** | Help keep flame wars under control. |
| **Rule 8** | Respect other people's privacy. |
| **Rule 9** | Don't abuse your power. |
| **Rule 10** | Be forgiving of other people's mistakes. |

Excerpted from the book *Netiquette* by Virginia Shea (Albion Books, 1994).

to-face setting. Taking advantage of their anonymity, some people seem to take a perverse joy in being as rude as possible, to the point that they drive people away. Flame wars are flames that are traded back and forth, often among multiple parties.

Other netiquette deals with certain Internet conventions that need to be learned in order not to inadvertently offend other users. For example, newcomers commonly type messages in all capital letters without realizing that by convention, this is commonly understood to mean that the writer is shouting. Without intending it, an e-mail writer using the all-caps style will be making people uncomfortable or even angry. Knowing the common rules of netiquette shown in Table 7-6 can help avoid this problem and other unintentional offenses.

**E-Mail Suggestions**  Some specific suggestions for composing and sending e-mail may help in using netiquette. The ease with which e-mail can be composed and sent makes it very easy to make mistakes that might be regretted later. There are several very important points to remember when writing and sending e-mail messages:

- Once sent, they cannot be retrieved.
- A permanent copy of an e-mail message probably remains somewhere on the Internet.
- E-mail is easily forwarded or copied.

For these reasons it is always a good idea to avoid sending any e-mail messages that have been written in anger or haste. It is better to save the e-mail, and then look at it again later when emotions have cooled. If the writer still feels that the e-mail should be sent, she still has that option. However, in most cases she will realize that sending the e-mail would not be a good idea, and may be something she would later regret. Once the *Send* button is clicked, it is too late to do anything.

Another factor to bear in mind is the ease with which e-mail can be copied or forwarded. An e-mail message criticizing someone could easily end up in that person's mailbox minutes after it is sent, after the original recipient forwards it.

# What's in a Name?

**BE CAREFUL IN WHAT YOU REVEAL** about yourself online. A recent study from the University of Maryland's engineering school shows that even sharing your first name or indicating your gender in an Internet relay chat room can subject you to unwanted attention and vicious personal attacks.

The original purpose of the study was to see whether talkative chat room users were more likely to be subject to aggressive technical attacks such as Trojan horses or computer worms. The researchers set up simulated users or "bots" in seven different chat rooms, primarily geared towards teenagers. One bot in each chat room had a feminine name.

The researchers were surprised at how many more responses the female user names were receiving. When they took a close look at the content, they were shocked at the sexually explicit and hostile nature of the private messages to the female names.

Male names such as "Bob" or "Jack" received an average of five—mostly innocuous—messages a day. The ambiguous names such as "Stargazer" or "Nightwolf" garnered up to 25. But the "Cathy"s and the "Irene"s were being bombarded with up to 163 mostly sexual or malicious messages a day. Although the researchers used bots, the responses were clearly coming from human chat room participants.

The disheartening message the researchers came away with is clear: If you're female, you'd better cover up your name and gender. The study may indicate that the Internet is evolving into a place where female voices and identity are being forced out of the conversation.

**Spam: Unwanted Communication**   An example of bad Net behavior is the significant and growing number of e-mail messages that are considered junk e-mail, or **spam**. The term *spam* refers to any type of unwanted message sent in mass numbers and/or repeatedly over the Net. Spam has become a major and growing problem that threatens the very usefulness of the Internet itself. In the single month of February 2006, in the United States, 150 million messages considered to be spam were blocked by ISPs and mail services. Many more messages still get through to our mailboxes, however. The current estimates are that less than 15 percent of all e-mail messages are legitimate. Lawmakers are contemplating further measures to control spam, since the e-mail servers that must receive all of this unwanted mail require billions of dollars worth of extra capacity just to process and screen the spam floods, which grow larger each year.

## Moderated Environments

Moderated environments are the answer for many people who want to avoid the seedy side of the Net. Many chat rooms, message boards, and mailing lists have a **moderator**, an individual with the power to filter messages and ban people who break the rules. Rules violations can be anything from hurling insults to simply straying off-topic. A moderator running a chat room on travel, for example, might warn or ban people for excessively discussing their favorite movies. Usually, a moderator has complete power over the situation and can ban people in any way he sees fit. If a moderator is too harsh, people might switch to another group.

## Net Neutrality

A common principle among networks is that of "network neutrality," often shortened to **net neutrality**. This concept is a doctrine of fairness that states that all net traffic shall be treated with equal priority, neither favoring nor ignoring one packet over another, no matter who the sender or receiver might be. This policy has several benefits, not the least of which is that it simplifies the job of the system to transmit data. It doesn't have to worry about "important" data; it is all the same and it simply passes on whatever it gets to its destination without the added burden of passing judgment upon the contents. The policy also provides for greater innovation, as a new Web page just put up on the Web is treated by the internal structure of the Internet with the same respect as the most popular site on the planet. This leveling of the playing field allows for new sites to grow rapidly.

## Privacy Issues

Privacy is a major concern for many users, particularly with e-mail communications and e-commerce transactions. Almost everyone is aware that e-mail messages can be intercepted and read by others. There is the real possibility that an employee's e-mail messages may be read by her supervisor, and under current law employers have a right to do just that. This practice is becoming more common as businesses discover employees spending time surfing the Web for personal reasons instead of performing their work. For more on employee monitoring, security, and similar topics, see Chapter 8.

## Copyright Infringement

Copyright law violations are frequent occurrences on the Internet. Much of the material found on the Web is copyrighted. Copying and using copyrighted items without permission is illegal, and most Web sites include a copyright notice that spells out general guidelines for how the site's content may be used. Nevertheless, copyright laws are frequently ignored, and violators sometimes end up in court.

Because existing copyright laws were written with printed materials in mind, Congress passed a new law in 1998 that addressed the major issues related to protecting digital content on the Internet, which can include text, videos, music, and many other file formats. Called the **Digital Millennium Copyright Act of 1998**, the law generally prohibits people from defeating software encryption programs and other safeguards that copyright holders have established to control access to their works. Entertainment companies have tried to protect their movies on DVD by including security codes, but hackers have already developed programs capable of cracking them. A key provision of the Digital Millennium Copyright

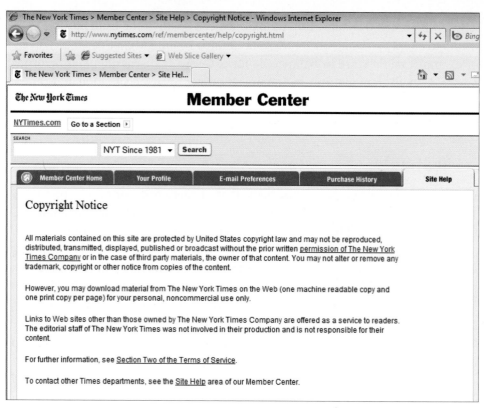

The copyright notice on The New York Times home page reminds visitors that the content of the site is copyrighted.

Act of 1998 makes the use and distribution of the security-cracking codes illegal, and imposes civil damages ranging from $200 to $2,500. Repeat offenders face criminal penalties of up to $1 million in fines, or 10 years in jail.

# OnThe**Horizon**

**THE INTERNET IS HAVING TROUBLE KEEPING UP** with the rapid increase in users and the increased workload created by the popularity of bandwidth-intensive applications such as music and video files. The broadband connections needed to enjoy these new applications are not evenly distributed. Several ongoing projects promise to provide solutions for these problems in the future. Once these connectivity problems are dealt with, people around the world will be able to enjoy the new Web services that are only a few short years away. These new services are only the beginning, and there are exciting possibilities even further down the line.

## Satellite Internet Connections

Broadband Internet connections do not serve many people living in remote or sparsely populated areas. Cable or fiber optic networks are very expensive to install and maintain, and ISPs are not interested in providing service to areas or individuals unless they think it will be profitable. One hope for people without broadband connections is provided by satellite TV networks. Remote ISPs connect to the satellite network using antennae attached to their servers. Data is relayed to and from ISP servers to satellites, which are in turn connected to an Internet backbone access point.

One drawback to satellite Internet connections is the high latency (time delay) caused by the extreme distance between satellites and receivers. A solution to this problem may be provided soon by airships, whose vastly lower altitudes would dramatically reduce latency. Located in the stratosphere approximately 12 to 13 miles above the earth's surface, the airships would be used to relay wireless communications signals, including broadband Internet. Latency would be reduced by a factor of 2,000 compared to orbiting geostationary stellites. Coverage area would be smaller, so multiple airships would be required to replace the footprint covered by a single satellite.

An Internet connection is an important way to stay connected wherever you are.

## Another Internet?

Internet2 is a research platform for the development of advanced high-speed Internet applications and technologies. A consortium of more than 200 universities working in partnership with industry and government, Internet2 enables large research universities in the United States to collaborate and share huge amounts of complex scientific information at amazing speeds, with the goal of someday transferring those capabilities to the broader Internet community.

Internet2 provides a testing ground for universities to work together and develop advanced Internet technologies such as telemedicine, digital libraries, and virtual laboratories. An example of such collaboration is the Informedia Digital Video Library (IDVL) project. Once implemented, IDVL will offer a combination of speech recognition, image understanding, and natural language processing technology to automatically transcribe, partition, and index video segments, enabling intelligent searching and navigation, along with selective retrieval of information.

The Internet2 consortium has partnered with Level 3 Communications to launch the Internet2 Network backbone, capable of supporting speeds of more than 100 Gbps. More can be learned about Internet2 by visiting the project's Web site at www.internet2.edu.

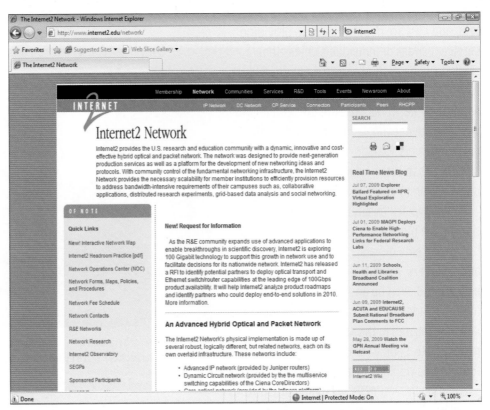

The Internet2 home page at www.internet2.edu is a link to a revolutionary type of Internet that will connect people quicker and more effectively through an ultra-high-speed network.

## Broadband Over Powerline

A new technology that transmits broadband Internet over powerlines has overcome several hurdles and is now being readied for wider use. Broadband over Powerline (BPL) lets any electrical outlet in a BPL-equipped electrical grid serve as a broadband Internet connection using low-cost plug-in adapters. BPL offers speeds comparable to cable Internet, but differs from cable in offering equal upload and download speeds. Since every electrical outlet is a potential Internet connection, computers in the same home or office can be networked without requiring a router. BPL benefits utility companies as well, letting them monitor line usage as well as allowing remote meter reading.

# Chapter**Summary**

*For an interactive version of this summary, go to this text's Internet Resource Center at www.emcp.net/CUT4e. A Spanish version is also available.*

## In what ways does the Internet create a global community?

Besides communications, the Internet can also be used for entertainment, e-commerce, research, and distance learning. Computers can be used for entertainment purposes, including playing games, gambling, listening to music, and even viewing movies and videos. **Electronic commerce (e-commerce)** refers to the Internet exchange of business information, products, services, and payments. E-commerce is commonly divided into two categories defined by target audience: business-to-consumer (B2C) and business-to-business (B2B). Search engines can be used to conduct research.

## What resources are needed to connect to the Internet?

An Internet service provider (ISP) is a company that provides Internet access. **Value added networks (VANs)** are large ISP companies that provide a connection to the Internet as well as additional content. There are two main ways for users to connect to the Internet: through **dial-up access** or by using a **LAN connection**. **Broadband**, or high-speed options, include cable, **digital subscriber line (DSL)**, wireless, and satellite connections.

## What does it mean to navigate the Internet?

To access and move about the Web, users need to know how to navigate using a browser. Web browsers locate material on the Internet using **Internet protocol (IP) addresses**. Every IP also has a corresponding Web address called a **Uniform Resource Locator (URL)**, which is a **pathname** describing where the information can be found. The Internet breaks files into many pieces of data, called packets, and sends them out over separate routes, a process called **packet switching**.

## How do you use the Internet but avoid unwanted information?

A **Web page** is the term for a single document viewable on the World Wide Web. A **Web site** includes all of the Web pages comprising the site. The first page displayed after a Web site is accessed is usually the site's **home page**. A **hyperlink** (also Web link, or link) is any element on the screen that is coded to transport viewers to another page or site. Web pages are usually created using **Hypertext Markup Language (HTML)**. **Extensible Markup Language (XML)** is a new and improved Web language that allows computers to communicate with each other directly. Web site designers frequently program using **Java** and Java applets. A **plug-in** is a mini-program that extends the capabilities of Web browsers in a variety of ways. Companies advertise on Web sites using **banners**, **blind links**, and **pop-up windows**. **WebRings** link sites devoted to a similar theme or topic.

## How do you find valuable resources on the Internet?

Search engines are based on the use of **keywords** (**search terms**). Advanced searching requires the use of logic statements known as **search operators** to refine searches and improve results.

## What are some newer ways to share information over the Internet?

**Peer-to-peer (P2P) file sharing** allows people to download material directly from other users' hard drives. **Internet telephony** provides free long-distance service. An alternative to downloading a piece of music or a video is to access it using **streaming** (also known as webcasting). Tiny video cameras called **webcams** allow conversations over the Web through live video transmission. **Audio mail** allows people to transmit not only text and pictures but also a recording of their voice.

## What are some challenges found within the Internet community and how are they handled?

Guidelines for good behavior, called **netiquette**, have been developed to encourage people to interact productively. **Spam** is a nuisance for Internet email users, and **flaming** is one of the most frequently encountered examples of rude Internet behavior. **Moderated** environments are another solution to inappropriate behavior.

Other concerns on the Internet include net neutrality, privacy, and copyright infringement. **Net neutrality** states that all net traffic shall be treated with equal priority. **Privacy** is a concern, particularly with e-mail communications and e-commerce transactions. Copyright infringement is a frequent occurrence on the Internet. The **Digital Millennium Copyright Act of 1998** generally prohibits people from defeating software encryption programs and other safeguards.

# KeyTerms

*Numbers indicate the pages where terms are first cited in the chapter. An alphabetized list of key terms with definitions (in English and Spanish) can be found on the Encore CD that accompanies this book. In addition, these terms and definitions are included in the end-of-book glossary.*

# Chapter**Exercises**

 *The following chapter exercises, along with new activities and information, are also offered in the Internet Resource Center for this title at www.emcp.net/CUT4e.*

## Tutorial > **Exploring Windows**

Tutorial 7 teaches different methods for copying and moving files and folders on your computer.

## Expanding Your Knowledge > **Articles and Activities**

 *Visit the Internet Resource Center for this title at www.emcp.net/CUT4e, read the articles related to this chapter, and complete the corresponding activities. The article titles include:*

- Topic 7-1: Internet Social Networks
- Topic 7-2: Streaming Media
- Topic 7-3: Browser Evolution
- Topic 7-4: Plug-ins, Applets, and ActiveX Controls

## Terms Check > **Matching**

 *For additional practice, go to the Internet Resource Center for this title at www.emcp.net/CUT4e for a chapter crossword puzzle.*

On the next page, write the letter of the correct answer on the line before each numbered item.

a. packet
f. e-commerce
b. HTML
g. browser
c. netiquette
h. banner
d. spam
i. zip file
e. keyword
j. dynamic routing

_____ 1. A common type of compressed data file.

_____ 2. Term used to find information using a search engine.

_____ 3. Business conducted using the Internet.

_____ 4. Unwanted messages sent in mass numbers and/or repeatedly over the Internet.

_____ 5. A program that allows users to retrieve information on the World Wide Web.

_____ 6. Small rectangular advertisements used to promote products and services on Web pages.

_____ 7. The method used to send packets by a variety of different routes to their final destination.

_____ 8. A code prescribing appropriate behavior for Internet users.

_____ 9. The programming language used to create most Web pages.

_____ 10. A fragment of data sent across the Internet.

## *Technology Illustrated >* **Identify the Process**

What concepts are portrayed in the drawing below? Write a paragraph explaining the process or processes this illustration represents.

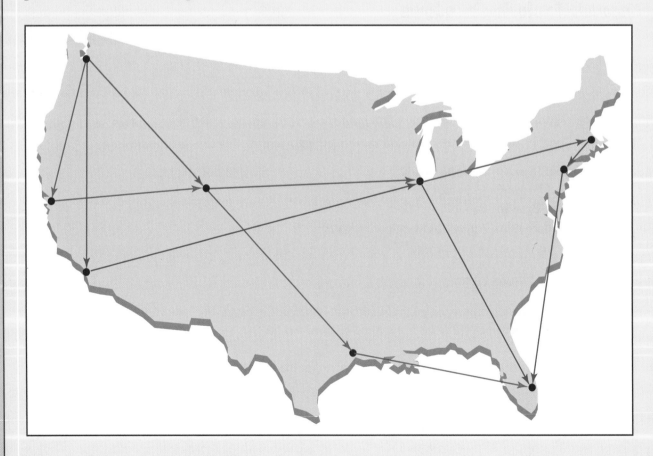

# Knowledge Check > **Multiple Choice**

  *Additional quiz questions are available on the Encore CD that accompanies this book as well as on the Internet Resource Center for this title at www.emcp.net/CUT4e.*

Circle the letter of the best answer from those provided.

1. The first screen visible when entering a Web site is called the
   a. Webmaster.
   b. home page.
   c. banner.
   d. hyperlink.

2. Of the following types of Internet connections, which generally provides the fastest speed?
   a. dial-up modem
   b. DSL
   c. wireless
   d. They are all about the same.

3. Files contained in e-mail messages are known as
   a. attachments.
   b. clip-ons.
   c. plug-ins.
   d. packets.

4. A type of ISP connection that provides high-speed access that might have to be shared with other users is a
   a. dial-up modem.
   b. DSL.
   c. cable modem.
   d. None of the above

5. HTML stands for
   a. High-tech Marketing Language.
   b. High-tech Markup Language.
   c. Hypertext Markup Language.
   d. Hypertext Marketing Language.

6. A file can be transported from a Web page to a PC by
   a. uploading.
   b. hacking.
   c. piracy.
   d. downloading.

7. ISP stands for
   a. international satellite phone.
   b. Internet satellite protocol.
   c. Internet service provider.
   d. international satellite provider.

8. Instant messaging is different from e-mail because
   a. you have to pay for the service.
   b. instant messaging is interruptive, like a phone call.
   c. there is only one provider of instant messaging services.
   d. All of the above

9. Telecommuting or telework involves
   a. avoiding the effort of commuting in a car to work every day.
   b. working online from home rather than in an office.
   c. a new and growing way for companies to reduce operating costs.
   d. All of the above

10. Why should users of chat rooms and instant messaging environments be wary of online strangers?
    a. Cyberspace is full of dangerous criminals.
    b. Users don't need to worry about it; people they meet online can't possibly harm them.
    c. The anonymous nature of online conversations mean that you don't really know with whom you are conversing.
    d. Police are everywhere online, listening for criminal intent.

## Things That Think > **Brainstorming New Uses**

In groups or individually, contemplate the following questions and develop as many answers as you can.

1. Cell phones, household appliances, vending machines, road systems, and buildings are just a few of the things that can be wired to the Internet for control and monitoring purposes. How will this change the definition of the Internet and how we think about it? What new applications might be possible, if roads can tell us what the traffic situation is, cars can tell how much fuel they have left, and VCRs can tell how much recording capacity remains?

2. Instant messaging (IM) technology has grown from a social medium to a business communications tool. Financial services and retail Web sites offer customers live "chat" with customer service representatives, and colleagues within an organization can informally meet whenever the need arises. How is this likely to evolve as video instant messaging becomes more popular? What additional benefits will businesses gain internally and externally with this technology?

## Key Principles > **Completion**

Fill in the blanks with the appropriate words or phrases.

1. The graphic persona of a player in a virtual reality game is called a(n) _____.

2. A small file stored on a Web surfer's hard drive that might be used to track behavior is called a(n) _____.

3. The part of a URL that comes last and identifies the type of organization is called the _____.

4. Another term used for telecommuting is _____.

5. A four-group series of numbers separated by periods represents a(n) _____.

6. An advertisement that occupies a rectangular portion of the screen is called a(n) _____.

7. Unwanted, repeated e-mail messages that are transmitted over the Internet are called _____.

8. The design feature that describes how packets are moved around the Internet by the best available route is called _____.

9. Web sites often ask for the user's approval before downloading and installing a _____ to provide additional functionality on a Web site.

10. A(n) _____ is a group of related Web sites that are linked together.

## Tech Architecture > **Label the Drawing**

The illustration below shows the path of a packet across the Internet. Label each step in the process.

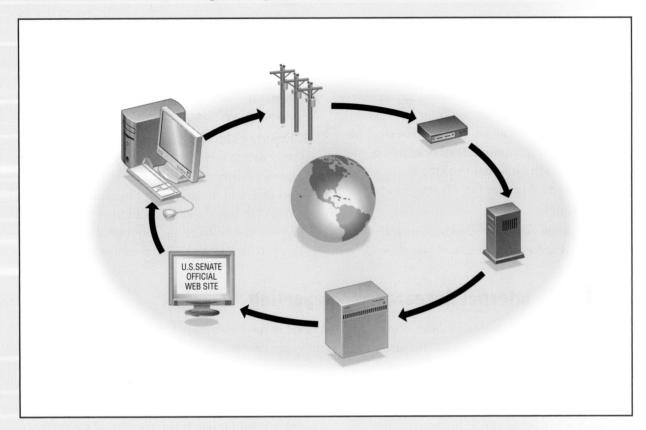

U.S.SENATE
OFFICIAL
WEB SITE

## Techno Literacy > **Research and Writing**

Develop appropriate written responses based on your research for each item.

1. Find at least four free-hosted Web site providers, such as www.geocities.com or www.homestead.com. Compare the features they support. Which ones have wizards that automatically build Web sites? Which allow form-based uploading? Which allow FTP client connections? Do any come with downloadable Web page editors? Visit some sites developed using these free hosts. Do they load quickly? Is there an excessive number of advertisements? Write a report comparing and contrasting free-host providers and decide which one you think is the best.

2. Use a free-hosted Web site provider to create and post a Web page that presents your resume to the world. The purpose of this site is to impress potential employers. At least one scanned-in image should be on the Web page.

Make sure your resume page has a title and subtitles for any sections. Add at least three hyperlinks that lead to other Web pages, such as links to the school you are attending or to one of your favorite Web sites.

3. Find out which ISPs are available in your area. Which one would best meet your needs? If you do not have access to a computer at home, assume you are researching this information for your school. For each ISP identify the services offered, including the equipment, type of server(s), and software used. Find out information on the cost for the service as well. Then create a chart in Excel or Word comparing the ISPs in terms of services offered and the cost. Present the information to your class using a PowerPoint slide show.

## Technology Issues > Team Problem-Solving

In groups, brainstorm possible solutions to the issues presented.

1. Do you believe that federal and state governments should invest heavily in the provision of Internet hookups for schools and libraries? Why or why not? If the government pays for Internet hookups, should it have a say in how schools and libraries use the Internet? Should high schools and colleges require that students use electronic versions of textbooks downloaded from the Internet once the technology is perfected? What are the advantages and disadvantages?

2. Many people use the Web to become self-employed or to telecommute. If you were to consider working from your home, what problems/advantages do you foresee? Is there more risk involved? More freedom? Less work or more work? What would be your greatest concern? Back up your answers by conducting research on this topic using the Web.

3. Experts claim that the shelf life of knowledge is only two to three years in many fields, including areas as diverse as medicine, technology, engineering, and history. How can distance learning and Web-based tools help address this issue? Given this problem, do you think diplomas should be stamped with an expiration date?

## Mining Data > Internet Research and Reporting

Conduct Internet searches to find the information described in the activities below. Write a brief report summarizing your research results. Be sure to document your sources using the MLA format (see Chapter 1, page 42, to review MLA style guidelines).

1. Research the pros and cons of using a wireless system to connect several home or office computers to the Internet. Include the approximate costs of cabling, hubs, installation, system speeds, convenience, and security. Research your answers and use supporting data from the Web. A good place to start looking for information about this equipment is www.shopper.com.

2. Research the availability and cost of cable modems and DSL services in your area. Could your home system benefit from these services today? How much more expensive is the connection when compared to dial-up modem systems? How much would it cost to install the service? How much faster and more reliable would it be? When comparing the costs, include the cost of a second phone line for a dial-up system, since the faster systems have the advantage of not tying up the phone.

3. Find a page with Flash animation on the Internet. Game advertisements from companies such as Disney, Sony, and Microsoft tend to use these frequently. Did the Web page ask you to download a plug-in? Are the resulting graphics superior? How much longer does it take to load a page with Shockwave graphics compared with one with simple HTML?

## Technology Timeline > Predicting Next Steps

Listed below is a timeline of some of the major events in the history of cybercrime. As you review the list, think of what major steps may occur next, both in terms of hacker actions and the government's response. Complete the timeline through the year 2015 with your predictions.

**1984** The press gets wind of several high-profile incidences of criminal security system breaking and uses the term hacker to describe such criminals.

**1986** The Electronic Communications Privacy Act and the Computer Fraud and Abuse Act pass Congress.

**1988** Robert Morris releases a worm that brings much of the Internet to a halt.

**1990** On January 15 AT&T's long-distance telephone switching system crashes, disrupting 70 million phone calls.

**1990** In May, Operation Sundevil commences. Sundevil was the code name for the government's sweeping crackdown on cybercrime.

**2000** In January hackers shut down Yahoo.com, Amazon.com, CNN.com, and eBay.com, among others, for one hour.

**2000** In March a 13-year-old hacker breaks into a government security system that tracks U.S. Air Force planes worldwide, damaging a "secret" system. The youth faces incarceration until age 21.

**2001** A cyberwar flares up between Chinese and American hackers after a U.S. Navy plane collides with a Chinese fighter aircraft, killing the Chinese pilot. Each side attacks thousands of sites in the other nation.

**2002** The FBI arrests three men who gained unauthorized access to credit reports and caused consumer losses of more than $2.7 million.

**2003** The Department of Justice, FBI, and Federal Trade Commission conduct a major cybercrime sweep called "Operation E-Con" that results in 130 arrests and $17 million in property seizures related to Internet auction scams, bogus investments, credit card fraud, and identity theft.

**2004** "Phishing" becomes the fastest growing Internet scam, in which crooks pretend to be a legitimate Web site or institution and request updates to your financial records.

**2005** Hackers favor the use of keystroke-logging technologies to steal sensitive information.

**2005** Hackers crack Microsoft's antipiracy system within 24 hours of its launch.

**2006** Jeanson James Ancheta pleads guilty to four felony charges for creating and selling botnets, thousands of computers infected with malicious code and turned into zombie computers to commit crimes.

**2009** An 18-year-old hacker going by the name GMZ cracks a Twitter staffer's password and gains access to high profile celebrity Twitter accounts.

## *Ethical Dilemmas >* Group Discussion and Debate

As a class or within an assigned group, discuss the following ethical dilemma.

The appeal of Internet chat rooms is often the anonymity that the medium provides. In minutes, you can create a user name, log in to a chat room, and discuss a variety of topics with relative strangers without others knowing your true identity. However, what are the consequences if the chat room sponsor shares your account information with your family, employer, or law enforcement authorities? What prevents the chat room sponsor from doing this? Would you have any recourse against the sponsor? Does this change your perspective on what you would say or not say in a chat room?

# CHAPTER 8

# Security Issues and Strategies

# CyberScenario

**WHEN JACK GOT THE BIG SALES BONUS** and the rest of us got a pat on the head, he made enemies. I was one of them, even though I kept smiling right through the meeting. I gritted my teeth for the rest of the morning, but soon he was out of the office for a few hours, and that was all the time I needed. I strode into his cubicle, popped a flash drive into the USB port on his computer, and installed a nifty little program. I could have sent the spyware disguised as an e-greeting card. He never would have known, but then he didn't always read his e-mail and I wanted to be sure. With the spyware software installed and set to fire up whenever he booted his machine, I headed back to my office and nuked some popcorn in the microwave. The show was about to begin.

First, I started up the viewer and ran through his machine with a fine-tooth comb. It was all there: a resume with a cover letter addressed to four company competitors, expense reports that included questionable items, and a few objectionable essays from some hate sites on the Web. Now down to the real business. I went online, using his login and IP address, of course. By this time I had the golden identity keys: his passwords, his social security number, his mother's maiden name—the works. I applied online for a few credit cards and went on a spending spree. I went out to some chat sites and wildly pumped stocks that I knew Jack owned, breaking trading laws, but who would know? I was about to try to get the attention of an FBI monitor in a chat room when poor old Jack returned to the office.

The real fun began when he logged in and I sat back to watch it all. The viewer software worked like a charm. He wrote a memo and I was there for every keystroke. He went online and I went with him. The popcorn needed more salt, but otherwise life was just fine.

## Risk Assessment

Jack's fictional peril outlined in the Cyber Scenario is unfortunately very real today. The spying technologies described in the scenario not only exist, but are used in the corporate and political worlds. Moreover, they represent only a small part of the total cyber crime problem, which includes the theft of corporate and personal data; criminals using the Internet to carry out crimes such as embezzlement and fraud; and the creation of viruses that disrupt the business operations of companies and organizations as well as destroy data, hardware, and software.

Because the topic of cyber crime is a large issue, this chapter narrows the focus to the security problems companies face, along with strategies and tools to address those risks.

In order to protect their systems adequately, organizations need to assess the level of security risk that they face. The two factors that help determine the level of risk are threat and vulnerability. **Threat** refers to the severity of a security breach, and **vulnerability** refers to the likelihood of a security breach of systems or data. Both of these factors can be plotted along a spectrum of low to high (see Figure 8-1). For example, low vulnerability means that a system is fairly well protected and a security breach is unlikely. An example of a high threat is a security breach that would make available hundreds of thousands of consumer credit card numbers. Plotting threats and vulnerabilities can help an organization set its priorities for addressing security concerns.

As we become increasingly dependent on computer systems to facilitate our jobs, our personal lives, and the infrastructures of our communities and country, the proper operation of computers grows correspondingly in importance. With the explosive growth of the Internet and networks in general, an enormous body of computers and data is now accessible by the general public—not all of whom are trustworthy. Companies today face security problems in three broad areas, each of which is discussed in this chapter:

Go to this title's Internet Resource Center and read the article titled "Protecting the Internet from Terrorists." www.emcp.net/CUT4e

- network and Internet security risks
- computer viruses
- hardware and software security risks

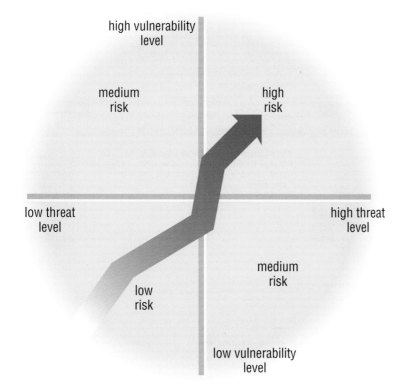

**Figure 8-1  Risk Assessment Matrix**
The higher the level of vulnerability and threat, the higher the level of risk.

# Network and Internet Security Risks

The Internet has been likened to the physical world of the last millennium, before it was explored on a large scale. Both represent vast new territories to investigate, with great opportunities for development that can benefit people individually and as nations. The physical world offered explorers large expanses of land, rich with natural resources. The Internet offers an ever-expanding body of information and the ability to communicate instantly 24 hours a day. Like the uncharted wilds, the Internet lacks borders, and it is this inherent openness that makes it so valuable and so vulnerable at the same time. Over its short life, the Internet has grown so quickly that the legal system has not been able to keep pace. Legal systems are not designed to adjust for rapid technological changes, and often a new technology is commonplace when laws and an enforcement body finally evolve to govern its use.

Security is a major concern, especially in electronic commerce transactions. Businesses selling products and services over the Internet have discovered that many potential customers are reluctant to use a credit card for payment. Stories abound about hackers penetrating computer systems and using stolen credit card numbers. To allay these fears, major retail companies have instituted sophisticated encryption systems that protect customers' financial information. The security risks networks and the Internet pose can be grouped into the following areas, each of which overlaps the others in terms of the technologies involved:

- unauthorized access
- denial of service attacks
- information theft

Electronic-commerce Web sites must use encryption measures to ensure the privacy and security of customer's credit card information.

## Unauthorized Access

Unauthorized access to a system is the most common security risk. Hackers carry out most cases of unauthorized access to computers and networks. A **hacker** is a computer expert that seeks programming, security, and system challenges. Some hackers exploit Web sites and programs with poor security measures in place. For more challenging sites, they use sophisticated programs and strategies to gain entrance. When asked, many hackers claim they like to hack merely for the challenge of trying to defeat security measures. They rarely have a more malicious motive, and they generally do not aim to destroy or damage the sites that they invade.

In fact, hackers dislike being identified with those who seek to cause damage. A **cracker** is a hacker with malicious or criminal intent. An annual survey that the FBI and the Computer Security Institute conducted in 2008 revealed that 29 percent of the participants experienced unauthorized access to their computers (see Figure 8-2).

Since the events of September 11, 2001, the government has taken an increasingly dim view of hacking in any form. Law enforcement now metes out much stiffer penalties to U.S. citizens caught hacking. Due to the proliferation of the Internet, however, many hackers now reside in foreign nations and are therefore more difficult to catch. Groups of international hackers are also becoming involved in **cyberwars**, attacking sites in a competing country when news events between two potential foes cause a flare-up of tensions. These cyberwars have yet to prove serious, but this may change in the future as we come to depend increasingly on the Net.

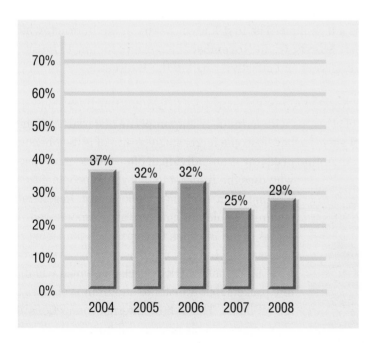

**Figure 8-2  Annual Percentage of Unauthorized Access to Computers**
Source: 2008 CSI/FBI Computer Crime and Security Survey,
http://i.cmpnet.com/v2.gocsi.com/pdf/CS/survey2008.pdf

A frequent security problem is the system backdoor, a vulnerability that programmers leave behind either accidentally or on purpose.

**User IDs and Passwords**   Most hackers focus on gaining entry over the Internet to a secure computer system by finding a working user ID and password combination. User IDs are easy to come by and are generally not secure information. Sending an e-mail, for example, displays the sender's user ID in the return address, making it very public. The only missing element then is the password. Hackers know from experience which passwords are common and they have programs (downloadable for free, of course) that generate thousands of likely passwords and try them automatically over a period of hours or days. Later in this chapter, the text will provide guidelines on how to create a safe password.

**System Backdoors**   Another unintentional entrance to networks and information systems is sometimes provided by programmers. A **system backdoor** is a test user ID and password that provides the highest level of authorization. The "backdoor" often is created innocently in the early days of system development to allow programmers and other team members access to fix problems. Through either negligence or design, the user ID and password are sometimes left behind in the final version of the system. People who know about them can then enter the system, bypassing the security, perhaps years later when the backdoor has been forgotten.

**Spoofing**   A sophisticated way to break into a network via the Internet involves spoofing. **Spoofing** is the process of fooling another computer by pretending to send packets from a legitimate source. It works by altering the address that the system automatically puts on every message sent. The address is changed to one that the receiving computer is programmed to accept as a trusted source of information. This type of attack was very successful in the earlier days of the Internet, but now defensive systems exist to guard against spoofing (see the information on firewalls in a later section). Software worms, described in the section on viruses, often use spoofing as a technique. The first-known worm on the Internet, which was created by Robert Morris, Jr., in November 1988, used spoofing to infect more than 6,000 core servers and effectively halted the Internet.

**Online Predators**   Another worry for many people is protecting their children from Web sites and chat rooms with harmful or inappropriate material. A problem that law enforcement agencies have become increasingly aware of is the phenomena of online predators. An **online predator** is an individual, often a child molester,

The best way for adults to protect children from inappropriate Internet content is by participating in Web surfing with their children.

who uses the Internet to talk young people into meeting them, exchanging photos, etc. In general, children should not have private, unmonitored access to the Internet. Organizations managing child access to the Internet often use a proxy system that is set up to make a URL check and which will disallow packets that transfer to and from Web sites that are off-limits. This is how Internet connections at elementary schools protect children from adult sites. A number of commercial software packages incorporate this feature for home use. Some of them also allow tracking of Internet usage so that parents can monitor which Web sites their children have visited.

# Shooting Dice on a PDA

**NEVADA WAS THE FIRST STATE** to approve the use of wireless handheld gambling devices inside hotel casinos. The casino industry had been eager to cater to its tech-savvy, PDA-obsessed clientele. Plus handhelds offer more gambling at no extra space cost for hotels that are devoting more and more footage to shopping, spas, elaborate pools, and clubs.

Nevada has put a list of restrictions on wireless gaming. Handhelds may only be offered in casinos that have at least 100 slot machines and provide at least one other gambling game. The handheld may only be used in public areas; hotel rooms and other private areas are off-limits. And they cannot be available overnight.

The PDAs offer a variety of games—bingo, poker, blackjack, and horserace betting—and can be activated by credit card. Customers can also check on activities occurring in and around the hotel, order food, and pay their hotel bill from their PDAs. Another plus: The system's GPS will direct the waiter with the pizza delivery to the correct lounge chair at the pool.

A biometric system that reads the user's fingerprint ensures that the intended gambler is using it, and encryption ensures security for the radio signals. The PDAs are programmed to stop working in any unauthorized areas.

The casinos don't expect to garner much additional revenue out of wireless gambling by on-premises patrons. But they have noticed that enormous profits are being made by offshore Internet gambling enterprises. The PDAs put them into a position to pounce when and if cybergambling becomes legal in the United States.

## Denial of Service Attacks

One type of computer crime generally attributed to organized hackers is known as **denial of service (DoS) attack**. This simple, but highly effective, form of attack by an organized worldwide team of hackers caused havoc for Yahoo.com, Amazon.com, CNN.com, and eBay.com over several days in the early part of 2001. In a DoS attack, one or more hackers participate, each running multiple copies of a program that simply asks for the same information from a Web site over and over again—not just a few times, but thousands of times a second. The system soon is flooded and is essentially shut down (see Figure 8-3).

To understand how a DoS attack operates, think of what has to happen when you click a link on a Web page or select a favorite Web site you wish to go to. Your computer sends a message to the host computer generally asking for the information stored on the home page. To respond to your request, the host computer sends the information across the Internet and your computer then displays it on the screen. This works fine if a reasonable number of people ask for the information simultaneously, but if thousands of requests are received, even by the fastest computers, things slow down. Have you ever gone to a Web site and had

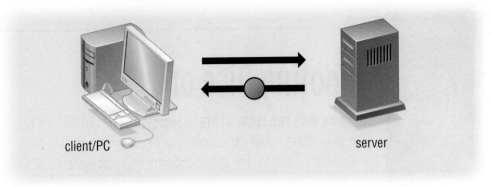

(a)

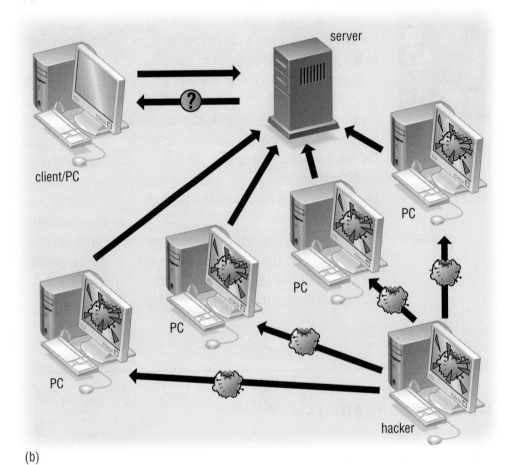

(b)

**Figure 8-3 Denial of Service Attack**

(a) Normally, when a computer makes a request of a server, the server is able to respond. (b) In a DoS attack, multiple simultaneous requests are made, thus overwhelming the server. As a result, the server cannot respond.

to wait a very long time for the page to load, even though it usually works quickly, and the other sites you have been surfing have popped right up? This is usually because many people are requesting the same information that you are. Imagine the system overload if thousands of requests are arriving each second.

## Information Theft

Information can be a company's most valuable possession. Think of a sales database, for example, listing all of a company's clients, with contact information and

The most valuable thing on a computer is the information stored there, such as credit card numbers, social security numbers, and passwords. These items need to be protected.

sales history. This database represents years of work and expensive research. A competitor who gains access to this information will have a huge advantage. He will know exactly how much to bid to gain a sale, which clients to call, and what products they like to buy.

Stealing corporate information, a crime included in the category of **industrial espionage**, is unfortunately easy to do and difficult to detect. This is due in part to the invisible nature of software and data. If someone steals a jetliner, it is easy to see that the plane is not in the hangar. With software, if a cracker breaks into a company network and manages to download the company database from the network onto a disk, nothing seems wrong. The original database is still in place, working the same way it did before. Even the disk containing the stolen information looks the same as it did when it was blank. For safety's sake, organizations regularly make many copies of their databases. Unfortunately, having multiple copies creates an additional security risk because it is difficult to track the copies. If an extra backup is made one day and simply vanishes, the crime often goes undetected.

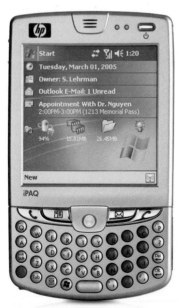

Wireless devices are easily connected to the Internet, which brings with it more security risks.

### Limited Security for Wireless Devices

The growing number of wireless devices has created a new opening for data theft. Wireless devices such as cameras, Web phones, networked computers, PDAs, and input and output peripherals are inherently less secure than wired devices. Home users in particular tend to not bother turning on security controls, such as requiring a password to surf the Web, on their wireless routers. A normal wired connection, such as a wire between a keyboard and a computer, cannot be as easily intercepted as a wireless

# Unwired & Unwary

**THE WIRELESS LIFE IS SO EASY.** Use the computer in the home office, move it to the patio, take it to the coffee shop. But wireless is making it easy, too, for eavesdroppers and hackers.

The trend toward wireless networking has grown exponentially in recent years. By the end of 2008, Wi-Fi services in trains, buses, and ferries increased 272% over the previous year. Yet there has not been a parallel increase in the use of security features to protect data from piracy.

In theory, domestic Wi-Fi networks come armed with a high degree of security. The wireless routers that are central to domestic Wi-Fi networks have several built-in protection features. Firewall software intercepts hack attempts, and encryption devices scramble data inside the network.

Such features only work, however, if users activate them. The process of setting up a home wireless system can be overwhelming. By the time users get to the complicated steps involved in securing the system—changing the default password, installing the security software, turning on the encryption device—many give up or do it wrong, leaving their network wide open.

Danger also lurks in "rogue hotspots." A laptop user may be sitting in a trusted wireless coffee shop, unaware that the latte drinker at the next table has equipment in his backpack that is jamming the legitimate base station and sending a stronger signal with a look-alike log-in. When the victim logs onto the rogue hotspot, his data is ripe for the taking.

Then there is "wardriving." Using a motorized vehicle and a laptop, wardrivers cruise the city streets in search of vulnerable networks. Using a GPS, an antenna, and software readily available on the Internet, they can collect information on wireless access points or break into a network.

Commercial networks are vulnerable as well. A quarter of the networks in New York, London, and Paris are unsecured, leaving them vulnerable to data theft and viruses.

Consumers and business users can protect their data by taking the time to figure out how to implement the safety features of their computer, software, and networks. But industry analysts say that industry should either make the protection features more user-friendly or build them into the wireless products, so it's not left to the end-user to put on the armor.

radio transmission. To intercept company e-mails on a wireless LAN, all a competitor need do is park a computer-laden van outside the building and listen. This is far easier than splicing into a network that is connected by wires.

One of the available security protocols for wireless networks is **Wired Equivalent Privacy (WEP)**, developed in conjunction with the 802.11 standard for wireless local area networks. Newer versions of WEP with enhanced security features make it more difficult for hackers to intercept and modify data transmissions sent by radio waves or infrared signals.

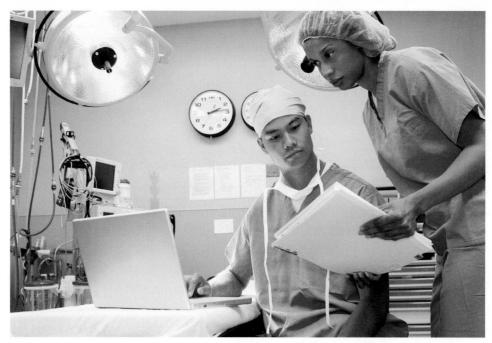

Many medical records are now stored electronically. By federal law, this information must be protected from the possibility of unauthorized access or data browsing.

**Data Browsing**   **Data browsing** is a less damaging crime that involves an invasion of privacy. Workers in many organizations have access to networked databases that contain private information about people. Examples include a college admissions staffer who has access to student transcripts, or an IRS employee who has access to citizens' tax returns. Out of curiosity, or occasionally malice, these employees "browse" through the private documents of famous individuals and personal acquaintances. Accessing this information without an official reason is against the law, but the information makes good lunchroom gossip. The IRS has had a particularly large problem with data browsing in recent years; in the late 1990s, browsing became so common and involved so many employees that it turned into a scandal. Some employees were fired and the rest were given specialized training in appropriate conduct.

## Computer Viruses

One of the most familiar forms of risk to computer security is the computer virus. Recall from earlier chapters that a computer **virus** is a program, written by a hacker or cracker, that is designed to perform some kind of trick upon an unsuspecting victim. The trick performed in some cases is mild, such as drawing an offensive image on the screen, or changing all of the characters in a document to another language. Sometimes the trick is much more severe, such as reformatting the hard drive and erasing all data, or damaging the motherboard so that it cannot operate properly. Worms are similar to viruses but work through a slightly different mechanism.

Worms are often confused with viruses, but they operate in quite a different fashion. Rather than adding itself to another program and waiting for a user to execute an attachment or open a file with a macro, a **worm** (also called a software

Tech Demo 8-1
Software Worms

# Beware Ransomware, the Newest Form of Malware

**RANSOMWARE IS THE TERM** coined for a malicious code that tries to extort cash from victims. In ransomware, a program will seize control of a computer until the user agrees to the attacker's demands. The extortion usually calls for the victim to transfer funds via e-Gold or other money transfer service.

In a new twist, the "Archiveus" program exhorts the victim to purchase a certain amount of pharmaceutical drugs from a Russian online drug store. Archiveus sneaks into a computer's "My Documents" folder, scrambles all the files and deletes the originals. An attached ransom text file lets the victim know that they can obtain a password to unscramble their files by purchasing from one of three overseas pharmacies.

In a similar vein, "Ransom.A" attacks a computer and then threatens to destroy one file every minute until the victim wires $10.99 via Western Union to a specified account.

"DigiKeyGen" finds its victims by appealing to baser instincts. It pops up as an advertisement promising access to a free pornographic Web site. Once downloaded, it covertly installs software that generates nonstop hard core ads. Then it coyly offers to sell the victim an anti-spyware program for $49.99 to clean up the mess.

Security software experts say that much of ransomware is more bark than bite. The key to unlocking files is usually somewhere in the ransomware file itself. In the case of Archiveus, an antivirus company cracked the code within weeks and put it online.

Even if it is a bluff, there are always victims in the first wave who fall prey to ransomware. Anti-spyware experts emphasize the importance of creating backups for systems and files—and to always be suspicious of something for nothing.

worm) actively attempts to move and copy itself. Operating in most cases on the Internet, a worm uses spoofing techniques to fool computers into accepting and executing a copy. The worm then transmits itself to other machines and performs its prime function, whatever that may be. Today, worms are commonly used as hacking devices. They seek out computer systems to break into and leave a route for later entry by a hacker or cracker.

Viruses and worms are a form of computer vandalism. They are destructive and attack victims randomly, often causing millions of dollars in damage. An interesting note is that computers running Microsoft Windows are more prone to viruses than those running the Mac OS. According to FBI profiling, the typical virus or worm creator in the past was a young, male computer science major working on a graduate degree. In some circles, the creation and release of a virus, like hacking, is a "rite of passage." Increasingly common, however, are viruses written by people for the purposes of selling a product that is basically without value. Another growing group of virus authors are people from other nations who are displeased for political and economic reasons and wish to lash out with viruses as a form of sabotage. Today, viruses and worms are being constantly created and defeated. The Internet has accelerated the rate of their creation and distribution, but at the same time it has helped speed up the distribution of defenses against them.

Many viruses today are transmitted as an attachment to an e-mail message sent over the Internet. When a user opens an attachment infected with a virus, the virus is installed on the computer and unleashed to do its damage. New viruses appear every day because they are easy to create and they can spread across the globe in a few days through the use of flash drives, e-mail, and network or Internet contamination (see Figure 8-4). In addition to the regular use of antivirus software, users can avoid viruses in e-mail by simply not reading spam, and certainly by never clicking on a link or downloading an attachment from an unknown source.

The battle against viruses is far from over; in fact, by some indicators it is getting worse. Data gathered by Commtouch, an anti-spam and virus detection company, shows spam accounted for about 72% of all e-mail during the first quarter

Tech Demo 8-2
E-mail Viruses

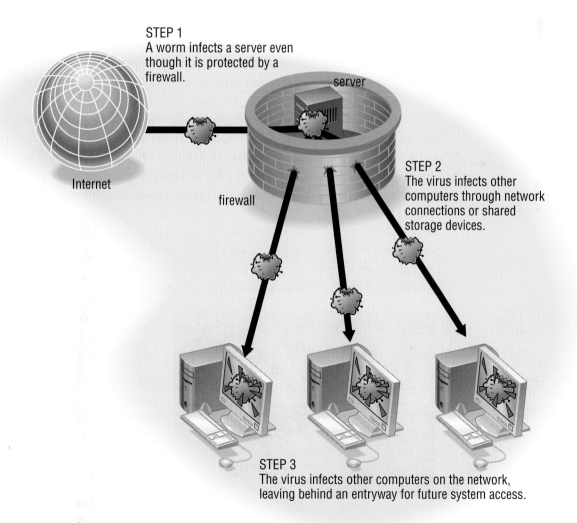

STEP 1
A worm infects a server even though it is protected by a firewall.

server

Internet

firewall

STEP 2
The virus infects other computers through network connections or shared storage devices.

STEP 3
The virus infects other computers on the network, leaving behind an entryway for future system access.

**Figure 8-4 The Virus Infection Process**
Viruses are often transmitted over the Internet and through shared devices such as flash drives.

of 2009, reaching as high as 96% in January. Infections of the Conficker worm reached more than 15 million computers between fall 2008 and spring 2009.

## Impact of Viruses

Hackers and crackers have developed a variety of viruses. Some virus creators are trying to express their creativity, and others are responding to increased anti-virus capabilities by finding new methods to inflict damage. These viruses have effects that range from annoying to catastrophic. Nuisance viruses, espionage viruses, and data-destructive viruses are the common types of viruses that may be encountered. Some of the signs of a virus infection are:

- When booting your computer, error messages are displayed requiring a reboot, or not allowing you to boot up at all.
- Some of your files become corrupted and suddenly don't work properly.
- A specific program, very commonly Microsoft Word, does not operate properly.
- Programs or files have suddenly vanished.
- Unknown programs or other files appear on your hard drive.
- Strange messages or images display on your monitor.
- Your system has less available memory or disk space than it should.
- A disk or volume name has been changed.
- Unexpected sounds or music are played at random times.
- You receive the same e-mail message repeatedly from the same people.

**Nuisance Viruses**   A **nuisance virus** usually does no real damage, but is rather just an inconvenience. In most cases, the purpose of a nuisance virus is to try to bully a computer user into purchasing a product. Often, the virus will be programmed to pop up a window every few minutes, warning the user that he or she must buy a certain piece of software to prevent some imaginary catastrophe.

**Espionage Viruses**   As you learned in the section on unauthorized access, some viruses are designed to create a backdoor into a system to bypass security. An **espionage virus** does not inflict immediate damage, but it allows a hacker or cracker to enter the system later for the purpose of stealing data or spying on the

A keystroke logger records keystrokes in order to provide a hacker or cracker with access to passwords and secured information at a later time.

work of a competitor. A common type of espionage virus is called a **keystroke logger** (also called a keylogger), which stores every typed keystroke on the hard drive. Later, a hacker can access this file and analyze it, looking for things such as credit card numbers and passwords to allow access to the accounts and financial instruments saved on the computer.

**Data-Destructive Viruses**   The most difficult part of a computer to replace is the data on the hard drive. The installed programs, documents, databases, and

Data-destructive viruses can eliminate computer data or make it unreadable.

saved e-mails form the heart of a personal computer, the portion that makes it *personal* and different from every other computer. A **data-destructive virus** is designed to destroy this data. Erasing or corrupting files so that they are unreadable is a common trick. Some viruses go for the easy route and simply attempt to format the entire drive, leaving it blank.

## Methods of Virus Operation

Viruses can create effects that range from minor and annoying to highly destructive, but how do they work? Where do they go on the disk and how do they become launched by another program? The following methods of operating and transmission provide another way to classify viruses:

- macro viruses
- varient viruses
- stealth viruses
- boot sector viruses
- Trojan horse viruses
- multipartite viruses
- logic (time) bomb viruses

**Macro Viruses**  A common method of operation for a virus is by a macro, a small subprogram that allows users to customize and automate certain functions. A **macro virus** is written specifically for one program, such as Microsoft Word, which then becomes infected when it opens a file with the virus stored in its macros. These applications will sometimes give a warning, asking if the macros should be activated or not. If the user clicks Yes and activates the macros in the infected document, they will then infect the application so that every file created or edited using that application on that computer will also be infected. Reinstalling the

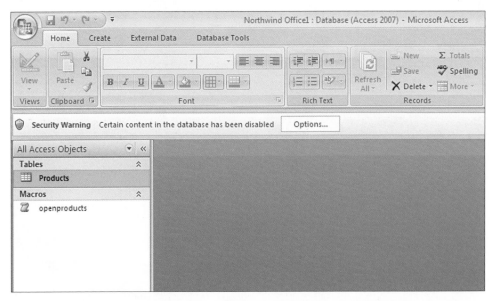

Microsoft Office applications will alert a user via the Information Bar if they detect a macro virus.

application will remove the virus, but the program will become infected again the moment it opens an old file containing the virus. The macro virus usually does little harm, but it can be difficult to remove.

**Variant Viruses** The viruses are becoming more sophisticated as well. In order to counter detection and prevention methods, the viruses are programmed to change themselves and their behavior to fool programs meant to stop them. These viruses come in many different "flavors" or change their behavior from one day to the next to avoid detection. This type of virus is called a **variant virus**.

**Stealth Viruses** A **stealth virus** tries to hide from software designed to find and destroy it. A stealth virus masks the size of the file it is hiding in by copying itself out of the file to another location on the victim's hard drive.

**Boot Sector Viruses** The **boot sector** of a hard disk contains a variety of information, including how the disk is organized and whether it is capable of loading an operating system. When a disk is left in a drive and the computer reboots, the operating system automatically reads the boot sector to learn about that disk and to attempt to start any operating system on that disk. A **boot sector virus** is designed to alter the boot sector of a disk, so that whenever the operating system reads the boot sector, the computer will automatically become infected.

Fortunately, most boot sector viruses can be easily detected since the size and nature of the boot sector of a disk are well known and normally do not change much. Antivirus software can identify any strange alterations, warn the user, and provide the option of removing the virus. The system cleans the disk by simply rewriting a normal boot sector onto it.

**Trojan Horse Viruses**   Like its namesake from a Greek legend, the **Trojan horse virus** hides inside another legitimate program or data file. These viruses are quite common with downloaded games and other types of shareware files such as screen savers. Sometimes, even downloaded movie clips and audio files can be infected. The downloaded file may install and run without a problem but, unknown to the victim, a virus is included in the software, installing itself with the other files. These viruses may cause damage immediately, or they may delay acting for a time.

To prevent a virus infection via the Trojan horse method, it is a good idea to download shareware programs from the original creator's Web site or a site the creator recommends. Other sites, such as fan sites, may be less monitored. The bottom line? Make sure you trust the Web site from which you are downloading software.

**Multipartite Viruses**   A **multipartite virus** utilizes several forms of attack. The name derives from this virus's ability to attack in several different ways. The virus may first infect the boot sector, and then later move on to become a Trojan horse type by infecting a disk file. These viruses are more sophisticated, and therefore more difficult to guard against. They are also more rarely encountered.

Named after the Trojan horse of Greek legend, Trojan horse viruses hide within legitimate programs but contain instructions that perform harmful actions.

**Logic Bomb Viruses**   A successful computer virus, like a successful biological virus, must spread before it kills the host. If a disease killed a person more or less instantly, it would not have a chance to infect more people. The same is true of a **logic bomb virus**, also called a time bomb virus, which typically does not act immediately, but rather sits quietly dormant, waiting for a specific event or set of conditions to occur. A famous logic bomb was the widely publicized Michelangelo virus, which infected personal computers and caused them to display a message on the artist's birthday. A destructive type of logic bomb virus that occasionally has been built into systems involves placing a virus within the company database and programming it to "explode" when the employee is marked terminated, thus destroying the database.

A logic bomb virus is a virus that works like a time bomb, waiting to explode at a specific time.

# Hardware and Software Security Risks

Although hackers, crackers, and viruses garner the most attention as security risks, companies face a variety of other dangers to their hardware and software systems. Principally, these risks involve types of systems failure, employee theft, and the cracking of software for copying.

## Systems Failure

A fundamental element in making sure that computer systems operate properly is protecting the electrical power that runs them. Power interruptions such as blackouts and brownouts have very adverse effects on computers. They can damage hardware and corrupt data. Steady, reliable power is one of the reasons why the U.S. West Coast and its Silicon Valley have hosted a major part of the growth in the computer industry.

A surge protector is used to guard against power spikes such as those caused by lightning. This type of protection is very important for home computers.

A simple power surge in the power grid, caused by phenomena such as lightning strikes, can damage computers. A sudden rise or fall in the power level, called a **power spike**, can cause poor performance or even permanently damage hardware. An inexpensive type of power strip called a **surge protector** can guard against power spikes and can also serve as an extension cord and splitter.

A much more vigorous power protection system is an **uninterruptible power supply (UPS)**, which provides a battery backup. Similar in nature to a power strip but much more bulky and a bit more expensive, a UPS not only provides steady, spike-free power, but also keeps computers running during a blackout. A constant, even flow of electricity is particularly important for a computer that functions as the database file server for a network, since a random loss of power can cause the system to corrupt files on disk. Unplug a system with a UPS and it will still keep running for several hours, without even a flicker, before the battery runs out.

An uninterruptible power supply (UPS) provides a battery backup as well as a constant, even flow of electricity.

## Employee Theft

Although accurate estimates are difficult to pinpoint, businesses certainly lose millions of dollars a year in stolen computer hardware and software. Often, in large organizations, such theft goes unnoticed or unreported. Someone takes a hard drive or a scanner home for legitimate use, then leaves the job sometime later, and keeps the machine. Sometimes, employees take components to add to their home PC systems. And occasionally, thieves break into businesses and haul computers away. Such thefts cost far more than the price of the stolen computers because they also involve the cost of replacing the lost data (if, indeed, the data is replaceable), the cost of the time lost while the machines are gone, and the cost of installing new machines and training people to use them. Mobile computing has created a whole new venue for computer theft as the devices are smaller and more easily taken. In response to this threat, employers are stepping up efforts to monitor employees, using security systems of the type outlined in this chapter's section on security strategies.

## Cracking Software for Copying

A common goal of hackers or crackers is to crack a software protection scheme. A **crack** is a method of circumventing a security scheme that prevents a user from copying a program, for example, a game. A common protection scheme for software is to require that the installation CD be resident in the drive whenever the program runs. Making copies of the CD with a burner, however, easily fools this protection scheme. It can also be fooled with a crack that involves copying extra files from the CD to the hard drive and redirecting the software to check the hard disk for these files instead of the CD. Some game companies are taking the extra step of making duplication difficult by scrambling some of the data on their original CDs, which CD burners will automatically correct when copying. When the copied and corrected CD is used, the software checks for the scrambled track information. If the error is not there, the software will not run.

# Security Strategies for Protecting Computer Systems and Data

Our increasing reliance on computer-based systems means a corresponding rise in computer security threats. If online banking and shopping are the norm, for example, it only makes sense that bank robbers and shoplifters would be online as well. The increasing complexity of the Internet and the constantly changing technologies also leave new gaps for cyber rogues to slip through.

Companies can adopt strategies to prevent computer vandalism, information theft, unauthorized access to networks, and damage from computer viruses. Perhaps the first line of defense is an awareness of the laws protecting an organization's data, hardware, and software. Physical property such as computers and peripherals are protected under standard theft laws. Federal legislation regarding information includes the Electronic Communications Privacy Act, which makes it illegal to intercept and make public any private communications over computer networks and telephone lines, and the Federal Computer Fraud and Abuse Act, which provides stiff penalties for breaking into a computer system or intercepting an electronic transmission to copy, alter, or destroy data.

Legal sanctions against those creating and spreading viruses have taken awhile to develop. Federal legislation has dealt mainly with offenses against government-owned computers and networks. Therefore, almost every state has adopted its own legislation to punish those who spread viruses. Virus creators can also be punished under statutes aimed at property damage rather than computer viruses specifically.

As the Internet has evolved and computer technology has become more sophisticated, IT managers, computer experts, and security specialists have developed a set of security strategies to prevent damage and losses, including:

Protecting computer systems from intruders requires strong security measures.

- physical security
- firewalls
- network sniffers
- antivirus software
- data backups
- disaster recovery plans
- authentication
- data encryption
- monitoring and auditing

## Physical Security

One of the most important ways to mitigate the risk of security breaches is to physically protect computing devices. Physical security has two major components: the location of devices and the use of locking equipment. Expensive or mission-critical equipment should be located in a controlled-access building or room. Biometric or security card access can be used to control who is authorized to enter a computing area. For notebook and laptop computers, locking cables should be used when they will be unattended. These cables, which connect to the computer, should be secured to a fixed point, such as a heavy desk or shelf.

## Firewalls

Developed originally to prevent security breaches such as spoofing and hacking, firewalls run on computers that are attached directly to the Internet, as was explained in Chapter 6. The firewall will generally allow normal Web browser

Locking cables can secure mobile computing devices to fixed objects to deter theft.

operations but will prevent many other types of communication. It works similarly to a door bouncer at a club who checks IDs before allowing customers in. The firewall checks incoming data against a list of known, trusted sources. If a packet does not fit the profile of anything on its list, it is rejected. If there is a special need for an additional piece of software that uses an unconventional route to transmit data into the system, the firewall's trusted list can be altered to allow it to accept the incoming data. Most employers have firewalls for their networks, which is why computer games and certain other consumer-type programs may not operate properly in the workplace.

Tech Demo 8-3
Firewalls

## Network Sniffers

A **network sniffer** is a software package that displays network traffic data. It shows which resources employees are using and the Web sites they are visiting. It can be used to spy and monitor, or to prevent unauthorized activity. Network sniffers can also be used to troubleshoot network connections and improve system performance. Most network administrators run one all the time, so keep in mind that somewhere, someone has the power to look over your shoulder. Although abuses of older technology such as telephones and written mail are forbidden by strict laws, online privacy rights are still emerging.

Go to this title's Internet Resource Center and read the article titled "Improving Home PC Security." www.emcp.net/CUT4e

## Antivirus Software

Because viruses often corrupt or erase data and open systems up to unauthorized access, antivirus software should be part of every computer system. This software is quite successful in detecting and cleaning off known viruses. The trouble with any antivirus software is that it can detect only viruses with known signatures. Newer viruses are harder to identify and remove. The Internet has helped greatly in this area, as it allows antivirus software to update itself over the Net. The process is normally free of charge and relatively painless for the user. If you use virus detection software, you should make it part of your routine to check for upgrades at least monthly. There are 10 to 20 new viruses reported daily, and your virus program must be upgraded constantly to protect against them. Antivirus software was covered in more detail in Chapter 4.

Go to this title's Internet Resource Center and read the article titled "Virus Detection and Prevention." www.emcp.net/CUT4e

## Data Backups

One of the crucial elements of any prevention scheme is to be prepared for the worst. What if a fire burned up your company's offices and computers? Do all employees have recent backups on hand to replace their critical files? Backing up data and placing the backup in a safe spot are necessary chores, because if antivirus software misses a bug or if a disaster occurs, you don't want to be left with nothing.

Organizations can choose from many backup schemes. Besides the obvious move of having a complete copy of programs and data in a safe place, companies tend to take additional measures, particularly concerning a primary database. If something goes wrong with the backup, a company could find itself out of business quickly. Organizations normally keep more than one backup of important databases and usually update them on a daily or weekly basis.

External backup appliances help protect system data.

A variation of the backup strategy is to create a **rotating backup** of perhaps seven copies of company data, one for each day of the week. When it comes around to the eighth day—for example, Monday morning—the administrator takes the previous Monday's backup and overwrites it, saving the new backup on an old tape and erasing the oldest copy. This scheme has several advantages. It saves time, as only one backup need be made per day. If the database is lost or corrupted, many copies exist, some of which may predate the beginning of the problem. For example, if a virus infects a database on Thursday and is not detected until the following Monday, it would be possible to reload Wednesday's version and therefore go back to a safe, clean copy with no virus in it.

## Disaster Recovery Plan

A **disaster recovery plan** is a safety system that allows a company to restore its systems after a complete loss of data. The elements of a typical disaster recovery plan include

- data backup procedures
- remotely located backup copies
- redundant systems

Besides backing up the data multiple times and storing backup copies in a different building, users can take other precautions for a big benefit when everything goes horribly wrong. These precautions include keeping extra pieces of critical hardware that can be quickly replaced in the damaged machine. Another safeguard is establishing redundant systems. One part of a **redundant system** might include having a fully mirrored hard drive that can be swapped with a damaged or corrupted hard drive, thereby keeping downtime to a minimum. A **mirrored hard drive** is one that contains exactly the same data as the original, and is updated automatically every time the original is updated. That way if one disk fails, the other can keep going with no loss of data. Many corporations have safeguards of this type to protect their critical databases.

# Authentication

**Authentication** is the proof that a user is who he says he is, and that he is authorized to access an account. The stronger the authentication mechanism, the more secure the system is. Common forms of authentication include personal identification numbers (PINs), user IDs and passwords, smart cards, and biometrics.

**Personal Identification Numbers**   An automated teller machine (ATM) card is issued with a PIN that the customer types into a numeric keypad. The card itself has an account number printed on it, and a magnetic strip with that same number encoded on it. Because only the owner of the card should know the PIN, access to the account is granted when the correct PIN is entered for the card that was inserted.

**User IDs and Passwords**   A major player in nearly every computer security system is the combination of a user ID and password. The user ID is the known portion of the combination, the identification of the user relative to which account the user is seeking access. The password is the core security element that is used as authentication. The user ID is generally publicly known. The password is the secret part, the part that any hacker or other type of cyber criminal seeks.

Since passwords are such critical elements to any security system, it is important to create one that is not easily guessed. Good passwords have two somewhat contradictory characteristics: They must be easy to remember and hard to guess. It is simple to think of a random string of letters and numbers that no one would ever guess, but while this password is definitely secure, it is not a good password. Passwords are of little use to a user who forgets them. Complicated passwords tend to leave the user no option but to write them down, which is a major breach of security.

On the other hand, it is just as easy to come up with passwords that are of no value because they are so obvious. These passwords err on the side of being memorable, but again provide little security because anyone could come up with them by guessing. For this reason, passwords that are identical to the user ID, or the name of the user, or some other familiar thing in the user's life are weak choices. Other types of ineffective, generic passwords are words such as *Password* or *Qwerty* (made by typing an obvious sequence of letters on the keyboard). To create a secure, memorable password, use one or two common or familiar words connected with a number or other symbol. Examples include the following:

- lightning72
- dog+wings
- justice&acquittal
- cow&duck5

An emerging technology called **single sign-on (SSO)** will help eliminate some of the security risks of weak passwords, as it will allow users to have just one user ID and password to access all applications and systems.

**Smart Cards**   Authentication to computer systems can also be provided by smart card technology. These cards are similar to security cards or badges that are used for access to buildings and secured areas. Some smart cards are swiped in smart

## COMPUTER RENAISSANCE MAN

# Alan Kay

**THE LAPTOP COMPUTER,** object-oriented programming, and modern windowing GUI all have their roots in the genius of Alan Kay.

Kay was working as a musician when he enlisted in the Air Force in 1961. The aptitude test pointed him to computers, and he was sent to work on an IBM mainframe. After completing his stint in the Air Force, Kay earned a bachelor's degree in mathematics and molecular biology from the University of Colorado. From there, he entered the University of Utah and was awarded a master's degree in electrical engineering. He completed his formal education with a PhD in computer science.

Kay's early employment experiences included serving as a professor with the Stanford University Artificial Intelligence Laboratory and as a lead researcher at the Xerox Palo Alto Research Center. While working at Xerox, Kay was heavily influenced by his observations of children using computers. Children did not have the patience for a computer that was difficult to use. They also seemed to learn better from text interlaced with pictures and sounds. Kay's team at Xerox came up with an easy-to-use computer model that incorporated lots of graphics and animation.

Another influence on Kay was his training as a biologist. He viewed the computer as a living organism consisting of individual, autonomous cells that cooperate to achieve a goal. This biological concept, and his lifelong interest in children and learning, led to the development of Smalltalk, the granddaddy of object-oriented programming languages.

Several other commonplace items of today's computing world owe their existence to Kay's vision. For example, at Xerox he built a model laptop with children particularly in mind. Called the Dynabook, the portable notebook used a flat screen, a stylus, a wireless network, and local storage. However, Kay could not convince Xerox management that the idea deserved funding.

In 1979, Steve Jobs and colleagues, who would later form the Apple Corporation, toured Kay's lab at Xerox. They were astounded by his ideas, including the mouse, the windowing interface using overlapping windows and icons, and the Smalltalk programming language. Kay eventually joined the Apple team in 1984, the year Apple Computer produced the user-friendly Macintosh that revolutionized personal computing.

Kay has earned numerous awards and distinctions, including the J-D Warnier Prix d'Informatique, the ACM Systems Software Award, the Computers & Communication Foundation Prize, and the Lewis Branscomb Technology Award. Additionally, he has been elected a fellow of the American Academy of Arts and Sciences, the National Academy of Engineering, and the Royal Society of Arts. He has served as a fellow at Xerox, Apple, and Disney and currently is president of Viewpoints Research Institute.

More than 40 years ago, Alan Kay conceived the idea of inexpensive, powerful computers, simple and entertaining enough for even a child. His motto, "The best way to predict the future is to invent it," helped pave the way to the personal computers of today.

A smart card in close proximity to a computer can authenticate a user and provide system access.

card readers, and others just need to be in proximity to the computer to authenticate the use and provide access to the system. These cards provide quicker access to systems than typing in a user ID and password, but there are security drawbacks since there is no proof that the person with the smart card is the owner of it.

**Biometrics**   A **biometric identifier** is a physical attribute that is unique to an individual and can be used to authenticate identity. Through a biometric authentication system, computers can effectively measure biometric identifiers such as a voice, a fingerprint, hand geometry, facial geometry, a retinal pattern, an iris pattern, and a handwritten signature. Many companies are now using biometric

Tech Demo 8-4
Biometic
Identification

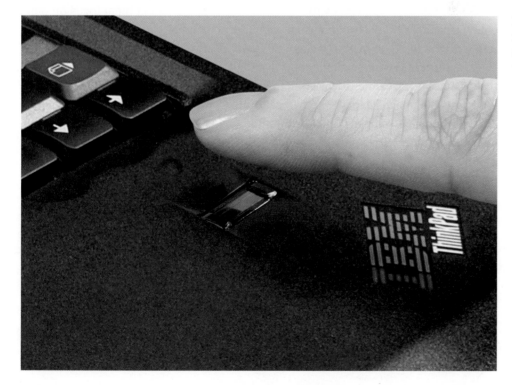

Notebook computers may have fingerprint scanners to recognize their users.

# Putting a Finger on Smell

**FINGERPRINT SCANNERS,** secure and convenient, are increasingly being used to screen employees and travelers in airports, to access safety deposit boxes, and to log on to computers. Also on the increase: fake fingers made of silicone, gelatin, and even Play-Doh. Biometric experts are constantly fine-tuning the scanners to stay one step ahead of those attempting to beat the fingerprint system.

A real human finger has its own distinct smell. Davide Maltoni at University of Bologna in Italy is exploiting that fact by combining a biometric reader with an electronic nose so that a perfect fingerprint match, if fabricated, would not pass the smell-test.

Electronic noses are currently used to monitor food quality, detect chemical leaks, and assess pollution levels. The e-nose contains a metal oxide film, which reacts to different gas molecules by changing its electrical resistance. Those changes are registered by electrodes. From the electronic signals it receives, the e-nose software is able to recognize smells it has been programmed to identify.

Testing his device with real fingers and an assortment of fake ones, Maltoni had a success rate of 92 percent. Once Maltoni fine-tunes his sniffer, fingerprints would need to not just read correctly, but smell correctly.

authentication systems to make sure that only authorized employees are allowed to enter secure areas, such as a research building. Biometric devices automatically recognize human beings in a variety of ways. Essentially, all of them focus on one characteristic or body part and use a computer to compare known patterns against a measurement taken by the device.

A **fingerprint scanner** simply makes a digital image of a person's fingerprint, just as an optical scanner turns a photograph into a GIF file. A computer then compares the image against a known set of fingerprint images stored in a database. If the image matches up, the system knows who is requesting access and can act appropriately. It is now a common security device on notebook computers.

A **hand geometry system** determines a person's identity by measuring the dimensions of a person's hand, which are unique to each individual. This system is touted as harder to fool than a fingerprint scanner, as it is more difficult to create a fake hand than a fake image of a fingerprint. The technology has actually been in use for some 20 years, having been introduced in the early 1980s at Shearson Hamill, an investment bank on Wall Street. Today's hand geometry systems take more than 90 measurements of the hand to build a profile for comparison purposes.

Through **computerized facial recognition (CFR)**, a computer recognizes a human face by comparing it with existing scans of photos in a database. These systems are popular, particularly in Las Vegas casinos, which are among the most camera-laden environments on earth. Everyone who enters the establishment is photographed and tracked automatically by numerous cameras from various angles. The face of each customer is then compared against a database of known cheaters. If there is a match, security personnel are alerted.

If you've ever looked closely into someone's eyes, you may have noticed that the iris is not a single, formless blob of color. Rather, it is a set of complex shapes that vary in color around the entire circle of the iris. Indeed, there are hundreds of details about irises that can be measured and which together form the unique patterns that are stored in an **iris recognition system**. Similarly, a **retinal recognition system** uses the unique patterns of blood vessels found on the back of the eyeball as identifiers.

Although relatively costly, iris and retinal recognition systems are highly effective. They are used primarily in high-security environments such as military installations and financial institutions. More recently, they are being piloted for use in airports in the United States. In Europe, the Amsterdam airport uses iris scanners to identify travelers, and officials may soon embed iris codes within passports.

A **voice verification system** employs a technology that been in use for several years. By measuring the pitch and timbre of a human voice, computers are able to recognize individuals. Simple systems require that a specific phrase be spoken for recognition to work. Newer, more advanced systems are much more capable, and can recognize voices even under difficult circumstances. Law enforcement agencies are developing systems that will identify known voices of criminals from among thousands of phone calls. The National Security Agency (NSA) monitors calls coming into and going out of the United States and uses computers to look for key phrases and voices being spoken to identify threats such as terrorists.

Historically, signatures have been used to authenticate documents. For years signatures have served as a low-tech way of verifying that someone is authorized

A CFR system can be used to compare a face against photos in an existing database.

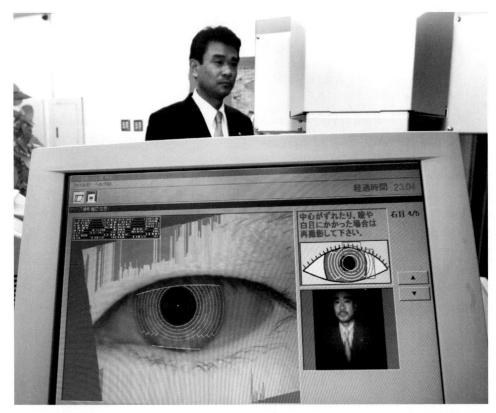

The unique patterns of human irises can be used to identify individuals.

Many university campuses use webcams as a security measure.

to sell a property, for example, or to write a check. A computer **signature verification system** works by comparing a scanned-in signature against a known database of signatures to determine if the signature is a forgery or if it is authentic. One of the keys to the technology is the measurement not only of the completed signature, but how it was created. The system takes into account the speed of each stroke, the pen pressure, the direction and length of strokes, and the delays and points where the pen is lifted from the paper. The combined measurements make forgery much more difficult.

## Data Encryption

To prevent people from spying on sensitive transactions, such as the transmission of a user name and password across the Internet, companies use data **encryption** to scramble the information so that it is unreadable before it is transmitted. The unreadable, encrypted text is called **ciphertext**. Data encryption schemes include an **encryption key** that is generated automatically and shared between the two computers that wish to communicate (see Figure 8-5). This security can also work with cell phones and other forms of communication devices. Without this key, it is very difficult to break the encryption code.

The FBI and the computer industry are at odds when it comes to encryption. Members of the e-commerce community argue that to continue expanding online banking and Internet purchasing options, more security will be required. They want to use longer, more complex encryption keys that make the encoded data more difficult to decipher. The U.S. government and the FBI in particular, however, want a limited level of encryption. Their goal is to provide some security for users, but if they get a warrant that allows them to "listen in," they want law enforcement to be able to crack the code at will. Both sides regularly lobby Congress on this issue.

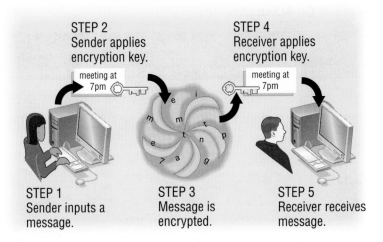

**STEP 2**
Sender applies
encryption key.

meeting at
7pm

**STEP 4**
Receiver applies
encryption key.

meeting at
7pm

**STEP 1**
Sender inputs a
message.

**STEP 3**
Message is
encrypted.

**STEP 5**
Receiver receives
message.

**Figure 8-5  Using an Encryption Key**
An encryption key is used to secure messages that are sent across the Internet.

**Encryption Methods**   Many different encryption methods may be used for coding and decoding data, and an encryption key may use more than one method. Table 8-1 illustrates four ways data can be encrypted.

The two basic types of encryption methods are secret key (also called private key) and public key encryption. With **secret key encryption**, both the customer and the business use the same encryption key to encrypt and decrypt the data. **Public key encryption** uses two encryption keys: a public encryption key that all authorized users know and a secret encryption key that only the sender and the receiver know. For example, a public key may be used to encrypt customer data being transmitted, and, upon receipt, a private key may be used to decrypt the data. A popular public encryption technology used to transmit data over the Internet is **RSA**, named for its developers, Rivest, Shamir, and Adleman.

**Encryption Protocols**   Several security and encryption technologies have been developed to ensure the protection and confidentiality of personal data and messages being transmitted over the Internet. Among the more used technologies are two cryptographic protocols called Secure Sockets Layer (SSL) and Transport Layer Security (TLS), its successor. Both protocols are substantially the same.

**Secure Sockets Layer (SSL)** is a cryptographic protocol that provides secure communications on the Internet for transmitting data such as credit card activities, e-mail, Internet faxing, and online banking. SSL uses two keys to encrypt data—a public key known to everyone and a private or secret key known only to the recipient of the message. SSL, first introduced in 1994 by Netscape, has become the de facto standard for e-commerce transaction security. It is supported by both Netscape Navigator and Internet Explorer and many Web sites use the protocol to obtain confidential user information, such as credit card and bank account numbers. URLs that use the SSL protocol start with https instead of http.

Another protocol for transmitting data securely over the World Wide Web is **Secure HTTP (S-HTTP)**. Whereas SSL creates a secure connection between a client and a server, over which any amount of data can be sent securely, S-HTTP is designed to transmit individual messages securely. SSL and S-HTTP, therefore, can be seen as complementary rather than competing technologies. Both protocols have been approved by the Internet Engineering Task Force (IETF) as a standard.

**Table 8-1  Ways Data Can Be Encrypted**

| Encryption Method | Word in Plaintext (English Format) | Word in Ciphertext (Coded Format) | Explanation |
|---|---|---|---|
| replace characters with different characters | COMPUTER | XMRCEYLZ | Each character is replaced by a different character. |
| insert an extra character after each character | JOHN | JBOBHBNB | The letter B is inserted after each character. |
| remove and store characters | INFORMATION | INFRMAION | Every fourth letter (O, T) is removed and stored. |
| switch characters | PAYMENT | APMYNET | Beginning at left, pairs of letters are reversed. |

## Monitoring and Auditing

Go to this title's Internet Resource Center and read the article titled "Surveillance Technologies." www.emcp.net/CUT4e

Companies realize that unauthorized access to systems and information may come from inside the company. Many companies have implemented monitoring of employees' online and offline activities while at work. Software packages used for monitoring include keyboard loggers (discussed earlier in the chapter) and Internet traffic trackers, which record the Web sites that employees visit for later auditing. Some employers also use video surveillance through webcams or closed circuit cameras to observe activities that occur around critical systems or data storage.

Unfortunately, our privacy laws are quite lax in the area of preventing video surveillance. In many states, there are essentially no laws preventing someone from videotaping even a person's most private moments without his knowledge. Court battles are under way and new laws are being written, but the process is slow and action is unlikely until there is a high-publicity case. In the meantime, employers are videotaping their employees and store owners are carefully watching customers. In many states, it is not illegal for employers to monitor the activity of their employees in many different ways. If there are restrictions, companies can easily get around them by having employees sign a waiver as a condition of employment, allowing the monitoring without consent. Many people don't realize what they are signing when they take that new job.

**Auditing** involves a review of monitoring data and system logins to look for unauthorized access or suspicious behavior. A security or audit officer typically reviews reports that keyboard loggers, Internet traffic analyzers, and usage of systems create. This officer is looking for abnormal patterns of behavior or login failures that suggest inappropriate access to data. This information is reviewed after it occurs, so it may provide supporting information in the case of an attack. It may also indicate areas of system vulnerability that need to be reviewed and improved.

# OnThe**Horizon**

**THE TOPIC OF SECURITY IS AT THE TOP** of legislative and corporate agendas due to concerns that criminal and terrorist organizations could exploit insecure communication networks, including the Internet. New developments in biometrics and cryptography show great promise in meeting coming security needs.

Biometric systems that can identify people automatically on the basis of fingerprints, speech, eye, and hand measurements are already in use, amd more sophisticated biometric technologies are just beyond the horizon. As computers become faster and our databases of biometric identifiers grow, the power of these systems to identify anyone, with or without his or her knowledge, grows as well. The initial release of Windows Vista will provide software developers with the capability of integrating biometric systems for the authentication of users, and industry observers predict that biometric authentication systems will one day be incorporated into all operating systems.

Cryptography, the process of transforming information into data that cannot be understood by unauthorized parties, has found a number of different communications applications, perhaps most importantly through offering a secure method for conducting financial transactions over the Web. Work on devising new and improved systems is ongoing and new applications that will enhance communications security are anticipated.

## Keystroke Dynamics

Taking keystroke logging to the next level is a biometric technology called keystroke dynamics. This involves the measure of a behavior that is virtually impossible for someone to falsify. Much like a signature, each person has a different pattern of typing on a keyboard. Besides speed and accuracy, the system also measures the dwell time, which is the amount of time a given key is depressed, and the flight time, which is the amount of time between strokes.

Keyboard dynamics is a software solution. When a user types, his or her typing rhythm is compared with a database of known users' typing rhythms. This could be used as an authentication technology to provide access to systems in combination with a user ID and password. It could also help companies that must comply with strict auditing guidelines

Shoulder-surfers watch your keystrokes to learn your network password or ATM PIN.

like Sarbanes-Oxley in financial services and the Health Insurance Portability and Accountability Act in health care. In this case, keystroke dynamics could also be used in monitoring and auditing processes to verify that the right person actually is using the user ID and password in use. A limitation of keystroke dynamics is the lack of uniformity among keyboards, which can cause variations in measurement.

### Merging Biometrics

No single method of biometric identification is capable of identifying every individual. Some people lack readable fingerprints, others have eye pigmentation that prevents successful iris scans, and facial recognition systems can be thwarted by superficial changes in appearance. To overcome these shortcomings, biometric researchers are now working on multimodal systems that combine different biometric identification methods into one system. Multimodal biometric systems assign probability scores for each biometric and combine them to offer much greater accuracy than systems dependent on a single biometric marker.

### Quantum Cryptography

One of the problems inherent in encryption is the fact that if somebody intercepts the randomly generated key, that person can then unravel the later encrypted transmission. Since the key must be sent and agreed upon by both ends of a connection (such as a secure connection between you and your bank account), that key is not secure. If a spying program gets that key, the security is broken for the duration of the connection.

Quantum cryptography is a new attempt to make even the starting keys secret. It is based on the physics principle that even observing a quantum phenomenon is enough to disrupt it. Using quantum devices to transmit light signals over fiber-optic cable, two parties that wish to send a secret message can exchange their unprotected key as normal to start the sequence. If anyone observes the key, the system will be disturbed, and both sides will be aware of the security breach. If no one observes the key, then the transmission will continue normally, with complete security. Quantum cryptography is still experimental, but government and industry are studying the technology as a means of ensuring secure transactions.

# Chapter**Summary**

## Why is risk assessment important when defining security strategies?

Organizations need to assess the level of security risk that they face in order to develop an effective security strategy. The two factors that help determine the level of risk are **threat**, the severity of a security breach, and **vulnerability**, the likelihood of a security breach of systems or data.

## What are the security risks on networks and the Internet?

Networks and the Internet are threatened by unauthorized access, denial of service (DoS) attacks, and information theft. Unauthorized access includes the work of hackers and crackers. A **hacker** is a computer expert who seeks programming, security, and system challenges. A **cracker** is a hacker with malicious or criminal intent. **Cyberwars**, or online attacks between countries, have the potential to cause as much damage as traditional wars. Hackers and crackers often use techniques such as vulnerable user IDs and passwords, **system backdoors**, and **spoofing**. **Denial of Service (DoS) attacks** are carried out by organized groups of hackers who run a computer program that repeatedly asks a Web site for information or access. Bombarding the site thousands of times a second means that legitimate users cannot access the site and thus are denied service. **Industrial espionage**, or stealing corporate information, is a type of information theft. Information can also be stolen through **data browsing**, which is an invasion of privacy. Lax wireless security can also provide information thieves with an entryway to systems with sensitive information

## What are computer viruses and worms and how do they attack computers?

Computer viruses may be classified as nuisance viruses, espionage viruses, or data-destructive viruses. **Nuisance viruses** are more annoying than damaging. **Espionage viruses** are meant to capture information to access systems at a later time. **Data-destructive viruses** may erase data or make it unreadable. Viruses may spread through e-mail, the Internet, or shared devices such as flash drives. There are a variety of methods under which viruses operate, including **macro viruses**, **variant viruses**, **stealth viruses**, **boot sector viruses**, **Trojan horse viruses**, **multipartite viruses**, and **logic bomb viruses**. A **worm** is similar to a virus, but it actively attempts to move and copy itself.

## What hardware and software security risks need to be considered?

Although hackers, crackers, and viruses garner the most attention as security risks, companies face a variety of other dangers to their hardware and software systems, including systems failure, employee theft, and cracking software for copying. A sudden rise or fall in the power level, called a **power spike**, can cause poor performance or even permanently damage hardware. An inexpensive type of power strip called a **surge protector** can guard against power spikes, and a more elaborate power protection system is an **uninterruptible power supply (UPS)**, which provides a battery backup. Employee theft includes employees taking hardware or software home for work purposes and never returning it and blatant removal of equipment for personal use or profit. Evasion of software protection features for copying is called a **crack**.

## What security strategies will protect hardware and software?

One of the best protections against any kind of data loss is to plan for the worst. This means asking the question, "What does the company need to keep if all data on the desktops or the network server were lost?" and then backing up these files on a regular schedule. Backup plans are part of an overall **disaster recovery plan** that also includes remotely located backup copies and **redundant systems**. Other security strategies include implementing physical security for computer systems, setting up firewalls to protect networks, using **network sniffers**, using antivirus software, using data **encryption** for sensitive transactions, and implementing strong authentication. Strong **authentication** methods include personal identification numbers (PINs), user IDs and passwords, smart cards, and biometrics.

# Key Terms

*Numbers indicate the pages where terms are first cited in the chapter. An alphabetized list of key terms with definitions (in English and Spanish) can be found on the Encore CD that accompanies this book. In addition, these terms and definitions are included in the end-of-book glossary.*

# ChapterExercises

## *Tutorial >* Exploring Windows

Tutorial 8 teaches you how to delete and restore files in the Recycle Bin and how to empty the Recycle Bin to maintain plenty of free hard disk space.

## *Expanding Your Knowledge >* Articles and Activities

 *Visit the Internet Resource Center for this title at www.emcp.net/CUT4e, read the articles related to this chapter, and complete the corresponding activities. The article titles include:*

- Topic 8-1: Protecting the Internet from Terrorists
- Topic 8-2: Improving Home PC Security
- Topic 8-3: Virus Detection and Prevention
- Topic 8-4: Surveillance Technologies

## *Terms Check >* Matching

 *For additional practice, go to the Internet Resource Center for this title at www.emcp.net/CUT4e for a chapter crossword puzzle.*

Write the letter of the correct answer on the line before each numbered item.

| | |
|---|---|
| a. Trojan horse | f. employee monitoring |
| b. hacker | g. cyberwar |
| c. biometric device | h. data backup |
| d. crack | i. surge protector |
| e. macro virus | j. firewall |

_____ 1. Protective software or hardware that is designed to prevent hacking and other attacks over a network.

_____ 2. The altering of a software product to remove copy protection.

_____ 3. A type of virus that hides within a data file or a program.

_____ 4. A method of infecting a file that affects a specific component of application software such as Microsoft Word or Microsoft Excel.

_____ 5. A critical and perhaps major component of any disaster recovery plan.

_____ 6. A device that helps prevent computer damage when there is a spike in the electrical power supply.

_____ 7. An individual who breaks into security systems, either out of curiosity or for the challenge.

_____ 8. A term used to describe an organized series of hacker attacks between citizens of different nations over the Internet.

____ 9. A machine or system that measures a human characteristic for purposes of identification.

____ 10. The legal practice of tracking Web-surfing habits, reading e-mail, and videotaping workers without their knowledge or consent.

## *Technology Illustrated* > **Identify the Process**

What process is illustrated in Part A of this drawing? What process is illustrated in Part B? Identify each and write a paragraph explaining how each process works, step by step.

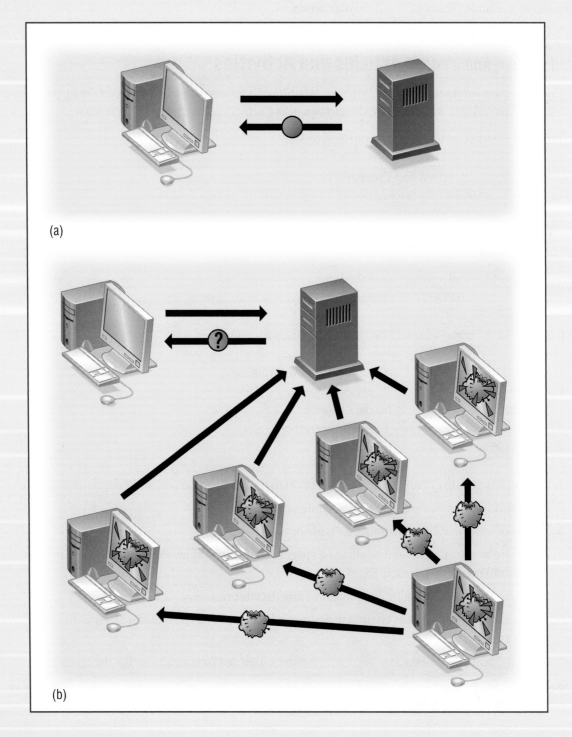

(a)

(b)

## Knowledge Check > **Multiple Choice**

  *Additional quiz questions are available on the Encore CD that accompanies this book as well as on the Internet Resource Center for this title at www.emcp.net/CUT4e.*

Circle the letter of the best answer from those provided.

1. A company's most valuable possession is often its
   a. information.
   b. software.
   c. applications.
   d. network.

2. A _____ is a work-around or an alteration of a program so that software copy protection is removed.
   a. logic bomb
   b. hacker
   c. crack
   d. software pirate

3. Passwords are a form of the security measure known as
   a. encryption.
   b. information.
   c. authentication.
   d. monitoring.

4. _____ measure a biometric identifier.
   a. Fingerprint scanners
   b. Hand geometry systems
   c. Computerized facial recognition (CFR) systems
   d. All of these

5. A _____ is a program that displays network traffic.
   a. network hacker
   b. network sniffer
   c. network hub
   d. firewall

6. What is the difference between a software virus and a software worm?
   a. A worm is bigger and uses more RAM.
   b. A virus works more slowly.
   c. A virus always destroys data.
   d. A worm actively tries to send itself places.

7. _____ eliminate(s) the need for users to remember user IDs and passwords for multiple systems.
   a. Single sign-on (SSO)
   b. A screen saver
   c. Password protection software
   d. Authentication

8. Which of the following is the most likely way to get a virus on your computer?
   a. Downloading a game from the Internet and running it.
   b. Acquiring it with software installations.
   c. Using another computer in your house that already is infected.
   d. Sending e-mail to your friends.

9. A powerful form of attack upon a Web site that is difficult to guard against and often involves an organized team of hackers is called
   a. virus attachments.
   b. spoofing.
   c. denial of service.
   d. worm armies.

10. A power supply for your computer that will keep it running smoothly during brownouts and blackouts is called a
    a. surge protector.
    b. UPS.
    c. power strip.
    d. firewall.

## *Things That Think* > **Brainstorming New Uses**

In groups or individually, contemplate the following questions and develop as many answers as you can.

1. Computers may soon be experts at identifying human faces, better at the task than even humans themselves. If a robot could perform this task, how might this be beneficial? What could a robot do if it could recognize human faces that it might not be able to do otherwise? What kind of new jobs does this open up for computers in the future?

2. Millions of e-mail messages are transmitted every day. The vast majority of them are personal or business-related. Some, however, indicate criminal intent. What if a program were able to read all of them, discern ones that were suspicious, and forward them to police for investigation? Would this be a beneficial system to employ or not? For more information, investigate the FBI e-mail monitoring system called Carnivore.

3. What are some new ways in which biometric identification systems can be used? Create a chart that lists several types of systems and a new application (or area) for each identification system.

## *Key Principles* > **Completion**

Fill in the blanks with the appropriate words or phrases.

1. A(n) _____ virus hides inside another legitimate program or data file.

2. _____ is a type of information theft that equates to an invasion of privacy.

3. The difference between a hacker and a(n) _____ is that the latter has malicious intent.

4. The process of fooling another computer by pretending to send packets from a legitimate source is called _____.

5. A(n) _____ is a physical attribute that is unique to an individual and can be used to authenticate identity.

6. The proof that a user is who he says he is, and that he is authorized to access an account is called _____.

7. A hardware problem that causes the electricity to surge and possibly damage data is called a(n) _____.

8. A plan to fix a system after a catastrophe is called the _____.

9. The act of one company seeking illicit information from another company is called _____.

10. A rare and sophisticated virus that attempts to hide from antivirus software by covering up its identifiable characteristics is called a(n) _____.

## Tech Architecture > Label the Drawing

In this illustration of how software viruses infect computers, identify each step.

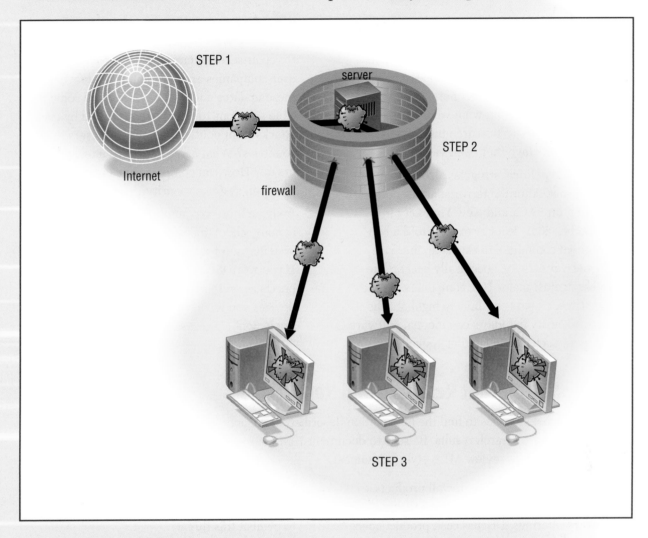

## Techno Literacy > Research and Writing

Develop appropriate written responses based on your research for each item.

1. Does your school monitor student and employee Web traffic? Find out what kind of surveillance, if any, is used at your school or workplace. Who is in charge of the surveillance system? Who decided to put it into place, and for what purpose? Does it apply only to students, or to employees as well? Are e-mails stored even after users mark them as deleted? Are security cameras hidden in the buildings?

2. How easy is it to acquire and use spygear? Find an advertisement for spy gear (minicameras, recorders, and spyware) and research the store or manufacturer. What kinds of products does it sell? Does it use suggestive advertising that indicates their products are suitable for voyeurism? Does the company make any attempt to discuss the ethical and legal implications of using their products? How much do their products cost, and how easy are they to use?

## Technology Issues > **Team Problem-Solving**

In groups, brainstorm possible solutions to the issues presented.

1. You find out that a coworker has been sending company e-mail addresses to a marketing company for a per-name fee. This company sells their mailing list to other businesses to use in sending unsolicited e-mail offers. How would this make you feel, and what would you propose to do about it? Research the current laws in your state. Have they been violated?

2. Worldwide political struggles also affect the Internet. After the terrorist attacks on Washington, D.C., and New York City in September 2001, security experts told a congressional committee to expect an increase in cyberwar activity, specifically hacker-like attacks against major U.S. companies. At the same time, experts continue to highlight the lack of security in today's commercial software packages, such as information systems software. Systems administrators find it difficult to keep up with software updates and patches to repair security cracks. In some cases, end-user companies are not taking advantage of these updates and patches. What are some possible solutions to the problems posed by cyber attacks from politically motivated users in other countries? What can software manufacturers do? How can companies be encouraged to maintain systems security?

3. Imagine there are numerous security problems at your school, including thefts, hacking into systems, and harassment in the parking lots. If you were given a budget and the power to purchase and install any computerized security devices you wanted, which ones would you implement at your school?

## Mining Data > **Internet Research and Reporting**

Conduct Internet searches to find the information described in the activities below. Write a brief report summarizing your research results. Be sure to document your sources, using the MLA format (see Chapter 1, page 42, to review MLA style guidelines).

1. Find information on two firewall products. Write a description that compares the two software offerings. Discuss cost, product specifications, and any limitations. If possible, find reviews of the products so you can judge which one is better or if they are equally effective.

2. With the current explosion of wireless technologies, what new security risks are we encountering? Find a story about a virus designed specifically for wireless systems. What tools might a wireless hacker use to invade networks remotely? What strategies might a company use to combat this threat?

3. Who is using facial recognition systems now? Find companies and organizations that are using facial recognition and explain why and how they use this technology. Would it make you feel more or less comfortable to know that a computer-driven system was identifying everyone at school or work? Why or why not?

## Technology Timeline > **Predicting Next Steps**

Since early civilizations, people have found it necessary to send secret communications that require a "key" of some kind to decode them. Data encryption has become particularly important with the evolution of the Internet, since companies and individuals routinely send private or secure information over the Net. Look at the timeline below outlining the major steps in the history of encryption techniques. Then research the subject and add at least two more steps to the timeline.

**5th century B.C.** Greeks use numbers to represent letters in sending secret messages.

**16th–18th centuries** Ruling monarchs use substitution-cipher techniques (letters to represent other alphabet letters).

**World War II** U.S. military uses the Navajo language to transmit secure communications.

**1950s–1960s** Encryption systems use keys and algorithms.

**1970s** Data Encryption Standard (DES) algorithm is introduced.

**1991** Pretty Good Privacy (PGP) is released as freeware and becomes a worldwide standard in data encryption software.

**1994** Netscape releases Secure Sockets Layer (SSL) technology.

**1999** Wired Equivalent Privacy (WEP) is ratified as a part of the IEEE (Institute of Electrical and Electronics Engineers) 802.11 standard.

**2002** Advanced Encryption Standard (AES) becomes a standard by the U.S. government.

**2004** The 802.11i extension to the Wi-Fi standard is ratified as an improvement over the WEP standard.

## Ethical Dilemmas > **Group Discussion and Debate**

As a class or within an assigned group, discuss the following ethical dilemma.

In August 2003, the school district of Biloxi, Mississippi, became the first district in the nation to install webcams in every classroom. The purpose was to deter crime and general misbehavior. Using the new technology, the school superintendent, principals, and security officers can view a classroom at any time from any computer throughout the school. This means teachers as well as students are "on stage" at all times.

Does this use of webcams constitute an invasion of privacy? If it reduces crime and instances of disruptive behavior, do the beneficial effects outweigh any possible ethical concerns? Is there a potential for misusing the technology? If so, how? Should all schools adopt the use of webcams?

# Database
# and
# Information
# Management

## Learning Objectives

> Explain how databases work and identify their basic structural elements

> Identify some common information systems that use databases

> Describe the elements of a database management system (DBMS) and their functions

> Discuss the different database classifications

> Explain how databases are designed

> Differentiate among methods of data processing

> Describe the areas of responsibility for a database administrator

# CyberScenario

**FATHER'S DAY WAS FAST APPROACHING** and Lenora still couldn't decide what kind of gift to buy her father-in-law. She was never really sure if he appreciated the cologne, neckties, or fishing gear she usually ended up buying. Hoping that he had taken her suggestion at Christmas to set up an online wish list, Lenora began to check some of the more popular wish list and gift registry services on the Internet.

Finding his wish list on her first try, Lenora began to peruse the items he selected. The range of choices was impressive, from books to camping supplies to artwork. She narrowed down the list by selecting her preferred price range and then began to read product reviews from other consumers. She then checked for recently purchased items and was presented with a hint to select a leather case and software for the GPS unit that someone else bought for him this week. Lenora smiled to herself as she pictured his surprise at her buying a useful birthday gift!

Next, she chose wrapping paper, customized a birthday card, and clicked the *Buy* button. The Web site informed Lenora of the total cost, and confirmed that the gifts would arrive on time. The entire shop-

ping experience had taken a mere 12 minutes. Lenora breathed a sigh of relief, knowing that this time she had bought her father-in-law gifts he was sure to like. Lenora's search illustrates how e-commerce transactions involve a series of online database interactions. The initial search for a product queries (asks) a database for information. A sales record is created in the company's database when a payment is made. That database then uses the customer's credit card number to access a bank database and electronically transfer funds to the retailer. Finally, the e-commerce site's database interacts with a shipping company's database to ensure that the purchase reaches the customer without delay.

## Database Basics

A **database** is a computerized system for storing information in an organized manner so that it can be searched for and retrieved when needed. Businesses, government groups, private organizations, and academic institutions all use databases, and they represent the dominant use of computing power in the business world

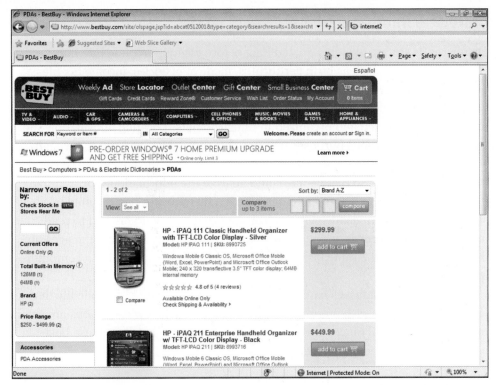

Electronic-commerce sites use databases to record price, sales, and other information about their products.

today. Without databases the Internal Revenue Service could not collect income taxes, the American Red Cross could not allocate funds, and colleges across the country could not operate efficiently. Schools use databases to store and handle grades, class schedules, tuition payments, library fines, and other records relevant to education. Colleges typically use enrollment trend reports to plan for new courses and to branch out into new academic areas. In these cases they might use not only their own database information, but also reports from national college associations and the federal government.

Databases are used for more than routine operations. Executives commonly consult company databases to aid in their decision making. If a company is considering opening a new branch office, managers and other strategic planners can carefully examine databases describing the purchasing habits of local consumers in order to choose the best location.

## Data vs. Information

The terms *data* and *information* are key concepts in understanding the importance of computerized databases. Recall from Chapter 1 that data is a collection of raw, unorganized (unprocessed) content in the form of words, numbers, sounds, or images. Data associated with other useful data on the same topic becomes information. The ability to associate or organize stored data in a variety of meaningful ways represents the power of database software. For example, an insurance company might store ZIP code information in its database, but a ZIP code alone is not particularly useful. However, when the ZIP code is associated with other data such as a name, address, or phone number, this set of organized data becomes information that can be used to locate and identify a customer.

## Historical Database Forms

Databases as storage systems existed long before computers came into being. Important records such as birth certificates, medical histories, income tax files, payroll records, and car license data were stored on paper before the first database software was developed in the 1950s and 1960s. These printed documents were usually collected and organized in filing cabinets. Locating information and structuring it for various purposes was possible, but it involved sifting through stacks of paper, identifying the desired data, and then writing or typing selected items on more paper so that people could analyze the information. For example, if a health department wanted to determine if a flu outbreak had resulted in a significant increase in deaths within a certain age group, workers had to read mounds of death records and manually note the causes of death and the ages of the victims. Today the same task could be executed in minutes using a computerized database.

Computerized databases have become so useful in all areas of public life that paper-based storage systems are rarely encountered. The few exceptions are small independent medical offices and some small retail shops, but even these businesses are rapidly moving to electronic systems.

## The Importance of Accurate Data

Databases are records of events or situations, so they must be continually updated to ensure that the data they contain is accurate. Consider, for example, the situation of an insurance company that maintains a database containing names, addresses, birth dates, and policy information. Several different departments in the company may share the database. Marketing sends out information whenever policy benefits change. They also send mailings to people who may be interested in new benefits. The accounting department uses the database for mailing billing

Go to this title's Internet Resource Center and read the article titled "The National Electronic Disease Surveillance System (NEDSS)." www.emcp.net/CUT4e

Paper forms served as a primitive type of database before records were computerized.

Inventory data and sales data must be accurate in order to manage a business.

notices. Company managers regularly generate reports, or information combined from linked database tables, to forecast new directions for the firm. If a policyholder moves to a new address, the database must be updated to reflect the change, or the information the company uses will be incorrect. Any inaccuracy will create an avalanche of problems throughout the different company departments and will reduce the quality of the data in the database.

Data quality is particularly important when considering that summarized information is often used for decision making. Every retail clerk, for example, helps tally store sales. Each entry is stored in a database that constantly tracks a store's current status. From the company's viewpoint this task is of vital importance. Sales information entered into the database allows managers to decide what supplies need to be ordered, and it provides a constantly updated snapshot of revenue.

## Levels of Data within a Database

The ability to organize and reorganize data for different purposes is due to two database characteristics: their vast storage potential and the way they organize data. Traditional databases organize data in a hierarchical fashion, containing information about entities in the form of fields, records, and files. Figure 9-1 illustrates this hierarchy.

 Tech Demo 9-1
Database
Structure

**Entities**  An **entity** is a person, place, thing, or event. Database files record information about different entities using fields, records, and files. A typical entity might be a sales transaction that describes products removed from inventory and the amount of money received for those products. Other examples of entities include student grades, traffic violations, and telephone records.

**Fields**  The smallest element of data in a database is a field. A **field** is a single value, such as a name, address, or dollar amount. A field generally has three attributes:

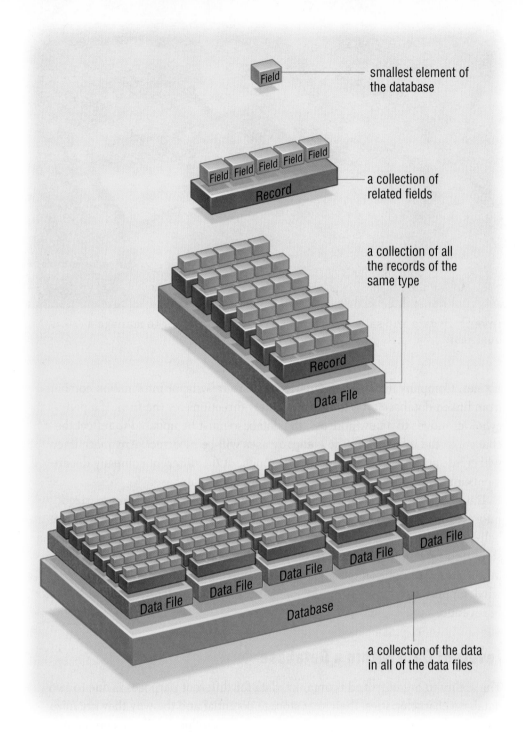

smallest element of the database

a collection of related fields

a collection of all the records of the same type

a collection of the data in all of the data files

**Figure 9-1 Traditional Database Hierarchy**
A traditional database, as shown above, organizes data in a hierarchy. The field is the smallest element. Fields are located within a record, and records are organized in a data file. The database is made up of a collection of data files.

- data type: usually numeric or text (numbers and letters)
- name: assigned by the person developing the database
- size: the number of characters that can be entered

A field called *FirstName* might have a size of 20 characters. The database automatically would truncate any name longer than 20 characters to fit into the field.

# Medical Records Go HITECH

**IMAGINE YOU'VE JUST MOVED** to a new city, and you need to see a doctor. What if your new doctor could access all of your medical records without waiting to receive them from your previous doctor's office? What if he or she could gain a thorough understanding of your health history instantly, just by clicking a mouse? That's exactly what the government thinks doctors should be able to do, and why it is helping to fund the creation of a massive new networked database—one that would contain the electronic health records of every American.

On February 17, 2009, President Obama signed the Health Information Technology for Economic and Clinical Health (HITECH) Act, which provides federal stimulus money to healthcare providers who adopt an electronic system for keeping patient medical records, and will likely carry penalties for those who do not do so by 2014. To receive funding, the provider's system must be interoperable, meaning the records can be viewed and shared by other providers. How exactly the records would be shared is still up in the air. While there has been talk of a national network, in which all the providers would have to agree on a standardized method of presenting information, some worry that this would create more problems than it solves. Instead, they envision a "network of networks," which would be similar to the system used to allow customers to access their bank accounts from any ATM across the world.

Because less than 10 percent of U.S. healthcare providers currently use electronic records, the task of creating this networked database is daunting and will take years to complete. However, the government believes that in the end, the system will save money, boost the economy, and most importantly, help Americans live healthier lives.

The most common data types are numeric and alphanumeric. **Numeric data** consists of numbers only. **Alphanumeric data** consists of letters, numbers, and sometimes special characters. Other types exist, such as logical yes/no fields, time and date fields, and memo fields, which allow unlimited character input. The more unusual data types include pictures, movies, and sound. Table 9-1 describes various field data types.

**Records**   A collection of related fields describing an event or situation is called a **record**. If a record covers mailing information, it would likely include fields for *name*, *address*, *city*, *state*, and *postal code*.

**Files**   A **database file** is a collection of records of the same type. When a database is designed and built, the designer must decide what records will be used, which fields will be in those records, and which data type and size each field will have. The record layout is used as the basis for each record in the table. For

### Table 9-1  Common Field Data Types

| Data Type | Description of Data |
|---|---|
| alphanumeric | textual information such as a person's name |
| numeric | numbers such as a count of inventoried products |
| logical | yes/no states such as "married" or "retired" |
| currency | dollar amounts such as a bank account balance |
| memo | lengthy text information, notes, or history |
| object | nontextual information such as pictures |
| hyperlink | connects a record to a Web address |
| date/time | allows only valid dates/times, such as November 12, 2007 |
| sequence (or autonumber) | integer that automatically increases whenever used; generally is used to make a primary key that automatically changes in order to be unique |

example, if a company's database has a record type called CUSTOMER, then there would be a record of CUSTOMER TYPE for each customer. All the records would use the same set of fields. When all the records of the same type are combined, they become a database file.

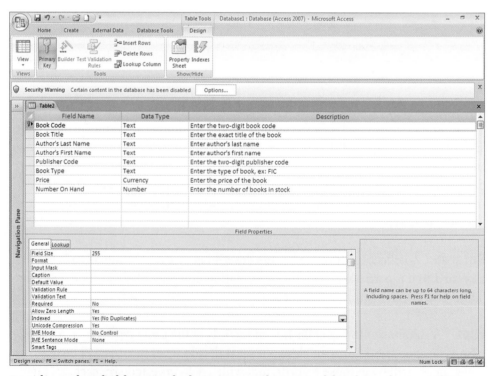

Deciding what fields to include in a record is part of database design. This screen is the design screen in Microsoft Access 2007.

# Databases and Information Systems

Networked databases allow businesses to save time and money by coordinating their operations. If each department in a business kept its own customer records, there would be duplicate entries, wasting time and causing confusion. If the different departments share a single networked database, information has to be entered only once, and it can then be accessed freely by anyone needing it.

The most common database application is an **information system**, which is a system of computer hardware, software, and operating procedures. Information systems are designed to meet the information needs of a company, such as tracking income and expenditures, recording transactions, sharing resources, and planning for future growth. A variety of information systems has evolved as software capabilities and market needs have changed over the years. This chapter provides a brief overview of information systems as they relate to databases.

## Management Information Systems

A **management information system (MIS)** is used to track and control every transaction through a database. A **transaction** is a business activity central to the nature of an enterprise. A transaction can be the sale of a product, the flight of an airliner, or the recording of a college course grade. A database stores the information that is at the core of any MIS system.

An MIS for an airline flight information display would need to handle flight numbers, gate numbers, and expected arrival and departure times. This information is available to the public and company employees to view. The data comes directly from a computer running an MIS. Every attendant at the ticket counter who enters data using a keyboard is communicating with the MIS. When a flight

Tech Demo 9-2
Web Databases

An airline's MIS would contain information about passengers, luggage, seat assignments, and flight arrival/departure times.

# Super-Secure Soccer

**THE GERMAN SPORTS ESTABLISHMENT** was proud and excited to host the 2006 World Cup Soccer Tournament. Yet with honor came the responsibility of protecting the large crowds gathered to watch the matches. Certainly no one wanted a repeat of the 1972 Munich Olympics, at which a group of Palestinian nationalists raided the Olympic village and killed 11 Israeli athletes.

But when the 64 games of the World Cup were over, no significant incidents had occurred—due no doubt in large part to the unprecedented security measures and the widespread use of databases to share information among agencies, venues, and security sites.

Operating 24 hours a day during the weeks in which the games took place, the National Information and Cooperation Center at the German Interior Ministry in Berlin monitored scores of computers fed from surveillance cameras in and around stadiums. Some of the cameras were equipped with biometric readers that could check the facial features of suspicious persons against a database of known soccer troublemakers. Thousands of tips from authorities in participating countries also contributed to the hooligan database. The computers also gathered and shared reports from police, Interpol, and intelligence services.

At the arenas, some of the 30,000 police officers on duty were equipped with wireless fingerprint devices that allowed them to instantly submit an optical scan of fingerprints taken from detained suspects into a central database at the German Federal Intelligence Service.

The 3.5 million ticket buyers had to provide name, address, date of birth, nationality, and ID card or passport number—more personal information than has ever been asked of a soccer fan. As fans entered the stadium, ticket takers scanned the RFID chips embedded in the tickets to look for matches in the database. The goal was to prevent entry to hooligans and known criminals, and also to thwart ticket scalping.

Germany took many other safety measures as well. Thousands of troops were on alert. Fifteen thousand private security specialists were hired for the games. Airspace over all the matches was closed. But the use of database and wireless devices were the hands-on technologies that helped deliver a safe and secure soccer scene for the 2006 World Cup in Germany.

finally does depart, another MIS run by the Federal Aviation Administration (FAA) uses radar systems to track its progress toward its destination.

## Office Information Systems

First popularized in the 1960s, the concept of an **office information system (OIS)** was billed as a replacement for paper-based information systems. An **electronic office** is an office that implements an OIS. Many people thought that the advent of electronic offices would lead to "paperless offices." Unfortunately, computer systems tend to generate more paper documents than their noncomputerized counterparts. This is in large part due to the ease with which printers can now churn out documents, as compared with the precomputer era when documents would have been typed manually.

The electronic office today is the norm rather than the exception. Most organizations of any size use a computerized OIS to manage their operations. For example, a shipping company OIS may hold records for every customer and corporate account and may use them to identify key clients. When an important client calls in, the receptionist can look him up in the database and immediately direct his call to the right agent. Clerks can also quickly access company work orders and check the status of any client orders.

## Decision Support Systems

A **decision support system (DSS)** is another common form of information system. Rather than simply tracking the day-to-day operations of a business, a DSS is designed to help management make decisions about an operation. A DSS might include a predictive model of the business that allows managers to work with "what-if" scenarios. If a business is considering expansion or the release of a new product, a DSS can help determine if the change would be likely to succeed or fail. The database could provide information on past performance, which the business owners could use to judge the cost of the expansion and any changes to revenue that might result.

## Factory Automation Systems

**Computer-aided manufacturing (CAM)** and **computer-integrated manufacturing (CIM)** are information systems that support factory automation. Generally, CAM refers to systems that run an assembly line directly, controlling the manufacturing process from the shop-floor level of conveyor belts and robots. CAM systems form a portion of a complete CIM system, a higher-level concept indicating a

CIM and CAM systems are used to automate manufacturing.

system that controls a manufacturing process from beginning to end. The database at the core of these systems stores information about factory operations, including counters that automatically add each item manufactured to inventory as it is made.

# Database Management System Software

**Database management system (DBMS) software** is software that allows a user to create and manage a computerized database. A DBMS also allows a user to create reports from stored data. IBM's DB2,, Oracle from Oracle Corporation, and Microsoft's SQL Server dominate the enterprise DBMS market. In the PC market, Microsoft Access is a widely used DBMS. In addition to maintaining the overall structure of the data, a DBMS has many other functions. Database keys, query tools, security elements, metadata, and backup and recovery utilities allow users to manipulate database data into information.

## Database Keys

A **key** is an attribute that can be used to identify a set of information and therefore provide a means to search a database. Within a database, fields are used as keys, and the designer designates the most important field in a record as the primary key. The **primary key** must also be unique, so it can be used to locate a record quickly. First names are poor keys because many people have the same first name. In a database that tracks traffic and parking violations, the state of registration plus car license plate number could be used as a primary key because no two cars registered in the same state can have the same license number. Phone, bank

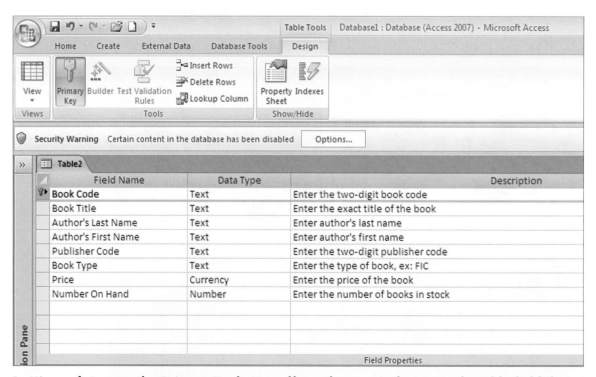

In Microsoft Access, the Primary Key button allows the user to designate the table field that will function as a primary key. To activate the feature, users select the desired table field and then click the Primary Key button on the Table Design toolbar.

## CEO, ORACLE CORPORATION
# Larry Ellison

**LARRY ELLISON, COFOUNDER AND CEO** of Oracle Corporation, is one of the most flamboyant and outspoken entrepreneurs of this century. Ellison is one of the richest as well. With a net worth of $50 billion and a financially successful company, he has reached the pinnacle of corporate success.

Among some of his friends and peers, Ellison may be considered an eccentric. It has been rumored that he once tried to purchase a Russian MIG fighter plane, but U.S. customs would not allow the plane into the country. In another incident, Ellison reportedly upset San Jose airport officials by landing his private jet after an 11 p.m. curfew, an action resulting in a $10,000 fine. To many of his fellow business associates, however, he is a business genius, a marketing whiz, and an avid promoter of simplified computing machines and network computers.

Oracle is the world's leading supplier of information management software, and the world's second-largest independent software company, boasting annual revenues of more than $9.7 billion. The company's diverse product line includes database software products, applications servers, software information management tools, and software suites for electronic commerce applications. Oracle's database software is the most widely used corporate database worldwide, and the company's product line continues to expand at a rapid pace.

account, credit card, social security, reservation confirmation, and work order numbers are commonly used as primary keys because they are unique. Primary keys are usually large numbers, but they may also be alphanumeric, like many drivers' license numbers.

It is possible to search a database without using the primary key, but it will be more difficult as other keys may not be unique and therefore may return a confusing array of results. This is why customers are usually asked to provide some form of unique identification when they call a company to inquire about a billing error or a product order. The requested information acts as a primary key, enabling the person assisting them to locate records quickly. If a service representative asked for a name, he would have to sort through records of everyone with the same name. This would waste time, as there could be thousands of duplicate names in a large database. Managing the enormous amounts of information in a database would be nearly impossible without primary keys.

Users may need to browse records to find the desired information when a record's primary key is unknown. **Data browsing** is the process of moving through a database file, examining each record, and looking for information. This strategy is also used when a search on a secondary key returns many results that must be sifted. Hunting through the best results returned by a search engine is a form of data browsing.

## Query Tools

Databases are stored in the form of data files until the system needs to perform **file processing** on the information. At that point, it is copied into RAM. Databases are sometimes too large to fit into RAM all at once, so only portions of the total data can be manipulated at any one time. To work with large amounts of data, database management systems come equipped with **query tools** that help users narrow down the amount of information that needs to be searched. A **query** allows users to ask questions designed to retrieve needed information. For example, a query combined with a report can be used to ask a grades database to list all students in the top 10 percent of academic achievement. The results could be used to print a report that would be the dean's list for that semester.

Requesting information involves the use of a query language. **Structured Query Language (SQL)** is the most popular database query language. It is simple when compared with a programming language, but it is also "structured," meaning that it is not as freeform as natural programming languages that mimic human speech. SQL is a very commonly supported query format and works with most databases in use today. Since it is standardized and so widely supported, SQL is often used to bridge communications gaps between database systems running on computers employing different operating systems.

The basic query command that SQL commands is the **SELECT command**, which asks a database to return records that match specified criteria. The command uses the keywords SELECT [fields] FROM [table] and specifies the table and fields from which the information is to be selected (see Figure 9-2).

Information from one query can be used to pull up data from more than one record source through a process called **joining**, which matches data from fields in various database files. This is usually done by matching up primary keys used as fields in one record to specify a relationship to another record. For example, if student names and grades were entered as separate records, "out of state" could be used as the primary key to find the grades of out-of-state students (see Figure 9-3).

## Security Measures

A DBMS also provides **security measures** to protect and safeguard data. Payroll, accounts receivable, and e-mail storage systems all contain sensitive information

```
SELECT    Student.FName, Student.LName, Student.StuID
FROM      StudentData
WHERE     Student.GPA>3.49
AND       Student.Enrolled="YES"
```

**Figure 9-2  Example of Structured Query Language**
This SQL statement could be used to search for the top students in a college, with "top" defined as those students with a grade point average (GPA) above 3.49.

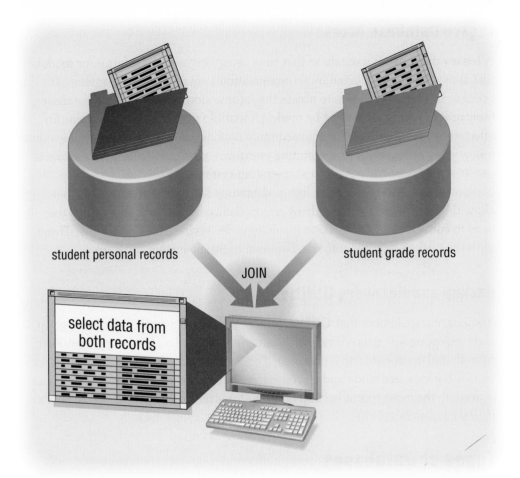

**Figure 9-3 Joining**
Joining matches data from fields in various database files. Both the student personal records and student grade records files would have a common student ID number field, allowing the information from both of these files to be returned in a single query.

that must be protected against theft, alteration, or deletion. Competitors, hackers, crackers, or disgruntled employees can do a great deal of harm if they are allowed access to critical company databases.

Maintaining data security is a critical issue for database administrators. Security methods include restricting access by requiring user identification and passwords. Usually only users with higher access levels can change data in a database, and only those with the highest level of access can change the format of the data itself.

## Metadata and the Data Dictionary

**Metadata** is information about data. **Data dictionary** is the term for a body of metadata. Metadata can be used for many things, but often describes the significance of various elements of a database. If a record field was called FNAME, metadata might describe this as being a text field with a maximum length of 20 characters, used for holding a person's first name. These characteristics might not be immediately obvious from the name FNAME. Designers, users, and administrators use metadata to manage databases.

### Legacy Database Access

A **legacy database** is a database that runs using languages, platforms, or models that are no longer supported by an organization's current database system. In order to be able to continue to access the information stored on these databases, their programming code must be made compatible with the newer system. An effective way to do this is to migrate legacy applications to operating systems that follow open or standard programming interfaces, which will allow a company to use its legacy applications on most operating systems.

Another option for accessing legacy databases is to use software tools that allow the data to be read directly by newer database systems. This avoids the need to convert the existing code to newer code, saving time and money. These tools are often integrated into database management system software.

### Backup and Recovery Utilities

Another major element that DBMS systems provide is a method for backing up and recovering lost data. Almost all companies keep sales, marketing, customer, payroll, and tax records on a database. To lose this data would be disastrous, so regular backups are made and stored safely. If a **recovery**, or restoration of data, is needed, the most recent backup is used. Important backup information is often stored in safes or off-site.

## Types of Databases

Databases are often categorized by the way they organize data (data models), or by their function (storing information for ongoing processes versus storing information for historical purposes).

### Databases Classified by Data Model

A **data model** defines the structure of information to be contained in a database, how the database will use the information, and how the different items in the database relate to each other. The goal of a database model is to identify and organize the database contents in a logical way.

The data model employed by a database is so central to the way it works that most databases are named after them. The data model chosen matters primarily to the database developer, as most data models can provide any kind of data or interface. Advanced data models tend to be more reliable and consistent, allowing for greater connectivity with outside systems. They also tend to be easier to work with and less expensive to develop and maintain. Common data models include flat file, relational, object-oriented, multimedia, and hybrids.

**Flat File Databases**  A traditional data file storage system that lacks the ability to interrelate data in an organizational structure is known as a **flat file database** — flat because the database contains only one table or file. These systems are simple and easy to use, but in general flat file systems are slower to respond because the records must be searched sequentially. They also consume more disk space than other types of databases. Flat files can be useful for finding information, but relational database systems offer faster, more comprehensive reporting capabilities.

| ID | User Name | Password | Last Name | First Name |
|---|---|---|---|---|
| 1 | mingdas | ×××××× | Solen | Mingda |
| 2 | kimmerr | ×××××× | Merrifield | Kim |
| 3 | klamoure | ×××××× | LaMoure | Keith |
| 4 | rosemh | ×××××× | Hettinger | Rose |
| 5 | gregjw | ×××××× | Winston | Greg |
| 6 | franklee | ×××××× | Lee | Frank |
| 7 | hwilson | ×××××× | Wilson | Hannah |
| (New) | | | | |

In a flat file database, a file is a collection of records. Each record is contained in a separate line, and fields are separated by a delimiter such as a comma.

**Relational Databases**   Most modern databases use a **relational database** model in which fields can be shared among all the files in the database, making it possible to connect them. In a relational database, a file is called a **table** (consisting of rows and columns), the record is called a **tuple**, and a field is called an **attribute**. Although many of the element definitions are the same as with a traditional flat file system, the primary difference concerns the organization of the tuples and their relationship to the table they are in.

Compared with flat file models, the most important advantage relational database models have is that information can be shared, extracted, and combined more easily among different tables. In a traditional system, an entity's address might be stored in several different records. If the entity's address information ever changes, address records would have to be updated in every location. If any record was overlooked, it would contain outdated information, meaning that any output using that record would be inaccurate. In relational databases, rather than having an attribute (field) called *address* repeated in many records, it would be stored once and shared among multiple tables. In a relational database, a single change to an attribute would change that attribute in all the tables at once.

**Object-Oriented Databases**   An **object-oriented database** stores data in the form of objects (units of object-oriented programming logic). Each object contains both the data related to the object (such as the fields of a record) and the actions that the user might want to perform on that object. A record object created for a payroll department might contain the salary of an individual, along with the calculations required to withhold taxes and print out a paycheck. Object-oriented databases allow for faster development and access times, speeding up database functions and making their development easier.

Go to this title's Internet Resource Center and read the article titled "Relational Database Design." www.emcp.net/CUT4e

Tech Demo 9-3 Relational Database

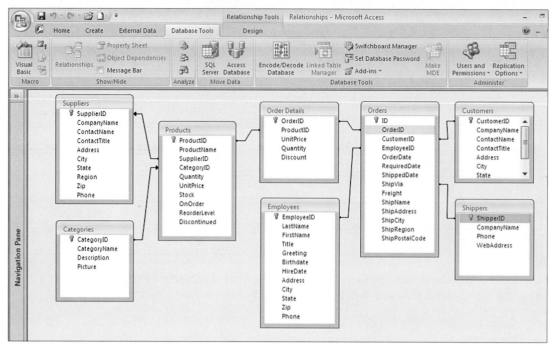

Microsoft Access shows the relationships between tables in a database. Attributes such as the customer number, customer's street address, and customer's phone number are stored in the Customers table while the customer number would also be found in the Invoice table when a purchase has been made.

**Multimedia Databases**   As computer storage and processing speeds continue to increase, so do the number of multimedia databases. In addition to the text and numbers a typical database model handles, a **multimedia database** allows the storage of pictures, movies, sounds, and hyperlinked fields. A multimedia employee database file, for example, could include snapshots of employees, along with recordings of their voices.

**Hybrid Databases**   A database is not limited to employing a single data model. Several different models may be used to allow more effective data handling. This type of database is called a **hybrid database**. A combination of relational and object-oriented database models is a popular form of hybrid database. Relational databases can handle only simple mathematical calculations, such as addition or subtraction, so users may have to use separate applications to perform complex functions. Combining relational and object-oriented data models allows for more sophisticated analysis within the framework of the relational database. The advent of the Web and the increasing availability of multimedia files is another factor increasing the popularity of this type of hybrid.

## Databases Classified by Function

The two major functional classifications for databases are operational databases and data warehouses. Operational databases are working systems that are continually being updated. For example, a supermarket may use an operational database that is updated every time a shopper purchases an item. In contrast, a data warehouse is a system from which data is extracted and analyzed by a company's staff

An information system used in a prison would combine alphanumeric prisoner data with a mug shot image in a hybrid database.

in order to make strategic decisions. A data warehouse typically is not modified or updated with new information.

It is possible for a database system to perform more than one function at the same time. Also, these classifications are not generally associated with a specific data model. Operational databases, for example, might use flat-file or relational structures. The list of database types is still evolving, and new classes may emerge in the future. Web databases are one example of a function classification that has evolved in recent years.

**Operational Databases** An **operational database** works by offering a snapshot of a fluid situation. These systems are called operational databases because they are usually used to track an operation or situation, such as the inventory of a store. Examples of operational databases include inventory tracking systems, such as that used at a large retail store. The store has products in stock and on the shelves for customers to purchase. As cashiers scan the bar codes on merchandise, the transactions automatically update a database that tracks the amount and location of each item in the store. When the stock of diapers or lawn chairs runs low, the database automatically orders more.

E-commerce Web sites are based on operational

The operational database at a nursery is updated each time an item is scanned at a checkout station.

databases. These sites allow users to place items in a virtual shopping cart and enter credit card and shipping information without ever talking to a person. This data is entered into a database, which is later used to track orders and payments.

# Biopirates Beware

**INDIA IS SEEKING TO PUT THE PRESSURE ON BIOPIRACY,** the practice of poaching the knowledge and resources of indigenous peoples. To protect its natural and cultural property, the country's National Institute of Science Communication and Information Resources has compiled a database of more than 100,000 traditional herbal medicines and thousands of plants and yoga positions. The database also contains millions of pages of ancient Indian text, national recipes, and Indian farming and architectural methods.

India has already turned back some biopirates. U.S. and European players tried to patent the medicinal properties of the spice turmeric and the Asian evergreen neem, but India won the legal battles to overturn the patents after proving that the medical properties were already well known in that country.

To combat further piracy, India and several other developing nations are urging the World Trade Organization to establish a system for controlling how native animals, plants, and lore are used to make pharmaceuticals or other products. The WTO wants laws that would require patent applicants to state the country of origin of any plant or animal used, to seek permissions from that country, and to share revenue from any resulting product.

Putting together a system to protect national property won't be easy. It would be an enormous task to track down the origins of particular ideas or biological organisms. Knowledge and tradition that have been passed down orally would be difficult to track to their roots. The development of a system that would assign property rights and establish ownership would require a Solomon-like ability to determine heritage. Nonetheless, India hopes that by establishing a database of national property, it has ammunition to fight outsiders who want to claim yoga or Darjeeling tea as their own.

Go to this title's Internet Resource Center and read the article titled "Data Warehousing and Data Mining." www.emcp.net/CUT4e

Depending on the amount of traffic that they receive, Web site databases may be distributed databases. A **distributed database** is spread across multiple networked computers, with each computer storing a portion of the total amount of data. These databases are valued for their ability to hold more information than any one computer can contain, and they are cheaply and easily expanded. Distributed databases offer advantages in cost, expandability, and storage capability. A major disadvantage is that they do not operate as quickly as mainframe or supercomputer databases, where all information is contained on one computer.

**Data Warehouses**   A **data warehouse** is used to store data gathered from one or more databases. Unlike operational databases, data warehouses do not change, delete, or manipulate the information they store. As their name implies, data warehouses function as vast storage places for holding information that can later be used in a variety of ways.

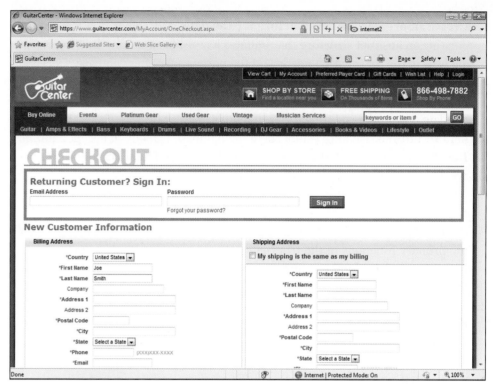

E-commerce Web sites use operational databases to store purchase information and customer information.

Law enforcement records are one example of a data warehouse, with vast collections of photographs and arrest records on file for reference or for statistical use. Companies also maintain data warehouses to test new ideas against past results. Many of the largest company databases contain information dating back to the 1950s. Companies are increasingly experimenting with these databases, using data mining techniques to sift through information and identify previously unnoticed trends. The strategy resembles survey work, but produces real results rather than estimating future behavior. Data mining systems often include elements of artificial intelligence.

# Planning and Designing Database Systems

Planning and designing a database system requires a combination of knowledge, skills, and creativity. This job is usually handled by a **systems analyst**. A systems analyst may also become responsible for administering the database after it is built. Like a structural engineer who designs buildings and draws blueprints, a systems analyst is an experienced specialist who can identify project needs and then design a structure or system to fulfill them.

## The Database Management Approach

The development and maintenance of database structures and applications employs a methodology called the **database management approach**, sometimes shortened to the database approach. Using the software tools of a database management system (DBMS), a systems analyst or database designer follows three broad steps in the planning process:

Data warehouses allow customer service representatives to suggest new products to customers based on their demographics and past behavior.

Tech Demo 9-4
Database Design

1. **Create an organizational structure for the data.** A designer first focuses on creating an abstract structure that imitates a real-life situation, drawing on an analysis of the information needs and the purpose(s) of the database. Decisions are made as to the kinds of records needed, the number of fields needed in each record, and how fields should be associated to form records. Choosing the data type and formatting for each field is another basic decision. With the field-record-file structure established, the database is ready to accept data.

2. **Design an interface that makes the database user-friendly.** Users do not need to understand a database's internal structure. Their most important consideration is that they are able to easily enter data and request information. A **front-end interface program** makes this possible. It interacts with the DBMS, the software that manipulates and manages the database. One of the primary functions of the front-end interface is to prevent erroneous data from entering the database. Figure 9-4 shows the relationship of the DBMS, the front-end interface, and the database.

3. **Set up reporting capabilities to allow for inquiry and response.** Because these functions represent the main database information analysis tools, they are a major focus of the designer's work. A DBMS typically includes reporting features, and the designer chooses how and where in the system the features can be used.

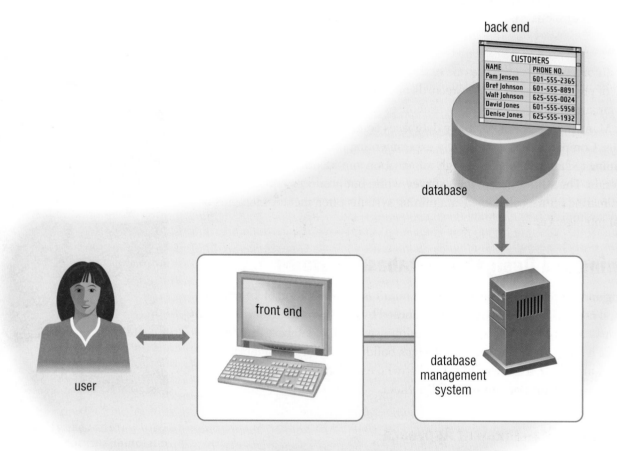

**Figure 9-4 Accessing a Database**
The user requests and enters data through the front-end interface program. The database management system manages the retrieval and update of the database itself.

# Database Objects: Tools in the DBMS

A **database object** is an element within an object-oriented database, such as a form, a report, or a data filter. Database designers use database objects to build the system interface and the reporting features.

**Forms**   A **form** is a template that allows users to enter data into the database. Forms perform the important jobs of detecting and preventing erroneous or incomplete data input. A form can be configured to allow the input and display of data in any fashion that the system designer sees fit. Forms can allow users to search through data, move to other forms, print reports, and make changes. Many jobs involve working with forms in a database, such as airline ticketing and hotel front desk work.

Forms are designed to let users input their answers to the form's questions or prompts. Default answers are included to ensure that the database has all the data required for its fields. Defaults are assumed input that will be utilized in the absence of entered input. Many software programs feature dialog boxes containing questions with default answers. If a user simply presses the *Enter* key, or clicks OK, the program will assume the default input for that question. For example, if a program asks "Do you wish to save before exiting?" and a user presses the *Enter* key, it will assume that the work should be saved, which is the default option.

**Reports**   A **report** is a formatted body of output from a database. Most reports are designed to be printed out for later review. Monthly phone bills, report cards, and grade transcripts are all examples of database reports.

A report can be generated by request or automatically. For example, credit checks are a type of database report that is not issued on a regular basis. Instead,

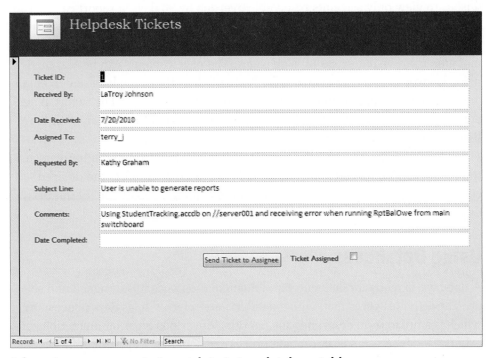

A form is an easy way to input data into a database table.

table

**Exam Summary Wizard**

**1. Select Exams**

☐ Select All

Chapter 1 , Always Available , Scored
Chapter 2 , Jan 29 2010 10:34AM to Jan 30 2010 10:34AM , Scored
Chapter 3 , Always Available , Scored
Chapter 9 , Always Available , Practice
Chapter 10 , Always Available , Scored
New Chapter 1 , Feb 16 2010 7:20PM to Feb 17 2010 7:20PM , Scored

*Hold the CTRL Key for Multiple Selections*

**2. Choose Viewing Options**

**Primary Sort**

Rank ▾   ● Ascending   ○ Descending

**Secondary Sort**

Cumulative Score ▾   ● Ascending   ○ Descending

[ Show Report ]

**Exam Summary**

| No. | Exam Title | Exam Type | Exam Date | Time Taken | Concept Score | Skill Score | Cumulative Score | Rank |
|-----|------------|-----------|-----------|------------|---------------|-------------|------------------|------|
| 1 | Chapter 9 | Practice | 21-3-2010 at 10:17 PM | 00:00:57 | 0 % (0/5) | 20 % (2/10) | 13 % (2/15) | 1/6 |
| 2 | New Chapter 1 | Practice | 16-2-2010 at 7:36: PM | 00:00:33 | 60 % (3/5) | 0 % (0/0) | 60 % (3/5) | 1/6 |
| 3 | Chapter 10 | Practice | 12-2-2010 at 1:20: PM | 00:00:17 | 70 % (7/10) | 0 % (0/0) | 70 % (7/10) | 1/6 |
| 4 | Sig Word Specialist Sample | Practice | 23-3-2010 at 3:31: PM | 00:00:26 | 0 % (0/10) | 20 % (8/40) | 16 % (8/50) | 1/6 |

A report is a formatted body of output from a database. It can be generated by request or automatically. This report was created from a database of an online assessment tool.

they are usually issued at the request of commercial firms or consumers. Other types of reports, such as paychecks, are generated automatically on regularly scheduled dates.

**Data Filters**   Some reports can be requested using filtering criteria, called a **data filter**, so that only a subset of the data is presented. For example, if a user wishes to view only accounts receivable overdue by 90 days, a report can be run filtering all accounts except for those overdue by that amount of time. Search engines on the World Wide Web are really data-filtering systems. Search engines maintain massive databases of Web pages. The page contents can be searched using keywords. If a user searches for "cat and dog" for example, a search engine would bring back pages containing the words "cat" and "dog." The report generated in this instance is the HTML Web page transmitted to the user, with the listed Web pages highlighted as blue hyperlinks.

In general, the more specific the data filter, the more limited and focused the result, and the greater the likelihood that the report offers the desired content. Creating good, effective data filters is an important goal of database designers.

## Using Databases

A database is ready for data entry and manipulation once it is designed and set up. The activities performed with a database are referred to as **data processing**, which is a broad term describing the handling of various types of interactions or events. Database users perform data processing activities as part of their job.

## Data Processing

The processing of database interactions can be set up using batch or transaction processing, or a combination of both of these methods.

**Batch Processing**   With **batch processing**, data processing occurs at a scheduled time, or when a critical point has been reached. Batch processing saves redundant effort by rearranging data all at once, rather than continuously. A database may only incorporate changed records at midnight each day, rather than whenever the new data was entered. Massive databases may take anywhere from several minutes to several hours to update. Batch processing streamlines the process by carrying out the work during off-hours. However, it can introduce some lag into the system, and users are sometimes informed that data will not appear until the day after it was entered. When this occurs, it is usually due to batch processing.

**Transactional Processing**   **Transactional processing** is more continuous and tends to be done with smaller databases or with operational databases that require all information to be very current. A **real-time system**, such as a factory automation or an air traffic control system, can't afford to wait until midnight to update. The data must be kept accurate down to the second in systems that provide data for these types of critical functions. In transactional processing, records of an "event" such as the purchase of an item, the construction of an automobile part, or the departure of a flight are sent to the database for processing one at a time.

E-commerce transactions use **online transactional processing (OLTP)**. These Web sites require fast, always-on processing. One of the great benefits of such systems is that they are effectively in business 24 hours a day. Credit cards are involved in most online sales transactions, and customers expect a quick response so that their orders can be processed.

An air traffic control system is an example of a real-time system. Data must be kept accurate and up to date as soon as a change occurs.

**Mixed Forms of Processing**  Transactional and batch processing techniques are often mixed in the same system. For example, in situations involving online orders, a transactional process may be used to handle credit card verifications, while batch processing may be used to handle work orders requesting that items be taken from inventory and delivered to customers.

## Database Users

Most people use databases only while performing their jobs, rather than being involved in database design or management. This does not mean that these employees do not have very important jobs. A great deal of effort goes into keeping a database accurate, and this requires constant maintenance. A database must be updated every time a bill is paid, an address is changed, or an order is placed. A **data entry operator** types data into databases and makes sure that it is accurate. Many others work with databases regularly as part of their jobs, including the accountants, executives, and salespeople of any organization.

Many operations are regularly performed on a database as a daily routine. For a situational model, consider a school's grades database. The system controls and maintains student transcripts for all the students of the institution, so records are constantly being added, modified, deleted, and sorted.

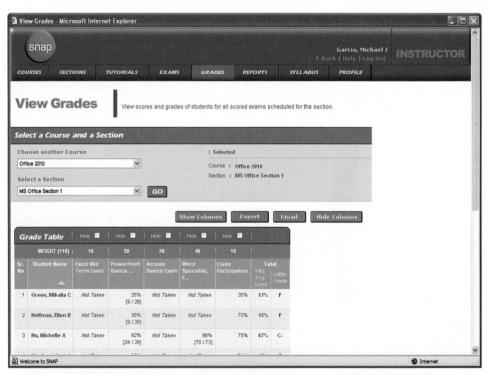

A student's grades are entered into a database and stored. The individual grades are used to create a report, or transcript.

## Adding Records

Adding records to the system is a common operation. If a student completes a course, a grade record is added to that student's transcript, listing the course taken, the date of completion, and the final grade received.

## Modifying Records

If a correction is needed to any prior entry, the record in question could be brought up and the change made on a form, such as a letter grade B being changed to an A. Personal information concerning students might also require changes, such as home and school addresses.

## Deleting Records

In the example of a college database, grade records are rarely deleted. Since a grade transcript database is really a data warehouse rather than an operational database, deleting a record does not make sense unless the grades were entered in error and need to be corrected.

## Sorting Records

Sorting is a critical function for any database, and involves arranging records in a particular order, such as alphabetically or numerically. When a record is added to a file, for example, the file must be sorted so that the results can be more easily searched. A phone book is an example of a set of printed data that is sorted alphabetically. It is easy to imagine how difficult it would be to find a specific phone number if the listing was not alphabetized. Sorting data in a database (based on the ordering of a key field) greatly reduces the amount of time it takes to find any one record.

Most database systems sort records automatically on the basis of their primary key. Social security numbers are used in many colleges as primary keys, as they are unique and don't require a student to learn a new number. However, sorting records by primary key isn't helpful if the primary key for a student is unknown. If a professor wished to change a grade for a student, but didn't know that student's social security number, it could take a long search to find that one record. In that case the database could be sorted by name, and the results searched to isolate the correct student.

# Database Administration

Many factors affect database performance, and thus the quality of the information generated. Database designers must consider each factor, and then ensure that corrections for possible problems are built into the system. Once problems occur, it is the job of the database administrator to solve them. A **database administrator** is responsible for maintaining and updating the database and the DBMS software. Larger systems require a team, or perhaps even an entire database and a department of people dedicated to the task.

Database administrators are responsible for keeping databases up and running to support a company's operations.

Go to this title's Internet Resource Center and read the article titled "Database Administration." www.emcp.net/CUT4e

A database administrator's duties are varied. Any changes in company policy often result in changes to the company database. If billing information sent to customers is supposed to have additional information, the appropriate report must be edited and tested. If a stand-alone system were changed to a networked system, the database must be set up to handle multiple users, and issues such as security and reliability must be thoroughly worked out.

Database administrators are critical players in the success of any organization, since they are largely responsible for preventing computer **downtime**, or time in which the system is unavailable. Consider an airline reservation system. If the computer system is down, the company cannot function. Customers do not like to be kept waiting, or to be told, "The computer system is down." Hearing that phrase usually means that a database administrator is working feverishly to solve a problem. Major factors that database administrators must be aware of include the corruption or loss of data; backup and recovery operations; database response times; record locking; and data integrity, contamination, and validation.

## Data Loss or Corruption

Data loss and data corruption are the most serious failures that can occur in a DBMS. Data loss occurs when data input can no longer be retrieved. **Data corruption** occurs when data is unreadable, incomplete, or damaged. Strategies for backing up data are the major method for recovering lost or corrupted data.

## Backup and Recovery Operations

A key part of any DBMS is a **backup and recovery plan**. Data can always be lost through power interruptions or equipment failure, so ensuring that data is backed up and recoverable is an important task for database administrators. To lessen the chance of accidental data loss, it is important that backup files are stored separately from original material.

Tape backups are a commonly used backup method, as tapes are cheap mass storage media that can be placed in a company safe for protection. They are common in the financial field because bank databases contain valuable and irreplaceable data. A bank cannot operate if it loses information related to customer accounts. In essence, a bank is a gigantic database, and all of its employees service that database. Since modern banks keep few account records on paper, any database failure would be a catastrophic event.

## Database Response Time

The length of time a database operation takes depends largely on the speed of the hard disk being used. The lag time between a user issuing a command and the database system taking action is called the **database response time**. Network conditions may also affect response time if someone is using a remote access method to perform database operations. This type of delay is magnified in the case of a distributed database, as several computers may have to work together to perform the entire operation. Figure 9-5 illustrates the lag that is often experienced in a distributed database.

Banks and other financial institutions commonly store critical data on backup tapes.

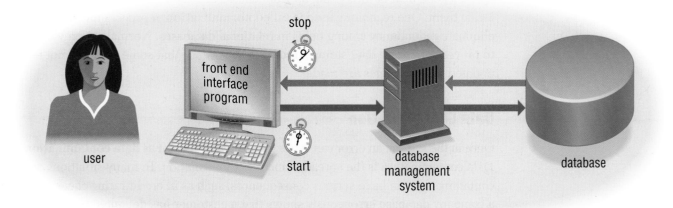

**Figure 9-5 Database Response Time**
Database response time is the lag time between a user issuing a command and the database system taking action.

## Record Locking

Many databases are designed to be used by more than one user at a time. This is usually achieved by networking computers so that information can be shared. Although there is no conflict when two users are viewing the same record, simultaneous attempts to update a record can cause a problem. **Record locking** is an automatic protection process that occurs when users attempt to edit existing records in a multi-user system. The system automatically checks to see if anyone else is working on the same record, and only allows one user at a time to edit or delete the record. During the process of changing a record, it is considered "locked," and the DBMS will generate an error message for any other users attempting to alter it at the same time.

## Data Integrity

The term **data integrity** (sometimes called data quality) is used to describe the accuracy of the information provided to database users. A system with high data integrity is obviously more valuable to users than a system containing a large percentage of errors. For example, a sales database with high data integrity will produce mailing lists with fewer incorrect addresses, increasing the percentage of sales material that reaches the intended targets and ultimately increasing sales.

**Redundancy**, or the duplication of data in several fields, is an enemy of data integrity. Having the same value in multiple places creates opportunities for error when changes are made. For example, if an address is entered in several database locations, any changes to that address would have to be entered in all the locations. Another example of this problem might occur if a person signs up more than once for the same account. Unless there were preventive measures in place, this could cause two separate records to be created. For example, a customer may get partway through an online purchase only to be disconnected. If the customer returns and repeats the process, two copies of the transaction may have been created, leading to duplicate products being delivered, and the customer charged for both.

Redundancy errors are difficult to weed out, and database administrators spend a good deal of time using up-front checks and data validation strategies to locate them. One technique used is called **normalization**, a process intended to eliminate redundancy among fields in relational databases. Normalization works to prevent duplicate data storage, reducing the chance that some data will not be updated when changes are made.

## Data Contamination

Once in the system, an error can cause a ripple effect known as **data contamination**. Data contamination is the spread of incorrect information. In many situations data contamination can have serious consequences, such as in credit rating checks. If a company database erroneously shows that a customer has defaulted on a credit purchase, it will eventually be reported to a credit agency. The customer could then receive a poor credit rating, and the company could be liable for any damages resulting from their mistake. Preventing data contamination is one of the goals of data validation.

## Data Validation

Among database administrators, the concept of data validation is summed up by the phrase garbage in, garbage out (GIGO). As explained in Chapter 1, GIGO means that bad input will result in bad output, which is why administrators use data validation methods to prevent bad data (garbage) from entering a system.

**Data validation** is the process of making certain that data entered into the system is both correct and complete. A database is only a reflection of reality, and it is not self-correcting. It is dependent on accurate input to maintain its validity, and therefore its usefulness. Because errors are far more difficult to detect and remove once they are in a system, the best way to ensure that a database is error-free is to prevent errors from being entered in the first place. Anyone who has ever tried to rectify a billing error will appreciate the difficulties involved in straightening things out once they go wrong.

There are a variety of techniques that designers or administrators can use to prevent false data from entering a system. Data validation checks are methods of restricting input so that false data cannot be as easily entered into the system. Validation methods include range, alphanumeric, consistency, and completeness checks.

**Referential Integrity**    **Referential integrity** involves a check to make sure that deleting a record in one table will not affect other tables. For example, if you were to delete the accounting department record in your database, then all the employee records that listed a key to the accounting department would have an invalid reference to a record that no longer existed. To make sure this doesn't happen, referential integrity confirms that when you delete a record other records are not depending on it for part of their data to be valid. To continue with our example, in order to delete the accounting department record without an error, you would have to first delete all the employees or move them to a different department before the database would allow the deletion of accounting.

**Range Checks**    A **range check** is a simple error-checking system usually performed on numeric data entries. For example, to reduce errors in birth date entries, a range check could be created specifying that no birth dates prior to 1890 be accepted, since it is very unlikely that anyone born before that date is still alive.

**Alphanumeric Checks**    When entering a value for a field, only certain characters may be allowed. An **alphanumeric check** allows only letters of the alphabet and digits to be entered. This would prevent users from entering incorrect characters, such as dollar signs ($), in a "customer home address" field.

Data validation requires complete and accurate input. This Access screen displays if the user tries to enter a null (zero) value in a database field.

**Consistency Checks**   A **consistency check** may be made against previously entered data that has already been validated. For example, a validation system will indicate an error if a user attempts to enter phone numbers or social security numbers that do not match previously validated information for these items.

**Completeness Checks**   A **completeness check** ensures that every required field is filled out. One of the greatest threats to data integrity is the natural human tendency to tire of entering data. This leads users to submit input before every field has been completely filled out. To prevent this, one of the first checks performed on any data entry is a check for completeness, meaning that valid entries were provided for every field marked "required." Incomplete records cannot be allowed into the system, such as credit card numbers without expiration date information.

# OnThe**Horizon**

**INDUSTRY OBSERVERS POINT TO SOME NEW TRENDS** that could mean more data for the dollar, less work for database administrators, and more efficient systems. These improvements will streamline operations and reduce costs, resulting in savings for customers and clients.

## Adaptive Database Management Systems

Database administrators (DBAs) are responsible for maintaining the security, integrity, performance, and functionality of the database systems they manage. Many of these tasks require the hands-on involvement of DBAs, but help is on the way through adaptive database management systems (DBMS) that can learn how to diagnose problems and perform repair and maintenance tasks automatically. If adaptive DBMS progress continues, databases of the future may be entirely self-managing.

## Improved File Organization Systems

Efforts are under way to create a new file organization system that bans the simple but tedious file folder directory tree. Newer systems will allow for easier file management with a more intuitive interface. As hard disks bloat into sizes of 100 gigabytes or larger, it is more important than ever to have a system that can locate every file simply and reliably. Newer designs will use virtual reality to let people organize documents and music, audio, and video files in more familiar ways. Imagine storing audio files in a virtual 3D structure like a CD rack, storing family photos in virtual photo albums that are organized on a shelf by date, filing documents in a virtual file drawer with no physical space limitation, and keeping task list items on sticky notes around your virtual house.

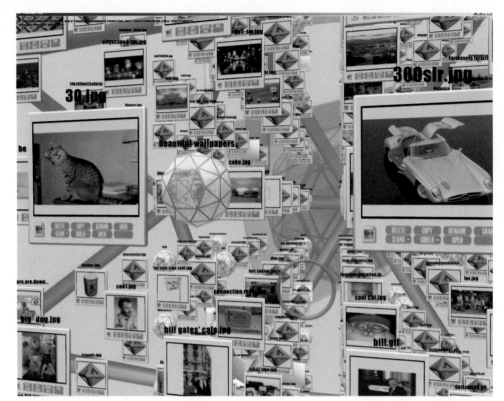

New file organization systems will look three-dimensional and resemble everyday settings.

## XML Databases

XML (eXtensible Markup Language) is a metalanguage, a type of computer language used to describe other languages. XML has been combined with HTML to produce the next generation of HTML, known as XHTML (eXtensible HyperText Markup Language). The increasing number of documents being written and stored in XML or XML-compliant languages such as XHTML has led to efforts to create and perfect XML databases.

In XML databases, the fundamental database structure consists of XML documents and elements, whereas in traditional relational databases data is stored in tables, organized in rows and columns. Using XML as a database structure means that XML documents can be stored in their entirety, instead of being broken down and stored in the different rows and columns of a relational database. XML documents can then be retrieved in their original format instead of being recreated from stored data.

One current disadvantage of XML databases is that they are memory-intensive, which often makes them slower to process information than relational databases, but this disadvantage is expected to become less of an issue as computer memory becomes increasingly less costly. While XML databases are ideal for working with XML documents, relational databases are more suited to storing numbers and text; thus XML databases will likely complement rather than supplant relational databases in the years to come.

# Chapter**Summary**

*For an interactive version of this summary, go to this text's Internet Resource Center at www.emcp.net/CUT4e. A Spanish version is also available.*

## What is a database and how does it organize information?

A **database** is a computerized system for storing information in an organized manner so that it can be searched for and retrieved when needed. Data associated with other useful data becomes information. The constant need to alter and amend masses of data is called database maintenance. Databases organize data in a hierarchical fashion, storing information about **entities** in the form of **fields**, **records**, and **database files**.

## How do databases help businesses manage information?

The most common database application is an **information system**, which is a system of computer hardware, software, and operating procedures. A **management information system (MIS)** is used to track and control every transaction through a database. A **decision support system (DSS)** is another common form of information system. **Computer-aided manufacturing (CAM)** and **computer-integrated manufacturing (CIM)** are information systems that support factory automation.

## How does database management system software work?

**Database management system (DBMS) software** controls databases. **Keys** are attributes that can be used to identify a set of information, and the designer designates the most important field in a record as the **primary key**. **Data browsing** is the process of moving through a database file, examining each record and looking for information. **Queries** allow users to ask questions designed to retrieve needed information. **Structured Query Language (SQL)** is the most popular database query language. A DBMS also provides **security measures** to protect and safeguard data. **Metadata** is information about data, and a **data dictionary** is the term for a body of metadata. Backup and **recovery** utilities provide a method for backing up and restoring lost data.

## What types of databases are available?

Databases are often categorized by the way they organize data (**data models**), or by their function (**operational databases** and **data warehouses**). Common data models include **flat file databases**, **relational databases**, **object-oriented databases**, **multimedia databases**, and **hybrid databases**.

## How are databases designed?

The job of planning and designing a database system is usually handled by a **systems analyst**. The development and maintenance of database structures and applications employs a methodology called the **database management approach**. Database designers use **database objects** to build the **front end interface program** and the reporting features. A **form** is a template that allows users to enter data into the database. A **report** is a formatted body of output from a database. Some reports can be requested using filtering criteria, called **data filters**, so that only a subset of the data is presented.

## What are the different types of data processing?

The activities performed with a database are referred to as **data processing**. With **batch processing**, data processing occurs at a scheduled time, or when a critical point has been reached. **Transactional processing** is more continuous, and tends to be done with smaller databases or with operational databases that require all information to be current. **Online transactional processing (OLTP)** is used at e-commerce Web sites requiring fast, always-on processing.

## How can databases help ensure high-quality information?

A **database administrator** is responsible for maintaining and updating the DBMS software. A key part of any DBMS is a **backup and recovery plan**, to recover data in the event of data loss or **data corruption**. **Tape backups** are a commonly used backup method. The lag time between a user issuing a command and the database system taking action is called **database response time**. **Record locking** is an automatic protection process that occurs when users attempt to edit existing records in a multi-user system. **Data validation** is the process of making certain that data entered into the system is both correct and complete. Validation ensures **data integrity** (or data quality) and protects against **redundancy**. Other validation checks include **range**, **alphanumeric**, **consistency**, and **completeness**.

# KeyTerms

*Numbers indicate the pages where terms are first cited in the chapter. An alphabetized list of key terms with definitions (in English and Spanish) can be found on the Encore CD that accompanies this book. In addition, these terms and definitions are included in the end-of-book glossary.*

# Chapter**Exercises**

 *The following chapter exercises, along with new activities and information, are also offered in the Internet Resource Center for this title at www.emcp.net/CUT4e.*

## *Tutorial >* **Exploring Windows**

In Tutorial 9 you learn how to customize some of the display settings in Windows to match your personal needs and preferences.

## *Expanding Your Knowledge >* **Articles and Activities**

 *Visit the Internet Resource Center for this title at www.emcp.net/CUT4e, read the articles related to this chapter, and complete the corresponding activities. The article titles include:*

- Topic 9-1: The National Electronic Disease Surveillance System (NEDSS)
- Topic 9-2: Relational Database Design
- Topic 9-3: Data Warehousing and Data Mining
- Topic 9-4: Database Administration

## Terms Check > **Matching**

 *For additional practice, go to the Internet Resource Center for this title at www.emcp.net/CUT4e for a chapter crossword puzzle.*

Write the letter of the correct answer on the line before each numbered item.

a. data contamination          f. database management system (DBMS)
b. primary key                 g. record locking
c. table                       h. query
d. multimedia database         i. field
e. data validation             j. redundancy

_____ 1. The smallest element of data in a database.

_____ 2. A question posed to a database.

_____ 3. In a relational database, the term used to describe what is called a file in other database models.

_____ 4. This feature allows only one person to use or modify a record at a time.

_____ 5. Errors that are multiplied and carried to other parts of a database, and possibly to other databases.

_____ 6. This type of database is used to handle video, graphic, and music files.

_____ 7. The field used to uniquely identify each record.

_____ 8. Two records containing identical information would be found using this type of check.

_____ 9. A set of tools that database designers and administrators use to structure the database system.

_____ 10. This is performed to prevent errors from entering a database.

## Technology Illustrated > **Identify the Process**

What process is illustrated in this drawing? Identify the process and write a paragraph describing it.

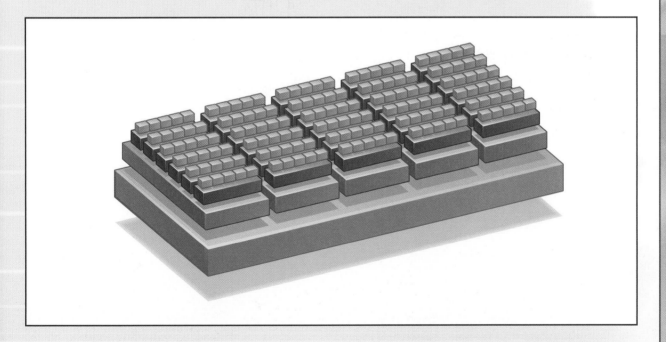

## Knowledge Check > **Multiple Choice**

  *Additional quiz questions are available on the Encore CD that accompanies this book as well as on the Internet Resource Center for this title at www.emcp.net/CUT4e.*

Circle the letter of the best answer from those provided.

1. Modern information systems are underpinned by
   a. databases.
   b. spreadsheets.
   c. word processors.
   d. operating systems.

2. Primary keys must be
   a. text.
   b. numeric.
   c. unique.
   d. All of the above

3. Which of the following allows users to enter data?
   a. reports
   b. queries
   c. forms
   d. primary keys

4. A(n) _____ is a collection of related fields.
   a. record
   b. database
   c. entry
   d. field

5. Which of the following fields would be the best choice for a primary key?
   a. birth date
   b. first name
   c. last name
   d. Social Security number

6. Microsoft's DBMS is called
   a. Paradox.
   b. SQL Server.
   c. DB2.
   d. Oracle.

7. Querying a large database to identify customer preference trends would be called
   a. maintaining a data dictionary.
   b. data modeling.
   c. data mining.
   d. database administration.

8. SQL stands for
   a. structured query language.
   b. static query language.
   c. statistical quality language.
   d. statistical query language.

9. Which of the following types of information systems would be useful for automating an office?
   a. CIM
   b. OIS
   c. CAM
   d. HTTP

10. Placing records into a logical order using their key fields is called
    a. listing.
    b. organizing.
    c. ordering.
    d. sorting.

## Things That Think > Brainstorming New Uses

In groups or individually, contemplate the following questions and develop as many answers as you can.

1. Web databases, such as those search engines use to catalog the Internet, are becoming increasingly intelligent in interpreting queries that nontechnical users write. Go to several search engines that boast of easy-to-use advanced searching techniques and try them out. What other developments do you think may help databases become more intelligent and thus more useful?

2. Smart guns have been developed and are being tested by law enforcement agencies. The guns detect a chip that must be in close proximity to the gun in order for it to fire. Peace officers wear the chip in the form of a wristband or a ring; their weapons will be rendered useless if they are ever wrested away from them. In the future, it is possible that these chips could be injected beneath the skin, making them impossible to remove. If this advance in gun safety becomes commonplace, what advantages or disadvantages do you foresee? Brainstorm possible uses for this technology in other areas.

## Key Principles > Completion

Fill in the blanks with the appropriate words or phrases.

1. Database administrators typically set up _____ plans to mitigate the consequences of lost data.

2. _____ is a standardized format for entering database queries.

3. When choosing the _____ for a database, the numbers or text must be unique.

4. Information about the data stored in a database is called _____.

5. _____ occurs when data is unreadable, incomplete, or damaged.

6. Matching data from fields in various record files, also called _____, is used when a database request requires data from more than one source.

7. The _____ is the person responsible for maintaining and updating the database and the underlying DBMS software.

8. The accuracy of the information provided to database users is referred to as _____.

9. A(n) _____ is the smallest element of data in a database.

10. _____ systems are slower to respond because all the records in the database must be searched sequentially.

## Tech Architecture > **Label the Drawing**

In this illustration, identify the numbered components of the screen shown below.

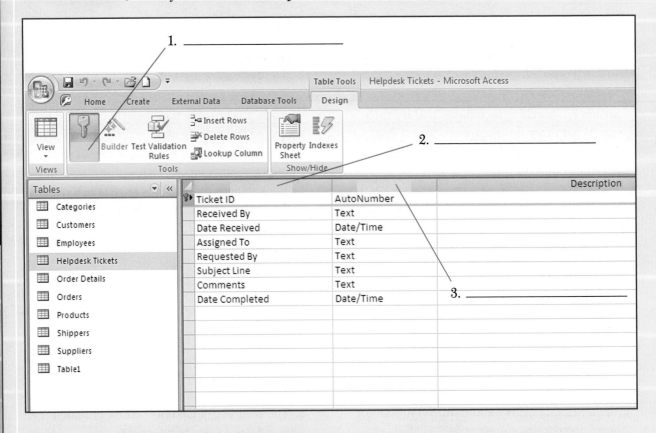

## Techno Literacy > **Research and Writing**

Develop appropriate written responses based on your research for each item.

1. What major features does Oracle's DBMS offer? Go to www.oracle.com and study their DBMS products. Do a Web search for other non-Oracle sources of information about Oracle DBMS products. Does Oracle offer any features that its competitors do not? Does Oracle allow prospective customers to download a free demo? Is their software aimed at home PC-type or professional users? Write a summary of the information you gather, including answers to these questions.

2. How would you design a database to describe this course? Create a database outline on paper with the entities that describe this course, including assignments, students, and grading. What types of records would you use? What fields would each record contain? What fields might be shared between records? Make sure that you identify the data type for each field. Do you think your database would be a useful resource for students and instructors if it was made available on a Web page? Would the content of your database pose any security risks?

3. Identify a business that is dependent on databases. Many businesses exist primarily to feed data into a database, process it, and retrieve it as valuable information. Can you think of a company in which practically every employee, and the very product of the business itself, is dependant upon a database? Describe in a written report how each employee interacts with the database, and show how the database forms the core of the overall operation of the organization.

## Technology Issues > Team Problem-Solving

In groups, brainstorm possible solutions to the issues presented.

1. In the near future, assume that most people will have access to high-speed Internet connections. You plan to run a dot-com service to provide downloadable music, e-books, and videos to the public for a fee. What kind of database would you use to do this? What kind of fee would you charge—a monthly subscription fee or a per use fee? How much do you think your customers would pay to download music?

2. You have been directed to price a database system for a network of ten workstations. A database license will be needed, along with two laser printers. You have technical staff able to perform the installation and setup, so you only need to price the software license and the printers. Research Web sites such as buy.com and gogocity.com to compare prices.

## Mining Data > Internet Research and Reporting

Conduct Internet searches to find the information described in the activities below. Write a brief report summarizing your research results. Be sure to document your sources, using the MLA format (see Chapter 1, page 42, to review MLA style guidelines).

1. It has long been a fear of privacy advocates that personal information will become a commodity, sold on the open market to the highest bidder. Investigate how companies obtain mailing lists and other customer information, and describe the kinds of companies that collect and sell this kind of information.

2. Electronic databases are the rule in most industries, but are not as common in some areas, such as medical records. Investigate the database situation at hospitals and medical facilities in your area. Do they use electronic databases, or are they still in the paper-file era? Are your medical records on the Internet? Do you think they will be some day?

3. With so much personal information stored in various Web databases, the crime of identity theft is on the rise. Research various online sources and write a summary that includes a definition of identity theft, statistics on the prevalence of identity theft, strategies for minimizing the risk of your identity being stolen, and the steps you should take if someone steals your identity.

## Technology Timeline > Predicting Next Steps

Look at the timeline below outlining the history of credit cards. Research this topic and try to predict the next logical steps by completing the timeline through 2020.

**1914** Western Union gives out metal cards providing credit privileges to preferred customers. These cards come to be known as "metal money."

**1924** General Petroleum Corporation issues the first "metal money" for gasoline purchases.

**1938** AT&T introduces the "Bell System Credit Card." Airlines and railroads soon reveal their own similar cards.

**1959** Many banks offer the option of revolving credit, allowing people to make monthly payments on balances owed, rather than having to pay them at one time.

**1966** Fourteen U.S. banks form Interlink, later known as Visa Card, a new association with the ability to exchange information on credit card transactions.

**2000** Smartcards grow dramatically in Europe and Asia, becoming the dominant form of electronic payment.

**2001** Disposable credit cards good for one-use-only become popular for online consumer purchases.

**2003** Orbiscom introduces ControlPay technology, which allows the primary credit card accountholder to control spending limits and locations for various family members.

**2004** PayPal reaches 50 million accountholders worldwide for its online payment service.

**2008** The average U.S. household carries about $8,700 in credit card debt.

## Ethical Dilemmas > Group Discussion and Debate

As a class or within an assigned group, discuss the following ethical dilemma.

Web sites often collect information about a user who has visited a site or has purchased something from the site. Sometimes this is accomplished by placing cookies on the hard drive of a user's computer that can be read the next time the user navigates to that site. Other times, a site requires a user to register some personal information in order to access "premium" features on the Web site. Many users offer this information without thinking about the privacy implications of sharing their personal data.

Because of consumer privacy concerns, more and more Web sites are posting a privacy policy, which typically indicates how they are storing site visitors' personal information, what they do with it, and whether they share it with other parties. However, they may also change this privacy policy from time to time or choose not to follow it. Have you noticed whether Web sites that you frequent have a privacy policy? Would you place more trust in a Web site that has a posted privacy policy? Would you no longer visit a Web site (or purchase from a Web site) if it did not have a privacy policy? Is it illegal or unethical for a company to change its privacy policy without notifying site users? What can you do if a company violates its own privacy policy? How would you recommend that privacy of consumer information be protected on Web sites?

# History of Computers Timeline

**AD 1625** The slide rule was invented around 1620–1630. The device consisted of an outer frame containing numbers. A sliding center piece, also containing numbers, could move horizontally—thus the name slide rule. By aligning two specific numbers, one on the frame and another on the center slide, the user was able to perform mathematical calculations, including multiplication and division.

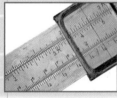

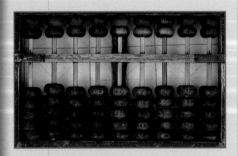

**300 BC** The abacus, believed to have been invented by the Babylonians between 500 B.C. and 100 B.C., is the earliest known calculating device. It and similar devices were used by early civilizations for counting. Interestingly, these devices are still used today.

**1642** Blaise Pascal, noted mathematician and scientist, built the first mechanical calculator, called the Pascaline. The device contained a series of eight rotating gears (or cogs). Each gear contained a set of 10 teeth representing the numbers 0–9. By turning the gear at the extreme right past the number 9 until it reached 0, the number 1 would appear in the next window at the left. Thus, the number 10 would appear in the two windows at the right, and so on. By rotating the gears, the user could perform basic mathematical operations, including addition, subtraction, multiplication, and division. Several of the Pascaline's features are in use today in devices like water meters and modern-day vehicle odometers.

| 300 BC | AD 800 | 1600 | | 1700 |
|---|---|---|---|---|

timeline not to scale

**1833** Augusta Ada Lovelace, the daughter of the British poet Lord Byron, held a lifelong friendship with Charles Babbage. A splendid mathematician and one of the few people who understood Babbage's vision, Ada created a program for Babbage's Analytical Engine. She is generally recognized as the world's first computer programmer and, in 1979, a modern programming language was named ADA in her honor.

**1801** Joseph-Marie Jacquard invents an automatic weaving loom that reads instructions from punched cards. A series of holes punched in each of a group of cards provided the loom with weaving instructions, including various patterns in the fabric. This technology was an early forerunner of modern computer-assisted manufacturing.

**1830** A British scientist and inventor named Charles Babbage begins developing plans for a device, called the Analytical Engine, which might be considered to be a computer in the modern sense of the word. Although never completed, the device was intended to use loops of Jacquard's punched cards to control an automatic calculator, which could perform mathematical calculations. Although this machine was designed as a "steam-driven" device, it was intended to employ several features later used in modern computers, including sequential control, branching, and looping. Babbage died before he could build a working model.

**1890** A step toward automated computation was the introduction of punched cards, which were first successfully used in connection with computing in 1890 by Herman Hollerith working for the U.S. Census Bureau. He developed a device, called the Tabulating Machine, which could automatically read census information punched onto cards. For example, using this technology the Census Bureau could easily determine the actual number of police officers in New York City. His idea came from watching a train conductor punch tickets. As a result of his invention, stacks of punched cards could be used as an accessible memory store of almost unlimited capacity and different problems could be stored on different batches of cards and worked on as needed. Hollerith's tabulator proved so successful that he started his own firm to market the device which eventually became International Business Machines (IBM).

1800                    1850                    1900

**1941** Konrad Zuse completes work on the world's first electronic computer, called the Z3. The Z3 was the world's first fully functional, program-controlled (freely programmable) computer. It was a binary computer using programs stored on punched tape. The device contained practically all features of modern-day computers.

**1944** Professor Howard Aiken of Harvard University along with support by IBM built an electro-mechanical machine, called the Mark I. The machine contained both mechanical and electronic parts. Data was stored electronically inside the device with the use of electromagnetic relays. Mathematical calculations were performed by the machine's mechanical counters. A moth caught in one of the machine's relays and discovered by Aiken's colleague Grace Hopper, gave rise to the term "computer bug."

**1942** At Iowa State University, Dr. John Atanasoff and Clifford Berry complete work on a device, called the Atanasoff-Berry Computer (also called the ABC). Although the ABC lacked program control and was not designed for general-purpose processing, it was a forerunner of today's modern computers.

**1945** In a brilliantly written paper, Dr. John von Neumann describes the stored program concept. His idea—that computer memory holds both data and stored programs—lays the foundation for all digital computers that have since been built.

**1943** Alan Turing and T. H. Flowers design the Colossus, a computer used by the British to crack German codes during World War II. Its existence remained a secret until the 1970s. Turing held that computers would in time be programmed to acquire abilities rivaling human intelligence, a concept now referred to as the Turing Test. The Turing Test became the basis for modern "artificial intelligence."

1940

1945

**1946** Professors J. Presper Eckert and John Mauchly build an all-purpose electronic digital computer, the Electronic Numerical Integrator and Calculator (ENIAC), which was used by the U.S. government for a variety of computing tasks. The ENIAC weighed 30 tons and covered 15,000 square feet. Eckert and Mauchly would later form a company to build and commercially market UNIVAC computers to the U.S. Census Bureau.

**1947** William Shockley, John Bardeen, and Walter Brattain invent the transistor (short for transfer resistance device). The transistor proved much more reliable than vacuum tubes used in earlier computers. This would lead to the development of smaller and faster computers and to many other small electronic devices including TVs, radios, and a variety of handheld electronic devices.

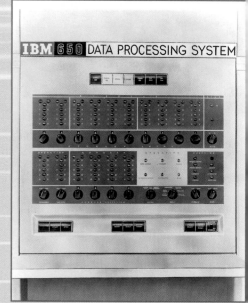

**1951** Remington Rand Corporation introduces the first commercial computer produced in the United States, called the Universal Automatic Computer (UNIVAC I). It was designed principally by J. Presper Eckert and John Mauchly. This computer gained wide acceptance after analyzing only five percent of the popular vote and correctly predicting that Dwight D. Eisenhower would win the 1952 presidential election.

**1953** IBM introduces its model 650 computer and expected to sell only about 50 of these machines but, because of its popularity, manufactured more than 1,000. Soon afterwards, IBM's model 370 established IBM as the world's dominant mainframe computer manufacturer.

1950                    1953

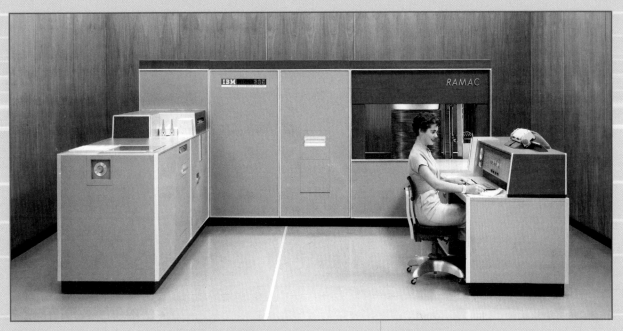

**1956** IBM's 305 RAMAC (Random Access Memory Accounting System) was an electronic, general-purpose, data processing machine that maintained up-to-the-minute business records. This was the first computer to use magnetic disk storage. The 305 RAMAC was one of the last vacuum tube systems designed and sold by IBM, and more than 1,000 of them were built before production ended in 1961.

**1957** John Backus at IBM introduces an efficient and easy-to-use programming language, called FORTRAN (Formula Translation).

**1957** The Soviet Union successfully launches Sputnik I, the world's first orbiting satellite. This event ushered in new scientific and technological developments and led to the creation of NASA. One such development was the first silicon-based computer chip, used on the Apollo landing craft to perform calculations for landing the craft on the moon.

**1958** Jack Kilby, a scientist at Texas Instruments, invents the integrated circuit which laid the foundation for future super-fast computers and large-capacity internal storage. Integrated circuits are now an essential component of computers and numerous other electronic devices.

**1960** Grace Hopper leads a team in the development of a high-level business application computer language, called Common Business-Oriented Language (COBOL). COBOL is one of the most widely used languages and uses English-like phrases. Programs written using COBOL can run on most business computers.

**1969** The United States Defense Advanced Research Project Agency (ARPA) establishes ARPANET, a wide-area network linking many colleges and research facilities for sharing information. ARPANET would become the predecessor of the Internet.

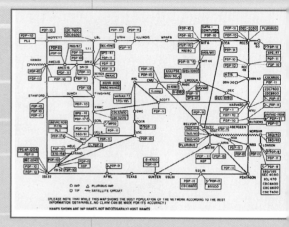

**1965** Dartmouth College professor John Kemeny and his colleague Thomas Kurtz develop the BASIC programming language that would become the most widely used language for personal computers. BASIC would enable students and other PC users to program their own computers.

**1970** The powerful UNIX operating system is developed at Bell Laboratories. Later versions of this operating system became widely used on large computers and formed the basis for operating systems for personal computers, including Linux and the Macintosh OS X. Among other uses, the power of UNIX has made possible the production of fascinating animated graphics, including those in the movie *Jurassic Park*.

**1970** A new generation of computers began to emerge featuring (Large Scale Integration (LSI) chips. LSI chips contained several thousand more electronic circuits than earlier chips. LSI chips lead to the development of smaller and more powerful electronic devices, such as pocket-size calculators.

1960          1965          1970

**1971** Ted Hoff, a scientist at Intel Corporation, develops the Intel 4004 microprocessor, a computer-on-a-chip microprocessor. The Intel 4004 spawned the beginning of the personal computer industry. Intel Corporation has become the world's leading producer of microprocessors.

**1971** A team of IBM engineers led by Alan Shugart introduce the first 8-inch memory disk, later called "floppy disk." Subsequent types of floppy disks would become standard storage media for large and small computers.

**1971** Cray Research founder Seymour Cray introduces the Cray-1, the world's first supercomputer capable of processing complex applications that less powerful units cannot handle. For example, modern supercomputers are needed to accurately forecast weather patterns and for processing complex mathematical applications, including NASA launches and military weapon systems development. Cray would go on to build other faster and more powerful supercomputers.

**1972** Hewlett-Packard introduces a series of scientific pocket calculators, including models featuring a variety of useful functions and capable of performing numerous mathematical computations. During the following years, smaller and more powerful pocket calculators have been developed.

**1972** The C programming language is developed at Bell Laboratories by a team led by Dennis Ritchie. The C language combined the best features and capabilities of earlier languages, including COBOL and FORTRAN, making C a useful and powerful language for both business and scientific applications.

**1973** Xerox's Palo Alto Research Center develops the Alto computer containing many of the features—a graphical user interface (GUI), windows, icons, a mouse, and pointers, and disk—that would be used years later in commercial personal computers.

1971                    1972                    1973

**1976–1977** In 1976, as a hobby club project to which they belonged, Steve Jobs and Steve Wozniak, later cofounders of Apple Computer Corporation, build the first Apple computer. The following year, Apple introduced the Apple II personal computer, capable of displaying text and graphics in color. The Apple II enjoyed tremendous commercial success, particularly among students and schools.

**1975** Dr. Robert Metcalf develops Ethernet, the first local area network (LAN), at Xerox's Palo Alto Research Center (PARC) in Palo Alto, California. Modern LANs allow digital computers of all types and sizes to communicate and share software, data, and peripherals. LANs are now used worldwide, thereby making it possible for computing resources to be shared and for users to enjoy the benefits of the Internet and World Wide Web.

**1978** Daniel Bricklin and Bob Frankston develop a powerful and compact spreadsheet program, named VisiCalc, for the Apple II computer. VisiCalc widely contributed to the commercial success of the Apple II and further Apple systems.

**1975** One of the first microcomputers, called the Altair, was introduced by Micro Instrumentation and Telemetry Systems (MITS). Available as kits needing assembly by buyers, the first machines had no keyboard, monitor, or software. The company received more than 4,000 orders within the first three months. Competing machines would soon begin appearing.

1975　　　　　　　　　　1976　　　　　　　　　　1978

**1980** IBM offers Bill Gates of Microsoft Corporation the opportunity to create the operating system for a personal computer being developed by IBM. Gates accepted and, with the development of MS-DOS, which IBM labeled PC-DOS, Microsoft achieves tremendous financial success.

**1980** Sony Electronics introduces the 3.5-inch floppy disk and disk drive. The disk drive and medium would become standard for millions of personal computers.

**1981** IBM introduces the IBM PC that quickly captures the largest share of the personal computer market and becomes the most widely used personal computer in business. It featured floppy drives and a version of the MS-DOS operating system, called PC-DOS, developed by Bill Gates and Microsoft Corporation.

**1981** The first known computer virus, called Elk Cloner, was written by a 15-year-old high school student for Apple II systems. Elk Cloner spread by infecting the Apple II's operating system, stored on floppy disks. When the computer was booted from an infected floppy, a copy of the virus would automatically start. When an uninfected floppy was accessed, the virus would copy itself to the disk, thus infecting it, too, and slowly spreading from floppy to floppy.

**1982** Intel Corporation introduces the 80286 microprocessor that would become the most common microprocessor for IBM-PCs and compatible computers.

**1982** Time magazine names the computer its "Man of the Year." Interestingly, the computer became the first object ever to receive the distinction. The publication officially recognized the importance of the computer, the use and popularity of which had already become widespread.

**1982** Compaq Computer Corporation is founded by Rod Canion, Jim Harris, and Bill Murto to build and sell 100-percent IBM-compatible computers. The company achieves immediate success.

1980    1981    1982

**1983** Lotus Development Corporation is founded by partners Mitch Kapor and Jonathan Sachs. The company, later acquired by IBM, develops and markets its best-known software product, called Lotus 1-2-3, which combines spreadsheet, graphics, and database programs in one package. Its relative ease of use and flexibility made it an enormous success and contributed to the acceptance of personal computers in business.

**1983** Microsoft announces Microsoft Windows, an extension of the MS-DOS operating system that would provide a graphical operating environment for PC users. With Windows, the graphical user interface (GUI) era at Microsoft had begun.

**1984** Apple introduces the first Macintosh computer. The easy-to-use Macintosh quickly became popular with its graphical user interface (GUI) and mouse.

**1985** Intel Corporation introduces the Intel 386 microprocessor. This microprocessor was first installed in PCs built by a startup company called Compaq Computer Corporation (later acquired by Hewlett-Packard). Compaq PCs were capable of running software developed for IBM-PCs, thereby giving rise to numerous types of PCs referred to as IBM-compatible.

**1985** The first CD-ROM players become available in the market. CD-ROM drives and discs would become important storage technologies for personal computers.

**1986** Microsoft Corporation has its initial public offering (IPO) of its stock. The stock was priced at $21 a share to open, but the first trade took place at $25.50 a share, an indication of the fierce demand for the stock. During the offering, Microsoft's initial offering of 3.095 million shares were traded, enabling Microsoft to raise more than $52 million. The initial 3.095 million shares are now worth more than $355 million.

**1988** Internet Relay Chat (IRC) is developed by Finnish student Jarkko Oikarinen. IRC enables users to communicate via the Internet in real time (almost instantly).

**1989** The first commercial Internet service provider, called The World, appears and begins offering dial-up service.

**1989** Intel Corporation introduces the Intel 486 microprocessor. This chip contained 1.2 million transistors and could execute one instruction per clock cycle. This was the first pipelining processor, meaning that begin executing the next instruction before finishing the execution of the previous instruction. Modern processors all have pipelining capability.

1983       1985       1988

**1990** Tim Berners-Lee invents the World Wide Web (WWW). Initially intended for use by scientists to share information, it evolves into widespread usage as a communications system for sharing information containing text, graphics, audio, animation, and video.

**1990** Tim Berners-Lee also invents and introduces the first browser, initially called WorldWideWeb, and later called Nexus so as to not be confusing with the Web. Unfortunately, this browser was not capable of displaying pages containing graphical elements, such as pictures.

**1994** Netscape Communications Corporation is founded by Jim Clark and Marc Andreesen. Their company soon introduces the Netscape Navigator browser.

**1994** Finnish programmer Linus Torvalds creates the Linux kernel, an operating system similar to UNIX, which he makes freely available across the Internet to other programmers for their enhancement of the system. Some computer manufacturers have now begun installing versions of Linux on computers they sell.

**1993** The U.S. National Center for Supercomputing Applications releases versions of Mosaic, the first Web browser capable of displaying both text, pictures, and various other images on the same page.

**1993** Apple Computer, one of the first companies to offer personal digital assistants (PDAs), introduces the Newton MessagePad. Shortly thereafter, several other manufacturers began offering similar products. Today, one of the most popular brands of PDAs is the series of Palm Pilots from Palm, Inc. PDAs are also called palmtops, hand-held computers, and pocket PCs.

**1995** Microsoft releases its Internet Explorer browser that eventually replaces Netscape's Navigator as the dominant browser.

**1995** James Gosling and colleagues at Sun Microsystems introduce Java, an object-oriented programming language that enables users to write one program that can be used on a variety of computers. Java has become widely used for developing Web pages.

**1995** Microsoft introduces Windows 95, a major upgrade of its popular Windows operating system. This upgrade was a combination of MS-DOS and Windows operating systems, and included numerous additional functions that resulted in millions of copies being sold.

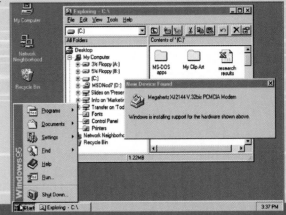

**1996** A group of universities launch Internet2, an advanced network for the research community that would enable institutions to develop new capabilities for possible use on the commercial Internet.

**1996** One-third of U.S. homes now have a personal computer and two-thirds of U.S. employees have access to personal computers. More than 250,000,000 personal computers are in use.

**1996** Microsoft releases a Windows upgrade, named Windows NT 4.0. This operating system is written for client-server networks. It quickly gains acceptance and is used by many businesses and organizations for implementing local area networks (LANs). This and other network software programs help usher in the Internet and World Wide Web.

**1996** A variety of products and technologies, collectively called WebTV, are introduced. Most WebTV products today consist of a small box that connects to a telephone line and television. It makes a connection to the Internet via a user's telephone service and then converts the downloaded Web pages to a format that can be displayed on a TV.

**1999** Palm releases its first handheld PC with wireless Internet access, called the Palm VII.

**1998** Under contract with the U.S. Department of Commerce, the nonprofit Internet Corporation for Assigned Names and Numbers (ICANN) assumes management of such basic Internet functions as the assignment of domain names and Internet addresses.

**1998** Microsoft begins shipping Windows 98, an upgrade version of Windows 95. Compared with the previous version, Windows 98 provides better Internet access, system performance, and improved support for new hardware and software. More than 10 million copies of this operating system are sold worldwide.

**1999** The BlackBerry, a wireless handheld device, is introduced. It provides access to e-mail, mobile telephone, text messaging, Web browsing and other wireless information services.

**1999** The approaching new millennium (year 2000) causes a worldwide scare because millions of older computer programs were incapable of correctly processing data based on the year 2000 and beyond. Reading only the last two digits, computers could not distinguish between the year 1900 and the year 2000. Business and governments spent billions of dollars rewriting software. Interestingly, the Y2K (year 2000) concern turned out not to be a significant problem.

**1997** Manufacturers began selling DVD players used for viewing movies stored on DVDs (digital video discs).

**1998** Apple Computer Corporation introduces and begins selling the iMac, an upgraded version of its Macintosh computer. The iMac quickly becomes popular among Macintosh loyalists.

**1997** The number of users connected to the Internet and Web exceeds 50 million. This number is rapidly increasing each day.

**1997** Intel Corporation introduces the Pentium II microprocessor containing 7.5 million transistors. With the chip's built-in MMX technology, the Pentium II can process audio, video, and graphics much more efficiently for applications involving movies, music, and gaming.

**1999** Microsoft Corporation begins shipping Windows 2000, Windows Me, and Office 2000. All quickly gained widespread acceptance and usage among PC users. Windows 2000 offers improved computer system performance. Office 2000 provides new features, including allowing users to create material and save it to a Web site. Windows Me, designed for home users, allows for editing home photographs and movies, share digital photographs, and create a home network.

1997          1998          1999

**2000** Intel Corporation introduces its Pentium 4 microprocessor chip that quickly becomes the most popular CPU for personal computers. An upgrade of its predecessor, the Pentium III, the Pentium 4 provides a processing technique, called hyperthreading, which greatly improves system performance in areas including image processing, video content creation, games, and multimedia. The Pentium 4 led to the rapid increase in the demand for computer video games.

**2001** Intel Corporation and Hewlett-Packard jointly produce the first 64-bit microprocessor (CPU), called the Itanium.

**2001** Microsoft releases its XP group of products, including Windows XP and Office XP. Windows XP provided users with increased security and an interesting aqua-type desktop interface. Improved speech and handwriting recognition was added, along with smart tags and task panes.

**2003** Microsoft launches Office 2003, a major upgrade of Office 2000. The popularity of all versions of Office is evidenced by the fact that there are now more than 400 million users worldwide.

**2003** Apple Computer enters the online music business with its iPod mp3 player and online iTunes venture. During the first year, Apple downloaded from its iTunes Web site nearly 20 million songs at 99 cents each. Other suppliers, including Wal-Mart, RealNetworks, Microsoft, and Sony, soon joined the competition to supply online music to subscribers.

**2000** Small, portable flash memory cards that plug into a computer's USB port and function as portable hard drives are introduced. USB flash drives are easy-to-use as they are small enough to be carried in a pocket and can plug into any computer with a USB drive.

**2002** A variety of new technologies appear in the marketplace. Digital video cameras and recorders allow users to make and edit high-quality videos. DVD writers/ recorders begin replacing older CD writers. DVDs can store up to eight times more data than the CDs they replace enabling users to store movies, photos, music, and more on a single DVD disc. The Tablet PC is introduced, a useful device for mobile users. Newly introduced LCD flat-panel monitors are an immediate hit among PC users.

**2003** The Recording Industry Association of America (RIAA), seeking to protect its music-producing membership, files numerous legal suits against computer users who offer copyrighted music over their peer-to-peer networks.

2000    2001    2003

**2004** IBM launches and tests the world's fastest supercomputer, called the BlueGene/L. Jointly developed by IBM and the U.S. Department of Energy's National Nuclear Security Administration (NNSA) and installed at DOE's Lawrence Livermore National Laboratory in Livermore, California, the BlueGene/L can perform 280.6 trillion calculations per second. It is the only computer ever to exceed a speed of 100 trillion calculations per second.

**2004** More than 69 million U.S. homes now use broadband connections, an increase of 35.9 percent over the previous year. The number of users having broadband connections in the workplace reaches 42 million, an increase of 21 percent over the previous year.

**2005** Smartphones have become the most widely used mobile device, surpassing PDAs and other mobile devices. More advanced smartphones provide users with cellular phone cap-ability, personal information management (such as appointment scheduling), electronic mail capability, Web browsing capability, music and voice downloading, and even picture capture and transmission.

**2005** Mozilla creates the Firefox browser and claims 10% of market. Recent versions of the free browser allow users to browse the Web and offers greater protection from viruses, spyware, and pop-ups.

**2006** The U.S. Department of Commerce reports that electronic commerce retail sales for the first six months of 2006 exceeded $51 billion. Almost any consumer product available in stores can now be purchased online.

**2006** Numerous cities and businesses begin offering citizens and customers economical broadband connectivity to the Internet. Locations, called "hotspots," are made available to users of notebook PCs, PDAs, and other mobile devices to connect to Wi-Fi access points. Some cities are developing city-wide access systems that allow for Internet access at any location within the city.

**2007** Microsoft Corporation introduces Windows Vista, an upgrade of its earlier Windows XP operating system for personal computers. Also, Microsoft launches its new Office 2007 software suite, an upgrade of the company's Office XP suite. Office 2007 provides greater security against unauthorized access and usage.

**2007** A JupiterResearch report based on a survey of just under 3,000 Internet users found that online users now spend about 14 hours a week, on average, surfing the Internet—the same amount of time they spend watching TV.

**2009** Microsoft releases Windows 7, the successor to Windows Vista.

**2010** Microsoft releases Microsoft Office 2010.

# Buying and Installing a PC

**S**HOPPING FOR A PERSONAL COMPUTER (PC) can be enjoyable, if you are well informed. Some shoppers think all personal computers are alike so their main objective is to find the cheapest one. Doing so can be a mistake. Many first-time buyers have discovered that the computer they purchased lacked components and features they needed. Avoid making this mistake by arming yourself with information and careful planning. This Tech Insight provides some useful guidelines to help you find the right desktop, notebook, or handheld PC and then install it.

## Buying a Desktop Personal Computer System

The decision to buy a PC represents a major investment in both time and money. Chances are that you will use your computer for at least three years, perhaps even longer. Before making the final purchasing decision, complete each step outlined in the following process.

### Step One: Identify Your Needs

Before spending your money, prepare a written list of your computing needs and how and where you will be using your new system. Answering the following questions will help you identify your needs.

1. Where will I use my new PC? If you will be using it only in your home or office, a desktop computer may be suitable. However, if you travel for business or if you need mobility in general, you should consider purchasing a notebook (laptop) computer weighing five pounds or less. See the "Buying a Notebook Computer" section for additional guidelines.
2. For what purposes will I use my computer? For example, will you use your PC to prepare letters and reports? Analyze numeric and financial data? Prepare visual presentations? Access the Internet? Listen to music? Create and work with graphics? List all possible uses since these will determine the software and hardware you need. Generally, if you will use multimedia and/or graphics programs, you will need greater storage and processing capabilities.
3. How long will I keep this computer? Try to estimate the number of years you will use your computer before buying the next one. If you expect to use your PC for several years, consider buying one that has expansion slots so you can add new components, such as a modem, printer, or add-on memory boards.

## Step Two: Establish a Budget

Ask yourself how much you can realistically afford to pay for a computer. Prices of desktop personal computers range from a few hundred to thousands of dollars. Faster and more feature-rich PCs are usually more expensive. Also, personal computers soon become obsolete. Within a few years you may need a faster and more versatile model.

## Step Three: Choose Software to Match Your Needs List

Every computer must have software, including system software and applications software. System software, such as Microsoft Windows or Mac OS, allows a computer to manage its computing resources, including the system unit and input and output devices. Most PCs come with the system software already installed. For general business or academic situations, Windows-based systems are more widely used, but for graphics applications, a Mac platform may be preferable.

Determine the total storage space and processing power you will need for the programs you intend to use. These calculations will drive your hardware choices. Note, too, that some PCs arrive from the factory with a software suite, such as Microsoft Office, already installed. The suite includes word processing, spreadsheet, database management, e-mail, and other applications.

## Step Four: Select the Hardware Components

Hardware refers to all of the equipment that makes up a personal computer system (see Figure 1): the system unit, input devices, output devices, secondary storage devices, and all peripheral devices,

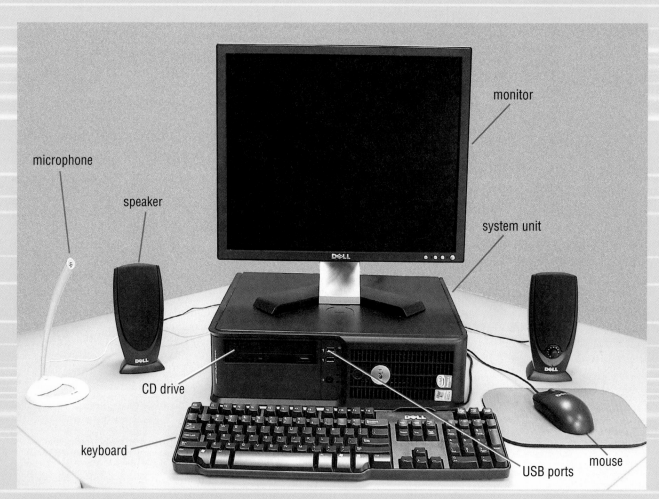

microphone

speaker

monitor

system unit

CD drive

keyboard

USB ports

mouse

**Figure 1  Hardware Components of a Personal Computer System**

A complete personal computer system includes not only the system unit, monitor, keyboard, and mouse, but also a printer and speakers and possibly a webcam.

such as printers. Following are some guidelines for selecting PC hardware components.

**The System Unit**   The system unit is typically a metal cabinet containing the essential components for processing information. Along with other standard components, the system unit contains a microprocessor, main memory (RAM), and slots for installing a graphics board, sound board, modem, or other peripherals. Hard disk drives, CD drives, and DVD drives are also housed in the system unit. Increasingly, PC manufacturers are not including a floppy disk drive in new computers.

- **PC architecture**. PC architecture refers to the design and construction of the PC and its system unit, and not all architectures are the same. For example, the architecture of an Apple Macintosh differs from that of an IBM or IBM-compatible PC. Therefore, software written for an Apple Macintosh PC may not run on an IBM or IBM-compatible PC. However, some newer Macintosh PC models can run both types of software. Although some users prefer a Macintosh PC, more software is available for IBM and IBM-compatibles.
- **Microprocessor**. Selecting the right microprocessor is extremely important. Processing speed, typically measured in gigahertz (GHz), is probably the first consideration. The higher the number of GHz, the faster the processor can access and process programs and data. If speed is important, consider choosing a microprocessor with a speed of 2.0 GHz or more. PCs containing microprocessors with speeds up to 3.0 GHz and higher are available.
- **Main memory**. Main memory (RAM) is needed for the temporary storage of programs and data while the data is being processed. Some application software requires a considerable amount of RAM to function properly, and newer software versions usually require more RAM than older versions. Newer desktop PCs typically come with 512 MB of RAM, or more. Make certain the PC has sufficient RAM to run the software you will be using. For example, if you will be working with newer, larger, and more complex applications, such as video and graphics editing, watching movies, or listening to music, consider buying a PC with 2 gigabytes (GB) of RAM.

- **Secondary storage**. What type(s) and amounts of secondary storage are you likely to need? Think of your hard drive as a storage cabinet. The more stuff you have, the more storage you need. Start with a hard drive with 80 GB. If you'll be storing many photos and tunes, move up to 160 GB. Storage capacity of newer hard drives go up to 500 GB. Most computers come with a CD drive and a hard disk drive already installed. A standard compact disc can store up to 750 MB of data, and certain DVDs provide even greater storage capacity. A hard disk drive contains one or more rigid storage platters and provides for the permanent storage of considerably more data. However, the disk itself cannot be removed from the drive. The storage capacity of a hard disk is an important consideration because it is used to store all system and application software, such as Microsoft Word. Typical hard disk capacities are 80 GB, 160 GB, and up to 500 GB.

  Other secondary storage devices and media are available. If you will use your PC to play movies, your purchase should include a DVD drive. If you will work with large files, consider purchasing a computer that includes a CD-RW drive. A CD-RW disc is a reusable high-capacity disc that allows you to store huge amounts of data and to erase data no longer needed. Flash drives are also easy to use and are portable.

A flash drive is an easy-to-use and portable secondary storage device that provides reusable memory.

- **Ports**. A port on a personal computer is a connection you can use to connect a device, such as a mouse or printer. A personal computer has internal ports and external ports. An internal port allows for the connection of components such as disk drives. External ports (see Figure 2) allow you to connect peripheral devices such as modems, printers, digital cameras, and mice. The number of available ports determines the number of devices and add-on boards that can be connected to the system unit.

  Older PCs typically have a serial port (for external modems), a parallel port (for printers), and maybe one or two USB ports. Newer computers, referred to as "legacy free," no longer include serial or parallel ports but instead include several USB ports. It is normal to find between four and eight USB ports on the back of the computer and two in front. A USB port connects various devices, including keyboards, mice, monitors, and printers. USB ports are particularly important if you need to connect a digital camera, connect to the Internet via a cable modem, or use a flash drive. A USB port located at the front of the system unit provides easy access if you will be plugging in a flash drive or connecting a digital camera.

  Some manufacturers label external ports to make it easy for users to locate where devices are to be connected to the system unit. For example, printer, mice, and keyboard ports are often labeled. Many new PCs come with instructions and diagrams that identify the ports to which specific devices are to be connected.

**Input Devices**   Typical input devices are a keyboard and a mouse, although other kinds of input devices are available. Most keyboards and mice operate similarly. However, there are slight differences in how each "feels" to the user. Before buying a PC, examine the keyboard and mouse for comfort and ease of use. Some sellers will allow you to exchange the keyboard or mouse that comes with the computer for a different one of comparable value.

**Output Devices**   Output devices produce output in either soft copy or hard copy form. Most PCs come with a monitor (for soft copy output), but you may have to purchase a hard copy device, such as a printer, separately.

- **Monitors**. Slim, lightweight, flat-screen liquid crystal display (LCD) monitors have virtually replaced the older and bulkier cathode ray tube (CRT) displays. The resolution of most LCD monitors is quite good and they take up less desktop space. There are wide differences among PC monitors, with resolution being perhaps the most important variable. Resolution refers to the clarity of the text and images being displayed on the screen. Higher resolutions, such as a resolution of 1,024 by 1,024 pixels, display text and images with exceptional clarity. High-resolution monitors are typically more expensive, but may be worth the extra cost.

  Monitor size is another important consideration. Viewing areas range from 15 diagonal inches to 21 inches and higher. Larger monitors are usu-

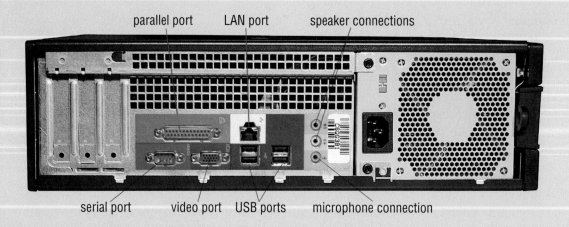

parallel port    LAN port    speaker connections

serial port    video port    USB ports    microphone connection

**Figure 2  System Unit Ports**

Ports are typically visible on the back of the system unit.

ally more expensive, but may be a priority if you work with graphics or if your vision is weak.

- **Printers**. Two popular types of printers are ink-jet and laser, both of which are versatile and capable of producing high-quality output in color. Examine a variety of printers and models and check the price, print speed, and output quality of each.

  Most ink-jet printers are quiet, produce high-quality output, and are relatively affordable, although the ink cartridges they use can be expensive. Print resolution is an important factor to consider. Some offer impressive resolution and can produce output of amazing color.

  Laser printers are fast and can produce high-quality output in both black and color tones. Color laser printers are more expensive than those using only black toner. The cost of color laser printers ranges from a few hundred to thousands of dollars.

  If you will print pictures or graphics, a photographic printer is preferable to an ordinary ink-jet or laser printer. Most photographic printers are reasonably priced and are capable of producing highly detailed and brilliantly colored photographs and graphics.

# Buying a Notebook Computer

A notebook (or laptop) computer is a portable personal computer that contains the components and

Notebook computers provide the same basic functionality as a desktop computer and are portable.

devices people use most often. However, various brands and models are available, and you should select the notebook that will match your list of needs, as described in the preceding section. Following are guidelines for buying a notebook computer.

## Compatibility

As a buyer, you have a choice between a Windows and Macintosh computer. If you already have a Windows desktop PC and will share programs and data between the two, consider buying a Windows notebook. If, on the other hand, you will be working with graphics applications, you may want to check out Macintosh notebook models. Regardless of the operating system you choose, make sure it is the most recent version available. If a new version will soon become available, you may want to consider waiting for the new version before making a purchase.

## Computer Size and Weight

Notebooks vary in weight from about four pounds to more than eight pounds. If you will be carrying it with you, a 7- or 8-pound computer can be quite burdensome so you should consider a notebook weight in the 4 to 6 pound range. For portability you will need a carrying case for your notebook computer. Some sellers offer a free carrying case with the computers they sell. If you will purchase a carrying case, choose one with separate compartments for storage media, such as CDs and DVDs. Make sure the case is lightweight and sufficiently durable to protect your computer.

## Processor

Consider notebooks with different processor speeds, and determine which speed will best fit your needs and your budget. Most users prefer a minimum processor speed of 1.6 GHz. For computer games, a faster processor makes playing games more enjoyable.

## Keyboard and Pointing Devices

Check out a variety of notebooks and the keyboard and pointing device each offers. Are you comfortable working on a small keyboard? Select a notebook that has a keyboard and pointing device that feels the most comfortable. You might decide not to use the built-in mouse but will use a wireless mouse instead.

### Display Screen

Before you buy, examine the size and clarity of the computer's display screen. Screens range from about 12 inches up to 20 inches, measured diagonally. Larger screens typically offer better viewing but they are heavier and usually more expensive. Also, some screens must be viewed directly whereas other types can be viewed from various angles. If you will use your notebook for displaying graphics or playing games, you may want a larger, active-matrix display screen.

### Disk Type and Capacity

Choose the type and capacity of disk drives. Will you need a hard disk drive? A CD-ROM or CD-RW drive? A flash drive? A notebook hard disk should have a minimum capacity of 40 GB. If you will use the computer to watch movies and/or listen to music, you will need speakers and a DVD drive.

### Internal Memory (RAM)

Internal memory capacity is an important consideration. Select a computer with at least 1 GB of RAM. Less RAM will limit the kinds of software you use and the applications you can run on your computer.

### Wireless Capability

Consider the option of built-in wireless capabilities. If you will travel and take your notebook with you, having wireless capability is essential. Many hotels, airports, restaurants, and other facilities now provide wireless access. To take advantage of wireless capability, you will need a built-in modem.

## Buying a Handheld Computer

The popularity of handheld computers has ballooned, particularly for mobile workers and people who want computer access anytime, anywhere. Depending on the specific handheld model, these lightweight, pocket-sized computers that fit in the palm of one's hand offer a range of features, including an appointment book, notepad, calculator, calendar, phone, video player, and music player.

Handheld computers offer organizer features such as an appointment book, notepad, calculator, and calendar. Additional software, including a word processing program, can be added to some models.

Many are Web-enabled, allowing owners to access information and to send and receive e-mail. Some handhelds also are preloaded with basic application software, including word processing and spreadsheet programs. Data entry and command selection are accomplished with a pen-like stylus or a built-in keyboard.

If you are in the market for a handheld, follow these guidelines to narrow the field of choices:

- Decide on how much you are willing to pay. Prices range from less than $100 to over $1000, depending on the type of handheld and the features offered. For example, a few hundred dollars will buy a handheld with a color 240 × 320 pixel touch screen, about 64 MB of RAM, and a 624 MHz processor. For a little more, you can get 124 MB of RAM, Wi-Fi, Bluetooth, and a color 480 × 640 pixel touch screen.
- Determine which applications you want to run on your computer. Read available literature and talk with other handheld users to get their opinions and suggestions. For business purposes, you may want programs such as Microsoft Word, Excel, and PowerPoint. For personal use, you may want MP3 capability in addition to the basic organizer functions.

A keyboard can be added to a handheld device to expand its functionality.

- Visit a computer retailer and ask a sales associate to demonstrate the various models available. With the employee's supervision, practice using the computer's touch screen and the device's keyboard and stylus (if available with the computer).
- Decide whether you want a color or monochrome (black and white) screen. Most users prefer color, and color-screen resolutions have improved markedly in recent years. A black-and-white display may be acceptable for buyers who will use only the calendar and appointment book features.
- Check out battery life and accessories. A long battery life may be a top consideration if your handheld is your only computer or your main work device. Think of the accessories you may need, such as an extra battery, battery charger, and carrying case for your computer. If you travel frequently, you may need a modem, removable storage, and a portable keyboard.
- Decide whether you need Internet access and wireless capability. Some handhelds come equipped with a modem and software that provides for wireless connections and Internet access. If you will need these capabilities, make sure the device you are considering offers them.

Before you make a purchase, learn whether the device is upgradeable so you can add additional capability in the future. Memory Sticks, for example, offer a quick and easy way to boost power and performance.

# Installing a Desktop Personal Computer

Because most notebook computers and handhelds are self-contained, the computer installation process mainly applies to desktop computers. Installing a new desktop PC requires following a few basic steps that should take less than an hour.

Prior to bringing your new PC to your home or office, or having it delivered, you need to decide where to position it. Estimate the total space the system will require. You will want to find a comfortable location near one or more electrical outlets. Avoid placing your PC where it will be exposed to direct sunlight or dampness. If your computer contains a dial-up modem and you will be connecting to an Internet service provider (ISP), your computer should be located near a telephone jack. If you will be using a cable connection, position your computer near the cable connection.

## Step One: Unpack Your Computer System

While unpacking your new computer and components, locate all items, including computer components, power cords and cables, manuals, assembly instructions and diagrams, and warranty cards. Keep these items together. Be sure to fill out all warranty cards and mail them to the respective manufacturers to register your purchase in case you need to return the computer or contact the manufacturer for technical assistance. Store the containers and padding materials in case you need to return the computer or a defective component to the manufacturer. As you continue unpacking, carefully place each component on your desk or table.

## Step Two: Connect the Components

After unpacking and placing the system unit at your workplace, look closely at the various ports on the front and back of the system unit. Usually, ports are labeled or color-coded to help you match each device with its port. Also, some manufacturers enclose written instructions and illustrations for connecting system devices. Locate these documents and carefully follow the instructions.

Because some system devices and peripherals, including the system unit, monitor, and printer,

A surge protector guards computer components from damage during electrical power surges.

require electrical power, each uses a power cord. Locate the cord for each device and plug it into the device. Some devices have a permanently attached cord.

You can protect components from damage that can result from power surges by using a surge protector. Plug the power cords into the device. Later, you will plug the surge protector into a wall outlet. (Caution: do not plug the surge protector into an electric outlet until you are ready to boot up the computer system.)

Each device that comprises your computer system needs to connect to the system unit by means of a cable. To connect a device, connect one end of the cable into the device itself and the other end into the appropriate port on the system unit (usually located at the back of the system unit). In addition to color coding cables and ports, some manufacturers package a color-coded chart or diagram showing how cables are to be connected. Typically, cable connectors are physically designed to fit a particular port.

### Step Three: Boot the Computer

After connecting all devices, plug the surge protector into a wall outlet, turn it on, and then turn on the computer. Check to make sure all components and devices work properly. If a device does not work, check first to see if the device is properly connected to the system unit, turned on, and plugged into the surge protector. If the computer, device, or component still fails to work properly, you can get help from an experienced user or from the seller's or manufacturer's Help Desk.

## A Final Word

Although prices are declining, a computer still represents a major expenditure, whether you are buying a desktop, notebook, or handheld PC. Do your homework. Ask for recommendations from friends or colleagues. Carefully examine various computer makes and models and then choose wisely. Chances are, the choice you make is one you will live with for a long time. Making the right decisions results in the purchase of a highly effective and efficient tool you will enjoy using in your home, at the office, in school, or on the road.

# Adding Software and Hardware Components to Your PC

**I**NSTALLING SYSTEM SOFTWARE, APPLICATION PROGRAMS, and hardware components with early PCs was difficult and cumbersome compared with the installation process for modern computers. In the past, users had to enter complex instructions. Thus, an experienced computer technician or other professional was needed to install the software or hardware properly. Today's computer manufacturers have made these activities easier by including installation instructions and diagrams with their products. Additionally, Microsoft Windows includes features that enable users to install software and hardware more quickly and easily. For example, the Windows Control Panel contains utilities for installing and removing application programs and hardware devices. In this Tech Insight you will learn how to install software programs and add hardware devices to your personal computer system.

Manufacturers such as Dell Computer preload most of their new PCs with the Windows operating system, some application programs, and basic hardware devices. Because most PCs use Windows, this Tech Insight assumes you are using a Windows-based computer.

## Installing or Upgrading the Operating System

Sometimes situations occur that require you to reinstall the operating system and application programs. An operating system (OS) contains programs that direct a computer's operations and programs that manage the computer's internal and external components. If Windows was not preinstalled on your computer, a CD-ROM containing the OS may have been included in the package, or you can purchase one at a computer store or at another retail outlet.

Installing the OS on your hard disk is relatively simple. With your computer turned off, insert the CD-ROM containing the OS into the CD or CD/DVD drive at the front of the system unit. Turn the computer on. A small ROM chip on the motherboard will search for an operating system and find it on the CD, along with a file of instructions for installing the OS. Installation instructions will be displayed on the screen. Follow the instructions to complete the process.

When a new version of the OS becomes available, you may want to install it on your computer, a procedure known as upgrading. To install the upgraded version, insert the CD-ROM containing the new version in the CD drive. Follow the instructions on your screen to install the new version. The installation should be completed in a few minutes.

## Installing Application Software

Application software enables users to perform specific types of activities and tasks for which computers were designed. The type of software purchased depends on the user's intended purpose, and there are application programs available for almost every need. The most widely sold type is productivity software that enables users to improve their efficiency at home and on the job. Examples of productivity software include word processing, spreadsheet, database, desktop publishing, presentation graphics, project management, and computer-aided design.

**TIP** System requirements for installing the software are usually printed on the software package or box. Among the requirements is the minimum amount of hard disk space (capacity) needed to house the software. Be sure your hard disk has enough unused capacity to store the software. If there is insufficient capacity on your hard disk, you will be alerted to this problem.

Most applications come on CDs or DVDs that run their Setup utility automatically when the disc is inserted into a PC. To install a new application, simply insert its disc and follow the prompts that appear. If AutoPlay is turned on for the CD or DVD drive and it is set to ask what you want to do with each disc, an AutoPlay dialog box appears. Click *Run autorun.exe* to allow the disc to run its automatic setup utility. If you are prompted for an administrator password or confirmation, type the appropriate password or provide confirmation.

If nothing happens when you insert a program disc, try manually activating the Autorun file on the CD as follows (in Windows Vista):

1. Click Start and click Computer.
2. Double-click the drive icon in which the CD or DVD is inserted.

If nothing happens after you do the preceding steps, you might need to browse the disc to find the Setup program. Follow these steps to locate the setup program:

1. From the Computer window, right-click the drive icon for the CD or DVD and choose Explore.
2. Double-click Setup.exe or Install.exe. If these files are not present, consult the documentation for the application to determine the name of the setup program file, and double-click on that file name.

After the software has been installed, you can access the program by clicking the Start button, the Programs option, and then selecting the program you installed, such as Word. (Note: The installation process is the same for almost all application programs.)

**TIP** If a previous (older) version of the software is already installed on your hard disk and you are installing an upgrade, only the needed parts of the newer version will be installed. Also, files you created using the older version will remain intact, allowing you to continue using those files.

Most software manufacturers include installation instructions with the software programs they sell.

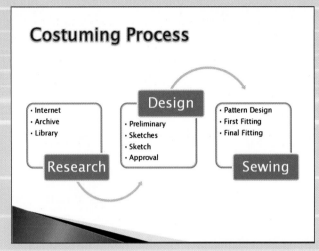

Presentation graphics is an example of productivity software.

# Connecting System Components

In addition to the system unit, your PC probably came with basic components such as the monitor, keyboard, mouse, and maybe a printer. These components are referred to as peripherals, because they are external (or peripheral) to the system unit. In the following sections, you will learn about device drivers and plug-and-play features and how to connect add-on peripheral devices to the system unit so that, collectively, all devices and components function smoothly as a computer system.

## Device Drivers and Plug-and-Play Features

Every device, whether it is a printer, disk drive, or keyboard, must have an associated driver program. A driver controls the device, translating commands between the device and programs that use the device so that it functions as intended. Each device has its own set of specialized commands that only the driver knows. Most programs access devices by using generic commands. A driver accepts generic commands and translates them into specialized commands for the device.

Some drivers, such as the keyboard driver, are included with the computer's operating system, because the manufacturer assumes you will use the keyboard that came with the computer. Other special devices, such as a scanner or joystick, may come with the device's driver program on a CD-ROM that you will need to load. The operating system will include drivers for a variety of devices, allowing the user to choose the needed ones. A filename of a

driver designed for use in a Windows environment often has a DRV file extension.

Some computer systems will configure devices and expansion boards automatically, a feature known as plug-and-play. With plug-and-play, a user should be able to plug in a device and use it immediately. Newer Apple Macintosh computers are plug-and-play systems, and both Microsoft and Intel use a technology called PnP (short for plug and play) that supports plug-and-play installation.

Your PC probably has the plug-and-play capability. Adding new components is simply a matter of plugging the devices into the appropriate ports on the back of the system unit.

## Locating System Unit Ports

The system unit contains several ports (see Figure 1). Many manufacturers label the ports, and some companies include an installation diagram with their computers. Additionally, cables that come with a computer usually will fit into only one port. These aids assist users in setting up a computer system.

## Connecting a New Printer

Most printers purchased for home or office use are either ink-jet or laser. Both types require a container of ink called a toner cartridge. If your printer came without a toner cartridge or a printer cable, you'll need to purchase these items.

Use the Autorun built into the application's CD to easily start the Setup program. Shown here is the AutoPlay dialog box in Windows Vista.

Installing a printer is a simple task. To connect the printer to the system unit and to a power source, complete the following steps:

1. With the power turned off, plug one end of the printer cable to the printer and the other end to the port located at the back of the system unit. Most printers are USB models, so they can connect to any available USB port on the PC.
2. Plug the power cord into the power connector on the printer and the other end into a surge protector.
3. Turn on the computer.
4. If Windows automatically detects the new printer and prompts you for its Setup disc, insert that disc and follow the prompts. If not, click Start and click Control Panel.
5. Click Hardware and Sound and then click Printers. Icons for the currently installed printer drivers will appear.
6. Click Add a Printer to open the Add Printer dialog box.
7. Click Add a local printer and then click Next.
8. Follow the on-screen instructions to complete the installation process.

# Installing Expansion Boards and Devices inside the System Unit

Most computers are shipped with printed instructions for installing internal components, expansion boards, and other devices inside the system unit. At some time you may want to add one or more of these components to increase your computer's capabilities. For example, you may want to install additional RAM capacity, a modem, or an extra CD or DVD drive. The instructions most likely include a section explaining the procedure for gaining internal access to the motherboard, expansion slots, and other components. Follow the steps carefully.

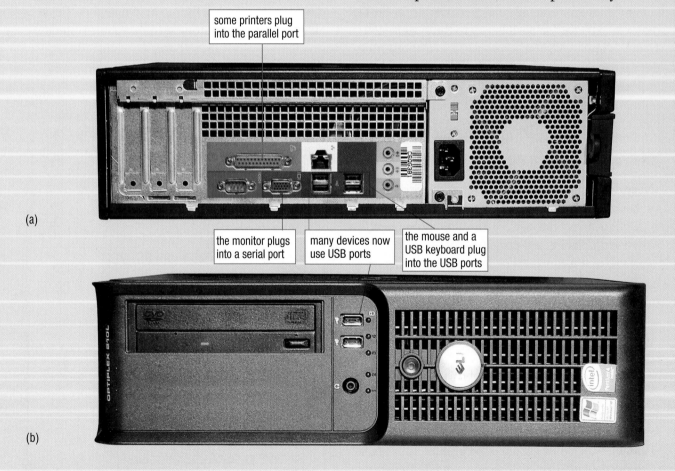

some printers plug into the parallel port

(a)

the monitor plugs into a serial port

many devices now use USB ports

the mouse and a USB keyboard plug into the USB ports

(b)

**Figure 1  Ports on a System Unit**

A variety of ports located on the system unit provide for the connection of peripheral devices, including monitor, keyboard, mouse, and printer. (a) Back of the system unit. (b) Front of the system unit.

A printer is one example of a peripheral device.

The Windows Add Printer dialog box allows for the installation of a local or network printer.

**TIP** Computer prices have declined significantly during recent years. If your computer is more than two or three years old, you may find it more cost-effective to purchase a new computer system with more capabilities and greater capacity than to upgrade your present computer.

## Precautionary Measures

Before attempting to install any device or circuit board inside the system unit, you should perform the following steps in sequence:

1. Turn off your computer and all other devices.
2. Ground yourself by touching an unpainted metal surface at the back of the computer (system unit) before touching anything inside the computer. While you work, periodically touch an unpainted metal surface to dissipate any static electricity that might cause damage to the computer.
3. Unplug the power cable to your computer and then press the power button to ground the system board.
4. Disconnect all devices connected to the computer, including the monitor, from electrical outlets or a surge protector to reduce the potential for personal injury or shock. Also, be sure to disconnect any telephone or communication lines from the computer.

An extensive variety of devices and circuit boards can be installed inside the system unit to render the computer more useful, including CD drives, DVD drives, graphics boards, sound boards, modems, and memory (RAM) boards. Unless you have training and experience in the installation of internal devices and circuit boards, you may want to have the work done by a certified PC technician who can perform and guarantee the installation. In such cases, ask questions and make sure the technician or company is one supported by the manufacturer of your computer. Additionally, only a certified technician should install or replace some components. For example, to replace a microprocessor in some computers you need a special tool designed for this purpose. Installing or replacing storage drives involves a series of complex steps that are probably better left to an experienced technician.

Unlike the installation of microprocessors, storage drives, and other components that may require the services of a service technician and typically involve a series of complex steps and special tools, installing expansion boards is relatively easy. Many users prefer to install one or more expansion boards, such as a RAM board, to enhance the computer's capabilities. The user's manual that came with your computer may contain instructions for installing various types of boards, including RAM boards. Also, manufacturers of expansion boards usually include printed installation instructions and illustrations in the package along with the board.

The installation procedures for various types of boards are quite similar. Chances are that after you have installed one kind of expansion board, you will find the installation of other kinds of boards even easier.

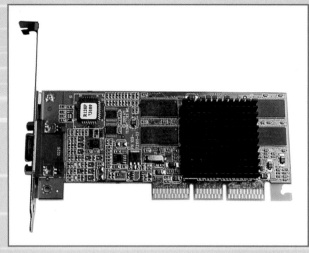

Additional components such as this video card can be installed to add extra functionality to a computer.

**Figure 2  Installing a RAM Board**
When inserting a DIMM module, the clip fits into the notch on the side of the DIMM. If inserted properly, it snaps into place easily.

### Installing a RAM Board

Older PCs came with a type of RAM called SIMM (single inline memory module). Newer Pentium PCs contain a type of RAM called DIMM (dual inline memory module). The user's manual supplied with your computer will specify the type in your system. The main difference in the way the two modules are installed is that SIMM modules are inserted into an expansion board at an angle and a DIMM module is inserted vertically. Assuming your computer uses DIMM modules, you can easily install an additional DIMM module by completing the following steps:

1. Study carefully the printed instructions and illustration(s) that came in the package along with the DIMM module. The illustrations or diagrams identify the slot where you will insert the module.
2. With the system unit panel removed to expose the motherboard, locate the slot where you will insert the module. (Note: Your computer should already contain at least one RAM module and may provide multiple slots for adding more RAM). Select an empty slot, perhaps the one closest to the already installed RAM module, although any available slot may be used.

3. Match the orientation of the DIMM module with the slot. The module will fit only one way because of notches in the slot.
4. Firmly press the DIMM module (board) straight down into the slot, until the clips on both ends fit over the notch in the DIMM module. The DIMM module fits properly if the clip snaps into place (Figure 2). (Caution: Do not exert too much pressure on the DIMM module. The module should easily snap into place when inserted properly.)

## A Final Word

A variety of software and hardware products is available to expand the capacity and functionality of your computer. However, you must decide whether to upgrade your old PC or purchase a new one with greater capabilities. Additionally, you need to decide whether you should perform the installation of new software or hardware or use the services of a trained professional. Consider the cost of an upgrade, the reputation of the prospective technician, and whether or not you feel competent in performing an upgrade.

# Working with PDF Files

**A** PORTABLE DOCUMENT FORMAT (PDF) FILE is a special type of document file. Similar to a word processing file, it is meant to be read and printed but not edited. PDF files are often used to distribute forms for users to fill out, such as tax return forms or user manuals for software products. If your organization is responsible for distributing a document that users are to download and print, but not alter, PDF files are very useful.

The copyright for the PDF format is held by a company called Adobe. Adobe is a large software company that markets many other products, such as Adobe Photoshop. They distribute a freeware product called Adobe Reader that allows users to open, read, and print PDF files, but not alter them.

Unlike normal files such as Web pages written in HTML, PDFs are designed to always print out correctly. Because HTML (Web page) files are flexible, a portion of the page may be deleted or a line may be split in half between two pages when the document is printed. This is the type of problem that PDF files are meant to correct. In addition, PDFs provide some security to your documents, and ensure a clean, readable, and printable document.

## Using Adobe Reader

Adobe Reader can be downloaded from www.adobe.com. This freeware program will allow you to do everything with PDF files except create and edit them.

Once Adobe Reader is installed, you can read a PDF file by simply double clicking it in Windows Explorer, or, if the PDF file is posted online, clicking the link to it and clicking the Open option when prompted. This will bring up the PDF file in your Web browser, usually in a new window.

Periodically, Adobe updates their file format and you will be prompted every time the Adobe Reader runs to upgrade your software. This upgrade is only needed to view files accurately that have been made with the latest version of Adobe Acrobat and that are using the newest features. If you want to upgrade, select features you wish to add and click on Update when the program prompts you. Usually, even if you don't update the reader, you will be able to view the file. This automatic update will happen only if you are online at the time.

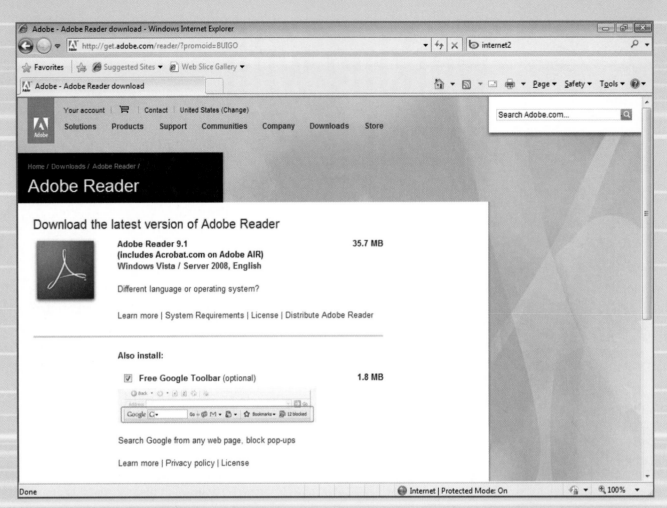

Adobe Reader can be downloaded for free from www.adobe.com.

**TIP** When you read a PDF file it can seem strange at first. PDFs are often used to hold very large documents, such as college course catalogs. Paging with the scrollbar on the right side of the page will often jump you far through the document, losing your place. Also, the text might seem tiny and unreadable. To resolve these issues, try clicking on the picture of a small hand at the top of the Acrobat Reader and then clicking and dragging the document to "grab" it and move around just a bit at a time to read the material. To switch pages, use the page up and page down keys rather than the scrollbar. If the text is too small to be read clearly, click on the zoom-in button at the top that looks like a magnifying glass with a plus sign (+) on it. Remember to click on the small hand button again after zooming in, or you will find yourself zooming more when you meant to click and drag. Experiment with the index and search features as well, if the document was created with them in place, they can be very useful.

## Identifying the Benefits of the PDF File Format

The PDF file format is similar to other data files stored by a variety of word processors. There are, however, several key differences that have made the file format so successful. As with other word processing file types, you can store text, images, and hyperlinks in the data files. You can edit them, track changes in them, print them, set them up as Web pages and everything else most other word processors do. So what is so important about PDFs? The strength of the format is in its security and document access controls. PDFs are built for professional users who need to share access with others at various levels. You can specify in a PDF file who is allowed to view and edit it, and you can track any changes on the basis of who made them. This kind of control is useful for important documents. For example, a business or organiza-

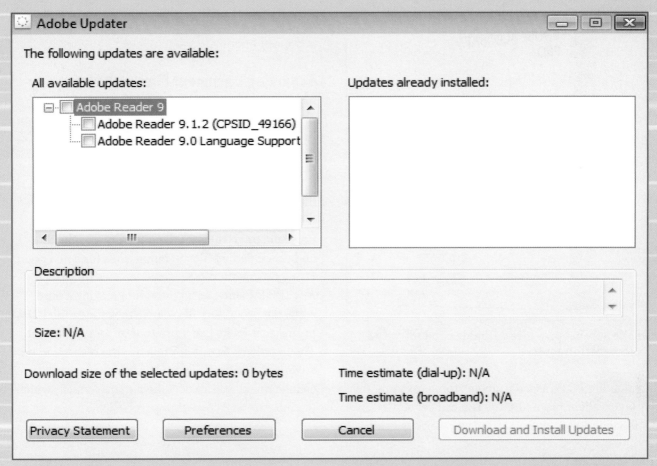

Adobe occasionally updates the Reader program and your system will prompt you to install the upgrade if it is available.

tion may want to restrict and track access to its legal contract.

In addition to sophisticated document controls, PDFs offer a level of usability unavailable in other file types. Rather than just being a body of text and images, a PDF (such as your school catalogue) can be set up with index tabs, searchable keywords, an index of important topics, etc. All of this makes a document more user friendly and therefore more useful.

# Creating New PDF Files

There are several ways to create new PDF files. The primary method would be to purchase Adobe Acrobat, the editor that is designed to create PDF files from scratch. Professional users who wish to create a lot of files in this format will find this product suits them well. If, however, you only wish to create a PDF occasionally, there are other methods that are easier and less expensive; these are outlined in the following text.

## Using the Adobe Acrobat PDF File Editor

Professional PDF users wanting access to the more advanced PDF features such as document access control and the creation of user-friendly features such as a tabbed index may need to purchase Adobe Acrobat. Acrobat is a program that saves files in the PDF format and allows access to all the more advanced features of PDF files. The license price for this software product is expensive as it is not really intended for home-users. Most Adobe Acrobat users are professionals working for corporations.

## Converting to PDF Online

One approach is to use a file conversion service such as the one operated by Adobe itself. In most cases, these services take a document format such as MS Word .doc or .docx files, image files, and Web pages (in .htm files) and convert it to a PDF file. These services operate on a subscription basis with a monthly fee for the conversions. They require no new software installation, and the first conversions are usually free. For purposes of sampling and

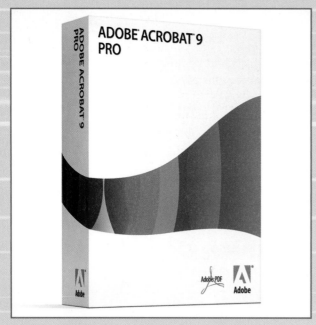

Adobe Acrobat provides valuable productivity and collaboration tools.

evaluating PDFs as a document storage system, this is an excellent place to start. You can get started in a few minutes at no cost. However, serious users

of PDF file formats will want to look into more advanced options.

## Exporting Document Files as PDFs

Adobe allows you to install a PDF converter as a "virtual printer." Also, Microsoft Office users can download an add-in for saving as PDFs directly from the Microsoft site. This exporting process is convenient for someone who wants to produce PDF files but does not want to learn a new software interface, pay for the full-featured Adobe Acrobat program, or go through the difficulty of uploading and downloading files to online sites for conversion. Using this method, you simply choose to "print" to a "PDF Printer" and instead of making a hard copy, the program will create a new file in the PDF format that looks like a printout of your document. The drawback to this approach is the restriction on advanced document features, such as file security, change tracking, and document management, which the full Adobe Acrobat supports.

PDF files can be converted online for a fee at sites such as www.adobe.com.

# Computer Ethics

**E**THICS ARE THE RULES WE USE to determine the right and wrong things to do in our lives. Most ethical beliefs are learned during childhood and are derived from our family, society, or religious tradition. Ethics are not the same as laws and regulations. Ethics are internalized principles that influence the decisions we make. A law is an external rule that, if violated, is punishable by society.

## The Source of Ethics

In many societies, ethics are based on what is thought to be God's, or a Supreme Being's, will. Another view alleges that ethics are based on eternal laws of unknown origin that do not change. Both these ethical viewpoints fall under the moral realism school of ethical thought. Moral realists believe ethical principles have objective foundations; that is, they are not based on subjective human reasoning.

Still other philosophers claim that ethics differ from society to society, from person to person, and from situation to situation. This school of ethical thought is

Ethics are not the same as laws, but ethics do inform the shaping of the laws. Laws are external rules that, if violated, are punishable by society.

Ethics come from numerous sources, including religious books and documents.

known as moral relativism, and is sometimes also referred to as situational ethics. Most ethical belief systems are based on one of these two schools of thought, or sometimes they are a mixture of these beliefs.

### Normative and Applied Ethics

The study of ethics can be divided into two main categories: Normative ethics and applied ethics. Normative ethics involves determining a standard or "norm" of ethical rule that underlies ethical behavior. Applied ethics refers to the application of normative ethical beliefs to controversial real-life issues. For example, while most cultures believe it is wrong to steal, some people may believe that the stealing of food by a starving person is ethically acceptable.

### Ethics and Technology

New technologies often create ethical dilemmas because they allow humans to act in new and unforeseen ways. Computer technology poses numerous ethical dilemmas. The adapting of traditional ethical thought and behavior to these issues has resulted in new interpretations of the old rules, and these new interpretations have, in turn, led to the formation of a new branch of applied ethics called computer ethics.

Early computers were large mainframe devices that a team of engineers and programmers maintained. Ethical decision-making involving computers and their capabilities was limited to the relatively small group of people involved in the design and use of these large mainframes.

Computer technology has advanced rapidly. Today, a majority of all U.S. households have at least one computer. The widespread availability of personal computers and the Internet means that millions of people are now faced with the ethical responsibilities inherent in controlling a powerful technology.

Three categories of ethical issues that have emerged with the evolution of computer technology are privacy protection issues, property protection issues, and personal and social issues. Privacy protection issues are issues involving the use and abuse of personal information. Property issues are those involving the use and abuse of property. Personal and social issues are those involving issues of personal morality or beliefs.

## Privacy Protection Issues

All people have information about their personal lives that they wish to keep private. In our society, we realize that there are times when we need to reveal personal information, such as when we apply for a job, a loan, or a credit card, or visit a doctor. Most people are generally willing to reveal information if it is absolutely necessary, and they expect that this information will remain closely guarded.

Unfortunately, the privacy that many people traditionally have taken for granted is being eroded as computer technology facilitates the gathering and transfer of information. In fact, any communication over the Internet makes us increasingly vulnerable to monitoring and data-gathering activities that can compromise our privacy. The cumulative effect of many different methods of gathering, processing, and sharing personal information could be disastrous, especially if such information falls into the wrong hands.

### Public Information Availability

A controversial privacy issue concerns the use of publicly available data. A wide range of personal information has always been available through public records such as birth records, drivers' licenses, and more. This information was scattered across a wide range of jurisdictions and often stored in dusty record books. Now, database companies have created electronic databases that can provide this information to anyone with access to the Web. Many people are justifiably worried this information may be misused.

## Threats to Privacy from Interception of Wireless Communications

Wireless communications devices such as cell phones and PDAs are extremely vulnerable to interception by others, partly because they transmit data into the air where anyone may intercept it. Wireless security is thus an important issue, and is becoming more so as the use of wireless devices increases. Unfortunately, traditional methods of computer security don't work well for wireless devices. For one thing, wireless devices often don't require authentication to ensure the identity of the user and the device. And encryption technology, while possible for use on wireless devices, places an undue burden on their already limited battery power and memory. Creating better security for wireless communications devices is a major challenge currently facing the computer industry.

## Commercial Threats to Privacy

One of the key threats to privacy comes from e-commerce activities. Since the earliest days of e-commerce, users have expressed serious concern about the potential abuse of personal data entered at Web sites. Buyers must provide certain information to pay for the goods or services purchased over the Internet. Many commercial sites also seek information about consumer preferences or buying habits. Once entered on the Internet, personal information can be used to create a consumer profile. A consumer profile contains information about the lifestyle and buying habits of an individual that marketers can use to more effectively target and sell their goods.

**Cookies** New tracking technologies allow organizations to gather personal data without the permission or even knowledge of consumers. One of the most controversial of these technologies is the cookie. A cookie is a small data file, placed on a computer's hard drive by Web sites with this programming technology. Cookies can remember passwords, user IDs, and user preferences and can automatically customize a site to those preferences during repeat visits. To accomplish this, cookies record information about the user's IP address, browser, computer operating system, and URLs visited.

**Global Unique Identifiers** Another tracking technology with the potential for misuse is the Global Unique Identifier (GUID), which is an identification number that can be coded into both hardware and software. The widespread use of GUIDs would eliminate any anonymity Internet users now enjoy. If GUID use becomes widespread, it will always be possible to track down the originators of unpopular or controversial messages or ideas, a severe blow to Internet privacy.

**Location Tracking** A third type of tracking device currently threatening the right to privacy is the tracking of cell phones and other types of handheld computers. Most cell phones are equipped with Global Positioning System (GPS) chips that can pinpoint the location of the cell phone within a few dozen feet. Although technologies such as this could be useful as navigation aids, to monitor the location of children or teenagers or to dispatch emergency services, there is a potential for abuse as well. Moreover, the use of location-based services is on the rise. Many businesses see great potential in installing wireless location systems in cars, handheld computers, and cell phones. Advertisements could thus be tailored exactly to a consumer's location. While such technology has many obvious benefits, its widespread use in society means that anyone could track you down or figure out where you are at any given time. This greatly worries privacy advocates, who are concerned that employers, creditors, and even stalkers could use the sensitive location data.

## Protection from Commercial Threats to Privacy

Consumer demands for privacy protection have led to several different kinds of responses in both the public and private sectors. The three types of responses are industry self-regulation, government regulation, and consumer self-protection.

**Industry Self-Regulation** Seeking to allay consumer privacy concerns, many commercial Web sites have adopted privacy statements. A privacy statement promises that an e-tailer will protect the confidentiality of any information a customer reveals.

However, some privacy advocates claim that industry self-regulation is not sufficient, and incidents such as online retailer ToySmart's attempt to sell its customer database in violation of its privacy statement demonstrate that privacy statement promises cannot always be trusted.

**Government Regulation** Passing new laws that protect consumer privacy has increasingly been viewed as the answer to the alleged failure of the Internet commerce industry to safeguard users. A number of bills to protect consumer privacy have been proposed at both the local and federal levels, but only one major piece of federal legislation has yet been passed. The Children's Online Privacy Protection Act (COPPA) of 1998 became effective April 21, 2000. This act prohibits the gathering and sharing of personal data of children under the age of 13 without the permission of parents or legal guardians.

COPPA protects children by prohibiting the gathering and sharing of personal information about children without permission of the child's parent or guardian.

Much of the debate over privacy legislation concerns whether consumers should have the right to choose to opt-in to receive cookies or opt-out to not receive cookies. Industry advocates prefer the opt-out feature, while privacy advocates worry that many consumers will be unaware of the need to opt-out or will not possess the computer skills to select that option.

**Consumer Self-Protection** You can take a number of steps to reduce the likelihood of your personal privacy being violated. First, make sure you conduct e-commerce transactions only on sites protected by encryption programs, such as Secure Sockets Layer (SSL), the most common protocol used for secure servers. Microsoft Windows Vista and Windows 7 support the newest version of SSL (version 3) and a newer protocol called Transport Layer Security (TLS).

Second, look for sites with privacy statements and read them carefully to see what protection the site offers. Sites that pledge compliance to third-party privacy programs offer an even higher level of security against potential abuse.

Third, set your browser either to warn you when cookies are going to be placed on the hard drive or to reject them altogether. You can also install software programs that allow you to accept or reject them as you see fit.

Fourth, never volunteer any more information than is absolutely necessary to complete an e-commerce transaction. Providing details about your lifestyle, habits, interests, or shopping preferences only increases the chance that this information will be passed on to third parties for marketing purposes.

Finally, Windows Vista and Windows 7 offer additional protection to Internet users. The Internet Explorer browser will run in a protected area so that cookies, spyware, and downloaded applications will be isolated from the main operating system.

## Governmental Threats to Privacy

According to the FBI, organized crime groups routinely use the Internet to conduct their activities. The FBI believes interception of these transmissions is essential. In fact, FBI statistics show that electronic surveillance has enabled tens of thousands of felony convictions. The FBI and other law enforcement agencies contend that if they are not allowed to monitor crime organizations under certain circumstances, society as a whole will suffer. They also worry that today's increasingly sophisticated encryption technology will provide criminals with powerful tools that law enforcement cannot counter. While many people understand the FBI's concerns, some critics believe government agencies themselves need careful policing to ensure that they do not step over the line and invade the privacy of innocent citizens.

## Workplace Threats to Privacy

Some employers use special software programs that monitor workers' behavior and read messages sent and received by employees. Many employees find this kind of monitoring of their work demeaning, and they question their employer's right to do it, yet there are no laws preventing electronic surveillance of employees in the workplace.

While at work, employees are using company property, and the company has the right to monitor the use of that property. Employers insist they are justified in such snooping in order to prevent employees from engaging in activities that could result in liability for the company. However, if a company has pledged to respect employee privacy, it must keep that pledge.

# Property Protection Issues

The convenience provided by linking computers through the Internet also creates some drawbacks. Computer viruses can travel around the world in seconds, damaging programs and files. Hackers can enter into systems without authorization and steal or alter data. In addition, the wealth of information on the Web and the increased ease with which it can be copied have made it simple for people to plagiarize. Plagiarism is using others' ideas and creations without permission.

## Intellectual Property

Intellectual property includes just about anything that can be created by the human mind. To encourage innovation and thus benefit society as a whole, our legal system grants patents to those who invent new and better ways of doing things. A patent awards ownership of an idea or invention to its creator for a fixed number of years. To encourage and protect artistic and literary endeavors, an author or an artist is awarded copyright to created material, allowing the right to control the use of the work and charge others for its use. Patent and copyright violation is punishable by law, and prosecutions and convictions are frequent. A recent and major threat to intellectual property rights posed by the Internet is the downloading of music, which was pioneered by the Napster Web site. The Napster program allowed computer users to share MP3 files, a digital file format for musical recordings. In early 2001, Napster went on trial for distributing copyrighted songs for free, and the company's actions were ruled illegal. The issue remains alive, however, as lawmakers and the recording industry struggle to define a fair, enforceable policy.

The Internet makes it easy to access and copy written works, photos, and artwork that may be copyrighted, and wholesale copying is illegal. However, it is legal to use a limited amount of another person's written material without permission as long as the use is acknowledged (cited), is for noncommercial purposes, and involves only the use of limited excerpts no more than 300 words of prose or one line of poetry. This right is called Fair Use and is dealt with under the U.S. Copyright Act, Section 107.

## Hacking, Viruses, and Phishing

Hackers (and crackers) who break into Web sites and cause them to slow down or even shut down have a direct effect on personal computer users. The greater danger associated with hacking into Web sites is identity theft, the theft of personal credit card information and other private data. Identity theft occurs when a hacker gains entry into a Web database and copies a person's social security number, address, and credit data. The hacker then uses the victim's personal data to apply for additional credit cards, a driver's license, and so on. Then comes the spending spree, and the victim ends up with a long list of unexpected bills.

Another way that individuals can lose control of their private information is by giving it away. Phishing is an activity characterized by attempts to fraudulently acquire another person's sensitive information, such as a credit card number. The term refers to the use of increasingly sophisticated lures to "fish" for users' financial information and passwords.

In a typical situation, the criminal sends an official looking e-mail or instant message in which the criminal masquerades as a trustworthy person or business. An unsuspecting individual is asked to enter a password, credit card number, or other personal data. Once the data has been submitted, the criminal uses the data to make credit card purchases, transfer funds from the victim's bank account, or engage in other activities.

Viruses create a different sort of damage, usually to the user's computer or to software running on it. A virus must enter disguised in another file (usually an e-mail attachment), which may be downloaded from the Internet. Viruses may also reside on storage media and even on legitimate copies of software programs direct from manufacturers.

Consumers can protect themselves from identity theft by dealing only with Web merchants who encrypt credit card numbers and other private data. Secure sites are indicated by an "s" following the "http" in the URL. It is important for users to protect themselves from phishing attempts by critically reading requests before responding with private information. Users should never provide sensitive, private information without confirming the legitimacy of the request.

The main precaution against viruses is to never open an e-mail attachment from an unknown source. The second strategy is to install an antivirus program, which, when activated, seeks out and destroys any known viruses found on a computer. To keep up with the proliferation of new viruses, the antivirus software needs to be continually updated. In addition, firewall software is recommended to protect any Internet-connected computer system from hackers.

# Personal and Social Issues

In addition to raising privacy and property concerns, computers have had an unanticipated impact on numerous personal and social issues. The solutions to these issues are often complicated because of a lack of consensus on what, if anything, should be done to deal with them.

## Gambling Online

Online gambling has proven to be a serious problem for many individuals and for society as a whole.

While gambling may be a pleasurable pastime for some individuals, it can become an addiction for others. Most gambling occurs at casinos, but the availability of online gambling is attracting growing numbers of gamblers, including both adults and teenagers who are prohibited by law from visiting brick-and-mortar casinos. Online gambling has become a $12 billion industry. The Internet gambling industry is based almost entirely outside the United States, though about half its customers live in the U.S.

## Protecting Freedom of Speech

The Internet contains material that would not be allowed in many jurisdictions if it were received by more traditional means, such as paper mail or TV. Examples of these types of materials are hate speech, cyberbullying, and pornography.

**Hate Speech Sites** The freedom of speech guaranteed by the U.S. Constitution allows great latitude in what a person can say. Consequently, a great number of Web sites contain written material that many would find offensive. This includes material inciting hatred against people of certain races, religions, or beliefs. Some hate speech sites use foul or inappropriate language, and even post dangerous material, such as how to make drugs or explosives.

**Cyberbullying** Texting or sending harassing e-mail messages or posting embarrassing photos is called cyberbullying. The problem affects students and people in the workplace. In the workplace it is called cyberstalking. The purpose is to harm another person's reputation or self-image. The National Crime Prevention Council states that half of all high school students report having been a victim of cyberbullying. The Council's research also shows an increase in this destructive online behavior. Some states have passed laws against digital harassment, and proposals to criminalize cyberbullying have been introduced in Congress. Some social networking sites are working to educate and protect the online community from this malicious form of digital conduct.

**Pornography Sites** Pornography is material containing sexually explicit images or script deemed unacceptable or harmful by society. Adult pornog-

# Appendix

**M**OST PEOPLE CAN USE A TELEVISION SET, operate a microwave oven, or drive an automobile, but few of us would consider attempting to repair the sophisticated electronics in each. Yet somehow we assume that computer problems are something that we should be able to repair without instruction or experience. Consider that all computers and their architectures are not alike, and that their repair methods and diagnostics are significantly different. The age of a system also impacts the repair techniques used. Indeed, for many systems produced fewer than five years ago, replacement parts exist in used markets only. Therefore, as in your TV, car, and microwave, there are many situations in which the diagnostics and work should be left to someone who has the experience and the hardware and software to accomplish the objective. There are, however, a number of items that can be checked by anyone to help ascertain if the nature of the problem requires an experienced technician. After all, in a comparable situation, it would be embarrassing to return to a store a camera that doesn't work only to find that the lens cap was not removed!

## Problem: The screen is blank—nothing is happening.

The most important first step is to be certain that the power is getting to the computer. Most computers and monitors have an LED light that glows whenever the power is on. If no power is getting to the computer, check the wall socket and surge protector in an attempt to verify current flow. Switching sockets into one that is known to work could resolve this possible problem.

## Problem: The start-up process is taking too long—or it can't seem to be completed.

Several actions take place between the time a computer is turned on and the appearance of the desktop and icons. A number of checks are performed during the power-on self-test (POST) on the system basic input output system (BIOS) to verify that all required parts, such as the keyboard, mouse, memory, and hard disk drive, are functioning normally. If they are not, a message will appear on the screen or a series of beeps will announce a problem. If a screen message shows the keyboard or mouse missing, it is possible that the cable has become loose from its connection or that the raw metal contact surfaces have become corroded. Repeated connection and disconnection of the device will usually correct the corrosion problem. Be very careful to examine the small contact pins that make the connection to verify that none are bent or damaged. These connectors are very delicate and force should not ever be required to plug them in.

Inexperienced users sometimes mistakenly disrupt the startup. During the starting or boot-up process, systems will sometimes send a message to press a key to enter setup, often the escape (Esc) key or the function keys F2 or F10. This is a part of the setup process that identifies the installed components in the computer. One of the best features of modern systems is the capacity for the system setup commands to be initialized by the installing software. Virtually all components now are recognized by the operating system when they are installed. This initialization process is "automatic" in the eyes of the user, but much takes place behind the scenes to keep the system setup correct and to maintain the Windows system file, called the registry, that governs all machine applications. Inexperienced users should avoid the setup location. If the system setup or registry becomes corrupted, it is again time to seek out experienced counsel.

## Problem: A message displays on screen saying there is a failure of the hard drive.

If the dreaded hard disk drive failure message appears on the screen, it may be a simple problem of a loose connection, or it could be an internal corrosion problem. In either case it should be left to experienced hands. This might be a suitable time to remind users that work that is worth saving is worth saving twice! If the data is critical, multiple backups are in order.

Internal components as well as peripheral hardware have a limited life expectancy. Most hard disks and CD drives will last typically five years, but failure can happen at any time. The cables that connect these devices are also subject to failure. The corrosion problem mentioned previously regarding metal surfaces can occur at any connection.

## Problem: The printer is not working.

Printer cables are particularly vulnerable to failure since they can get moved either deliberately or accidentally. If printing problems cannot be corrected by working with the cables or by reinstalling the printer driver software provided by the manufacturer, then a new printer may be in order. It comes as a surprise to many users of inkjet printers that units up to about $300 in cost are essentially disposable. Replacement often costs less than labor and repair, and a newer printer will likely have superior capabilities.

## General Guidelines

- Take notes that describe your problem. In order to help a diagnostician locate a problem, it is helpful to be able to describe exactly what is happening. If the system "beeps" you should note how many times and identify if it is in a pattern. If system diagnostic error messages appear on the screen, write them down.
- When installing new hardware or software, make changes one at a time. In this way, if a problem occurs you should be able to back up one step to bring the system back to life.
- Ask for assistance rather than dive into something for which you are not trained. Sometimes your attempt to fix a problem can make things worse than they were originally. As you observe the work and diagnostics of others, you will begin to develop your own experience base, increase your confidence, and be able to attack more serious problems the second time they occur. You would not be likely to tear into a problem with your microwave oven for lack of knowledge; your computer deserves at least the same amount of respect.

# Introductory

## 4TH EDITION

# COMPUTERS

## UNDERSTANDING TECHNOLOGY

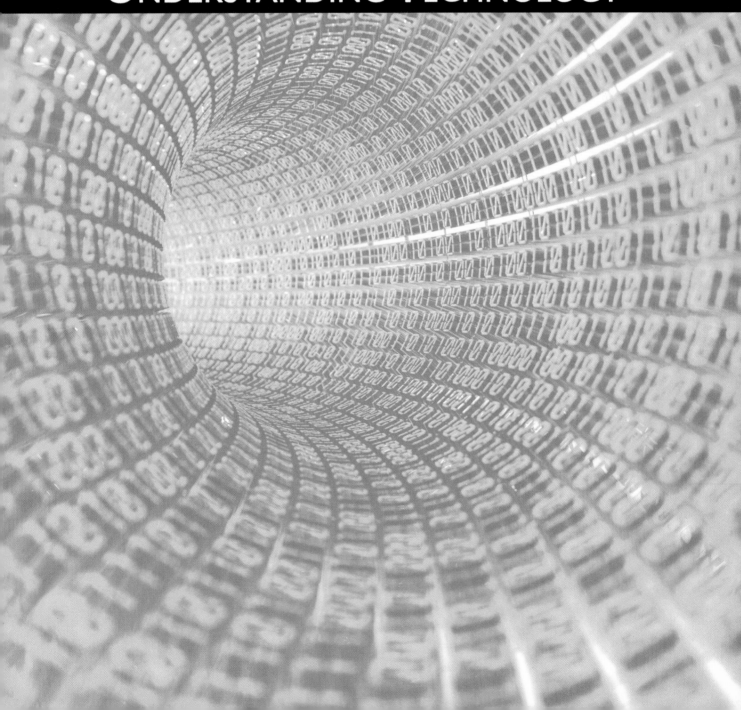

# Windows

## Starting Up and Shutting Down a PC

This tutorial describes how to start up and log on with a user name and password to a Windows PC with the Windows 7 operating system installed. The tutorial also explains the shut down procedure to correctly power off the computer when you have finished your tasks.

### Starting Up and Logging On

During the installation of Windows 7, the setup routine includes a process to create a user name and password to log on to the computer. You will need to know the user name and password created (if one was created) for the PC you are using before proceeding. The first screen that appears after turning on the power, or moving the mouse to re-activate a system that is in standby mode, is called the Welcome screen.

When you click the icon for the user name that you want to use to log on to the computer, the icon enlarges and a password text box appears if the account requires a password. The remaining user names disappear from view. If you attempt to log on with an incorrect password, Windows 7 displays the password hint if one was created with the user account.

**TIP** In, out, up, down—what does it all mean? Logging on means connecting to the computer; logging in is the same thing, just different wording. Logging off means disconnecting, and logging out is the same thing.

### Steps

To log on at the Windows 7 Welcome screen:
1. Click the icon for your user name.
2. Type your password if a password is required and then click the right arrow button or press Enter.

> In an environment where multiple users access the same computer, such as in a school, logging on (and off) is important for tracking purposes. On a network, logging on also connects the computer to the network using settings and permissions that are set up especially for that user. For example, there might be certain locations on a file server that become accessible through the network when a certain user logs on, but not when some other user logs on.

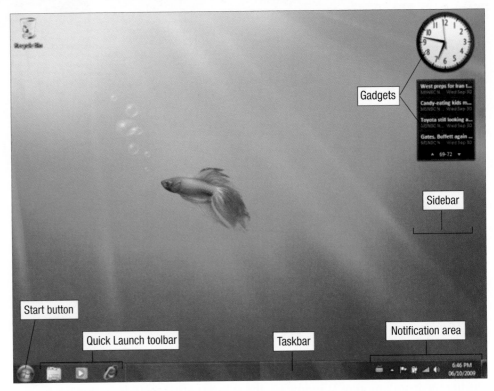

**Figure 1  Windows 7 Desktop**

**TIP** Previous versions of Windows provided the ability to turn off the display of the Welcome screen; however, in Windows 7, the Welcome screen cannot be turned off.

The Windows 7 desktop appears when you successsfully log on (see Figure 1). The desktop shown displays the default background using the Windows 7 theme. Your background may be different since other pictures are available. On the desktop, icons to launch programs are available as well as the Taskbar. The Taskbar is the horizontal bar along the bottom of the screen and is used to manage application windows. Gadgets appear along the right side of the screen (your Gadgets may be different).

## Logging Off

Logging off and shutting down are two separate operations, although shutting down also logs you off. Logging off indicates the user no longer requires the computer. The user's programs and documents are closed and the Welcome screen redisplays; logging off does not shut down the PC.

## Steps

To log off:

1. Click the Start button.
2. Point to the right-pointing arrow button next to the Shut down button in the right pane.
3. Click Log off.

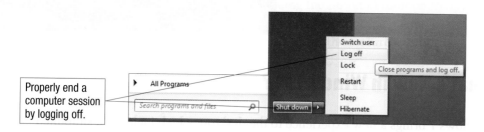

Properly end a computer session by logging off.

You can also use a feature called Fast User Switching to enable multiple users to be logged on at once to the same PC. This could be handy when one person is working on the PC and someone else comes up and wants a turn "just for a second." Instead of logging off as in Step 3 above, click *Switch user* and allow the other person to log on temporarily. Switch user leaves the original user's programs and data files open, whereas logging off closes them all.

## Restarting and Shutting Down

In addition to logging off, you can also restart the PC, or you can shut it down completely. Restarting can help if you are experiencing errors or problems with Windows' operation. Shutting down completely is a good idea when you are going to be away from your PC for a while (say, 24 hours or more).

## Steps

To shut down or restart:

1. Click the Start button.
2. Click Shut down (to completely power off the computer).
3. To restart your PC, point to the right-pointing arrow button next to the Shut down button and then click Restart.

Click the Start button, point to the right-pointing arrow beside Shut down, and then click Sleep to place the computer in Sleep mode. In Sleep mode, all of your work is automatically saved, the screen is turned off, and the computer is placed in its lowest power state. A light on the outside of the computer case blinks or turns yellow to indicate sleep mode is active. Reactivate the computer by pressing the Power button or by moving the mouse. After logging on, the screen will be exactly as it was when you activated Sleep mode.

4. Scroll through the resulting Help topic window, and click on a link that interests you (for example, Windows Firewall).

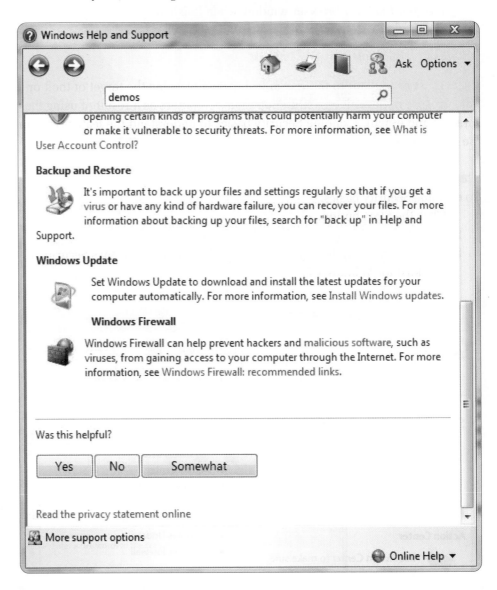

5. Close the Windows Help and Support window.

## TUTORIAL **3**

7. Click

8. Click

### From a Fi

If you see ar
are browsing
associated w
ment tasks s

**Steps**

To run the V

1. Click t
2. Click (
3. Double
   instruc
4. Doubl
5. Double
   pane t
6. Click (
   appear
7. Double

8. Click the
   to close
9. Click the
   to close

Seem like a
DVD that is nc
tents and start

## Running Applications

A primary function of Microsoft Windows is to run applications. Without applications, there would be no reason for any of its other features, such as networking, file management, and online connectivity. There are many ways of running an application; as you work in Windows you will choose the method that is the most appropriate for a given situation.

### From the Start Menu

The Start menu provides a convenient, central organizing location for shortcuts that run most of the installed applications.

**Steps**

To open the WordPad application from the Start menu:

1. Click the Start button.
2. Click *All Programs*. The options in the left pane are replaced with the All Programs submenu.
3. Click *Accessories* in the left pane. The Accessories option in the submenu expands to show a list of accessory programs.
4. Click *WordPad*. The WordPad application opens.

> **Prior versions of Windows opened a cascading side menu when you clicked options from the Start menu. Windows 7 replaces the left pane or expands options in the left pane as you click menu options. Notice the Back option at the bottom of the menu that you can use to return to the previous menu.**

5. Click the Close (X) button in the top right corner of the WordPad window to close it.

**TIP** See Tutorial 11 to learn how to customize the Start menu.

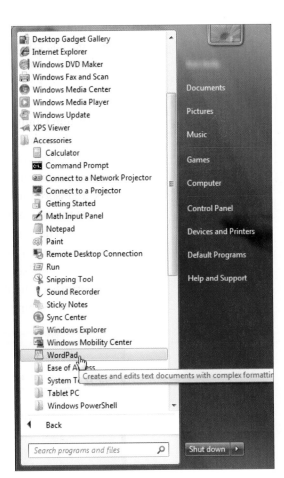

## Working with a Window

Almost all content in Microsoft Windows 7 appears in frames called windows. Each application runs in its own window, as does each file management interface such as the Computer or Documents option.

In Tutorial 3 you saw two types of windows. The window for WordPad was an application window, and the window for Computer was a file management window. In this tutorial, you will explore what you can do with windows after opening them.

### Three Window States: Maximized, Minimized, and Restored

Every window is in one of three states at any given moment:

- Maximized: Fills the entire screen
- Minimized: Hidden except for its icon on the taskbar
- Restored: Open and visible, but not full-screen

You can switch among these three states with the buttons in the upper right corner of the window—not the X (that button is for closing the window)—but the other two. Why are there only two buttons, when there are three states? The Restore Down and Maximize buttons never appear simultaneously; a window has one or the other based on its current state.

When a window is restored, the buttons look like in Figure 2. When a window is maximized, the buttons look like in Figure 3. When a window is minimized, it appears on the Taskbar as in Figure 4.

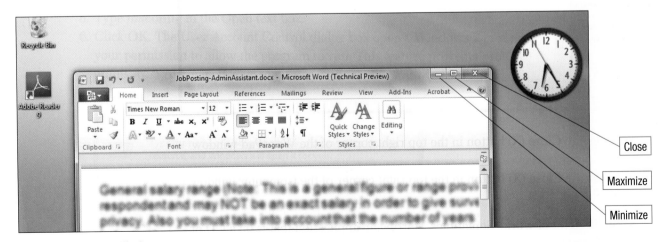

**Figure 2 Restored Window**

## Steps

To see the action of these buttons:

1. Open any computer window. (The window shown in Figure 3 is for a Word 2010 program.)
2. Click the Maximize button in the computer window. (If the computer window is already maximized, Step 2 is not necessary; proceed to Step 3.)
3. Click the Minimize button in the computer window. The window disappears except for the Computer button on the taskbar as in Figure 4.
4. Click the Computer button on the taskbar. The window reappears, in maximized form.
5. Click the Restore Down button in the computer window. The window returns to its nonmaximized size.
6. Click the Close button in the computer window. The window closes.

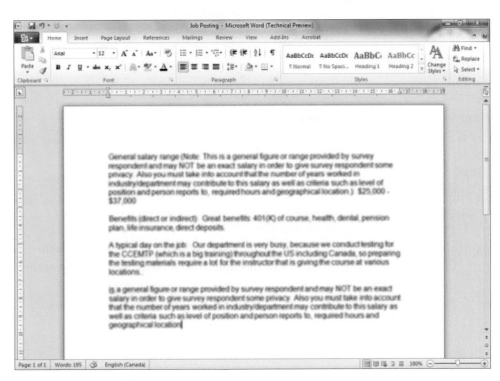

**Figure 3  Maximized Window**

**Figure 4  Minimized Window**

## Move and Resize a Window

When a window is restored, there's some "breathing room" around it on the desktop. You can move the window around on the desktop, and/or you can change its size.

To move a window, drag the window's title bar to the desired location. (The title bar is the horizontal bar across the top of the window, see Figure 5.)

To resize a window, drag the top, bottom, left, right, or corner border in the desired direction. Many people drag the bottom right corner of a window to resize the window's length and width simultaneously; however, you can drag any edge.

Figure 5  Window Showing the Title Bar

### Steps

To move and resize a window:

1. Reopen a computer window.
2. Point to the title bar of the window.
3. Hold down the left mouse button and drag the title bar to move the window to a different location on the desktop. Release the mouse button at the desired location.
4. Point to the bottom right corner of the window until the mouse pointer changes shape to a diagonally pointing double-headed arrow.

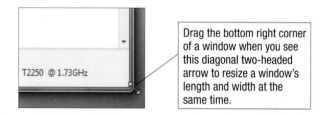

Drag the bottom right corner of a window when you see this diagonal two-headed arrow to resize a window's length and width at the same time.

5. Hold down the left mouse button and drag to change the window's size to approximately one-half the window's original length and width. Then release the mouse button.
6. Resize the window again, this time making it so large that it almost takes up the entire screen.
7. Close the computer window and then reopen it. Notice that Windows remembers the computer window's previous size and location.
8. If desired, move and/or resize the computer window to suit your preferences.
9. Close the computer window.

# Windows

## Browsing Disks and Devices Using the Computer Feature

The Computer feature is the central location in the Windows interface for browsing disk contents. The window lists all available local drives (and may also show network drives to which the computer has access).

### Steps

To open a Computer window:

1. Click the Start button.
2. Click *Computer*.

By default the Computer window appears with two panes (see Figure 6). At the right is the List pane with icons depicting the drives available on the computer. The Navigation pane is at the left showing the Favorites, Libraries, Homegroup, Computer, and Network lists. Any list can be opened or closed by clicking the up-pointing or down-pointing arrow to the left of them. Using the Computer list you can view the organizational structure of the disks, including all levels of folders.

**Figure 6  Panes in the Computer Window**

**TIP** Folders are logical units that help users more easily manage the great number of files stored on a disk. In the next tutorial you will learn how to create and rename folders. Generally, you create a folder in which you will save related documents and keep them separate from other nonrelated files. For example, you could create a folder in which to place all of the documents created for a specific project. You can create folders within a folder to organize your work in a hierarchical structure.

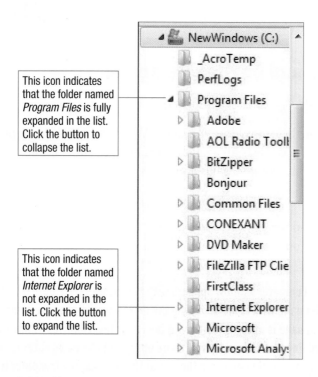

This icon indicates that the folder named *Program Files* is fully expanded in the list. Click the button to collapse the list.

This icon indicates that the folder named *Internet Explorer* is not expanded in the list. Click the button to expand the list.

**Figure 7 Folder List**

## Browsing Disk Content

To view the contents of a disk, double-click the desired disk icon in the Computer window. The folders and files the disk contains appear in the List pane of the Computer window. To view the contents of a specific folder, double-click the folder name in the list.

If the Folders list is expanded in the Navigation pane, you can also browse the disk contents by clicking the folder name in the Folders list (see Figure 7). Double-click a folder name in the Folders list to expand the list and show the folders within that location. The list of drives and folders is commonly called a *folder tree* because the fully expanded hierarchy resembles the branches on a tree. When a "branch" of the file hierarchy is fully expanded, a black downward pointing diagonal arrow appears next to the folder name in the Folders pane; a white right-pointing arrow indicates the folder list is not expanded for that folder name. Click the white or black arrow to either expand or collapse the folder list.

## Moving Back and Forward

Each time you click a different drive or folder name, the list is replaced in the List pane with the new items. To return to a previous display, click the Back button. After you click the Back button, the Forward button becomes available; clicking Forward returns the display to the list before you clicked Back.

Back button

Forward button

## Moving Folder Levels

The folder structure of a drive can be many levels deep. The path to the top level of the disk is represented by a path statement that starts out with the drive letter and then lists the folders that you would travel through to arrive at that location (see Figure 8). For example:

C:\NewWindows (C:)\Windows\System

The above statement represents the path to the System folder, which is stored within the Windows folder, which is stored on the C: drive, which is stored on the Computer. The folder name to the left of another in the path—or above it in the folder tree—is called its *parent folder*. The folder names within a parent folder are its *child folders*.

When you move up one level, you move to the immediate parent folder of the current folder. For example, to go up one level from the above path, you would go to:

C:\NewWindows (C:)

To move to a previous level in the path and display the contents of the folder, click the folder name in the Address bar of the Computer window.

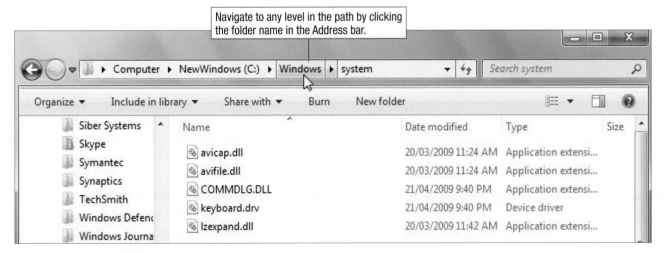

**Figure 8  Sample Folder Path**

# Windows

## Creating and Renaming Folders

Have you wondered how all those folders came to exist on your disk or other storage medium? Windows itself created several of them on the computer's main disk drive, including Windows, Program Files, Libraries, and more. Other folders are created when you install new software.

You also can create your own folder names. These can be used as organizers for storing files you create or acquire, such as digital camera pictures, word processing documents, and applications and data that you download from the Internet or receive as e-mail attachments.

### Creating a New Folder

A new folder can be created only in relation to an existing folder (or a drive's root folder), so you must start the folder-making process by displaying a particular location's content in the List pane of the Computer window (refer to Tutorial 5). Whatever location is currently displayed becomes the parent folder for the new folder you will create.

**TIP** Each drive's top level is its root folder. An analogy: When you walk into an office building, you first go into the lobby. At that point you are not in any particular office—you are simply in the building. The root folder of a drive is like that lobby. You're not in a folder yet—you're just "in the drive."

### Steps

To create a new folder:

1. Open the Computer window, navigate to the folder window and display in the folder window the folder in which you want to place the new folder. (For example, display the contents list for the folder named *My Documents*.)
2. *Right*-click the mouse in a blank area of the List pane, point to New, and then click *Folder*. A folder icon appears with a text box containing the text *New Folder*. The default name New Folder is automatically selected indicating you can begin typing the name you want to assign to the folder.

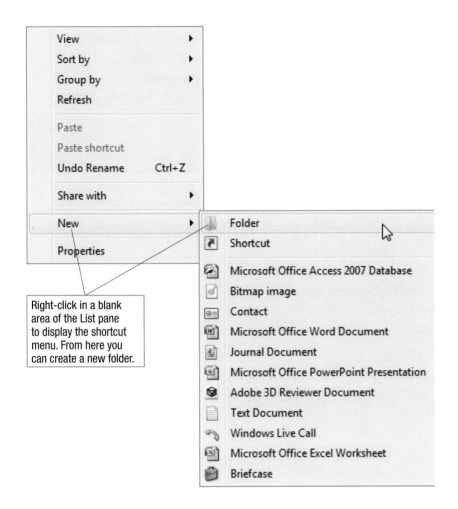

Right-click in a blank area of the List pane to display the shortcut menu. From here you can create a new folder.

3. Type the name that you want to assign to the new folder.

> **Folder names can be up to 255 characters and can include spaces and most punctuation symbols (but not reserved symbols such as \*, \, /, or ?). Windows will let you know if you have entered a prohibited character. Even though long names are possible, most people prefer to keep folder names relatively short (under 12 to 16 characters or so) to make it easier to refer to them and to make the display more tidy.**

4. Press Enter. The new folder name is accepted and appears next to the folder icon.

 TermProject

## Renaming a Folder

You can rename folders any time. However, use caution when renaming folders. If you rename a folder that a certain application relies on to operate, the application might not work anymore. When evaluating whether a folder can safely be renamed, ask these questions:

- Does the folder contain only data files, such as word processing documents, spreadsheets, and so on? If so, you can rename it safely. However, if a certain application has a default Save location set up for its data files, you may need to change it to the new folder name within that application.

- Is the folder stored within the Windows or Program Files folder? If so, do not rename it, or some application will probably stop working.
- Is the folder used to store the operating files for an application, or is it stored within the Windows or Program Files folder? If so, do not rename it, or the application will probably stop working.

### Steps

To rename a folder:

1. Click the folder once to select it.
2. Press F2. The name becomes editable.

WindowsProject

3. Type a new folder name, or edit the existing name by inserting and/or deleting characters.
4. Press Enter.

You can also *right*-click an existing folder name in the List pane, click *Rename* at the shortcut menu, type the new name, and press Enter to rename a folder. Using the context-sensitive shortcut menu alleviates the need to remember function keys.

# Copying and Moving Files and Folders

In previous tutorials you learned how to use a Computer window to view disk content and create folders within the file system. Now that you know how the file system is organized, you are ready to start manipulating folder content.

You can move and copy files and folders to other locations—that is, to other disks or storage media such as a USB flash drive, or to other folders within the same disk. You might move a file to archive it on another storage medium, or copy a file to create a backup copy in another folder or storage medium.

## Moving/Copying Using Drag-and-Drop

One easy way of moving or copying is to select and drag the file or folder to the desired location. The desired location must be visible (or at least an icon for it must be visible) either in a window or in the Folders list.

### Steps

To move or copy a file or folder using drag-and-drop:

1. Open a Computer window.
2. If the Computer list is not expanded in the Navigation pane, click the right-pointing arrow to the right of Computers to display the list. Next, expand the Windows folder to display that list, and finally, expand the Users folder to display that list. The Navigation pane will look like the pane at the right.
3. Display in the List pane the file(s) and/or folder(s) you want to move or copy.
4. Expand the folder tree as needed (refer to Tutorial 5) so that the destination disk or folder's icon is visible on the tree. If necessary, consider resizing the window to view a larger Folders list.
5. In the List pane, select the file(s) and/or folder(s) you want to move or copy.

> **To select multiple contiguous files or folders at once, click the first file or folder name and then hold down the Shift key while clicking the last file or folder name. For a non-contiguous selection, hold down the Ctrl key as you click individually on each desired file or folder name.**

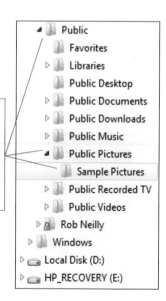

Double-click folder names in the hierarchy to expand the list until you find the location of the file(s) or folder(s) you want to move or copy.

# Windows

## Customizing the Start Menu

The Start Menu can be customized by rearranging, adding, and deleting application shortcuts.

### Pinning a Shortcut to the Start Menu

You might have already noticed that the applications you use most often appear in the left pane of the Start menu. The shortcuts in this area change depending on your usage (see Figure 9).

Notice also that above these changing shortcuts are two or more additional shortcuts: at least one for Internet and one for e-mail. These are shortcuts to the e-mail and Web programs you have configured as the default applications. You can place other shortcuts in this top section of the left pane as well, to make a program's shortcut a permanent part of the Start menu's top level. This feature is known as pinning the shortcut to the Start menu.

### Steps

To pin a shortcut to the Start Menu:

1. *Right*-click the application's icon.
2. Click *Pin to Start Menu* at the shortcut menu.

### Steps

To unpin a shortcut:

1. *Right*-click a pinned shortcut.
2. Click *Unpin from Start Menu* at the shortcut menu.

**Figure 9   Start Menu**

## Reorganizing the All Programs Menu

When you click Start, *All Programs*, the left pane is replaced with a menu containing shortcuts for installed applications. Some of these have their own folders (submenus); others appear directly on the first level of the All Programs menu.

To delete a shortcut from the All Programs menu, *right*-click the shortcut, click Delete (see Figure 10), and then confirm the action at the dialog box that appears. Deleting the shortcut does not uninstall the application; it simply removes its shortcut. You can still start the application using other shortcuts (for example, on the desktop) or by browsing for the executable file in a Computer window.

For more extensive reorganization, open the All Programs menu in a Computer window. From there you can create new folders (which will be submenus) for organizing. This works because All Programs is actually just a folder on your hard disk and the shortcuts on the menu are merely shortcut icons stored within it.

**Figure 10  Right-clicking the Start Menu**

**TIP** In some school settings, customization options are prevented unless you are logged on with a user account that has administrator privileges.

### Steps

To open the All Programs window:

1. Click the Start button.
2. *Right*-click All Programs and then click *Open All Users*. The Start Menu items open in a Computer window.
3. Double-click the *Programs* folder name. The contents of the All Programs menu appears in the List pane.

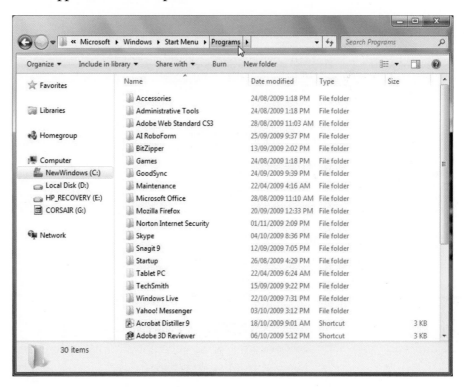

4. Add, delete, arrange folders and shortcuts, burn files to CDs, and do other operations as desired. You learned in earlier tutorials how to create and delete folders and how to move and copy files.

5. Check the results of your customization by opening the Start, All Programs menu. When you are finished customizing the menu, close the Computer window.

## Choosing Which Items to Show

In the right pane of the Start menu are icons for commonly used shortcuts such as Documents, Pictures, Music, Games, Computer, Control Panel, and so on. You can use the Start Menu Properties dialog box to control which of these icons appear in the right pane and whether the item appears as a submenu or a shortcut to a folder.

### Steps

To define the Start Menu right pane content:

1. *Right*-click the taskbar and click *Properties* at the shortcut menu. The Taskbar and Start Menu Properties dialog box open.
2. Click the Start Menu tab.
3. Click the Customize button. The Customize Start Menu dialog box opens.
4. In the Start menu list box, scroll through the list of items and select the desired setting for each menu option. For example, you can make the Control Panel not appear at all, display as a link (the default setting), or display as a menu.
5. Click OK to close the Customize Start Menu dialog box.
6. Click OK to close the Taskbar and Start Menu Properties dialog box.

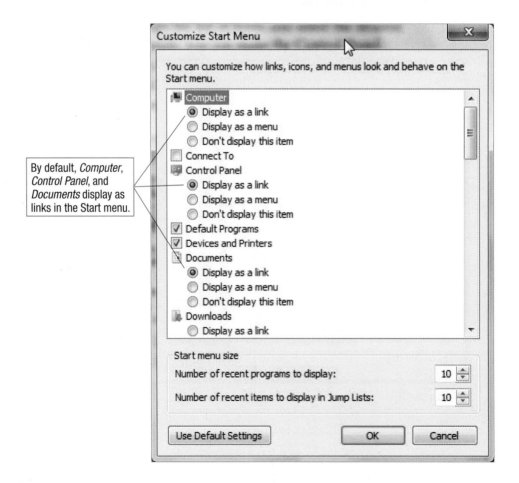

By default, *Computer*, *Control Panel*, and *Documents* display as links in the Start menu.

# Playing Music and Movies

Windows Media Player is a music and video player application that is provided with Windows 7. Windows Media Player plays a wide variety of music and movies in various file formats including the popular MP3, WMA, WAV, MOV, and AVI formats.

**TIP** Windows Media Player does not support all audio and video compression formats in use; however you can install a codec (a piece of software that acts as a converter) that will allow Windows Media Player to play a file that is not recognized. See the Help system in Windows for information on third-party add-on applications for the player.

## Playing an Audio CD

To play an audio CD, simply insert the CD in the appropriate drive. The music will start playing automatically. The first time you play a music CD you may need to set the AutoPlay option at a pop-up dialog box; however, once set the option becomes the default for all future CDs. If for some reason, the music does not begin to play, open the Windows Media Player window to start the CD.

### Steps
To start or restart an audio CD with Windows Media Player:

1. Click the Start button and click *All Programs*.
2. Click *Windows Media Player*.
3. In the left panel, click the name of the CD (x:), where x is the drive letter for the drive containing the CD.
4. Click the Play button to begin playing the first track. (Note: As the CD plays, a graphic in the Media Player window may move in response to the music.)

The Now Playing tab also displays a track list. From this screen (see Figure 12) you can:

- **Play a track out of sequence.** Double-click a track in the list to begin playing it immediately.
- **Skip a track.** Click the Next button while a song is playing to skip the track.
- **Play Next, Previous, Pause, or Stop the player.** Use the buttons at the bottom of the window. These are standard buttons for any player device.

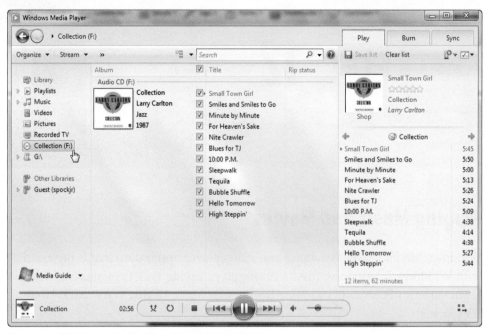

**Figure 12  Windows Media Player Now Playing Tab**

## Playing a DVD Movie

Most computers that have a DVD drive also have extra software that works with that drive to play DVD movies. One popular brand is WinDVD. Such software is usually more full-featured than Windows Media Player, so you may prefer to use it if it's available. However, in the absence of a third-party DVD movie player utility, Windows Media Player will serve.

**Figure 13  AutoPlay Dialog Box**

### Steps

To play a DVD movie using Windows Media Player:

1. Insert the DVD movie in the DVD drive. In most cases, the movie will begin playing automatically. If this is the first time a DVD movie has been inserted, the AutoPlay dialog box (shown in Figure 13) appears, in which you choose the AutoPlay option. Once set, the selected option becomes the default for all future DVDs.
2. Click Play DVD Movie using Windows Media Player. Notice the check box *Always do this for DVD movies* is selected by default.

# Windows

## Burning to a CD or a DVD

Most new computers have at least one drive that can write content to either a CD or a DVD. Windows 7 has functionality built in to use these drives for writing ("burning") a CD or DVD. You may also elect to use a third-party application such as Nero or Easy Media Creator, which include additional features and capabilities.

Nearly all writable CD/DVD drives can use either CD-recordable (CD-R), DVD-recordable (DVD-R), CD-rewritable (CD-RW), or DVD-rewriteable (DVD-RW) discs. CD-R and DVD-R discs are cheaper but can be written to only once. CD-RW and DVD-RW discs are more expensive, but the contents can be changed after the initial write.

## Creating a Data CD

The CD is a great medium for creating backups of important files and digital pictures. A CD can hold about 700 MB of data while a DVD can hold up to 4.7 gigabytes of data.

### Steps

To copy files to a writable CD:

1. Insert a blank CD-R in the drive. Depending on whether AutoPlay defaults have been set in the Control Panel, a blank window may appear in which you specify the files to copy (see Step 5). Otherwise, proceed to Step 2.
2. At the AutoPlay dialog box, click *Burn files to disc using Windows Explorer*.

3. Type the title text you want to assign to the CD in the *Disc title* text box at the Burn a Disc dialog box and then click Next. Leave the choice *Like a USB flash drive* checked, as this allows you to save, edit, or delete files on the CD at any time.

4. Windows formats the disc to prepare the disc to receive data. A progress bar indicates the format progress. When the formatting is completed, a blank Computer window will appear in which you specify the content to be burned to the disc. If an AutoPlay dialog box appears instead, click the *Open folder to view files using Windows Explorer* button.

5. Do either of the following:

- Navigate to and select the file(s) and/or folder(s) using standard Windows selection techniques (Shift + click contiguous files; Ctrl + click noncontiguous files), *right*-click within the selection, point to *Send To*, and then click the appropriate drive containing the blank CD.
- To copy multiple file(s) and/or folder(s), navigate to the desired source locations in the Navigation pane, and use the Copy and Paste routines you learned in Tutorial 7 to copy the content to the CD drive. As you paste each selection, Windows copies the source files to the CD.

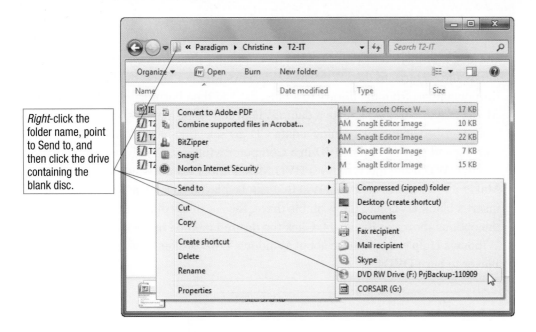

*Right*-click the folder name, point to Send to, and then click the drive containing the blank disc.

6. A progress bar indicates the estimated time for copying. Wait for the files to be written to the CD. Try not to use the computer while it is writing, to minimize the possibility of write errors. When the CD is finished, if the window displays the CD contents in the List pane, close the window.

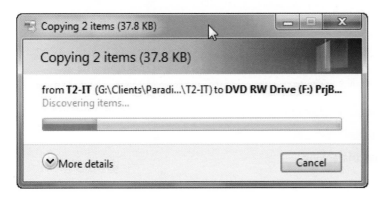

7. Eject the disc using the button on the drive. The disc session will close. This process takes a few seconds to complete since Windows has to finalize the disc preparation and close the session before the CD is ready for use.

**TIP** By default, Windows 7 uses the Live File System to burn files, meaning you can copy files to the disc at any time rather than creating a master list and burning all of the files at once. If the CD may be used in older computers, use the Mastered format to avoid compatibility problems. See Windows Help for information on the Mastered format.

**TIP** What does it mean to rip a CD? You can copy tracks from an audio CD to the computer with Windows Media Player. Once ripped, the songs become files on your computer which you can play back from the library. Be careful that you do not violate copyright laws when copying music files.

## Burning a DVD

Burning information to a DVD offers more options than for a CD. You can burn music and pictures to the DVD using Windows Media Player, by dragging and dropping items from the library to a burn list and then burning the DVD from the Media Player window. Create a data DVD by following a process similar to the one described above for burning a data CD (by selecting files and/or folders and copying and pasting to the DVD in a Computer window). Finally, you can create a video DVD using the Windows DVD Maker application. Using Windows DVD Maker allows you to create a DVD that can be played back on a TV. When you insert a blank DVD into the writable drive, the AutoPlay dialog box appears with the options shown in Figure 14. Click the desired method to create the DVD. Use Windows Help to learn more about Windows DVD Maker or Windows Media Player to burn DVDs.

**Figure 14  AutoPlay Dialog Box**

**TUTORIAL 14**

# Windows

## Using the Action Center

The Windows Action Center provides the current status of several security features in one window (see Figure 15). Windows displays alert icons in the notification area of the taskbar when a problem is detected with a security setting. For example, if the Windows Firewall has been turned off, the red security alert icon 🗵 displays. A yellow alert icon 🚩 appears for other types of less serious security issues.

### Steps

To open the Windows Action Center:

1. If it is present, double-click the security alert icon in the notification area. Otherwise, click the Start button, click *Control Panel*, click the <u>System and Security</u> hyperlink in the Control Panel window, and then click <u>Action Center</u> in the Control Panel, System and Security window.

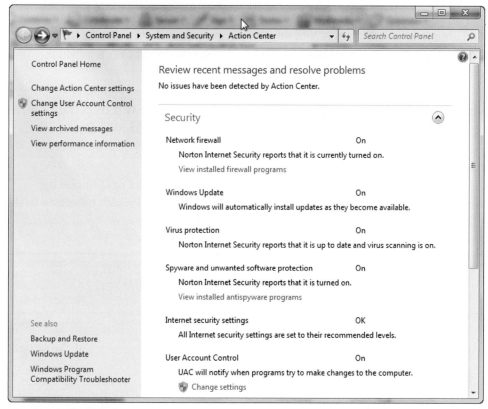

Figure 15  Windows Action Center

## Preventing Unauthorized Access with a Firewall

A firewall can include software or hardware. Firewalls prevent hackers or other malicious software from accessing your computer through the Internet or via a network. Windows includes a software firewall by default and turns the firewall on. Firewalls other than Windows may be installed on the computer you are using meaning the Windows Firewall may be turned off, but the system may still be protected. In this case, you should check the third-party firewall to make sure it is operating correctly.

## Automatically Updating Windows 7

By default, Windows searches for critical and recommended updates to your computer, downloads the updates from Microsoft, and installs them each day. If you prefer you can change the update setting to:

- download updates but install only after you have reviewed the update list and discarded those you do not want.
- check for updates and let you decide which ones to download.
- never check for updates.

## Protecting Your PC from Malware

One of the most important actions you can take to protect your computer and your data is to install and update reliable antivirus and antispyware software. These applications contain lists of virus and spyware definitions that identify malware and provide the means to remove the unauthorized object and fix the damage (when possible). New computer viruses and spyware are created daily. Most applications automatically check for updates and install them weekly. Antivirus and antispyware software is sold on a subscription basis which means you buy the license for a certain period of time, after which you need to pay a renewal fee to maintain the updates.

Windows 7 includes the antispyware application Windows Defender that operates in real time to protect your PC from pop-ups and security threats caused by spyware. However, an antivirus program is not included with Windows 7. At the Action Center, if no antivirus software is detected, Windows provides a button to assist you with finding a program (see Figure 16).

Clicking the Find a program button links you to a Web site maintained by Microsoft with links to popular antivirus programs, many of which offer free trials before you have to buy the application license.

**Figure 16   Windows Defender Find a Program Button**

## Internet and User Account Control Settings

The last option at the Windows Action Center indicates if Internet security and User Account Control settings are at the recommended levels. By default, Internet security is set to medium-high, which means you will be prompted before downloading potentially unsafe content from the Internet and unsigned Active X controls will not be downloaded. User Account Control causes a dialog box to pop up requiring your authorization to continue with a change that will affect your computer's operation or change settings that affect other users. In some cases, you may be prompted to enter an administrator password to continue the operation.

## Maintaining Your Computer

Operating a computer is similar to operating a motor vehicle—after a certain period of time the vehicle requires a tune-up to optimize the vehicle's performance. In the same way, a computer requires a "tune-up" periodically to clear the hard disk of temporary files and improve performance.

Part of your regular computer maintenance should also include checking for Windows Updates and ensuring your anti-virus and antispyware software definitions and subscriptions are up to date. Recall from Tutorial 14 the Windows Action Center provides a one-stop window to perform these checks.

## Deleting Temporary Files with Disk Cleanup

As you surf the Internet and work with data files, temporary files are created on your hard disk which are not removed when you have finished your work. The Disk Cleanup utility frees up space on your hard disk by finding and removing these temporary files. As well, the utility can empty the Recycle Bin and removes any system files that are no longer needed.

### Steps

To perform a disk cleanup:

1. Click the Start button.
2. With the insertion point positioned in the *Start Search* text box, type **disk cleanup**.
3. Click *Disk Cleanup* in the results list at the top of the left pane.

Type the name of the program you want to find in the Start Search text box to save time browsing the menu structure.

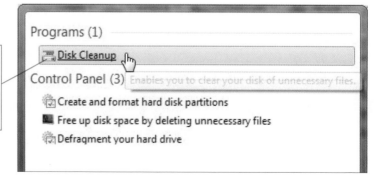

4. At the Disk Cleanup: Drive Selection dialog box, choose the drive you want the temporary files removed from and click OK. Disk Cleanup begins by calculating how much disk space can be freed. When finished, the Disk Cleanup for [computer name] appears in which you can specify which files to delete.

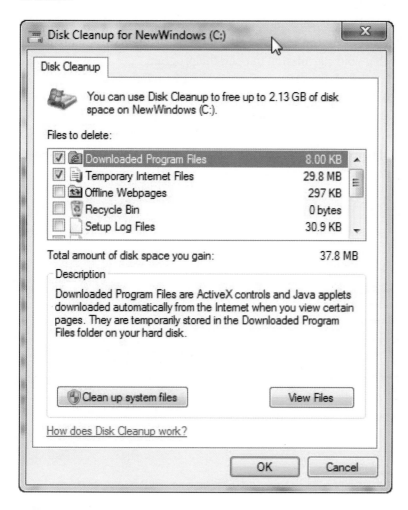

5. At the Disk Cleanup Options box, click OK to proceed with the removal of files, or select or deselect the options that you want to retain and then click OK.
6. Click Delete Files at the next dialog box to confirm you want to permanently delete the files. A progress bar displays as the program removes the files.

## Improving Performance using Disk Defragmenter

As you add and delete files to and from your computer, the hard disk becomes fragmented with gaps where files were deleted. A fragmented disk slows down the computer's performance. Defragmenting the hard disk rearranges the data so that the hard disk operates efficiently. By default, Disk Defragmenter is scheduled to run each week; however, you can defragment manually if you have been performing a large amount of file maintenance, or if you have disabled the automatic operation.

### Steps

To defragment the hard disk:

1. Click the Start button.
2. With the insertion point positioned in the *Start Search* text box, type **disk defragmenter**.
3. Click *Disk Defragmenter* in the results list at the top of the left pane.
4. Click Continue at the User Account Control dialog box (if it appears), requesting your permission to open the program.
5. From the list of disks that appears in the List pane, select the disk you want to defragment. Click the Defragment disk button. The defragmentation process may take anywhere from several minutes to more than an hour to complete depending on the amount of fragmentation on your hard disk. While the process is working, you can continue doing other tasks on the computer.

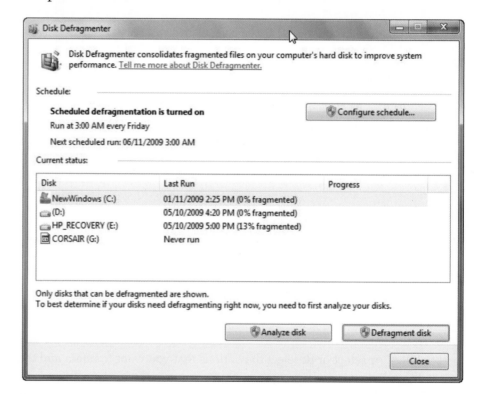

# Internet

## Browsing the Web Using Web Addresses

The Internet is a collection of computers around the world connected through telephone lines, cables, satellites, and other telecommunications media. The World Wide Web, called the Web, is a part of the Internet that contains Web pages consisting of text, sounds, video, and graphics that link to other related Web pages. These links are called hyperlinks. Many Web pages are stored in a language called HTML (Hypertext Markup Language) that can be viewed on any computer regardless of the operating system platform (Macintosh, Windows, UNIX, Linux, and so on).

To connect to the Internet and view Web pages you will need the following resources:

- A computer with Internet access
- Browser software, such as Internet Explorer, Firefox, or Netscape, that provides the interface for viewing Web pages

In the steps that follow, you will explore Web sites on the Internet using Web addresses in Microsoft Internet Explorer version 8.0 operating in the Windows 7 environment. If you are using another operating system, Web browser, or a different version of Internet Explorer, you may need to alter these instructions slightly.

### Steps

1. Click the Launch Internet Explorer browser icon in the Quick Launch toolbar next to the Start button, or click the Start button and choose *Internet Explorer* from the Start menu.

   **If you are completing this tutorial using your computer at home, you may need to enter your user name and password and click OK to connect through a dial-up connection to your Internet service provider (ISP).**

   **The Internet Explorer window appears with the configured home page displayed in the window as shown in Figure T-1. (The default Web page shown when Internet Explorer first opens may vary from the U.S. Government page shown.)**

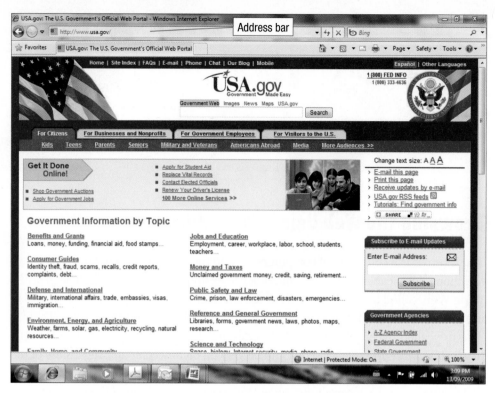

**Figure T-1  Internet Explorer Window with U.S. Government Web page**

2. Move the mouse pointer over the current entry in the Address bar, and then click the left mouse button.

> **Clicking the left mouse button selects the entire address and changes the white arrow pointer to an I-beam which indicates you can type text and/or move the insertion point using the arrow keys on the keyboard.**

3. Type **usatoday.com** and then press Enter. The USA Today home page appears in the window.

> **The entry in the Address bar is called a URL (Uniform Resource Locator). URLs are the addressing method used to identify Web pages. After pressing Enter, notice the browser automatically inserted *http://* in front of the address you typed. The letters *http* stand for Hypertext Transfer Protocol, which is the communications standard used for transferring data within the Web.**

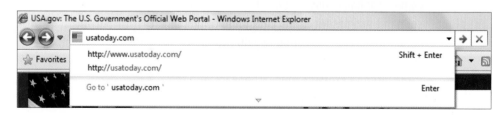

4. Move the mouse pointer over items beside the word **Essentials**, which appears directly underneath the main USA TODAY blue banner at the top of the page. Notice the pointer changes shape to a white hand with the index finger pointing upward, and the menu items (Games, Lotteries, Video, etc.) change to a light blue text when you hover over them with the mouse.

5. Hold the mouse pointer over the word Photos, then make a selection from the drop-down menu by clicking the left mouse button (for example, Day in Pictures). In a second or two, a new window will open that shows *The day in pictures* page.

6. Scroll through The *day in pictures* page and click X to close that window when you're done. From the main USA TODAY page in the original window, click the Back button to return to the previous Web page you were viewing.

7. Click the Forward button on the toolbar to redisplay the main USA TODAY page (the page viewed prior to clicking the Back button).

8. Notice the down-pointing arrow to the right of the Back and Forward buttons on the toolbar. Click the down-pointing arrow and then click a Web site name in the drop-down list to jump to a page previously viewed.

9. Click the mouse pointer in the Address bar, type **microsoft.com**, and then press Enter.

10. Click one of the hyperlinks on the Microsoft home page to jump to a topic that interests you.

11. Continue exploring Web pages by typing URLs in the Address bar, clicking hyperlinks, as well as the toolbar Back and Forward buttons.

12. When you have finished exploring the Web, click the Close button at the right end of the Title bar to exit Internet Explorer. If necessary, disconnect from your ISP if you are not continuing on to Tutorial 2.

Back button

Forward button

Close button

# Internet

## Conducting a Basic Web Search

In the previous Internet tutorial, Web sites were explored by keying the Web address (URL) for a specific company. Another method used to find information is by entering a keyword or a phrase and then browsing through a series of Web pages that were found. Several search engines are available to assist users with locating Web sites by topic. A search engine is a company that uses specialized software to continually scan the Web to index and catalog the information that is published. These companies have created Web sites where the user begins a search by typing the word or phrase about which they would like to find information. The search engine then lists the Web pages that contain the word or phrase as links, which are called hits. Some search engines maintain category indices where the user clicks through a series of categories and subcategories until they reach the desired list of Web pages.

In this tutorial, you will find information on the Web by entering keywords and then conduct another search by browsing through a list of categories.

### Steps

1. Start Internet Explorer and then maximize the Internet Explorer window if it is not already maximized. If necessary, connect to your ISP and enter your user name and password.
2. Locate the Instant Search Box in the top right corner of the browser window.

> **The Instant Search Box allows you to execute a search using a search engine at any time, no matter what Web page you are currently on. Internet Explorer 8 uses Bing as its default search engine. This is indicated by the text *Bing* in the Instant Search Box.**

3. Click once in the Instant Search text box (the default text will disappear), immediately type **space station facts**, then press the Enter key. A list of hyperlinked Web pages displays in the Internet Explorer window that Bing

has indexed to the phrase you typed. *Note: If a dialog box appears asking you to enable Auto Complete, click No.*

4. Click one of the links in the Internet Explorer window to view a related Web page.

5. Click the Back button to return to the search results list and then click another link to view another Web page.

> **Another way to search for information is to use a search engine's category index. In the next steps, you will type the URL for a search engine and then browse the category index.**

6. Click once on the URL currently displayed in the Address bar.

> **Clicking on the URL in the Address bar highlights it; anything you type next replaces the URL.**

7. Type **yahoo.com** in the Address bar and then press Enter.

> **Yahoo! is a popular search engine that maintains category indices and can also be used to search for a topic by keywords.**

8. Click the More hyperlink above the *Search* text box at the top of the Yahoo! page and then click *Directory Search on the next page.*

9. Scroll down the Yahoo! Web page and then click the Science hyperlink.

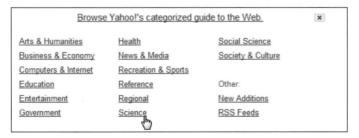

10. Scroll down the Yahoo! directory page for the Science category and then click the Space hyperlink.

- **Oceanography@**
- **Paleontology@**
- **Physics** (1895) NEW!
- **Psychology@**
- **Space** (1700) NEW!

11. Scroll down the Yahoo! directory page for the Science > Space category and then click the Space Stations hyperlink.

- **Space Environment** (73)
- **Space Physics** (29)
- **Space Stations** (54)
- **Spacecraft** (513) NEW!
- **Web Directories** (7)

12. Click <u>International Space Station (ISS)</u> on the Space Stations category page.
13. Click one of the links that is of interest to you on the International Space Station category page to read about this international project.
14. Click the Back button on the Internet Explorer toolbar, click another link from the International Space Station category page, and then view the Web page.
15. Close Internet Explorer.

If necessary, disconnect from your ISP if you are not continuing on to Tutorial 3.

| URLs for Other Popular Search Engines | |
| --- | --- |
| Excite | http://www.excite.com |
| Google | http://www.google.com |
| WebCrawler | http://www.webcrawler.com |

# Conducting an Advanced Web Search

The number of Web sites that an individual will see in a list as the result of a search request can be overwhelming. It is not uncommon to see thousands of hits result from searching by a few keywords. The challenge when searching for information on the Internet is to reduce the number of hits to the smallest possible number. Including a search operator with the keywords refines a search by limiting the sites that are displayed based on where or how the keywords are placed. Search operators vary among search engines, so it is best to view links to advanced search information for a search engine prior to using operators.

In this tutorial, you will find information on the Web using Boolean operators, specifying a time period, and filtering by a domain in an advanced search page.

## Steps

1. Start Internet Explorer. If necessary, connect to your ISP and enter your user name and password.
2. Type **google.com** in the Address bar and then press Enter.

   **Search engines are constantly adding and removing Web pages from their databases and directories and changing their search page design. Therefore, the results you achieve throughout this tutorial may differ from what is shown in the figures or what is mentioned in the text.**

3. Type **tesla** in the search text box and then click the Google Search button. In a few seconds, linked Web pages display; the total number of sites found from searching the index provided at the top of the search results list. The search engine has found over 3,500,000 results for "tesla," including the rock band Tesla, the scientist Nikola Tesla, and Tesla Motors. *Note: Search engine listings change daily so the number of results you receive will likely differ from 3,500,000.*

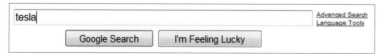

4. Scroll down the search results list and read the titles and descriptions of the Web pages found.

   **In the next steps you will refine the list to display only those pages that contain information about the scientist Nikola Tesla.**

5. Scroll to the right of the text search box and then click the <u>Advanced Search</u> hyperlink.

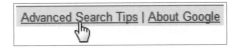

6. Click the <u>Advanced Search Tips</u> hyperlink near the top of the page.

<u>Advanced Search Tips</u> | <u>About Google</u>

7. In the Google Web search box at the top of the page, type in **advanced search operators** and press Enter. Click the hyperlink that says <u>Google search basics: Advanced Search</u>. Scroll down the page and click the <u>Print-and-save Google Cheat Sheet</u> hyperlink.

Types of advanced search operators include:

- <u>Include search</u>
- <u>Synonym search</u>
- <u>OR search</u>
- <u>Domain search</u>
- <u>Numrange search</u>
- <u>Other advanced search features</u>

<u>Complete list of advanced operators</u>

<u>Print-and-save Google Cheat Sheet</u>

8. Read the information about the options available for the Google search engine.

**When you type multiple words in the Google search box, all words are used to find results as if all your words were separated by the word AND. The more words you type, the more precise your search. You can also precede a word with a minus sign to exclude that word from the results. Let's specify "Nikola" and omit results with the words "band" or "motors."**

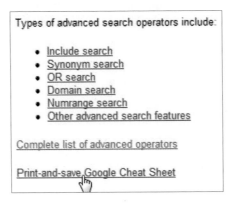

| OPERATOR EXAMPLE | FINDS PAGES CONTAINING... |
|---|---|
| vacation hawaii | the words **vacation** and **Hawaii** |
| *Maui OR Hawaii* | either the word **Maui** or the word **Hawaii** |
| *"To each his own"* | the exact phrase **to each his own** |
| *virus –computer* | the word **virus** but NOT the word **computer** |
| *+sock* | Only the word **sock**, and not the plural or any tenses or synonyms |
| *~auto loan* | loan info for both the word **auto** and its synonyms: **truck, car,** etc. |
| *define:computer* | definitions of the word **computer** from around the Web. |
| *red * blue* | the words **red** and **blue** separated by one or more words. |
| I'm Feeling Lucky | Takes you directly to first web page returned for your query. |

9. Click in the Address bar, type google.com, and press the Enter key to return to the Google search page.

> **Typing google.com in the Address bar takes you directly to the Google search page, which is quicker than clicking the browser's back button several times.**

10. In the Google search box, type **nikola tesla -band -motors** and click the Google Search button. *Note: Take care to type the hyphens (or minus signs) immediately before band and motors.*

> **Your search results have been filtered. Instead of over 3,500,000 results, you now have approximately 1,600,000. While that may seem like a lot, the majority of results should relate to the scientist and not the band or motor company. In the next steps, you will further refine your search by specifying a time period for published information and a domain filter.**

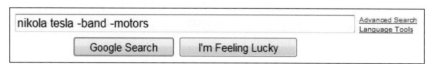

11. Click the <u>Advanced Search</u> link to the right of the text search box. Your search terms are pre-filled for you. Notice *nikola tesla* appears in the *all these words* text box while *band motors* appears in the *any of these unwanted words* text box.

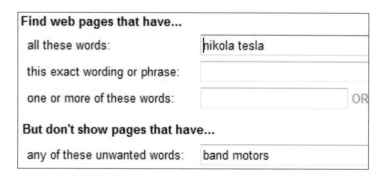

12. Scroll down the <u>Advanced Search</u> page, and click the <u>Date, usage rights, numeric range, and more</u> hyperlink. In the Date: section, click the down pointing arrow next to the (how recent the page is) text box and choose *past year* from the list menu.

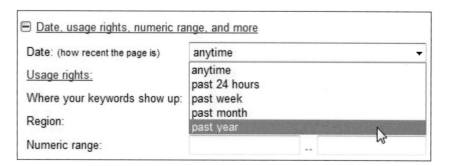

13. Locate the *Search within a site or a domain* section and type **pbs.org** in the text box. (This section is directly above the Date section.)

**This will filter your search results further to include only Web pages from the pbs.org domain that have been updated in the past year.**

| Search within a site or domain: | pbs.org |
|---|---|
| | (e.g. youtube.com, .edu) |

14. Click the Advanced Search button. Your search results will be filtered to a handful of results, and the results should be more relevant to your search terms. *Note: The number of your results may vary. If you do not return any results, click Advanced Search and change the return Web pages updated in the textbox to "anytime."*

15. Close Internet Explorer. If necessary, disconnect from your ISP if you are not going on to Tutorial 4.

# Internet

## Shopping on the Web

The ability to shop at any time throughout the day, browse a variety of products within minutes, and compare prices among vendors with just a few mouse clicks is making online shopping a popular choice. **E-tailing**, the selling of retail goods on the Internet, is what most individuals think of when the term **e-commerce** is used. Companies that brought e-tailing to mainstream popularity are Dell Computers and bookseller Amazon.com. Most e-tailers use secure Web site servers that automatically encrypt personal data such as a credit card number as it is transmitted. This provides protection for both the consumer and the e-tailer. A secure Web site is indicated with a URL that begins with *https* rather than *http*. Encryption involves the use of Secure Sockets Layer (SSL) technology that scrambles information into an unbreakable code before it is sent over the Internet. To indicate that an active Web site is secure, Internet Explorer, Firefox, and Netscape display an icon of a closed lock on the right side of the Address bar.

In this tutorial, you will browse an e-tailer's secure Web site and identify the security and privacy features.

### Steps

1. Start Internet Explorer. If necessary, connect to your ISP and enter your user name and password.
2. Type **newegg.com** in the Address bar and then press Enter.

   **Newegg is an online retailer specializing in computer gear.**

3. Click any one of the items shown on the home page.

   **Clicking an item takes you to a details page where you can learn more about the item.**

4. Click the ADD TO CART button. *Note: In the next steps you will proceed to check out in order to look at the visual clues that identify a secure Web server. However, you will not complete an actual transaction.*

5. Click the View Shopping Cart link, and then click the Checkout button. The shopping cart summary page displays and shows you the one item you have placed in your shopping cart.

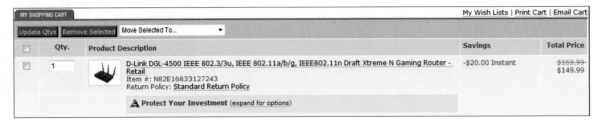

6. If necessary, scroll to the bottom of the page and click the Checkout button. The login page appears for existing members to log in.

> **New shoppers to the Newegg Web site without an account can create an account from this page.**

7. Locate the identifying features of a secure server. The URL begins with *https* and the closed padlock icon appears on the right side of the Address bar.

8. To find out more about Newegg's security, click the Newegg.com logo to return to the home page and then click the *Help & Info* tab near the top of the browser window. In the next screen, type **security** in the Search FAQ text box and press Enter.

> **Security is not just about keeping credit card information safe but is also about protecting a buyer's personal information. If an e-tailer does not have a link to a page that informs the buyer how information is stored and shared, then the site should be avoided.**

9. Close Internet Explorer. If necessary, disconnect from your ISP if you are not going on to Tutorial 5.

Cavaet Emptor!
The trading principle, "Let the Buyer Beware" is just as applicable to electronic commerce as it is to face-to-face shopping. Buyers need to be prudent about verifying product and vendor reliability. The Better Business Bureau's site at http://www.bbb.org is a great place to start.

# TUTORIAL 5

# Internet

## Downloading Information from the Web

If you find a Web site that contains information on a topic that you want to save for future use, you can either print a hard copy of the Web page(s) or you can save it as a file on your computer. If you want to save only a portion of the text on the Web page, select the text with the mouse and then copy it to the Clipboard. Once the text is stored in the Clipboard, it can be pasted into WordPad or Microsoft Word and then saved as a document. A graphic or another multimedia component on a Web page also can be downloaded and saved as a file.

In this tutorial, you will save an entire Web page as a file, select text from a Web page to copy and paste, and then save a graphic image as a file.

### Steps

1. Start Internet Explorer. If necessary, connect to your ISP and enter your user name and password.
2. Type **loc.gov** in the Address bar and then press Enter.
3. Click the <u>AMERICAN MEMORY</u> link, and then click the Go button.

4. At the American Memory home page, click the <u>Today in History</u> link.

5. Click the Page button on the Standard toolbar and then click Save As.

**To successfully save the page, you will have to determine three options: the folder location in which the file will be saved, the name of the file, and the type of file. You will determine these three settings in the next few steps.**

6. If you don't see a list of locations on the left side of the Save Webpage dialog box, click the Browse Folders button at the bottom of the dialog box.

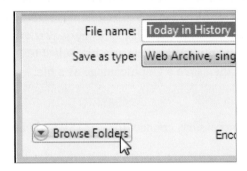

7. On the left side of the Save Webpage dialog box, select *Desktop* (in the Favorites section).

**This sets the download location to your desktop as indicated in the Save Webpage dialog box's Address bar. This will make it easy to find your file once it has been downloaded.**

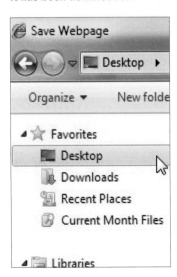

8. Verify that the *File name* text box reads *Today in History [today's date]* and that the *Save as type* option is *Web Archive, single file (*.mht)*, and then click the Save button.

   **A progress box briefly appears as the Web page elements are downloaded and saved locally. To view the Web page at a later time, start Internet Explorer and press [CTRL]+[O]. Click the Browse button in the Open dialog box, navigate to the drive and/or folder where the Web page is stored, and then double-click the Web page name in the list box.**

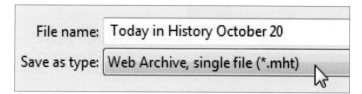

9. With Today in History still the active page, position the mouse pointer slightly left of the first character in the first paragraph of text until the pointer changes to the I-beam pointer and then drag the mouse down and right to the end of the first paragraph as shown. *Note: Your text will vary from the text shown if you are viewing Today in History on a date other than October 20.*

I-beam pointer

> I leave you with undefiled hands, an uncorrupted heart, and with ardent vows to heaven for the welfare and happiness of that country in which I and my forefathers to the third or fourth progenitor drew our first breath.

10. Click the Page button on the Standard toolbar and then click Copy.

    **The selected text is saved to the Windows Clipboard. To save the text permanently, open a software application such as WordPad or Microsoft Word, paste the text, edit or format as required, and then save it as a document.**

11. Click the Start button, click *All Programs*, click *Accessories*, and then click *WordPad*.

12. At a blank document window, click the large Paste button in the Clipboard group on the Home tab.

13. Click the Save button on the toolbar to open the Save As dialog box. Change the drive and/or folder if desired, then type **Today in History** in the *File name* text box, and click the Save button.

14. Click the WordPad button and then click *Exit* to close the document and exit WordPad.

    **When WordPad closes, you should automatically be returned to the Internet Explorer window. If necessary, click the button on the Taskbar representing Internet Explorer to restore the window.**

15. Click Back on the toolbar to return to the American Memory home page.

16. Move the mouse pointer over any of the photographs in the main part of the page and then right-click. Click *Save Picture As* from the shortcut menu.

A graphic does not have to be saved as a file. Right-click a picture on a Web page and Copy it to the Clipboard. Paste the image into a document using the Edit, Paste command if you simply want to copy an image and do not need it saved as a separate file.

17. At the Save Picture dialog box, navigate to your desktop or other storage location as you did when you saved a Web page previously in this tutorial.
18. With the default name in the *File name* text box, click the Save button.
19. Close Internet Explorer. If necessary, disconnect from your ISP if you are not continuing on to Tutorial 6.

# Internet

## Reference Resources on the Web

A search engine can return a large number of hits as the result of a search request by keyword(s) or phrase even when search operators are included to reduce the list of Web pages. Although using the Internet to locate information is fast and very accessible, extra time needs to be taken to assess the reliability and accuracy of the online information. Information on the Internet can comprise opinions, stories, statistics, or facts. The context with which information is presented may be designed to inform the reader or persuade the reader to accept an opinion or buy a product or service. A considerable amount of time to filter through the hits to find the credible information can be avoided by using one of the many reference resources available on the Web. Reference resources are portals to information that has been evaluated prior to being linked through the resource site.

In this tutorial you will use two reference resource sites to locate information about global warming and earth sciences on the Internet.

### Steps

1. Start Internet Explorer. If necessary, connect to your ISP and enter your user name and password.
2. Key **lii.org** in the Address bar and then press Enter.

   **The Librarians' Internet Index contains over 7,800 Internet resources selected and evaluated by librarians. The index was originally funded by the U.S. Institute of Museum and Library Services and is now maintained through funding from the Library of California.**

3. Click in the Search text box, type **"global warming"**, and then click the Search LII button. *Note: Be sure to include the opening and closing quotes.*

4. Scroll through the list of Web links found. Click one of the links that interests you.
5. If a new window popped up with your search results, close it and return to the window with your original search results. Otherwise click the Back button on the Internet Explorer toolbar to return to your original search results listing. Scroll down the page until you see the *Warnings from the Ice* category of links. Under that paragraph, click the <u>Regions of the World</u>

hyperlink. On the resulting search page, click the Polar Regions hyperlink. This narrows your search results to global warming in the polar regions. Scroll through and examine the links on the Polar Regions page.

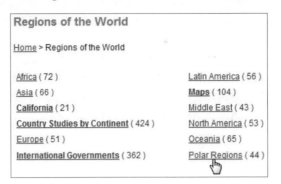

The Librarians' Internet Index and the Internet Public Library are just two of many reference resources. Go to your favorite search engine page and type reference resources to find more!

6. Type **ipl.org** in the Address bar and then press Enter.

**The Internet Public Library is hosted by the *iSchool* at Drexel College of Information Science and Technology. The site contains a rich resource of library services to Internet users.**

7. Click the Science hyperlink on the left side of the page.

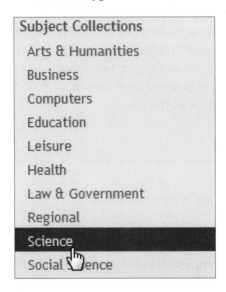

8. Click the Earth Sciences hyperlink in the main area of the page. Scroll down the page if necessary to see the link.

9. Scroll down the list of Internet resources provided for the Earth Sciences category and then click a link to a site that interests you.

10. Close Internet Explorer. If necessary, disconnect from your ISP.

# GLOSSARY

**3D modeling program** a program that allows users to create the illusion of depth in objects drawn on the computer

**3G** third-generation cellular technology that allows for the transfer of voice and nonvoice data

**802.11 protocol** a protocol for wireless LAN technology that specifies an over-the-air interface between the wireless client device and a server, or between two wireless devices, approved by the IEEE in 1997; also called Wi-Fi

**802.11a protocol** revision of the 802.11 protocol for wireless LAN technology, approved in 2001, which offers transfer rates of up to 54 Mbps when devices are at a range within 60 feet of the primary access point or hub, 22 Mbps at longer distances

**802.11b protocol** first major revision of 802.11 protocol for wireless LAN technology, approved in 1999, relatively low cost and with a faster transfer rate of 5.5 Mbps to 11 Mbps at a range up to 250 feet; popular in home and small office wireless networks

**802.11g protocol** approved in June 2003, this protocol for wireless LAN technology operates in the same frequency range as 802.11b but with transfer rates similar to 802.11a

**802.11n protocol** latest revision of the 802.11 protocol for wireless LAN technology, approved in 2009, which offers transfer rates up to 600 Mbps and can operate at 2.4 GHz (like 802.11g) and/or 5 GHz (like 802.11a) frequency range

# A

**Accelerated Graphics Port (AGP) bus** a bus that increases the speed at which graphics (including 3D graphics) and video can be transmitted and accessed by the computer

**acceptable use policy (AUP)** a set of guidelines schools and other organizations develop to inform their internal users about standards of computer and Internet behavior and the procedure for reporting violations

**access time** the time a storage device spends locating a particular file

**active-matrix display** a type of monitor display in which separate transistors control each color pixel, allowing viewing from any angle; also called thin-film transistor (TFT) display

**adapter** an electronic circuit board that can be inserted onto the motherboard inside a computer to add new capabilities to a computer; examples include sound cards, graphics cards, and network interface cards; also called an expansion card

**address** a specific location in memory where an instruction or data is stored; the computer assigns an address to each location so the instruction or data can be quickly located and retrieved when needed

**adware** software that tracks the Web sites that a user visits in order to collect information for marketing or advertising

**algorithm** a series of precise steps to solve a given programming problem

**alpha product** a prototype of software under development used by the development team for testing purposes

**alphanumeric check** a check made by database input forms to make sure that the value entered into a field contains only letters or numbers

**alphanumeric data** data that contains letters and numbers; may contain special characters

**American Standard Code for Information Interchange (ASCII)** a coding scheme used on many personal computers and on various midrange servers

**amplifier** an electronic device that receives signals along a network, amplifies the signals, and resends the amplified signals along the network; also called a repeater

**analog signal** an electronic signal composed of continuous waves transmitted at a certain frequency range over a medium, such as a telephone line

**android** a term used to describe a robot designed to seem human

**antivirus software** a software program for personal computers that seeks out and destroys any viruses found on a computer

**applet** a small application program, generally one created using the Java programming language, that performs specific functions; used to extend the capabilities of Web pages

**application developer** a person whose job it is to adapt software for use within a new system

**application development** the use of commercial software to develop an information system for a specific organization

**application programmer** a professionally trained programmer who specializes in developing new application software or updating existing application software

**application programming** software development that specializes in creating new or updating existing application software

**application software** programs that enable a user to perform specific tasks; examples of programs include word processors, database programs, spreadsheets, and desktop publishing

**applied ethics** the application of normative ethical beliefs to controversial real-life issues

**arithmetic/logic unit (ALU)** the part of the central processing unit (CPU) that carries out the instructions and performs the actual arithmetic and logical operations on the data; can perform arithmetic operations such as addition, subtraction, multiplication, and division and can also compare data items

**artificial intelligence (AI)** the science of using computers to simulate intelligent mental activities or physical behaviors such as problem solving, learning, and natural language processing

**assembly language** a low-level programming language that is derived directly from the binary instructions (machine language) understood by the CPU

**asynchronous transmission** a data transmission method in which control bits surround each byte of data; an extra bit, called a start bit, is added at the front of the character to signal its beginning and another bit, the stop bit, is added at the end of the character to indicate its end; and there is also the error checking bit called a parity bit

**attribute** the term for a field in a relational database

**audio** data relating to sound, including speech and music

**audio data** relating to sound, including speech and music

**audio input** the process of entering (recording) speech, music, and/or sound effects into a computer

**audio mail** sound attachments that can be sent with e-mails

**audio perception** the capability of a computer system to hear sounds in its environment and to understand what it is hearing; speech recognition is one example of this technology

**audio port** connects a sound card to external devices such as speakers, microphones, and headsets

**auditing** a review of monitoring data and system logins to look for unauthorized access or suspicious behavior

**authentication** the process of identifying an individual based on a user name and password

**automated clearinghouse (ACH)** an automated entity established for the purpose of transferring funds electronically from one account to another account

**auxiliary storage** a type of storage that consists of devices and media used to record information and data permanently so it can later be retrieved, edited, modified, displayed, or printed; also called permanent storage, secondary storage, or external storage

**avatar** a virtual body given to a player in a game in order to create a virtual reality

**AVI file format** a Windows movie media format, identified with an .avi extension

# B

**backup and recovery plan** developed by database administrators to ensure that data is backed up regularly and can be recovered in the case of loss

**backup utility** software that allows the user to make copies of the contents of disks or tapes

**bandwidth** the amount of data that can travel over an analog medium

**banner** a type of advertisement that takes up an approximately one-inch-high slice of a Web page; clicking on the banner activates a link to a vendor's site

**bar code reader** an electronic device that uses photo technology to read the lines in a bar code; the lines and spaces contain symbols that the computer translates into information

**BASIC** a programming language designed in the 1960s as a learning language for new programmers; acronym for Beginner's All-purpose Symbolic Instruction Code

**basic input/output system (BIOS)** a program that boots (starts) a computer when it is turned on and controls communications with the keyboard, disk drives, and other components

**batch processing** the accumulating of a large amount of data to process at once, rather than doing it immediately, as requests come into the system

**bay** a site within the system unit where a device such as a hard disk drive or CD-ROM drive is installed; also called a storage bay

**beta testing** one of the last steps in software development that involves allowing outside people to use the software to see if it works as designed

**beta version** a prerelease version of a piece of software distributed so that users can test it to evaluate features and to identify any existing bugs

**binary numbers** base 2 numbers written as strings of 1s and 0s

**binary string** sequence of binary symbols

**biometric identifier** an identifiable physical trait that can be measured by a biometric device and used to identify individual people

**bit** the smallest unit of data a computer can understand and act on; an abbreviation for binary digit

**bit depth** the number of bits used in a graphics expansion board to store information about each pixel; also called color depth

**bitmap** a storage technique in which scanned text or a

photo is stored as a matrix of rows and columns of dots

**bitmap-based graphics program** a computerized process of displaying images in which the program treats the image as a large collection of pixels, each of which is stored in its own memory location; the image is created by specifying the color of each pixel; also called a raster image-based graphics program

**bits per second (bps)** the number of bits (the fundamental digital unit, which can be either a 0 or a 1) that can be transmitted in a second's time; the usual measure of bandwidth

**blind link** a hyperlink that directs a Web browser to an unexpected result or location, such as a link that triggers an undesired download

**blog** frequently updated journals, or logs, containing chronological entries of personal thoughts and Web links posted on a Web page

**blogosphere** the collective world of all blogs, also referred to as Web-based journals or logs, containing chronological entries and Web links

**Bluetooth** a wireless technology that offers short-range connectivity with other Bluetooth devices through a small, temporary network that can transmit both voice and data

**boot drive** the disk drive that houses the operating system

**booting** the procedure for starting or restarting a computer

**boot sector** part of a hard disk that contains information about how the disk is organized and whether it is capable of loading an operating system

**boot sector virus** a virus designed to alter the boot sector of a disk so that whenever the operating system reads the boot sector, the computer will automatically become infected

**breadcrumbs** Internet navigation tool that defines a location within the hierarchy of a Web site

**bridge** hardware and/or software that allows for communication between two networks that are similar

**broadband** high-speed Internet connection

**broadband medium** a communications medium capable of carrying a large amount of data at fast speeds

**browser** software that allows users to move from one location to another on the Web and to access and retrieve Web pages; also called a Web browser

**browsing** accessing and moving about the Web using a browser; also called surfing

**buffer** a temporary storage place to which part of data to be displayed, printed, or transmitted is written

**bug** a term Grace Hopper coined meaning any kind of computer error

**bus** a collection of tiny wires through which data, in the form of 0s and 1s, is transmitted from one part of the computer to another

**business intelligence (BI)** the information gained from the effective use of online analytical processing (OLAP) systems

**business systems analyst** a highly trained professional who specializes in business information systems analysis, problem identification, and solution planning and who serves as a liaison between nontechnical business people and programmers

**business-to-business (B2B) electronic commerce** buying and selling of products and services between businesses over the Internet

**business-to-consumer (B2C) electronic commerce** buying and selling of products and services between sellers and customers over the Internet

**bus topology** a type of network topology in which all computers are linked by means of a single line of cable, called a bus, with two endpoints

**bus width** a measure of the size of a bus; determines the number of bits the computer can transmit or receive at one time

**button** a graphical element that, when selected with the mouse or keyboard, causes a particular action to occur within a software program

**byte** a combination of eight bits (0s and 1s) that represents a letter of the alphabet, a number, or a special character inside a computer; there are enough different combinations of bits (0s and 1s) in an 8-bit byte to represent 256 different characters

# C

**C** a programming language developed in the 1970s; newer versions are used to write most of the software sold to the public

**C#** a new version of the C++ programming language under development by Microsoft

**C++** an object-oriented version of the C programming language developed in the 1980s

**cable modem** a special type of modem that provides fast transmission speeds

**cache memory** a dedicated holding area in random access memory (RAM) in which the data and instructions most recently called from RAM by the processor are temporarily stored

**CardBus** a type of expansion board (card) developed for use with small computers such as notebooks and laptops; it replaced the PC card

**carpal tunnel syndrome** the condition of weakness, pain, or numbness resulting from pressure on the median nerve in the wrist; the syndrome is associated with repetitive motion, such as typing or using the mouse

**CASE tool** a software tool that aids in the project management of software development

**cathode ray tube (CRT) monitor** a large, sealed glass tube housed in a plastic case; formerly a common type of monitor for desktop computers

**CD burner** a device that uses lasers to record and read data to and from an optical disc; also called a CD-R drive

**CD drive** a drive that can read nearly any kind of data recorded on an optical disc, including text, graphics, video clips, and sound

**CD-R** an optical disc technology that allows a user to write data onto a compact disc; can be written on only once, cannot be erased, but can be read from an unlimited number of times; acronym for compact disc–recordable

**CD-R drive** a drive that uses lasers to record and read data to and from an optical disc, including text, graphics, video clips, and sound; also called a CD burner

**CD-ROM** an optical disc technology in which data is permanently recorded on an optical disc and can be read many times, but the data cannot be changed; acronym for compact disk–read-only memory

**CD-RW** an optical disc storage technology that uses an erasable disc on which a user can write multiple times; acronym for compact disc–rewritable

**cell** in a spreadsheet, the intersection of one row and one column into which text, numbers, formulas, links, or other elements may be entered; a 10- to 12-square mile area with its own antenna to receive and send cellular telephone signals

**cellular technology** an increasingly popular technology that allows people to communicate anywhere in the world without having to be connected via wired phone lines or cables

**central processing unit (CPU)** the part of a computer that interprets and carries out instructions that operate the computer and manage the computer's devices and resources; consists of components, each of which performs specific functions; also called the microprocessor or processor

**certificate program** intensive education courses offered primarily by large IT companies such as Microsoft and Cisco intended to train an individual for a particular job working with a specific type of product

**chart** a visual representation of data that often makes the data easier to read and understand; displays data in graphical rather than numerical form

**chat room** an online area, provided by an online service or an Internet host, where people can meet, exchange ideas and information, and interact socially

**check box** a dialog box feature that indicates an option a user can turn on or off; an option activated by clicking and

thus adding a check mark; usually one of several options that can be selected

**Children's Internet Protection Act (CIPA)** legislation requiring public schools and libraries to install Internet filtering software on their computers

**Children's Online Privacy Protection Act (COPPA)** legislation aimed at protecting children under the age of 13 from privacy violations

**chip** a thin wafer of silicon containing electronic circuitry that performs various functions, such as mathematical calculations, storage, or control of computer devices

**ciphertext** unreadable, coded information produced by the process of encryption from user's personal or financial information; ensures that consumers' privacy rights will not be violated when they enter data to complete online transactions

**client** a smaller computer, terminal, or workstation capable of sending data to and from a larger computer (host computer) in a network

**client/server architecture** a type of network architecture in which a personal computer, workstation, or terminal (called a client) is used to send information or a request to another computer (called a server) that then relays the information back to the user's client computer, or to another computer (another client)

**clip art** professionally designed graphic images sold for use in word processing and other types of documents; collections are sometimes included in a software program

**clock cycle** the time between two ticks of a computer's system clock; a typical personal computer goes through millions or even billions of clock cycles per second

**closed system** a hardware or software system that must be serviced and supported by the original vendor

**cluster** a group of two or more sectors on a disk; the smallest unit of storage space used to store data

**coaxial cable** a type of wire that consists of an insulated center wire grounded by a shield of braided wire

**COBOL** a business application–oriented language developed in the 1960s; acronym for Common Business–Oriented Language

**coding** a term programmers use to refer to the act of writing source code

**cognitive science** a broad discipline dedicated to the study of the human mind

**cold boot** process of starting a computer by turning on the unit's power switch

**collaboration software** programs that enable people at separate PC workstations to collaborate on a single document or project, such as designing a new automobile engine; also called groupware

**color depth** the number of bits used in a graphics expansion board to store information about each pixel; also called bit depth

**command-line interface** a user interface, like the one created by the DOS operating system, that makes use of typed commands

**comment** a note programmers write in the source code; helps later readers comprehend the meaning of the program or line of code

**commercial software** programs intended for businesses or other organizations with multiple users

**Common Gateway Interface (CGI) script** a program used on Web sites to allow the tracking of traffic and the production of dynamic Web pages

**communications (COM) port** a port (opening) for connecting devices such as the keyboard, mouse, and modem to a computer; a port that transmits data one bit at a time; also called a serial port

**communications device** a device that makes it possible for a user to communicate with another computer and to exchange instructions, data, and information with other computer users

**communications medium** a medium, such as a telephone line, used for carrying data or information between computers and networks

**communications satellite** a solar-powered electronic device that contains a number of small, specialized radios called transponders that receive signals from transmission stations on the ground called earth stations, amplifies the signals, and then transmits the signals to the appropriate locations

**communications software** software that allows your properly equipped computer to communicate with other similarly equipped computers; software used to send and receive electronic messages, visit various Web sites, locate and retrieve information stored on other computers, electronically transmit large files, and much more

**compact disc (CD)** a plastic disc 4.75 inches in diameter and about 1/20th of an inch thick; uses laser technologies to store information and data

**compiler** a type of language-translating software that translates an entire program into machine language before the program will run; each language has its own unique compiler

**completeness check** a database accuracy element that requires every field to be filled in completely

**computer** an electronic device capable of interpreting and executing program instructions and data and performing the required operations to produce the desired results

**computer codes of ethics** standards for ethical use of computers put forward by computer professional organizations

**computer engineering degree** an educational degree focusing on hardware design

**computer ethics** the adapting of traditional ethical thought and behavior to issues involving computers and computer technology; computer ethics is a newly formed branch of applied ethics

**computer graphic special effects (CG FX)** special effects created for movies with computer graphics

**computer information systems (CIS) degree** an educational degree that is application-oriented, requiring both business and computer science courses; students learn programming, usually aimed at application development with existing software products rather than the creation of new software products

**computer science degree** an educational degree focusing on writing, or programming, new software

**computer system** system unit along with input devices, output devices, and storage devices

**computer-aided design (CAD) software** a sophisticated kind of productivity software providing tools that enable professionals to create architectural, engineering, product, and scientific designs

**computer-aided manufacturing (CAM)** a computer information system that directly manages factory production

**computer-integrated manufacturing (CIM)** a computer information system that manages production and connects the factory floor to every level of management

**computerized facial recognition (CFR)** a computer system capable of comparing facial images with a database of known individuals, thereby recognizing people

**connectivity** refers to the ability to link with other programs and devices

**consistency check** a database check that ensures data is accurate by checking it against known data

**consultant** an individual or a company with highly skilled IT workers that completes projects for other organizations

**consumer profile** a set of information about customers' lifestyle and buying habits that marketers use to target and sell their goods more effectively

**context-sensitive Help message** a help message that "senses" the user's needs based on what the user is doing

**control unit** the part of the CPU that directs and coordinates the overall operation of the computer system; interprets each program instruction in a program, and then initiates the action needed to carry out the instruction

**cookies** small programs placed on a computer's hard drive by Web sites designed to remember passwords and user IDs, avoiding the necessity of having to enter this data each time the site containing the cookie is visited

**coprocessor** a special type of dedicated processor designed to perform certain kinds of processing, such as processing large amounts of numerical data

**copyright** the legal protection of an individual's or business's original work, such as applications software, music, and books, that prohibits others from duplicating or illegally using such work or products; an artist or author whose work is copyrighted has the right to charge others for its use

**core** the essential components of a microprocessor's central processing unit (CPU)

**crack** the altering of a software product to remove copy protection

**cracker** a hacker with malicious or criminal intent

**crash bug** a run-time error that causes a program to stop running, or crash

**credit account** a customer's promise to pay for online purchases upon receipt of a periodic statement from the seller; when online purchases are made, each purchase is charged to the customer's credit account

**credit card** a small plastic card with a metallic strip containing owner information that enables the owner to make online and in-store purchases on credit

**crossover** a new design created as a result of combining the most successful variations (mutations) of potential design solutions

**cross-platform compatibility** the capacity of a software package to run on more than one operating system/type of computer

**cross-platform operating system** an operating system capable of being used on more than one type of computer

**cryptographic coprocessor (crypto-coprocessor)** a chip designed specifically to provide encryption and related processing

**custom program** a specialized software program a programmer writes to meet a company's special requirements; also called customized software

**customer relationship management (CRM)** all aspects of interaction a company has with its customers and suppliers; can help companies keep track of customers, develop detailed consumer profiles, and offer customers just the products they want to buy

**customized software** a specialized software program a programmer writes to meet a company's special requirements; also called a custom program

**cyberbullying** the destructive online behavior of texting or sending harassing e-mail messages or embarassing photos for the purpose of harming another person's reputation or self-image

**cyberwars** attacks by groups of international hackers who attack sites in a competing country

# D

**data** raw, unprocessed information

**data browsing** a type of information theft that equates to an invasion of privacy; the process of moving through a database file, examining each record, and looking for information

**database** a computer application in which data is organized and stored in a way that allows for specific data to be accessed, retrieved, and used

**database administration** a combination of application development, technical support, and technical training; includes maintaining and fixing databases

**database administrator** a critical job that involves the continuous management of a database management system (DBMS)

**database approach** a procedure for the development of databases; also called database management approach

**database file** a collection of related records

**database management approach** a procedure for the development of databases; also called database approach

**database management system (DBMS)** software that allows a user to create and manage a computerized database, and to create reports from stored data

**database object** an element within an object-oriented database, such as a report or a table

**database response time** the length of time it takes a database to respond to a request from a user; a critical measurement in rating the performance of any database

**data compression** a process of shrinking the storage size of a body of data by removing redundant information

**data contamination** the spread of incorrect information throughout a database and into other databases, diminishing the usefulness of the systems

**data corruption** the process of data becoming unreadable, incomplete, or damaged

**data-destructive virus** a virus designed to destroy data either by erasing or corrupting files so that they are unreadable or by formatting the entire drive so it is blank

**data dictionary** a descriptive listing of all the data values in an information system

**data entry operator** a person whose job it is to keep the information in a database current and accurate

**data filter** a condition that narrows down a large list of records

**data integrity** a measurement of database correctness and validity; also called data quality

**data mining** a technique programmers use to collate and extract meaningful data from a data warehouse; data mining software allows data warehouse users to see as much data detail or summarization as they need to aid them in making decisions

**data model** defines the structure of information to be contained in a database, how the database will use the information, and how the different items in the database relate to each other

**data modeling** provides a simulation of a real-world situation built into a software application; users can input numeric data into "what-if" scenarios to predict future outcomes

**data processing** the actions performed through transactions with a database; also called information processing

**data quality** a measurement of database correctness and validity; also called data integrity

**data register** a reserved location in main memory for storing data being processed or being used in a specific processing application

**data transfer rate** the speed at which data is transferred from memory or from a storage device to the CPU

**data validation** a strict process that ensures the entry of valid data into a database

**data warehouse** a collection of related databases that have been stored together so that needed data can be retrieved, analyzed, and readily available for decision making

**dead code** any source code within the final version of a released software product that is "commented out" and therefore not part of the actual working program

**debit card** resembles a credit card and, like a credit card, is used as an alternative to cash when making purchases

**debugger** a utility that helps a programmer remove errors from software

**decision statement** the decision points in a program and the different actions that can be performed depending on conditions

**decision support system (DSS)** an information system designed to model possible future outcomes and thus aid in the decision-making process of corporate management

**decoding** the activity of translating or determining the meaning of coded instructions

**default option** an option that has been programmed into a program by the software publisher under the assumption that that option is the one most likely to be chosen

**defragmenting** the process used by a defragmenter utility to reorganize files and unused disk space allowing the operating system to locate and access stored files and data more quickly

**deliverable** a document, service, hardware component, or software program that must be finished and delivered by a certain time and date in order to keep a project on schedule

**demodulation** the process of changing an analog signal into a digital signal

**denial of service (DoS) attack** a form of online attack, usually performed by hackers, in which a Web site is brought down by overloading it with false requests for data

**design specification** a document that specifically states how a program development project will be completed

**desktop** a screen on which graphical elements such as icons, buttons, windows, links, and dialog boxes are displayed

**desktop computer** a personal computer system designed to fit on the top of a desk

**desktop publishing (DTP) software** a type of software that enables a user to produce documents that closely resemble those done by printing companies

**dexterity** hand-eye coordination

**diagnostic utility** a utility program that assesses a computer's components and system software programs and creates a report identifying problems

**dialog box** an element in a graphical user interface that displays a rectangular box providing information to a user and/or requesting information from a user; usually displays temporarily and disappears once the user has entered the requested information

**dial-up access** a method for accessing the Internet in which a user can connect to the Internet using a computer and a modem to dial into an ISP or online service over a standard telephone line

**dial-up modem** a modem (electronic device) that converts digital signals into analog form so they can be sent using an analog communication medium

**digital** composed of discrete bits (1s and 0s) understood by computers

**digital cable** a technology capable of offering a wide selection of TV stations, typically more than 200, with the capability of expanding to 2,000 stations

**digital camera** a type of camera that records and stores images, including people, scenery, documents, and products, in a digitized form that can be entered into and stored by a computer

**digital cash** a system that allows a customer to pay for online purchases by transmitting a number from one computer to another computer; issued by a bank, each digital cash number represents a specified amount of real money

**digital divide** a term created to describe the gap between those who have access to computers and the Internet and those who do not

**digital ink technology** process in which a digitizer (a grid of tiny wires) is laid under or over an LCD screen to create a magnetic field that can capture the movement of a special-purpose pen and record the movement on the LCD screen; the effect is like writing on paper with liquid ink

**digital media** a digital form of media that can be stored on a computer

**Digital Millennium Copyright Act of 1998 (DMCA)** legislation updating copyright protection to bring it in line with the technical changes brought about by computer technology that generally prohibits people from taking action to break down software encryption programs and other safeguards that copyright holders have established to control access to their works, including DVDs, software, and digitized books and music

**digital subscriber line (DSL) Internet service** a high-speed Internet connection using telephone lines

**digital versatile disc (DVD)** an extremely high-capacity optical disc; also called a digital video disc (DVD)

**digital video recorder (DVR)** a digital TV cable box that allows for pausing and rewinding of live TV and quick, easy, intelligent TV recording for later viewing

**digitizing** the process of converting analog information to digital information; sometimes referred to as going digital

**digitizing pen** an electronic pen device, resembling a standard writing pen, used with a drawing tablet to simulate drawing on paper

**direct access** a storage technique that allows a computer to immediately locate and retrieve a program, information, or data similar to the way music stored on a CD-ROM is accessed

**direct thermal printer** a printer that uses heat to transfer an impression onto paper

**disaster recovery plan** a safety system that allows a company to restore its systems after a complete loss of data; generally includes procedures for data backup, remotely stored backup copies, and redundant systems

**disk defragmenter** a utility program that scans hard disks and reorganizes files and unused disk space, allowing the operating system to locate and access files and data more quickly

**disk pack** a vertically aligned group of hard disks mounted inside a disk drive on a large computer system; when activated, electromagnetic read/write heads record information and/or read stored data by moving inward and outward between the disks

**disk scanner** a utility that examines hard disks and their contents to identify potential problems, such as bad sectors

**disk toolkit** software that contains utility programs that let users identify and correct various problems on a hard disk

**display device** the screen, or monitor, of a personal computer; also called a monitor

**display window** a rectangular area of the screen used to display a program, data, or information

**distance learning** the electronic transfer of information from a college or publisher's host computer system to a student's computer at a remote site and the transmission of required responses from the student's computer to the host computer system; a course presented in this manner is called an online course

**distributed database** a relatively new type of database model where databases function in a networked environment, with each computer storing a portion of the total amount of data in the network

**distribution management system** a common application of information systems involving the transportation of goods from the manufacturer to the customer

**divide-and-conquer approach** a methodology for software development that breaks down large problems into small ones, and then tackles the smaller problems first

**docking station** a laptop computer accessory that provides additional ports plus (typically) a charger for the laptop's battery, extra disk drives, and other peripherals

**document object model (DOM)** a version of HTML that allows object-oriented Web page development

**documentation** any written manual, specification, or commentary upon a computer system

**domain name** a portion of an Internet address, such as .com or .edu, that is used to segment Internet addresses into broad categories

**domain suffix** the last part of a URL, identifying the type of organization hosting the site

**dot pitch** the distance between the centers of pixels on a display

**dot-com company** a Web-based e-commerce company with a Web site in the .com domain

**dot-matrix printer** an impact printer that forms and prints characters in a manner similar to the way numbers appear on a football scoreboard

**dots per inch (dpi)** a measurement in which resolution (text and image quality) is expressed as the number of dots occupying one square inch

**Double Data Rate SDRAM (DDR SDRAM)** a type of random access memory (RAM) chip that can transfer data twice as fast as SDRAM because it reads twice as much data during each clock cycle

**download** to transmit data, such as a digitized text file, sound, or picture from a remote site to one's own computer via a network

**downtime** time during which the system is unavailable

**draft quality** a print quality acceptable for most in-house needs, but not for professional-looking documents

**drawing program** software that provides an intuitive interface through which a user can draw pictures, make sketches, create various shapes, and edit images

**drawing tablet** a tablet with wires under the surface that, when used with a digitizing pen, allows the user to create and capture drawings that can be entered and stored on a computer

**driver** a small program that enables the computer to communicate with devices connected to it, such as a keyboard or a printer

**drop-down menu** a menu containing various lower-level options associated with main menu options; also called pull-down menu

**dual-core processor** a central processing unit (CPU) chip that contains two complete processors along with their cache memory

**dumb scanner** a scanner that can only capture and input a scanned image; once entered into a computer, the image cannot be edited or altered

**DVD drive** a drive that uses lasers to record and read data to and from a DVD

**DVD-R** an extremely high-capacity disc capable of holding several gigabytes of data, such as a movie or the entire contents of a telephone book listing every resident in the United States; acronym for digital versatile disc–recordable

**DVD-ROM** an extremely high-capacity disc capable of holding several gigabytes of data, such as a movie or the entire contents of a telephone book listing every resident in the United States; acronym for digital versatile disc–read-only memory

**DVD-RW** a type of DVD that allows recorded data to be erased and recorded over numerous times without damaging the disc; acronym for digital versatile disc–rewritable

**Dynamic HTML (DHTML)** a general term used to describe a variety of new features in HTML programming that allow for more responsive, graphically interesting Web page development

**Dynamic RAM (DRAM)** a type of random access memory (RAM) chip that eventually loses its contents without a continuous supply of electrical energy

**dynamic routing** a capability of the Internet to send a given packet via a different route depending on traffic circumstances

# E

**earth station** transmission stations on the ground

**e-commerce venue** a Web site where e-commerce transactions occur

**educational and reference software** programs that facilitate learning, such as software designed to enable a user to learn algebra, or that provide reference information, such as encyclopedias and dictionaries

**electronic check (e-check)** a payment method that directly initiates an electronic transfer of funds from the customer's checking account to the merchant

**electronic commerce (e-commerce)** a set of business Internet technologies in which business information, products, services, and payments are exchanged between sellers and customers and between businesses

**electronic data interchange (EDI)** companies' use of computer networks to buy, sell, or otherwise exchange information with each other electronically

**electronic data processing (EDP)** an old term for an information system

**electronic funds transfer (EFT)** a general term for the transfer of money over the Internet

**electronic mail (e-mail)** a text, voice, or video message sent or received remotely, over a computer network or the system by which such a message is sent

**electronic office** an information system dedicated to automating an office environment; also called an office information system (OIS)

**electronic signature (e-signature)** a code attached to an e-mail that uniquely identifies the sender of the message

**electronic wallet (e-wallet)** a software application that stores a user's personal, credit card, and shipping information; the application may store one set of user information or multiple sets that allow a user to choose which credit card or shipping information will apply to a certain purchase

**e-mail** a text, voice, or video message sent or received remotely, over a computer network or the system by which such a message is sent; short for electronic mail

**embedded computer** a specialized computer, usually housed on a single chip, that is part of a larger system, device, or machine

**encryption** the process of converting readable information, or plaintext, into unreadable information, or ciphertext, to prevent unauthorized access and usage

**encryption key** a special type of encryption code used to encrypt (encode) information

**entertainment software** category of programs that includes interactive computer games, videos, and music

**entity** a person, place, thing, or event in a database

**ergonomics** the study of the interaction between humans and the equipment they use

**espionage virus** a virus that does no damage, but allows someone to enter the system later for the purpose of stealing data or spying

**e-tailer** an individual or company that carries out business-to-consumer e-commerce over the Web

**Ethernet protocol** a bus topology type protocol that many local area networks use

**ethics** rules we use to determine the right and wrong things to do in our lives

**e-ticket** an airline ticket purchased over the Internet

**executable statement** a statement within a program that, when run by the program, performs an action

**executing** the CPU process of performing an operation specified in a program instruction

**execution time (E-time)** the time required for the arithmetic/logic unit to decode and execute an instruction and store the result

**executive support system (ESS)** an information system tailored to the needs of upper management

**expansion bus** a motherboard component that provides for communication between the processor and peripheral devices

**expansion card** an electronic circuit board that can be inserted onto the motherboard inside a computer to add new capabilities to a computer; examples include sound cards, graphics cards, and network interface cards; also called an adapter

**expansion slot** an opening in a computer motherboard where an expansion board can be inserted (installed)

**expert system** a sophisticated decision support system (DSS) data model that attempts to model an expert's knowledge of a topic

**exporting** the process of saving a data file with a different file format

**ExpressCard** a type of expansion board (card) developed by PCMCIA for use with small computers such as notebooks and laptops; it has replaced the PC card and CardBus in popularity

**Extended Binary Coded Decimal Interchange Code (EBCDIC)** a coding scheme used mainly on large servers and mainframe computers

**Extensible HTML (XHTML)** a scripting language comprised of elements of HTML and XML, used in Web page programming

**Extensible Markup Language (XML)** a scripting language that not only defines the content of a Web page but also organizes data so that computers can communicate with each other directly, without human intervention

**external modem** a modem that works in the same fashion as an internal modem, but is a stand-alone device connected by cable to a computer's motherboard

**external storage** a type of storage that consists of devices and media used to record information and data permanently so it can later be retrieved, edited, modified, displayed, or printed; also called permanent storage, secondary storage, or auxiliary storage

**extranet** a network that makes certain kinds of information available to users within the organization and other kinds of information available to outsiders, such as companies doing business with the organization

# F

**facsimile machine** an electronic device that can send and receive copies (facsimiles, or faxes) of documents through a telephone line; also called a fax machine

**Fair Use** the right by law to use copyrighted materials under certain conditions

**fax** an electronic document that is transmitted or received over a telephone line using a fax machine or fax/modem board

**fax/modem card** an expansion card that serves as a modem and provides many of the features of a stand-alone fax machine

**fax program** software needed to send and receive a fax; allows users to compose, send, receive, print, and store faxes

**feasibility study** a study conducted to investigate how difficult a project might be to complete and how much it might cost

**fetching** the CPU process of retrieving instructions or data from memory for execution

**Fiber Distributed Data Interface (FDDI)** a type of network software for ring networks dispersed over a large area and connected by fiber-optic cables; the software links the dispersed networks together using a protocol that passes a token over long distances

**fiber-optic cable** a cable consisting of optical fibers that allows data to be transmitted as light signals through tiny hair-like glass fibers

**field** in a table created by a database management system application, a location into which one kind of information about an entity, such as name or address, is entered; the smallest element of data in a database

**file** a named body of data that resides on a storage medium

**file allocation table (FAT) file** a section of a disk that keeps track of the disk's contents

**file compression** the process of shrinking the size of a file so it occupies less disk space

**file extension** a period (.) and a set of characters following a file name that identifies the type of file

**file manager** an operating system function that performs basic file management functions, including keeping track of used and unused disk storage space and allowing a user to view stored files and to format, copy, rename, delete, and sort stored files

**file processing** manipulation of the data within a database

**file server** a special type of computer that allows other computers to share its resources

**file specification** an optional additional element in a URL, following the domain suffix, that indicates the name of a file or file folder

**File Transfer Protocol (FTP)** a transmission standard that enables a user to send and receive large files, such as reports, over the Internet

**filtering program** software that can prevent access to sites, keep track of sites visited, limit connection time, record keystrokes, prevent downloading, and allow users to view only those sites that have been accessed

**financial electronic data interchange (FEDI)** a form of EDI technology used to transmit payments and associated remittance information electronically among a payer, payee, and their respective banks

**find** a software program feature that allows a user to quickly locate a number or a particular type of text within a file

**fingerprint scanner** a biometric device that reads, records, and recognizes fingerprints

**firewall** software and hardware systems that place an invisible wall around the internal network, protecting it from unauthorized material from the Internet

**fixed storage medium** a storage medium that is built into the system unit during the manufacturing process

**flaming** the act of transmitting negative comments to someone via the Internet

**Flash** a commonly used format for online, downloadable movies, created by Adobe

**flash memory** a type of read-only memory that can be erased and reprogrammed quickly, or updated; also called flash ROM

**flash ROM** a type of read-only memory that can quickly be erased and reprogrammed quickly, or updated; also called flash memory

**flat file database** traditional data file storage system that lacks the ability to interrelate data in an organizational structure because it contains only one table or file

**flat-panel display** a type of computer monitor that allows display units to be smaller, thinner, and lighter so they can be used with small computers, such as notebook computers, personal digital assistants (PDAs), and other devices

**flowchart** a graphic representation of a programming algorithm

**foot mouse** a foot-controlled mouse that allows a user with carpal tunnel syndrome or other hand or wrist injuries to use a computer

**form** in a database management system, a document used for entering information to be stored in one or more linked records

**FORTRAN** a programming language developed in the 1960s and used primarily for the solving of math and science problems; acronym for FORmula TRANslator

**forum** an Internet application consisting of an electronically stored list of messages that can be accessed and read by anyone having access to the bulletin board; a user having access can post messages, read existing messages, or delete messages; also called a message board

**frame** a single still image; many frames, shown together in rapid succession, create the illusion of movement

**frame rate** the number of frames that a system is capable of producing and displaying per second; if this rate falls much below 20 frames per second, video begins to appear choppy

**freeware** a computer program that is provided free to users by its creator but for which the creator usually retains the copyright

**frequency range** a span of changes reflected in the transmission of voice or sound signals

**front-end interface program** the interface program of a database, through which the user enters data and requests information

**full-duplex transmission** the simultaneous transmission of information or data in both directions at the same time

**function** a section of code containing instructions for a specific purpose; also called a routine

**functional specification** a document that describes what an information system must do, but not exactly how it is supposed to do it

**fuzzy logic system** an artificial intelligence term that relates to the use of inexact conditions and criteria

# G

**Gantt chart** a chart that identifies beginning and end times of tasks required for the completion of a system development project

**garbage in, garbage out (GIGO)** a database related proverb meaning that if errors are entered into a database, it will produce erroneous output; also refers to all situations involving incorrect user input into a computer

**gateway** hardware and/or software that allows communication between dissimilar networks

**general-purpose computer** a computer that allows the user to perform a range of complex processes and calculations

**genetic algorithm** an artificial intelligence design concept that uses tiny, evolutionary changes to solve a problem by trying many solutions, testing them, and selecting the best, then trying more variations of the best survivors of each successive generation

**geosynchronous orbit** the path of a satellite orbiting the earth at the same speed as the earth's rotation, making the satellite appear stationary when viewed from the ground

**GIF file format** a file format, indicated with a .gif extension, that provides compressed bitmap images with limited animation capability; acronym for Graphics Interchange Format

**gigabyte (GB)** unit of memory equal to 1,073,741,824 bytes

**Global Unique Identifier (GUID)** an Internet tracking device using unique identification numbers that can be coded into both hardware and software

**gold release** the published, generally available version of software

**grammar checker** a part of a program or a stand-alone application that automatically searches for errors in grammar, usage, capitalization, or punctuation and suggests correct alternatives

**graphic data** still images, including photographs, mathematical charts, and drawings

**graphical user interface (GUI)** a computer interface that enables a user to control the computer and launch commands by pointing and clicking at graphical objects such as windows, icons, and menu items

**graphics** computer-generated pictures produced on a computer screen, paper, or film, ranging from a simple line or bar chart to a detailed, colorful image or picture; also called graphical image

**graphics and multimedia software** software that allows users to work with graphics, video, and audio files

**graphics card** a circuit board residing on the motherboard inside the system unit that converts the digital signals produced by the computer into analog signals and sends them through a cable to the monitor; also called a video card or video adapter

**graphics coprocessor** a chip designed specifically for processing image-intensive applications, such as Web pages and computer-aided design programs

**graphics tablet** a flat tablet used together with a pen-like stylus or a crosshair cursor; to capture an image, the user grasps a stylus or crosshair cursor and traces an image or drawing placed on the tablet surface

**grid** a matrix formed by the intersections of rows and columns, as in a spreadsheet

**groupware** communications software that allows groups of people on a network to share information and to collaborate on various projects, such as designing new products or preparing employee manuals; also called collaboration software

# H

**hacker** an individual who attempts to break into computer security systems

**hacking code** writing code without carefully planning and structuring the program

**half-duplex transmission** a transmission method in which transmissions can flow in both directions but not at the same time

**hand geometry system** a biometric device that recognizes individuals based on the structure of their hands

**handheld computer** a personal computer small enough to fit into a person's hand; also called handheld, pocket PC, or palmtop

**hard copy** a permanent, tangible version of output, such as a letter printed on paper

**hard disk** a magnetic secondary storage medium consisting of one or more rigid metal platters (disks) mounted on a metal shaft and sealed in a container, called a disk drive, that contains an access mechanism used to write and read data

**hard drive** a device for reading and writing to the magnetic storage medium known as a hard disk; consists of one or more rigid metal platters (disks) mounted on a metal shaft in a container that contains an access mechanism

**hardware** all physical components that compose the system unit and other devices connected to it, such as a keyboard or monitor; items peripheral to the computer itself

**hardware design** the specifications of computer hardware such as CPUs, video cards, and memory chips; as a career, it is part electrical engineering and part programming and requires advanced skills

**hertz** a unit of measure that refers to the number of cycles per second

**high-definition television (HDTV)** television technology that uses digital signals instead of analog signals to display high-quality pictures on the screen; a screen with more lines and more pixels for a higher resolution

**high-level language** an English-like computer language used for writing application programs

**hi-jacker** a program that directs a Web page visitor's browser to a different Web address than the visitor intended to go to; usually directs visitors to advertisements

**home page** the first page usually displayed when a user accesses a Web site; often contains links to other pages at that site or to other Web sites

**host computer** a large and powerful computer to which smaller computers are connected in a network, and which manages all user activity occurring on the network; also called a network server

**hot plugging** the procedure of disconnecting one device and connecting another device to a computer while the computer is still running

**hot swapping** the capability of switching back and forth among various types of PC cards while a notebook or similar computer is running

**hotspot** a location that has one or more wireless access points

**hub** an electronic device used in a local area network that links groups of computers to one another and allows computers to communicate with one another

**hub-and-spoke topology** a network topology in which multiple computers and peripheral devices are linked to a central computer, called a host, in a point-to-point configuration; also called a star topology

**hybrid database** a type of database that combines more than one data model

**hybrid topology** a combination of networks having different topologies, such as a star network and a ring network

**hyperlink** an address that links to a document or to a Web page; also called a Web link

**hypertext document** a Web document created using a Web language, such as HTML or XML, that contains one or more hyperlinks (links) to other Web documents or sites

**Hypertext Markup Language (HTML)** a set of codes specifying typefaces, images, and links within text, used to create pages for the World Wide Web

**Hypertext Transfer Protocol (HTTP)** the communications standard used to transfer documents on the World Wide Web

**hyperthreading** a technology developed by Intel that allows its series of microprocessors to execute multi-threaded software applications simultaneously and in parallel rather than processing threads in linear fashion, thereby greatly increasing processing speed

# I

**icon** a graphic symbol that represents a software program, command, or feature

**identity theft** the stealing of an individual's personal information, such as social security number and/or credit card numbers, via hacking into a database on the Internet

**if-then statement** a decision statement in a programming language that decides upon two or more possible courses of action

**image-editing program** software that allows a user to touch up, modify, and enhance image quality

**immersiveness** a measurement of how convincing a virtual environment is, how "immersed" the user feels in the virtual reality

**impact printer** a printer that prints much like a typewriter, by striking an inked ribbon against the paper

**implementation** the phase of a project in which the actual work of putting the system together is done, including creating a prototype and completing the programming

**importing** the act of loading a file that uses a different data file type than the application normally requires

**individual application software** programs individuals use at work or at home

**industrial espionage** the stealing of corporate information

**Industry Standard Architecture (ISA) bus** the most common type of expansion bus that allows devices such as a mouse or modem to communicate with the processor

**inference engine** a software component of an expert system that processes input and a knowledge base to make logical conclusions

**infinite loop** a software bug that involves the creation of a loop with no endpoint, and which may cause the computer to crash

**information** data that has been processed to make it useful for a specific purpose, such as making a decision

**information processing** the actions performed through transactions with a database; also called data processing

**information processing cycle** a cycle during which a computer enters, processes, outputs, and/or stores information

**information system (IS)** a system involving hardware, software, data, people, and procedures that is usually used to help manage a company

**infrared technology** a communications technology that provides for line-of-sight wireless links between PCs and other computing devices, such as keyboards and printers

**ink-jet printer** a nonimpact printer that forms images by spraying thousands of tiny droplets of electrically charged ink onto a page; the printed images are in dot-matrix format, but of a higher quality than images printed by dot-matrix printers

**input** data that is entered into a computer or other device or the act of reading in such data

**input device** any hardware component that enables a computer user to enter data and programs into a computer system; keyboards, point-and-click devices, and scanners are among the more popular input devices, and a desktop or laptop computer system may include one or more input devices

**instant messaging (IM)** a form of communicating online in real time that includes a pop-up window that alerts a user when a message is received

**instant messaging (IM) software** software that allows for communicating online in real time that causes pop-up windows to interrupt users when a message is received

**instruction register** a memory location (register) where instructions being used for processing are stored

**instruction time (I-time)** the amount of time required to fetch an instruction from a register

**integrated circuit** a small electrical device consisting of tiny transistors and other circuit parts on a piece of semiconductor material; also called a microprocessor chip

**Integrated Services Digital Network (ISDN) line** a special digital telephone line that can be used to dial into the Internet and transmit and receive information at very high speeds, ranging from 64 kilobits per second (64,000 bits per second) to 128 kilobits per second; a line that requires the use of a special ISDN modem

**integrated software program** software that is packaged together and is designed to work together seamlessly

**intellectual property** creative endeavors that are claimed as the personal property of the person who created them

**intelligent agent** a program or interface to a program that behaves intelligently, attempting to make complex operations easier and faster for a user by employing artificial intelligence techniques

**intelligent scanner** a scanner that uses optical character recognition (OCR) software to create an image that can be manipulated (edited or altered) with a word processor or other application program

**interdependence** the relationship between businesses and the outside vendors who help create, market, and distribute their products

**interface** a plug-in slot on a computer to which you can connect a device, such as a printer or, in the case of accessing the Internet, a telephone line; also called a port

**internal modem** a type of modem inserted into an expansion slot on the computer's motherboard

**Internet** a worldwide network of computers linked together via communications software and media for the purpose of sharing information; the largest and best-known network in the world; also called the Net

**Internet Protocol (IP)** a set of standards for the sending and receiving of information over the Internet

**Internet Protocol (IP) address** a numeric address, similar to a phone number, that locates a specific computer on the Internet; URLs are translated to IP addresses when connections are made

**Internet service provider (ISP)** an organization that has a permanent connection to the Internet and provides temporary access to individuals and others for free or for a fee

**Internet telephony** a combination of hardware and software that allows two or more people with sufficiently good connections to use the Internet to make telephone-style calls without long-distance telephone charges; also called Voice over IP (VoIP)

**interpreter** a type of language-translating software that reads, translates, and executes one instruction at a time

**intra-business electronic commerce** a Web-based technology that allows a business to handle transactions that occur within the business; although no revenues are generated, increased efficiency enables the business to save money by lowering its operating costs

**intranet** a network normally belonging to a large business or organization that is accessible only by the business or organization's members, employees, or other authorized users

**iris recognition system** a biometric device capable of identifying individuals through the unique patterns of their irises

# J

**Java** a third-generation programming language used to write full-scale applications and small applications, known as applets, for use on the World Wide Web

**Java Virtual Machine (JVM)** part of the Java programming language that converts the general Java instructions into commands that a device or computer can understand

**JavaScript** a scripting language developed by Sun Microsystems

**joining** a process that allows a query to pull up data from more than one record source by matching data from fields in various record files

**joystick** an input device (named after the control lever used to fly fighter planes) consisting of a small box that contains a vertical lever that, when pushed in a certain direction, moves the graphics cursor correspondingly on the screen; it is often used for computer games

**JPEG file format** a file format, identified with a .jpg or .jpeg extension, for still images

**jump drive** a storage device that plugs into a USB port on a computer or other mobile device; also called a USB drive, thumb drive, or pen drive

**just-in-time (JIT)** a strategy that provides for the manufacture of products in time for delivery, and for the delivery of products at the exact time they are needed

**just-in-time (JIT) distribution** computerized distribution management system that allows companies to produce products to match market demand in order to shrink inventories and increase profits

# K

**kernel** an operating system program that manages computer components, peripheral devices, and memory; maintains the system clock and loads other operating system and application programs as they are required

**key** an attribute that can be used to identify a set of information and therefore provide a means to search a database

**keyboard** an electronically controlled hardware component used to enter alphanumeric data (letters, numbers, and special characters); the keys on most keyboards are arranged similarly to those on a typewriter

**keylogger** a program that stores keystrokes in a file such as a credit card number or password for later analysis; also called a keystroke logger

**keystroke logger** a program that stores keystrokes in a file such as a credit card number or password for later analysis; also called a keylogger

**keywords** words used to tell a search engine what information to look for on the Web; also called search terms

**kilobyte (KB)** unit of memory equal to 1,024 bytes

**knowledge base** a specially structured database of information an expert system uses to make intelligent decisions

**knowledge engineer** an individual who creates knowledge bases

# L

**label printer** a small printer designed to print adhesive labels

**land** flat, unburned area on a compact disc

**landscape format** a printing format in which a printed page is wider than it is tall

**language translator** a special type of program needed to translate (convert) high-level language programs into machine-language programs so they can be executed by the computer

**laptop computer** a computer small enough to be placed on a lap or carried by its user from place to place; also called a notebook computer

**laser printer** a nonimpact printer that produces output of exceptional quality using a technology similar to that of photocopy machines

**law** an external rule that if violated, is punishable by society

**legacy database** an older database that has been updated and maintained for years, and which may contain helpful, undiscovered information

**legal software** programs designed to help a user analyze, plan, and prepare a variety of legal documents, including wills and trusts

**letter quality** a print quality preferred for important business letters and documents; available with a variety of printers including laser printers

**level 1 cache memory** a type of cache memory that is built into the architecture of microprocessor chips, providing faster access to the instructions and data residing in cache memory

**level 2 cache memory** a type of cache memory that, in current processors, may be built into the architecture of microprocessor chips; on older computers, it may consist of high-speed SRAM chips placed on the motherboard or on a card inserted into a slot in the computer

**level 3 cache memory** a type of cache memory that is available on computers that have level 2 cache, or advanced transfer cache, and is separate from the microprocessor

**line printer** a line printer is a high-speed printer capable of printing an entire line at one time

**Linux** an operating system based on AT&T's UNIX and developed by a Finnish programmer named Linus Torvalds; original version is a nonproprietary operating system and is available for free to the public

**liquid crystal display (LCD)** a display device in which liquid crystals are sandwiched between two sheets of material

**local area network (LAN)** a computer network physically confined to a relatively small geographical area, such as a single building or a college campus

**local area network (LAN) Internet connection** a way to connect to the Internet by connecting users to an ISP on a direct wire at speeds 20 or more times faster than can be achieved through a dial-up modem

**local bus** a high-speed bus that connects devices such as disk drives to the CPU

**locomotion** broad movements such as walking

**logic bomb virus** a virus that is triggered by an event or the passing of a certain time; also called a time bomb virus

**logic error** in programming, an incorrect instruction stated in correct syntax

**looping** the process of repeating instructions in a computer program

**low-level language** a computer language that is closer in form to the thought processes computers use and less like natural language such as English, written in binary language consisting of 1s and 0s; language also called machine code

# M

**machine code** a computer language that is closer in form to the thought processes computers use and less like natural language such as English, written in binary language consisting of 1s and 0s; also called low-level language

**machine cycle** a cycle a computer uses during which four basic operations are performed: (1) fetching an instruction, (2) decoding the instruction, (3) executing the instruction, and (4) storing the result

**machine language** a program consisting entirely of 0s and 1s that a computer can understand and execute quickly

**Macintosh OS** the first profitable graphical user interface released with Apple's Macintosh computers in 1984; it later became a model for other GUIs

**macro** a sequence of instructions designed to accomplish a specific task and generally executed by issuing a single command

**macro virus** a form of virus that infects the data files of commonly used applications such as word processors and spreadsheets

**magnetic disk storage** secondary storage that provides for the storage of programs, data, and information on a magnetic storage medium, such as magnetic tape

**magnetic storage device** a storage device that works by applying electrical charges to iron filings on magnetic storage media so that each filing represents a 0 or a 1

**magnetic tape storage** a type of secondary storage for large computer systems that uses removable reels of magnetic tape; the tape contains tracks, each of which contains metallic particles that are magnetized, or not magnetized, to represent 0 and 1 bits

**mail server** a computer used to facilitate the sending and receiving of electronic mail messages

**main memory** addressable storage locations directly controlled by the central processing unit (CPU) used to store programs while they are being executed and data while it is being processed; also called primary storage

**main menu** a horizontal or vertical bar in a software program that shows the highest-level command options; also called menu bar

**mainframe computer** a large, powerful, expensive computer system capable of accommodating hundreds of users doing different computing tasks

**malware** malicious software

**management information system (MIS)** an information system that turns raw data into information so that managers can make knowledgeable decisions

**markup language** a set of specifications describing the characteristics of elements that appear on a Web page, including headings, paragraphs, backgrounds, and lists

**megabyte (MB)** unit of memory equal to 1,048,576 bytes

**memory access time** the amount of time required for the processor to access (read) data, instructions, and information from memory

**memory card** a flash memory storage device similar to a USB flash drive; used in digital cameras, digital video cameras, printers, portable music players, cell phones, and other handheld devices

**memory resident** a characteristic describing programs, including operating systems, that remain in memory while the computer is in operation

**mental interface** systems that read the minds of their users by monitoring brainwave activity and react by controlling the computer

**menu** an onscreen set of options from which a user can make selections by clicking the option with a mouse or by typing one or more keystrokes

**menu bar** a horizontal or vertical bar in a software program that shows the highest-level command options; also called main menu

**merchant account** an account in which money is held until an online transaction has been completed and that requires e-tailers to pay a monthly fee to maintain this account plus a commission on each transaction

**message board** an Internet application consisting of an electronically stored list of messages that can be accessed and read by anyone having access to the bulletin board; a user having access can post messages, read existing messages, or delete messages; also called a forum

**metadata** information that helps explain the nature of other data

**metalanguage** a language for describing other languages

**metropolitan area network (MAN)** a wide area network limited to a specific geographical area, such as a city or town

**micro payment** a software system that enables buyers to purchase low-cost items such as newspapers over the Internet

**microcomputer** a single-user computer capable of performing its own input, processing, output, and storage; also called a personal computer (PC)

**microprocessor** the part of a computer that interprets and carries out instructions that operate the computer and manages the computer's devices and resources; consists of components, each of which performs specific functions; also called the central processing unit (CPU)

**microprocessor chip** a small electrical device consisting of tiny transistors and other circuit parts on a piece of semiconductor material; also called an integrated circuit

**microwave system** a communications technology that transmits data in the form of high-frequency radio signals through the atmosphere from one microwave station to another microwave station, or from a microwave station to a satellite and then back to earth to another microwave station

**midrange server** a powerful computer capable of accommodating hundreds of client computers or terminals (users) at the same time; also known as a minicomputer

**mirrored hard drive** a drive containing duplicate data from another hard drive so that if one fails, the data is not lost

**mobile commerce (m-commerce)** the carrying out of e-commerce activities through the use of small portable computers such as wrist or handheld computers

**modem** a hardware device that translates signals from digital to analog and from analog to digital, making it possible for digital computers to communicate over analog telephone lines

**modem card** enables computers to communicate via telephone lines and other communications media

**modem port** connects a modem card to a telephone line; the cable used to connect to a telephone line is a standard telephone cable with an RJ-11 connector

**moderator** an individual charged with maintaining order and civility in a virtual environment, such as a chat room

**modular code** code created in modules, with each module handling separate components of a program

**modularity** a measurement of how well written software is, based upon how well divided the source code is into modules

**modulation** the process of changing a digital signal into an analog signal

**monitor** the screen, or display device, on which computer output appears

**moral realism** a school of ethical thought that believes ethical principles have solid objective foundations and are not based on subjective human reasoning

**moral relativism** a school of ethical thought that believes ethical principles are not absolute and unchanging, but subjective and variable from society to society, from situation to situation, or from individual to individual

**motherboard** the main circuit board inside a personal computer to which other circuit boards can be connected; contains electrical pathways, called traces, etched onto it that allow data to move from one component to another

**mouse** an input device that, when moved about on a flat surface, causes a pointer on the screen to move in the same direction

**mouse pad** a rubberized pad with a smooth fabric surface that facilitates use of a mouse

**mouse pointer** a type of cursor resembling a small on-screen arrow, movements of which correspond to movements made with a mouse

**MOV file format** an Apple movie media format, identified with a .mov extension

**MP3 file format** a file format for storing digital sound files using a data compression system

**MPEG file format** a commonly used file format, identified with an .mpeg (or .mpg) extension, for storing compressed video files; the movie equivalent of the MP3 music format

**MPEG2 file format** the high-quality movie format DVD players use

**multi-core processor** a central-processing unit (CPU) chip that contains more than two separate processors on a single chip

**multifunction device (MFD)** a piece of equipment that provides a variety of capabilities including scanning, copying, printing, and sometimes faxing

**multimedia** the use of sound, images, video, and text mixed together to create a work or presentation

**multimedia authoring software** program that allows a user to create stand-alone multimedia products

**multimedia database** a database model that allows the storage of pictures, movies, sounds, and hyperlinked fields

**multimedia developer** a graphic artist, digital sound editor, or animation specialist who creates and enhances Web content with images, sounds, and movies

**multimedia development** the use of computers to create and enhance Web content with images, sounds, and movies

**multipartite virus** viruses that have the ability to attack in several different ways

**multitasking** the ability of an operating system to run more than one software program at a time; the use of different areas in Windows RAM makes this possible

**multithreading** a carefully designed program that enables several threads to execute at the same time without interfering with each other

**multi-user computer system** computer that can accommodate many users concurrently

**multi-user operating system** an operating system designed for use with large computer systems and capable of handling several users at the same time

**Musical Instrument Digital Interface (MIDI)** a type of data file for instrumental music

**mutation** random variations in the designs genetic algorithms generate

# N

**narrowband medium** a communications medium capable of carrying a smaller amount of data at slow speeds

**native format** a file format that is specific to the application being used

**natural interface** an interface between human and machine that more closely approximates the normal communications between people

**natural-language interface** an interface that allows programmers to describe what they want a computer to do using natural (human) language rather than writing programs in highly structured programming languages

**navigation** the science of moving a mobile robot through an environment

**Net** short for Internet, a worldwide network of computers linked together via communications software and media for the purpose of sharing information; the largest and best-known network in the world

**net neutrality** a principle of even-handedness in the treatment of all network traffic

**netbook** a portable computer, smaller in size than a full-size notebook, designed for e-mail and Internet access

**netiquette** rules directing polite behavior online

**NetWare** an operating system developed by Novell, Inc. for microcomputer-based personal computers; largely replaced by Open Enterprise Server (OES)

**network** a group of two or more computers, software, and other devices that are connected by means of one or more communications media

**network administration** the operation and maintenance of a company network, including a LAN, WAN, network segment, intranet, and/or interactions with the Internet

**network administrator** the person whose job it is to oversee and maintain a company's network

**network architecture** the way a network is designed and built, just as an architect might design a new building or other facility

**network firewall** a combination of hardware and software that screens all communications entering and leaving networked computers to prevent unauthorized access

**network interface card (NIC)** expansion board that allows a computer to be networked

**network operating system (NOS)** an operating system in which a network server controls the flow of messages from client computers and also provides services such as file access and printing

**network port** connects a computer system to a local area network

**network server** a large and powerful computer to which smaller computers are connected in a network, and which manages all user activity occurring on the network; also called a host computer

**network sniffer** a software package that displays network traffic data such as which resources are being used or which Web sites are being visited

**network topology** the way computers and peripherals are configured to form networks

**neural network** an artificial intelligence technology that mimics the way nerve cells are connected in the human brain; information is supplied to the neural network to train it to recognize certain patterns, resulting in a program capable of making predictions, such as weather forecasts and fluctuations of stock values

**niche information system** an information system focused on a particular set of customers, for example a system designed for dental offices; also called a vertical market package

**node** a component connected to a network server, such as a personal computer or a printer

**nonimpact printer** a printer that uses electricity, heat, laser technology, or photographic techniques to produce output

**nonprocedural language** a programming language, such as a scripting language, that explains what the computer should do in English-like terms but not precisely how the computer should do it

**nonresident** a characteristic describing a program that does not reside in memory while the computer is running, but instead resides on a storage medium, such as a hard disk, until needed

**nonvolatile memory** a type of computer storage specifically designed to hold information, even when the power is switched off

**normalization** a process performed in a relational database to eliminate duplication of data (redundancy)

**normative ethics** determining a standard or "norm" of ethical rule that underlies ethical behavior

**notebook computer** a computer small enough to be placed on a lap or carried by its user from place to place; also called a laptop computer

**nuisance virus** a virus that usually does no real damage but is rather just an inconvenience

**numeric data** consisting of numbers only

# O

**object** a programming term indicating a single element that contains both data and the code to manipulate the data

**object-based graphics program** a program that creates pictures by means of creating, editing, and combining mathematically defined geometric shapes; also called vector-based graphics program

**object linking and embedding (OLE)** a feature of Windows operating systems and applications that allows material from one application to be imported into a document created in another application and linked in such a way that when the material is updated in the originating application, it is automatically updated in the application into which it has been imported

**object-oriented database** a database that stores data in the form of objects; each object contains both the data related to the object and the actions that the user might want to perform on that object

**object-oriented programming (OOP)** a basis for programming language design developed in the 1980s

**office information system (OIS)** an information system dedicated to automating an office environment; also called an electronic office

**online analytical processing (OLAP) system** software that focuses on providing better ways to analyze the mass of data in large databases and massively distributed data systems, such as the Internet, in order to produce more useful results

**online auction** a peer-to-peer online transaction venue where consumers can place items for sale, bid on auctioned items, or (in some cases) buy items outright; an example is eBay

**online banking** the process of using a computer, a modem, and an Internet connection to conduct routine banking transactions; through this service, a user can make arrangements with the bank that will allow the user to pay bills, transfer funds among various accounts, and transact other financial activities

**online catalog** a virtual presentation of information about products and services similar to a traditional paper catalog; online catalogs can include multimedia such as voice, animation, and video clips

**online gambling** using a computer and Internet access to gamble online

**online predator** an individual who attempts to influence underage young people by conversing with them online

**online shopping** using a computer, modem, browser, and Internet access to locate, examine, purchase, sell, and pay for products over the Internet, either locally or worldwide

**online shopping mall** a collection of stores found at a single Web site sharing an electronic marketing environment, including servers, software, and payment systems

**online store** similar to a walk-in store, a seller's Web site where customers can locate, examine, purchase, and pay for products and services; also called a virtual store

**online storefront** an e-tailer's home page, a computerized version of a brick-and-mortar retail store, on which the e-tailer lists or shows products, descriptions, and prices of the merchandise

**online superstore** online stores that offer an extensive array of products, from candy bars to household appliances

**online transactional processing (OLTP)** a form of transactional processing used at e-commerce Web sites that require fast, always-on processing

**Open Enterprise Server (OES)** currently most popular and widely used operating system, developed by Novell, Inc. for microcomputer-based personal computers; it has replaced Novell's earlier NetWare operating system

**open system** a system that can be altered by a company's IT staff or by a third party

**Open Systems Interconnection (OSI) Reference Model** a set of communications protocols defined by the International Standards Organization based in Geneva, Switzerland, and adopted by the United Nations; also called OSI model

**open-source software program** software whose programming code is owned by the original developer but made available free to the general public, who is encouraged to experiment with the software, make improvements, and share the improvements with the user community

**operating environment** an onscreen visual interface on top of an underlying DOS kernel that makes using a computer easier

**operating system (OS)** a type of software that creates a user interface and supports the workings of computer devices and software programs that perform specific jobs

**operational database** a database that aids in the daily operations of an organization

**optical character recognition (OCR)** software that allows a captured image to be manipulated (edited or altered) with a word processor or other application program

**optical disc** a secondary storage medium on which data is recorded and read by two lasers: a high-density laser that records data by burning tiny indentations, or pits, onto the disk surface, and a low-intensity laser that reads stored data from the disk into the computer

**optical mouse** a type of mouse that contains no mouse ball and instead uses a light-based sensor to track movement; can be moved around on nearly any smooth surface, except glass, and thus no mouse pad is required

**optical reader** a type of optical scanner installed by many retailers at checkout stations

**optical scanner** a light-sensing electronic device that can read and capture printed text and images, such as photographs and drawings, and convert them into a digital form a computer can understand; once scanned, the text or image can be displayed on the screen, edited, printed, stored on a disk, inserted into another document, or sent as an attachment to an e-mail message; also called a scanner

**option button** a type of button used with a graphical user interface and resembling buttons on a standard radio that enables you to choose from among a set of options; also called a radio button

**OS/2** an operating system produced by IBM in response to the popularity of Microsoft Windows and the Apple Mac OS operating system

**output** information that is written or displayed as a result of computer processing; also the act of writing or displaying such data

**output device** any hardware device that makes information available to a user, such as a monitor or printer

**output medium** any medium or material on which information is recorded, such as paper

**outsourcing** hiring a third party to handle a project, usually a consultant or a systems integrator

# P

**packaged software** programs created and sold to the public on a retail basis by software development companies

**packet switching** the process of breaking up a message into parts called packets and directing the packets to their final Internet destination, where they are reassembled

**painting program** software that allows a user to create images in bit-map form and also to color and edit an image one bit at a time

**Palm OS** an operating system produced by Palm, Incorporated for use with the company's handheld personal digital assistants (PDAs)

**parallel port** a slot (opening) for connecting printers, scanners, and other devices; a parallel port can transmit data eight bits at a time

**parallel processing** a processing action in which two or more processors work concurrently on segments of a lengthy application, thus dramatically increasing processing capability

**parallel transmission** a transmission method in which a group of 8 bits representing a single byte plus one bit called a parity bit are transmitted at the same time over separate paths

**parity bit** an extra bit added to a byte, character, or word to ensure that there is always either a predetermined even number of bits or an odd number of bits; if data should be lost, errors can be identified by checking the number of bits

**password** a secret code of letters and numbers used to prevent access to a computer system by unauthorized people

**patent** an award made to inventors that allows them ownership of their invention; an inventor whose work is

patented has the right to charge others for the use of the invention

**pathname** the entire URL (Web address) describing where information can be found

**PC card** a type of expansion board (card) developed for use with small computers such as notebook and other small computers; also called a PCMCIA card

**PCI Express bus** a computer bus standard for attaching peripheral devices to a computer's motherboard, providing faster data transfer rates than the original Peripheral Component Interconnect (PCI) bus

**PCMCIA card** a type of expansion board (card) developed for use with small computers such as notebook and other small computers; also called a PC card

**PDF file format** a popular platform-independent file format, identified with a .pdf extension, for the storage of high-resolution printable documents; PDF documents may contain text, graphics, video, and sound in the QuickTime video format

**peer-to-peer architecture** a network design in which each PC or workstation composing the network has equivalent capabilities and responsibilities

**peer-to-peer (P2P) file sharing** a way to use the Internet that allows people to download material directly from other users' hard drives rather than from files located on Web servers

**peer-to-peer online transaction venue** a Web site forum that allows individuals to sell, buy, trade, or share goods with each other over the Internet

**pen computer** a computer equipped with pattern recognition circuitry so that it can recognize human handwriting as a form of data input

**pen drive** a storage device that plugs into a USB port on a computer or other mobile device; also called a USB drive, jump drive, or thumb drive

**performance monitor** a set of operating system instructions that monitor the computer system's overall performance

**Peripheral Component Interconnect (PCI) bus** a type of bus that allows for the connection of sound cards, video cards, and network cards to a computer system

**peripheral device** a device, such as a printer or disk drive, connected to and controlled by a computer but external to the computer's central processing unit (CPU)

**perl** a popular script language that is similar to C, but with powerful text-processing abilities; acronym for Practical Extraction and Report Language

**permanent storage** a type of storage that consists of devices and media used to record information and data permanently so it can later be retrieved, edited, modified, displayed, or printed; also called secondary storage or auxiliary storage

**permanent storage medium** a storage medium on which information and data can be permanently recorded, such as a compact disc or a hard disk, either built-in or external

**personal computer (PC)** a single-user computer capable of performing its own input, processing, output, and storage; also called a microcomputer

**Personal Computer Memory Card International Association (PCMCIA) modem** a modem that can be inserted into a PCMCIA slot in a notebook or other portable computer

**personal digital assistant (PDA)** a handheld, wireless computer, also known as a handheld PC or HPC, used for such purposes as storing schedules, calendars, and telephone numbers and for sending e-mail or connecting to the Internet

**personal finance software** programs that assist users with paying bills, balancing checkbooks, keeping track of income and expenses, and other financial activities

**personal firewall** a software-based system designed to protect a personal computer from unauthorized users attempting to access other computers through an Internet connection

**personal information manager (PIM)** software that helps users organize contact information, appointments, tasks, and notes

**person-to-person payment system** an Internet service that allows consumers to transfer money through a credit card or a bank account

**petabyte (PB)** a unit of memory measurement equal to approximately 1 quadrillion bytes

**petaflop** a measure of speed equivalent to 1 quadrillion calculations per second

**phishing** an activity characterized by attempts to fraudulently acquire another person's sensitive information, such as a credit card number

**photo printer** a unique high-quality ink-jet printer designed to print high-quality color photographs in addition to other types of print output

**pipelining** a technique for improving microprocessor performance that enables the computer to begin executing another instruction as soon as the previous instruction reaches the next phase of the machine cycle

**pit** a tiny indentation burned by laser into the surface of a compact disc to represent information, data, or programs

**pitch** the quality of sound reflected in the sound's loudness, intensity, and clarity

**pixel** the smallest picture element that a computer monitor or other device can display and from which graphic images are built

**plagiarism** the unlawful use of another's ideas or written work

**plaintext** readable information entered into a computer that is then converted to ciphertext, or unreadable, coded information in the process of encryption

**platform** compatible computers from one or more manufacturers; the two popular platforms for personal computers are PC and Macintosh

**plotter** a hard-copy output device used to output special kinds of hard copy, including architectural drawings, charts, maps, diagrams, and other images

**plug-in** a downloadable software addition, often used to distribute additional Web browser capabilities

**polling protocol** a network protocol that continually polls all workstations to determine if there are messages to be sent or received by each workstation

**pop-up blocker** a browser feature that blocks Web page pop-up windows

**pop-up window** a screen that jumps into the foreground of a Web page, usually during surfing; these windows are oftentimes advertisements

**port** a plug-in slot on a computer to which you can connect a device such as a printer or other periferals; also called an interface

**portable computer** a computer small enough to be carried around

**portable printer** a battery-powered, small, lightweight printer that mobile workers easily can transport and use with various types of computer and communications devices such as notebook computers, personal digital assistants (PDAs), and smartphones

**portal** a Web site that offers a variety of Internet services, such as search engines, news, weather, sports, yellow pages, and online stores and shopping malls

**portrait format** a format in which a printed page is taller than it is wide

**Post Office Protocol (POP) server** a special type of server that holds e-mail messages until they are accessed and read by recipients of the messages

**postage printer** a small printer designed to print postage stamps

**power-on self test (POST) chip** a chip containing instructions that check the physical components of the computer system to make certain they are working properly when the computer is turned on

**power spike** a jump up or down in the level of power provided to a computer system, potentially damaging the hardware

**power supply** a source of electrical energy that enables the computer to function

**presentation graphics software** an application program that allows one to create a computerized presentation of slides

**primary key** a database key that uniquely identifies every record in a table

**primary storage** addressable storage locations directly controlled by the central processing unit (CPU) used to store programs while they are being executed and data while it is being processed; also called main memory

**printer** the most common type of hard-copy output device that produces output in a permanent form

**print server** a type of server that allows multiple users to share the same printer

**print spooling** a printing technique in which a document to be printed is placed in a buffer instead of being sent to the printer; the document is held in the buffer until the printer is ready to print it, thereby enabling the printer to print at its own speed and free the CPU to perform other tasks

**privacy statement** an e-tailer's written promise that the merchant will protect the confidentiality of any information revealed by a customer

**problem-solving process** the use of a logical series of steps in order to analyze a problem and find a solution

**processing** the manipulation of data by the computer's electrical circuits

**processor** the part of a computer that interprets and carries out instructions that operate the computer and manage the computer's devices and resources; consists of components, each of which performs specific functions; also called the central processing unit (CPU)

**procurement** the activity of searching for, finding, and purchasing materials, supplies, products, and services at the best prices and assuring that they are delivered in a timely manner

**product developer** a company that manufactures new hardware and software products for the general market

**productivity software** programs that allow users to perform specific tasks, such as creating documents, preparing income tax returns, managing finances, sending and receiving messages over the Internet, and designing new products; software that enables a user to be more "productive"; sometimes referred to as application software

**program** a set of instructions to be executed by a computer; types of programs include applications and operating systems

**programming language** a coding system, containing smaller vocabularies and simpler syntax than human (natural) languages; coding language used to write programs

**programming language generation** a group or type of programming language that was developed at the same time, in a particular chronological order

**project management software** category of programs that allow a user to plan, design, schedule, and control a

project, thus facilitating the effective and efficient management of complex projects

**project plan** an estimate of how long a project will take to complete, along with an outline of the steps involved and a list of deliverables

**prompt** a symbol, character, or phrase that appears on-screen to inform the user that the computer is ready to accept input

**proprietary software** software owned by an individual or business that cannot be used or copied without permission; software that does not adhere to open standards but instead uses algorithms, protocols, file formats, and so on that were developed exclusively for the software by its developers to fulfill a certain purpose

**protocol** a set of rules and procedures for exchanging information between network devices and computers

**prototype** an initial "demo" version of a product or information system that allows people to get an idea of the final product's capabilities

**pseudocode** programming code that is more English-like than a programming language, and therefore easier to read, but is more structured and simplistic than English; algorithms often are written in pseudocode

**public access network (PAN)** a wide area network operated and maintained by a large company, such as AT&T, MCI, or Sprint, that provides voice and data communications capabilities to customers for a fee

**public key encryption** a form of data encryption that uses two encryption keys, a public encryption key known by all authorized users, and a secret encryption key known only by the sender or the receiver

**pull-down menu** a menu containing various lower-level options associated with main menu options; also called a drop-down menu

**pure-play e-tailer** a company that depends on e-commerce as its single marketing and sales channel

# Q

**quality assurance (QA)** the task of making sure that products meet quality standards before being released to the public

**query** a request for information from a database; allows users to ask questions designed to retrieve needed information

**Query by Example (QBE)** a standard for querying, or asking for particular information from, a database management system

**query tools** tools in a database management system that help users narrow down the amount of information that needs to be searched

# R

**radio button** a type of button used with a graphical user interface and resembling buttons on a standard radio that enables you to choose from among a set of options; also called an option button

**random access memory (RAM)** a computer chip or group of chips containing the temporary, or volatile, memory in which programs and data are stored while being used by a computer

**range check** a database validity check that makes sure a field value entered by the user is within specified limits

**rapid application development (RAD)** a set of techniques and practices designed to increase the speed of software development

**raster image** an image composed of a collection of black, white, or colored pixels; the most commonly used file format is the Tag Image File Format (TIF or TIFF)

**raster image–based graphics** a computerized process of displaying images in which the program treats the image as a large collection of pixels, each of which is stored in its own memory location; the image is created by specifying the color of each pixel; also called a bitmap-based graphics program

**read-only memory (ROM)** a computer chip on the motherboard of a computer containing permanent, or nonvolatile, memory that stores instructions

**real-time dialog** conversation taking place in the present moment; usually referring to Internet chat rooms

**real-time system** an information system that is in communication with real-world events directly and must operate fast enough to keep up with those events; examples include CAM, traffic control, and elevator systems

**record** in a table created by a database management system application, a row providing information about one entity, such as an individual or organization; a collection of related fields describing an event or situation

**record locking** a process a database uses to ensure that errors do not occur when two users access the same record

**recovery** a restoration of data from a backup

**reduced instruction set computing (RISC)** a shortened set of instructions that increases the speed and performance of a microprocessor

**redundancy** the duplication of data in different locations within a database

**redundant system** a duplicate system that is part of a disaster recovery plan; one part of a redundant system might be a mirrored hard drive that could be used to replace a damaged or corrupted hard drive

**referential integrity** a data validation test confirming that if a record is deleted from a database, no other record's validity will be affected

**refresh rate** the number of times per second a monitor's screen is redrawn

**register** a component of the arithmetic/logic unit (ALU) that temporarily holds instructions and data

**relational database** a type of database in which various tables can be linked (or related) in a way that allows retrieval of data from more than one table; tables must have a common data field, such as a product number

**removable storage medium** a secondary storage medium, such as a flash drive or a CD-ROM, that a user can remove and replace with another medium

**repeater** an electronic device that receives signals along a network, amplifies the signals, and resends the amplified signals along the network; also called an amplifier

**repetitive motion injury** a category of injury that involves the overuse and subsequent damage of joints and nerves

**report** a database output that is often printed, such as a utility bill or a school transcript; a formatted body of output from a database

**request for proposal (RFP)** the solicitation of a plan for an information system sent to possible suppliers, inviting them to send representatives to determine what is required before quoting a price

**resolution** a measurement of the sharpness of an image displayed on a computer monitor or other output device; measured in dots per inch (dpi), both vertically and horizontally, with higher resolution achieved by more dpi

**retinal recognition system** a biometric device that uses the unique retinal patterns of individuals to identify them

**ribbon** an interface device in Microsoft Office 2007 that groups commands in a tab format instead of a menu bar

**ring topology** a network topology in which there is no host computer, each computer or workstation is connected to two or more other computers and/or periferal devices and communications are passed in one direction from the source computer to the destination; if one computer or periferal is not working, it is bypassed

**robotics** the science of creating machines capable of independent movement and action

**rotating backup** a system of maintaining multiple backup copies of data in which the oldest copy is erased and reused every time the system is backed up

**router** a hardware device that connects two or more networks

**routine** a section of code containing instructions for a specific purpose; also called a function

**RPG** a programming language commonly used in business environments; an acronym for Report Program Generator

**RSA** a popular public encryption technology used to transmit data over the Internet; named for its developers, Rivest, Shamir, and Adleman

**run-time error** program mistake that occurs when an application is running

# S

**sampling** the process of measuring the pitch, frequency, and volume of a sound

**scanner** a light-sensing electronic device that can read and capture printed text and images, such as photographs and drawings, and convert them into a digital form a computer can understand; once scanned, the text or image can be displayed on the screen, edited, printed, stored on a disk, inserted into another document, or sent as an attachment to an e-mail message; also called an optical scanner

**screen projector** a device that captures the text and images displayed on a computer monitor and projects those same images onto a large screen so the audience can see the text and images clearly

**scripting language** a large variety of languages that are interpreted rather than compiled; scripting languages are often used to write special functions into Web pages, as the transmission of a script is faster than a binary plug-in

**scroll bar** a rectangular bar at the side or bottom of a window that enables a user to see and work with other portions of the document by moving the small arrows at the tips of a scroll bar or by dragging the small box between the two arrows

**search engine** a software program that enables a user to search for, locate, and retrieve specific information on the Internet about any topic

**search operators** logic statement used by search engines to locate information on the Web; three of the most common are AND, OR, and NOT

**search terms** words used to tell a search engine what information to look for on the Web; also called keywords

**secondary storage** a type of storage that consists of devices and media used to record information and data permanently so it can later be retrieved, edited, modified, displayed, or printed; also called permanent storage, auxiliary storage, or external storage

**secret key encryption** an encryption method in which both the customer and the business use the same encryption key to encrypt and decrypt the data

**sector** a numbered section or portion of a disk similar to a slice of pie on which programs, data, and information are stored

**Secure HTTP (S-HTTP)** a protocol for transmitting individual messages securely over the World Wide Web

**Secure Sockets Layer (SSL)** an encryption protocol used for secure servers commonly found on sites that involve financial transactions, such as the use of credit card information

**security measures** methods used by a database management system to protect and safeguard data

**SELECT command** the basic query command supported by SQL, which asks a database to return records that match specified criteria

**semiconductor** a type of material that is neither a good conductor of electricity (like copper) nor a good insulator (such as rubber) and therefore does not interfere with the flow of electricity in a chip's circuits; most commonly made of silicon, a type of purified glass

**sequential access** a storage technology whereby stored data can be retrieved only in the order in which it is physically stored, just as musical selections on a cassette tape are recorded and accessed one after the other

**serial port** a port (opening) for connecting devices such as the keyboard, mouse, and modem to a computer; a port that transmits data one bit at a time; also called a communications (COM) port

**serial transmission** a data transmission method in which all the bits (0s and 1s) that compose the data are transmitted one bit after another in a continuous line

**server** a computer and its associated storage devices that users access remotely over a network

**shareware** software developed by an individual or software publisher who retains ownership of the product and makes it publicly available for a small "contribution" fee

**shopping agent** software that works for shoppers by locating Web sites that offer products specified by a user and does comparison-shopping to find the best bargain; also called a shopping bot

**shopping basket** a virtual location where a customer electronically places products for purchase at an online shopping site; also called a shopping cart

**shopping bot** software that works for shoppers by locating Web sites that offer products specified by a user and does comparison-shopping to find the best bargain; also called a shopping agent

**shopping cart** a virtual location where a customer electronically places products for purchase at an online shopping site; also called a shopping basket

**signature verification system** a biometric device that recognizes individuals via their handwriting

**Simple Mail Transfer Protocol (SMTP)** a communications protocol installed on the ISP's or online service's mail server that determines how each message is to be routed through the Internet and then sends the message

**simplex transmission** a directional protocol that allows transmissions to flow in only one direction; that is, messages can be either sent or received but not both

**single sign-on (SSO) technology** a security design that eliminates the problem of users having an ID and password for each application or system they access

**single-user computer system** computer that can accommodate a single (one) user at a time; the type of personal computer system found in homes and in small businesses and offices

**site analysis** a business or organization's ongoing evaluation of an e-commerce Web site and its activity

**site license** a contract that allows an organization to load or use copies of a piece of software on a specified maximum number of machines

**situational ethics** another name for the school of ethical thought called moral relativism

**slide** a document created using presentation graphics software that may contain text, graphics, images, sound, and other elements that can help capture and hold an audience's attention

**slide show** a group of slides compose a presentation; a slide show may include any number of individual slides

**smart card** a small plastic card that stores personal and financial data on a tiny microprocessor embedded in the card; when the card is inserted into an electronic card reader, information on the card is read and updated when appropriate

**smartphone** a device that allows users to transmit and receive phone calls as well as e-mail messages and photos and browse through Web sites

**social networking services** the means for online communities of people who share interests to meet and interact; most are based on personalized Web pages and provide message boards, instant messaging, and other user-defined content

**soft copy** a temporary version of output, typically the display of data on a computer screen

**software** programs containing instructions that direct the operation of the computer system and the written documentation that explains how to use the programs; types include system software and application software

**software development** the creation of new software products for commercial sale; includes systems programming, application programming, multimedia development, and quality assurance

**software development life cycle (SDLC)** the phases involved in the process of creating, testing, and releasing new software products

**software engineering** the organized, professional application of the software development process by programmers and software engineers

**software piracy** the act of copying or using a piece of software without the legal right to do so

**software suite** a combination of applications programs (usually integrated) bundled as a single package; may contain applications such as word processing, spreadsheet, database, and possibly other programs

**software worm** a program that actively transmits copies of itself over the Internet, using up resources and causing other problems; also called a worm

**Solaris** a variation of the UNIX operating system designed for use on Sun servers

**sort** a feature of many application programs, such as word processing programs and database management systems, that enables the user to organize selected information in a particular way, as, for example, alphabetically or by date

**sound card** a type of expansion card that allows voice input by means of a microphone and sound output via speakers

**sound digitizing card** a computer hardware component capable of reproducing sound from a variety of digital file types

**source code** a computer program written in a programming language, but not yet turned into executable machine language by a compiler

**spam** an unsolicited e-mail message sent to computer users by a business or individual to promote products or services; similar to junk mail

**spam blocker** a utility program that allows users to block incoming unsolicited e-mail messages sent to computer users by a business or individual to promote products or services

**speaker-dependent program** a particular speech recognition program whereby the computer captures and stores your own voice as you speak words slowly and clearly into the microphone

**speaker headset** a miniature version of larger speakers frequently used with portable devices, including music CD players

**speaker-independent program** a particular speech recognition program that contains a built-in vocabulary of prerecorded word patterns; the computer can recognize only spoken words that match a word contained in the built-in list of vocabulary words

**speakers** computer devices that output sound; applications for which speakers are particularly important include computer games, multimedia distance learning programs, audio e-mail, and videoconferencing

**special-function keyboard** a type of keyboard designed for specific applications involving simplified, rapid data input

**specifications** a detailed set of requirements for a software product to be developed

**speech recognition program** a computer program capable of recognizing and capturing spoken words; usually speaker-dependent

**spelling checker** a part of a program or a stand-alone application that automatically searches for spelling errors and suggests correctly spelled alternatives

**spoofing** a practice by which a program masquerades as a legitimate source of data on a network in order to get a remote computer to accept its transmissions

**spreadsheet software** a productivity program that provides a user with a means of organizing, calculating, and presenting financial, statistical, and other numeric information; used to manipulate numbers electronically instead of using a pencil and paper

**spyware** software that tracks the activity of Internet users for the benefit of a third party

**standard operating procedure (SOP)** a set of instructions describing how to perform a task

**star topology** a network topology in which multiple computers and peripheral devices are linked to a central computer, called a host, in a point-to-point configuration; also called a hub-and-spoke topology

**start bit** a bit that signals the beginning of a character during asynchronous transmission

**Static RAM (SRAM)** a type of random access memory (RAM) that is faster and more reliable than the more common dynamic RAM

**statistical quality control (SQC) system** a methodology manufacturing companies use to maintain quality by vigilantly performing statistical analysis upon their production error rates

**stealth virus** a rare and sophisticated virus that attempts to "hide" from antivirus software by covering up its identifiable characteristics

**stereoscopic vision** vision that allows depth perception and the detection of movement

**stockless inventory distribution** a model for distribution management that involves daily deliveries to the customer

**stop bit** a bit that signals the end of a character during asynchronous transmission

**storage** a permanent recording of information, data, and programs on a permanent storage medium, such as CD-ROM, so they can be used again and again

**storage bay** a site within the system unit where a device such as a hard disk drive or CD-ROM drive is installed; also called a bay

**storage device** a hardware component that houses a secondary storage medium; also called secondary storage or storage medium

**storage medium** a material, such as an optical disc, on which data is recorded (stored)

**storage register** special areas of main memory used to store program instructions being executed and data being processed

**storing** the activity of permanently saving instructions and data for future use

**storyboard** sketches of the pages or frames as they will appear in the final work; used to plan sequential page-based multimedia or movie-based multimedia

**streaming** an alternative to downloading a piece of music or a video; sends a continuous stream of data to the receiving computer, where it is immediately displayed; also called webcasting

**structured programming** a set of procedural rules for creating software that is written in a readable, standardized format, and which is broken into coherent structures

**Structured Query Language (SQL)** a standard for querying, or asking for particular information from, a database management system

**style** a special shortcut feature that allows text to be formatted in a single step

**style error** an error in writing source code that does not keep the program from working, but does make it more difficult to read

**stylus** a sharp, pointed instrument used for writing or marking

**supercomputer** fastest, most powerful, and most expensive type of computer designed for multiple users

**supply chain** a series of activities a company performs to achieve its goals at various stages of the production process; the value added at each stage contributes to profit and enhances the product's value as well as the company's competitive position in the market; also called a value chain

**support contract** a contract that allows users to contact the systems house for technical support, training, and sometimes on-site troubleshooting

**surfing** accessing and moving about the Web using a browser; also called browsing

**surge protector** a type of power strip that contains electronics that try to modulate and "smooth out" spikes in the power supply

**switch** a small hardware device that joins multiple computers together within one local area network (LAN)

**synch byte** bytes of data signaling the beginning and end of blocks of data during synchronous transmission

**Synchronous DRAM (SDRAM)** a high-speed, dynamic random access memory (DRAM) technology that can synchronize itself with the clock speed of the microprocessor's data bus

**synchronous transmission** a transmission method that provides a fast and efficient way of sending data in which blocks of bytes are wrapped in start and stop bytes called synch bytes

**syntax** the structure of a language

**syntax error** an error that violates the rules of a programming language; a compiler lists syntax errors when it attempts to translate a program from source code into machine language

**system backdoor** a secret, sometimes forgotten entry point into an otherwise secure system; oftentimes left behind by the original programmers, accidentally or on purpose

**system bus** connects the processor (CPU) to main memory, providing the CPU with fast access to data stored in random access memory (RAM)

**system clock** a small electronic chip inside a computer that synchronizes or controls the timing of all computer operations; the clock generates evenly spaced pulses that synchronize the flow of information through the computer's internal communications channels

**system development life cycle (SDLC)** a series of steps culminating in a completed information system; planning, design, implementation, and support

**system software** a type of software consisting of a set of programs that control the operations of a computer system, including starting the computer, processing applications, formatting disks, and copying files; software that controls all components and devices that compose the computer system

**system unit** the main part of a personal computer system that contains the motherboard and other components necessary for processing information

**systems analysis** the process of gathering requirements and developing a design for systems of distribution management, office information, management information, decision support, executive support, and factory automation

**systems analyst** the person whose profession it is to study and evaluate computer operations and procedures used to accomplish specific goals in order to plan and design a database system; may also be responsible for administering the database after it is built

**systems integrator** a company that specializes in installing, customizing, and supporting information systems

**Systems Network Architecture (SNA)** a networking program that uses a polling protocol for transmitting data; workstations are asked one by one if they have a message to transmit

**systems programmer** a professionally trained programmer who specializes in the development of systems software as opposed to application software

**systems programming** a highly specialized area of software development that involves writing instructions in C++, JavaScript, or other programming languages to accomplish a succession of tasks

# T

**T line** a permanent connection between two points set up by a telephone company and typically leased by a business to connect geographically distant offices; always active and dedicated for use only by the leasing business that pays a monthly fee for use of the line

**T1 line** a high-speed telephone line that allows for both voice and data transmission and can carry data at a speed of 1.544 megabits per second

**T3 line** a high-speed telephone line capable of carrying data at speeds of up to 44.7 megabits per second

**tab** a subset of options, each of which is labeled as if it were a manila folder within a file drawer; the name of the subset of options is displayed in a tab at the top of the folder; clicking on the tab brings the particular group of options to the front of the dialog box

**table** in relational databases, a file consisting of rows and columns

**tablet PC** a type of notebook computer that has a liquid crystal display (LCD) on which the user can write using a special-purpose pen, or stylus

**tactile perception** the science of making a computer understand what it is touching

**tape cartridge** a secondary storage technology used with personal computers mainly for backing up the contents of a hard drive; the tape is housed in a small plastic container (the cartridge) that also contains a tape reel and a take-up reel

**tape drive** a device that records and reads data to and from a reel of magnetic tape; many large businesses and organizations use this sequential-access storage medium for backing up important programs and data

**tax preparation software** programs designed to aid a taxpayer in analyzing federal and state tax status and to prepare and transmit tax returns

**technical sales** a career involving educating potential customers about a product so that they want to buy it

**technical servicing** the installation and maintenance of hardware and software

**technical support** a career that involves responding to customers' phone and e-mail requests for assistance with computer-related products

**technical training** a career that involves teaching individuals how to use computer systems

**technical writing** a career that involves writing user manuals, training materials, and textbooks for hardware and software products

**technician** the person whose job is to repair and maintain computer equipment and systems and install software on a company's computers

**telecommunications** the combined use of computer hardware and communications software for sending and receiving information over communications media, including phone lines and other types of media

**telecommuting** an Internet application that enables workers to perform their work activities at home instead of at the workplace by using their computers, communications software, and a telephone line; also called teleworking

**teleworking** an Internet application that enables workers to perform their work activities at home instead of at the workplace by using their computers, communications software, and a telephone line; also called telecommuting

**template** a previously created and stored form

**terabyte (TB)** a unit of memory measurement equal to approximately 1 trillion bytes

**teraflop** a measure of speed equivalent to 1 trillion calculations per second

**terminal** an input/output device, consisting of a keyboard and monitor, typically used with multi-user computer systems; also called dumb terminal

**terminator** a device in a bus topology that absorbs signals so they do not reflect back down the line

**testing harness** a standard set of tests that a software product must pass before being released to the public

**text** output consisting of characters and numbers that can be used to create words, sentences, and paragraphs

**text box** a type of dialog box used for typing information that will allow the computer to continue or complete a task

**text data** alphabetic letters, numbers, and special characters, typically entered to produce output such as letters, e-mail messages, and reports

**texture** a bitmap used to cover the surface of a virtual object in a virtual environment such as a game

**...rmal dye sublimation printer** a printer that produces ...es by heating ribbons containing dye and then diffus- ... dyes onto specially coated paper or transparencies; ...d a thermal dye transfer printer

**...e transfer printer** a printer that produces ...ating ribbons containing dye and then diffus- ...to specially coated paper or transparencies; ...mal dye sublimation printer

**thermal printer** an inexpensive printer that uses heat to transfer an impression onto paper; category of printer that includes direct thermal, thermal wax transfer, and thermal dye transfer printers

**thermal wax transfer printer** a printer that produces images by adhering a wax-based ink onto paper

**thin-film transistor (TFT) display** a type of monitor display in which separate transistors control each color pixel, allowing viewing from any angle; also called active-matrix display

**threat** a factor of risk assessment based on the severity of the effects of a security breach

**throughput** a measure of a computer's overall performance

**thumb drive** a storage device that plugs into a USB port on a computer or other mobile device; also called a USB drive, jump drive, or pen drive

**time bomb virus** a virus that is triggered by an event or the passing of a certain time; also called a logic bomb virus

**title bar** a rectangular area at the top of a window in which the window's name is displayed

**token** an electronic signal

**token ring protocol** a type of protocol that sends an electronic signal, called a token, carrying both an address and a message around a token ring network quickly

**toner** an ink-like powder used in a laser printer

**toolbar** a type of menu on which sets of icons are displayed that represent actions unique to the software and ones frequently employed by users; the number and kinds of icons often vary among programs and among different versions of the same program

**top-down design** envisioning a programming project in its entirety by viewing larger elements and then the smaller elements contained within them; often documented using an outline format

**touch pad** an input device that enables a user to enter data and make selections by moving a finger across the pad; also called a track pad

**touch screen** an input device that allows the user to choose options by pressing a finger (or fingers) on the appropriate part of the screen

**trace** electrical pathway etched onto a motherboard that connects internal computer components

**track** a numbered concentric circle on a magnetic disk, or groups of lines along the length of magnetic tape, along which programs and data are stored

**track pad** an input device that enables a user to enter data and make selections by moving a finger across the pad; also called a touch pad

G-27

**trackball** an input device consisting of a plastic sphere sitting on rollers, inset in a small external case, or in many portable computers, in the same unit as the keyboard; the user moves the ball with her fingers or palm to position an onscreen cursor

**transaction** a business activity central to the nature of an enterprise, such as the sale of a product, the flight of an airline, or the recording of a grade

**transactional processing** a type of data processing that is done continuously, as each activity occurs; used with smaller databases or with operational databases that require all information to be very current

**transceiver** a device that sends messages along the bus in either direction

**Transmission Control Protocol/Internet Protocol (TCP/IP)** protocol that governs how packets are constructed and sent over the Internet to their destination

**transponder** a device contained in a communication satellite that receives signals from transmission stations on the ground

**Transport Layer Security (TLS)** a newer encryption protocol used for secure servers; it may replace SSL

**tree diagram** a diagram that shows the links between the planned pages of hypertext page-based multimedia

**Trojan horse virus** a computer virus that gets the victim to install and use it by masquerading as a legitimate program

**true color** a term that refers to a graphics device using at least 24 bits to represent each pixel so that up to 16 million unique colors can be represented to accommodate the complex shades and hues of our natural world

**trusted operating system (TOS)** a security-hardened version of a standard operating system

**tunneling** a security technology a virtual private network uses to safeguard data that enables one network to send its data via another network's connections

**tuple** a record in a relational database

**turnkey system** an information system that is tailored to the customer's needs and thus is easy to use

**tutorial** a form of instruction in which students are guided step by step through the learning process

**twisted-pair cable** a communications medium consisting of two independently insulated wires twisted around one another: One of the wires carries the information while the other wire is grounded and absorbs any interference that may be present on the line

# U

**Unicode** a data coding scheme that can accommodate a larger array of letters and symbols than ASCII; uses two

bytes, or 16 binary digits, and can represent 65,536 separate characters

**Uniform Resource Locator (URL)** an Internet address; also called Universal Resource Locator

**uninstaller** a utility program for removing (deleting) software programs and any associated entries in the system files

**uninterruptible power supply (UPS)** a device that provides a battery backup for a computer in the event of a blackout

**Universal Product Code (UPC)** a type of code printed on products and packages consisting of lines and spaces that a computer translates into a number; the computer then uses this number to find information about the product or package, such as its name and price, in a computerized database

**Universal Serial Bus (USB) port** a type of port that is widely used for connecting high-speed modems, scanners, and digital cameras to a computer; a single USB port can accommodate several peripheral devices connected together in sequence

**UNIX** an operating system developed by programmers at Bell Laboratories originally designed for large computer systems including minicomputers, mainframes, and supercomputers

**USA PATRIOT Act** antiterrorism legislation enacted in 2001 that allows law enforcement agencies to eavesdrop on private telephone messages and to intercept and read e-mail messages sent by individuals and groups

**USB flash drive** a storage device that plugs into a USB port on a computer or other mobile device; also called a thumb drive, jump drive, or pen drive

**User Access Control (UAC)** a protection system in Windows Vista that prompts the user for administrator-level credentials whenever an operation is attempted that might affect system stability or security

**user ID** a unique combination of characters (letters and numbers) identifying an individual computer user; also called a user name

**user interface** a set of instructions that allow the software to communicate with the user and, in turn, the user to communicate with the software; the manner in which the user enters data and commands and in which information and processing options are presented is controlled by the program's interface

**user name** a unique combination of characters (letters and numbers) identifying an individual computer user; also called a user ID

**utility program** a type of program that performs a specific and helpful task, such as checking for viruses, uninstalling programs, and deleting data no longer needed

**utility software** programs that perform specific tasks, such as managing a monitor, disk drives, and printers and removing viruses

# V

**value added network (VAN)** a network in which a business uses the facilities of large communications companies to provide subscribers with additional services, such as providing subscribers with access to various network databases, electronic mail, and online advertising and shopping venues

**value chain** a series of activities a company performs to achieve its goals at various stages of the production process; the value added at each stage contributes to profit and enhances the product's value as well as the company's competitive position in the market; also called a supply chain

**variable** in a computer program, a data object used to hold values such as numbers or text

**variant virus** a virus that can alter itself to prevent anti-virus software from detecting it

**VBScript** a script form of Visual Basic that can be used to create sophisticated Web pages

**vector-based graphics program** a program that creates pictures by means of creating, editing, and combining mathematically defined geometric shapes; also called object-based graphics program

**vertical application software** a complete package of programs that work together to perform core business functions for a large organization

**vertical market package** an information system focused on a particular set of customers, for example a system designed for dental offices; also called a niche information system

**video** consists of motion images, similar to those seen on a television or movie screen

**video and audio editing software** software that allows users to create and modify recorded video and audio clips

**video card** a circuit board residing on the motherboard inside the system unit that converts the digital signals produced by the computer into analog signals and sends them through a cable to the monitor; also called a graphics card or video adapter

**video data** moving pictures and images, such as a video-conference, film clip, or full-length movie

**video digitizing card** a piece of hardware that allows users to capture and digitize video images and sound from such sources as television, videotape recorders, and camcorders

**video editing software** software that allows users to edit sound and video and output it in various digital formats

**video input** an input technology that occurs by using a special type of video camera attached to the computer and plugged into a video capture card in an expansion slot, which converts analog video signals into digital signals

**video port** a port (connection) for connecting a monitor to the system unit; the port may be built into the computer's system unit or provided by a video card placed in an expansion slot

**video streaming** a fast method of distributing video clips over the Internet without having to download the entire file before viewing; since video files tend to be very large, allows viewers to begin watching content within a few seconds as opposed to a long waiting period that would be required for a full download of the file

**virtual private network (VPN)** a type of wide area network (WAN) whereby a company has each branch office set up a local Internet connection through which company networking traffic is routed; uses encryption and other security technologies to ensure that only authorized users can access it and that the data cannot be intercepted

**virtual reality (VR)** a game-like form of interface that puts the user into a very realistic alternate world; used for 3D design work and gaming

**virtual store** similar to a walk-in store, a seller's Web site where customers can locate, examine, purchase, and pay for products and services; also called an online store

**virus** a program that is designed to harm computer systems and/or any users, typically sent via e-mail

**Visual Basic (VB)** a language developed by Microsoft in the 1990s that is popular with programmers who want to rapidly develop Windows interface software

**visual perception** the science of making a computer understand what it sees with an electronic eye (camera)

**voice input** technology that allows users to enter data by talking into a microphone connected to the computer

**voice output** technology that allows spoken words and sounds to be heard via a computer's speakers

**Voice over IP (VoIP)** a combination of hardware and software that allows two or more people with sufficiently good connections to use the Internet to make telephone-style calls without long-distance telephone charges; also called Internet telephony

**voice recognition program** programs that recognize pre-programmed words stored in a database; usually speech independent

**voice verification system** a biometric device that recognizes people via their voice patterns

**volatile memory** a type of computer memory whereby stored instructions and data are lost if the power is switched off

**vulnerability** a factor of risk assessment based on the likelihood of a security breach

# W

**warm boot** process of restarting a computer while power is on; clears the memory and reloads the operating system

**wave file format** a noncompressed file type, identified with a .wav extension, used to reproduce any kind of sound

**wearable computer** a type of computer that can be worn on a person's body, thereby providing the user with access to mobile communicating capabilities and to information access via the Internet

**Web administrator** the person who is responsible for developing and maintaining a Web site; also called a Web master

**Web authoring software** software that helps users develop Web pages without learning Web programming

**Web browser** software that allows users to move from one location to another on the Web and to access and retrieve Web pages; also called a browser

**webcam** a digital video camera that captures real-time video for transmission to others via a Web server or an instant messaging tool

**webcasting** an alternative to downloading a piece of music or a video; sends a continuous stream of data to the receiving computer, where it is immediately displayed; also called streaming

**webconference** an online conference between two or more participants at different sites, using computer networks and webconferencing software

**webconferencing software** programs that make webconferencing applications possible

**Web hosting service** a company that allows individuals or other companies to use their Web server to store Web pages; examples include Internet service providers, communications companies, and online shopping malls

**Web link** an address that links to a document or to a Web page; also called a hyperlink

**Webmaster** the person who is responsible for developing and maintaining a Web site; also called a Web administrator

**Web page** an electronic document stored at a location on the Web; the document can contain text, images, sound, and video and may provide links to other Web pages

**Web page trap** a Web page specifically built to fire advertisements at users in a bewildering array in order to keep them from leaving the site

**WebRing** a managed ring of links between Web sites that allows a surfer to move through many topically similar sites

**Web site** a collection of Web pages associated with a given topic or company on a single host system

**wide area network (WAN)** a network that spans a large geographical area

**Wi-Fi** a protocol for wireless communication that specifies an over-the-air interface between the wireless client device and a server, or between two wireless devices; also called the 802.11 protocol

**Windows 7** Microsoft's 2009 release of the Windows operating system for personal computers; it offers many usability and performance updates including the Aero interface and an improved taskbar

**Windows 2000** a Microsoft operating system designed for use with business desktop and notebook computers and containing the power as well as many of the features of the earlier Windows NT Server

**Windows 2000 Server** a Windows-based operating system specifically designed for use on a network server

**Windows Defender** a protection system in Windows Vista and Windows 7 that monitors for and defends against spyware and adware

**Windows Firewall** a protection system in Windows Vista and Windows 7 that blocks other computers from gathering information or communicating with the system via unused network ports

**Windows Mobile** an operating system, similar in appearance to the Windows XP operating system, used for personal digital assistants, smartphones, and handheld PCs

**Windows NT Server** one of Microsoft's earlier entries into the client/server market that supports multitasking operations

**Windows Server 2003** Microsoft's server operating system that is available in four editions: Standard, Enterprise, Datacenter, and Web

**Windows Server 2008** the server version of Windows Vista, designed to help IT professionals manage and maintain Windows-based networks; it includes a Network Access Protection tool that enables an IT administrator to define health requirements for the network, to restrict computers that do not meet these requirements from participating in the network, and to deploy installations and patches remotely

**Windows Vista** Microsoft's 2007 release of the Windows operating system for personal computers

**Windows XP** an operating system from Microsoft Corporation, released in 2001 and designed for fast, powerful computers with lots of memory and hard disk space

**Wired Equivalent Privacy (WEP)** a security protocol for wireless networks

**wireframe diagram** a graphic created using three-dimensional vector techniques to show the underlying structure of a three-dimensional object on a two-dimensional surface

**wireless access point** a hardware device that transmits a wireless network signal to Wi-Fi-enabled devices

**Wireless Application Protocol (WAP)** a protocol commonly used with low-bandwidth, wireless systems, such as cell phone networks

**Wireless Markup Language (WML)** a standardized language included in the Wireless Application Protocol (WAP) that converts an HTML-coded page to Wireless Markup Language (WML), removes the graphics, and then sends the text to the wireless device, where it is displayed on the device's screen

**wireless service provider (WSP)** a business that provides wireless Internet access to subscribers using wireless Internet devices

**wizard** a programming feature that guides a user through a series of steps which allow the user to select content and layout options to be applied to a file

**word** a group of bits or bytes that a computer can manipulate or process as a unit

**word processing software** a type of computer application that allows the user to create, edit, manipulate, format, store, and print a variety of documents, including letters, memos, announcements, and brochures

**word size** the number of bits a processor can interpret and execute at a given time

**workstation** a high-performance single-user computer with advanced input, output, and storage components that can be networked with other workstations and larger computers

**World Intellectual Property Organization (WIPO)** a specialized agency of the United Nations dealing with intellectual property rights

**World Wide Web (WWW)** a global system of linked computer networks that allows users to jump from one site to another by way of programmed links on Web pages; also called the Web

**worm** a program that actively transmits copies of itself over the Internet, using up resources and causing other problems; also called a software worm

**write once, read many (WORM) disk** a type of optical laser disk that provides very high capacity storage that companies often use to store huge amounts of data, particularly images

**WYSIWYG** stands for "what you see is what you get"; the layout and content of the actual Web page can be seen within the Web authoring software

# Z

**zipped file** a compressed file format, commonly used for the quick downloading of large files over the Internet

# INDEX

DDR3, 79
DDR SDRAM (double data rate SDRAM), 79
Debian, 157
decision support systems (DSS), 409
decoding, 70–71
default options, 167
defragmenting, 186–187
demodulation, 258
denial of service (DoS) attacks, 363–364
dense wave division multiplexing (DWDM), 291
Desai, Roger, 238
desktop computers, 24–25. *See also* personal computers (PCs)
desktop publishing (DTP) software, 208, 213
desktops
    GUIs, 164–165
    Microsoft Windows Vista, 159
diagnostic utilities, 185
dialog boxes, 169
dial-up access/service, 320–321, TI: A10
dial-up modems, 258
dictionaries, 230
digital, 5
digital cameras, 57–58, 233
digital divide, TI: E7
digital harassment, TI: E6
digital information, 6
digital ink technology, 25–26
digital interactions, 2–5
Digital Light Processing (DLP) projectors, 112
Digital Micromirror Devices (DMDs), 112
Digital Millennium Copyright Act (DMCA), 343–344
digital music distribution, 327–328
digital photography
    cameras, 57–58, 233
    dots per inch (dpi), 58
    printers, 120, TI: B5
Digital Picture Frame, 58
Digital Subscriber Lines (DSLs), 263–264, 323
digital television, 111–112
digital versatile disc-read-only memory (DVD-ROM) discs and drives, 135–136, 137
digital versatile disc-recordable (DVD-R) discs and drives, 136, 137
digital versatile disc-rewritable (DVD-RW) discs and drives, 136–137
digital versatile (or video) discs (DVDs) and drives, 130, 137, TI: A12, TI: A13, TI: B3
digitizing pens, 53
DigKeyGen, 368
DIMM (dual inline memory module), TI: C6
direct access, 126
directional protocols, 285
direct thermal printers, 118
disabled persons: accessibility, TI: E8
disaster recovery plan, 378
disk defragmenters, 186–187
disk packs, 138
disk scanners, 186
disk toolkits, 187
display devices. *See* output devices

display windows, 165–166
distance learning, 202, 316, 318
distributed computing, 242
distributed databases, 418
docking stations, 86
document formatting, 211
domain names, 324
    suffixes, 324, 325
dot-com companies, 324
dot-matrix printers, 114–115
dot pitch, 109
dots per inch (dpi), 55, 58
Double Data Rate SDRAM (DDR SDRAM), 79
download, 306
downloading, 305–306
downtime, 426
dpi. *See* dots per inch (dpi)
draft quality printing, 115
DRAM (dynamic RAM), 79
drawing programs, 231
drawing software, 231–232
drawing tablets, 53
drivers, 160–161, TI: C3
drop-down menus, 166–168
DTP. *See* desktop publishing (DTP) software
dual-core processors, 76
dual inline memory module. *See* DIMM
dumb scanners, 55
DVD-ROMs (digital versatile disc-read-only memory) discs and drives, 135–136, 137
DVD-Rs (digital versatile disc-recordable) discs and drives, 136, 137
DVD-RWs (digital versatile disc-rewritable) discs and drives, 136–137
DVD (digital versatile or video) discs and drives, 130, 137, TI: A12, TI: A13, TI: B3
Dynabook, 380
Dynamic RAM (DRAM), 79
dynamic routing, 327

# E

EarthLink, 106
earth stations, 267
EBCDIC, 64–65
e-business. *See* business-to-business (B2B) electronic commerce
Eckert, J. Presper, 62–63, TI: A4
e-commerce. *See* electronic commerce (e-commerce)
editing
    audio, 233
    images, 233
    text, 210
    video, 233
educational software, 229–231
E Ink Imaging Film, 142
electronic commerce (e-commerce), 315–316
    amount, TI: A14
    database interactions and, 400, 423
    groceries, 304
    operational databases and, 417
    privacy threats, TI: E2–E5
    security, 360

Electronic Communications Privacy Act, 375
electronic devices, 2–3
electronic mail (e-mail), 235, 288–289, 305–306
electronic noses, 382
Electronic Numerical Integrator and Computer (ENIAC), 62, TI: A4
electronic offices, 408–409
electronic paper, 142
Ellison, Larry, 411
e-mail, 235, 288–289, 305–306
embedded computers, 6, 33
employee privacy, 377, 386, TI: E5
employee theft, 374
encryption, TI: E3, TI: E4, TI: E5
    keys, 384, 385, 388
    methods, 385
    protocols, 385
encyclopedias, 230
e-noses, 382
Enquire, 313
entertainment: Internet, 312–315
entertainment software, 228
entities, 403
ergonomics, 110
e-shopping. *See* electronic commerce (e-commerce)
espionage viruses, 370
Ethernet, 262, 288, TI: A8
Ethernet protocol, 288
ethics, TI: E1–E9
executing, 71
execution time (e-time), 72
expansion buses, 86
expansion boards, installing, TI: C4–C6
expansion cards, 83–84
expansion slots, 83
exposed bays, 67–68
ExpressCards, 84
Extended Binary Coded Decimal Interchange Code (EBCDIC), 64–65
Extensible languages, 329–330
Extensible Markup Language (XML), 329–330
external modems, 258, 259
external ports, TI: B4
external storage, 124, 126–140
extranets, 275–276

# F

facsimile/fax machines, 121–123
factory automation systems, 409–411
FAT (file allocation table) files, 129
fax, 121
fax/modem cards, 122–123
fax programs, 123
Federal Computer Fraud and Abuse Act, 375
fetching, 70
Fiber Distributed Data Interface (FDDI), 288
fiber-optic cables, 256, 262–263, 291–292
fields, 217, 403–405, 415
file allocation table (FAT) files, 129
file compression utilities, 187
file conversion services, TI: D3–D4
file extensions, 125

wireless application protocols (WAPs), 289–291
wireless communications
    access points, 268, TI: A14
    capability, TI: B6
    networks, 34, 334
    technology, 268
wireless devices
    eyewear, 27
    gaming, 363
    headsets, 52
    increasing use of, 33–34
    privacy threats, TI: E3–E4
    security, 365–366
    types of, TI: A13
wireless fidelity. *See* wireless communications
wireless service providers (WSPs), 268, 322, 323
wizards, 209, 222
word, 74
word processing software, 208–211
word size, 74
workplace privacy, 377, 386
workstation, 28
World of Warcraft, 312–313
World Wide Web (WWW), 12. *See also* Internet; Web
WORM, 140
worms, 362, 367–368
Wozniak, Steve, 106, 107, TI: A8
write once, read many (WORM) disks, 140
WYSIWYG, 234

## X

Xerox Corporation, 142
Xerox Palo Alto Research Center (Xerox PARC), 262, 380, TI: A7, TI: A8
XML (Extensible Markup Language), 329–330
XO communications, 291

## Y

Y2K, TI: A13
Yahoo! Inc., 308, 317
Yang, Jerry, 317
yottabytes (YB), 80

## Z

Z3 (electronic computer), TI: A3
zettabytes (ZB), 80
zipped files, 305–306
z-learning, 240–241
Zuse, Konrad, 22, TI: A3

# IMAGE CREDITS

**Chapter 2.** Page 46: (top) Corbis, (left) Eric K. K. Yu/ Corbis; Page 47: Artiga Photo/Corbis; Page 48: (top) © Paradigm Publishing, Inc., (bottom) Saed Hindash/Star Ledger/Corbis; Page 49: (top) Ramin Talaie/Corbis, (bottom) Encore; Page 51: Courtesy of Microsoft Corporation; Page 52: © Lian-Li Industrial Company, Ltd; Page 53: Courtesy of Wacom Company, Ltd., © Microsoft Corporation; Page 54: Roger Ressmeyer/ Corbis; Page 56: (clockwise from top left) Courtesy of Hewlett-Packard Company, Reuters/Corbis, Courtesy McKesson Provider Technologies; Page 57: (top) Rick Friedman/Corbis, (bottom) © Eastman Kodak Company; Page 59: (top) Roy Morsch/Corbis, (bottom left) © Sintec Corp., (bottom right) © Paradigm Publishing, Inc.; Page 61: (top) Ramin Talaie/Corbis, (bottom) Larry Williams/ Corbis; Page 63: Bettmann/Corbis; Page 67: © Paradigm Publishing, Inc.; Page 68: © Lian-Li Industrial Company, Ltd; Page 69: Courtesy of ASUSTek Computers Inc.; Page 78: William Whitehurst/Corbis; Page 82: James Leynse/Corbis; Page 83: (top) istockphoto.com/jackson gee, (bottom left) © NVIDIA Corporation, © Creative Technology Ltd, istockphoto.com/Marc Dietrich; Page 84: (left) © Cisco Systems Inc., (right) Courtesy of PCMCIA/Expresscard and the Rabbit symbol are trademarks of PCMCIA; Page 85: © Paradigm Publishing, Inc. Page 88: (top) Digital Art/Corbis, (bottom) © 2005 Business Wire; Page 89: © Virtual Devices, Inc.;

**Chapter 3.** Page 100: Roy McMahon/zefa/Corbis; Page 101: Corbis; Page 102: (top) Corbis, (bottom) Toru Hanai/Reuters/Corbis; Page 103: (left) Monica M. Davey/ epa/Corbis, (right) Jim Craigmyle/Corbis; Page 104: (top) Albert Gea/Reuters/Corbis, (bottom) T & L/Image Point FR/Corbis; Page 105: Samsung Electronics/Handout/ Reuters/Corbis; Page 106: Lou Dematteis/Reuters/Corbis; Page 110: (top to bottom) Najlah Feanny/Corbis, Forestier Yves/Corbis Sygma, Courtesy of Apple Inc.; Page 112: © Microsoft Corporation; Page 115: (top) © Printronix, (bottom) © Hewlett-Packard Company; Page 118: (top) © Hewlett-Packard Company, (bottom) © Canon Inc; Page 119: © Hewlett-Packard Company; Page 121: (top to bottom) © Primera Technology, © DYMO, © Canon Inc; Page 122: (top) © Canon Inc, (bottom) © Panasonic Corporation; Page 123: (top) © CNET Networks Inc, (bottom) Corbis; Page 126: Royalty-Free/istockphoto.com; Page 127: (top left to right) Courtesy of Western Digital Corp., (bottom) Courtesy of Dell Corp.; Page 129: Courtesy of Maxell Corporation Inc.; Page 130: (top) © Paradigm Publishing, Inc., (bottom) © Maxell Corporation Inc.; Page 135: (left) © Memorex Products Inc, (right) © ePerformance; Page 142: Courtesy of Plastic Logic Limited 2007.

**Chapter 4.** Page 154: Don Mason/Corbis; Page 163: Courtesy of Apple Computers; Page 170: Lynn Goldsmith/Corbis; Page 177: Courtesy of Red Hat, Inc. © 2006 Red Hat Inc. All rights reserved; Page 178: Kim Kulish/Corbis; Page 180: Microsoft product screen shot reprinted with permission from Microsoft Corporation; Page 182: Courtesy of Palm, Inc.; Page 183: (top left to right) © Hewlett-Packard Company, © Motorola, Inc., (bottom) © 1995-2009 Symantec Corporation. **Chapter 5.** Page 202: (left) Courtesy of the University of Phoenix © University of Phoenix, (right) A. Sneider/zefa/Corbis; Page 203: © istockphoto.com/Marje Cannon; Page 204: Adobe products box shots reprinted with permission from Adobe Systems Inc., Courtesy of Corel Corp.; Page 207: © 2009 WebMediaBrands. All rights reserved. Reprinted with permission from http://www.internet.com; Page 209: © Devan/zefa/Corbis; Page 212: Digibarn Computer Museum; Page 213: Erik Freeland/Corbis Saba; Page 214: © Paradigm Publishing, Inc.; Page 221: Corbis; Page 224: Jim Craigmyle/Corbis; Page 225: Corbis; Page 226: © istockphoto.com/Jill Fromer; Page 227: (left) istockphoto.com/christine balderas, (right) Courtesy of Quicken Willmaker Plus 2010 © Nolo; Page 228: Robert Glabraith/Reuters/Corbis; Page 229: By permission. From Merrriam-Webster OnLine Dictionary © 2009 by Merriam-Webster, Incorporated (www.merrriam-webster. com); Page 231: Courtesy of Apple, Inc.; Page 232: Louis Fabian Bachrach; Page 234: © Pinnacle Systems, Inc.; Page 235: Corbis; Page 236: Lars Langemeier/A.B./ zefa/Corbis; Page 237: Screen shots © Google Inc., and are used with permission; Page 239: Adobe product screen shot reprinted with permission from Adobe Systems Inc.; Page 240: Jon Feingersh/Corbis; Page 241: Varie/Alt/Corbis. **Chapter 6.** Page 254: Corbis; Page 262: Nogues Alain/Corbis Sygma; Page 264: Digital Art/ Corbis; Page 268: © Cisco Systems Inc.; Page 269: Corbis; Page 280: (top) © Cisco Systems, Inc., (bottom) istockphoto.com/Arkadiusz Stachowsla; Page 282: (left) istockphoto/com/Marc Dietrich, (right) © Cisco Systems, Inc.; Page 286: Jagadeesh NV/Reuters/Corbis; Page 290: James Leynse/Corbis. **Chapter 7.** Page 304: (top) Helen King/Corbis, (bottom) Corbis; Page 307: Screen shots © Google Inc. and are used with permission, AOL, AOL. com, AIM, AIM Express, the Running Man and Triangle Logos are registered trademarks of AOL LLC; © Kim Kulish/Corbis; Page 309: ROB & SAS/Corbis; Page 310: Erik Freeland/Corbis; Page 311: © 2003-2009 PhysOrg. com; Page 312: © 2009 UCAR, Vaughn Youtz/ZUMA/ Corbis; Page 313: Louie Psihoyos/CORBIS; Page 314: © Paradigm Publishing, Inc.; Page 315: © Apple Inc.; Page 317: © Kim Kulish/Corbis; Page 319: Courtesy of the

# SOURCES

**Chapter 1.** *Page 17:* Sandrasagra, Mithre J. "Development: Digital Divide Becoming a Vast Chasm," *Inter Press Service News Agency*, September 14, 2005. December 2006 http://ipsnews.net/news.asp?Idnews =30263; *Page 22:* Zuse, Horst. "The Life and Work of Konrad Zuse," *EP Online*. December 2006 <http://www.epemag.com>; *Page 24:* "Q & A: Sabeer Bhatia," *Red Herring*, May 15, 2006. December 2006 <http://www.redherring.com>; *Page 27:* "Electronic Contact Lenses for Better Vision," *MedGadget*, January 17, 2008. October 2009 <http://www.medgadget.com/ archives/2008/01/electronic_contact_lenses.html>; "Bionic Contact Lenses," *ScienCentral*, February 22, 2008. October 2009 <http://www.sciencentral.com/ articles/view.php3?type=article&article_id=218393067>; Nusca, Andrew. "With electronic contact lenses, bionic eyesight could become reality," *Smart Planet*, September 2, 2009. October 2009 <http://www.smartplanet.com/ business/blog/smart-takes/with-electronic-contact-lenses- bionic-eyesight-could-become-reality/566/>; *Page 28:* Graham-Rowe, Duncan. "'Fly-by-Wireless' Plane Takes to the Air," *New Scientist*, May 16, 2006. December 2006 <http://www.newscientist.com/channel/tech/dn9176. html>; *Page 30:* The Biography Channel. **Chapter 2.** *Page 52:* "Brain-controlled Device Could Help the Disabled," *Mail&Guardianonline*, March 7, 2006. December 2006 <http://www.mg.co.za/articlePage .aspx?articleid=265991&area=/>; *Page 54:* <http:// www.intel.com>; *Page 63:* O'Connor, J. J., and E. F. Robertson. *John Presper Eckert*. December 2006 <http://www-history.mcs.st-andrews.ac.uk/Biographies/ Eckert_John.html>; O'Connor, J. J., and E. F. Robertson. *John William Mauchly*. December 2006 <http://www-history.mcs.st-andrews.ac.uk/Biographies/ Mauchly.html>; *Page 70:* Crothers, Brooke. "Samsung: PRAM to push mobile battery life," *Nanotech: The Circuits Blog*, September 29, 2009. October 2009 <http://news.cnet.com/8301-13924_3-10363035-64 .html>; Nusca, Andrew. "Samsung's 'melting' memory chips could boost mobile phone battery life by 20%," *Smart Planet*, September 30, 2009. October 2009 <http:// www.smartplanet.com/business/blog/smart-takes/ samsungs-melting-memory-chips-could-boost-mobile- phone-battery-life-by-20/1226/>; *Page 74:* Peale, Cliff. "Firm Implants ID Chips," *The Cincinnati Enquirer*, February 14, 2006; McIntyre, Liz, and Katherine Albrecht. "Wisconsin Bans Forced Human RFID Chipping," *News With Views*, June 1, 2006. December 2006 <http://newswithviews.com/McIntyre/Liz6.htm>; "VeriChip," *Wikipedia*. December 2006 <http://en .wikipedia.org/wiki/Verichip>; *Page 77:* Johnson, George. "The Nobels: Dazzled by the Digital Light,"

*The New York Time*s, October 15, 2000; Glanz, James. "3 Men Vital to Internet Share Physics Prize," *The New York Times*, October 11, 2000; Crissey, Mike. "Texan's Microchip Speeds Info Age." December 2006 <http:// www.news.excite.com/news/ap/001010/19/nobel-reax>; Texas Instruments Company Overview, 2006. December 2006 <http://www.ti.com/corp/docs/kilbyctr/jackstclair. shtml>. **Chapter 3.** *Page 106:* "Steven Jobs Biography," *A&E Television*, July 2006. December 2006 <http://www .biography.com/search/article.do?id=9354805>; *Page 124:* Garreau, Joel. "Tongue in Check," *The Washington Post*, May 24, 2009. October 2009 <http://www .washingtonpost.com/wp-dyn/content/article/2009/05/21/ AR2009052104697.html>; Thibodeau, Patrick. "*Star Trek*-like universal translator a step closer," *ComputerWorld,* June 30, 2009. October 2009 <http:// www.computerworld.com/s/article/9135019/_i_Star_ Trek_i_like_universal_translator_a_step_closer>; *Page 134:* Adhikari, Richard. "HP's Web-Connected Printer Could Be a Game-Changer," *TechNewsWorld*, June 23, 2009. October 2009 <http://www.technewsworld.com/ story/67401.html?wlc=1245924419>; *Page 140:* Lewis, Jim. "Robots of Arabia," *Wired*, November 2005, pp. 188–195. **Chapter 4.** *Page 157:* McConnachie, Dahna. "Debian Gives Linux a Bhutanese Touch," *LinuxWorld*, June 22, 2006. December 2006 <http://www.linuxworld. com.au/index.php/id;1239885333;fp;2;fpid;1>; Noronha, Frederick. "Computers Can Now Speak Bhutan's Dzongkha," *NewKerala.com*, June 21, 2006. <http://www .newkerala.com/news3.php?action=fullnews&id=11689>; *Page 159:* "IBM Builds Super-fast Transistor," *CNN. com*, June 20, 2006. <http://www.cnn.com/2006/TECH/ ptech/06/20/ibm.chip.reut/index.html>; Needle, David. "IBM has world's Coolest Chip," *InternetNewsBureau. com*, June 20, 2006. December 2006 <http://www.inter- netnews.com/dev-news/article.php/3614586>; *Page 170:* "William H. Gates," *Microsoft*. December 2006 <http://www.microsoft.com/billgates/bio.asp>; *Page 178:* <http://www.dataworks.biz/Linux/LinusBio.htm>; "About Linus Torvalds," *Linux Online!* December 2006 <http://www.linux.org/info/linus.html>; *Page 181:* Tweney, Dylan. "Here Comes a Google for Coders," *Wired News*, February 17, 2006. December 2006 <http:// www.wired.com/news/technology/0,70219-0.html>; "Demo—The Premier Launchpad for Emerging Technologies," <http://www.demo.com/demonstrators/ demo2006/63003.html>; "Krugle Enterprise," *Krugle*, October 21, 2009. October 2009 <http://www.krugle. com/products/index.html>. **Chapter 5.** *Page 206:* Graham- Rowe, Duncan. "Operate on a Heart Without Missing a Beat," *New Scientist*, February 27, 2006. December 2006 <http://www.newscientist.com/article.ns?id=mg1892540

6.800&print=true>; *Page 212:* Shepherd, Robert D. *Introduction to Computers and Technology*, Paradigm Publishing: October 1997; *Page 230:* Pilon, Mary. "Anti-plagiarism Programs Look Over Students' Work," *USA Today*, May 22, 2006. December 2006 <http://www.usatoday.com/tech/news/2006-05-22-plagiarism-digital_x.html>; *Page 238:* "MoSoSo," *Wikipedia.* <http://en.Wikipedia.org/ wiki/MoSoSo>; "Campus Wireless Rave," *Red Herring*, June 5, 2006. December 2006 <http://www.redherring.com/Article.aspx?a=17123&hed=Campus+Wireless+Rave>; Terdiman, Daniel. "MoSoSos Not So So-So," *Wired*, March 8, 2005. December 2006 <http://www.wired.com/news/culture/0,1284,66813,00.html>; Kharif, Olga, and Peter Elstrom. "Connections, the Wireless Way," *Business Week*, June 29, 2005. December 2006 <http://www.businessweek.com/technology/content/jun2005/tc20050629_3438_tc024.htm>; Home Page, *Rave Wireless.* December 2006 <http://www.ravewireless.com>.

**Chapter 6.** *Page 262:* Shepherd, Robert D. *Introduction to Computers and Technology*, Paradigm Publishing: October 1997; *Page 270:* "Watering Crops in the Wireless Age," *New Scientist*, February 25, 2006; McCabe, Bruce. "Profits from Our Big Bots to Go Offshore," *Australian IT*, June 27, 2006. December 2006 <http://australianit.news.com.au/articles/0,7204,19570437%5E31923%5E%5Enbv%5E15309,00.html>; *Page 279:* Dignan, Larry. "Cisco Brings James Bond Briefcase to Disasters," *eWeek.com*, June 25, 2006 <http://www.eweek. com/print_article2/0,1217, a=181836,00.asp>; "IT Lends a Helping Hand; An Interview with NetHope's Edward Granger-Happ," *CIO Insight*, January 28, 2005. December 2006 <http://www.cioinsight.com/print_article2/0,1217 ,a=143549,00.asp>; *Page 283:* Weinberg, Neal. "Matt vs. the Volcano," *Network World*, June 26, 2006. December 2006 <http://www.network world.com/news/2006/062606widernet-volcano.html>; *Page 286:* "Chambers, John T," Britannica Book of the Year, 2001, *Encyclopedia Britannica Premium Service*, June 21, 2006. December 2006 <http://www.britannica.com/eb/article-9344721>; John T. Chambers Executive Profile, *CEO Central Home*, December 2006 <http://www.surferess.com/CEO/html/ john_chambers.html>.

**Chapter 7.** *Page 308:* "Google Milestones," *Google*, January 2006. December 2006 <http://www.google.com/intl/en/corporate/history.html>; "Google Corporate Information: Management," *Google.* December 2006 <http://www.google.com/intl/en/corporate/execs.html>; Elgin, Ben. "Larry Page and Sergey Brin: Information at Warp Speed," *Business Week Online*, December 27, 2004. December 2006 <http://www.businessweek.com/magazine/content/ 04_52/b3914014_mz072.htm>; *Page 313:* "Tim Berners-Lee," <http://www.w3.org/People/Berners-Lee>; *Page 317:* <http://www.metroactive.com/papers/metro/01.11.96/yahoo-9615.html>; Deutschman, Alan. *The Weaver Group*, January 4, 2005. December 2006 <http://www.rickweaver.net/index.php?src=news&prid=7&category=Resources&search=filo%20yang#>; Kopytoff, Verne. "It Started as 2 Guys in a Trailer; Yahoo Stands as One of Internet's Biggest Success Stories," *San Francisco Chronicle*, February 28, 2005. December 2006 <http://www.sfgate.com/cgi-bin/article.cgi?f=/c/a/2005/02/28/BUGJUBGR5D1.DTL&hw=yahoo+verne+kopytoff+trailer&sn=002&sc=990>; *Page 322:* <http://www.aircell.com/index.php?option=com_content&task=view&id=129&Itemid=336>; <http://www.gogoinflight.com/>; <http://www.shephard.co.uk/news/2303/>; <http://www.flightglobal.com/articles/2009/06/09/327637/panasonic-sets-pricing-scheme-for-exconnect-connectivity.html>; *Page 330:* O'Reilly, Tim and Jennifer Pahlka. "The Web Squared Era," *Forbes*, September 24, 2009. October 2009 <http://www.forbes.com/2009/09/23/web-squared-oreilly-technology-breakthroughs-web-2point0.html?feed=rss_technology>; *Page 334:* Marks, Paul. "Cities Race to Reap Rewards of Wireless Net for All," *New Scientist*, March 28, 2006. December 2006 <http://www.newscientist.com/article.ns?id=mg18925446.000&print=true>; White, Bobby. "Cities Shop for Lower Prices in Wi-Fi: Free," *The Wall Street Journal*, June 20, 2006; *Page 342:* "Female-Name Chat Users Get 25 Times More Malicious Messages," *UM Newsdesk*, May 9, 2006. December 2006 <http://www.newsdesk.umd.edu/scitech/release.cfm?ArticleD=1273>; "Study: Chat Rooms Hostile to Girls, Women," *NPR Future Tense*, May 10, 2006. **Chapter 8.** *Page 363:* "Wireless Games Coming to Vegas 2.0?," *The Show Buzz*, May 4, 2006. December 2006 <http://www.showbuzz.cbsnews.com/stories/2006/05/04/games/main1586047.shtml>; *Page 366:* Graham-Rowe, Duncan. "Wireless Boom Is Hackers' Heaven," *New Scientist*, January 22, 2005. December 2006 <http://www.newscientist.com/channel/tech/dn6894.html>; Bernard, Allen. "Wi-Fi Security Still a Major Issue," *Wi-Fi Planet*, May 30, 2006. December 2006 <http://www.wi-fiplanet.com/tutorials/article.php/3609866>; <http://www.muniwireless.com/2008/11/05/icomera-reports-272-percent-increase-in-wi-fi-use-on-public-transport/>; *Page 368:* Krebs, Brian. "Ransomware Rising," *The Washington Post*, May 8, 2006 <http://blog.washingtonpost.com/securityfix/2006/05/ransomeware_rising_1.html>; "Spyware Program 'Blackmails' Computer Users," *NewScientistTech*, May 31, 2006 <http://www.newscientisttech.com/article.ns? id=dn9247&print=true>; "Extortion Virus Code Gets Cracked," *BBC News*, June 1, 2006. December 2006 <http://news. bbc.co.uk/1/hi/technology/5038330.stm>; *Page 380:* Gasch, Scott. "Alan Kay," September 2003. December 2006 <http://ei.cs.vt.edu/~history/GASCH.KAY.HTML>; "Alan Kay Biography," *Hewlett-Packard*, October 15, 2003. December 2006 <http://www.hp.com/hpinfo/newsroom/feature_stories/2002/alankaybio.html>. **Chapter 9.** *Page 405:* "Blumenthal open letter seeks support for ONC's health IT plans," *Healthcare IT News.* August 20, 2009. October 2009 <http://www.healthcareitnews.com/news/blumenthal-open-letter-seeks-support-oncs-health-it-plans?Page=0,1>; Twiddy, David. "Work begins on a national e-health record network," *KTUU/Associated Press*, September 30, 2009. October 2009 <http://

www.ktuu.com/Global/story.asp?s=11230792&clienttype
=printable>; *Page 408:* Blau, John. "Security Scores Big at
World Cup Tourn-ament," *PC World*, May 26, 2006.
December 2006 <http://www.pcworld.com/article/
id,125910;psgr,1/article.html>; *Page 411:* Home Page,
*Oracle Corporation* <http://www.oracle. com>; and other
Web sources; *Page 418:* Bellman, Eric. "India to WTO:
Help Us Protect Herbs, Tea, Yoga," *The Wall Street
Journal*, December 19, 2005. December 2006 <http://
yaleglobal.yale.edu/display.article?id=6638>.